MICHAEL MacCAMBRIDGE
AMERICA'S GAME

Michael MacCambridge is the author of *The Franchise: A History of* Sports Illustrated *Magazine*, and the editor of the bestselling *ESPN SportsCentury*. He worked for eight years as a columnist and critic at the *Austin American-Statesman*, writing about movies, music, and popular culture. The father of two children, Miles and Ella, he lives in St. Louis.

Acclaim for Michael MacCambridge's

AMERICA'S GAME

"First-class reporting and writing. . . . Author Michael MacCambridge earns As across the board in this outstanding book. This book, like its author, has style and substance."   —*The Dallas Morning News*

"Welcome to the National Football League, a cultural artifact that causes thinkers to commit sociology. Michael MacCambridge plumbs these depths in his fine new book. . . . It is a rip-roaring epic of American business."   —George Will, *Newsweek*

"Superb . . . one of the best. . . . A big winner in terms of content, good writing and analysis."   —*The Washington Times*

"[A] fascinating [and] provocative history."   —*The Austin Chronicle*

"MacCambridge presents a compelling account of how foresight and fortune (good and bad) conspired to make the NFL the nation's most successful sports enterprise."   —*The Boston Globe*

"A well-written, thoroughly enjoyable history."   —*The Baltimore Sun*

"MacCambridge's portraits of the key characters in football are riveting and the details overwhelming. The perfect pick for the die-hard NFL enthusiast."   —*The Sporting News*

"Well-written and ridiculously well-sourced, *America's Game* demonstrates an understanding of both the game and the nation in which it is played. . . . It's a history text and a fine one at that."

—*Palm Beach Post*

"An interesting and entertaining and knowledgeable [read]. . . . [The] game descriptions are riveting."

—*Houston Chronicle*

"With a fan's passion and an insider's knowledge, *America's Game* . . . is as factual as it is dramatic."

—*San Antonio Express-News*

AMERICA'S GAME

MICHAEL MacCAMBRIDGE

ANCHOR BOOKS

A DIVISION OF RANDOM HOUSE, INC. ★ NEW YORK

AMERICA'S GAME

The Epic Story of How Pro Football
Captured a Nation

The Library of Congress has cataloged the Random House edition as follows:
MacCambridge, Michael.
America's game: how pro football captured a nation / Michael MacCambridge.
p. cm.
Includes bibliographical references and index.
1. Football—United States—History—20th Century. 2. National Football League.
I. Title.
GV954.M32 2004
96.332'64'0973—dc27
2004052003

Anchor ISBN-10: 0-375-72506-7
Anchor ISBN-13: 978-0-375-72506-7

Author photograph © Suzy Gorman
Book design by Carole Lowenstein

www.anchorbooks.com

For the home team,
Danica, Miles, and Ella

CONTENTS

December 28, 1958

A s the sun went down over Yankee Stadium, a series of thunderclap roars filled the sky, and the crowd surged forward, raucous and intent. The arc lights shone down on the field, highlighting the condensation floating above the surface, shimmering off the dark blue helmets of the New York Giants, and bathing the white uniforms of the Baltimore Colts in an ethereal glow.

While the two teams slugged it out through the fourth quarter, raising dust with every tackle across the hard dirt infield, the fans grew louder, colder, and more desperate. The Longines clock on the big scoreboard above the end zone showed just 1:56 remaining in the 1958 National Football League championship game, with the Giants leading, 17–14. At that instant, New York's star running back, Frank Gifford, was on one sideline, in an uncharacteristic rage, yelling that he'd made a first down on the previous play. Across the field, big Colts defensive end Gino Marchetti sat up on a stretcher, still in uniform, legs bundled under blankets on the sideline, looking like some vet shot down on the battlefield. The makeshift tourniquet around Marchetti's just broken ankle was the only concession he'd made to his injury. As the Colts' medical staff tried to transport him to the locker room, he barked that he was going to stay right there until the game was over.

Sam Huff and the Giants' defense took the field for a last stand in the chilled darkness, greeted with another magnificent roar by the Giants fans. At the same moment, from across the field, the Colts' Johnny Unitas—his face set in its customary portrait of gaunt, stoic purposefulness—trotted slowly toward the Baltimore huddle. Unitas exuded an infectious confidence but it didn't come from any commanding physicality. His body was ungainly, his legs mere thin stalks, and his football pants seemed too tight, riding high on his wide, bony hips. But beneath the brush cut flattop and high, pale brow, he possessed the cool, surveying eyes that could take the measure of teammates and opponents alike. Bending slightly forward at the waist, his hands placed softly on his hip pads, he peered in at his teammates.

"We got 86 yards and two minutes," he said with a voice of flat authority. "Let's get to work."

Yankee Stadium, and 45 million sports fans watching NBC's national telecast, looked on with rapt fascination. The game pitting the Giants, the league's marquee franchise, against the young Colts squad led by their quietly charismatic quarterback, had taken on the aspect of grand struggle.

Rather than opening with a short gainer, Unitas began the drive with a long pass, which fell just beyond the outstretched arms of Lenny Moore. Two plays later, he converted the crucial third down by hitting Moore over the middle of the field for 11 yards. With fresh life, he found his rhythm, calling a series of deceptive plays, each going counter to what the Giants' defense expected. When New York's defense cheated to the outside, Unitas looked instead over the middle for his end Raymond Berry—the precise craftsman of fakes and feints who would set a record for receiving yards in a championship game. And as the clock dipped into its final minute, he connected three times with Berry in the center of the field, gaining 62 yards. The last completion moved the ball to the Giants' 13-yard line, with 20 seconds left, no timeouts remaining, and the clock still running. The Colts' field goal unit scrambled onto the field and set up without a huddle, snapping the ball at the :07 mark. The inconsistent Steve Myhra, who'd missed a similar chip shot earlier in the game, kicked it between the goalposts to tie the game at 17.

With that, the 1958 NFL championship game guaranteed its place in the realm of sports legend. It already boasted a classic match-up, pairing the glamorous Giants with the exciting, upstart Colts. It had the requisite controversy that would spark countless barroom arguments: did Gifford make enough for the first down or didn't he? And when the last seconds of the fourth quarter elapsed, a crucial third element was added to the mix, as the game entered a dimension of uncharted territory in spectator sports. The National Football League had been in existence since 1920 and playing championship games since 1932. And while a rule had been in place since 1947 stipulating sudden death overtime in the event a playoff game ended in a tie, such an event hadn't occurred before.

"What happens now?" said a weary Pat Summerall to captain Kyle Rote on the Giants' bench. "Now," said Rote, "I think we play some more."

Up in the booth, where Giants broadcaster Chris Schenkel and Colts play-by-play man Chuck Thompson were sharing the call for NBC, Schenkel pointed out that pro football was about to experience its first venture into sudden death, with the two teams continuing play until the tie was broken.

"John!" yelled Weeb Ewbank, the short, rotund Colts coach, scanning his sideline for Unitas. "There's another coin flip—go out there for Gino." Marchetti, the Colts' team captain, obviously couldn't make it to the center of the field with his broken ankle. So Unitas went to midfield, and listened quietly as the referee explained the simple and unforgiving rules of the NFL's first sudden death overtime to decide a championship game: first team to score wins.

At the 50-yard line, Unitas called tails and the referee's coin toss landed heads. As Huff informed the referees that New York wanted to receive, Unitas looked distracted and restless, his gaze cast downward and his black high-top cleats casually kicking the dirt. With the word that the home team would get the ball first, a different sort of applause rolled through the stands of Yankee Stadium. It wasn't the throaty, predatory cannonade that had greeted many of the day's events, but instead an exhortative cheer, more wishful than confident. After the kick, the Colts' defense stopped New York on three plays, and the Giants had to punt.

Out came Unitas again, all business, angular jaw set. The twenty-five-year-old quarterback, who just three seasons earlier had been cut by the lowly Pittsburgh Steelers, possessed an unexcitability in times of intense pressure that teammates found both reassuring and inspiring. Moving with a dour, relentless efficiency, he continued mixing his plays beautifully. He'd fire off passes with his distinctive stoop-shouldered motion, the follow-through so exaggerated that it concluded with his right hand bent sharply at the wrist, all his fingers pointing toward the ground.

But the passes were accurate. And when the Colts' ground game sputtered early, at third-and-15 on their own 25, Unitas improvised with brilliant daring and surprising quickness. Fading back to his right, he was set to release to Lenny Moore on a curl pattern down the right sideline, but as the protective pocket of blockers began to collapse around him, he pulled the ball back down and started scrambling. With Giants linemen careening toward him, Unitas shuffled to his left, moved back toward the line of scrimmage, then went left again. By this point, the Colts receivers had seen him scrambling and broken off their routes, moving back toward the ball. But Unitas, still sliding left to elude another pursuer, extended his left arm forward, motioning to Raymond Berry to move further back down the field, past the first-down marker. Then he threw a dart to Berry, for just enough yardage to keep the drive alive. With the Giants' defense now on its heels, and middle linebacker Sam Huff cheating back to help his overmatched secondary, Unitas crossed it up again with a trap play to fullback Alan Ameche, who rumbled for 22 yards. Two plays later came a daring slant pass—rifled at such a dangerous angle that it sailed between the helmet ear hole and raised arm of Huff—that found Berry down at the 8.

The 20,000 or so Colts fans who'd bused in from Baltimore were now in a frenzy, many of them rocking the bleachers in the end zone, imploring their heroes to bring home the victory.

And in that pressurized instant around the country, 45 million Americans watched their television screens go black. Then this message appeared:

Please Stand By
PICTURE TRANSMISSION HAS BEEN
TEMPORARILY INTERRUPTED

The rocking of the Colts' fans had disconnected a cable down on the sidelines, causing NBC to lose its picture before Berry's catch. After the play, Unitas called a timeout, and after arriving at the Baltimore sideline asked Ewbank what he had in mind. "Just keep it on the ground," said the coach. "We can kick a field goal from here."

The quarterback took the field again, unaware that the TV audience was in the dark, and gave his teammates their next assignment. As the team clapped hands to break the Colts' huddle, a jowly, middle-aged civilian, with a look of deranged glee on his face, rushed onto the field and for a time eluded the three New York City policemen who were in hot pursuit. As the crowd roared at the break in tension, the man was hemmed in close to the Colts' huddle, and placed in handcuffs.

Moments later, the picture returned throughout the country, and from the control booth in the back of a van in the parking lot outside the stadium, NBC producer Ted Smith exhaled loudly with relief. Newspapers would report the next day that an NBC technician had managed to reconnect the cable and restore the picture. But it would be a long time before anyone outside the NBC offices found out that the apparently drunken fan who ran onto the field during the delay was actually a stone-sober NBC business manager named Stan Rotkiewicz, who'd been working down on the sidelines as a statistician. While he couldn't save the game for the Giants, he had saved it for the rest of America. His intrusion gave NBC enough time to find the disconnected cable and repair it, missing just one more play, a run into the line that gained one yard.

When NBC got its picture back, it was second down at the seven, and the Giants' linebackers inched close to the line of scrimmage for another ground assault. But Unitas defied convention again; he found end Jim Mutscheller open on the right sideline, and lofted a perfect, feathery toss over Mutscheller's shoulder, with the big end's momentum after the catch carrying him out of bounds inside the one-yard line. There was still murmuring in the press box about the apparent danger of such a pass when, on the next play, a run up the middle called "16 power" in the Colts' playbook, Ameche took Unitas's handoff and burst untouched into the end zone—a concert of photographers' bulbs leaving the flash of time forever frozen in history—to score the touchdown that ignited pandemonium on the field and rang down the curtain on pro football's watershed game. The Colts' fans stormed the field, tore down the goalposts, and celebrated their city's first championship in major professional sports.

Later, in the locker room, as a jubilant Unitas reacted with uncharacteristic glee to the news that he'd won a Corvette as the game's most valuable player, reporters wanted to talk about the final drive. Someone asked him about the pass to Mutscheller. "What if it had been intercepted? It could have been run all the way back for a touchdown."

"When you know what you're doing," he said, turning serious, "they're not intercepted."

That day, America found a new icon in Unitas, and a new passion in professional football. He was invited onto that evening's live broadcast of *The Ed Sullivan Show*, but declined the invitation and the $300, he explained, because he wanted to be with his team. Ameche gladly went in his place, to be greeted by Sullivan and the country.

Three days later, Castro's forces would overthrow Cuba. But on December 28, 1958, America witnessed the beginning of its own revolution—and this one would be televised. Like a rebel army seizing the seat of power, pro football had announced its insurgency with an epic football game at the most hallowed ground in baseball, the House That Ruth Built.

By the end of the Colts-Giants game, a seismic shift in the American sports landscape had clearly begun. In another decade, after another New York football team and its charismatic leader stunned the sports world, football was no longer the rebel, but the new king. And baseball was no longer America's national pastime.

————————

In the great books of history, it will go down as little more than a cultural footnote: in the second half of the twentieth century in the United States, pro football's popularity as a spectator sport grew to eclipse that of Major League Baseball.

But within the narrow stratum of American popular culture, the rise of pro football and relative decline in the popularity of Major League Baseball seems more momentous, a demarcation between past and present, not merely in sports but in the culture itself. This is true for several reasons, among them the speed with which pro football surpassed baseball, and the fact that well into the 1950s, so few people saw it coming.

To say that baseball was the number one sport in America at the end of World War II is to imply a hierarchy where none existed. Baseball towered above the sporting landscape like a colossus, the unquestioned National Pastime, the only game that mattered. Most fans had come to accept baseball's primacy as something immutable, as much a part of the natural order of things as air and water.

"Whoever wants to know the heart and mind of America had better know baseball," wrote Jacques Barzun in 1954. Barzun's words earned him a place in *Bartlett's*, and were still being quoted enthusiastically a half-century later. But in the span of two generations in postwar America, pro football became a truer and more vivid reflection of the American preoccupations with power and passion, technology and teamwork, than any other sporting institution in the country.

As pro football rose in stature and popularity through the '60s, it was logical to look for the simplest explanation to account for such a startling change. Many critics viewed pro football's rise as the inevitable sign of the quickening (and perhaps coarsening) of the culture or, at the very least, a simple product of one sport being better on television than the other.

Indeed, it was on television that the differences between baseball and football were most evident. The writer James Michener's *Sports in America* marveled at football's "almost symbiotic" relationship with television, and in 1970, when the sport became a hit on prime-time television, its incursion into the entertainment culture freed all sports to follow suit.

By the early '70s—when even the sport's announcers had become part of the American celebrity culture, and the Super Bowl attained the status of unofficial holiday in the nation's civic culture—the change had come. In the space of eleven years, between 1961 and 1972, the percentage of Americans saying that pro football was their favorite sport rose 15 points, from 21 percent to 36 percent, while those who said baseball was their favorite sport decreased 13 points, from 34 percent to 21 percent. This is a striking shift in any realm, but particularly remarkable in this one. For most people, a favorite sport was chosen at an early age and kept throughout a lifetime. And yet during the '60s, Americans changed those core loyalties in astonishing numbers.

So there became a myth, too frequently told in America, that pro football arrived fully born on December 28, 1958, a bolt out of the blue, and proceeded to roll across baseball on the sheer, self-evident power of its magical telegenic power.

But to argue football's inherent superiority on television is to insist that apples are better than oranges. Baseball telecasts framed the relevant central drama of batter vs. pitcher more completely and dramatically than a football telecast could document the complex and interdependent action of the twenty-two players in action on the field at any one time. And baseball, with its built-in commercial breaks at the end of each half-inning, was at least as well suited structurally to the medium as football. That football possessed more action than baseball was an observation often made, but insufficient to adequately explain its rise over all other sports. Basketball offered more fluidity and intimacy, hockey more speed and violence.

Equally unsatisfactory was the argument that football excelled on TV primarily because it satisfied some deep-seated bloodlust of the American sports fan. The first sport deemed perfect for television was boxing, with its theatrical intimacy, its brutal and at times bloody action, and its built-in commercial breaks every three minutes. Yet the story of boxing in the twentieth century is the story of the moth to the flame, of a sport perfectly suited for television that was all but destroyed because of it.

Television was surely a vehicle for change, and one that pro football exploited masterfully, but the medium alone cannot explain the rise of the message. So how did it happen, so swiftly and decisively? The beginnings of an answer can be found in the long-held American love of sports competition, and the unique structure of professional football.

Freedom of association is a powerful thing. Every organization in America is someone's version of utopia. The National Football League in its ascendance was the perfect, egalitarian vision of commissioner Pete Rozelle. A lifelong fan and former public relations executive, the Jesuit-trained Rozelle understood that leagues were most likely to succeed financially when they lived up to the ideals of a higher cause—fair play.

More than any other person, Rozelle engineered the game's transformation, as Colts lineman Art Donovan put it, "from being a localized sport based on gate receipts and played by oversized coal miners and West Texas psychopaths to a national sport based on television ratings." The changes Rozelle brought about, as well as the policies he preserved, reflected this philosophy. Central to his leadership was a thorough understanding of the principles and practices of mass communication. His mastery in tailoring the NFL's image for a broad middle-class audience helped make the game more appealing, both in person and on television. In short, Rozelle sold sports as they'd never been sold before—as a sophisticated passion, rather than a trivial juvenile pastime.

In 1961, the National Football League's owners voted to sign a national television contract with CBS, and share the revenues from that deal equally among all of its teams, regardless of market size or national appeal. This was important at the time, when the individual team television revenues were wildly disparate and made up a sizable portion of a team's income. It would become crucial in the decades ahead, when television exploded into the largest source of revenue in professional football.

While there was much media smirking over the league's "socialist" financial structure, the idea of a league sharing revenues while in the greatest capitalist society on earth wasn't a contradiction to Rozelle. His reasoning, passed down from his predecessor, Bert Bell, and the grizzled elder owners of the league, held that though profits were important, the sport must take precedence over the business. The self-evident truth that Rozelle stressed repeatedly was that the business of sports would be most successful if the competition was as equitable as possible. So the business model that emerged through the '50s, '60s, and '70s viewed the league's teams not as a number of restaurants vying for supremacy on a single street, but instead a chain of restaurants, with every franchise across the country competing among themselves to be the best, but each dependent on the survival of the whole to truly prosper.

Nearly as important to the growth of the sport in the '60s was the arrival of the American Football League. In the century's most tumultuous decade, the "other league" spawned its own distinct culture, one of combative yet collegial competitiveness. Built on the same foundation of equal opportunity (it had shared TV revenues equally from its beginning in 1960) and intense rivalry among teams, the AFL opened up the game offensively, and opened doors previously closed in pro football, not just to players, coaches, and entire cities, but to ideas, races, even cultural sensibilities.

A revolution needs both a mastermind and a catalyst. In the thirteen months following the 1958 Colts-Giants game, pro football would get each, in Rozelle and AFL founder Lamar Hunt. First separately, then together, they would be instrumental in bringing about a new era in American sports. The eventual merger between the leagues that was consummated in the hectic, cloak-and-dagger days of the spring of 1966 was more complex and treacherous than anyone but a few insiders realized. The irony was that in spending seven years trying to destroy each other, the feuding leagues unwittingly accelerated the growth of the sport as a whole. The war between the leagues brought a level of intrigue that the game had never possessed before, kept football on the sports pages throughout the off-season, and hastened innovation and integration. When the leagues finally merged, the whole was stronger than the sum of its parts.

The peace settlement also brought about a merger of two very large ideas. It was Rozelle's articulation of the NFL's vision of competitive balance (not just in revenue, but in competition, collaboration, and corporate outreach) aligned with Hunt's vision of widespread and wide-open opportunity—a sort of benign, solipsistic Texan arrogance which assumed that every big city in the country would want its own professional football team (and ought to get one)—that would eventually meld over the turbulent, antagonistic '60s. The result of this mixture would change the face of sports, television, and the way America spent its Sunday afternoons.

Pro football's rise also tapped into larger social themes—none more important than the advance of blacks in postwar America. On VJ Day in 1945, there were no African-Americans in the country's major professional team sports. A year later, four blacks broke the color barrier in pro football, months before Jackie Robinson made his celebrated debut with the Brooklyn Dodgers. By the kickoff of the 2004 season, more than 70 percent of the players in the NFL were black, with an even higher percentage starting and starring for their teams. (At the same time, just as in America as a whole, African-Americans found fewer opportunities at the highest levels of the industry. There was movement in the past decade to improve this condition, and sincere effort by many in the league. But for much of the twentieth century, at least, the color-blind meritocracy of the game stopped at the edge of the field.)

There was also a sense in which the interior world of pro football—with its draft, salary cap, revenue sharing, stacked scheduling (giving the best teams the more difficult schedules the following season), and "equity rule" (dictating that any device used on the sidelines by one team be made available to the other as well)—was a reflection of the best impulses of American egalitarianism. It was inevitable that some franchises would still prosper in this atmosphere, but it would be much harder to dominate, and every franchise, if it placed intelligent people in charge of football operations, had a measure of hope that was all but impossible amid the Darwinian economic disparity of Major League Baseball.

Pro football succeeded ultimately because it struck a resonant chord in the American psyche. In a time of increasing alienation and urban flight, when a sense of community was dissipating, it unified cities in ways that other civic enterprises could not.

What no one could have counted on, though, was the sheer degree with which sports fans began to care about, and build their lives around, their respective pro football teams. The NFL became a reality unto itself, one that far transcended its domain of Sunday afternoons and, later, Monday nights. From Dallas to Los Angeles, Cleveland to Baltimore, New York City to Kansas City, modern American men found a truth and beauty in pro football that was more reliable, more sharply defined, than almost any other aspect of their lives.

Like the best of the arts, pro football worked on multiple levels. For the loyalists, there was the fortune of the home team. For neutral or casual fans, there was action, skill, suspense, and violence. For gamblers, the wagering proposition. For those with a deeper interest, the game could exist on a larger canvas—as a morality play; a cultural metaphor; a crucible of values in which teamwork, sacrifice, and dedication were rewarded, while selfishness, cowardice, and sloth were harshly punished. What those who were contemptuous of sports misunderstood was not merely that a middle-class sports fan might revere football to the same degree that an inveterate theatergoer revered Shakespeare, but that he might do so for many of the same reasons.

This was, to be sure, disquieting to many. There was much in the NFL to comfort admirers and detractors alike. Its proponents hailed its competitiveness and ecumenical popularity, as well as its emphasis on teamwork and interdependence. Critics saw a remorseless world full of impersonal corporate decision making and casual, crippling brutality. In truth, pro football had become, more than either side cared to admit, a reflection of the country's double-edged culture itself: big, slick, fast, exciting, competitive, dangerous, and unforgiving.

At the dawn of the twenty-first century, pro football stood alone as the apotheosis of modern American sport, a financial and cultural dynasty, both tempted and plagued by greed and always in danger of overstretch. At the same time, it was a mass media juggernaut responsible for the ten most-watched television programs in history, and one of the few solid pieces of common ground left on the increasingly balkanized map of modern American popular culture.

By that point, the myth had become accepted truth. Pro football's success had come to seem preordained, the natural result of a faster, more technological society, attracted to the action and violence delivered by television's all-seeing eye. In part, of course, its success was due to all of these things.

But a closer examination of the sport's rise in postwar America provides compelling evidence that pro football's domination was hardly inevitable, the keys to its success numerous and complex. And the tidal change that altered American sports didn't begin with the classic 1958 title game, or Lamar Hunt's naive, inspired idea to form a new league in 1959, or Pete Rozelle's unlikely arrival as commissioner in 1960. Instead, the seeds had been sown earlier, as far back as the '40s, when baseball was king and the country was at war.

AMERICA'S GAME

Going West

B undled in a heavy winter coat and sporting a beaverskin hat, Daniel Farrell Reeves dug his hands into his pockets and marched from the gate bordering the stands out onto the field in the cavernous Cleveland Stadium. In a matter of hours, his Cleveland Rams would take the field to play the Washington Redskins for the championship of the National Football League. But as he surveyed the field in the numbing chill of this overcast morning two days before Christmas, Reeves could see nothing on the gridiron but thousands of bales of straw, and a small army of men laboring to move them. This was pro football in 1945.

Compact and slender, no more than 5-foot-8 and 140 pounds, Reeves was a man of reserved nature but wry wit. In four seasons, he had grown accustomed to the perennial financial losses—"Irish dividends," as he called them—common to owning a pro football team. But the 1945 season had been uniquely rewarding and frustrating. Reeves had returned home just two months earlier, after a three-year tour of duty with the Army Air Corps, to what would become a season-long victory celebration. America's triumph in World War II had been officially consecrated during August two-a-days, and the long lines that greeted the end of gas rationing dissipated by the season-opening win over the Chicago Cardinals. Just one season after the 1944 squad lost six of its last seven games, the Rams rebounded to become the surprise of the NFL, and win their first Western Conference title. In early December, rookie quarterback Bob Waterfield, soon to be named the league's Most Valuable Player, was profiled in *Life* magazine. And though the article spent less time on Waterfield than his wife—Hollywood bombshell Jane Russell, star of Howard Hughes's "sex western" *The Outlaw*, which censors still hadn't allowed to be screened in the U.S.—the mere thought that a player for the Cleveland Rams would merit space in *Life* seemed to Reeves a miracle in itself.

After the Washington Redskins beat the New York Giants in the regular season finale, Reeves's dream match-up was set. For the title game, the Redskins would make their first trip to Cleveland in eight seasons, bringing along their famed 110-piece marching band to perform a special Christmas-themed halftime show. Interest was high for the match-up between the rookie Waterfield and perennial All-Pro Slingin' Sammy Baugh. And so Reeves had bravely decided to move the championship game from the Rams' regular stadium, the deteriorating League Park, with its cramped capacity of 30,000, to Cleveland Stadium, which seated 80,000.

Six days before the game, the National Weather Service had forecast a major winter storm hitting the Cleveland area in midweek, so the Rams had spent the early part of the week searching for enough bales of straw to cover the tarpaulin, to prevent the field from freezing. It was general manager Charles "Chile" Walsh who finally located 9,000 bales of straw from around Elyria, and had it delivered to the stadium at a cost of $7,200. In the days leading up to the game, eighteen inches of snow fell on Cleveland, leaving the stadium resembling an arctic snowscape, with drifts piled several feet high in the aisles.

On Sunday morning, the Rams lined up 275 workers, many of them off-duty city employees, to remove the bales. While the Rams were responsible for the field, the city of Cleveland was responsible for the stadium and the parking lots, which were left unshoveled. Despite the weather and conditions, the Associated Press projected the game would draw 50,000, and the *New York Times* wrote that "a crowd of better than 40,000 is almost certain with a capacity audience of 77,569 possible in case the forecasters are wrong."

But when the lights were turned on at Cleveland Stadium at 6:30 the morning of the game, the temperature was eight degrees below zero. Marching in mucklucks from the Clevelander Hotel a little before eight, Reeves balefully noted the unpassable streets. There was no parking in the two blocks closest to the stadium, since that area was overrun with snow. And taxi service wasn't running to the stadium, another skirmish in the war between the Rams and Arthur McBride, owner of the Zone/Yellow Cab Co. and the new Cleveland entry in the All-America Football Conference, which would begin competition in Cleveland the following fall.

By 10:30 that morning most of the 9,000 bales had been cleared off the field. But the trucks that were to transport them away had trouble gaining purchase on the still clogged city streets, leaving the workers no choice but to place the straw against the walls surrounding the playing field. Behind the benches, just in back of the end zones, and stacked more than ten bales high at the walls, the sea of straw was parted so the game could be played.

Cleveland Stadium had rarely looked so empty as on this day, when only 32,178 turned out. When former Rams business manager Manny Eisner and his wife walked into the stadium about an hour before kickoff, there were already people filing out, succumbing to the cold. In the stadium ticket office, Lou Isaacson was more prepared than most. Dressed in three pairs of socks, knee-high brogan work shoes, two pairs of pants, two sweaters, and two coats, he sat in the unheated box office for four and a half hours, and sold two tickets.

In financial terms, Reeves had already resigned himself to the realization that his share of the gate wouldn't even pay for the cost of buying, transporting, and removing the bales of straw. But as the kickoff neared, none of that mattered. Up in the press box, Reeves was nervous and amiable, greeting writers and VIPs, accepting congratulations for signing Waterfield to a three-year contract the day before. "The stars are making so much money now, I call them 'Mister' and they just call me 'Reeves,' " he said. When the game began, the joking ended, and Dan Reeves suffered in silence, as he'd done every game day since 1941, when he'd bought the team. He paced nervously, far removed from his wife, Mary, the rest of his family, and his closest friends. It was not a time to be jovial or even social. It was time for football.

Down on the field, the game sounded different, victim to the noiseless vacuum of severe cold. There was little kibitzing between the teams, and almost none of the concussive, amplified smack that so often accompanied the heavy hitting of professional football. The quality of play was still sharp, but on a day when the temperature was zero degrees at kickoff, the players felt the pain more than heard it, each tackle accompanied by heavy breathing and dull, muffled thuds. The crowd sounded different as well, its applause muted by layers of gloves, the cheers rising curt and thin in the icy air.

Even in the '40s, people argued about whether the pressure of football built character or revealed it. But Reeves had long ago learned how capricious the game could be, how random its deciding factors. On this frigid Sunday, he watched Sammy Baugh's pass from the Redskins' end zone hit the goalpost and fall back into the end zone, for what was then an automatic safety. After Waterfield threw the first of two long touchdown passes for the Rams, his extra point attempt was partially blocked, with the ball careening toward the crossbar, hitting it, and dribbling weakly over. Baugh's freak safety and Waterfield's wounded conversion had been the difference in the 15–14 edge the Rams nursed into the fourth quarter.

By that time, the windows of the Cleveland Stadium press box had fogged over, and most of the writers covering the game had abandoned their typewriters and gone outside into the biting cold, cursing as they bundled up to face the brutal wind, but drawn to the finish of the frantic battle below. Reeves himself was outside when he saw the play that decided the game. With the Redskins nearing midfield in the closing minutes, running back Steve Bagarus made an end run to the right, then reversed field and broke free, running in a sweeping arc to the far sideline, with two Rams in hot pursuit. The first slowed him down and the second, Waterfield (who in addition to being the star quarterback was also the team's best defensive back), made a desperate lunge and extended his left arm before hitting the ground. The contact was scant—Waterfield's hand barely nicked the toe of Bagarus's trailing foot—but it was just enough to knock the runner off his feet and save a touchdown. The Rams' defense stiffened from there and the Redskins missed a field goal attempt.

Moments later, the game was over and the Cleveland Rams were world champions. The hardiest fans stormed the field to tear down the goalposts in celebration, while the rest of the crowd headed for shelter and celebration into Cleveland's bars, restaurants, and dance halls. In the locker room, where the players massed for the traditional celebratory championship candid photograph, head coach Adam Walsh hugged his brother, Chile Walsh, and announced, "I knew you were champs back there at Bowling Green! I knew it! I knew it!"

NFL commissioner Elmer Layden greeted Adam Walsh, his old college roommate at Notre Dame, with a hug and a handshake. Then Layden presented Reeves with the league's Ed Thorp Memorial Trophy, given annually to the NFL champion. "I've been used to losing for so long," said Reeves, with tears in his eyes, "that I wasn't counting on anything until it was all over."

As Reeves returned with friends and family to his suite at the Clevelander Hotel, his jubilation was tempered by the private realization that his time in

Cleveland was near its end. Reeves had lost more money in earlier years, but in the season in which his team had marched to the world championship, it still lost $64,000. And the prospects for box office improvement were dim, since the rival All-America Football Conference would begin play the following season, with a franchise in Cleveland that seemed to be the strongest in the league.

Reeves had decided, win or lose, that when the NFL held its annual meeting in January, he would insist on fulfilling his goal, stated for years in private sessions with the owners, to move his franchise to Los Angeles. This time, he was determined: Dan Reeves was heading west, or else Dan Reeves was leaving football.

———

By the end of World War II, the unique personality and character of the National Football League had begun to develop. The NFL owners comprised a particularly hidebound and tightly knit fraternity, loath to accept outsiders, reluctant to change the often circuitous, inefficient manner in which proceedings were conducted. Many could remember the league's earliest years, when it was perceived to be—and for the most part was—a haphazard assemblage of pickup games and hired hands making weekend pay.

The Bears' legendary coach and owner George Halas had been there from the start, present at the creation of the league, one of sixteen men in Ralph Hay's Jordan and Hupmobile showroom in Canton, Ohio, in August 1920. That meeting, called by the league's first president, Jim Thorpe, laid the foundation for what would be called the American Professional Football Association, and two years later renamed the National Football League, though it had no franchises west of Chicago or south of Washington, D.C.

Its next president, elected in 1921, was the tireless Columbus promoter Joe F. Carr, who presided over the league's dark ages, in which thirty-five franchises folded in the league's first ten seasons. At that 1921 meeting, Halas moved the Decatur Staleys to Chicago, where a year later he renamed them the Bears, and the Green Bay Packers and Earl "Curly" Lambeau entered the league. In 1925, they were joined by New York bookmaker Tim Mara, who bought the New York Giants for $2,500, reasoning that any franchise in New York City ought to be worth that much.

In 1932 and 1933, the rest of the inner circle came on board. First there was George Preston Marshall, the bombastic Southern laundry man, who bought the Boston Redskins in 1932, moving them to Washington, D.C., five years later. In 1933, "Blue-Shirt Charlie" Bidwill, Chicago businessman and diehard Bears fan, bought the crosstown rival Chicago Cardinals, though those closest to him knew the Bears were still his favorite club.

Then there was Philadelphia's Bert Bell and Pittsburgh's Art Rooney, who'd met at a horse track in the late '20s, and whose franchises joined the league in 1933, the same year that the Pennsylvania state legislature relaxed its blue laws, allowing sporting events on Sundays. De Benneville "Bert" Bell, the son of a Pennsylvania attorney general, was a blueblood aristocrat with a common touch, who spent much of the '20s roaring his way through his inheritance. The raconteur Art Rooney, son of a corner tavern owner in Pittsburgh, was a delightfully egalitarian personality in his own right. Rooney's team was called the Pirates throughout the '30s, before changing its name to the Steelers in 1940.

For most of the '30s and '40s, these seven men—Halas, Lambeau, Mara, Marshall, Bidwill, Bell, and Rooney—*were* the National Football League. The '30s brought hard-earned growth, with liberalized passing rules, the introduction of a two-division system with an annual championship game (Marshall's idea), and the first college draft (the brainstorm of Bell), all introduced under Carr's watch. Through the decade, the game retained its slangy sense of barnstorming informality. Pittsburgh head coach Johnny Blood once missed a game because he simply forgot it was on the schedule. Most players fit practices during the week around their regular jobs, others came into town on the weekends and played for less than $100 a game.

The tight band of owners fought like brothers, but persevered in the face of several rival start-ups, the indifference of much of the American sporting public, the condemnation of many in college football, and the failures of several of their partners. Those who remained were cautious, inherently suspicious of change, and not eager to test their horizons.

In 1936, the Cleveland Rams, who had struggled through a season with the failing rival American Football League, called NFL president Joe Carr to apply for an expansion franchise in the NFL. Carr came to Cleveland, met owner Homer Marshman, and invited him to come to the next meeting to apply for membership.

"So in December 1936," recalled Marshman, "I went to the NFL meeting in Chicago and made my presentation. They told me to sit down and wait. Next, a man from Houston made his presentation. They thanked him and told him to leave. I thought that was very impolite since I was allowed to remain. Next, a man from Los Angeles made a pitch for Los Angeles. They excused him, too. I couldn't understand it, because their presentations were every bit as good as mine. As soon as the two others had left the room, George Preston Marshall jumped up and said, 'I move we give it to Cleveland.' Everybody agreed. It was set up. They had decided on us in advance. They wanted to keep the teams in the east and midwest."

After Carr's death in 1939, the league limped along with former Dayton owner Carl Storck as acting president. The obese, unprepossessing Storck, known as "Scummy" during his playing days, had a habit of opening each league meeting by sitting at the head of the table with a gavel in front of him and to either side a box of chocolates, from which he would regularly graze during the discussions. In 1939 and again in 1940, owners tried to interest others in the job. George Halas offered it twice to *Chicago Tribune* sports editor Arch Ward, the creator of baseball's All-Star Game and football's College All-Star Game, the *Tribune*'s annual season-opening exhibition between the defending NFL champions and a team of just-graduated All-Americans. In December of 1939, George Preston Marshall of the Redskins and Dick Richards of Detroit approached FBI director J. Edgar Hoover about the position.

Storck's resignation in 1941, ostensibly due to failing health, allowed the owners to rescue themselves from their rudderless state and bring in a new leader, changing the name of the office from president to commissioner, and investing it with broad powers, similar to those enjoyed in baseball by Judge Kenesaw Mountain Landis. At Ward's suggestion, the league summoned Elmer Layden, still a sports legend from his days as one of Notre Dame's Four Horsemen. Throughout World War II, Layden held forth at his office at 310 South Michigan Avenue in downtown Chicago, aided by publicity director George Strickler.

Layden was well regarded in amateur football circles, and his hiring was meant to bring about a change in the pro game's reputation, making it more legitimate in the eyes of the public. But his effect proved largely cosmetic, and even those slight alterations didn't come easily. It took Layden four years to push through a rule requiring that all players wear stockings during games. His other cherished innovation was ordering officials to wear color-coded shirts (referees in black-and-white, umpires in red-and-white, head linesman in orange-and-white, and the field judge in green-and-white), a scheme that veteran official Dan Tehan ridiculed as a "circus on parade." Little else changed under Layden. There was still incessant bickering and politicking, and issues were often determined by a test of stamina as much as any guiding principle. Those who left the marathon sessions for some sleep might find the issue had been decided, not in their favor, by the time they returned the next morning.

And most teams kept losing money. Four seasons after joining the league, Marshman sold the Cleveland Rams to twenty-eight-year-old New York stockbroker Dan Reeves. Reeves was one of the keen, restless obsessives absorbed by the sport and science of football, a sportsman who found in the game a beguiling combination of action, violence, camaraderie, and strategy not duplicated in any other segment of American life save the military when at war.

Born rich, Reeves was neither flamboyant with money nor particularly obsessed with increasing his wealth. Though he had played football at Newman Prep in New Jersey as a boy, he didn't like to hit or be hit. He was not aggressive by nature. But like many men before him, and millions more to follow, Daniel Reeves loved the game of football for reasons he could neither articulate nor fully understand. With the wealth to do whatever he wanted, Dan Reeves wanted to buy a football team. Asked by a writer in 1941 to explain why he'd purchased the Rams, Reeves replied, "Doesn't every boy dream of owning a football team?"

The son of a grocery store magnate, Reeves was in a better position than most to realize his dreams. Upon buying the Rams, Reeves frankly explained to his fellow owners that he hoped to move the club to Los Angeles at the earliest opportunity. That, Reeves emphasized, was a place where the sport could grow and prosper. Before the season was over, his hopes and plans, like that of most other Americans, would have to be put on hold.

———

The final Sunday of the 1941 season saw the Redskins hosting the Philadelphia Eagles before a crowd of 27,102 (including the young naval officer John F. Kennedy) at Griffith Stadium, when a messenger found Federal Bureau of Investigation assistant director Edward A. Tamm in his seat, and escorted him to the stadium switchboard. There Tamm was patched into a call with FBI chief J. Edgar Hoover and a special agent in charge of the bureau's Honolulu office. The agent in Hawaii held his phone up to the window of his office so that Hoover and Tamm could hear the bombs and explosions at the U.S. Army base in Pearl Harbor.

On that Sunday, December 7, 1941, at the three stadiums where NFL games were being played, it was the football writers who learned the news before almost anyone else. The clattering Associated Press wire, which delivered updates from the league's other games on its fat roll of pulp paper, interrupted its staccato reports with the phrase "CUT FOOTBALL RUNNING" and then delivered the bulletin about the Japanese attacking Pearl Harbor.

Within weeks of the attack, President Franklin Delano Roosevelt addressed the dominant question on the minds of sports fans across the country.

"I honestly feel that it would be best for the country to keep baseball going," he wrote in a January 15, 1942, letter to Judge Landis. "There will be fewer people unemployed and everyone will work longer hours and harder than ever before. And that means that they ought to have a chance for recreation and for taking their minds off their work even more than before. Baseball provides a recreation which does not last over two hours or two hours and a half, and which can be got for very little cost. And, incidentally, I hope that night games can be extended because it gives an opportunity for the day shift to see a game occasionally."

There was no mention, either in FDR's letter to Landis, or in any of his other pronouncements at the time, of what the future might hold for professional football, or any other sport. Like such rickety and parochial pursuits as pro basketball and hockey, the sport was left to its own devices, less dismissed than simply ignored. Though it had already developed a following in big cities, pro football lagged behind even college football in terms of national prestige. The most respected publication in the sport was the weekly St. Louis newspaper *The Sporting News,* which was known as "the Bible of Baseball" but ignored football until 1942, when it began devoting a single page of coverage to other sports in season.

And although it was football that had been disrupted by the war—the NFL title game between the Bears and Giants drew just 13,341 people two weeks later—much of the national sporting press could respond only in terms of baseball. "Japan was never converted to baseball," argued *The Sporting News* in its December 11, 1941, editorial. "They may have acquired a little skill at the game, but the soul of our national game never touched them. No nation which has had as intimate contact with baseball as the Japanese, could have committed the vicious, infamous deed of the early morning of December 7, 1941, if the spirit of the game ever had penetrated their yellow hides."

As the nation rallied to the war effort and the government reaffirmed the indispensability of baseball, the very existence of the National Football League remained in doubt. By May of 1942, 112 of the league's 346 players (32 percent) had been drafted into the armed forces, and there was little hope that they would be replaced by college graduates. From the league's Chicago office, Layden worked to keep his league together, and prove its worthiness to the American effort. "While we believe professional football has a definite place in the recreational program of a nation at war," said Layden, "nothing connected with it should or will be permitted to hinder the war effort." Average paid attendance, which had topped 20,000 for the first time in 1941, fell to 16,144 in 1942. Despite the losses in fans and personnel, the league gave more than any other sports organization to aid the war effort, contributing $680,000 in 1942 alone.

But the manpower drain worsened and, even with rosters cut from thirty-three men down to twenty-five, there was speculation in the spring of 1943 that only three of the league's eight clubs would be able to field a team for the season ahead. The Rams—with just eighteen players left, and both Reeves and minority partner Fred Levy in the service—were allowed to suspend operations for the 1943 season. Two months later, the league announced it would go into the season with eight teams, after the Pittsburgh Steelers and Philadelphia Eagles merged for the season, to form the "Steagles." Across the league, talent was scarce. "We held tryouts at Cubs Park," recalled Halas, "and signed up anybody who could run around the field twice."

In 1944, the Rams returned to action, the Eagles fielded their own team, but the Steelers had to merge again, this time with the depleted Chicago Cardinals. That amalgam, known as "Card.-Pitt." in the standings, and "the Carpets" around the league, lost all ten of its games.

The owners, always thrifty, became penurious during the war years. For games in New York City, the Eagles traveled by coach train on the morning of the game, to avoid hotel expenses, and ate their pregame meal in the Bronx at Horn & Hardart, the chain of coin-operated Automat delicatessens. When the Steelers came to New York, they did stay at a hotel; but instead of chartering a bus to the game, a team official would give each Steeler a nickel to take the subway to the Polo Grounds, and another nickel, in the locker room after the game, to return.

So the league fought manpower trouble, declining gates, and travel restrictions for the balance of the war. And it operated in the shadow of baseball, even in its oddities. The NFL's one-armed player (Jack Sanders, who lost part of his left arm in an explosion at Iwo Jima) received only a fraction of the attention of baseball's one-armed player (the St. Louis Browns' Pete Gray). Over the course of the war, 638 NFL players served their country, 355 as commissioned officers, and nineteen players died in combat.

For all that, pro football exhibited a remarkable resiliency. Attendance, after falling in 1942, rebounded with a smaller schedule of forty games in 1943 and, by 1944 topped a million for the fourth time in league history. The NFL's fractious owners had persevered, hung together, and retained hope that with the end of the war, their prospects might brighten. Instead, by the end of 1944, they were preparing to face another, more direct challenge, the greatest in the league's history.

During the war, the league received several applications from prospective owners in Los Angeles, none of whom were more persistent or serious than the urbane actor Don Ameche. In 1942, Ameche fronted a Hollywood group that presented the league with a novel proposal. Realizing that travel restrictions would be a prohibitive barrier to a Los Angeles franchise during the war, Ameche's group offered to base the team in Buffalo for the balance of the war, then move it to Los Angeles. Though Arch Ward argued his friend Ameche's case privately with both Layden and the Bears' Halas, he couldn't convince them or the larger group that the time was right to expand.

"We owners were a tight little group," recalled Halas. "We had gone through a lot together. We had helped one another. . . . We liked things the way they were. We did our best to keep things that way. Looking back I can see how our closed door was certain sooner or later to produce trouble for us."

From his bully pulpit as the author of the *Tribune's* "In the Wake of the News" sports column, and with the support of *Tribune* publisher Colonel Joseph McCormick, Ward was the most influential sports editor in the country. When his friend Ameche was turned down, Ward was livid. His anger became the seed for the NFL's newest challenge.

On June 4, 1944, in St. Louis, Ward gathered a group of investors from around the country to organize a new professional football league that would challenge the NFL directly for players and fans. He announced the formation of the All-America Football Conference a month later, to banner headlines in the *Chicago Tribune*. The league planned to begin in 1945 in eight or ten large cities, including Cleveland, Chicago, New York, and Los Angeles. "All clubs are financed by men of millionaire incomes," wrote Ward, "who are prepared to engage in a battle of dollars with the National Football League, if necessary." Shortly thereafter James "Sleepy Jim" Crowley, one of Layden's partners in the Four Horsemen backfield, was installed as commissioner. The All-America Football Conference was a logical step, argued Ward, who noted that baseball's American League was founded twenty-four years after the National League, and that the NFL had just completed its twenty-fourth season.

At first, the established league's attitude was dismissive. "I did not realize there was another league," said the Redskins' George Preston Marshall, when asked about the AAFC, "although I did receive some literature telling about a W.P.A. project."

But the AAFC's legitimacy was soon clear. In February of 1945, the new franchise in Cleveland announced that Ohio State coach Paul Brown, by then serving his war duty by coaching a football powerhouse at Great Lakes Naval Academy, would coach the Cleveland franchise after the war. Three months later, the AAFC held a meeting in Chicago, and Brown and Chicago Rockets owner John L. Keeshin were appointed to represent the AAFC in seeking a meeting with Layden to discuss "working agreements on a players' draft, players' salary limits, schedules, inter-league games, anti-raiding policies, etc."

When the *Tribune* called the NFL offices for comment about the delegation, Strickler argued to Layden that he should make some kind of statement explaining why he wouldn't meet with Brown and Keeshin. "All I know is what I read in the newspaper," Layden told the press. "There is nothing for the National Football League to talk about as far as new leagues are concerned until someone gets a football and plays a game."

The off-the-cuff comment, extensively reported at the time, would be an element in Layden's eventual undoing. At a football luncheon attended by both Crowley and Layden later in the spring, the AAFC commissioner opened his remarks with a football under his arm, saying, "Look, we have a football." More than a year later, the quote and its rejoinder were still reverberating. Paul Brown was one of several AAFC figures photographed with dozens of footballs, next to the inevitable caption, "Hey, Elmer, Now They've Got a Ball."

Though the war forced the upstart league to delay its launch, announcing early in 1945 that it wouldn't begin play until 1946, the AAFC owners were better financed than those in the NFL. And Ward's influence garnered them plenty of publicity.

So for the NFL, the 1945 season had the air of both prelude and valediction. The giddy postwar aura of triumph and possibility was there, but it coexisted alongside a deeper and broader sense of crisis, that the league's very existence was again on the line. The tension would lead to the extraordinary events in the first month following the 1945 season, marking the dawn of the modern age of pro football, expanding the horizons of American sports, and setting the stage for the NFL's rapid ascent over the next quarter century.

Among the cantankerous NFL owners, frequent rumbling about Elmer Layden's performance had existed for years, and were exacerbated by the rise of the AAFC. Many felt that Layden didn't have the stomach for a good fight, especially one with his friend Arch Ward. But as late as the title game in Cleveland, his job was considered secure. Then came the news that Dan Topping, owner of the NFL's Brooklyn Dodgers, was taking his team out of the league and joining the AAFC. Topping, who also owned the New York Yankees in baseball, was one of the NFL's wealthiest and most visible owners. Layden had been unable to settle the squabble over Sunday home dates between Topping and Giants owner Tim Mara.

The NFL's 1946 annual meetings were scheduled to start Friday, January 11, at the Commodore Hotel in New York City. They in fact began the night before that, when a group of owners gathered at the Commodore and agreed among themselves not to renew Layden's contract. The Redskins' George Preston Marshall had arrived in New York vowing, "Layden will be reelected over my dead body." The next day, when Layden banged the gavel to begin the meetings, he did so to an empty conference room. Returning to his hotel room, he received official word later that the owners had voted on his ouster.

"Layden was forced out," Strickler explained years later, "because he had not been able to bring himself around to using [his] power. Poor Elmer really never got out of college. He had been brought up on and could not break away from the amateur approach to football. . . . He was just beginning to catch on when they dumped him."

For their new commissioner, the owners drafted one of their own: Bert Bell. By the end of the war, a series of financial setbacks had forced him to sell the Eagles and take a minority position with Art Rooney's Pittsburgh franchise. Among the best-liked owners in the league, Bell also was the only one of the inner circle willing to give up his ownership stake to take the job. With his partner Rooney remaining as the owner of the Steelers, Bell accepted the owners' offer of the $20,000-per-year job.

He was presiding on Saturday morning, January 12, when the 1946 annual meeting officially got underway, with Marshall formally nominating Bell for the position he'd already accepted.

Then it was time for the owners to hear from the Rams. As Dan Reeves sat quietly at the conference table, general manager Chile Walsh made a passionate case that the league should allow the Cleveland Rams to move their operations to Los Angeles.

Walsh reminded the owners that the Rams had suffered daunting financial losses during the war, and lost money even in their championship season. They now faced a challenge from the AAFC's Cleveland contingent, likely to be the most formidable entry in the new league. After years of planning for California, they had a chance of being able to play in the Los Angeles Memorial Coliseum and had also, as a fallback, inquired about the Cotton Bowl in Dallas. But the team, and the league, needed to go to California now, Walsh argued, or else cede the entire territory to the two AAFC teams—the Los Angeles Dons and San Francisco 49ers—which would begin play in the fall of 1946.

Eight votes were needed to approve a transfer, but as in years past, consensus could not be reached. Six teams supported the move, three were opposed, and the Green Bay Packers abstained. As the voting was completed, Dan Reeves stood up and spoke for the first time during the meeting. "And you call this a national league?" he asked. "I suppose Texas doesn't interest you, either?"

Halas, speaking for those opposed, explained that the owners didn't want to face the exorbitant costs of traveling outside the league's geographical area.

"If that's your final word," Reeves said, turning to leave, "then I am no longer a member of the National Football League. Consider the Cleveland Rams out of pro football."

This wasn't the first time, nor would it be the last, that an owner had stormed out of a league meeting. But with the gravity of Reeves's complaint, and the fresh memory of Topping's defection weighing heavy on the occasion, Bell called a recess to his first meeting as commissioner. Halas, Bidwill, and Marshall were dispatched to Reeves's hotel suite to bring about a truce. Their initial entreaties were ignored, as Reeves retreated to his bathroom and shouted, at one point, "It's either Los Angeles or Dallas, or nothing."

With that, the three other owners began discussing a way to accommodate Reeves while addressing concerns over the heightened travel expenses of West Coast trips. At 2:00 p.m., when the meetings reconvened, they'd talked both Reeves and their partners into supporting the move provided Reeves agreed to offer all visiting teams an extra $5,000 above and beyond the $10,000 road team guarantee, for all games in L.A. That afternoon the National Football League became America's first truly national sports league, with franchises from coast to coast.

As Reeves left the Commodore, he was beaming over the pending move. "Now I just need to ratify the decision with my family." In fact, he was less concerned with the response of his wife and children than with the reaction the Rams would get three days later in front of the Los Angeles Coliseum Commission, which had effectively banned pro football from its stadium for more than twenty years.

———

The NFL's record book shows a team in Los Angeles for a single season in 1926. In fact, the Los Angeles Buccaneers never played in Los Angeles. They were based in Chicago, largely because they couldn't get permission to use the Los Angeles Coliseum, where Red Grange had played in front of 75,000 fans in his barnstorming tour with the Chicago Bears the previous winter. Since then, there had been an unofficial ban on pro teams at the Coliseum, whose governing commission—comprised of three representatives from city, county, and state government—was brimming with alums of Southern Cal and UCLA, two schools conscious of maintaining college football's primacy on the West Coast.

Reeves had positioned himself to break that ban. Months earlier, he had lined up an exhibition game at the Coliseum, to be played between the Rams and Redskins in August 1946, with proceeds going to the Los Angeles Times Charities. With that foot in the door, he felt that the move would get a measure of support from Los Angeles political leaders. What complicated matters was the other professional football applicant, Ameche's Los Angeles Dons of the AAFC, who also wanted a contract to play at the Coliseum.

For his part, Reeves had moved cautiously in the press, stating carefully that the matter shouldn't be seen as one that pitted college football against pro football, or one pro league against another. "If the Coliseum commission wants to let another club in, that will be all right. With the California climate, and lights in the Coliseum, there is no reason the whole thing can't be worked out to everyone's satisfaction."

When Coliseum Commission chairman Leonard Roach arrived at the stadium for the hearing that Tuesday afternoon, January 15, 1946, he was approached by three members of the black press, Halley Harding of the *Los Angeles Tribune* and Herman Hill and J. C. Fentress of the *Pittsburgh Courier*, the leading black newspaper of the era, which promoted a "Double V" during the war, signifying victories over fascism and imperialism in the war, and over racism at home.

As with major league baseball, pro football was segregated at the time, not by rule or law, but by practice and custom. Numerous blacks had played with the town and factory teams of the league's early years, but since the 1933 season—when the black running back Joe Lillard played for the Chicago Cardinals and a tackle named Ray Kemp saw action with Pittsburgh—not a single black player had received so much as an invitation to training camp, even during the desperate manpower shortages during the war.

While the canard that blacks couldn't compete with whites was preserved in baseball by segregation throughout the minor leagues, the myth of white superiority was harder to maintain in football, where blacks were starring for integrated college teams across the country, excelling not just in exhibitions (as in baseball) but throughout the season and in high-profile bowl games.

Few players had shone as brightly as UCLA's Kenny Washington in the late '30s. Washington led the nation in total offense in 1939 and Bob Waterfield

later described him as "the best football player I ever saw." Though a scoreless
tie against Southern Cal in 1939 prevented UCLA from going to the Rose
Bowl, Washington received a standing ovation from the sellout crowd of
103,000 at the Los Angeles Coliseum, a scene that prompted syndicated
columnist and future TV star Ed Sullivan to write, "I have never been so
moved emotionally, and rarely so proud of my country."

Jackie Robinson, who had been Washington's backfield mate at UCLA,
later called him "the greatest football player I have ever seen. He had everything needed for greatness—size, speed and tremendous strength. Kenny was
probably the greatest long passer ever."

Despite the acclaim and the accomplishments, Washington wasn't selected
in the 1940 NFL draft. In an "open letter" sent over the airwaves that year,
NBC broadcaster Sam Balter asked NFL owners why none of them chose the
player that most experts agreed was "not only the best football player on the
Pacific Coast this season, but the best of the last ten years and perhaps the best
in all that sport's glorious football history—a player who had reduced to absurdity all the All-American teams selected this year because they did not include him—and all know why."

When he traveled to Chicago to play in the College All-Star Game in August 1940, Washington's performance prompted New York Daily News columnist Jimmy Powers to call on New York owners Tim Mara and Dan Topping to
bring him into the league. "He played on the same field with boys who are
going to be scattered through the league," wrote Powers. "And he played
against the champion Packers. There wasn't a bit of trouble anywhere." After
the game, Washington recalled that the Bears' Halas asked him to stick around
Chicago for a week, "and he'd see what he could do for me. I waited for about
a week and then was told that he couldn't use me." For the next six seasons,
Washington spent much of his time playing for Paul Schissler and the Hollywood Bears in the Pacific Coast League, where he injured his knee so badly he
couldn't qualify for active military duty. For the balance of the war, Washington played sporadically for the Hollywood Bears and traveled on the USO
tour, making stops from Alaska to the Burma Road.

So when Roach arrived for the commission meeting, Harding and his colleagues were ready, with the argument that those in the black press would be
opposed to opening up the Coliseum if the pros continued to exclude athletes
who, in Harding's words, "happen to be colored."

"Well, fellows," said Roach. "I am against Jim Crow, not only in pro football but in all other forms." Roach said the group should select a representative, who would speak at the hearing.

At 2:45, in a packed conference room on the second floor of the Coliseum's small administration building, the meeting was called to order by Roach. The first order of new business was the use of the Coliseum for professional football, and prepared statements were delivered by Chile Walsh for the Rams and general manager Lloyd Wright of the Dons, after which Roach asked if anyone else had anything to say.

At that, the immaculately dressed Harding rose to his feet and addressed the gathering, with a calmly eloquent oratory about the injustice of racial segregation in sports. He spoke first of the long history of Negro athletes in pro football, invoking the names of Fritz Pollard, Paul Robeson, Sol Butler, and Duke Slater, all standout professionals in the NFL of the '20s, who were later excluded from the league.

Harding pointed out that blacks had been excluded from the NFL for more than a decade, and he blamed the Redskins' segregationist owner George Preston Marshall for keeping the racial barrier up on a league-wide basis. Then he cited the case of UCLA's Kenny Washington, and argued that it was "singularly strange that he had never been signed by any team in the National League." Before finishing, Harding reminded the meeting that blacks had fought for American freedoms overseas, and now deserved those same freedoms at home.

As Harding sat down, an electric silence filled the room. Commission member Roger W. Jessup asked if it was true that no team in pro football would play with or against "our Kenny Washington." Another board member, John Anson Ford, praised Harding for his stand.

Asked to respond to Harding's speech, Chile Walsh at first repeated what others in the league had long claimed—that there was no written rule against blacks playing in the NFL. But then he went a crucial step further.

"Kenny Washington is invited by me at this moment to try out for the Los Angeles Rams team," Walsh said. He added, "I will submit a gentleman's agreement that if you can deliver me Buddy Young on completion of his graduation from the University, I will sign him." Young, then preparing for his senior season at Illinois, was considered one of the country's best running backs. Two weeks later, the commission voted unanimously to approve the Rams' petition.

And so on May 4 as promised, the Rams signed Washington to a three-year contract. Later in the summer they signed another black player, his Pacific Coast League teammate Woody Strode, an end from Illinois. Neither would have much of an impact on the game. Washington's knees had been ravaged more than anyone knew. Strode, at thirty, also was past his prime (and already well along on his career in acting). But that fall, the two men would make the team, and play, without a major public racial incident, effectively reintegrating the NFL.

So in a matter of days in January 1946, the National Football League had moved west, at a time when Major League Baseball's horizons were still bound by the Mississippi River. And the league integrated, with little national fanfare, at a time when Jackie Robinson was still toiling in the minor leagues for the Dodgers' AAA farm club, the Montreal Royals.

In July, the Los Angeles Rams reported for training camp. Though a movie star owned the rival Dons, the big stars were with the Rams. Waterfield's marriage to Russell had made plenty of headlines, and teammate Tom Harmon had taken up with Hollywood starlet Elyse Knox.

That summer, the Rams held their training camp at Compton Junior College, a few miles south of downtown Los Angeles, and site of one of the most powerful junior college athletic programs in the country. Each of Los Angeles' six major dailies covered the early days of camp at Compton, with predictably suggestive asides about Waterfield's wife ("I venture to say," wrote the *Times*'s Vincent X. Flaherty, "that if Daniel Farrell Reeves can promote Russell into assuming that billboard posture of Sabbath afternoons, he will pack the whole coliseum and will have wild young men spilling over the walls").

The most prominent of L.A. sportswriters, *Times* editor Paul Zimmerman, showed up to file as well. He was one of many to be impressed by the crack job done by the Rams' publicity staff, which was aided by personnel from Compton, including a lanky, tanned, amiable student assistant, who seemed particularly adept, dispatching the daily news briefings, always willing to help the writers with whatever they needed.

"That kid you've got is good," Zimmerman mentioned to Goldie Holmes, Compton's athletic director, at camp one day. "What's his name?"

Holmes informed him that the young man who delivered the hot coffee, made sure the press releases were free of typos, and was even then working on the paste-up pages for the Rams' intrasquad game program, was a well-mannered, whip-smart Compton College student, recently back from the war, by the name of Pete Rozelle.

2

The Organization Man

At 8:30 in the morning, Monday, July 29, 1946, at the Alpha Xi Delta sorority house on the campus of Bowling Green University, forty-nine football players sat in seven neat rows of desks, arranged in alphabetical order. The name of each player was written on masking tape, affixed to the front-facing backrest of each chair, so the speaker standing in front of the room could tell at a glance who was missing or late. On this morning, all the seats were filled, and had been for several minutes.

Standing in front of the classroom, dressed in brown pleated slacks, a crisply pressed white T-shirt, and a baseball cap, Paul Brown looked out at the assembled players and, as the second hand swept across the 12, began his first address to the Cleveland Browns football team with the words, "Call me Paul."

His voice was an arid, Midwestern tenor, free of accent or flamboyance, but tinged with an edge of precise rectitude, and the clipped cadences of a former English teacher, which he was. "We will be the most amateur team in professional sports," he vowed. "I don't want fellows who are strictly professional. I don't want you to think of the money you'll be making; rather I want you to think of the game first and the money second. We'll start just as we started when I coached at Massillon. It'll be just like it was there, at Ohio State and at Great Lakes, and those of you who were with me at those places know exactly what I mean. We'll coach the pro team the same way we coached the others.

That means we'll start on the ground floor with fundamentals." That meant the afternoon session would be devoted not to the first practice but instead a lecture instructing the team how it would conduct its practices, followed by a test run through calisthenics.

In an era when most pro football training camps were ragged, casual affairs, Brown's approach was not a departure so much as a counterattack, a repudiation of a quarter-century's worth of business-as-usual in the sport.

Later that morning, the assistant coaches distributed green three-ring binders, and Brown explained that all the plays and terminology they would learn in the weeks ahead would be copied down by each player. "Everything we do, everything expected of you, will go in here," he said. "I will call in the notebooks without warning. They will be graded. A sloppy notebook means a sloppy player. Star or rookie, you will be gone."

The remainder of Brown's morning speech summarized the unprecedented social contract between a professional football coach and his players. In it, he laid out the rules that his players would be expected to live by, not just during training camp but throughout the season.

"Don't set up any love nests in Cleveland," he warned. "We're going to find out where you live. If you sneak out after bed checks you'll be fined and you'll read about it in the paper, and I'll be the first to tell your wife. Keep your wives out of football. Don't have your wife talk football with other wives. It breeds trouble. I don't want one wife complaining to the wife of the quarterback that her husband is being overlooked as a pass receiver.

"I ask you to wear a sport shirt to dinner. At the table, keep the meal enjoyable . . . it's no place for pigs. . . . Try to avoid cliques. Know all your teammates. Class always shows."

And in closing, the purposeful man gave his team a clear goal.

"I want this team to be the darling of professional football," he said. "We're starting from scratch, and I want you to think in terms of being the best. We'll settle for nothing less than a winner. When you think of baseball, you immediately think of the New York Yankees. When you think of golf, Bobby Jones comes to mind. When you think of boxing, it's Joe Louis. One of these days when people think of football, I want them to think of the Cleveland Browns."

What would in fact happen, in the coming years, was that when people would think of football, they would think of Paul Brown. The head coaching job in Cleveland, which he'd accepted in the spring of 1945, was the last in an audacious series of jumps that had taken him from a just-graduated newlywed, coaching at an obscure prep school in 1931 to the pinnacle of his profession, in just fifteen years. For the next decade, his team would dominate professional football and his methods would reshape it. The program that he set in place in Cleveland was the culmination of an adult life spent viewing football not as a sport but a field of study, worthy of the fine and close attention of academic inquiry. Others would have to learn to do the same if they hoped to compete.

————

Massillon, Ohio, lay just eight miles to the west of Canton, connected by the old State Highway 30 and the kind of fraternal competition between close communities that has fueled sports rivalries for ages. Canton in the early twentieth century was both a political hotbed (hometown to President William McKinley) and an industrial center, full of steel mills and other factories. Its neighbor Massillon, where Paul Brown grew up, was a bustling steel town and port city, lying on the heart of the old Ohio & Erie Canal, which connected the Ohio River and Lake Erie. Brown's parents, Lester and Ida, had moved to Massillon, for Lester's job as a telegrapher and chief dispatcher on the Wheeling & Lake Erie Railway.

Young Paul Brown was just 120 pounds when he went out for the Massillon Washington High School football team in the August prior to his freshman year. By his junior year, he was the starting quarterback, a 140-pound package of preternatural authority and intelligence. During his senior season, Brown was suggesting substitutions, and head coach Dave Stewart was listening. "He was like a banty rooster, full of authority and self-confidence," said Stewart. "When he was my quarterback, his voice rang with inspiration as he called the plays. The kids believed in him and he ran them like a Napoleon."

By the time he'd graduated from college, at Miami University in Oxford, Ohio, Brown had begun to doubt whether he really wanted to fulfill his father's wishes of becoming a lawyer. Instead of law school, he accepted a teaching job at Severn, a naval preparatory school in Maryland, where he'd also be able to coach the football team.

His course was set. Within two years, he returned to Massillon as head coach, and proceeded to turn the moribund program into the premier football power in the state, compiling an 80-8-2 record over nine seasons. It was during these years that Brown's innovative coaching techniques, and his competitive urge to acquire quality players, began engendering both respect and resentment. Len Dawson, who'd later play for Brown in the pros, recalled growing up in nearby Alliance, Ohio. "There were rumors back in high school that he'd have telephone repair people coming over here to our practice facilities at Alliance High School to see what we were doing."

One key to Brown's success was his ability to elicit a community-wide dedication to the game. The booster club drew 2,500 fans to the regular Monday night dinners. In his final season at Massillon, 1940, the Tigers drew 182,500 people to their ten games.

Late that year, the most visible coaching job in the state opened up, and Paul Brown was named the head football coach at Ohio State. He found instant success, going 6-1 his first season, then winning the national championship in 1942. He was perfectly suited for the college life, with its strict schedules, malleable athletes, and frenzied school spirit, and with the football team at the absolute center of the school's social whirl.

In 1943, with many of his front-line players drafted or enlisted in the military, Brown suffered his first losing season as a coach, capped by a painful blowout loss to Michigan. The lesson he learned, of the ultimate importance of personnel—"You've got to have a phenomenal animal"—would remain with him for the rest of his career. The next year, 1944, he entered the service himself, taking what was to be a temporary leave from Ohio State. He was placed as the athletic director and football coach of the Great Lakes Naval Station outside Chicago, where in two years he led the school to upset wins over several national powers.

He also developed a reputation as a man who was not to be trifled with. He abstained from drinking from the first day of training camp until the end of each season, also giving up gin rummy and golf during the campaign. "Paul was a stickler for details," remembered Marion Motley, who first played for Brown at Great Lakes. "Paul was sitting on a train one Sunday afternoon at the same time me and another player, a young kid, were sitting in another train on the same track. We were going out on liberty. This kid I was with didn't see Paul. But Paul saw him. The kid had a cigarette in his hand. On Monday morning, Paul fired the kid. They sent him to Iwo Jima, I think."

Many Ohio State fans were surprised in 1945 when Brown announced that he was taking a job coaching a pro team, and a fledgling one at that. But those who knew him best understood his smoldering resentment over his perceived mistreatment at the hands of the school administration and athletic director Lyn St. John (whom, Brown felt, welcomed him back to his old job with less enthusiasm than was warranted). Then, too, there was Cleveland entrepreneur

Mickey McBride's pitch: a $1,500 a month retainer for the remainder of the war, a $25,000 salary commencing with his discharge from the navy, and a 5 percent stake in the team.

But what Brown found irresistible was the opportunity to create his own team, from the ground up, and then concentrate exclusively on football. Rather than fitting in practices for students who were spending most of their time taking college classes, or preparing for naval training, his players would take classes in football, and prepare solely for football games.

To appreciate what a revolutionary Brown was in the '40s, it helps to understand not just the sport's humble beginnings but its brutal, and at times sluggish, development. For twenty-five years, George Halas and some of the more enlightened caretakers of the game had been seeking to rescue football from the worst excesses of its own inherent brutality, the monotonous repetition of roughneck factory workers engaging in monster scrums—a delight for the factory workers, but less interesting for spectators. In the '30s, the sport was, in the words of historian Robert Smith, locked in "the thralldom of tradition that seemed to have doomed it to remain, especially if the field were wet, a slam-bang, grunt-groan, pull-devil, pull-baker affair that was occasionally less fun to watch than an honest wrestling match."

The forward pass rules, liberalized in 1933, had helped, and the innovations of T formation mastermind Clark Shaughnessy, with Ralph Jones's man-in-motion wrinkles (which moved more action away from the congested center of the field), had brought a greater element of strategy and grace to the game. As personified by the Bears' epochal 73–0 rout of the Redskins in the 1940 NFL title game, and the Shaughnessy-coached Stanford team's 21–13 win over Nebraska in the Rose Bowl weeks later, football took on an aspect of artful dodging, with quarterbacks like Stanford's Frankie Albert duping teams with nimble spins and well-concealed fakes.

The T helped to civilize the game further because it put an even greater emphasis on skill and speed over raw strength. Quarterbacks had a wider array of faking options, and with the quickness in getting the ball-carrier to the hole, blocking became a more nuanced process of delaying or interfering with a defender rather than flattening him. Personnel were still crucial, but strategy and tactics mattered as well. And the glimpses of this game, while still rough, encouraged the sort of spectacular action and dense strategy that was rarely combined in any single sport.

While Halas and Shaughnessy worked on tactics, Brown was convinced that the principles of organization, never observed in a systematic way in the sport, could make the difference. In this way, he was part of a civilizing continuum, helping to bring intelligence, skill, and strategy to the game.

Throughout the war, as the T formation gained prominence in playbooks at every level of football, coaches everywhere were scrambling to adjust and understand it. Brown, like so many other single-wing coaches at the start of the '40s, was forced to play catch-up. He coached the single-wing throughout his time at Ohio State but upon arriving at Great Lakes, decided to experiment with the T, and spent some time attending Bears practices.

Brown was still in the military when he accepted the Cleveland job, but through assistant John Brickels he engaged in a remarkably comprehensive recruitment of talent, searching far and wide to find the "high-class people" he was looking for to fill his football team. The circumstances were extraordinary; Brown could not have built up such an arsenal of players limited by the strictures of a draft in an established league. Nor, under a less benevolent and less wealthy owner, would he have been able to offer the salaries and monthly retainers that McBride was willing to pay.

While colleges waited for their stars to return to campus, Brown sought out players who'd played for him or against him, and wrote them to ask them to consider turning pro. The letters he sent came as part of the standard military mail call, small slips in the mountains of information, care packages, mash notes, and correspondence that crisscrossed the globe during World War II. The letters bore the return address of the new franchise, 405 N. Leader Building in downtown Cleveland, and contained a personal letter from Paul Brown. The offers that accompanied the contracts weren't just generous, but unique: a retainer for players of $250 per month for the balance of the war, a signing bonus of as much as $2,500, and salaries up to $7,500.

Brown didn't march out and try to sign a dream team of All-Americans. He had kept a dossier on the players he coached and played against at Massillon, Ohio State, and Great Lakes, and these were the primary contacts he used to assemble his squad. He started with his quarterback. Brown was convinced that to run the T effectively, a team needed a quarterback who was both a natural leader and an all-around athlete. When the time came in 1945 to start assembling a pro team, Brown sought for his quarterback "an artist throwing the ball; a particular kind of guy; a quick thinker; a finesse man." Typical of his vision for the game, the man Brown had in mind for his T formation quarterback had never played the position before.

The only loss Brown's Ohio State team suffered in 1941 was an upset at the hands of Pappy Waldorf's undermanned Northwestern team. The key play was engineered by Otto Graham, the Wildcats' star tailback. With the score tied, Graham took a deep snap from his tailback position in the single-wing, and followed a wall of blockers toward the left on what looked like an end run. Stopping nimbly and squaring his shoulders, Graham threw a long touchdown pass across his body and down the right sideline. Brown never forgot it, and he sensed that Graham possessed the ideal blend of skills for the position.

With a shock of close-cropped black hair and thick eyebrows that set off a sharply handsome face, Graham was a terrific athlete and model student, clean as milk, who seemed to excel at everything he pursued. Invited to Northwestern on a basketball scholarship, he was also a multi-instrumentalist adept at the piano, the violin, the cornet, and the French horn, which he played for one year in the Northwestern student orchestra.

After graduating early, Graham went to Carolina Pre-Flight, as part of the navy's V-12 flying program, where he was contacted by Brown, who signed him to a $7,500 contract, with a $250 monthly stipend during the balance of his time in the military.

Once Graham was signed, Brown cast a wide net for players in service around the globe. Lou Groza was working with a medical battalion stationed on Mindoro, preparing for the invasion of the Japanese mainland, when he received Brown's contract offer. Groza had impressed Brown with his placekicking skills before joining the service after his sophomore year, and soon after signing his contract received two footballs by mail. Without any goalposts, Groza worked on perfecting his accuracy, spending hours at a time aiming for a spot at the very top of a tree. In the Philippines, where Lin Houston's company commander had to witness his signature, he looked at the contract and said, "Kid, if you don't sign it, I will. You'll be making more than me, and you're only a private." Brown would also court Dante Lavelli, who served nearly three years with the 28th Infantry Division, where he fought in the Battle of the Bulge.

Though each player's original freshman class had graduated, Lavelli, Houston, and Groza—along with Gene Fekete and George Cheroke—all had college eligibility remaining at Ohio State. It was inevitable that the players Brown was recruiting would return as much more mature and less credulous than they'd been as schoolboys. When the news came that Brown was signing players with college eligibility left, his separation from Ohio State developed into outright antagonism.

"Ohio State is counting itself exceedingly fortunate in having Paul Brown eliminate himself from the university picture," wrote St. John in a letter published in Ohio State's monthly alumni magazine and reported in the Cleveland newspapers.

"Keep in mind that I am the same Paul Brown whom they claimed to have offered $15,000 annually to remain there a year ago," Brown shot back a day later. "Maybe the series of events that followed my leaving might give some insight as to why I really left. St. John is a bitter foe of pro football and I seem to be in the middle of the two."

With the Rams' move to Los Angeles, Brown had the Cleveland market all to himself. By the middle of the summer, the team was even bearing his name. An early name-the-team contest had resulted in the club announcing, in the spring of 1946, that it would be known as the Cleveland Panthers. But when the owner of a failed minor league franchise of the '30s claimed rights to the name, Brown decided to ditch it. "We don't want to have any association with a loser," he said, ultimately agreeing to let the team use the most common name suggested by the fans, Cleveland Browns.

Brown didn't wait until the players arrived at Bowling Green. His letter, sent two months prior to the opening day speech, outlined what they could expect.

"Regardless of how good a friend of mine you might be or how much of a football name you might have, it means nothing when it comes to making this football team. To make the squad you must earn the right. . . .

"We will take our football players on the lean and hungry side. Our team is based on SPEED. I feel certain that you will know what I'm talking about when we get down to work."

To help him, he'd assembled a staff of six assistants, the largest in pro football. The last addition to the staff was Blanton Collier, the veteran high school coach from Paris, Kentucky, whom Brown had met at Great Lakes. The two men seemed particularly well suited, with the gentle, amiable Collier—a classic teacher in the true sense of the word—bringing just as much intellectual curiosity to the pursuit of coaching as Brown.

At Bowling Green, the regimen quickly set in: a fire bell rang at 7:00 a.m. to wake the players, breakfast was served at 7:30, practice was at 9:30, lunch at noon, more practice at 3:00 p.m., dinner at 6:15, meetings to follow after, players in the dormitory at 10:00 p.m., in bed by 10:30.

Brown was hardly the first coach to run organized practices, or to give chalk talks, or to use film study, or to station men in the press box during games. But in each of these areas, his attention to detail was more thorough than anyone else in professional football. And because he'd carefully selected his players, and paid them well, he had a willing squad to work with, a group of players more talented to begin with than any other in the AAFC.

On the third day of practice, Brown installed his first play, an off-tackle run. From then through the next three weeks, the schedule remained the same. In the evening, the team would take notes on a running play, which would be installed and practiced the next morning. The afternoon meetings would explain the passing play, which then was inserted that afternoon. The evening session would review the progress and assignments of that day, then introduce a new running play to be installed the next morning.

Brown drew from outside accepted football practices to prepare and judge his players. From the military, he adapted the army intelligence test, a twelve-minute, fifty-question multiple-choice examination given to players at the beginning of training camp. He'd later become the first coach in pro football to conduct psychological testing, designed to reveal not raw intelligence but drive, determination, and the ability to sacrifice for the good of the group. (These early attempts in this area provided specious results.) Intent on building a fast team, he began timing players in the 40-yard dash, rather than the 100, reasoning that the 40 was a more meaningful measure of true football speed, about the distance a player would cover on a punt.

"There was a total positive attitude in everything Paul did," recalled Blanton Collier. "Everything was planned to the minutest detail. For the first four or five years of the eight I was with him in Cleveland, each player and coach wrote everything that was in the playbook. I mean, we sat there and wrote down what he dictated to us. Each coach had to write out what he was going to teach. Then you dictated that to the players and they wrote it in longhand. That meant drawing up every play that went into our system. Nothing was left to chance."

When the Browns reported to camp in late July, there were no black players on any AAFC roster. Marion Motley, Brown's star fullback at Great Lakes, had written a letter to Brown in the spring of 1945, asking for a tryout, but received a note telling him the team had enough running backs. Bill Willis, an All-America lineman at Ohio State under Brown, had written him the previous fall, and Brown said he'd contact him later. After not hearing from Brown for nearly a year, Willis agreed to play with the Montreal Alouettes in the Canadian Football League, though he had not yet signed a contract.

Willis was preparing to leave for Canada when he got a call from Paul Hornung, the *Columbus Dispatch* sports editor and friend of Brown's, requesting that he come to the Browns' camp. "We'll try him at guard and if he proves that he hasn't lost his old fire and speed, we'll definitely sign him," Brown told the *Cleveland Press.* "He'll do us a lot of good if he still has it. He was like a black panther when he was playing for me at Ohio."

Willis still had it. He reported to camp on August 6 and his impact was felt instantly. As the Browns began scrimmaging that day, Willis, lined up just off the shoulder of center Mike "Mo" Scarry, came off the ball so quickly he consistently reached Graham before the quarterback could pivot away from center. Scarry charged that Willis was jumping offside, but after Brown and his assistants kneeled on hands and knees so they could look straight down the line of scrimmage, they confirmed his charge was legal.

Later in the month, Brown arranged for Motley to show up at Bowling Green and "ask" for a tryout. This was another contrivance, as Brown had asked a friend of his in Canton to contact Motley and drive him to camp. For the fullback, married and supporting a family of four, it may have been a last chance at carving out a life outside a steel mill. He didn't waste it.

Brown later claimed that he had decided, even before Branch Rickey signed Jackie Robinson to a contract in August 1945, that he wanted both Willis and Motley on his team, and that he waited until training camp had already started to summon them to reduce the pressure each man would face. While his orchestration of their signing was certainly calculated, his claim seems difficult to square with other facts. As Dan Daly and Bob O'Donnell relate in *The Pro Football Chronicle,* Willis was signed at a time when the Browns had not a single guard with professional experience, and Motley came to the Browns after fullback Gene Fekete had been hurt in a scrimmage and another fullback, Ted Fritsch, had asked to be released so he could return to the Green Bay Packers. Brown never informed Willis or Motley of his plans, and because of that came close to losing Willis to the CFL. Years later, Brown would remark to the writer Mickey Herskowitz that it had been Collier who was agitating for him to bring in Motley.

Whatever the motivations, the method did result in less scrutiny being placed on either Willis or Motley—as well as less criticism being directed at Brown than if he'd taken a more publicly active position, similar to Rickey's, or even Reeves, who'd announced the signing of Washington and Strode months earlier.

With the last two key players in camp, the Browns continued to build toward the regular season in a calm, methodical fashion. Brown had too many quality players for the thirty-three-man roster. Rather than waive them to other teams in the AAFC, he devised a secret plan with owner McBride by which several players who had been cut would land jobs with the Zone/Yellow Cab Co., with schedules arranged so that they could report to League Park in Cleveland, where the Browns practiced. Thus was born the "taxi squad" in pro football. During the Rams years, Cleveland had gained a reputation as a bad football town. But the steady drumbeat of publicity that Brown's name engendered had raised interest to record levels, guaranteeing weeks in advance that the Browns' first game would be played in front of the largest crowd for a regular season game in pro football history.

Less than a year after losing a champion with which they never developed a bond, Cleveland's fans now seemed prepared to embrace an untested startup team as their own.

———

The AAFC season opener was played on a Saturday night, September 5, at Cleveland Stadium, and drew 60,135 fans, nearly equalling the Rams' home attendance for the entire 1945 regular season. The fans saw a smartly dressed Browns team—brown jerseys with orange numerals, outlined in white block-shadow, white pants, and shiny white helmets—storm onto the field as the marching band of 120, including bandleader George "Red" Bird's 30 Marching Majorettes, serenaded them with brassy music.

The game was covered by *Life* magazine and other representatives of the national press, who left duly impressed with the new league and its marquee team. "About $10,000 worth of fireworks were exploded," wrote Jimmy Powers in the *New York Daily News*. "A leggy chorus of devastating beauties knocked the customers dizzy with intricate midfield ballet work that can be compared only to New York's Radio City Rockettes. A new automobile was given away as a door prize. . . . A midget [Tommy Flynn, the team's "Brownie" mascot] led a swing orchestra through the latest hit parade and two French chefs with white mushroom hats appeared in the press box and proceeded to carve giant roasts of beef."

The game itself was an embarrassing mismatch. Faster, stronger, and much better prepared, the Browns coasted to a 44–0 victory over the Miami Seahawks.

The Browns outclassed their opposition, rolling through their first six games by a combined score of 149–20, and it wasn't until their seventh game, at home against the Los Angeles Dons, that they trailed at halftime. Motley stormed through the Dons for touchdown runs of 47 and 68 yards in the second half, en route to a 31–14 win. Dons coach Dudley DeGroot (who the year before had coached the Redskins to the NFL title game) remarked that Motley was "the greatest I've ever seen. A fullback that can run that fast when he gets out, and won't be tackled by only one man, when you have that you have something."

The Browns had something else: a passing attack more sophisticated than any other team in the league, and a willingness to throw in any situation, at a time when many coaches were still adhering to the belief that teams should never throw within their own 20-yard line, and some teams still punted or quick-kicked rather than try to advance the ball on third-and-long. Graham took over the starting quarterback job from Cliff Lewis after three games, and went on to earn All-League honors as a rookie. After two losses in the middle of the season, the Browns rolled through the rest of the regular season schedule without being pressed, finishing 12-2 and drawing a professional record of 339,962 fans for the seven regular season home games.

While Graham was the natural team leader at quarterback, the offensive key to the team was Motley, who forced defenses to bunch up for the run, leaving them more vulnerable to the pass. On the other side of the line, Willis was just as dominant, seeming to play the game in a different gear than other linemen.

During the opening rout of the Seahawks, Miami was as confounded by Willis's speed as Mo Scarry had been upon Willis's arrival in training camp. Reports circulated of Willis's quickness, marking the first of countless occasions in the postwar era in which a black player's excellence in pro football was attributed to athletic ability. But Willis was in fact small for the position, at 6-foot-2, 210 pounds; the key to his rush was his attention to the minutest movements in the center's fingers, and a series of sluicing swim moves to evade blocks that made him one of the canniest linemen of his era.

When the Browns traveled to Miami to face the woeful Seahawks later in the season, Motley and Willis stayed back in Cleveland because of a Florida state law that prohibited whites and blacks from competing on the same field. (The Browns routed the Seahawks again, 34–0.) Motley and Willis encountered racism in virtually every game they played. "There were times in games when I'd be punched by an opponent after a play, or called a black S.O.B.," recalled Willis. "Lou [Groza] and Lou Rymkus, another lineman, said to me, 'Don't let anybody excite you. If there's trouble, tell us. We'll handle it.' I never had to say anything. We were in the trenches together and they'd know. And the two would take care of the guy. It was comforting to have teammates like that, believe me."

"That kind of crap went on for two or three years," said Motley, "until they found out what kind of players we were. They found out that while they were calling us 'niggers,' I was running for touchdowns and Willis was knocking the shit out of them. They stopped calling us names and started to catch up with us."

The team's organizational innovations didn't end with training camp. With the largest coaching staff in pro football, Brown could afford to spare one assistant, Red Conkright, to serve as an advance scout, traveling on weekends to the game of Cleveland's next opponent. Conkright's scouting reports were incorporated into the weekly game plans that Brown distributed to the team. Writing it up and mimeographing it Tuesday night to be handed out at Wednesday's meetings, the "Brown News" could run up to twenty-five pages.

While Conkright's analysis was given plenty of weight, Collier's input frequently was crucial. At Great Lakes, Collier's scouting and game plan abilities had been instrumental in the team's upset of Notre Dame in 1943. He was equally effective in the pros; after the Browns suffered their first loss of the 1946 season, a 34–20 defeat at the hands of San Francisco, Collier devoted extra time to dissecting films from the game. Two weeks later, when the teams met again in San Francisco, Cleveland shut down the 49ers and Frankie Albert, 14–7.

Cleveland's practices during the week were the least physical in the sport. Pro teams typically gave their players Mondays off, but Brown gave his players Monday and Tuesday off, allowing the staff more time to review the previous game and assemble the scouting report for the next opponent. Wednesdays and Saturdays called for short run-throughs. Thursday and Friday were the busiest days, with extensive film study and game plan meetings in the morning, and practices in the afternoon. Each practice—scheduled at 1:00 p.m. to coincide with kickoff times on Sunday—began with tackling drills, but no other significant physical contact. "A coach who scrimmages doesn't know how to teach," Brown said, keenly aware that virtually every other coach in the game scrimmaged at least once a week during the season.

As in training camp, Brown attempted to cast his influence far beyond the field. "Paul was the one who originated the Tuesday rule," said Otto Graham. "No sex with your wives after Tuesday night. . . . 'Save yourself for the game,' he'd tell us. We kidded about that. I guess it shows the morality of that time. Paul didn't recognize that sex existed outside the marriage. I kept asking him, 'What about the single men?' and Paul never answered."

During the season, the night before home games, he brought the Browns together in the Hotel Carter. The team would eat dinner together, then attend a movie before returning to the hotel for the night, with a kiss good night to wives and girlfriends (invited to the movies, but excluded from the dinner) in the Carter lobby. On the road, Brown followed the same procedure, and discouraged sightseeing. "This is a business trip, nothing more, nothing less," he said.

On game days, the team was rested and focused, having been spared any rigorous physical contact during the week, and after spending much of the last twenty-four hours before kickoff together. The pregame speeches were terse and usually dispassionate. Brown might say, "Say your prayers, and let's get going," and leave it at that.

The first AAFC championship game, played against Dan Topping's New York Yankees (who had been renamed after bolting from the NFL after the 1945 season), would prove another example, as if one were needed, of Brown's absolute authority.

After the team returned from its regular-season-ending 66–14 win at Brooklyn, lineman and team captain Jim Daniell hit the town with Lou Rymkus and Mac Speedie. Pulling up behind a police car, Daniell laid on the horn in an attempt to have the officer move. When the officer got out of his car to investigate, the ensuing confrontation landed the belligerent Daniell at the station, on a drunk-and-disorderly charge. The next morning, as the team gathered in the locker room after practice, Brown confronted Daniell in front of the team.

"Is what I read in the paper true?" Brown asked. Daniell confirmed that it was.

"Fine," said Brown. "Turn in your suit."

"Don't you want to hear my side of the story?" asked Daniell.

"No, you're through."

Daniell was kicked off the team less than forty-eight hours before the AAFC championship game. Rymkus and Speedie, both key starters, were let off with a stern warning.

"We were a young team and Paul had us in the palm of his hand after that," Otto Graham later explained. "We thought, if he could do that to Jim

Daniell, he'd do it to anyone. Daniell's backup was a lineman who was just about as good as Jim. But I didn't realize that until later. What Paul did was get a message across to us, and not hurt the team, either. For years, veteran players told rookies about the day Paul Brown cut Jim Daniell, and that just made him even bigger and more powerful in the eyes of the young players."

The game itself was a tightly fought contest, with the Yankees, though outgained 315 yards to 146, laboring heroically, to lead 3–0 after a quarter and 9–7 at the end of the third period, before Graham led the Browns on the game-winning drive late in the fourth quarter. At the end of the game, with the 40,000 in attendance storming the field, Brown's players lifted their coach to their shoulders and marched him into the locker room. His players' winning shares were $931.57, with the deposed Daniell voted a full share.

Afterward, Brown seemed more relieved than thrilled, remarking, "It was a long afternoon." But he was satisfied with his first year of professional football, and not reluctant to discuss the implications. "For the players' sake, too," he said, "I'm tickled with that victory. But my satisfaction is in proving that the same ideas and ideals that won in high school and college can win, too, in pro ball. That makes me happy."

———

One more important element of the game would change under Brown in that first year. Prior to 1946, it was common for head coaches and their assistants to take four to six months away from football, working off-season jobs in the winter and spring. Brown was convinced that if he could pay his assistants enough to work year-round, as they did at the largest college programs (where recruiting made it a necessity), there was an edge to be gained in doing so.

After the season, Blanton Collier headed home to his house in Kentucky with films from all fifteen games of the 1946 season, a hand-crank projector and a special viewer that would allow him to magnify part of the picture and examine a single player on the film one frame at a time. Squirreling himself away for long days and evenings in an upstairs room in the family's home, Collier examined every Cleveland player's performance on every play of the previous season.

Collier's job was twofold. First, he would combine the grades of each player on each play to come up with a percentage of made and missed assignments—he and Brown determined that a player needed to complete his assignment at least 80 percent of the time to be successful.

The second was the grand analysis that Brown had dreamed of, and that Collier executed. By cataloguing each play the team called, Brown and Collier could see how a particular play had done over the course of the season.

One example: The team's "24" play, an off-tackle slant with the left half-back, was run 27 times during the 1946 season, gaining a total of 102 yards, or 3.77 yards per carry. Three of the plays resulted in touchdowns. On the reasoning that a perfectly executed play should always result in a touchdown, the other 24 were considered failures. Collier's careful analysis revealed the reasons for each instance in which the play didn't result in a score ("Four times when the left tackle made a poor block on the opponents' right tackle. . . . Once when the left halfback hit the hole too wide").

The results, compiled in a thick report that Collier submitted to Brown late in the spring of 1947, was the most extensive performance analysis done in the history of football to that date, and it gave the Browns a secret window to their own offensive personality. Brown, suitably proud of the report, referred to it as his "flaw-finder."

And in the zero-sum world of football coaching, the flaw-finder and the information it revealed was a key component in keeping the Browns ahead of the crowd. During the 1947 and 1948 seasons, the team would lose just one game, in the process winning two more league titles.

As in every other industry, the methods that were the most successful in football were widely copied. "When everyone else had two assistants in '46, he had six," said Lou Spadia, the vice president of the 49ers. "And so in '47, everyone else had six. No one ever put their team up at a hotel the night before a home game. Shit, he does it and now everyone else has to do it."

By 1948, Brown had become the most influential coach in America. His annual coaching clinic in Cleveland was attended by more than 2,000 coaches, and his speeches to this group amounted to a football manifesto.

"You must earn morale, you can't make it or develop it," said Brown. "Morale comes from the coach. You must be an all-out person. You have to love the game, show interest in it, work hard at it. You have to feel it; it has to come from the heart. Your wife should support you, and she should be concerned about how much time you put in on it. I compare it to the commitment that is made when a person decides to become a priest. You have to be a football crackpot; there are no shortcuts."

In the audience, a group of football crackpots looked on, assiduously taking notes, spreading the Brown philosophy. Though the AAFC's future was murky, the success of Paul Brown was guaranteed. He had recast football in his image.

Brown's words at that first training camp—about wanting to be the most amateur team in professional football—would be oft-quoted. What he'd accomplished, though, was in some ways the opposite. With precious few pep talks or appeals to emotion, he had taken a game dominated by near-amateurs, and instilled it with a sophisticated, professional air. Or as he himself would put it in a less guarded moment, "We're getting the guesswork out of football. We're making a science out of what is called a game."

3

"Let Bert Do It"

I n their time of crisis, confronted with the specter of Arch Ward, Paul Brown, and an AAFC bankrolled by multimillionaires, the NFL owners had selected as their new commissioner a cash-poor blueblood who had been, arguably, the worst head coach in league history, mustering just 10 wins in five-plus seasons.

But what the owners were looking for in 1946 wasn't a celebrity figurehead or a polished boardroom presence or a proven winner with an aura of genius. They instead sought a fighter, someone who didn't need to be sold on the virtues of their sport, or briefed on the intricacies of its problems. And in the indefatigable presence of Bert Bell, they found their beacon of hope, a man whose unquenchable love for football was so close to blind adoration as to make no difference. "His mission in life was football," said George Halas. "He had a sure instinct for conducting the business of the game."

Bell still bore vestiges of his old self, the playboy raconteur of the '20s with slicked-back hair, by now silver, and an estimable paunch, neatly draped in blue serge suits during the fall and winter, and tan gabardine in the summer. His voice was a thing of wonder, a deep, growling baritone that projected through office walls and over static-filled phone lines. He was a voluble man of motion, generally heard before seen. And he was what pro football needed most at the time: a true believer.

His hiring came at a critical moment, and not only because of the challenge of the AAFC. The league was in danger of imploding, beset by factional rivalries and legislative paralysis, a result of ten strong-willed men, each with definite ideas about why their beloved sport was losing so much money.

Even worse than the yelling and arguing were the intractable, soul-deadening stalemates, when long stretches of time went by in which nothing was said, when the only sound in the room was two or more men fuming. While numerous gatherings deteriorated to these standoffs, the league's annual meetings were particularly brutal because they involved the perennial exercise in argumentation, the drawing up of the coming season's schedule.

The schedule itself—the selection of opponents and the sequence of games—was a crucial element in each team's home game ticket sales, which in turn were the single most important revenue source for each club. So from the earliest days of the league, owners devoted days and days to obdurate, petulant haggling over the competing claims on the coming season's schedule.

With the ten-team league separated into two divisions in 1933, the only definitive rules were those that stipulated that every team should play a home-and-home series against every other team within its division. But that would account for just eight of each team's twelve games. Beyond that, every owner wanted his own advantage; every team in the East wanted the Bears to visit; every team in the West wanted the Redskins to visit. And each team wanted to go on the road to play teams that drew well, because visiting teams got a 40 percent share of the gate, after allowing for stadium rental.

This issue was, in a real sense, why a league office was needed in the first place: an impartial arbiter to determine qualifications, league games, rules, procedures, and, when possible, to help generate publicity on behalf of the entire enterprise. In theory, it was the league's job to mediate these disputes and find equitable solutions to problems such as the schedule. In reality, Layden and Joe Carr before him had found this difficult, if not impossible, to do.

"The owners who had the staying power were the ones who came away with the decent schedules," said Art Rooney. "The guys who snuck out to get some sleep or go night-clubbing wound up getting murdered the next season because when they weren't there to defend themselves, we'd give them all the dates we didn't want." Even those who stuck around to fight often felt victimized by cronyism and the perception that the oldest franchises looked out for themselves to the exclusion of others.

So owners learned to dread the annual meetings, and the battles that would invariably follow. Minutes from meetings in the '40s often included the shorthand euphemism, "There was a general and lengthy discussion on the problems of the game schedule." Entire sessions might consist of this notation alone. Or, from the 1948 meeting, a notation that beginning with the evening of January 15, "discussion on the schedule took place from 3:50 to 7 PM, 8 PM to 2 AM, 10:45 AM to 1:45 PM and 2:55 to 6 PM." On one occasion, after three days of debate resulted in a schedule finally being placed in its entirety on a chalkboard, the Redskins' George Preston Marshall—angry that he hadn't gotten either of the swing home games he coveted—walked up to the chalkboard and quickly erased the entire chart, eliciting curses and howls, since no one at the meeting had yet committed the schedule to paper.

It was hoped that the well-liked Bell could bring some equanimity to the proceedings, but both the 1946 and 1947 meetings deteriorated into the usual protracted discussions, in which nothing was settled. Wellington Mara, son of Giants owner Tim Mara, was just then getting his first taste of league meetings. "The schedules would always take several days and Bert always found time to be politic," said Mara. "All the clubs were very jealous of the schedules and no one trusted anyone. After a while, people started walking out of the league meetings and saying, 'Let Bert do it.' "

And for the next dozen seasons, Bell did.

Though he endeavored to meet each team's specific needs, his scheduling was guided by an overall philosophy. "Weak teams should play other weak teams while the strong teams are playing other strong teams early in the year," he once explained. "It's the only way to keep more teams in contention longer into the season." That his intent was to help teams at the box office was undeniable. But the function of Bell's machinations was to make the league more competitive, and to keep more teams in the race longer into the season.

Each off-season, Bell would devote himself to this task, often to the exclusion of all others, and spend hundreds of hours fashioning dozens of different prospective schedules, while juggling the various commitments, requests, blackout dates, and other variables. Sitting at his dining room table, he worked with a huge cardboard placard, laid out in a grid fashion, with team names running along the top and game dates running down the side. Next to the board would be dozens of dominoes, borrowed from his sons, Bert Jr. and Upton, each with a team name Scotch-taped on the back, along with several books of paper matches. When Bell wanted Philadelphia to play at Washington on a certain date, he'd find the date on the left-hand side of the board, and on that line he'd place a domino with Philadelphia's name on it into the two-inch-square box below Washington's heading. On the same line, he'd then place a match into the box under Philadelphia's heading, to indicate the Eagles had been assigned a road game that week.

For weeks on end, Bell would fill out numerous schedules in this fashion, drinking coffee and sipping grape juice, breaking only for dinner at seven and, later on, his nightly constitutional to Davis' Drugstore a few blocks away in downtown Narberth, the Philadelphia suburb where he lived. Armed with a small container of chocolate ice cream, he would return to his schedules and work late into the night, taking phone calls with a long extension cord, copying off possible schedules on smaller pieces of cardboard when he was finished. He would then weigh each against the others, noting minor adjustments among the countless different combinations, before presenting one or more to the assembled owners.

There were other factors besides the schedule that contributed to the change, but Bell's intention of keeping the league more balanced was soon realized. From 1937 to 1946, the Packers and Bears from the Western Division and the Giants and Redskins from the Eastern took nineteen of the twenty spots in the NFL championship game. Beginning with 1947, that would change, with even longtime doormats like the Eagles and Cardinals rising to the top. As caretaker of and ambassador for the game, Bell quickly developed a mind-set in which the league was only as healthy as its weakest team. His son Upton would recall him returning home after Sunday games and proudly calling upstairs to his wife, Frances, "Mother, guess what? It's week four, and they're all still in the race."

———

Those in Bell's social circle had expected different, grander things. He was the squire of a Philadelphia Main Line family whose father, John Cromwell Bell, was among the most prominent lawyers in the Philadelphia area, and the Pennsylvania state attorney general from 1911 to 1915. The elder Bell, who played football at Penn in the 1880s, was chairman of the school's athletic council, was second in seniority to Walter Camp on college football's seminal Football Rules Committee, whose reforms saved the sport in 1906.

De Benneville Bell was born February 25, 1895; because there were many "De Benneville Bertrams" in his lineage, he was known as "Bert" from an early age. "If you don't think I had to fight to get people to call me 'Bert,' " he told one reporter, "then I must have dreamed all those schoolyard battles." He grew up muscular and affable, and by all accounts unspoiled by this luxurious upbringing. Bert starred in football, baseball, and basketball at the Haverford School outside of Philadelphia, but when speculation rose about him going to one of the emerging football powers outside the state, his father immediately and publicly quashed it. "He'll go to Penn," John C. Bell told a newspaper reporter, "or he'll go to hell." Bell indeed went to Penn in 1914, majoring in English and playing football for three years as quarterback. In 1916, Penn went 7-2-1 and accepted a bid to the Rose Bowl. Bell started at quarterback in the game, January 1, 1917, where unbeaten Oregon prevailed, 14–0. After a two-year stint with an army medical unit in France, he returned to captain Penn's football team in 1919, graduated in 1920, and returned that fall as an assistant for Penn head coach John Heisman, where he remained on staff through 1928.

Though he worked nominally as a stockbroker during the '20s, Bell spent the decade living a life not unlike the romanticized cinematic visions of the '20s, frequenting nightclubs, dancehalls, and speakeasies, tooling around town in a cherry-red Marmon roadster and a coonskin coat, playing with equal vigor the stock market, the gambling halls, and the horses, devoting the month of August to the summer season at Saratoga. On summer Saturdays in Chelsea, when his father would leave for Philadelphia to attend church services the following morning, Bert Bell would often throw a party, hosting his eclectic assemblage of friends—ranging from entertainers like Bob Hope and Cesar Romero to blue-collar acquaintances from the resort town.

After a series of financial setbacks, Bell was working for his father, managing the Ritz-Carlton Hotel on Broad Street. It was there he met the musical comedy actress and former Ziegfeld dancer Frances Upton, a sweet, vivacious dazzler with a dramatic streak and a staunch moral fiber, a perfectly complicated Catholic beauty of the modern age. Between starring roles in such Broadway hits as *Whoopee!*, with Eddie Cantor, Frances Upton often performed sets at the Ritz's small, swanky rooftop lounge. Doting on Frances, the smitten Bell would wait until she finished her performance, then escort her to a nearby Catholic church where a mass was held at two in the morning for late-shift printers and newspaper workers. While the daily communicant Frances went inside, Bert remained outside on the street, reading the paper, joshing with the police officers, and watching the nightlife. One summer night when Bert professed his undying love to Frances, she told him she could never marry a drinking man. Surrounded by friends, he ordered one last drink and downed it, then vowed to her he would never touch alcohol again. By all accounts, he didn't; they were married January 4, 1934.

The previous summer, Bell had borrowed $2,500 from his fiancée and, along with his former Penn teammate Lud Wray, headed a syndicate that bought the NFL's defunct Frankford Yellow Jackets franchise, a pro power in the '20s that had gone bankrupt during the 1931 season. Renaming the team the Eagles, after the eagle logo on the National Recovery Administration's emblem ("We Do Our Part"), Bell and Wray took over the club and rejoined the NFL for the 1933 season.

It was clear from the day he bought the Eagles that Bert Bell had found his calling, and in the coming years he would serve as owner, coach, trainer, general manager, ticket-taker, and janitor. Walking along the Jersey shore during their honeymoon, Frances looked up to the clear night sky and said to Bert, "Gee, look at the moon." He gazed up at the night sky and smiled. "Frances," he said, "I only wish I had a punter who could kick that high."

The Eagles were not immediately embraced by the city. Even though his playing costs were modest—Bell paid some players as little as $15 per game—stadium rentals were steep, the team drew poorly, and the losses were alarming. Over their first three seasons, the Eagles lost more than $80,000 and the partnership went bankrupt after the 1935 season. When the team was put up for auction in 1936, Bell was the only bidder, buying out his partners for $4,500, and installing himself to replace Wray as head coach. By that time, Bell had already made a lasting contribution to pro football.

After two seasons with the Eagles, it had become apparent to Bell that the league was becoming dangerously stratified. The three perennial contenders—the Bears, Packers, and Giants—were the only clubs that flirted with profitability, while the remainder of clubs were rarely in contention and suffered heavy losses. The best players coming out of college were, naturally, more inclined to sign with teams where their earning power and chances of success were high.

Bell had been particularly discouraged by his fruitless efforts to sign Stan "King Kong" Kostka, a brawny fullback who'd transferred from Oregon to Minnesota in time to play for the Gophers' first national championship team in 1934. After contacting Kostka by phone, Bell took a train from Philadelphia to Minneapolis, and they met in the lobby of a hotel. Kostka said the best offer he'd received from another team was $3,500, and Bell offered $4,000. Hedging, Kostka said he wanted an hour to consider it. When they met later, Kostka was still noncommittal. After Bell increased his offer to $6,000, Kostka still balked, and after further flirtations later signed with the NFL's Brooklyn Dodgers. Bell returned to Philadelphia discouraged, and convinced the whole system needed to be fixed. "I made up my mind that this league would never survive unless we had some system whereby each team had an even chance to bid for talent against the other," said Bell.

His reasoning led to the radical proposal he floated the following spring, during the league meetings of 1935. "Gentlemen, I've always had the theory that pro football is like a chain," he told his fellow owners. "The league is no stronger than its weakest link—and I've been a weak link for so long that I should know. Every year the rich get richer and the poor get poorer." Bell suggested that the dominance of the Giants, Bears, and Packers meant that the league's other teams were at a functional disadvantage in recruiting new players. "Here's what I propose," he said. "At the end of each football season, I suggest that we pool the names of all eligible college seniors. Then we make our selections in inverse order of the standings—that is, the lowest-ranked team picks first. We do this round after round until we have exhausted the supply of college players."

There's no record that Bell used the word "draft" in this proposal, but when the motion was approved, reporters quickly called a spade a spade, and the NFL draft was born. The Bears and Giants, who had played in both of the league's first two scheduled title games in 1933 and 1934, had the most to lose from such an arrangement. But both Halas and Tim Mara went along with it. "People come to see a competition," Mara explained. "We could give them a competition only if the teams had some sort of equality, if the teams went up and down with the fortunes of life. Of course, that meant that no team would in the future win a championship every third year and people would start saying, 'What's happened to the Giants? They aren't the team they used to be.' That was a hazard we had to accept for the benefit of the league, of professional football and everyone in it."

The Eagles went 2-9 in 1935, earning Bell and the Eagles the dubious right to select first in the league's first "annual selection meeting," held February 8, 1936, at the Ritz-Carlton in Philadelphia. Bell selected Chicago halfback Jay Berwanger, winner of the inaugural DAC Trophy, presented by the Downtown Athletic Club of New York City to the best player east of the Mississippi. (A year later, after the death of Bell's former coach, DAC director John Heisman, the trophy was renamed the Heisman Trophy, and players across the country became eligible.) But Berwanger chose not to turn pro and, in fact, the Eagles were unable to sign any of their nine selections in that first draft.

Though it would take at least a decade before scouting systems became sophisticated enough to have any success at reliably identifying pro prospects, Bell's concept was a crucial element in equalizing talent and competition throughout the league. He was not to profit, however, from his own innovation. Starting with his first season as sole owner and head coach in 1936, Bell's Eagles finished fifth, fifth, fourth, fourth, and fifth in the five-team Eastern Division.

In the face of these persistent failures, his enthusiasm never wavered. He'd beat the streets, often buttonholing fellow members outside Philadelphia's Racquet Club, or leaving a packet of tickets behind the bar at Lew Tendler's

Saloon, close to the Ritz. He'd even been known to stand on an island in the middle of rush-hour traffic on Broad Street to hawk tickets at passing cars. But the losses mounted, and by the end of the 1940 season Bell was in another financial crisis. "Bert was a guy that just squandered his money," said one family friend. "I mean he was a good person and he wasn't out drinking or doing any of that kind of stuff. But he just didn't have control of his money."

The Steelers' Art Rooney would bail him out of his crisis, through a complex series of procedures. First Rooney sold the Steelers to New York millionaire Alexis Thompson, then put up a stake to buy a half-interest in the Eagles. Then, Rooney and Bell swapped franchises with Thompson, along with the players themselves. Historian Bob Carroll, founder of the Professional Football Researchers Association, summarized it thusly: "Bert and Art brought the Eagles to Pittsburgh and renamed them the 'Steelers.' Meanwhile, Thompson took the Steelers to Philadelphia and renamed them 'Eagles.' Most of the former Philadelphia players wound up in Pittsburgh and [vice versa]. As late as 1945 the Steelers were officially owned by the Philadelphia Football Club, Inc. . . . Just about everybody ignores the technically correct descent, and it's probably best that they do. I mean, how convoluted do you want your pro football history to be?"

Asked about the deal years later, Art Rooney could only throw up his hands. "Things were different then," he said. "Money was tough to come by."

So in 1941, Bell and Rooney were running the Steelers, with Rooney serving as general manager and Bell coaching yet again. A picture from the period shows Bell, proudly standing on the field, in a fedora and T-shirt, "Pittsburgh Steelers Football Club" neatly stenciled across the chest, whistle around his neck, two-tone buckskin shoes peeking out beneath khaki slacks. After beginning the 1941 season with an 0-2 record, a morose Bell returned to Pittsburgh and suggested to Rooney that the team make some deals.

"People in Pittsburgh are tired of our deals," said Rooney, chomping his ever-present cigar. "They always backfire."

"What do you think we should do?" asked Bell.

"Bert," said Rooney, "did you ever think about changing coaches?" Bell heeded his friend's advice and retired from coaching for good, moving to the Steelers' front office, where he and Rooney would soldier on through World War II. Combined with his ignominious five years in Philadelphia, Bell compiled a 10-46-2 record in the NFL. His .190 winning percentage is the worst in NFL history among coaches with five seasons or more experience.

When the war ended and the time came to replace Layden, Bell was the insider who was quickly chosen. "Those guys—Halas, Marshall, Bell, Rooney, Mara, Bidwill—those six pretty much were the guys that ran the show," said Dan Rooney, who grew up watching his father's enduring friendship with Bell. "And so when they were ready to make a change, they just came to the conclusion that Bert could do it. Bert could go back to Philadelphia and run the league. And it was an obvious choice from the standpoint of what they wanted to do: make one of their own, who could become available, the commissioner. I mean, you know, Halas couldn't become available, Marshall couldn't become available. Bert was one who could."

————

"Pro football has growing pains," wrote John Lardner in *Newsweek* in 1945. "The end of the war may be the event which will build the sport into national proportions both geographically and commercially, just as the end of the last war gave pro players their original impetus and made them begin to think of organization and respectability." In this, Lardner proved prophetic. The country was mobilizing for a series of broad social changes each of which, in its own way, would benefit pro football.

More than 16 million Americans had joined the armed forces during World War II, and 12 million of them—about two thirds of all American men between the ages of eighteen and thirty-four—were still in uniform when the war concluded in August of 1945. Within a year, nine million of them had moved to civilian life. Many would take part in the GI Bill of Rights, signed in 1944, which in addition to providing aid for housing and business start-ups, provided returning vets with monthly stipends to cover educational expenses. When the program ended in 1945, nearly two million had gone to college with GI Bill assistance. Almost 500,000 Americans graduated from colleges in 1950, compared to 216,500 in 1940. That sweeping change affected campus life and campus athletics, and it surely affected the quality and quantity of football players eligible for the NFL's draft.

Salaries increased sharply in pro football and, for the first time, there was something of a decent living to be made. Even pedestrian players returning from the war in 1945 made more than the annual per capita disposable income in current dollars of $1,074.

Television research, which had been virtually suspended with the beginning of American involvement in World War II, was again a top-priority issue for businesses, and sales in the U.S. would increase exponentially in the years ahead. The effects of the baby boom would solidify the growth of spectator sports in the '60s and '70s, but even in the late '40s, it was clear that Americans were going to have more free time and more spending money. By the end of the decade, the U.S. accounted for 7 percent of the world's population and 42 percent of its income.

With this postwar prosperity as a backdrop, and a nation embracing its pastimes in a return to normal, the NFL's and AAFC's "war between the leagues" was a big story. From the moment he assumed office, Bell was prepared to fight. And he did so initially by refusing to discuss the challengers. Upon taking the job in January 1946, he said, "Sure I recognize there's a rival professional league in operation, trying to take our players and buck us at the gate. But I expect to be so busy with the affairs of the National League that I will have no time to think about the other circuit." He moved the league offices from Chicago, where Layden was based, to New York and, after wearying of the daily commute, in 1948 to Philadelphia, first to a spot near the University of Pennsylvania campus, then to Center City Philadelphia, in an office building at 1518 Walnut Street.

The challenge of the AAFC was as formidable as expected. Arch Ward's league was an unusual upstart, because it brought so many advantages that rival leagues in the past hadn't enjoyed: by the end of 1946, Paul Brown was probably the best-known pro football coach in America and his organization was justly celebrated; Ward's role in the formation of the league and his influence throughout the country meant that the new league would have little trouble getting press.

The AAFC possessed a roster of owners who were much wealthier than their NFL counterparts. The new league had real estate magnates like Mickey McBride, Anthony J. Morabito in San Francisco, with vast holdings in the lumber business, trucking company owner John L. Keeshin in Chicago, and the Los Angeles syndicate fronted by Don Ameche, MGM head Louis B. Mayer, and Benjamin Lindheimer, a millionaire sportsman who owned horse tracks. Arrayed against those forces, the NFL could offer only stability and tradition. The league's decision to continue operating during the lean days of World War II thus proved crucial. Had it suspended operations during the war, then tried to resume on equal footing with the AAFC in 1946, the war between the leagues might have been much more of a toss-up.

As it was, the NFL was more popular than ever in 1946. With the lifting of travel restrictions, it resumed its barnstorming exhibition schedule, with the Redskins opening in Los Angeles, playing in front of 68,188 at the first Los Angeles Times Charity Game, and playing games across the Southeast. The league broke its all-time attendance record in the regular season, averaging more than 31,000 per regular season game.

But for all the success at the box office, the season was less successful in the public perception. The AAFC took its share of headlines, with Paul Brown and the Cleveland Browns featured in virtually every magazine in the country that covered sports, including *Time, Life,* and *Newsweek.* The College All-Star Game, the annual exhibition opener between the defending NFL champion and a squad of college stars, took on a different meaning with the Ward-orchestrated AAFC challenge to the NFL. Many NFL owners were convinced that AAFC teams were offering an invitation to the All-Star Game for those who signed with the new league, which helped to explain why forty-four of the sixty All-Stars were headed to the new league. Harder to explain was the final score, a 16–0 win for the All-Stars over the Los Angeles Rams.

But the greatest crisis was an internal one. The 1946 campaign found the Giants and Bears back on top of their respective divisions. Midway through the season, New York shut out Chicago, 14–0, in a championship preview, then coasted to the Eastern Conference title. Yet the week before the title game, on the streets in New York, it was the Bears who were installed as 10-point favorites over the Giants. This raised the suspicion of New York detectives, who eventually uncovered an attempt to fix the 1946 NFL championship game.

Back in Philadelphia on the eve of the game, Bell received a late-night call from New York mayor William O'Dwyer, who had called Giants running back Merle Hapes and quarterback Frank Filchock to Gracie Mansion, where he and city detectives interrogated them. Filchock insisted he hadn't heard a word about a proposed fix, while Hapes admitted to the bribe attempt, from Sidney Paris, a convicted felon who'd served four years for mail fraud, and had joined a group of Giants boosters at an Elks Lodge gathering in New York City in late November. Paris had spent the intervening weeks befriending Hapes and Filchock, taking them out to the Copacabana, buying them drinks, offering them jobs in the off-season, then had proposed, a week earlier, that each man could become rich by making sure that the Giants lost by at least 10 points in the title game. Faced with that evidence, and with just hours to go before the game, Bell suspended Hapes but agreed to let Filchock play.

Under suspicion still, Filchock played valiantly the next day and though he threw six interceptions in the 24–14 loss, few questioned that he had tried his best. But in subsequent months, as the case went to court, Filchock later admitted that he had been approached by gamblers as well. It would turn out that while both players turned down Paris's proposals, neither reported the case to the league, leaving the impression in the informed circles of underworld gambling that the fix was in. Bell suspended both players indefinitely.

At the January 1947 meetings, owners gave the commissioner the latitude to suspend for life any player or team official involved in a game-fixing attempt. Hapes and Filchock were suspended indefinitely; Hapes, reinstated in 1954, never played in the NFL again, while Filchock, reinstated in 1950, threw three passes for the Baltimore Colts that season and retired.

Bell's action was decisive and crucial to public confidence. Coming on the heels of the Brooklyn basketball point-shaving incident, in an era when corruption was widespread in boxing, and the 1919 Black Sox World Series scandal had occurred in most fans' lifetimes, the threat of game fixing was pervasive and severe.

Bell was convinced that the league needed to do more. In announcing the Hapes and Filchock suspensions in April 1947, he stated, "Professional football cannot continue to exist unless it is based upon absolute honesty. The players must be not only absolutely honest; they must be above suspicion. In short, the game and its players must be kept free from corruption, from all bribes and offers of bribes and from any possible 'fixing' of games." Two months later, Bell announced that with the beginning of the 1947 season, the league would publish in advance of each game a list of players who were injured and would be unable or unlikely to play. (This would be the precursor to the detailed injury lists that would become a staple of midweek agate type in the '70s.) With the move, Bell struck a blow for fairness and open information and also, paradoxically, made the first in a series of moves that would increase betting interest in and gambling on pro football. It was certainly in the NFL's interests to guarantee the public that the game was honest and conducted fairly, and distributing names of injured players furthered that cause. But it also gave those inclined to bet more information with which to place their wager as well as greater confidence that they were betting on an honest competition.

Bell was hardly a prude about gambling. A good deal of the money that built the league had come from it—Tim Mara had been a bookmaker on the lawn at Saratoga, Art Rooney owned a horse track and was a skilled horse player (faithfully reporting his winnings to the IRS), and the Bidwills owned a track, and made a fortune in the printing of pari-mutuel tickets. Bell's philosophy was distinctly not one of pretending that gambling didn't exist, but rather that it must be monitored by the league. His preoccupation was that people, whether they gambled or not, be reassured that the game was clean and beyond reproach.

Having won for the time being a battle for public confidence in the honesty of the game, Bell and the league returned their attention in 1947 to the war of attrition with the AAFC. With salaries skyrocketing in 1946 and 1947, it seemed that deeper pockets might be decisive. The only teams to show a profit in 1946 were the two league champions, the Browns in the AAFC (showing a profit of $10,553.89) and Halas's Bears. The AAFC owners were prepared to lose money, and they did. In that inaugural 1946 season, the San Francisco 49ers lost $51,000. Franchises in New York, Chicago, and Los Angeles—fighting in markets with established NFL teams—each suffered greater losses. For all that, the league was developing a following, not just in Cleveland, but in Buffalo, Los Angeles (where the Dons initially outdrew the Rams on the strength of star Glen Dobbs and a better record), and San Francisco, where the 49ers were playing an exciting brand of football, with former Stanford quarterback Frankie Albert leading Buck Shaw's slick T formation attack.

Yet Bell's strategy remained the same. When private overtures were made by Ben Lindheimer for the leagues to meet after the 1946 season, Bell declined to meet. Publicly, as well, he refused to recognize the league in any meaningful way. When asked about the AAFC, his standard answer was, "No comment." When the annual *Pro Football Illustrated*—a picture-filled staple of concession stands throughout the league—chose to preview both the NFL and the AAFC in 1947, the publication was banned from NFL stadiums.

The AAFC owners would realize that the NFL's owners were more resilient than they had hoped. Though the teams in Brooklyn and New York had hurt the Giants, neither could gain a foothold of its own. The Chicago Rockets were doomed in what became the three-team market of Chicago, especially when the Cardinals rose up to win the NFL title in 1947 and advance to the title game again in 1948. At one point that season, the increasingly desperate Arch Ward requested a private meeting with Brown and asked him to "send" Otto Graham to the Rockets for the good of the league, reasoning that the quarterback, raised in nearby Waukegan, would be a boon to the Rockets' woeful attendance. This elicited a predictable response. Ward biographer Thomas B. Littlewood wrote that "the coach fixed the sports editor in his cold stare, issued an emphatic 'no,' and that was the last of that."

Throughout the 1947 and 1948 seasons, as losses continued to mount in both leagues, there was some back-channel communication. By the beginning of 1949, columnist Stanley Woodward noted that the AAFC was "being held together principally by Ward's skill and generosity in spending other people's money."

But the real problem was more fundamental—a lack of competition had dampened interest in the AAFC in every city. Cleveland had been the dominant team in the AAFC from day one, and their superiority was becoming so accepted, it began to hurt the gate throughout the league. After dropping a game to the Los Angeles Dons on October 12, 1947, the Browns went nearly two years without another loss, winning the title with a 12-1-1 record in 1947, sweeping through the 1948 schedule at 14-0, then beginning the 1949 season at 4-0-1 before the 49ers ambushed them in San Francisco, 56–28, on October 2, 1949.

Browns players from that era would long remember their coach's speech after the streak finally ended with the loss to the 49ers. Returning to their hotel in Los Angeles, where they'd remain for another week to play the Dons, some expected Brown would be conciliatory. They soon found out otherwise. "There's a bus outside waiting to take you through the movie studios," he announced to the team. "Have fun. I don't see how you can. Not after the way you played against San Francisco. I'm telling you this and it's cold turkey. If those of you who fell down on the job don't bounce back against Los Angeles, I'll get rid of you. I mean that exactly. I don't care who you are, or how important you may be. I'll get rid of you. If anyone thinks I'm kidding—just try me. That's all."

The speech was successful both in the short term (no players joined the studio tour) and in the long term (the Browns routed the Dons, 61–14, the next weekend and didn't lose again en route to their fourth straight AAFC title).

By this time, many in the press were speculating about the Browns "wrecking the league" with their persistent excellence. By that 1949 season, even the Cleveland fans were growing bored. After setting pro attendance records in 1946 (averaging 48,556 per home game) and again in 1947 (56,108), the team tailed off during its undefeated season of 1948 (45,517) and saw attendance drop steeply during 1949 (31,600). It was a curious dilemma—a team hurting itself with success—but Brown was steadfast in his commitment. "Don't worry about the fans," he told his team. "Whether there's 100 or 100,000, I want you to score as many points as you can."

While Cleveland steamrolled through the AAFC, the NFL was seeing tight competition. In 1947, the Cardinals edged the Bears by a game for the Western Conference title, then beat Philadelphia, 28–21, for their only NFL title. The Eagles, whose fortunes had begun to turn shortly after Bell sold his stake, went on to play in and win the next two league titles, shutting out the Cardinals, 7–0, in 1948, and the Rams, 14–0, in 1949.

Finally, in December 1949, after two days of negotiations at Philadelphia's Racquet Club, the AAFC capitulated, to terms not much better than what they'd turned down a year before. Just two days before the Browns were to play the 49ers in what would become the last AAFC title game, the "merger" between the NFL and AAFC was announced, with the new league accepting just three teams, the Browns, the 49ers, and the Baltimore Colts (who'd agreed to pay Marshall a $50,000 territorial rights fee). Originally the new league was to be known as the "National-American Football League." But the flawed semantics couldn't survive the off-season. Less than three months later, Bell announced that the league would continue to be called the National Football League, and that only the conferences would change their names, from East and West to National and American (even those labels would last for just three years; the Eastern and Western conference designations returned in 1953).

Brown and Marshall had developed a mutual dislike during the earlier truce talks, and at the first meeting of the joint league, in the winter of 1950, they tangled again. Marshall wanted the Browns designated a "swing team" in the realigned, thirteen-team NFL, with a schedule that would have them playing each of the other teams just once. Brown fought it bitterly, threatening to pull out if the Browns were so designated. Bell acted as the conciliator, ultimately making Baltimore the swing team. Brown would remember the Washington owner as an "obnoxious" man who "insulted your intelligence and had a great habit of sleeping most of the day and showing up at the meetings late in the afternoon. We then had to stop the proceedings to brief him on all that had been accomplished. By that time all of us were pretty tired and ready to adjourn, but he was rested and mentally sharp. That was when he tried to work some of his little deals."

For all the discussion about which club would be the swing team, the most important decision at the league meeting involved not divisional structure but rules. Following the AAFC's lead in lifting limitations on substitutions, the NFL announced that it would allow unlimited substitutions in the 1950 season. This was a less obvious decision than it seems in retrospect. Many who wrote about and coached the games in the late '40s thought that unlimited substitution would hurt football. When Red Blaik used two platoons for Army in 1948, he was widely criticized; during a game with Stanford at Yankee Stadium, the Cadets were booed each time they changed units. But that game was a 43–0 blowout, and Bell was confident—with the leveling influence of the draft—that such mismatches would be rare at the pro level, where competitive balance was honed to a keener edge than in the wildly divergent college ranks.

In the long term, unlimited substitution would bring about the end of football's renaissance men, the two-way players, who would no longer play every down, but instead be used on one side of the ball or the other, depending on where a coach thought they'd be most helpful. In the short term, this meant that Brown could continue the practice he'd devised in 1949, of calling the plays himself, and shuttling them in by way of alternating guards. Impervious to the criticism this drew from writers, and the terse but compliant response afforded him by his quarterback, Graham, Brown was convinced that calling the plays from the sidelines—with input from Collier and other assistants in the press box—would afford him more control and make the play calling more reliable and scientific.

For Bell, the merger, by any name, came as a personal triumph. In the four years he'd been commissioner, he'd stabilized the league, ameliorated some of its most heated bickering, helped bolster the league's reputation, and fought off its greatest challenge. The league meetings didn't get any less contentious—it still wasn't uncommon to have lengthy discussions and a deadlocked vote on questions as minor as whether to take a dinner break—but with Bell as the commissioner, the spirit of the assemblage was more of brothers than antagonists.

For all Bell's efforts, there was still a question about whether the sport of pro football could ever prosper. What Joe Carr had said before dying in 1939 still largely held true: "No owner has made money from pro football but a lot have gone broke thinking they could." In 1948, the Philadelphia Eagles were NFL champions, defeating the Chicago Cardinals, 7–0, in the title game. They still lost money for the year, and while some of that could be pegged to the war between the leagues, it remained true that pro football had always been a high-risk enterprise with a narrow profit margin. In 1948, the Eagles had revenues of $624,782, with 86 percent of that sum coming from ticket sales. The radio and television rights to their games brought in $20,975, or 3 percent of revenue, which was less than they earned for their exhibition schedule, where they brought in $48,042. Their expenses were $709,920, the primary cost being player payrolls, which accounted for $268,819. In a booming postwar economy, playing in a large stadium, in a major East Coast market, the world champions lost $85,000.

And yet, there was hope. Despite the losses, which had by the late '40s become routine, there were signs of optimism. The Bears' income passed $1 million in 1948, and as the effect of the Browns was being felt throughout both leagues, more clubs began conducting business on a year-round basis. The American economy was booming and as the postwar culture began to take shape, it was clear that all Americans would have more leisure time, and many would spend much of that watching sports.

The National Football League had ridden out a decade-long storm, its primacy and viability intact. And though the business was small and losses were often great, the league was nearing a point in which it could seek some stability, after nearly a decade in which its very existence was threatened.

Through it all, Bert Bell presided over the game, the cheerful ambassador and tough policeman who, through the sheer force of will, made sure that pro football would be in a position to thrive in the years ahead.

The writer John Steadman remembered Bell vividly from this period, walking into a press room filled with reporters covering an annual league meeting in Philadelphia, carrying the religion of pro football with his typical room-filling exuberance. "Who wants chicken sandwiches?" bellowed the commissioner. "Who wants chocolate ice cream? Who wants beer? Order what you want, boys, it's on the Eagles. They made all the money this year."

4

Going Deep

Inside the dimly lit visitors locker room in the bowels of Birmingham's Legion Field, Paul "Tank" Younger sat on a wooden bench, too tired to pull his jersey over his shoulder pads, too spent to ask one of his Grambling College teammates for help. It was late afternoon, January 2, 1948, and the Tigers had just lost a hard-fought game, 27–21, to Central State (Ohio) in the Vulcan Bowl, the annual postseason classic billed as "the Rose Bowl for black colleges."

Younger was a strapping, quietly confident bull of a man, 6-foot-2, 220 pounds, with a calm demeanor, and a fierce work ethic. Though only a junior, he was already regarded among the loose confederation of writers and coaches who followed the black colleges as the best player in black college football. He'd run for 1,207 yards and 18 touchdowns that season, and passed for 11 more.

Dejected and quiet, Younger's expression didn't change when Grambling's clubhouse attendant walked up to him and said, in a low voice, "Tank . . . there's a man here to see you."

Younger asked him what he wanted.

"I don't know. Says he's looking for you."

"Well," said Younger, "tell him he'll have to wait."

The attendant looked perturbed, and as his eyes searched the floor for words, he interjected a clarification.

"Man's a *white* man," the attendant added. "Says he's with the Los Angeles Rams."

Younger sighed, and stood up, and followed the attendant to the door of the locker room, where amidst the postgame bustle stood a short, wiry man, sporting a wrinkled suit and an easy smile.

"Tank, I'm Eddie Kotal of the Los Angeles Rams," he said, greeting Younger with a handshake. "I've been watching you."

Kotal explained to Younger that he was the Rams' college scout, and that he spent most of his year traveling the country watching college football players, to help the team decide who to take in the annual NFL draft. Kotal often found himself explaining his occupation, since he was at the time the only person in the country with such a job, the first full-time, traveling scout in all of pro football. He had read and heard about Younger, was familiar with his feats, and asked him if he might be interested in playing pro football someday. Younger answered that he certainly would be. The two men spoke a few minutes more and, before leaving, Kotal promised, "I'll stay in touch with you—and I'll be watching."

At the time Kotal met Younger, there were only four blacks in the National Football League. Each came from a major college, and had been offered jobs after their war service was up. There had yet to be a black selected in the National Football League draft. The dozens of historically black colleges that populated the Southeast and Atlantic Coast were ignored by pro football. Not a single player from any of the schools had ever been offered a tryout with a pro team. Conventional wisdom held that no one "at that level of competition" could play in the pro game.

The blinkered mind-set was consistent with the state of scouting in pro football at the time, a haphazard pursuit that head coaches and assistant coaches took up in their spare time. In the early winter, they would make several calls around the country, to coaching cronies and others in football, to gather recommendations. They'd show up to the drafts in February armed with some notes and preseason football annuals—*Stanley Woodward's College Football* and *Street & Smith's College Football* were two perennial favorites—and select players about whom they knew precious little.

Meanwhile, in Los Angeles, the Rams were executing the blueprint for the future of pro football scouting. Dan Reeves was the first owner to recognize not just the importance but also the potential of scouting. He hired Kotal in 1946, and together they implemented a system of scouting that dwarfed in scope anything ever attempted. Kotal was a full-time employee who was away from the office 200 days a year, driving from campus to campus, combing the country in the spring and the fall to develop a network with coaches and to see as many potential pro football players as he could find.

And what stuck with Tank Younger after his meeting with Kotal, what made him shake his head and whistle to himself in sincere amazement, was the plain fact: the first full-time scout in pro football had come to Birmingham, just to watch Grambling College's Paul "Tank" Younger—and he was only a junior.

So complete was the willful ignorance among the rest of the NFL teams about players in black college football that the Rams didn't even use a pick for Younger in the twenty-five-round draft held in February 1949. But shortly thereafter, Kotal stopped at Grambling to sign Younger to a free agent contract, making him the first player from a historically black school to be signed by a pro football team.

What was nothing but a line of agate in most newspapers was a historic occasion for the black colleges, a harbinger of hope for the future of integration in sports. In July, before Younger left for the Rams' training camp, Grambling coach Eddie Robinson sat down with him and methodically explained what Younger might expect: a cold shoulder from many of his teammates, late hits and dirty play from opponents, and likelihood of racial slurs wherever he turned. "You have to let it go in one ear and out the other," Robinson implored, looking into Younger's eyes. "You have to make the ball club."

In this, Robinson was unusually adamant, emphasizing that the stakes went beyond Younger and a professional football career. "Tank, if you go up there and you don't make it, there's no telling how long it'll be before somebody else gets a chance," said Robinson. "They'll be able to say, 'We took the best you had to offer, and he wasn't good enough.' "

The success of Dan Reeves's scouting system was not yet apparent to the rest of the league, but by 1949 it would propel the Rams into their first of three consecutive NFL championship games, and solidify Reeves as the league's premier innovator in what would increasingly be viewed as the most important element in pro football management: evaluation of college football players. After hiring Kotal in 1946, Reeves began to assemble a dossier on every senior in the country. Kotal would then set out by car in the beginning of the spring, at about the time teams began their spring practices, and would hit most of the major universities in the months ahead. While many in the Rams' office suspected he took advantage of his expense account and lack of supervision ("apparently there were a lot of good prospects up by Vegas," said one fellow Rams employee), Kotal unquestionably delivered the goods. After returning in the late spring to spend two months going over reports and providing analysis, he would hop back in his car and crisscross the country once more, from the early days of school's preseason training camps through the end of the year, watching games on Saturday, taking Sunday to travel, then hitting anywhere from five to ten schools per week, where he would talk with coaches, look at game film, get 40-yard dash times and as much other information as he could muster. After a dinner often spent alone, Kotal would return to his hotel room to write more reports.

Meanwhile, the club had more than 100 bird dogs around the country—mostly college head and assistant coaches, who filled out biannual reports for $100 a year. In Los Angeles, the Rams also hired a number of high school coaches to come in nightly and watch film of potential prospects.

At the same time, a staff of assistants in the Rams' offices sent out questionnaires to every school in the country, asking for the raw data and coaches' comments to provide a dossier on each true prospect. The reports from the coaches across the country came into a small room in the Rams' offices, where they would be sorted, collated, alphabetized, and placed into a series of chunky three-ring binders. Behind the desk in Reeves's office at the Rams' headquarters was a giant map of the United States, divided into six sections. Within each section was a series of pushpins showing every four-year college in the country that played football. From this haystack of data came the occasional needle of vital, original information. Part of the routine was to send personnel sheets to players as soon as they were identified as prospects in their junior year. One sheet that came back to the Rams' office late in 1948 was from Oregon quarterback Norman Van Brocklin. The young passer was considered one of the nation's top prospects, and ideally suited for the frequent passing of the T formation offense. Kotal, reading over Van Brocklin's questionnaire one night, fixed upon one of his fill-in-the-blank answers: under the heading "When will you graduate?" Van Brocklin had scrawled in "49 ma?" Following up on the lead, the Rams discovered that Van Brocklin was ahead in his studies and might be able to graduate in three and a half years. Armed with that information, they selected him in the second round of the 1949 draft, to yelps of protest from other owners in the league, when the pick was announced at the draft in Chicago.

But Van Brocklin was indeed able to finish his studies early—finding the last class he needed in a summer session at Swarthmore—and Bell approved the selection, allowing Van Brocklin to join the Rams in 1949, where he would quickly press the All-Pro Waterfield for playing time.

It wasn't just scouting in which the Rams paced the league. For much of the '50s they were among the NFL's prime innovators in strategy, marketing, design, and public relations. Success at the box office would take longer.

Saddled with the obligation of the extra $5,000 guaranteed to all visiting teams, plus the major expenses of moving the franchise from Cleveland and the war of publicity and words with the rival Dons of the AAFC, Reeves suffered staggering losses in his early years on the coast. In 1946, the club posted a disappointing 6-4-1 record and lost $161,000, after which Reeves fired both of the Walshes and committed himself to the constant supervision of the franchise, assuming the general manager's role. New coach Bob Snyder was unable to reverse the trend in 1947, while the Dons continued to outdraw the Rams, and the Rams lost $184,000, forcing Reeves to bring in partners.

Facing a fifth season of losses exceeding $50,000, he was in danger of falling victim to the government's "hobby" law, which stipulated that anyone who lost more than $50,000 five years in a row could no longer write off those losses as a business expense and, further, would have to pay a tax on the total amount deducted in the previous years. Reeves took in three partners, including wealthy UCLA alum Ed Pauley, Jr., a Democratic Party power and oil businessman who was an avid sportsman. (UCLA's basketball arena, Pauley Pavilion, would eventually bear his name.)

Each of the investors paid just $1 for a stake in the team, agreeing to bear a portion of any future losses. Though Reeves's total share had dipped to just 30 percent by 1949, he wasn't worried. His old Cleveland partner and close friend Fred Levy still controlled 20 percent, and all the partners signed an agreement giving Reeves final say on football decisions unless partners controlling a majority of the shares opposed him.

Even as the losses accrued, Reeves's changes were already bringing the Rams to the verge of success, both on the field and at the box office. In the offseason of 1947, he'd fired his public relations man, Maxwell Stiles, because there had been grumbling among the other papers that Stiles was leaking stories to his friends and colleagues at the *Long Beach Press-Telegram*.

Through a friend of one of the partners in Reeves's stock brokerage, Reeves received a recommendation of Tex Schramm, then a twenty-six-year-old sports editor of the *Austin American-Statesman*, who'd recently graduated from the University of Texas on the GI Bill. He'd grown up in Southern California and a few years earlier had done some work for the *Los Angeles Times*.

The young Tex Schramm was not yet the force of nature that he would become in later decades, but even in his college years he had made quite an impression as a gruff, handsome, whip-smart young journalist who was a decent writer, an excellent reporter, and—a rare thing in Texas—an avid fan of pro football.

Reeves invited Schramm to Los Angeles for an interview, and was immediately impressed with the young man's wit and maturity. At a salary of $4,000, Schramm accepted the job and moved with his wife, Marty, from Austin back to the Los Angeles suburb of San Gabriel, not far from where Schramm had played high school football in Alhambra.

Schramm's assignment was a grinding one, but typical of what pro football teams did to get press coverage in the era. The five daily newspapers in Los Angeles were competitive, but understaffed, and most couldn't afford a daily beat reporter for both pro football teams. On many days during the season, the Rams' publicist had to write the stories himself, altering the leads slightly at each newspaper. Even columns occasionally had to be fabricated out of whole cloth, often in the style of the writer. This was particularly painful in the case of writers like John B. Old, whose hackneyed style was amplified by his own personal index card file of clichés.

In that first season, Schramm improved everything he touched, from the amount of coverage the Rams received in local papers and the number of write-ups generated in other cities, to the quality of the clipping service the team used for its scrapbook and the quality and readability of its game programs (which around the league at that time consisted of little more, in Schramm's words, than "a bunch of head shots with a Coke ad in the middle").

After Reeves and Kotal agreed that they needed to do more to scout the hundreds of small colleges around the country, it was Schramm who came up with the inspired idea of getting scouting tips for free, through the ruse of "Tom Harmon's Little All-America Team." Using the Michigan star and former Rams player as a beard of sorts, the Rams sent out "voting ballots" to coaches at every small school in the country that played football, asking them to name the five best players they played against. That gave them early lines on such future Hall of Famers as Andy Robustelli, from tiny Arnold College in Connecticut, and Dick "Night Train" Lane from Scottsbluff Community College in Nebraska.

By 1949, Schramm was promoted from the PR job, and given the title assistant to the president, and began performing many of the duties of a traditional general manager. As his replacement, he hired his old friend Tex Maule, another atypically avid pro football fan from Texas, whose eclectic background had included time as a circus trapeze artist and a merchant seaman. Each man knew enough about football to provide valued help with Reeves's relatively comprehensive draft preparation, and helped the Rams further distance themselves from the rest of the league.

Then, too, there were instances of pure serendipity. One of the players on those Rams teams was Fred Gehrke, a halfback from Utah, who had first played with the Rams when the franchise was in Cleveland in 1940, then spent the war working as an aviation artist for Northrop Engineering, rejoining the club in 1945. Gehrke, an art major in college, was fascinated with the idea of painting a logo on the Rams' drab brown leather helmets. When he tried to explain the idea to Bob Snyder, the coach couldn't even understand what he was talking about. Showing a sketch of a helmet with a ram's horn to Schramm, Gehrke explained the concept again and, with Schramm's encouragement, brought a helmet home. Working in his garage, he painted the entire outer surface of the helmet blue, and then painted the outline of a ram's horn on each side. Filling in the outline with bright gold paint, Gehrke created an eye-catching effect unlike anything ever seen before on a helmet. It wasn't so literal as the painting of a ram, or as realistic as a drawing of an actual ram's horn. Instead the graceful rendition was a representational, nearly experimental, depiction of a ram's horn, spiraling out from the front brim, sweeping up across the crown of the helmet, and looping back down to an upturned tip by the ear hole. It was a work of modern art on the side of a football helmet.

Dan Reeves loved it, and dispatched Gehrke back to his home to paint every helmet that the Rams owned, paying him $1 per helmet plus expenses. When the team took the field for the traditional exhibition opener at L.A. Coliseum against the Redskins in August of 1948—blue jerseys with gold numerals, blue-and-gold helmets gleaming under the night lights—they were greeted by extended, appreciative applause. As an aesthetic statement, Gehrke's helmet design was a masterpiece of pop art. As a utilitarian move, it was equally successful, making the team and its players instantly recognizable, and starting a revolution of helmet design that would, in the coming years, be felt at every level of football. Decades later, the popular artist LeRoy Neiman would say of the Rams' helmet design, "It is the most effective pop art symbol in all of sports. It captures the very purpose of the helmet—to ram someone. How satisfying it must be, for the artist, to see his art functioning every Sunday."

After the disappointing 6-6 record in 1947, the Rams hired Clark Shaughnessy to be the team's "technical adviser," working as an assistant to head coach Bob Snyder.

Throughout the '40s, the mercurial Shaughnessy was regarded as the reigning genius of football strategy as well as, perhaps, a less-than-balanced man, one who seemed so preoccupied with the strategies and tactics of the game that the rest of the world seemed to escape his notice.

After stops at Maryland and Pitt during the war, he took his first full-time pro job in 1947 as an assistant with the Washington Redskins, and was summoned to Los Angeles after that season, at the behest of Snyder, who had played for the Bears when Shaughnessy was advising the team. Reeves was so dazzled by Shaughnessy's brilliance that he fired Snyder in the preseason, and named Shaughnessy the head coach. Taking advantage of his newfound authority, Shaughnessy soon began an extensive series of changes designed to modernize the attack. He held two-a-day practices throughout training camp, even practicing in the morning on days when the team was playing an evening exhibition game.

As the tactics grew more complex, so did the terminology that accompanied them. And Shaughnessy's lexicon was the most extensive in the sport. Offensive formations were based on a combination of directional signals and the commands that plowing farmers gave to their mules. An end out wide to the right side was "east," to the left side was "west." The left halfback in motion to the right was "gee," the right halfback in motion to the left was "haw." For blocking, he used a combination of mnemonic cues, what he called "memory hooks," and masculine (for blocks on linemen and linebackers) and feminine (defensive backs) names. From these formulas came a blinding array of blitz, pass rush, and secondary coverage calls that could be as simple as "Green Tornado" or as complicated as "Brown Stash Mutt Purple Jack Shuffle Right Wheel Left." (Though his complex vocabulary wouldn't survive, many of its principles—especially the homonyms and mnemonic cues—would carry into the modern day.)

When Tank Younger showed up to training camp in 1949, he was presented with the full-frontal assault of Shaughnessy's complex terminology. Told to study and learn the thick book with its obscure and intricate lexicon, he was initially intimidated. Younger had experienced nothing like it at Grambling, where Eddie Robinson's simple playbook contained a reverse play known as Douglas MacArthur ("I shall return"), and little rhyme or reason in the numbering system used to determine nomenclature. The first night of camp, Younger went to the pay phone at the end of the hall in the Redlands

College dorm, and called Robinson, who provided reassurance and an explanation. Though he didn't use much of Shaughnessy's system, Robinson was familiar with the terminology, and helped Younger find the logic within it.

Back at Grambling, Younger's tryout was considered so vital that Robinson had started subscribing to all of Los Angeles's daily newspapers. Each afternoon during that late summer, Robinson and Grambling athletic news director Collie Nicholson went to the university library, to parse the sports pages for clues to Younger's progress. They celebrated one September morning when they read a staff story in the *Los Angeles Times*, which noted that "Younger, the continually surprising Negro, virtually nailed down the No. 1 right-half position with his vicious blocking and running."

Younger lived up to his promise. In the Rams' first exhibition game, at home in the Los Angeles Times Charity Game against the Redskins, he was introduced with the Rams starters and as the PA announcer introduced "Tank Younger, Grambling College" he burst forth in a full sprint from the Coliseum tunnel and received a rousing cheer from the crowd of 90,000. That night, he found himself at linebacker, trying to keep up with the Redskins' fleet back Dick Sandifer. When Sandifer broke free past Younger on a pass route, the rookie simply jumped and tackled Sandifer, bringing an inevitable defensive penalty. On the sidelines, Shaughnessy brought Younger over and berated him for the foul. "But Coach," said Younger, "you told us if we thought someone was getting away from us, to just tackle him to save a touchdown." Shaughnessy looked at him for a moment, then turned to the Rams' trainer and said, "Wipe this boy off and get him back in the game." Tank Younger went back in, knowing he'd made the team.

In that 1949 season, the Rams became the most dangerous team in the league. The mother lode of draft talent matured quickly, with Van Brocklin earning playing time at quarterback and Younger starring on both sides of the ball, as a fullback and linebacker. Heisman winner and Army legend Glenn Davis completed his Army commitment, giving the team a gifted receiver out of the backfield. Vitamin T. Smith was drafted from tiny Abilene Christian, and instantly made a contribution in the backfield.

Shaughnessy's 1949 team also boasted an array of speed never before seen in pro football, with six school sprint champions on the roster, five of whom had recorded sub-10.0 times in the 100-yard dash. The key acquisition was the signing of Elroy "Crazy Legs" Hirsch, the game-breaking halfback who had grown tired of the struggles in the AAFC with the Chicago Rockets and jumped to the Rams. Shaughnessy treated Hirsch with great care, putting him on a daily five-mile running regimen to strengthen his injured leg, and fitting him with a lightweight but strong helmet of molded plastic (which would within three years become the industry standard, replacing leather helmets) to prevent concussions. Hirsch found a new position in Los Angeles. Shaughnessy moved him out of the backfield and away from the line of scrimmage, as the league's first true flanker back, offset from the line of scrimmage and several yards wide of the tight end. With Bob Shaw staying at the end of the interior line, and Tom Fears split out on the other side, the Rams became the first team to use three ends consistently, and since all three were talented, opposing teams had trouble containing them. In their last six regular season games, en route to winning the Western Conference title, the Rams scored more than 40 points four times.

But on the morning of the 1949 title game, as rain approached monsoon-like conditions in Los Angeles, much of that speed was neutralized. In a storm that Younger would characterize as "a Louisiana frog strangler," Greasy Neale's Eagles shut down the Rams' attack, and emerged with a 14–0 win, their second straight title. Among those in attendance that day, sitting high up in the press box, keeping to himself, making precise, detailed notes, was Browns assistant Blanton Collier. The "merger" with the AAFC had been announced days earlier, and Paul Brown was already hard at work on the next season.

———

"The worst team in our league could beat the best team in theirs," huffed George Preston Marshall about the upstart AAFC and the three teams who would be joining the NFL in 1950. The schedule for the 1950 season was announced in April, and Bert Bell had done his work well. On the eve of the opening Sunday slate of five games, the season would kick off with a single game Saturday night, September 16, at Philadelphia's Municipal Stadium, with the two-time defending NFL champion Eagles playing host to the four-time AAFC title-holder Browns. It was dubbed by many in the press as "The World Series of Pro Football."

During the exhibition season, the Browns swept through the NFL's lesser lights in a way sure to guarantee attention and resentment, averaging 35 points per game en route to a 5-0 record. The finale was played at War Memorial Stadium in Buffalo, a merciless rout of the Steelers that was never as close as the 41–31 final score would indicate. As the teams headed to the locker room at halftime, Steelers defensive end Bob Davis yelled at the Browns, "This isn't football! You guys ought to join the Celtics!"

The Steelers discovered what the rest of the league would know soon enough: Cleveland's personnel was excellent, and it had developed a pass offense that, if not ahead of the Rams in speed or sophistication, was more precisely calibrated. The NFL hadn't seen anything like the Browns' precision "comeback" patterns, with Dante Lavelli and Dub Jones snapping off their down-and-out routes by taking sharper angles to the sidelines, coming back to Graham's passes in a way that made it nearly impossible to defend.

In the opener, the Browns would confront what many regarded as one of the NFL's all-time great squads. The Eagles' offense was anchored by star running back Steve Van Buren, a classic bruiser instrumental to the team's back-to-back titles. The key to coach Greasy Neale's "Eagle" defense was beefy middle guard Bucko Kilroy, who lined up over the center and controlled the holes to either side, allowing the other four linemen to concentrate on containing outside runs. It was widely felt, especially after the Eagles shut out the Rams in the 1949 title game, that the "Eagle" defense was impregnable to the pass.

In front of 71,237 fans, the Browns kicked off and held the Eagles on three plays, forcing a punt, which Cleveland's Don Phelps returned 64 yards for a touchdown, only to have the play called back by a clipping penalty. Graham threw three straight incompletions on that first possession, each revealing in its own way. With the Browns sending running back Rex Baumgardner in motion, to be picked up by a linebacker, the Eagles consistently put defensive halfback Russ Craft on right halfback Dub Jones, who was coming out of the backfield and running 10-yard square-out routes to the sidelines. Graham didn't throw to Jones, but noticed that Craft was covering him more closely each time, inching up toward the receiver in hopes of a possible interception.

When Cleveland got the ball again, now down 3–0, Graham called a similar pattern, with Baumgardner again drawing the attention of the linebacker, and Dante Lavelli and Mac Speedie drawing the safeties with curl patterns in the middle of the field. Jones again ran a square-out, but this time, when Craft charged toward the sideline for an interception, Jones shifted his route to an out-and-up, and was far behind Craft streaking down the sidelines when he caught Graham's expertly lofted 59-yard touchdown pass.

Surreptitiously, the Browns were also widening their running lanes. Early on in the game, Cleveland came to the line of scrimmage with their linemen spaced a few inches further apart than usual. They'd hold that spacing for a while, then widen again a few plays later. Since both the Philadelphia defensive tackles tended to line up just off the outside shoulder of the offensive guard across the line of scrimmage, the Eagles' blind adherence to this alignment widened the gaps between their two tackles, where only Bucko Kilroy was operating. Philadelphia paid the price on trap plays that sprang the bruising Marion Motley for big runs.

A Motley fumble deep in Browns territory gave the Eagles a chance at changing the momentum. But after Cleveland stoned the Eagles four times inside the Cleveland five-yard line, the rout was on. The Browns led 14–3 at the half en route to a resounding 35–10 win.

After the game, Neale churlishly dismissed the Browns as "a team that does nothing but pass," but among the Eagles players, there were few excuses. A dismayed Russ Craft said, "We just never played against a team that threw to a spot as well as Cleveland. We would be on top of their receivers but they caught the ball anyway because it was so well timed. It was like trying to cover three Don Hutsons . . . impossible . . . impossible."

Bert Bell entered the Browns' locker room beaming, congratulating Brown for his part in the win, and calling the Browns "the best-coached football team I've ever seen."

For the rest of the season, the Browns were in the crosshairs, as the established league tried to find a way to beat them. While the two other AAFC entries, the Colts and the 49ers, stumbled to a combined 4-20 record, the Browns carried the flag for the defunct league, going 10-2 during the 1950 regular season. The only team with any success against them was the New York Giants, who, under the exacting leadership of veteran coach Steve Owen, had devised a defense to counteract the Browns; it looked similar to a 6-1, except that the two ends were decoys, who often peeled away at the snap into short zones, to prevent the Browns' short passes to the shallow areas behind the line. Behind them came four defensive backs, arranged in a wide arc, with the cornerbacks playing closer to the line of scrimmage and the safeties in the center of the field further back. The defense, known as "the umbrella," was directed on the field by an AAFC refugee named Tom Landry, a cool, analytical defensive back with little speed but a professor's sense of calm rationalism and a comprehensive knowledge of the Browns' personnel. Sometimes the ends would drop into coverage, at other times they would rush the quarterback, and this mixture of looks confounded Otto Graham and frustrated the Browns' short passing game. In the teams' first meeting, Graham couldn't complete a single pass in the first half.

Losing both games to the Giants, Cleveland wound up tied with New York for the Eastern Conference championship. In the playoff game, the Browns prevailed in a 9–7 struggle, with three Groza field goals providing the margin, and earning the team a berth in the NFL championship game in its first season in the NFL. Across the country, ready in waiting, were the Los Angeles Rams, who had run through another season of dominating performances.

———————

The loss to the Eagles in the 1949 championship game had led to another eventful off-season in Los Angeles. In February, assistant coach Joe Stydahar came to Reeves with news that his old teammate Gene Ronzani had been named head coach of the Green Bay Packers, and wanted Stydahar to be his top assistant. Before giving Stydahar permission to leave, Reeves asked for forty-eight hours to work out details. When Stydahar returned two days later, set to say his goodbyes, Reeves greeted him by saying, "Joe, you are the new head coach of the Los Angeles Rams." The stunning turn of events, firing Shaughnessy, football's most famous innovator, for an assistant coach who was well liked but unversed in the intricacies of the Rams' attack, left Stydahar speechless and his former mentor uncharacteristically bitter. Asked for his reaction to the news, Shaughnessy said, "Stydahar coach of the Rams? Why, I could take a high school team and beat him." (To those closest to the team, the shocking decision was less surprising. Shaughnessy's eccentricities had continued unabated, and as the playbook grew thicker each week, even the good soldier Waterfield had bridled near the end of the 1949 season.)

Stydahar was a player's coach but an old-school footballer, whom Pat Summerall once described as "the only man I have ever known who could smoke a cigar, chew tobacco and drink whiskey at the same time." In an attempt to replace Shaughnessy's technical expertise, Stydahar hired his former Bears teammate, Hampton Pool, then an assistant coach at Santa Barbara Junior College. A keen tactician in his own right, Pool wound up devising much of the game plans for both offense and defense for the Rams.

Reeves's other major decision over the off-season would have broader implications, as it involved an embrace of the emerging technology of television. Though World War II brought technical experimentation to a halt, research and testing began in earnest following the war, when in 1946 DuMont and NBC aired nine hours and thirty minutes of prime-time programming each week, with nearly four hours of that devoted to sports programming. The most popular of the early sports shows was *The Gillette Cavalcade of Sports*, owned by the razor manufacturer and broadcast on NBC. Gillette had been one of the earliest believers in the potential of TV, already having realized huge market share gains due to sports broadcasts on radio. The *Cavalcade* was a weekly boxing show from Madison Square Garden. The format of boxing, with plenty of action taking place in a small, well-lit area, was perfectly suited to television and the medium's limitations at the time, which tended to make any medium or long shots unrecognizable. The popularity of boxing on television grew quickly, prompting one writer to remark "the passionate affair between television and professional fighting turned into an orgy."

The makers of Gillette sensed what others in the business would soon find out. Sports on television fueled the wholesale purchase of sets. NBC producer Harry Coyle recalled, "When we put on the World Series in 1947, heavyweight fights, the Army-Navy football game, the sales of television sets just spurted." In a postwar boom that saw car sales mushroom, television purchases did the same, jumping from 7,000 sets in 1946 to 14,000 in 1947 to 172,000 in 1948. Sales still lagged on the West Coast because the coaxial cable required to feed broadcasts through a network hadn't made it over the Rocky Mountains, leaving stations in California forced to run shows from networks later, after they had been converted to film or kinescopes.

While boxing was dominating the airwaves, Major League Baseball was moving gingerly to embrace the new medium, and often meeting disastrous consequences when doing so. After winning the NL pennant in 1948, the Boston Braves sold the rights to televise all their home games in 1949 and 1950, and nearly all of them in 1951 and 1952. By the end of the contract, despite having a contender in three of those four seasons, their attendance had dropped from 1,455,000 in 1948 to 281,278 in 1952, and they were soon on their way out of town. The Cleveland Indians were among baseball's powers in the same period, but after televising many of their home games for eight seasons, they'd seen their attendance drop 67 percent. Overall attendance in Major League Baseball dropped from nearly 21 million in 1948 to 14.3 million in 1953.

And if television hurt the majors, it's fair to say that it nearly killed the minor leagues. From an all-time high of 42 million in 1949, attendance would drop to 13 million by the end of the '50s. Fans wouldn't travel downtown to see minor league baseball when they could watch the big clubs on their home television or at the corner tavern.

All this would seem obvious after the fact, but the patterns were not yet so clear in 1950. With the Browns set to join the NFL that season, Paul Brown offered the exclusive television sponsorship rights to the Browns' games to Cleveland Gas and Electric for $5,000. "They said that seemed high," he recalled. "I had to convince them. They gave me the money, but it was more to humor me than anything else."

The Rams, who had lost money even as they advanced to the championship game in 1949, were searching for any way they might increase revenues. The Admiral Television Company approached the team with an offer to broadcast all their home games. (Live broadcasts of road games back to the West Coast remained a technical impossibility.) Reeves was ambivalent about the risk to the home gate, which had averaged nearly 50,000 per game in the 1949 season. Ultimately, the Rams struck a unique deal with Admiral. After Schramm spent some time researching league attendance records, the team calculated that they could fairly expect a 10 percent increase in attendance, and added a provision to the contract stipulating that any attendance short of a 10 percent increase would be compensated by Admiral. That August, as the high-powered Rams were providing glimpses of their offensive potential (scoring 70 points against Baltimore in a game in San Antonio), ads were running in the Los Angeles papers promising live pro football in the home.

After losing a closely fought opener at home to the Chicago Bears, the Rams won eight of their next nine games, during which they unveiled the most potent 1-2 passing attack in pro football history. In a year when the rest of the league's teams averaged 176 yards per game passing, Waterfield and Van Brocklin averaged 294 yards per game, throwing for a combined 29 touchdowns in 12 games. The team would set twenty-two scoring records that season, averaging 38.8 points per game, an NFL record that still stood in 2004.

Defenses facing the Rams confronted an array of problems. Tom Fears was the league's best possession receiver on one side, the flanker Hirsch a fleet, dexterous burner on the other side. And they were joined by Bob "Seabiscuit" Boyd, a blazing fast end who had been a freshman at Compton Community College when the Rams began their first training camp in 1946. The rookie caught only 17 passes in 1950, but his speed made him a terror to cover, especially when he came into the game as a third end in Pool's three-receiver sets.

In a three-game homestand in October, the Rams rolled to 163 points, then scored 88 during their next two road games. By the end of the 1950 season, the Rams' aura of glamour was felt throughout the country. It owed to the spectacular quality of their passing game, the celebrity of minority owner Bob Hope, the cachet of the team's Beverly Hills address, a fan base studded with Hollywood executives and stars, even the Gehrke-designed helmet (which by 1950 was even shinier, with the design baked into the plastic shell, saving Gehrke from repainting the helmets each week).

Of course, having a few movie starlet wives didn't hurt: Waterfield was still often referred to as "Mr. Jane Russell." Tom Harmon, married to actress Elyse Knox, quit the game in 1947 after two injury-plagued seasons, but by 1949, another Heisman winner, Glenn Davis, joined the team. His wife, Terry

Moore, was also in the movies. And then there was Hirsch, whose movie star looks—strong jaw, sweeping shock of hair—got him on the silver screen, where he starred as himself in *Crazylegs*, the 1953 biopic that featured several Rams in smaller roles.

And yet for all this, despite the success, excitement, and national reputation, it was a horrible season at the box office, with the Rams suffering an attendance decline of nearly 50 percent, from 49,854 per game to 26,804. No conclusion could be reached other than that televising home games was directly responsible for the loss in attendance. After a 51–14 rout of the Green Bay Packers clinched a playoff showdown with the Bears for the Western Conference title, the Admiral Television experiment came to an end. The playoff win over the Bears, played in Los Angeles but not broadcast on local television, drew 83,501, and fairly rang the death knell of home television for the Rams and, as it would turn out, the rest of the league. Following the season, Admiral paid $307,000 to the Rams to cover the cost of the attendance drop. "This was back," noted Schramm, "when $300,000 was a lot of money."

———

The 1950 championship game match-up had an eerie sense of déjà vu, with the Cleveland Browns playing host to the Rams. For Reeves, Waterfield, and the rest of the Rams, it was their first return to Cleveland since winning the world title in 1945. For the Browns, it was a chance to complete their quest for an NFL title and, in so doing, reassert the validity of each of their four previous AAFC crowns.

In subfreezing conditions, with a cruel thirty-mile-an-hour wind coming in from Lake Erie, the game was played in front of a modest Christmas Eve crowd of 29,751 at Cleveland Stadium.

The two potent offenses slashed back and forth throughout the game, overwhelming two capable defenses. Midway through the fourth quarter, Graham converted two fourth downs into first downs, and completed a long drive with his fourth touchdown pass of the day, to move the Browns to within 28–27. After a Cleveland stand, the Browns got the ball back with just over five minutes left and moved steadily downfield. Graham had just gained a first down on a quarterback draw when linebacker Milan Lazetich hit him from behind, forcing a fumble recovered by the Rams at their own 22-yard line with just 3:16 to play.

"It was the lowest moment of my life," Graham would say later. "Honestly, I was more devastated at that moment than I was a few years ago when the doctor told me I had cancer." As he reached the sideline, Graham's head was bowed in dejection, preparing for a grilling from his coach. But instead of criticizing, Brown put his hand on his quarterback's shoulder and told him, "Don't worry, Otts. We'll get the ball back for you and win this thing yet."

The Browns held and, with 1:50 left and no timeouts, they took over at their own 34. On the first play, Graham called a keeper, gaining 14 yards. Three completed passes later, the Browns moved the ball to the center of the field, and Groza kicked a 16-yard field goal with 16 seconds left, to give Cleveland the 30–28 win.

Though Waterfield had completed 18 of 22 passes for 312 yards, Stydahar called upon the stronger-armed Van Brocklin (who broke his rib in the Chicago game a week earlier) to make the last desperation throw. After a return to the Rams' 46, Van Brocklin's long bomb to Glenn Davis was grasped by both Davis and Browns defensive back Warren Lahr at the Browns' five-yard line, before Lahr emerged from the scuffle with the ball in the end zone as the clock struck :00, and Cleveland's fans stormed the field in jubilation.

"It was terrible," said Graham. "We didn't know for several seconds what the referee was going to call. We were sure Lahr had intercepted. But what if they gave Davis the ball and a touchdown? And what if they called it a safety or something?"

It was the game that Brown would later call the greatest he'd ever seen, and in the locker room he was unusually ebullient, shouting, "What the hell was the final score?" The Cleveland Browns had been in existence for five years and won five championships, but this win made them, for the first time, undisputed world champions. Bert Bell, making another postgame visit to the Browns' dressing room, as he'd done after the opener in Philadelphia, called it "the greatest football game I've ever seen." And when he found Brown, he reached out to embrace the coach and said, "You are the greatest team to ever play football."

Whatever else coaches, players, and other observers thought of the 1950 title game, one fact was obvious: at a time when there were only fourteen blacks in the National Football League, nine of them were on the field playing for the two teams in the championship game. Pro football would never be the same. In the coming years, the sport wouldn't merely reflect the changes in society, it would help bring them about.

The first generation of players to integrate the game after the war had encountered fierce resistance; many had been emotionally and physically scarred by the experience. The Rams' Jim Hardy would long remember his friend and teammate Kenny Washington enduring constant verbal abuse and late hits and sucker punches in a 1947 game in which he scored three touchdowns for the Rams. Later, when the two men were alone, Washington said, quietly and matter-of-factly, "Sometimes, it's hell to be a Negro, Jim."

"I'll never forget the hurt in his eyes," said Hardy. "But his statement wasn't one of self-pity by any means. It was simply a social comment, and he was alone, and there wasn't any way to comfort him."

Similar events were occurring, on and off the field, throughout pro football. "When Joe Perry joined us, I couldn't get a cab for him in Baltimore in '47," said the 49ers' Lou Spadia. "He couldn't stay with us, which he understood. And I was assigned the job of getting him out to this black doctor's home. And we were standing outside the Lord Baltimore Hotel and I'd wave for a cab to come, and the cab would come by, and we'd start to get in and the cab driver would say, 'I'll take you, but not the nigger.' Finally I had to call the doctor, and he came down and got him."

But by the early '50s, the integrationist movement in sports was reaching a second phase. The writer Gerald Early has noted that, after spending time fighting with the integrated U.S. forces in the Korean War, black veterans returning to the United States "found segregation intolerable." The same thing would happen in pro football in the coming years, where teams integrated on the field were not so easily split apart off it. It would be decades before the last vestiges of institutional racism disappeared, but with the arrival of Paul Brown's Cleveland team in the NFL in 1950, and the emergence of stars like Younger, as a representative of the long-ignored black schools, a new era was dawning, and the minds of scouts, coaches, and owners around the league were beginning to change. A game predicated so much on an environment of pure competition could not long ignore an obvious edge offered by the best black players.

————

A year later, the Rams and Browns would meet again for the NFL title, this time in Los Angeles. The season had provided the first hint of commercial success for the Rams, who blacked out home games and saw attendance spike back up to 43,813 per game.

Waterfield and Van Brocklin, evenly splitting the duties again, combined for 26 touchdown passes, 17 of which went to Hirsch, who had one of the great receiving seasons in history, averaging 22.7 yards on each of his league-leading 66 catches. The Browns were, if anything, even stronger than the 1950 team, going 11-1 and thumping the Rams, 38–23, in an early-season game in Los Angeles.

As the teams prepared for their title game rematch at the Coliseum, the Rams suddenly faced a dire public relations crisis. It had been the team's policy, throughout earlier seasons, to give free tickets to the family members of the media covering the games. But the league, hoping to further establish its own legitimacy as a major league organization, stipulated that no complimentary tickets could be given out for championship games. (There were good reasons for this: since the players themselves got 70 percent of the gate in prize money, any free tickets necessarily took money out of their own pocket.) Presented with the news that family members wouldn't receive free passes for the title game, the Los Angeles print media banded together. Schramm remembered one writer telling him "if that was the way we were going to be, we weren't going to see the word 'Rams' in the newspapers for the next seven days." Faced with this challenge, Schramm convinced Reeves to buy 300 tickets that could then be handed out as media comps. That crisis averted, the game received the expected buildup, drawing a crowd of 57,522 at the Coliseum.

They would see another classic, entertaining and closely fought throughout. Early in the fourth quarter, just three plays after the Browns had tied the game at 17, Van Brocklin threw 20 yards downfield to the streaking Fears, who caught the ball just as he split defenders Cliff Lewis and Tom James at midfield, and brought it all the way in for the game-winning 73-yard touchdown reception. Afterward, Dan Reeves wryly noted that the second title was so sweet, it was probably worth the fortune he'd lost getting it. And that he was pleased, this time, to be staying put in a city that had embraced his team.

The game was a watershed of sorts. It was the first national broadcast of an NFL championship game, with the coaxial cable finally connecting both coasts in 1951. (The 1949 title game was televised live only on the West Coast.) The DuMont network paid $95,000 for the rights for the dream rematch, and concluded a season in which Bell had charted the league's future course.

Greeted with the Rams' disastrous attendance with home games televised in 1950, Bell had decreed in 1951 that the teams in the league could not sell broadcast rights to home games, and must black them out instead. That brought an inevitable challenge from the U.S. Justice Department, which charged restraint of trade and filed a complaint that would take two years to work its way through the courts. The decision, handed down by U.S. District Court Judge Allan K. Grim in Philadelphia on November 12, 1953, was momentous. Though Grim disallowed constraints in certain peripheral areas, prohibiting the blacking out of radio broadcasts, he preserved the league's right to black out telecasts of home games, and all other league games when the home team was playing at home.

Television riches did not immediately flow to the National Football League. There would be more trouble to come, and there were still a scant few teams making regular profits. But with the example of the Rams' ill-fated home television policy in 1950 as a prod, and the Grim decision as a covenant, pro football's policy toward television had been established. While baseball continued to thrash about without a policy, the NFL had succeeded in realizing another means of revenue, and figured out how to do so without threatening its most important source of income, the gate. That combination was a crucial one, setting the stage for the league's steep ascent through the next two decades.

5

Baltimore

"There has been a lot of talk in recent years to the effect that professional football is a dying sport in this country," wrote *Sport* magazine in an unsigned editorial in the October 1952 issue. "Pro football never has been able to sell itself completely to the fans who are so wild over the collegiate version of the sport. Many people stubbornly insist upon regarding football as a rah-rah game which isn't the same when you take away the rah-rah."

The view that the pro game remained a marginalized sport, inferior to its college counterpart, was still commonly held in the early '50s, and was somewhat understandable, in light of the upheaval the league endured since the dissolution of the AAFC. Attendance was stagnant, still unable to match the average crowds of 30,000 that had turned out in 1946 and 1947, and a franchise failed in each of the first three seasons of the decade. It was the darkness before the dawn in the growth of pro football. And when the league's itinerant orphan franchise finally found a home in 1953 it was, oddly enough, right back where it started the decade, in abject failure.

When the NFL and the AAFC announced their "merger" in December 1949, it was clear that the Browns and 49ers, the league's two most successful teams, would be joining the NFL. But the identity of the third team was less obvious. Only seven clubs had played in the AAFC's final campaign, and because of the presence of NFL teams in New York, Chicago, and Los Angeles, there was no chance that any of the AAFC franchises in those cities would be chosen. That left either the Buffalo Bills or the Baltimore Colts. Buffalo had the strongest support, and the better team—having played for the AAFC title in 1948 and in a playoff game in 1949. But NFL owners were leery about bringing in a city with such severe winters; others felt it wasn't large enough to support pro football.

So the selection was Baltimore, despite a 1-11 record and $90,000 in losses in 1949, prompting the team's original owner, Bob Rodenburg, to throw in the towel. Somehow, the dismal Colts still drew 23,000 fans per game in 1949—nearly equaling the NFL's average attendance for that season—at a time when attendance was down 30 percent throughout the AAFC, due to Cleveland's dominance. Adding three teams created a nightmare in scheduling with the thirteen-team league, since an odd number of teams meant one club would be out of action each week.

Trucking magnate Abraham "Shorty" Watner, a man with a gift for gab and euphemism (he once referred to the cemetery he owned as a "series of underground bungalows"), stepped in to buy the Colts franchise, vowing, "I will underwrite the team for two years, I will take any losses and I will give all profits to worthwhile local charities. Baltimore is in the big leagues to stay!"

But after another one-win season, in which the team averaged barely 15,000 per game, Watner turned the club over to the league and the Colts were dissolved, their players drafted off among the remaining twelve franchises. In response, the city of Baltimore filed suit against Watner and the NFL.

A year later, after the New York Yanks stumbled to a 1-9-2 record in the 1951 season, and owner Ted Collins (better known, and much more profitable, as singer Kate Smith's manager) decided to give up his franchise, Bell invited Baltimore representatives to the 1952 meetings. But most NFL owners were unconvinced, after the dismal performance in 1950, that Baltimore would support football. Instead, the owners uncharacteristically looked to a new market in the Southwest.

Into the picture, with stereotypical Texan pride, came Giles and Connell Miller, sons of the founder of the Texas Textile Mills, and would-be entrepreneurs determined to turn the game on its head with a flow of schemes that would match the state's grandiose reputation. The franchise, granted in January 1952, would be called the Dallas Texans, and the Miller brothers crowed about possible innovations: players introduced to the Cotton Bowl crowd on horseback; a gun holster design sewn onto the team's game pants; substitutes running on the field carrying the Texas state flag, presenting it to the player being replaced, who would then transport it back to the sideline.

None of those ideas were realized, nor were the wishful-thinking rumors, published in the *Dallas Morning News* just days after the Texans' purchase was announced, that the team was "going to trade the three Negro players for one outstanding performer." But how a still segregated city would react to an integrated team was a hot topic; as difficult as it was for the home team's black players and fans, it was worse for visitors, as Dallas's Jim Crow laws maintained segregation in all the city's hotels.

To handle publicity for the new team, the Miller brothers recruited Tex Maule to come to Dallas as the team's PR man, with a guarantee that he could, as Schramm had in Los Angeles, work his way up to general manager duties. (Back in Los Angeles, Maule's position as publicist had been filled when Schramm hired Pete Rozelle, the Compton College student who'd helped with the Rams' first training camp in California in 1946.)

Shortly after arriving in Dallas, Maule found a wayward circus masquerading as a football team. The coach was the vastly entertaining but overmatched Jimmy Phelan, whose love of football was often eclipsed by his love of horse racing (he called off one practice before a game in Los Angeles to take the team to Del Mar). Practices were barely organized recess periods for adults, with Phelan drilling his quarterbacks and backs while the linemen mustered impromptu volleyball games using the goalpost crossbar for a net. After his years with Reeves and Schramm and the sophisticated Los Angeles system, Maule was horrified to see a team run so shabbily.

The Texans' season opened at home on September 28, 1952, against the New York Giants, expected to be a sizable draw because of the presence of SMU alums Kyle Rote and Fred Benners. But the game was the third one in the Cotton Bowl in as many days—SMU faced Duke Friday night, Texas A&M played Oklahoma A&M Saturday—and the pros drew just 17,499 fans for their opener.

In the following weeks, as dire reports filtered back to the league offices in Philadelphia, it quickly became apparent that pro football in Texas was a fiasco. Typical of the underwhelming response that greeted the pro game in Dallas was the decision by one paper, the *Fort Worth Press,* to assign a twenty-year-old writer to the Texans' beat. "I remember the Texans vs. the 49ers, and Hugh McElhenny running wild in the rain," said Bud Shrake, who took breaks from his homework while attending classes at TCU to cover the Texans. "And I remember looking down from the press box—and could not see one single fan in the stands. Those few who were in attendance had gathered under the overhang to get out of the rain. Art Donovan and Gino Marchetti were joking in the locker room that if the fans gave 'em any shit they could go into the stands and whip the whole crowd."

The Texans played what would turn out to be their final home game in the Cotton Bowl November 9 against the Los Angeles Rams, in front of a crowd generously listed as 10,000. Prior to the game, Tex Schramm received a call from Bell in Philadelphia, ordering him, "Don't you leave that office until you get your check."

And so it ended quickly. The Dallas Citizens Council refused a bailout loan of $250,000, and after Giles Miller placed an SOS to Bell—wiring him on November 12 that the team could no longer operate—the league took over the Texans. The players practiced for the last time in Dallas on Thursday, November 13, after which they boarded a plane—bade farewell by a weeping Giles Miller, who had lost $225,000 in less than a season—and departed to Detroit, for a 43–13 loss to the Lions.

The team never returned to Dallas, but instead, with a chastened Bell and the league assuming control of the franchise, was based for the rest of the season in Hershey, Pennsylvania, the bucolic company town that was the site of the Eagles' training camp, an annual exhibition between the Colts and Eagles, and a frequent stopover for West Coast teams on an East Coast jaunt.

While trying to determine what to do with the Texans, Bell had another problem on his hands, the pending suit from the city of Baltimore, over the Colts' short-lived one-year stay in the NFL. Sensing a settlement was not imminent and hoping to solve two problems at once, Bell announced December 3, 1952, that the city of Baltimore could inherit the Texans' franchise, provided they could sell 15,000 season tickets in the next month. The city immediately swept into action, holding all manner of dinners, drives, and auctions to raise the funds. It was one of the early signs of a phenomenon that pro football would see frequently in the coming decades: sports fans convinced that the very existence of a franchise gave the city itself a measure of national prestige and identity. By early January, the drive had sold 15,755 season tickets and raised $300,000.

Though Baltimore had achieved its goal and had $300,000 in the bank, it still didn't have an owner. Bell had been pestering his summer neighbor in Margate City, New Jersey, the mercurial millionaire Carroll Rosenbloom, to take the club. Rosenbloom began his career working in his father's Marlboro Shirt Company, then made his own millions during World War II with the Blue Ridge Manufacturing Co., which made denim for military work uniforms. He had played on one of the Penn football teams for which Bell was an assistant coach, and though he was fond of his old mentor, he insisted that he was too busy with his other interests. But Bell kept leaning on his old friend, insisting Rosenbloom was the only man who could give the franchise the stability that the city deserved. Bell finally settled the impasse with his usual mixture of decisiveness and gruff charm. Calling Rosenbloom on the night of January 11, Bell said, "Carroll, you're the new owner. I just announced it."

The sales terms were accommodating, requiring only $25,000 of the $200,000 price tag up front, and the rest of the payments scheduled to be paid, without interest, over the next eight years. Rosenbloom relented, and agreed to assume 51 percent ownership of the franchise (with four Baltimore businessmen taking the other 49 percent), provided Bell could find him a general manager to handle the day-to-day affairs of the club. Bell chose Don Kellett, the director of operations at WFIL-TV in Philadelphia. Baltimore was back in the business of pro football.

Instead of the old silver-and-green, the Colts wore blue-and-white, as had the Texans. In fact the capes the players wore on the sidelines were the same as those worn in Dallas, with a Colts patch sewn onto the back, covering the word "Texans." The team got off to a 3-2 start, proving again the wisdom of Bell's balanced scheduling philosophy, only to lose its last seven games, being outscored 45–2 by Los Angeles and 45–14 by San Francisco on the season-ending West Coast swing. Despite the poor performance, attendance was good, as the Colts drew more than 30,000 fans per game.

At the end of the season, first-year coach Keith Molesworth was reassigned to the scouting department and Rosenbloom ordered Kellett to search carefully to find the best coaching candidate in the game. No one within pro football was surprised when Kellett came back with the name of Browns assistant coach Blanton Collier.

Paul Brown was in a sullen mood by the time New Year's Day 1954 rolled around. For the third season in a row, his Browns had lost the NFL title game. After the 24–17 rematch loss to the Rams in 1951, the Browns suffered bitter title game defeats to Buddy Parker and his Detroit Lions, who beat Cleveland 17–7 in 1952 and prevailed 17–16 in 1953. The Browns still had been to the title game in every season of their existence, but with the rise of the hard-hitting, hard-drinking Lions, pro football had a different prototype for success, a throwback club that had all the talent of the Browns, but none of their stuffy discipline. As an answer to "Automatic Otto" Graham, the Lions came up with Bobby Layne, the commandeering quarterback from Texas. "When Bobby said block, you blocked," said teammate Yale Lary. "When Bobby said drink, you drank."

Yet beneath the surface, the Lions' system showed signs of Brown's influence. When Parker took over in 1951, he followed Brown's lead of shorter, less physical practices, as well as the custom of gathering the team in a hotel the night before home games. Just like Brown, Parker developed his playbook from Shaughnessy's system from the Bears in the early '40s, then simplified to the extreme.

It was the mind-set that Brown had brought to the game earlier—how to do things more efficiently than opponents—that led Parker to introduce the principles and pace that would come to be known as the "two-minute offense," a hurried-up, scaled-down set of plays in the closing minutes of each half, designed to make maximum use of sideline patterns to conserve the clock, signals at the line to avoid huddling after each play, and judicious use of timeouts. "I had noticed how so many teams let down the two minutes before the half, and the last two minutes of a game," said Parker. "It seemed you could get things done then that you couldn't in the other 56 minutes of play. So we drilled on it. Every day."

In the title game rematch at Detroit, Cleveland led much of the way despite Graham's worst day as a pro (he was 2-of-15 passing), but the Lions got the ball on their own 20 with 4:10 to play, trailing 16–10, and Layne drove them down the field for a 17–16 win.

Brown, still coping with the anguish of his third straight title game setback, gave Colts GM Kellett an icy reception when Baltimore called about Collier. As Carroll Rosenbloom would explain later, "Well, Paul Brown didn't want Collier to leave and refused to give me permission to talk to him. I went to see Bert about that and he assured me I had a perfect right to do so, whether Brown wanted me to or not, as long as it was a step up. So I talked to Blanton, who was scared to death of Paul Brown and did not want to be a head coach at that time, which was strange."

After a conflicted Collier asked to have his name removed from consideration for the job, Rosenbloom soon received advice from Browns minority owner Davy Jones that another Browns assistant, Weeb Ewbank, also would make a fine head coach. With Bell already having clarified the policy of interviewing assistants, there was nothing Brown could do to stop Ewbank from talking with the Colts, or leaving when the job was offered a week later. When he was first contacted by Baltimore, Ewbank knew nothing of the Colts' recruitment of Collier, so he asked Brown whether he could talk to the team. "If I don't let you, you'll never forgive me," said Brown.

Brown feared that if coaches fully versed in the Browns' system took his organizational techniques to other teams, Cleveland would lose much of its edge. He was right to be fearful.

Ewbank began by doing things exactly the way the Browns did them. In the spring of 1953, the Colts and Browns swung a fifteen-player deal, and players like Don Shula and Bert Rechichar, who had played under Brown in Cleveland, recognized in the Ewbank system in Baltimore the same terminology, the same practice structure, the same attention to detail, as they'd seen in Cleveland. While many had seen him as a foil for some of Brown's occasional barbs, Ewbank was no rube, and possessed a quiet confidence in his own coaching skills. Upon accepting the Colts job, he predicted that within five years Baltimore would have a world champion.

Art Donovan had heard that Ewbank had a reputation around the league as "a tremendous coaching talent and a rat bastard." He was inclined to agree after his first meeting with Ewbank in Baltimore, when the coach informed him he'd have to lose thirty pounds prior to training camp. But Donovan was starved for winning, and he responded, flourishing under the meticulous coaching of Ewbank.

As it happened, Collier wouldn't remain long with the Browns. Just days later Paul "Bear" Bryant left the University of Kentucky to take over the head coaching job at Texas A&M, and the school sought Collier. It was the one job that the Kentuckian Collier would consider at the time, and on February 11, 1954, after meeting with Brown at his winter home in Fort Myers, and a sleepless night of consideration, Collier accepted the job.

But he did so with a heavy heart, as a letter he wrote to Brown a few days later made clear. "The personal depth of our relationship I cannot discuss in a sane manner," Collier wrote. "As always, I choke up like some kid, so you will have to guess at the extent of my feelings. As to the technical phase of our relationship, I want you and everyone else to know that anything I have ever done in football is a result of the opportunities you have given me."

While Brown felt abandoned, all was not immediately lost. In the short term, the aging Graham would carry the Browns back to the summit, and the team routed Detroit, 56–10, in the 1954 championship contest, as Graham threw three touchdown passes and ran for three more. The Browns took a 35–10 halftime lead and never faltered. He walked off the field, accepted the MVP award, and announced his retirement.

––––––––

While the Browns—a model of consistency—were facing the prospect of life without their leader Graham, the Rams were trying to figure out why their talented club could be so frustratingly inconsistent. Much of the tumult started at the top, where coach Joe Stydahar, so fatigued after the 1951 championship that he was hospitalized for stress, grew convinced that his longtime friend and key assistant Hamp Pool was trying to undermine him. After losing 37–7 to the Browns in the 1952 season opener, Stydahar went to Reeves with an ultimatum, that either he or Pool had to go. Reeves declined to fire Pool, so Stydahar quit, and Pool—who was already drawing up game plans for both the offense and the defense—became the new head coach of the defending champs. After an 0-2 start, Pool settled the team and the Rams won eight straight, before losing to Detroit in a playoff for the Western Conference title.

In 1953, they swept the Lions, but suffered two close losses to their archrival, the San Francisco 49ers, costing them the division title. The all-California games were becoming a major attraction, drawing a pro record crowd of 77,648 in 1952, breaking that record with a crowd of 85,865 to the L.A. Coliseum in 1953, and breaking it again in 1954, as 93,553 watched the two teams tie, 24–24.

In those years, Schramm grew to admire the organizational vision of Reeves, while at the same time loathing his weaknesses. There were times when Reeves was brilliant, a keen, focused executive, at once wry and reserved, able to pinpoint a problem and work doggedly until a solution emerged. And then, inevitably, there would come a night when Schramm would get a call from Reeves, phoning from Kiernan's or some other nearby tavern, his voice lilting but slurred, asking casually if Schramm might want to join him on the next plane to Ireland. "And he'd be gone, just like that," said Schramm. "Nobody would hear from him for days on end. It was the most maddening damn thing."

Schramm soon recognized that, whatever else his talents and defects were, Reeves was a binge drinker with a dark soul and an unhappy marriage. His drinking made an already stressful situation in Los Angeles all the more volatile, and Schramm was convinced that his boss was drunk when he ordered the firing of Pool after the 6-5-1 season of 1954. Indeed, by the time of the Pool firing, Reeves was about to hire his eighth coach in fifteen seasons. But the Pool firing wasn't without basis: while undeniably a skilled tactician, Pool had lost the support of some of the players and had a difficult, standoffish relationship with the growing L.A. press corps (despite PR man Pete Rozelle's frequent entreaties to be more accommodating to the writers).

After the firing, Reeves asked Schramm to begin a nationwide hunt for the best coaching prospect he could find. Schramm called Bud Wilkinson at Oklahoma, Red Blaik at Army, Red Sanders at UCLA, and heard one name over and over again. "Everybody I spoke to talked about this guy Sid Gillman at

Cincinnati," said Schramm. "There were rumors that the only reason he hadn't gotten a bigger job offer was because he was Jewish. Well, that wasn't a problem for us."

There were plenty of rumors about the hyper-competitive, irascible Gillman, and some of them were true. He really did spend hours on end in the dark in his office, not just watching films but splicing them into different thematic reels, looking at how players from different teams executed the same moves or pass patterns. He actually had sent one of his assistants, Jack Faulkner, out to the campus of the University of Nevada in the summer of 1948 posing as a walk-on to earn a spot on the team and collect information about Cincinnati's season-opening foe. And though they would develop a civil relationship in later years, Paul Brown was convinced that Gillman had once sneaked away from a speech at one of Brown's clinics and pilfered a playbook from the team's coaching office.

Gillman looked like the put-upon father of some '50s-era situation comedy. In his natty suits and trademark bow tie, pacing the sidelines, chain-smoking, and barking behind his Wayfarer sunglasses, he emanated a kind of flinty cosmopolitanism. Like so many others in the sport, Gillman was a football obsessive. Unlike them, however, he seemed to have countless other paths he might have chosen. The son of a movie theater owner who grew up in Minneapolis, the gifted musician was seemingly bound for law school, but before he left for college, he fell in love with football, then played his last two years of college under Ohio State's legendary Francis "Close the Gates of Mercy" Schmidt. Schmidt's innovative offensive ideas awoke in Gillman a kind of consuming intellectual curiosity, and Gillman stayed on after graduation to work as Schmidt's assistant.

Preparing to embark on his honeymoon, he convinced his bride, Esther, to go to Chicago to watch the College All-Stars practice instead, and shortly thereafter, even as the couple was living as frugally as possible, Gillman spent $15 to buy a used 35mm projector that would allow him to watch game film. He also arranged to have his father, uncle, and brother smuggle football film clips from the newsreels at the Minneapolis theaters they managed. On the Sunday morning of the Pearl Harbor attack, Sid Gillman was already in his office, watching game film for the next season.

By 1954, he'd amassed a long list of rivals, as well as a 50-13-1 record. Dan Reeves was impressed, and hired him.

Gillman took the use of film study to new areas, separating game films into isolated reels for offense and defense, then cutting those further to concentrate on specific plays and situations. With his background in movie theater production, he understood not just how to operate a projector but how to cut and splice film. Squirreled away in his office with a film cutter and a handheld splicer, he'd cut a piece of film, stick a piece of masking tape to it, scrawl a rushed label onto the tape, then tape it onto any flat surface in his office. Gillman's work with film became so intense that the Rams eventually hired a full-time assistant in charge of film, a Southern California cinematographer named Mickey Dukich, who brought an electric splicing machine that allowed Gillman to work faster and in more organized form. Suddenly, he could quickly assemble a reel of all the down-and-out routes that Tom Fears ran in a previous season, or all of the Bears' plays from a certain formation. Instead of merely seeing a diagram of a play written by their coach on the chalkboard, Gillman's players were now able to see themselves, and others, repeatedly on film, using the repetition of visual evidence as the first step to teaching. Watching the previous season's film of the Rams' games, Gillman was amazed by the array of moves used by Tom Fears. "We were just beginning to understand how 'moves' are made by a receiver," he'd explain later. "Fears was one of the greatest 'move' men in the history of the game. He didn't have much speed, but he could turn 'em on their heads. We studied Fears and we began to coach what he was doing."

In his first season, 1955, Gillman's Rams were a charmed, inspired squad. Though his offense was considerably less explosive than Pool's 1954 squad (scoring 54 fewer points, rushing for 307 fewer yards, and passing for nearly 1,000 fewer yards than the previous season), Gillman's team was sound and competitive. And with a late charge, they won the Western Conference title. In a gleeful Rams locker room, Gillman allowed himself a bit of a boast. "Where has this been all my life?" he exclaimed. Schramm fixed him with a look and warned him, "Sid, it's not always going to be this easy."

And it wasn't. A week later in the NFL title game, the Browns rolled over the Rams, 38–14. It was a perfect coda for Otto Graham, whom a desperate Brown had coaxed out of retirement at the beginning of the 1955 season, after Cleveland lost to the College All-Stars at the start of a 1-5 exhibition season. After looking rusty in a season-opening loss to the Redskins, Graham was brilliant the rest of the season, then masterful in the title game victory. The win fulfilled a vow Graham had made to Brown four years earlier when, walking off the field after Cleveland's 24–17 loss to the Rams in the 1951 title game, he told his coach, "I'll make this up to you, Paul, I promise you that." Graham retired for good after the 1955 season; he had played ten seasons and led Cleveland to ten championship games, winning all four in the AAFC and three out of six in the NFL.

Brown knew that his team would no longer have a free ticket into the title game, as it had in the past. A competitive shift had occurred in the larger, post-AAFC version of the NFL, as Brown's organizational mastery was now widely imitated. And as other teams began employing some of the same principles, they also began seeking their own distinct advantages—the Rams with their scouting system, the Lions with their simplified schemes and two-minute offense—and the margin of error afforded the Browns became smaller and smaller.

With Collier at Kentucky and Ewbank across the sidelines in Baltimore, Brown's network of top-notch aides was diminishing. Though they would be replenished with quality assistants, he would never again in Cleveland assemble a staff in which he had the same level of confidence and comfort.

Ewbank and Gillman arrived as head coaches at a time when the modern, recognizable two-platoon form of professional football—at once violent and cerebral, increasingly reliant on the passing game and the dueling strategies of opposing coaches—began to reach critical mass. The game as played in 1955 had changed substantially from what it had been even five years earlier: faster, more wide-open, and played at a higher level of specialization and expertise than ever before. Free substitution became a permanent part of the rulebook in 1950, and by the middle of the decade, the two-way player was becoming an anachronism, and the onset of the distinctly modern American concept of specialization was in full bloom. Players now confined themselves to either offense or defense, and were afforded the luxury of focusing on a particular discipline during practice; they also remained fresher physically during the games, which were thus played at a higher intensity level. The emphasis on speed by a few teams in the late '40s began to be felt throughout the league as well. But these developments were obscured by the growing awareness of the game's often casual brutality. "Never have the pros played better, more exciting football," wrote Melvin Durslag in *Sports Illustrated* in 1955. "Never have division races been tighter nor games more unpredictable. Yet hanging like a pall over the otherwise brilliant play are two nasty words: 'dirty football.' "

Reports of growing violence, cheap shots, and "hatchet men" had been building for some time before a sensationalistic *Life* cover story—"Savagery on Sunday"—in the fall of 1955. By the time the jury found *Life* guilty of libel—awarding Eagles Bucko Kilroy and Wayne Robinson $11,500 each—the league's reputation had undergone a serious beating. A year later, the Bears' Ed Meadows executed a brutal late hit on Bobby Layne, in the game that helped Chicago edge Detroit for the Western Conference title. A few weeks later, *Sports Illustrated* began a Q&A with Bert Bell following the 1956 season with the leading question, "Do you believe that pro football is dirty and getting dirtier?"

Even as the discussion of the game's violence was at its shrillest, the sport was becoming safer. The catalyst of one important change can be traced to a Cleveland game against San Francisco in 1953. Late in the second quarter, after scrambling for a first down, Otto Graham's face was slashed on a savage late hit by the 49ers' Art Michalik. It took fifteen sutures inside Graham's mouth, administered without novocaine at halftime, to close the wound. In the second half, while completing 9 of 10 passes to rally the Browns to victory, Graham wore an inch-thick piece of clear plastic to protect his mouth. Later in the season, the Riddell sports equipment company came up with a plastic shield that wrapped around the helmet, but the shield grew brittle and often cracked in cold weather. (Graham disliked it because he couldn't spit under it.)

That led to another innovation from Paul Brown. At the end of the season, he visited Riddell's offices in Chicago, and described to technical consultant G. E. Morgan what he wanted: "Give me something that will fit across the front of a helmet and will be about as big as my little finger, with tensile strength. I want it so it can withstand a stray foot, or a deliberately thrown fist or elbow, and take away the inclination to punch someone. But keep it light enough to weigh less than an ounce." With that description to work on, Morgan and his team of engineers invented the BT-5 (the BT stood for "bar tubular"), a single gray bar composed of rubber and plastic that the Browns began wearing on their helmets in 1954. While modified facemasks had been fashioned before, this was the first one to be mass-produced. The faceguards caught on quickly, and became common in the NFL within the next two years. (Brown, incidentally, had a contract with Riddell that paid him a royalty for every mask sold, bringing him millions in the decades ahead.)

The other significant change was written into the rules in 1955, and while it seemed merely a minor modification at the time, it proved to have a powerful civilizing influence. Instead of defining a tackle as both bringing down a runner and stopping his forward progress, the new rule stipulated: "If a player touches the ground with any part of his body, except his hands or feet, while in the grasp of an opponent and irrespective of the grasp being broken, the ball is declared dead immediately." The immediate result of the rule was that it stopped much of the vicious close-in fighting that took place after tackles had been made, as runners tried to struggle free and keep running. It also curtailed the routine piling on that took place at the end of tackles, with defenders continuing to jump on a runner long after he was downed. "The pileup is where most players are injured," said Greasy Neale in 1954. "It's intentional and can be avoided. That's vicious football."

It would be a while before public perception caught up with the reality of the changing nature of the game. The combination of safety, speed, and unlimited substitutions, along with the influence of Cleveland's relatively cerebral style and the Rams' wide-open attack, meant that the game would inevitably become more complex. And with that, the role of coaches and personnel scouts would become more important than ever.

In 1955, after Ewbank had spent a year at the helm in Baltimore, having built up one of the most extensive networks of scouts in the country, the Colts opened the draft by winning the "bonus choice," a lottery system by which all the teams in the league were guaranteed to get the top pick in the draft once every twelve years. The draft itself was becoming one of the most important dates on the NFL calendar, with teams following the Rams' lead and devoting more time and resources to preparing for it.

The Colts' investment in scouting was still financially modest, the team paying a loose collection of college assistants $50, plus a sport shirt from Rosenbloom's Marlboro Shirt Company, for their annual reports. In that 1955 draft, the Colts used the first pick for All-American quarterback George Shaw of Oregon. The team was still not well known nationally, and when the time came for him to negotiate, Shaw had to ask the Colts what their colors were.

At a time when rosters were at thirty-three and only three to five rookies might be expected to make a team, the Colts' first six selections, and twelve rookies overall (including three free agents) made the 1955 squad. It seemed that they had found their starting quarterback, center, and running backs for the next ten years. Alan "The Horse" Ameche, from Wisconsin, quickly won the starting running back job, along with L. G. "Long Gone" Dupre of Baylor. Dick Szymanski, a center from Notre Dame, looked to anchor the line, and the quarterback, Shaw, who went on to win Rookie of the Year honors in 1955, was deemed a can't-miss prospect.

While teams like the Rams and Colts were taking a more systematic approach to scouting, other clubs still lagged behind. It wasn't uncommon, when the draft was held in Philadelphia in the late '50s, for teams' scouts to show up with a few magazines and news clippings and park out by the pay phones at the Warwick Hotel lobby. "Guys would come in with rolls of quarters, because in those days you didn't have credit cards to make telephone calls," said Gil Brandt, who did scouting work for the Rams at the time. "So they would have a pick coming up, and they'd run out to the pay phone and drop two dollars and twenty-five cents in—*ding, ding, ding*—and call Pappy Lewis of West Virginia. 'Hey, Pappy, who is the best offensive lineman you played against last year?' And that's how this kind of stuff took place, as recently as the late '50s."

Typical of the mind-set at the time was that held by the Steelers, who had the bonus pick for the 1956 draft. Head coach Walt Kiesling, a longtime Steeler on his third tour of duty as coach, had received a rousing recommendation from a fellow coach about a Colorado State player named Gary Glick, projected to be a defensive back in the pros.

As the scouting continued, in meetings with Steelers owner Art Rooney, and his sons Dan and Tim, Kiesling kept returning to the recommendation. "Kiesling kept pulling this letter out," remembered Dan Rooney, "and he keeps saying, 'We need a defensive back. This kid would be terrific.' It's a bonus pick! And we never send anybody out to see him. We never did anything. Talked to him on the phone, the kid was wonderful—you know, why wouldn't he be? I mean, he might have been a good fifth-round pick, but to take him as the first guy in the country . . ."

When the draft was held the weekend following Thanksgiving, and the Steelers announced their selection—"Gary Glick, Colorado State"—the veteran *Pittsburgh Press* newspaper writer Bob Drum marched over to the Steelers' table and said, "Harry Stick! Where the fuck did you get this guy?"

In the aftermath of the draft, Dan Rooney called the school to get film of the player, something that the Steelers' coaching staff had neglected to do. When it arrived a week later, Dan invited his father up to the Steelers' scouting office to watch the film with him. "But my father wouldn't go. He said, 'I'm busy.' So we go off to the eighth floor, where we've got our personnel office,' and we put the film on. And it's like, the smallest college that you could imagine, dogs running out on the field. So we come back down into my dad's office, and nobody says anything. And I remember my father saying, 'He didn't look very good, right?' "

While the Steelers were still shooting blanks, many of the other clubs were hitting a higher percentage. In the first round that same year, the Colts selected fleet future All-Pro Lenny Moore, from Penn State, who would go on to add a measure of explosiveness to an already strong attack. The Browns' scouting system continued to thrive as well, as Cleveland added nine players who'd have NFL careers in 1955, and eight more in 1956.

But with teams in such close quarters, with competition honed to a sharper edge than before across the league, every single personnel decision took on greater importance. And a seemingly minor one that Brown had made a year earlier, in August of 1955, would come back to haunt him.

———

From its earliest days, one of the credos of football was that deprivation bred toughness. Coaches believed that boys with the most difficult childhoods made the best football players. They were built of tougher stuff, more willing to administer and accept pain, more willing to sacrifice for the good of the whole, to find a familial bond in football.

John Unitas was one of the tough ones. He had been just five years old when his father died of pneumonia in 1938, leaving him and his three siblings to be raised by their mother, Helen, who took over the family's coal delivery business in Pittsburgh, and got other work on the side, from cleaning offices to accounting.

So Unitas quickly learned the value of work, earning a quarter at a time by shoveling two tons of coal into his neighbors' cellars. Prematurely stoic, and undersized until a growth spurt in high school, he was best known at an early age for being an excellent dribbler in basketball and terribly shy away from the fields and courts. He could be jovial, even a cutup, but it happened only with close friends and never in a large social setting, where he maintained a kind of quiet, barely polite detachment. On many a Friday night, Unitas would pick up his sweetheart, Dorothy Hoelle, and take her and her friend to the gymnasium for a school dance. He would drop them off, then wait in the parking lot for a couple of hours; he didn't care for dancing, or crowds, but he was determined that he would fulfill his obligations and escort his girlfriend to the dance.

Unitas didn't see his first professional football game until September 1950, when his coach, Max Carey, brought him to the Browns-Eagles game that opened the season in Philadelphia. At the time, he was a 5-foot-10, 135-pound junior quarterback at St. Justin's. Under Carey, he would blossom in his junior season, beating out senior Dan Rooney, then attending the local power, St. Cecilia's, for All-City quarterback.

A year later, Unitas had grown an inch and gained ten pounds, and was again an All-City performer. But there was little to indicate that he was going to make it even as a college quarterback. He was dismissed as too small during a tryout at Notre Dame (the Irish assistant sent Carey a letter saying he thought Unitas would get hurt playing college football). Indiana expressed, then lost, interest. He failed the entrance exam at Pitt.

The lone school of consequence interested in Unitas was the University of Louisville, where he earned a starter's job midway through his freshman season and went on to lead a consistently undermanned team through two winning seasons, before an academic scandal resulted in fifteen players transferring from Louisville. With the decimated squad, Louisville won just five games in Unitas's last two years, and the modest buzz from pro scouts all but vanished. Still, Browns assistant Dick Gallagher told Unitas he'd be drafted by Cleveland if he was available in the later rounds. Instead, Pittsburgh took the hometown boy in the ninth round of the 1955 draft.

That summer of 1955, Unitas reported to training camp for his hometown Pittsburgh Steelers. It was a rude awakening. At the Steelers' training camp in Olean, New York, he was overwhelmed by the cliquishness of the veterans, who after a few days started calling him Clem, after the country hayseed character Clem Kadiddlehopper created by comic Red Skelton. The hazing he might have expected; the lack of professionalism he didn't. When Unitas asked for the daily whites—socks, T-shirt, shorts, and an athletic supporter that players wore under their uniform in practice—the Steelers' trainer told him to rummage for them himself from what was lying in a large pile on the floor of the locker room. After morning practices, a player had to hang his soaked whites on a big hook by his locker, hoping the clothes would dry by the afternoon session. When Unitas asked about getting his ankles taped before practice, he was told that players didn't get taped unless they were hurt.

Steelers head coach Walt Kiesling found little to like in Unitas, particularly since competition was so intense on the thirty-three-man roster, and with starter Jim Finks, versatile Ted Marchibroda (who also handled the punting duties), and fellow rookie Vic Eaton, Kiesling paid Unitas little mind. Through five exhibition games, Unitas never took a snap.

Meanwhile, Art Rooney's sons were going crazy. "His accuracy was incredible," recalled Dan Rooney, who by then was overseeing the training camp while his father spent the month of August at horse tracks. "I'd watch him throw for hours and it made me sick to think Kies wasn't giving him a look. My brother, Timmy—he was fifteen then—wrote my father a letter telling him Unitas was not only the best passer in camp but probably the best passer in football but the coaches weren't giving him a fair shot. My dad wrote back from Aqueduct or someplace and said, 'Why don't you leave the coaching to the coaches?' "

Kiesling's mind was made up; he found Unitas thick and withdrawn, too slow to grasp the Steelers' playbook, that he set up too slowly in the pocket, and couldn't find secondary receivers. On September 5, a full three weeks before the beginning of the regular season, Unitas was cut. When Kiesling called him into his office to tell him he was being released, a bristling Unitas was defiant, openly challenging the decision. "Y'know, it'd be different if I screwed up," Unitas told him, "but you never gave me an opportunity to play."

"Unitas was totally ignored," said Dan Rooney. "They never did anything with him. It wasn't a question of misjudging him. They would have had to judge him first. But they never did a thing with him."

Unitas received bus fare back to Pittsburgh, but hitchhiked home instead, where Dorothy (by now his wife) was waiting with news that she'd bought tickets for their families to see the Steelers' opening home game the following week. That evening, they sat around in their living room, neither speaking, neither quite sure what to do next.

Within a day, his old high school coach, Max Carey, would provide consolation and direction. The Browns, without the retired Otto Graham, had lost to the College All-Stars, and were clearly desperate for quarterbacking help. Carey persuaded Unitas to send Paul Brown a telegram, asking for a tryout in Cleveland. (Unbeknownst to Unitas, Art Rooney had called Brown at the behest of his son. "Dan says this Unitas is a good lookin' kid," he said. "Maybe you guys should pick him up.") By that time, though, Brown had already made his move, coaxing Otto Graham back for one more season. Brown wired Unitas back, telling him that since Graham was returning for one final season, the Browns wouldn't need any help at quarterback that year, but if he wanted to, Unitas was welcome to come to training camp with the Browns the following July.

With that shred of hope, Unitas kept his dreams alive. He spent the next few months working construction in Pittsburgh, spending six days a week as the "monkey man" atop a pile driver, part of a road construction crew laying the foundation for a mill in Aliquippa. On Thursday nights he'd drive to the rock-strewn dirt field next to Arsenal Street School, and play with the Bloomfield Rams, a semipro team that played once a week in the Steel Bowl Conference, an array of Industrial Belt semipro clubs. At $6 per game, Unitas was playing football. Paid in cash by team owner Chuck Rogers in the basement of Parise's Dairy, just across the street from the field, Unitas brought his $6 home to his wife, telling her, "Dotty, don't spend this on bills. Spend it on something nice for yourself."

By the end of Weeb Ewbank's second season with the Colts in 1955, only twelve players remained from Keith Molesworth's Colts squad of 1953. Baltimore's team was younger, bigger, faster, more talented, and, with a 5-6-1 record, starting to show signs of coming together. During that fall of 1955, Ewbank received a postcard from Pittsburgh, unsigned but addressed to him, which read, "There's a boy in sandlot ball here, playing for the Bloomfield Rams, who's worth looking at. His name's John Unitas." He later mentioned Unitas to Colts GM Don Kellett, who also had him on a list of possible free agents. One of the few places the team felt secure was at quarterback, with bonus pick George Shaw coming off his impressive Rookie of the Year season in 1955. But when backup quarterback Gary Kerkorian told Kellett that he was planning to retire so he could attend law school, the GM began combing the free agent lists, and came across the name of Unitas, whom Ewbank had mentioned earlier.

In February 1956, Kellett called Unitas. What would go down in legend as an 80-cent phone call was actually two 84-cent long-distance calls, one in the afternoon, when Dorothy Unitas told Kellett her husband wasn't home from work yet, and another later in the evening, when Unitas answered the phone. Kellett invited him to come work out for Ewbank the following week, with the understanding if he passed muster then, he'd be invited to training camp, and offered a $7,000 contract if he made the team.

While some teams, most notably the Rams, had started using movie cameras as a technical aid during practices, the Colts didn't have such equipment. When Unitas and some other free agents came for their workout, they played on an unmarked field next to the Clifton Park pool in Baltimore, and an assistant snapped still photos of all the players, to study for later evaluation.

"We took pictures of John under center, and again when he set up and right at the last when he followed through," recalled Ewbank. "That was the thing we noticed right away, the way he followed through. It was exceptional. The pictures showed it clearly. His arm went through so far that he turned his hand over like a pitcher. . . . When he followed through his fingers turned over and you could see the back of his hand."

Ewbank told Unitas to work on keeping the nose of the football up on short passes, to get more loft on his long passes, and to be in camp in July. Unitas could have held out and gone to the Browns' camp, but the Colts were more aggressive, and Cleveland hadn't been in touch since Brown's short note the previous August. With only one proven quarterback in Baltimore, Unitas sensed his chances for success were better there. Thus would the relative fortunes of the Cleveland Browns and Baltimore Colts be forever changed.

From the first day of Colts training camp, that July 1956 in Westminster, Maryland, Unitas realized that he'd found a home. He felt welcomed by the Colts, comfortable in an environment that was much more nurturing for players. Dick Nyers, a rookie kick returner, met him at the airport and drove him to the Colts' offices, where they got a ride to training camp. In the locker room, the whites were rolled up and waiting by each player's locker. When the veterans arrived days later, Unitas found a completely different atmosphere. "These guys would take you aside and try to work with you and help you," he said. "George Shaw was happy to help me with anything I asked of him. You could see Gino Marchetti taking a defensive end and showing how to work. You never got any of that kind of treatment in Pittsburgh." Unitas still didn't cut a very convincing figure on the football field. The Giants had first faced him in that 1956 preseason, and Unitas appeared so ungainly trotting out onto the field that day that Giants quarterback Charlie Conerly looked over to Frank Gifford on the New York sideline and said, "Look at that goofy sonofabitch."

But as would be said about him hundreds of times after then, they noticed that Unitas got the job done. The first glimmer came in the team's annual blue-white intrasquad scrimmage in Hershey, Pennsylvania. Shaw had been out with the flu, and Unitas started for the white-jersey second squad, passing for three touchdowns. Late in the game, the staff asked him to switch to a blue jersey, to try to rally the team, which he did, as the game ended 20–20. On the closing drive, he made his first pass to the Colts' second-year end Raymond Berry.

The two men came from vastly different backgrounds—Berry's father had been a coach at the Paris, Texas, high school—but they shared a relentless desire to master the game. With Unitas, there was the endless perfection of the technique that Ewbank constructed on his carefully annotated four-page sheets of quarterback's instructions. Concerned about his tendency to throw the ball too low, Ewbank during one training camp took to stringing a volleyball net up across the scrimmage line, and having Unitas throw his arsenal of passes over it.

But it was not all instruction. Unitas possessed qualities that were unteachable and inimitable. Teammates and opponents alike soon noticed his absolute fearlessness in the face of a pass rush, his willingness to hold on to the football before releasing a pass until the last possible instant, and to do so without flinching. He also had a habit, on deeper routes, of deceiving defenders by rolling his shoulders as if winding up for a pass, away from the side of the field he intended to throw to, then rolling them back toward his chosen receiver. More deceptive than the standard pump-fake, the move impressed Ewbank enough for him to try to teach it to the other quarterbacks. But it required a dexterous, loose-jointed coordination, and no one else on the team could master it.

If Unitas was a diamond in the rough, Berry was a self-polished stone. Decades before it became common in pro sports, he'd developed his own elaborate set of habits and methods, which set him apart from anyone on the team. "He went to bed at half past eight, to make sure he got enough sleep," remembered Unitas, "and when he got a pair of uniform pants that fit just the way they should, he insisted on hand-washing them himself, so they wouldn't be given out to some other player after laundry was done. He carried a football with him every place he walked the camp grounds, so he would get the feel of the ball and keep his fingers supple enough to catch any passes that might be thrown to him." Berry would develop, both on his own and later in 1958 with the help of receivers coach Bob Shaw, an arsenal of eighty-eight distinct maneuvers designed to elude defenders. And in training camp and throughout the season in practices, as the shadows grew longer and the light grew dimmer, Unitas and Berry could be found out on the field for thirty minutes or more after all of their teammates had gone inside.

The Colts were 1-2 when they traveled to Chicago on Sunday, October 21, to face the Bears in Wrigley Field. Leading the game 20–7, Colts quarterback George Shaw was injured, tearing ligaments being tackled by Chicago defensive tackle Fred Williams. Unitas came in and the first ball he handed off was a fumbled exchange, leading to a touchdown. His first pass was intercepted by the Bears' J. C. Caroline, and returned for a touchdown. The Bears ran away with the game, 58–27. But the next week, Unitas led the club to a 28–21 win over the Packers, and there was evidence to suggest that the team was rallying around him.

Ewbank would remember Unitas taking control almost instantly, and having both the will and the presence to be able to stridently criticize his teammates if they weren't performing. "Goddammit, this is no fun back here," Unitas would say. "You should try throwing that ball, the way you're letting them through."

On November 11, 1956, Unitas led the Colts into Cleveland, where Baltimore won, 21–7, in a homecoming of sorts for Ewbank. It was the Colts' first win over Cleveland in seven games, dating back to the AAFC. When an elated

Ewbank trotted across the field to shake hands with his old mentor, Brown wasn't there.

Later that week, back in Baltimore, equipment manager Fred Schubach wondered aloud when George Shaw would return from his injury. The big defensive end Gino Marchetti fixed Schubach with a look, and said, "He's never going to be the quarterback again. Unitas is the quarterback."

6

On Any Given Sunday

Shortly after a rain-drenched day in early October 1955, when the New York football Giants drew a crowd announced as 7,000 to the Polo Grounds for a game against the Chicago Cardinals, owner Tim Mara received a call from Bert Bell in Philadelphia. The commissioner told him that two un-named Texas oilmen were willing to pay $1 million for the Giants—but only if they could move the team's games to Yankee Stadium.

Mara wasn't selling, but he was intrigued by the prospect of a new venue. The Polo Grounds, with its elongated dimensions, lacked the amenities or ca-chet of Yankee Stadium. But what had kept the Giants from considering a move earlier was Mara's ongoing war with Yankees owner Dan Topping, which dated back for more than a decade, when Topping owned an NFL franchise. Thirty years earlier, Tim Mara had mused that any franchise in New York ought to be worth $2,500. After Bell's call, he consulted with his sons, Jack and Wellington, and conceded that if someone was willing to pay $1 million for putting the Giants into Yankee Stadium, they probably should consider doing it themselves. Jack Mara made the overtures and, early in 1956, the Giants signed a contract to play their games across the Harlem River, in the Bronx.

While pro football was gathering momentum throughout the '50s, and crowds were growing in Baltimore and Cleveland and Los Angeles, the most striking changes in the decade occurred in New York City, where a confluence of trends contributed to a greater profile for the sport than it had ever enjoyed.

After Steve Owen's twenty-three-year tenure as head coach ended with a 3-9 mark in 1954, the Giants handed the job to the laid-back Arkansan Jim Lee Howell, who presided over an 8-4 turnaround in 1955. In 1956, the charmed first season in Yankee Stadium, the Giants went 8-3-1 and were at home when they won their first title in twenty years, blowing out Chicago, 47–7, on a frigid, slippery field.

All over the city that fall, players who for years had been ignored or made to feel inferior to their baseball counterparts were getting the sort of VIP attention that had previously been the sole province of baseball players. "I could tell a difference even then," said halfback Frank Gifford of the city's change in attitude in the wake of the 1956 success. "All of a sudden instead of going to the dumps on the West Side, somebody would be inviting you to dinner at Toots Shor's or '21' or Al Shack's or Rose's or Manuche's, it was just a different world."

———

The dawning age of specialization could be seen in the Giants' success, off the field as well as on. Many on the team credited the team's resurgence to the dynamic assistant coaching combination of Vince Lombardi, who ran the offense, and Tom Landry, in charge of defense. Head coach Jim Lee Howell was a delegator; Giants linebacker Sam Huff would say he "never once saw him draw a play up on a chalkboard."

Visiting Howell at work in 1958, Red Smith wrote, "Mostly he is the administrator and the coordinator, and that apparently is the way to do the job today. If the question is offense, Howell says, 'Ask Lombardi about that.' Defense? Tom Landry is the man to see. U.S. Steel does fairly well on that plan, but it is unorthodox in football and therefore suspect by some."

Tactically speaking, the two assistants had much in common. Both were students of the expanding science of film study, not just for evaluating their own players but for finding clues to an upcoming opponent's philosophy and patterns.

Though they were the two best-known and most respected assistants in pro football, Lombardi and Landry were never close. The Catholic Lombardi was voluble and fiery, a man of vast charm but profane tirades, whom Landry nicknamed "Mr. High-Low" for his radical mood swings. Landry, a self-proclaimed born-again Christian who had flown bomber missions in World War II, was balding, detached, and self-collected, an industrial engineer who loved the solitude of extended study sessions. Gifford saw "a lot of competition" between Lombardi and Landry, and viewed it as a logical progression of the increasingly specialized units themselves. "We didn't like [the defense] very much, and they didn't like us much. And didn't really care. We were cliquey." The antagonism was felt on both sides of the ball, especially when New York's offense was sputtering. Sam Huff, marching off the field after another defensive stand, had been known to mutter to his offensive counterparts taking the field, "Now get in there and hold 'em."

Lombardi, who came to the Giants in 1953 from assistant coaching jobs at Army and Fordham, ran the offense with a mixture of fundamental willpower and unusual mental gymnastics. He convinced the Giants to bring a Polaroid camera up to the press box, to provide overhead views of the defensive alignments, which were then shuttled down from the upper deck by Wellington Mara, who put the pictures inside a sock weighted with a rock, then lowered them on a string to the sideline. In 1956, he took to beginning games with his backup quarterback, Don Heinrich, in the starting lineup, then spending the first two or three series conferring with his number one quarterback, Charlie Conerly, about the defensive alignment and the plays that might work best. Then, after a quarter or so (or even, on one occasion, as long as three quarters), he would insert his "starter."

Lombardi also incorporated the intricacies and exquisite logic of "rule blocking," a system in which each offensive lineman's assignment on a particular play was dependent upon the alignment of the defender in front of him (an alignment that could, of course, change in an instant prior to the snap). An offensive guard's assignment might be different if the man across from him was shaded to his right shoulder than if the same man was four inches over, "face-up" on his nose. One of the assistants on Red Blaik's staff at Army described rule blocking as "a combination of Sanskrit, algebra and infantry tactics," but it quickly became standard procedure in the NFL, where Sid Gillman in L.A. was another proponent and innovator.

Most of all, Lombardi was a motivator, who used his intensity to alternately intimidate and placate his players, driving them to higher levels of performance. While Landry was unquestionably a brilliant tactician, his spare, ascetic style left many of his players cold. "He never made a comment about, 'You're playing well' or 'You're playing terrible' or 'You're not doing anything,' " said Pat Summerall, traded from the Cardinals to the Giants in 1958. "He just said, 'You didn't do what I told you' and that was his simple way of correcting and praising. 'You did what I said, so we won.' "

The cornerstone of the Landry defense was the belief that finding patterns in a team's play in previous games could help determine their likely play selection in future games. Carefully charting the film he was watching not just for different formations and plays, but the frequency of plays and types of calls in certain down-and-distance situations, Landry likely became the first coach in the game to intensively document an opponent's tendencies to construct a game plan. For his players, Landry converted this information into a series of reads or "keys," in which they responded to a certain formation or initial player movement with a countermove based on a team's likely play-calling history in the two or three earlier games Landry had studied on film.

What had emerged from Owen's umbrella defense was Landry's modern variation, called the 4-3-4, or, simply, the 4-3. In this setup, the middle guard moved three to five yards behind the line of scrimmage, and became the middle linebacker. Huff, in that position, was the leader of the defense, and one of the league's first purely defensive stars.

In an age when offenses were starting to spread out, the 4-3 offered defenses more lateral mobility. And when Landry rubbed his stomach on the sidelines, the linebackers, instead of lying in wait for the play to develop, would charge into the backfield. The "blitz" or "red dog" became one of the pro game's signature plays, an instance of the defense taking a gamble on a par with the long bomb by the offense.

Brown's innovations had upped the ante of general organization and planning throughout the league; the machinations of Landry and Lombardi (along with a handful of other innovators, like Pool and then Gillman in Los Angeles and Brown and Collier in Cleveland) would make the game's strategy and tactics even more complex. And with the title in 1956, the Giants were on the front end of that change, and would begin a glorious run that would last for nearly a decade.

But it was not so much the Giants themselves as the reaction *to* the Giants, building throughout the late '50s and early '60s, that indicated pro football had turned a corner.

For the advertising community in New York, brimming with young, active execs and consultants tuned into the faster pace of the new media, football held a visceral tug that other sports couldn't match. The word they spoke about most often was "action," and Madison Avenue's interest translated beyond Sunday afternoons. For the first time, there were commercial opportunities presenting themselves to players. Charlie Conerly, the Giants' quarterback, became friends with longtime Giants season ticket holder Jack Landry, an executive with Philip Morris, who helped him line up an endorsement deal with Marlboro cigarettes. Frank Gifford landed a television pregame show and a news broadcasting spot. Gifford also was recruited by an energetic ad agency exec named Homer Groening for the Jantzen sportswear campaign, a major print push that included athletes like Bob Cousy and Ken Venturi, but significantly, no baseball players, since Groening wasn't a fan. (Homer Groening's son, Matt, would go on to a career as a cartoonist and creator of *The Simpsons*.)

The large, loud crowds that came to cheer the Giants on Sunday were not just avid but also knowledgeable. They began cheering not only for the offensive backfield stars but also for the Giants' defense, shouting "DEE! FENSE! DEE! FENSE!" during important stands, or repeatedly chanting the names of Huff or Robustelli. Like fans in Cleveland and Green Bay and other cities, bundling up to spend an afternoon in ridiculously cold weather became a perverse point of pride, and a sign of commitment and devotion.

Pro football had become, in the same vein as baseball, a sport for serious fans. And, at the same time, it was becoming the flip side of baseball—often urgent while baseball was often relaxed, strictly regimented where baseball was at times meandering. Attending a baseball game asked less of the fan, was never quite the ordeal that football—with the frequent exhortations, concerted clapping, chants, and stomping, attempting to sway both sides—had become. While college fans had the identification for the alma mater to spur them on, the relationship with a professional team and its fan base was a more synthetic one. Yet the evidence, around the country in the late '50s, was that it was growing rapidly.

The league's surge in popularity didn't come in a vacuum, however, nor without resistance. It is difficult to exaggerate the casual contempt with which spectator sports were held in the collective consciousness of many cultured Americans in the early 1950s. Though the games were clearly gaining popularity across age groups and social classes, the mere act of fandom still was frowned on by much of the cultural elite. Before *Sports Illustrated* launched in 1954, an executive at Time Inc. wrote in a memo that the likely audience for such a magazine would be made up of "either juveniles or ne'er-do-wells."

But that advice wasn't heeded, and *SI* itself would later help to change the perception of the games themselves. In 1956, the magazine began running regular stories by Tex Maule, who, after leaving the Rams for his ill-fated stint as PR man for the Dallas Texans in 1952, worked as a columnist on the *Dallas Times Herald*, then came to New York to become the new magazine's pro football writer in 1956. Maule was hardly the best writer at *Sports Illustrated*, but he was among the most expert, a writer with strong connections throughout the league, who was as intrigued as many fans with the point and counterpoint of gridiron strategy. He was, almost unique at the time, a writer who could divine many of the intricacies of the modern game without either mocking the process or making light of his inability to fathom it. Almost imperceptibly at first, more clearly later, the public began to understand that the game was not all a matter of brute force. Television helped that cause, in giving fans a better view of the action than they might have at the game. And *Sports Illustrated* contributed as well, with Maule treating the game and the league with a seriousness it hadn't always received in the national press.

There were still stories arguing whether the pro game was more entertaining than the college one, but by the late '50s, few people were questioning the pros' proficiency. "I believe we began to convince people that pro football was a logical extension of college football," said Carroll Rosenbloom, "a way for them to continue to follow their college heroes, who otherwise would have graduated and never been heard from again. Take Alan Ameche [the club's 1955 first-round draft choice from Wisconsin]. They wanted to keep seeing him, and millions could, all over the country." Attendance, which had averaged 23,196 for the sixty games of 1949, increased every year during the '50s, and by 1959, the league was averaging 43,617 for its seventy-two games.

––––––––

Presiding over the league's ascendance, with an ever more assured hand, was Bert Bell. By the beginning of the decade, he was viewed as nearly indispensable by the owners.

"We're as much concerned about his health as Republicans are about the health of the president," said George Preston Marshall in 1954. Early that year, when Bell collapsed at the Racquet Club in Philadelphia, his doctors were worried about his diet and schedule, telling him to cut down on his cigarette smoking and hours. As his health worsened and pace quickened in 1957, Bert Jr. began to worry as well. In February of 1959, Bell suffered a mild heart attack, and convalesced at Lackinaw Hospital just outside Philadelphia, vowing to cut back on cigarettes, eggs, fat, and steaks. Before the league meetings that spring, league treasurer Austin Gunsel furtively contacted several owners asking them—at the behest of Bell's physician—to avoid the marathon late-night sessions that typically marked previous league meetings.

Though he had matured in the job, and learned when to apply pressure and when to act as conciliator, Bell's operational style had changed little. He never flew, taking Pullman trains for road trips. In his office, he sat behind a massive mahogany desk, with burn marks all around the edges of the desktop, a product of Bell's placing lit cigarettes on the desk during many of his lengthy telephone discussions. From the office at Bala Cynwyd (pronounced bal-uh kin-wood), just across the street from the Philadelphia city limits, to the phone with the long extension cord in the front room at his home in the Narberth neighborhood where he had lived since 1950, he routinely ran up long-distance expenses in excess of $10,000 per year.

After more than a decade in Center City Philadelphia, Bell decided the league office should be moved out of the city limits—where the onerous wage tax lopped off 1.5% of every worker's income. The league chose a modern building, close to a train stop, in Bala Cynwyd. The new office put Bell even closer to Narberth.

Even in the last half of the '50s, with the sport on the rise, the league office was still a modest operation. Secretaries had come and gone, and by 1958, when Bell's twenty-six-year-old son, Bert Jr., began working as a clerk in the office, there was no dedicated secretary. The office was instead filled with one-finger typists, not a major problem since almost all of Bell's correspondence was by telephone. Once, asked by a lawyer to see his correspondence with CBS, Bell replied, "I've never had any correspondence with CBS. All our deals are made by telephone." CBS executive Edgar Scherick, who dealt with the commissioner extensively throughout the '50s, recalled, "Bell himself ran the whole goddamn league out of his kitchen. . . . He'd call me up every morning, just as I was soaping myself up in the shower, and we'd work out our arrangements by telephone."

The league's legal counsel was Bert's brother, Jack Bell, the Pennsylvania Supreme Court justice. Austin Gunsel, formerly of the FBI, was the treasurer and the league's de facto director of security, who began the league policy of putting an ex-FBI agent on retainer in each league city. Joe Labrum, who'd attended Penn with Bell, was the league's publicist. Rounding out the office was Mike Wilson, director of officials, and Harry Standish, Jr., the league's director of personnel (and Bell's brother-in-law, married to the sister of Bell's wife), in charge of approving player contracts. Standish kept a series of 3 × 5 note cards on every player's contract, each one beginning with his handwritten words, "This boy was . . . ," before a recitation of the round the player was drafted in, how much he signed his contract for, and what bonuses were in his contract. In many ways, Standish's contract note cards were the most sophisticated organizational tool in the office. There was no receptionist, no central file clerk, no typing pool. Many reporters would find, when calling the league offices in the '50s, that Bell himself might answer the phone. Even when he didn't pick up the office phone, he gave the staff instructions to patch all calls for him directly through.

Because of Bell's success, the league's rapid attendance growth, and rising revenues, much dissent was muffled in the name of progress. Some owners resented the scheduling. Others felt that Bell had a natural bias for his closest friends among the owners. When the Bears' Ed Meadows bludgeoned Bobby Layne in the 1956 game that decided the Western Conference title, many saw the lack of a fine as being a sign that Bell was in George Halas's hip pocket. West Coast teams perceived a clear regional bias. "It was the old guard, and every ruling would be in favor of them," complained Tex Schramm, with the Rams at the time. "That shit got old fast." But owners who strongly disagreed with Bell either couldn't muster the support to defeat him on key issues, or else eventually capitulated out of a combination of respect and peer pressure.

"When he wanted to get something done," said the Colts' Carroll Rosenbloom, "and he wasn't getting his way, Bert would sit there and slowly take out his false teeth and lay 'em on the table. His face would pinch up and he would look sooooo old, so tired, and he would start to cry. He was a great crier. George Preston Marshall would be walking up and down, screaming and exhorting everybody, and finally they would see that Bert was crying and somebody would say, 'For Chrissakes, George, siddown, you're annoying Bert.' "

––––––

"The Fifties was a decade in which everybody became watchers instead of doers," said Tex Schramm. "Television meant the end of minor league baseball as we had known it and also minor league entertainment. Why pay to see a stage show with one big name and no other talent, when you could turn on your TV and watch the best entertainers in the world? I think this also signaled the end of regionalism. People started thinking more on a national scale." Leaving behind what he viewed as a chaotic owners situation with the Rams in 1957, where Reeves and his partners were not communicating, Schramm spent the end of the decade in the eye of the CBS Sports storm, as the popularity of television and sports began to change. Schramm joined as the lieutenant of Bill MacPhail, for whom CBS Sports had become something of a personal fiefdom. In MacPhail, CBS found a man perfect for the moment. He'd paid his dues, as a public relations man working for the lowly Kansas City Athletics in 1955, and though he initially felt like college football would be a better buy (because of the pageantry, tradition, and sex appeal of cheerleaders), he was alert and open enough to recognize the emerging appeal of pro football, as well as the untapped potential of the Sunday afternoon telecast.

The number of television sets in the country had grown from 172,000 in

1948 to 25 million in 1954, the same year that the oversize perennial photo-journalism weekly *Life* lost 21 percent of its circulation over a six-month period. It was clear that television would transform the culture, but few knew exactly how, and the thought that it would change the perception of and the profile of sports was scarcely recognized. Certainly, television featured plenty of sports in its early incarnations. But as viewers around the country gravitated to sets, usually at the corner tavern, they were watching either boxing or staged sports, like wrestling or Roller Derby. Among team sports there was widespread anxiety about the effect of television on the crucial gate that was the lifeblood of sports leagues.

At CBS, the young, affable executive MacPhail (who had the title of president of CBS Sports, though at the time no such distinct entity existed) toiled with little support. "CBS had no reason to fool with sports," MacPhail said of the period. "CBS was so number one, overall, that its prime time was inviolate. There was no way I could get programming in there. I was the fifth wheel, the necessary evil. CBS would spend hundreds of thousands of dollars to develop prime-time pilots it would never use—and then ask, 'Why do we have to do the goddamn Gator Bowl?' "

Within much of the sports world, the aversion was mutual, as many executives recoiled from the medium's effect on the box office. In Brooklyn, Dodgers owner Walter O'Malley looked at his team's books and realized the club was making essentially the same money in the early '50s as it had made during the war. "TV money was much larger of course," he recalled, "because we were televising nearly all of our games. Our attendance at the ballpark was drastically down. And our radio income was down. We were standing still, even though we had won five pennants in those years. Five of them and we'd have been positively bankrupt in five more years if we had stayed in Brooklyn. An old and dear friend of mine, the late Frank Shaughnessy, who used to be president of the International League, liked to say, 'Radio whets the appetite. Television satiates it.' That was what happened in Brooklyn, you see. Our people were TV-sated."

While baseball struggled to make sense of its predicament, the NFL moved quickly to embrace television on its own terms. Supported by the Grim court decision to allow the league to black out games in markets where NFL games were being played, the NFL by the mid-'50s had codified its television policies. The blackout helped the home gate, and the telecasting of all road games back to a team's home city increased interest in the team and, in turn, helped promote the home gate as well.

By the early '50s, the network schedules were full of news and game shows in the morning, soap operas in the afternoon, and entertainment in prime time. One time slot resistant to programming was Sunday afternoon, which quickly became known as "the ghetto" within the TV industry. For much of the '50s, the schedule was dominated by CBS's Emmy-winning *Omnibus,* a broad cultural show that featured such highbrow entertainment as Chekhov plays, the Metropolitan Opera staging *Die Fledermaus,* or Orson Welles as King Lear. Pro football would soon change that.

In 1956, though NBC held the championship game, all twelve NFL teams had individual deals with CBS or its affiliates. During that 1956 season, Bell continued building the series of arrangements that would define the relationship between television and football in the future. In a memo sent out to the league's twelve franchises in August 1956, the commissioner advised the clubs, "This year the Columbia Broadcasting System (CBS) and the local sponsors will present to the public all our games on television, giving us our greatest opportunity to sell the National Football League and professional football. Everyone must do all in his power to present to the public the greatest games in football combined with the finest sportsmanship."

While each team negotiated its own deal independently, Bell had the right to approve all the deals. The key to the marketplace was Rule 4(b) in the standard National Football League team's television contract, which stipulated that no game be broadcast into the home territory (within seventy-five miles) of a team playing at home that particular day.

Under Bell, the television networks were prohibited from showing injuries or fights. This was not a mere verbal agreement, but a stipulated element of the standard contract ("CBS News shall instruct its cameramen and camera crews to make every reasonable effort to avoid training any television camera on any fights among or injuries to the players") that Bell insisted upon. "I never would and never have questioned the right of a reporter to write about anything he sees in an NFL game," he explained. "Reporters are free to say anything they want. They're doing a job for the public. However, in the matter of television and radio we are doing a job for the public, a job of showing them the best football in the world. We don't want kids sitting in the living room to see their heroes trading punches. That doesn't teach good sportsmanship."

The announcer Bob Wolff would recall receiving a late night call from Bell just hours after a Colts-Redskins game in August 1955. "Just checking you out," Bell told the young announcer. "Good call, good excitement, but a couple of flaws. You called tonight's game an exhibition game. We don't play exhibition games. We play hard-fought pre-season games. Get it? Once you said, 'The runner was tripped coming through the line.' Bob, this is a tackling game.

These guys don't go around sticking out their legs to trip people. A final thing. In the last quarter, you wrestled a fullback to the ground. Bob, that's another sport. We're football. Otherwise, good job."

The system was rudimentary, but it worked. In 1949, league television rights had totaled $75,000. By the late 1950s, it was a multimillion-dollar enterprise that, because it was so astutely managed through the blackout rules, was contributing to annual records in attendance.

"I don't believe there is any honesty in selling a person a ticket and then, after you've taken his dollars, decide to put the game on television, where he could've seen it for nothing," said Bell. "As long as I have anything to do with this league, home games won't be televised, period." The numbers were hard to argue with, as average attendance at NFL games increased from 23,356 in 1950 to 43,617 by 1959.

Even the national press was starting to take note. At the Associated Press bureau in New York City, two young writers—Don Weiss and Jim Kensil—sensed the game's increasing significance, and fought with the AP Sports chief, Ted Smits, to get more coverage. As the sport's popularity increased through the mid-'50s, Weiss would often look at the daily sports story budget from the AP and shake his head at the lack of football features. The material that did run was hard to come by, since the NFL's publicity chief, Labrum, was not particularly sophisticated. "Even if you would call to Philadelphia," said Weiss, "you never got any information that amounted to anything. Anything you developed you developed on your own. Even that didn't get much reception because the powers that be at the time weren't sure that the readers wanted it." But that marginalization began to change after the Giants' title in 1956, and by the 1958 season, Weiss and Kensil were heartened by the broader staffing and priority placed on the sport. "The '58 season was a catalyst that opened the AP's eyes to professional football," said Weiss. "We staffed that later part of that season to a greater extent than anything we had ever done before."

As the 1958 season built to its climax, with the league bound for its ninth consecutive season of rising attendance, the NFL clearly was as healthy as it had ever been. The game's franchises, save for the Chicago Cardinals (in the shadow of Halas's Bears), had stabilized. Television revenues were good and getting better. The challenge from the AAFC was long past, and an early '50s salary war with the Canadian Football League had been effectively pushed off, with an infusion of cash and the league's higher profile. Antitrust questions from Congress had been muted, if not stilled.

"A combination of things is responsible for the mounting interest in pro football," Bell said that fall. "First, and foremost, the nation's press, radio and television annually give us $50 million worth of free publicity and promotion that General Motors couldn't buy. Secondly, we're giving the paying public what it wants—entertainment. I say that a pro game is the best show on Earth. Moreover, the keen competition lends an element of suspense. There isn't any such animal as a weak sister in our league anymore. You knock my brains out this Sunday and I knock your brains out the next time we meet. Do you realize that of the first 54 games played [this season], 32 of them were won by the so called underdog?"

The commissioner's oft-repeated adage—"On any given Sunday, any team in our league can beat any other team"—was proving true. But the league was offering more than mere competition. With the championship race building in intensity throughout the season, the league was taking advantage of the episodic nature of its weekly schedule. Crucial games were being discussed in offices on Mondays, and coming match-ups were being anticipated throughout the week. And what would occur in the final weeks of the 1958 campaign would build to the sort of crescendo that would eloquently announce the sport's arrival at the shoulder of baseball's popularity.

————

The three central figures in the serial drama that would conclude the 1958 season—and help send pro football's popularity soaring into the '60s—had all joined the league within the previous three seasons. Johnny Unitas had signed with the Colts in the spring of 1956; the same year saw the rookie campaign of the Giants' Sam Huff, the hard-nosed tackle from West Virginia, whom Tom Landry would quickly convert to the new position of middle linebacker in his 4-3. Joining them in the headlines a year later, as the best player on the other best-known team of the era, was the incomparable Jim Brown of the Cleveland Browns.

Going into the 1957 draft, held November 27, 1956, Paul Brown was suffering through his first losing season as a pro coach, as well as his first year without Otto Graham. He was desperate for a quarterback, and possessed the sixth overall selection in the first round.

Green Bay won the bonus choice, and went for Heisman Trophy–winning quarterback Paul Hornung; the Packers also had their own pick at number four and took tight end Ron Kramer. Drafting second and needing a running back, the Rams selected Southern Cal running back "Jaguar" Jon Arnett, the hometown attraction who was seen as one of the top two running back prospects along with Syracuse's Jim Brown. Decades later, many were still regretting the decision. "The scouting department, and all our graders were for Jim Brown," said the Rams' cinematographer, Mickey Dukich, who helped compile and collate scouting reports close to the draft. "The grade points were for Jim Brown, but [Rams co-owner] Ed Pauley wanted the local boy."

The two quarterbacks that most interested Paul Brown were Stanford's John Brodie, who went third to San Francisco, and Purdue's Len Dawson, selected fifth by Pittsburgh.

With the two quarterbacks gone, Paul Brown selected Jim Brown, and in so doing, found more than he could have hoped for. Brown's impact as a runner was immediate, and powerful. Instantly, he would dominate the position in pro football. At 6-foot-2, 230 pounds, he was a fast, intimidating, angry runner who delivered as much punishment as he sustained. He'd take off from his three-point stance, moving with a power and purpose, take the ball from the quarterback, and burst forward with a brutal confidence, running in a coiled position with his head up. Then, at the point of contact, when other runners would cover up or try to fall forward, Jim Brown exploded. Tucking the football tightly to his gut, he'd lower a shoulder toward his tackler, and swing his free arm into his opponent's chest with a stunning forearm shiver. After a touchdown run against the Steelers in the Browns' first exhibition in 1957, Brown came to the sidelines, where Paul Brown sought him out and said simply, "You're my fullback."

Huff was already a young star of the vaunted Giants defense when he had his first meeting with Jim Brown in a 1957 game that would leave Huff with an indelible memory: "It was early in the third quarter, and here came Jim Brown through a hole and there I was to meet him. I hit that big sucker head-on and my headgear snapped down and cut my nose and my teeth hit together so hard the enamel popped off. He broke my nose, broke my teeth, and knocked me cold. I woke up in the training room with an ice pack on my head and my nose bleeding. My teeth were killing me. I always took great pride in those teeth; in fact, people always used to tease me about my nice, big smile. Well, it wasn't so nice anymore. I was lying there and my tongue was going all over these rough edges and I was screaming, 'My teeth are gone, my teeth are gone!' "

In Jim Brown, Paul Brown had found the greatest single force he would ever marshal as a football coach, as well as the most difficult personality—one at least as strong-willed as his own. The conflict and tension between the blessing and the challenge would define the rest of the coach's career in Cleveland.

Brown confounded many of the racial stereotypes of the day. He was neither surly nor jovial. He was a team player, but one who was fully aware of his value to the team. And while he embraced many of the notions of team unity on the field, he was unquestionably his own man off it, where in his rookie season he purchased a light purple-and-white Cadillac convertible, which he parked next to the Browns' practice field at League Park. He was the sort of man, to borrow the Southern expression of the period, who took guff from no one.

He would at once bridle against Brown's remedial methods of discipline and uniformity, while recognizing that those same methods were color-blind, unlike those of so many other coaches. "Paul's dictatorship discouraged cliques, and discouraged racial prejudice," Brown recalled. "His rules were not to be questioned, by anyone. We all had to abide by them equally. That was very pleasing to me."

But Jim Brown had seen the behavior of black sports stars like Jackie Robinson, Joe Louis, and Jesse Owens, and he'd vowed that he would not capitulate. "Jackie had to do it," he said. "Jackie had to play a role because of the plan that they had, and he made a vow to Branch Rickey, to play that role. That was not his nature; if he did not have to do it for the betterment of the whole, he would not have done it. Joe Louis was a nice man that was kind of like that anyway; Jesse Owens was obviously that way. My attitude was, in no way was I going to be that way. . . . In no way did I ever feel that I would accept discrimination."

The two strong-willed men would inevitably clash, but in the short term, the arrival of Jim Brown brought about an instant renaissance for the Browns. Cleveland went 9-2-1 to win the Eastern Conference title in Brown's rookie year of 1957, when he led the league in rushing with 942 yards on 202 carries. (Rick Casares, the runner-up, carried two more times that season, and gained 242 fewer yards.)

Jim Brown was even better in 1958, gaining an NFL record 1,527 yards, averaging 5.9 yards per carry and scoring 17 touchdowns to lead the league in scoring. By the eighth game of the season, he broke the existing all-time season yardage and touchdown records (both held by Steve Van Buren). Cleveland jumped off to a 9-2 record and went into Yankee Stadium for the regular season finale on December 14 against the 8-3 Giants, needing a win or a tie to wrap up their second straight conference title and Paul Brown's eighth in nine NFL seasons.

On the first play from scrimmage, Brown broke for a 65-yard touchdown run, to give Cleveland a 7–0 lead. But it was his only score of the day and, in a blizzard, the Giants rallied, eventually tying the game at 10. Then in the last minutes, Summerall came on to kick the winning field goal, estimated at the time at 49 yards, though no one really knew, since the standing snow had obscured the yard lines.

All season long, the Giants—many of them living in the residential apartments at the stately Hotel Concourse Plaza ("The business and social center of the Bronx"), just up 161st Street from Yankee Stadium—had felt like a team of destiny, and the unlikely regular season finale win against Cleveland only heightened the sensation. In Cleveland, several players grumbled about Paul Brown's decision before a field goal attempt at the end of the third quarter that would have given the team a 13–3 lead. Brown called time out, then ran a fake field goal, which was stuffed. "From that point on, Paul never had quite the same respect from the players," said *Cleveland Press* beat writer Bob August. "The Giants suddenly became a big issue."

Though the Browns returned for a rematch the following week, they were a spent team. Falling behind early, they gave the ball to Brown just seven times for eight yards. The Giants won the game, and the Eastern Conference title, 10–0. It was Cleveland's first shutout loss since 1950, when Owen debuted his umbrella defense.

The match-up was set. Because the site of championship games rotated on an annual basis, the 1958 title game would be played in New York, with the Eastern Conference champion Giants playing host to the upstart Western Conference champion Baltimore Colts. Landry had prepared them for the game with his usual attention for detail. But while against the Browns he could work off the rather predictable tendencies of Paul Brown, Unitas was calling the plays for Baltimore and, as events would show, he had a mind all his own.

Yankee Stadium was not quite sold out for the game, partly due to weather concerns, partly due to a newspaper strike that had minimized coverage surrounding it. But around 15,000 Colts fans journeyed to New York from Baltimore, and their presence gave the game a tension even in the stands, where the Baltimore faithful made nearly as much noise as the Giants fans.

It was, of course, a game for the ages, and Weeb Ewbank made a pregame speech that was worthy of the moment. In the locker room beforehand, he singled out fourteen of the Colts' thirty-five players, each of whom had been released or traded by another team in the league. "Pittsburgh didn't want you, but we picked you up off the sandlots," he told Unitas. To cornerback Milt Davis, he said, "Detroit didn't want you, but I'm glad I got you." Spying guards Art Spinney and Alex Sandusky, Ewbank said, "You couldn't play offensive end, and you were too small for defensive end, but we made offensive guards out of you." Ewbank even alluded to himself being a castoff, the second choice for the Colts after Blanton Collier had taken his name out of consideration. The purpose of the speech was obvious, but it was effective nonetheless. Many of the Colts were still angry over Charlie Conerly's remarks, published in his wife's weekly column in a New York tabloid, about how the Giants "outgutted" Baltimore in their regular season meeting.

The Colts came out and were sluggish in the first quarter, hurting themselves with two turnovers and a blocked field goal, but when Gifford fumbled on a pass attempt deep in his own territory, Baltimore capitalized quickly to go up 7–3 early in the second period. After a long Giants drive ended in another Gifford fumble, at the Colts' 14, Unitas executed a long, masterful drive that at the close of the half ended with a perfect pass to Berry between two defenders, giving the Colts a 14–3 lead.

The third period was played at a desperate pitch by the Giants. On the first drive, Sam Huff hit Raymond Berry after he was already out of bounds, a hit so flagrant that Ewbank responded with a punch to Huff's jaw. The two men were separated, and neither was ejected—in fact, there was no penalty on the play. But the Colts' drive stalled. Later in the quarter, Baltimore drove down to the Giants' three, where on first-and-goal, New York's defense stiffened and held for three downs. On fourth-and-goal at the two, with a chance to put the game away, Ewbank kept mediocre placekicker Steve Myhra on the sidelines, and let Unitas make the call. The play was "428," a little used fullback option calling for a pitchout wide to Ameche, who would take two steps as if on a sweep, then pass to Jim Mutscheller in the end zone. The play was executed perfectly and Mutscheller was wide open. But Ameche hadn't heard the "4" in Unitas's play call, so he thought he was running the Colts' regular "28" pitch play and kept the ball, where he was tackled for a four-yard loss. It was the first real moment that the Giants' fans had to cheer, and three plays later, the offense responded with another one of those absurd plays they'd been making in crucial situations all season long. Conerly, in the game since late in the first quarter, hit Rote on a deep pass down the center of the field. Defensive back Andy Nelson tackled Rote at the 25, jarring the ball loose, but the Giants' Alex Webster, trailing the play, picked the ball up and brought it to the 1. The Giants, outplayed all day, scored on the next play to trail by just 14–10, and the momentum had switched sides. After stopping Baltimore on three plays, lightning struck again, with Conerly hitting end Bob Schnelker for 17 and then 46 yards, then finding Gifford open on the sideline, where he brought it in for the go-ahead touchdown.

The incredible din only heightened the sense of urgency, and it was three more possessions before Unitas led Baltimore out for the game-tying drive. One key play, on a second-and-10 situation, found Berry lined up on the left side, as the primary receiver on a 12-yard square-out pattern. But one of the silent signals the two players had established over the years was that if a linebacker came out wide to face up on Berry, the receiver would change his route to a quick slant pattern. The secret switch came decades before "sight adjustments" were common in the NFL, and it worked perfectly as Unitas hit Berry for 25 yards, with 1:04 left. On the next two passes, he found Berry again, first for 15, then for 22 yards. At that point, the Colts field goal unit came out and Myhra kicked the game-tying 20-yard field goal.

The exquisite tension of overtime, culminating with Ameche's touchdown run to give the Colts the 23–17 win, was watched by 45 million Americans on television, including President Eisenhower at his Gettysburg retreat. To many in the league it felt like the culmination of a long journey. Bell was in the press box afterward, tears of joy in his eyes, shaking hands with John Steadman and saying, "I never thought I'd see a day like today."

In the Giants' locker room, the dominant emotion, next to disappointment, was awe at Unitas's otherworldly composure. "Everything we expected him to do, and what you absolutely believed he would do, he didn't do," said the Giants' safety Emlen Tunnell. "He did exactly the opposite. Those of us who have been around knew we had been beaten by a better man."

Even the losers, though saddened by the defeat, were exhilarated by the classic game. Giants owner Tim Mara would die only weeks later (with his sons Wellington and Jack succeeding him), but every day throughout early January, he'd show up at the Giants' office at the usual seven o'clock and find another dozen or so new season ticket orders. "He'd say, 'We're gonna sell out next year,' " Wellington Mara said. "He died on a real high."

The Colts headed home to Baltimore, and more proof of pro football's impact. There perhaps has never in American sports been anything quite like the scene that took place on the tarmac of Friendship Airport in Baltimore that night. As the crowd, estimated to be at least 30,000 by local police, pushed out of the terminal and onto the macadam to wait for the victorious Colts, the planes taxied to a distant hangar in the far east of the runway, where the players and coaches got into two buses (an ambulance took the injured Marchetti directly to a hospital). The first bus drove over to the crowd for a series of scheduled victory interviews and was engulfed by the mob, prompting the second bus to peel away from the scene and take an alternate route to Baltimore, since the highway leading to the airport was clogged with fans.

The police cruiser escorting the bus to the interview platform was similarly swamped, and as revelers jumped on the roof of the police car, they demolished it. By the time WBAL-TV announcer Joe Croghan cut his microphone to seek cover, there were dozens of people on top of the bus and a huge throng surrounding it, with everyone leaning forward for a glimpse of their heroes, and those on top of the bus jumping and stomping in a rhythmic, chanting cacophony. Inside the bus, according to the *Baltimore News-American*'s John Steadman, the players "watched in disbelief at what was going on around them and listened to the pounding on the roof. . . . The crowd wouldn't allow itself to be restored to calm and order. Some fans were knocked down in the melee, women lost hats and even their shoes as the crowd moved back and forth, similar to a storm-tide that had grown violent and wicked. In the front of the bus, Kellett and Ewbank agreed they should not attempt to get off but should wait out the turbulence. 'They'll tear us to pieces,' said Ewbank. '. . . We can't stand here all night. But I guess this is what they have been waiting and longing for.' "

When the bus was finally extricated from the crowd, there were more than a dozen people, mostly teenagers, still on the roof. At a roadblock outside the airport proper, the bus stopped and the police herded fourteen more off their perch atop the bus. Temporarily taken into custody, some were pushed into the back of a police car. "I just want to meet some Colts," exclaimed one teen and, eventually, Unitas got out of the bus and went back to greet the boys, who were released without charges. Much had been written, in October 1957, of how the Milwaukee Braves' trip to the World Series had put the Wisconsin city in the national consciousness, but such a claim had never been made for a football championship. But in the shining closing weeks of the 1958 season, pro football had achieved a kind of transcendent visibility, the fruits of which were reaped by the ecstatic city of Baltimore. Assessing the mob scene at the airport later, Steadman could only resort to superlatives. "Berserk Baltimore fans, many of them," he wrote, "had gone temporarily insane."

———

In the 1958 title game, pro football had arrived as a viable alternative to baseball, not merely as the most popular sport, but the one that best defined America. And in Unitas's high-tops and laconic manner, the game—and the country—had discovered a sports metaphor for the Cold War era. With the two long drives in the 1958 title game, and the endless dissection of the pressure and strategy surrounding those marches that circulated through the press afterward, the myth of the quarterback as "field general" was virtually complete, refashioned in the image of Unitas's distinctive style.

Sammy Baugh and Sid Luckman were seen as great athletes and leaders, but little was written about their roles in the mind games of football. Otto Graham, the most successful quarterback of the '40s and early '50s, was famous for *not* calling the plays in Paul Brown's system. Then came Unitas— stoic and fearless and unflappable, with a sixth sense for reading defenses and correctly guessing what opponents might do in a certain situation.

Unitas's style hadn't changed in three years. But instead of being perceived as goofy, he was suddenly the standard for what quarterbacks ought to look like. Millions of boys around the country started scrunching up their shoulders to simulate Unitas's pinched profile in shoulder pads, and throwing with the elongated, fingers-down follow-through that they'd seen Johnny U display on television.

By the time the Colts won their second straight title, after the 1959 season, Unitas had become an authentic American archetype, the virtual definition of a certain kind of honorable American manhood, as much of a keystone figure as Bogart's hard-boiled characters or Sinatra's hard-luck crooner. Except, of course, there was no script and no reshoots, and when Unitas got up from a blow that broke his nose and gashed his mouth, as happened against the Bears in 1960, he refused to come off the field, and threw a game-winning touchdown on the next play. The quality fans were seeing was similar to what Hemingway called grace under pressure and what test pilots referred to as "the right stuff."

By the end of the '50s, a growing number of Americans, especially those in NFL cities, were becoming transfixed with the game. The New York Giants' publicist Don Smith observed that the temper of football crowds by the end of the decade was "violently partisan and devoutly involved. They did not wander about in search of hot-dog vendors during the play, nor go visiting among friends in other sections, as baseball fans would do. They yearned openly to participate in the struggle and would invariably jump to their feet whenever a particularly long run or forward pass seemed about to erupt." In Smith's view, what had kept fans away from pro football in the past was less apathy than "sheer ignorance, too often fostered by certain sportswriters, who did not believe the professional game could be as thrilling as the college version. When television began to allow fans to see for themselves, they recognized that they had been missing a great spectacle, and one in which it was easy to involve one's self, heart, soul, voice and paycheck."

Over the coming years, few would become as involved as a mild-mannered fan from Dallas, Texas, who on December 28, 1958, was just another television spectator, one of the tens of millions of Americans watching the Colts and the Giants into the late afternoon. While others put off dinner or long rides home, he had delayed his trip to the sports arena in Houston, where he'd traveled to watch the Southwest Conference Holiday Basketball Tournament. The diffident young Texan, heir to a billionaire oilman, had spent much of the previous few months casting about for a major league baseball team or professional football team to buy, never really quite sure of his direction.

By the end of that afternoon, though, Lamar Hunt was sure. After seeing Alan Ameche plunge over for the game-winner in overtime, he sat on the hotel bed and realized that his mind had been made up. "My interest emotionally was always more in football," Hunt said. "But clearly the '58 Colts-Giants game, sort of in my mind, made me say, 'Well, that's it. This sport really has everything. And it televises well.' And who knew what that meant?"

7

"A Light Bulb Came On"

The best ideas are common property.
SENECA

While the appeal of pro football grew in the '50s, the universe of pro football did not. There remained only 432 jobs in the country for professional football players, just thirty-six spots on each of the NFL's twelve teams. There was little turnover from one year to the next, competition for spots was fierce and often arbitrary, and coaches possessed all the power.

"The NFL in the '50s was this brutal, Darwinian, biological, survival-of-the-fittest environment," said Jack Kemp, the strong-armed backup quarterback from Occidental College drafted by the Detroit Lions in 1957. For unheralded players like Kemp, who showed talent and the potential to play at the NFL level, there was always the elusive question of opportunity. Lions coach Buddy Parker thought enough of Kemp to trade for him after he left Detroit for Pittsburgh in 1957. But in the 1958 preseason, when the Steelers traveled to Los Angeles to play in front of a crowd that included dozens of his friends and family, Kemp boomed a punt deep instead of following Parker's orders to kick it out of bounds. After the kick was returned for a touchdown, Kemp sheepishly returned to the sidelines, where a seething Parker released him on the spot. "Kemp, you're going to be a great punter in this league someday," said Parker. "But not for the Pittsburgh Steelers. You're cut."

Shortly thereafter, Kemp landed on the taxi squad of the 1958 New York Giants, and was hoping to stick with the Giants the following season. But when they drafted All-American quarterback Lee Grosscup in the 1959 draft, he wasn't invited to camp. After a short stint in the Canadian Football League in 1959, he signed with the San Francisco 49ers, and was suited up for his first game in San Francisco when he was ruled ineligible—after a protest was filed by Paul Brown—because he'd already played in the CFL that year. In three seasons of professional football, Kemp threw 18 passes in the NFL.

It was a closed shop for owners as well. As the league's attendance, revenues, and profile grew through the 1950s, dozens of businessmen called on Bert Bell to inquire about a new franchise in the NFL. The one with seniority was the crusty Minneapolis insurance executive Ole Haugsrud, who'd owned the Duluth Eskimos in the 1920s, and still held an "option contract" to have the first chance at a franchise if the league ever decided to put a club back into Minnesota. Minneapolis was growing in the 1950s, but the group to which Haugsrud belonged, Minnesota Sports, Inc., received little encouragement from Bell, who told Haugsrud in April 1959 that he saw no chance for the league's expansion into the city.

The Minneapolis group was hardly alone. In the '50s, representatives from Seattle, Buffalo, New Orleans, Denver, and Miami all heard nearly the same thing. The NFL wouldn't completely rule out expansion (to do so would invite scrutiny from the government's antitrust division), but as Bell wrote to Denver Bears general manager Bob Howsam in May 1958, "I do not believe there will be any expansion in the National Football League until at least 1961, if there is any even at that time."

This stasis came at a time when the pace of commerce and culture was quickening in remarkable ways. Advertising itself was reaching new heights. American companies had spent $5.7 billion on advertising their products in 1950, but would spend $11.9 billion a decade later. Consumer spending also was way up; the eight suburban shopping centers in the U.S. in 1946 had grown to more than 4,000 by the end of the '50s. Interest in football was clearly up as well, as attendance had increased to record highs during every year of the decade.

The league did consent to form a committee to study the issue of expansion in 1958, but the committee of the whole never met, and soon was pared down to Art Rooney and George Halas. The true prospects for expansion were bleak. A unanimous vote was required to approve any new team. Washington's George Preston Marshall was a staunch opponent on general principle, and the Chicago Cardinals were opposed out of self-interest. The lowly Cardinals, who lost 100 games and nearly $1 million over the decade, were considering a move and wanted to keep all options open. The downtrodden club, once owned by the late Charles Bidwill, by now belonged to his widow, Violet, and her new husband, St. Louis businessman Walter Wolfner. For the Cardinals, located on the South Side of Chicago, in the shadow of George Halas and the Bears, second best was a way of life.

Since telecasts of NFL games were blacked out when a team was at home, and since the Cardinals or Bears were at home nearly every week, the lucrative Chicago TV market was nearly bereft of pro football on television. Bell had been hoping for years that the Wolfners would sell their franchise or move elsewhere, to give their club a chance to succeed.

In the absence of any movement from the expansion committee, and with the continued presence of two teams in the Chicago market, expansion seemed dead in the water. And so when Lamar Hunt called Bert Bell's office in the spring of 1958 to inquire about an expansion franchise in the NFL, Bell told him pretty much the same thing he'd told people in Seattle, Orange County, Houston, Atlanta, New Orleans, and Minneapolis for years: "Call the Wolfners."

———

At age twenty-six in the spring of 1958, Lamar Hunt was as polite and mild-mannered as he was rich, which is to say absurdly so. A shade under six feet, with a smallish head, chestnut brown hair carefully parted and combed, and jet-black horn-rimmed glasses, he looked and acted like a healthful, earnest accountant. He was genial but so unassuming as to seem almost meek. In short, he was an inversion of every stereotype that ever existed about Texas oil tycoons and their offspring.

Born in 1932, Lamar was the son of the self-made oil billionaire Haroldson Lafayette Hunt, whom *Fortune* magazine described in 1948 as the world's wealthiest man. H. L. Hunt was a larger-than-life figure whose gambling and courtship of women were conducted along the same general dimensions as his architectural instincts. From the age of six, Lamar Hunt grew up in the sparsely settled development of White Rock Lake, just outside Dallas, in a house modeled after George Washington's Mount Vernon, though, typical of the scale of his father's ambition, twice the size.

Perhaps in a response to his father's tumultuous private and public life, Lamar Hunt made a conscious effort, from an early age, to blend in, to be polite, to be one of the crowd. When alone, he would invent his own games, intricate solitaire pastimes with clear rules and precise record keeping.

He was a decent athlete, though never physically imposing, and after attending high school at the Hill School in Pottstown, Pennsylvania, he returned to Dallas and Southern Methodist University. His college football career was not distinguished; he was a third-string end, behind Raymond Berry, and saw only twenty minutes of action over his three years on the varsity, not enough to earn a letter.

Forrest Gregg, an All–Southwest Conference lineman at SMU a year behind Hunt, faced off against him daily in practice. But for more than a year, until another teammate told Gregg about visiting Hunt's parents' home and swimming in the Hunts' backyard swimming pool, Gregg had no idea that his teammate came from wealth. "That's how smart I was and how unassuming Lamar was," said Gregg. "You'd never know. He wore the same thing I did, which was penny loafers, and socks we stole from the athletic department, SMU T-shirts, and blue jeans. That was him and he was one of the guys. I always appreciated that about Lamar." On less affable men, this parsimony could seem either soulless or mean-spirited. But most of Hunt's friends viewed it as an eccentric if unshowy thriftiness.

After graduating with a geology degree from SMU in 1956, Hunt joined Hunt Oil Co., and quickly realized that he possessed neither the temperament nor interest to follow his father and brothers in a life devoted to the oil business. Instead, he was animated by what he would later describe as "a passion for show business or entertainment or the sports business—they're all interchangeable in my mind." With the trust fund from his father and a gently reckoned optimism, Lamar Hunt set out to make his own mark, proceeding all the while with a quiet air of absolute discretion, consistent with the circumspect nature of a young man who was "horrified" the first time he saw his name in the paper. Over the next two years, he traveled extensively, following his curiosity about sports, learning the specifics about financing football and baseball teams.

Late in 1958, Hunt began hearing rumors of a third major league in baseball, and he joined as a minority investor a group trying to secure a franchise for the Dallas–Fort Worth area. Branch Rickey had described a new baseball league as "inevitable" in May 1958, and began informally fronting the organization some months later. Hunt traveled with the group to New York to hear Rickey speak late in 1958, and remembered Rickey being a "very convincing person, a very reasonable person—he wasn't a flamboyant salesman or anything like that."

But football had always been Lamar Hunt's first love, and by the beginning of 1959 he'd grown determined to find a pro football team.

He'd been negotiating with the Wolfners for months, with no more success than any of the Cardinals' other frustrated suitors. In February 1959, Hunt traveled one final time to discuss a deal, this time in Miami, where the Wolfners spent their winters. Hunt had offered a variety of different scenarios in which he could move the team down to Dallas and eventually retain a controlling interest. But by the time of his last visit, Walter Wolfner seemed newly intent on staying in Chicago, and was driving a hard bargain.

"Do you know Bud Adams?" Wolfner asked at one point. Hunt said he didn't, and Wolfner explained that Adams, an oil millionaire from Houston, had also been interested in acquiring the team. Others had approached him as well, he boasted, mentioning the potential ownership group in Minneapolis and Denver. But he wasn't budging. The team would stay in Chicago, he vowed, and would be controlled by the Wolfners.

Hunt shook Wolfner's hand, and wished him the best of luck. Then he took a cab to the Miami airport and boarded an American Airlines flight to Dallas. The four-engine propeller plane took more than four hours to get from Miami to Dallas, and en route on that winter evening, Hunt glumly considered the fact that he was no closer to owning a football franchise than he'd been a year earlier, when he'd first placed a call to Bert Bell.

Sitting on the plane, Hunt began to synthesize the disparate bits of information that he'd received over the previous months: Bud Adams in Houston. A group in Denver, likely led by Bob Howsam. An ownership group in Minnesota. Every one of these people wanted the Cardinals to move to their city. But the Cardinals wouldn't sell, and the NFL wouldn't expand anytime soon.

And then, it was as if, Hunt would say later, "a light bulb came on."

Why not go see THOSE people and put together a new football league?

Hunt had long had a habit of taking copious notes on whatever paper was available, and many of his brainstorms had been sketched out on the back of envelopes or in the margins of magazines. But with this bolt of inspiration, he knew he needed more. He asked a stewardess for some stationery, and hurriedly sketched out the plans on three sheets of onionskin writing paper with an American Airlines letterhead. Under the heading "ORIGINAL 6; FIRST YEAR'S OPERATIONS," he began outlining the particulars of a prospective new league. He had looked at the Cardinals' financial statements (the club had lost nearly $220,000 during the 1956 and 1957 seasons alone), and so knew enough about the economics of football to come up with a prospective profit-and-loss statement for a hypothetical pro team.

Writing in short, neat printing strokes, Hunt finished his outline, drawing up provisions for owners, even making rough estimates on the costs of equipment and the revenue from ticket sales. By the time the plane arrived in Dallas, Hunt's idea seemed fully formed. He drew up a rough schedule for the first season, going so far as to sketch out the likely weekends the regular season would begin and end.

And then, typical of his operating style, Lamar Hunt told no one.

In the coming weeks, though, he started to look at the entire sports universe with fresh eyes. From his office, he began accumulating background information on the prospects of virtually every large city in the United States. Within weeks, he became convinced that his idea was perfectly timed. If Major League Baseball, with sixteen franchises and slumping attendance, was in need of expansion—as Rickey persuasively argued—then there was an even greater necessity for expansion in pro football, with but twelve franchises and rising attendance in each year of the '50s.

Still moving cautiously, Hunt called Bell in March 1959, to inquire again about the possibility of an expansion team in the NFL. Bell reiterated that the league couldn't consider expansion until resolving the Cardinals situation. He added that the league was not at all impressed with Dallas, because of the poor performance of the Texans in 1952, and that its first commitment was to the city of Buffalo. After Hunt pressed further for an appointment with the expansion committee, Bell suggested he call George Halas, then vacationing at the Arizona Biltmore in Phoenix. But Halas was no more accommodating. When Hunt suggested he come visit Halas to "throw my hat in the ring," Halas dissuaded him, and called it a waste of time, adding that "expansion is probably a long way off."

With that clear indication that the NFL was staying put, Hunt began to seek out potential owners for a new league. His first prospect was Kenneth S. "Bud" Adams, also the son of a Texas oilman and much more in keeping with the traditional stereotype of Texas millionaires. Adams progressed from a burly youth who played football at Kansas to a heavyset adult best known for his distinct flair in office decoration. In his subterranean office in downtown Houston, next to the tasteful displays of Native American art, Adams had a cage full of rare doves, a lily pond, and an indoor barbecue pit. He had been known as "Jabber" at his college prep school, and his Texas patois was both cocksure and elusive, wholly unintelligible to some from the North. One of Adams's peers would later say, "To be honest it took me about two or three years to understand a single word of whatever the hell it was Bud was saying.

He always seemed to be talking out the side of his mouth, not so much figura-
tively as literally."

The two men had never met, but Hunt called Adams and asked if he could
join him for dinner, during which Hunt characteristically spoke about everything except football. Finally, as Adams was driving him back to Houston's
Hobby Airport to catch a flight to Dallas, Hunt mentioned that he was interested in starting a new football league. "If I could come up with some other
franchises, would you come in?"

"Hell, yes," said Adams.

Hunt told him he'd be in touch. Over the following weeks, he was greeted
with equally enthusiastic responses in Denver and Minneapolis. "We folks
here in Minnesota have been trying to get a franchise for some time," wrote
Ole Haugsrud later, "but it seems as though the National League does not care
to move or expand."

Feeling he needed a franchise in Los Angeles and New York, Hunt began
casting about for prospects in those cities. Through friend and former tennis
star Gene Mako, he was introduced to Barron Hilton, son of hotel magnate
Conrad Hilton; in New York, Continental League backer Bill Shea suggested
that Hunt contact the popular football announcer Harry Wismer, instantly
the best-known (and, as it would turn out, least stable) member of the
prospective ownership group.

At this point, another man might have called a press conference and announced the new league. But Lamar Hunt was not one for splashy shows of
Texas bravado. His next step would be characteristic of the reticence that
would later be seen, by his detractors, as a sign of deviousness, and by his
friends as proof of his modest demeanor and methodical business style. His
friend David Dixon, a New Orleans businessman who'd been working to bring
pro football to that city, said of Hunt, "Lamar is the best super-rich guy I've
ever known. But by his family practices, he's very secretive, a lot of times un-
necessarily so." Hunt himself would later admit, "I possibly have an indirect
way of finding things out."

This was certainly the case with his next actions. On June 2, 1959, Hunt
flew to Philadelphia for a lunch with Bert Bell, and they went to one of Bell's
favorite restaurants, the Tavern in Narberth, along with Bert Bell, Jr., and the
Eagles' Joe "Jiggs" Donoghue. After plenty of the usual Hunt small talk, with
no mention of his own plans for a new league, Hunt finally mentioned that he
was still interested in bringing an expansion franchise to Dallas. Bell reiterated
that the NFL wouldn't consider expansion until the league solved its "Chicago
problem" and achieved a greater measure of competitive balance. "My dad

told him they weren't ready for expansion," said Bert Bell, Jr. "He wanted the bottom teams to win three or four games, some amount of games, before they were ready for expansion."

After the meal, Bell called Hunt over to the corner of the restaurant and said, less vexed than perplexed, "What in the world did you come up here for? What in the world do you want?" Hunt repeated his interest in expansion and Bell reiterated, "The owners are not interested in any kind of expansion, they have no expansion plans, and it's just a lost cause as far as Dallas is concerned." Then Bell added, "As far as I am concerned, I don't believe they will *ever* vote to expand."

Satisfied he'd exhausted all avenues with the NFL, Hunt returned to Dallas and began firming up his plans for the new league. The next month, before making any announcement, he sent an emissary—the former TCU great Davey O'Brien, one of Bell's favorites during his early years coaching the Eagles—to approach Bell, on behalf of the prospective new league. "I was at least intelligent enough to know that I did not want to start a war," said Hunt. O'Brien called on Bell and explained that a new league was being formed and sought his blessings, without revealing any of the investors or potential cities, but adding that the group hoped Bell might even consider serving as commissioner of the new league. Bell declined, but wished them luck and, before O'Brien left, added, "Incidentally, tell that young friend of yours in Dallas that he can come to me for advice any time."

But it was Bell himself who made the next call. On July 26, the commissioner phoned O'Brien and explained that he was due to testify before Congress, part of the NFL's long and as yet fruitless efforts to gain legislation that would provide the sport with the same antitrust protection as baseball. The Subcommittee on Anti-Trust Monopoly, part of the Judiciary Committee in the U.S. Senate, was sure to ask him about expansion, Bell explained. He wanted O'Brien to ask if it might be okay to mention the proposed new league. And so on July 28, while Bell entertained a subcommittee with his folksy dissertation on the state of pro football, Lamar Hunt sat silently in the back of Room 318 of the Senate Office Building, listening while his idea for a new football league was announced to the world. He couldn't have asked for a better salesman than Bert Bell.

"The more football there is and the more advertisement of pro football, the better off we are," Bell told the committee. "We are in favor of the new league." He added that he considered the years of the NFL's rancorous war with the AAFC were "a great thing for pro football. Every newspaper was arguing who was the best and they would keep it in the papers." Michigan Senator Philip Hart interrupted Bell to point out that many of the owners didn't consider the AAFC's challenge a great thing for the sport at the time. "I know," Bell replied. "But I can't help what the owners think. I know what it did. I will tell you this is great and I have talked it over with every owner and not one of them has an objection to it, not one of them."

Bert Bell may not have been the most sophisticated man alive, but he knew how to tell a group of politicians what they wanted to hear. In fact, he hadn't spoken to any of the other NFL owners about the new league before speaking to Congress, but he did call George Halas the day after the speech, telling him that he thought the league was nebulous and might never get off the ground. That same evening, Hunt and O'Brien visited Bell at his summer home in Margate, New Jersey, arriving after ten o'clock and sitting for a freewheeling discussion until almost two in the morning. Bell was jovial and helpful, repeated that he was too busy with other things to entertain the thought of running a new league, but peppered Hunt with helpful advice. He particularly urged the new league to go with eight teams in the first season, rather than six, on the grounds that eight was necessary for scheduling purposes, and it also allowed a league to plausibly split into two divisions, bringing about a useful rationale for a championship game at the end of the season.

"All of you will enjoy this," Bell told Hunt at one point, "and all of the owners will get to become good friends down through the years. However, there is one thing that will separate you: when you start to fight over players." Hunt thanked him for the advice and promised to stay in touch. Three days later, on August 3, the day after his twenty-seventh birthday, Lamar Hunt joined Bud Adams in Adams's Houston office to announce the start of the American Football League.

"I really liked Bert Bell," Hunt said. "I really thought we could all get along." Hunt would later characterize this opinion as "one of the more naive thoughts in the history of American sports."

The first meeting of the new league—which voted to call itself the American Football League—was held August 14, 1959, in the Imperial South Suite on the twentieth floor of the Chicago Hilton. They were sportsmen in the classic sense of being wealthy fanatics, and adjourned early so all in attendance could make it to Soldier Field to watch the College All-Star Game. Within days, the league lined up another franchise owner, Ralph Wilson, a Detroit insurance executive and minority owner of the Lions, who wanted to place a franchise in Miami, but ultimately settled on Buffalo, because of stadium availability. (The issue of stadiums became something of a theme. In Minneapolis, Houston,

Miami, and Seattle, the university stadium that the league wanted to play in was unavailable. The conflict ultimately caused the Seattle group, which Bell had personally recommended to Hunt, to drop out.)

On a Saturday afternoon, August 29, Hunt realized it was not going to be as easy as he'd hoped. He was at his home in Dallas, trimming shrubs in and around his rose garden when the phone rang. It was an Associated Press reporter who asked him for his response to the news out of Houston: at a press conference before the Steelers-Bears preseason game, George Halas and Art Rooney had announced that the NFL *would* be expanding, with plans to award franchises the following January, to begin competition in 1961. When asked to name the two most likely cities for their expansion, they cited Houston and Dallas, where the man in line for the Dallas NFL franchise was the diminutive, sharp-tongued Clint Murchison, Jr., like Hunt a son of an oil millionaire.

When he heard the news that Saturday, Hunt remained outwardly calm, and asked for a few moments to compose a response. He called back the reporter in a matter of minutes, after writing out a press release while sitting on his bed. As he read the statement his voice was even and forceful. "Everybody has been knocking on their door for years and they've turned everybody down. It is obvious what they are trying to do, and it can get them into trouble. . . . They're trying to knock out Dallas and Houston, but this doesn't change our plans at all and we're moving ahead. We'll be adding our seventh and eighth teams this fall."

When Hunt called Bell the following Monday, the commissioner protested that the matter was largely out of his hands. "What can I do?" he said. "They want to expand. How can I stop them?" Bell remained reassuring both privately (he sent Adams a copy of the NFL by-laws, to help the AFL construct its constitution) and in public. "There are plenty of players," he said to a reporter in September. "There are 250 kids graduating from college every year with pro football ability. We keep about five per team, a total of 60. That leaves 190 unemployed in football."

But with the prospect of the NFL coming into the AFL's two anchor cities, many more observers thought that Hunt's quest had gone from daring to foolhardy. To some, continuing with the new league seemed pointless if the NFL were coming to those cities anyway.

"If Adams and Lamar Hunt insist on war, then they themselves and the cities they represent will be the losers," wrote the *Houston Post*'s Jack Gallagher the week after the Halas and Rooney announcement. "From here it would appear that the wisest move the AFL can make at this time is to disband."

———

The 1959 season, which would see Unitas and the Colts march to another championship, kicked off with Bert Bell in his element, ruling pro football with his unique air of backslapping rectitude, ever vigilant to the good of the game.

After fourteen years on the job, and at the age of sixty-six, Bell was ready to slow down. He'd already envisioned the third act of his football career: he would retire at the end of the 1959 season and buy the Eagles, so he could return to the ownership ranks, ending his career in the NFL as he began it, side by side with Rooney and Mara and Halas. Secretly, Bell had struck an agreement to buy the Eagles through his negotiations with his friend Joe Donoghue, part of the One Hundred City Brothers consortium that had purchased the Eagles from Alexis Thompson in 1949. Bell had secured financing for a $900,000 loan through the Philadelphia National Bank, and was set to sign the loan on Wednesday, October 14. It would be a gift to himself for all his hard work, and to his sons, Bert Jr. and Upton, who would be able to carry on the family involvement with football.

Bell's plan was still a well-kept secret on the morning of Sunday, October 11, 1959, when he woke up, read the newspapers, ate breakfast with Frances, then attended morning mass at St. Margaret's Church. From there, he and Bert Jr. drove to Franklin Field. Outside the gates, father and son split up so the commissioner could use the ticket office telephone, to check once more on any late line movements, then go down to the field to greet the game officials.

The columnist Jimmy Breslin saw Bell that morning outside the stadium and witnessed the commissioner being approached by a former player. "A guy who needed a haircut and had on a suit that has little fray marks on the cuffs came up the walk and Bert went over to meet him. He said hello to the guy and gave him a ticket to the game. And, with that clenched-fist way of staking you all class guys have, he slipped something in the fellow's hand. 'Get me on the phone Monday,' Bert said to the guy. 'We'll get something done.' "

Bell didn't often spend his games in the press box or with owners. Instead, he preferred to sit in the stands with season ticket holders. He changed seats once during the game, moving in the second half to get into the shade on the warm fall Sunday. Chatting casually with old friends during breaks, he raptly watched the tense finish of the game between two teams he'd once owned, on the very field where he'd been a college quarterback at Penn. And there, with about two minutes left in the game, Bert Bell collapsed from a massive heart attack.

One writer said, "It was like Caruso dying in the third act of *Pagliacci*." Red

Smith wrote, "It was almost as though he were allowed to choose time and place."

But it soon became clear that this was far from being the case. Two days after his father's death, Bert Bell, Jr., received a call from Philadelphia National Bank informing him that "the Eagles deal was off." He knew of no such deal, but found out subsequently about his father's plans.

While Bell's death was a tragedy for the family, it also came at a crucial, precarious moment for the league. When the owners met after the Bell funeral in Philadelphia, it was clear that treasurer and acting commissioner Austin Gunsel, well liked around the league, might be the early-line favorite to replace Bell. But a new commissioner wouldn't be elected until the annual meetings the following January, and until then, there was only a breach. In Dallas, an alarmed Lamar Hunt quickly realized that, with Bell gone, all bets were off.

The furtive, unofficial offers began not long after Hunt's league was formally launched. Even as the NFL was outflanking the AFL, announcing plans to place teams in its two flagship cities, it was constantly sending emissaries to negotiate a truce that would have instantly brought Hunt and Adams what they'd wanted in the first place—franchises in the NFL.

In September, Hunt and Barron Hilton met with Ed Pauley, Jr., at the Beverly Hilton. "Mr. Pauley's pitch seemed to be centered around telling us how sure the American Football League was to fail," said Hunt, "and how I would end up supporting all the teams, and that he and his dad felt it could be worked out so that Bud Adams and I could get a franchise. In fact, they were convinced then that I *was* supporting all the teams. . . . But he was primarily pointing out that Bud Adams and I could get a franchise in Dallas and Houston and they would take Barron into the Rams ownership and the American Football League would fold up its tent." Hunt, having committed to the other owners, wouldn't forsake them.

He'd have numerous chances to reconsider that stance. In the aftermath of Bell's death, Halas took a more aggressive role in trying to broker a deal that might bring Hunt and Adams into the NFL, and in so doing kill any chance for a competing new league. The talks were revived in late October, when the NFL's own expansion plans in Houston were hurt by Rice University's announcement that it wouldn't allow its stadium to be used by any pro teams. Though Hunt listened to and discussed offers, he never wavered.

The AFL had recently lined up its eighth franchise—Boston, with an ownership group led by Billy Sullivan, a former Notre Dame football publicity director—when it gathered in Minneapolis the weekend of November 21–22 for the first AFL draft. On the eve of the draft, as the owners sat in a banquet room at the Cedric Adams Hotel waiting to begin their regularly scheduled evening meeting, Harry Wismer burst through the door, visibly agitated, carrying a newspaper under his arm. Someone asked Wismer if he was ready for dinner.

"Yes!" he shouted, slamming the paper on the conference table. "And this is the last supper!" Pointing to Max Winter of the Minneapolis group, he added, "And he's Judas!"

The headline of the next day's edition of the *Minneapolis Star-Tribune* read "MINNESOTA TO GET NFL FRANCHISE" and detailed the back-channel negotiations by Halas on behalf of convincing the Minneapolis group to bolt the AFL in favor of the NFL. While the Minneapolis group had not been the very first to join the new league, they were considered a crucial franchise in the upper Midwest, and had played a vital role in the league's early formation. Their abdication to the NFL, expertly engineered behind the scenes by Halas, was a major blow to the AFL, and a victory for the older league, which seemed likely to approve expansion to Dallas and Minneapolis-St. Paul at its annual meetings in January.

Conducted amid the hangover of the Minneapolis defection, the AFL's first draft, held November 23, proceeded with an air of anxious uncertainty. The teams began with "territorial" selections—Houston took LSU's Billy Cannon, Dallas selected SMU quarterback Don Meredith, Notre Dame fan Wismer chose to take Irish quarterback George Izo. The thirty-three-round draft that followed was not so much a draft as a lottery. Since some teams hadn't even begun to hire personnel departments yet, it was decided that a committee of personnel men would get together and pick a master list of players, which then would be drawn by lot.

It would be two more months before the league would find an eighth franchise to replace Minneapolis, and the choice of Oakland was one of necessity, since Los Angeles owner Barron Hilton was threatening to drop out if he didn't have a natural geographic rival on the West Coast. The Oakland ownership group was led by Chet Soda, an ebullient Oakland businessman fond of calling everyone he met "Señor." At the press conference announcing the new team, Soda showed up with a beatific smile and distributed sombreros to many in the press corps, before announcing that the winner of the name-the-team contest was "the Oakland Señors." This prompted perhaps the most animated public display shown toward the team all year, as the nickname was roundly panned. Within a few weeks, the club relented, opting for the nickname Raiders instead.

But the franchise, and seven others, persevered. And when the American Football League's first season kicked off, with the Boston Patriots facing the Denver Broncos on September 19, 1960, in front of 21,597 at Boston University Field, it marked a new era for pro football, one that also ushered in the Dallas Texans, Houston Oilers, Los Angeles Chargers, New York Titans, Buffalo Bills, and Oakland Raiders. That the American Football League had survived, bloodied but unbowed, long enough to see its first season was a credit in large part to Hunt's ingenuity and steady hand, the loyalty he commanded from owners like Adams and Hilton, and the indefatigable public relations work of the league's first commissioner, World War II flying ace Joe Foss. As the face of the league, Foss made hundreds of speeches in his first year in office, logging 200,000 air miles—most of which he piloted himself—pushing the AFL message to Rotary and Kiwanis clubs that gladly listened to the spiel so that they could meet a genuine war hero. Foss had no experience in football administration; when he was hired in 1959, he'd seen just two pro football games in person and a few dozen on television. But his frontier enthusiasm and plainspoken frankness was a winning combination. Of the NFL's moves to usurp Dallas and Minnesota, Foss said, "They certainly haven't been wasting any sweetness on us."

The lingering animosity that both sides felt would not quickly be forgotten. Hunt was loath to criticize, but felt he'd been blindsided by the older league, and at the very least outfoxed by Halas. And the representatives of the NFL found Hunt too earnest by half, a schemer whose tactics—coming to meetings with his lawyer, calling a meeting with Bell after he'd already decided to start the AFL—were designed with a lawsuit always in the back of his mind. In their view, Hunt had never really wanted to start his own league, but simply use the threat as a negotiating ploy.

But this was unfair. The very men who cursed Hunt for the headaches he caused the NFL would have been thankful for his behavior had they been with the other AFL owners, on the outside looking in. Hunt's loyalty and ethics were proven numerous times, as he repeatedly turned down the opportunity for NFL franchises because some of his partners would have been frozen out. But his methods were open to question, and this secretiveness caused more trouble than it prevented. Hunt's reticence, his workmanlike methodology all would hurt his relationship with the NFL's owners, who couldn't help but wonder about his real objectives. And yet, a central fact remained: prior to the formation of the AFL, there were no specific discussions about expansion in the NFL. Within weeks after the formation of the league, George Halas and

Art Rooney were announcing plans to expand in two cities by 1961 and two more by 1962.

Of course, Hunt's persistence and Foss's enthusiasm, alone, wouldn't have kept the AFL solvent for long. Five different leagues had attempted to challenge the NFL over the previous forty years, and there were three other start-ups in the works in 1959. But the American Football League that began play in 1960 had an advantage that none of the others were afforded. The ultimate saving grace was the new league's TV deal, negotiated in the spring of 1960. It wasn't just the fact of the TV contract, but the kind of contract that the league negotiated that would make all the difference. And that was a story in itself.

The genesis of the idea that would transform the landscape of American professional sports was first publicly proposed—and roundly dismissed—at the annual meeting of organized baseball, held in Scottsdale, Arizona, in 1952.

The unwelcome messenger bringing tidings of the future was baseball's reigning iconoclast, Bill Veeck, the owner of the St. Louis Browns. Standing before a collection of major and minor league executives, Veeck rocked the gathering with a portentous warning about the future of baseball and television, and a radical proposal about how to confront it.

"It is my contention that the Browns provide half the cast in every game they play," said Veeck. "Therefore, we're entitled to our cut of the TV fees the home club receives for televising our games. Morally, I know I am right, and I plan to fight this thing to the end."

The principle that Veeck pointed to was a simple one. Since every major league game involved two competing clubs, and since the selling of television rights required no investment on the part of the home club, he reasoned it was only fair that those rights fees be split equally in each market between the home and visiting clubs. He proposed that teams retain only 50 percent of their TV revenue, with the other 50 percent going into a general pool to be divided equally among all the league's teams. The response to this idea ranged from "barely polite" applause, in the words of one attendee, to heated outrage. Afterward, Dodgers owner Walter O'Malley labeled Veeck "a damned Communist" for his suggestions.

Veeck was affably defiant in the face of the criticism. "Under this system they want to continue the rich clubs get richer and the poor clubs continue poor. With all that television money they're getting the Yanks can continue to keep outbidding us for talent. They've signed $500,000 worth of bonus players in the last couple of years, paying for 'em out of the TV money we help provide. We poorer clubs are helping cut our own throats. None of us is ever going to catch up with the Yankees at that rate."

Veeck's measures were defeated in Arizona, but he found a more sympathetic audience in Philadelphia, where Bert Bell read about the meeting and telephoned Veeck to hear more details. The NFL's evolving policy on television was already more clearly defined than baseball's, with Judge Grim's 1953 decision having ratified the home blackout policy. Baseball had no set policy, and nowhere near the sharing of revenues; in the American League, visiting teams still received 28 cents from every ticket sold, just as they had for fifty years. Meanwhile, visiting teams in the NFL shared 40 percent of gate receipts, after accounting for the home team's rental fee. Bell sensed quickly that, like the draft and the NFL's 60-40 home-visitor gate split, revenue sharing of television receipts could provide another mechanism to equalize the opportunity for each of the NFL's clubs to field a competitive team. While blacking out telecasts of home games helped the gate in all markets, Bell had grown increasingly concerned with the disparity between the league's largest and smallest markets. In 1953, the Rams would earn nearly $100,000 for TV rights, while the Packers were barely clearing $5,000 for their rights. Despite his strong influence on league affairs, Bell was unable during the remainder of the 1950s to convince the owners to pool all their resources in a manner similar to what Veeck envisioned.

But Veeck's idea was far from dead. By 1958, it found another receptive listener, fellow baseball maverick Branch Rickey, who joined forces with New York developer Bill Shea, and began to drum up support for the Continental League, a "third major league" for baseball that would bring the sport to a handful of previously ignored markets, as well as partially remedy the wrenching exit of the Dodgers and Giants from New York.

In Rickey's presentations to potential investors, he outlined a television strategy that was an even more radical extension of Veeck's plan, with teams keeping just one third of their TV revenues, and putting the other two thirds into a pool to be shared equally. "It has been reported that the American League club in New York City in 1959 realized a gross income of one million four hundred thousand dollars from radio and television," he noted in one speech. "The Washington club in the same league took in approximately $125,000, yet the Washington club plays eleven games at Yankee Stadium. How can Washington ever expect to compete in the competitive market for player contracts where money is king? Any rule or regulation that removes or tends to remove the power of money to make the difference in playing strength is a good rule. The American League cannot help itself at this point. Neither can the National League. The proposed new third major league has provided in its Constitution for the pooling of two-thirds of all television receipts from what-ever source from all clubs."

The Continental League never came to be, but the efforts of Rickey forced major league baseball into its first round of expansion since the turn of the century. The sport was as resistant to his television ideas as they'd been to Veeck's, yet even as Rickey was being pushed to the sidelines, the stage was set for a lethally ironic turnabout. Veeck's very concept, embraced by Rickey, and explained to Hunt, was about to become a cornerstone of a new football league.

On the plane to Miami, just weeks after hearing Rickey's Continental League proposal, Hunt had copied out the exact television revenue-sharing plan espoused by Rickey (33 percent to the team, 67 percent shared equally with the other clubs in the league), which itself was a refinement of the original plan offered by Veeck (50-50).

Over the next few months, Hunt and his partners settled on an easier, more elegant way to accomplish the same goal: a single network package, negotiated by the league office on behalf of all its teams, to be divided equally by all teams. For whatever reason, the idea of equalizing television revenues as a means to equalizing competitive opportunity appealed to the son of one of the wealthiest men in the world. In 1959, it seemed a mere detail in a large, sprawling plan, but its significance would be borne out in time.

After neither NBC nor CBS expressed the slightest interest in a deal, Hunt decided to approach ABC, distant third among the major networks, without a sports division. The actual negotiation was left to the canny agent Jay Michaels (whose son Al would one day become the best-known play-by-play man in football), of the Music Corporation of America, and MCA president David A. "Sonny" Werblin. In early June, Werblin and ABC's Tom Moore met for a dinner at "21," and hammered out a five-year, $8.5 million deal, which would pay each club more than $170,000, then graduate to higher levels in subsequent years, provided that advertising targets were met. In the deal was an explicit provision that each team would get the same amount from an overall league deal, regardless of how many of their games reached "national" audiences.

That ABC was in the market for sports broadcasting was a happy accident, itself a result of a cautionary tale. Boxing, a staple of Friday night television since the inception of the medium, was finally canceled by NBC after the 1960 spring season. Gillette, which had spent $8 million advertising its products on the *Gillette Cavalcade of Sports,* took its advertising budget to ABC. Suddenly, the "Almost Broadcasting Company" had a mother lode of ad revenue, needing only to find the programming to go with it.

There was one other bit of good fortune for the AFL in the deal. ABC, having no internal sports division, contracted out with Edgar Scherick, the former CBS executive who formed his own company, called Sports Programs Inc., in 1957. Scherick's top producer was an avid, imaginative fan named Roone Arledge, who had a vision of football broadcasts as a dynamic kaleidoscope of action, color, and detail. In a memo to Scherick outlining his plans for ABC's college football coverage in the spring of 1960, Arledge wrote, "Heretofore, television has done a remarkable job of bringing the game to the viewer—now we are going to take the viewer to the game!! We will utilize every production technique . . . to heighten the viewer's feeling of actually sitting in the stands and participating personally in the excitement and the color."

Arledge would bring many of the same techniques to the AFL broadcasts. What he realized, before almost anyone else in the TV industry, was that the games could be not only a great spectator sport or a great television sport, but great *television.* And by observing many of the conventions of dramatic television, the game could be made more involving to the viewer. Arledge's influence wasn't noticed right away, but it would animate the early days of the AFL broadcasts, providing skillful, exciting coverage of a youthful, freewheeling league. And in the first year of ABC's coverage, the main innovation Arledge brought was cutting straight from the punter to the receiver, rather than following the flight of the ball in the air, so that fans at home avoided seeing an ocean of empty stadium seats, a technique that would eventually be known, within the industry, as "AFL coverage." The AFL, for its part, boasted that unlike the older league, it would televise fights and injuries, citing their news value. (Within a few years, the NFL would eventually relax its restrictions as well.)

The AFL's innovative contract, dividing money equally, would allow even the shakiest of franchises some revenue to stem the tide of losses. The package itself would be a vivid testament to Rickey's philosophical cornerstone—"*Any rule or regulation that removes or tends to remove the power of money to make the difference in playing strength is a good rule*"—of the rationale for revenue sharing.

Without ever having played a game, each of the eight teams in the American Football League entered the 1960 season guaranteed to earn more in television revenues than five of the venerable, established franchises in the

National Football League. This development did not go unnoticed at the NFL offices, where the ideas of Veeck—adapted by Rickey and reshaped by Hunt— would soon find another crucial adherent.

It would be years before the impact was obvious, but by the beginning of 1960, the concept had already begun to change the landscape. As modified further, into the even simpler formula adopted by the AFL, and later by the NFL, Veeck's idea would help launch and sustain a new football league, spur the existing one to greater heights, sharpen the competitive balance of both, and eventually hasten the end of baseball as the national pastime.

8

The Siege

As the owners and general managers arrived at the Kenilworth Hotel in Miami Beach for the NFL's annual meetings in January 1960, the National Football League stood at a crossroads. The agenda was packed: the explosive issue of expansion loomed over the proceedings, as did the inevitable conflict over the alignment of the divisions should expansion come to pass. The league had to hammer out a policy against a new rival league, address the elusive possibility of a joint TV contract with CBS, and help decide the fate of the Chicago Cardinals. But before any of these questions could be resolved, the NFL had to select a successor to Bert Bell. The agenda was so long that many viewed the pending vote for the new commissioner as more of a preliminary than the main event.

In this case, the preliminaries would last for eleven days.

The meetings convened in executive session, four days before their official beginning, with a bitter parliamentary debate between George Halas, accompanied to the league meetings for the first time ever by his lawyer, and George Preston Marshall, who brought *his* lawyer, and an endless string of objections to the mere discussion of the expansion question. That, and the introductions of the four cities seeking franchises—Murchison's Dallas entry, the AFL defectors from Minneapolis-St. Paul, plus bids from Miami and Atlanta—took much of the first three days.

It was assumed and widely reported that the new commissioner—whose election would require a supermajority of 75 percent of the clubs voting—would be either Austin Gunsel or Marshall Leahy. Gunsel, acting commissioner since Bell's death, was the league's treasurer, an ex–FBI man and longtime aide to Bell, who was well versed in his mentor's management style—though he lacked Bell's magnetism—and content to keep the league office in suburban Philadelphia. But many felt he was a pale echo of Bell, and lacked the stature to be elected commissioner. "Too much like a policeman" was the horse-track assessment of Gunsel from the Cardinals' Stormy Bidwill.

Out on the West Coast, support was brewing for the 49ers' bright, well-liked lawyer Leahy, who had been instrumental in handling the legal details when the NFL absorbed the remnants of the All-America Conference a decade earlier. The forty-nine-year-old Leahy was respected as one of the rising executives of the league, but he had publicly insisted prior to the meetings that he would only accept the job if he could move the league offices to San Francisco, where he was raising five daughters.

It was Wednesday afternoon, January 20, before Gunsel turned the gavel over to the Eagles' Joe Donoghue, and left the room, along with Leahy, so the owners could vote on the next commissioner. The two men sat on the couch in the Kenilworth lobby, where many of the two dozen or so writers in attendance eagerly vetted them for information. Hours passed and the wait grew more awkward for both men.

Inside, the discussion deteriorated into a generational and geographic struggle, a battle between the league's supposed "old guard," who wanted to retain a system similar to Bell's leadership, and a "new guard" of far-flung teams that wanted a greater voice in league business. On the second ballot, eight votes came in for Leahy, three votes for Austin Gunsel, and one abstention, from George Halas. The 49ers' co-owners, Vic and Tony Morabito, had expected to carry the day when they secured Art Rooney as the eighth vote for Leahy. "George Halas, in my presence, promised Vic Morabito that, 'If you get eight votes, I'll be your ninth,' " said GM Lou Spadia. "So the eighth vote was Art Rooney. So Vic got up, walked over to Halas. And Halas wouldn't even acknowledge his presence, wouldn't answer him. Vic kept saying, 'You said you'd be our ninth.' And Halas was just mum."

After another vote yielded the same result, Paul Brown strode over to Halas and said, "C'mon, George, one more vote and we have this thing licked." At that point, Carroll Rosenbloom spoke up, warning, "George, if you vote for Leahy, you can forget about expansion."

This threat was a potent one—even with an amendment to the league constitution, expansion would need the vote of ten teams to pass. Since the Redskins and Cardinals would oppose any such vote, Halas knew he couldn't afford to lose even one more team in support of it. More concerned about expansion than about the identity of the next commissioner, Halas was holding on to his vote so as not to alienate either side for the expansion vote that would follow. The meeting moved through eight more ballots without any significant change, adjourning to the next day.

By the end of Thursday's debate, and six more ballots, there were a "Solid Seven" franchises backing Leahy: San Francisco, Los Angeles, Green Bay, Detroit, Cleveland, the Chicago Cardinals, and the New York Giants. Pittsburgh's Art Rooney had gone back to the other side, and joined Marshall, Rosenbloom, and Philadelphia's Frank McNamee among those insisting they didn't want the offices moved any further west than Chicago, where Elmer Layden had presided. And Halas continued abstaining, on each and every subsequent vote.

That's how it remained for much of the next week, as the stalemate in Miami Beach became a national public relations nightmare. As the days dragged on, *Miami Herald* columnist Jimmy Burns wondered if the owners had been influenced by the Miami Chamber of Commerce's slogan "Stay through May." League PR director Joe Labrum had to file stories for more than one soused writer. Meanwhile, Marshall Leahy, fed up with the stalemate and perhaps convinced that leaving the scene would be a wise tactical maneuver, checked out of the Kenilworth, leaving a San Francisco forwarding address and his name in nomination. But through seven more ballots on Sunday, there was no change.

Bert Bell had once told Bert Jr. that if anything ever happened to him, the man best qualified for his job would be Paul Brown. But stoked with a drive to return his Browns to the top, Brown had no interest in an administrative position, rebuffing both private and public draft efforts. At one point, on Sunday evening, Eagles president Frank McNamee stood up and said, "Gentlemen, Marshall Leahy is a very fine man, but there is *no way* we are going to have the league office west of the Mississippi. Now, the press is laughing at us because we can't make a decision. We all know there's a man in this room who is qualified, and would do a hell of a job." Then, casting his eye down at Brown, McNamee asked, "Paul . . . will you take the job?"

Brown paused to look around the table for a moment, then said, "Only if the league offices are west of the Mississippi." The room erupted in laughter and soon broke for another recess in what was by then beginning to look like an interminable siege.

A vote was taken Monday morning, and another that night, the twenty-second ballot overall, after which the positions remained locked in and tempers had frayed. "If Jesus Christ himself came down here, you people would still insist on Leahy!" shouted Rosenbloom.

The next morning, Tuesday, January 26, Wellington Mara and Dan Reeves reached the conclusion that their man Leahy could not win, and they were only prolonging their frustration by insisting upon him. They then began to put together their own list of possible compromise candidates, topped by the Packers' new coach, Vince Lombardi, who'd lifted the team from the doldrums to a 7-5 record in 1959. Lombardi had returned to New York for a speaking commitment, so Mara and Reeves decided they should approach Packers president Dominic Olejniczak to see if he'd be willing to allow Lombardi's name to be put up to a vote. As Reeves and Mara sat on the couch in the Kenilworth lobby, which looked out onto the swimming pool, they dispatched Wellington's brother, Jack Mara, to privately broach the subject of drafting Lombardi with Olejniczak, who was then out by the pool.

From their vantage point on the couch, they couldn't see the conversation, but a few moments after Jack went to speak to him, a furious Olejniczak jabbed the door open and marched straight toward the bar, and ordered a drink.

"Well," said Reeves, looking at Mara. "Scratch Lombardi off the list."

They had already considered and dismissed some of the other names and were by then left with just one possibility. Sitting there silently, looking at the fourth name on the list, Wellington Mara said, "Dan, it's got to be Pete."

"I think you're right," said Reeves. "I hate to lose him, but I think he'd do a great job."

And with that, the movement to draft Pete Rozelle as a compromise candidate began. Reeves had suggested Rozelle first, according to Mara, but had done so with some reluctance. But the more Reeves considered it, the more certain he became that Rozelle could be just the man to lead the NFL into the next decade. His GM was skilled and savvy, and had done a remarkable job bridging the gulf between Reeves and his co-owners.

"I know he's young," mused Reeves. "But that could help—he doesn't have any enemies."

In fact, Rozelle, though still the league's youngest general manager at thirty-three, was more prepared for the job than even Reeves could have imagined.

———

When the eighteen-year-old Pete Rozelle left for the service in 1944, his father, Ray, bought one of the prefab military scrapbooks so popular at the time, offering prideful, worried parents an outlet to catalogue their son's military duty and progress. The book included a series of fill-in-the-blank prompts to provide depth and dimension to the lives of young men heading off to war.

Ray Rozelle filled out Pete's personal history in his precise, dashing print, noting that his oldest son graduated with high honors from Compton High School on June 15, 1944. He listed Pete's accomplishments as: "Basketball, tennis, sports editor, Tartar Shield [the school newspaper]; Sports editor, Dar-U-Gar [yearbook], 1st Place Award, sportswriter, by Helms Foundation." In the personal record page, Ray Rozelle then filled out his son's pastimes. "Favorite pastime: *Baseball.* Favorite sport: *Basketball.* As spectator: *Football.* Hobby: *Sports.*"

In earlier generations, only the monied classes could immerse themselves in sports as youths. For others, games were a carrot: for rural kids who'd viewed sport as a lone refuge from a long day of work, or for the urban underclass, who saw it as a way out. Yet even as Pete Rozelle grew up during the Depression, he found himself part of a new American middle class, free to choose his own passions and preoccupations. And his choice was clear. "Sports was really my life," he'd say of his childhood.

Alvin Ray Rozelle, oldest of the two Rozelle boys, had been born in 1926 in Lynwood, California, one of America's first true suburbs, and nicknamed Pete by an uncle at an early age. His father, Ray Rozelle, was a courtly, gentle man, who grew more taciturn after the failure of his grocery store, the Pacific Market, during the Depression. Pete's mother, Hazel Healey Rozelle, was the demonstrative sort, "an actress who never got to be an actress," in the words of her granddaughter, prone to wearing long strapless gowns to almost any social occasion, the sort of woman who colored the food green for St. Patrick's Day. Pete grew up precociously bright, an avid reader with an agile mind and a love for sports, which filled his days. At the family's modest stucco home at 3205 Lynwood, his younger brother, Dick, would recall "Pete hardly being around the house—he always had something going on."

The childhood lesson that would make the biggest impression upon him came during a Sunday School retreat as a ten-year-old—decades later, Rozelle would remember a camp counselor explaining "character is what you are, and reputation is what people think you are, and reputation is thus every bit as important as character." Pete would allow later that he'd "always worked very hard and tried not to alienate any more than necessary." But treating others well wasn't merely a trait with Pete Rozelle. It eventually became something like an organizing principle. "He avoided fights," said his seventh-grade classmate Bill Evans. "He was never in trouble because he knew how to negotiate his way out of it. Not that he was a sissy—it was just that he disliked strife."

At Lynwood Junior High, Pete was the smallest boy on the varsity basketball team, but was also the student body president in the fall of 1941. In the fall of 1942, he entered eleventh grade at Compton High School, which shared a handsome campus of cream deco-styled buildings with Compton Junior College (the school district was then on a "6-4-4" system, putting eleventh and twelfth graders at Compton High School on the same campus as the freshmen and sophomores of Compton Junior College).

As an athlete, Pete was more a participant than star, lettering twice in basketball in junior high, and twice in tennis. But by high school, his aspirations as a sportswriter were clear. Ray had bought a Royal typewriter for Pete a few years earlier, and by the 1943 school year, Rozelle had a column on the sports pages of the *Tartar Shield*. First called "Pete's Repetes" and later "Sports in Review," his still purplish sportswriting prose was emerging in those years. ("Eddie Suggett's Tartar hickory stick nine was very unhospitable to the visiting Pepperdine college ball club last week as they fashioned out a wild 15–12 trackmeet score over the Waves.")

The school's athletic star was four-sport letterman Edwin "Duke" Snider, who had played football for Pete's uncle Joe Rozelle at Enterprise Junior High. Peppering the *Los Angeles Times* high school correspondent John de la Vega with reports of Snider's exploits, Rozelle helped his friend make the *Times*'s second-team All-City, and helped bring a raft of baseball scouts as well. By then, Rozelle had found work during weekends on the sports desk of the *Long Beach Press-Telegram.* The impression shared by virtually all who met Rozelle in those years was not merely that he was likable, but that he seemed mature beyond his years, still boyishly enthusiastic but self-possessed, someone who treated all people with respect and a warm kindness.

By high school, the war effort was increasing, and there were antiaircraft guns and searchlights stationed up and down Century Boulevard. Rozelle was as transformed as any of his classmates by the prospect of world war. "Our country needs you and me," he wrote in an English class paper. "We must answer the call. If we do, then through our efforts and the grace of God in heaven we will win this war and save for the world the democratic ideals for which we stand."

And yet, there was still the sprawling backyards and the next round of games. There were home movies, shot in the summer of 1944, with Pete in the front yard of his friend Daily Childs's house, lanky and freshly scrubbed, beaming in pleated slacks, a long-sleeve shirt, and a Compton letterman's cardigan, playing baseball soft toss with high school classmates Childs and Louie Joseph. At the end of the short segment, with cars lazily rolling past on the residential streets of Lynwood, the three boys spontaneously formed a football formation, with Rozelle snapping the baseball to Joseph and then going out for a pass. Then Pete Rozelle got on his bicycle, smiled sheepishly for the camera, and rode off into the late afternoon twilight. That glimpse would encapsulate much of the golden promise of Pete Rozelle's youth.

Nothing in his two years of military duty would change it. Rozelle registered for Selective Service on his eighteenth birthday, March 1, 1944, and took his pre-induction physical just two months later. By then, he'd grown to a gangly six-foot and 140 pounds, with an army physician noting Rozelle's brown hair, blue eyes, light complexion, and a small mole on his right cheek. Reporting for active duty July 29, 1944, Rozelle spent eighteen months aboard the oil tanker USS *Guardoqui* in the Pacific, working his way up to yeoman second class, handling all the clerical duties aboard the ship, even working on a ship newsletter. Later, after the war, he spent a few more months aboard another ship, the USS *Audrain*, early in 1946, waiting for his decommissioning.

His high school friend Max Patterson saw him when the *Guardoqui* docked at Treasure Island in San Francisco. Rozelle told him about a recent trip into port, when it was left to Rozelle, the only yeoman on board, to assign liberty to half the sailors. "They were all climbing my frame, saying 'Pick me, pick me,' " Rozelle related. "You know, Max, that's the first time in my life I've ever had any power. And I *loved* it."

Rozelle, who saw no battle, was decommissioned in 1946, and returned home largely unchanged by the experience. "When he came back, it was just like he'd been to summer camp," said his younger brother, Dick. "He took everything in stride."

In May 1946, Rozelle returned to civilian life and his parents' home in Lynwood, ready to begin junior college. He had already lined up the job as Compton's student athletic news director, so he dropped by the Rams' offices and introduced himself to Bill John, the business manager who'd traveled with the team from Cleveland. Rozelle secured a job to help out around the Rams' training camp, and wound up working so many hours that John would eventually challenge them. Rozelle was unfazed. "Pay me whatever you want to pay me," he said. By the end of the summer, he'd been hired by John to put together the Rams' programs for the 1946 season, at $50 per game. Throughout the camp he was a constant presence, ever-watching and ready to help, soaking in the sights and sounds of professional football. When *Sport* magazine came to Compton for a cover story on Tom Harmon and his Hollywood starlet wife, Elyse Knox, the photographer created a fans-in-the-stands tableau with Harmon, fully decked out in his uniform, sitting in the front row with his arm around Knox. At the edge of that cover shot, a partially obscured Rozelle can be seen, sitting two rows behind Harmon, broad smile on his face.

When the team offered him tickets for the Rams game against the College All-Stars in Chicago, Rozelle set out with his friend John Lehman. They spent a week in Evanston, rooming at the YMCA, and Pete spent much of his time with Jane Coupe, a poised, comely art student he'd met during an earlier stop in Chicago. Rozelle returned not just smitten but deeply in love. Jane eventually followed him to California, where three years later they were married.

In the spring of 1948, Rozelle was working as the Compton undergraduate athletic news director when he met Pete Newell, the basketball coach at the University of San Francisco. Newell was down in Compton scouting talent at a junior college tournament and was impressed by the young Rozelle's professional air. "When you'd go scout somebody, you were lucky to get a seat," said Newell. "But Pete had hot coffee for us, he had all the statistics. He was so far ahead of what anyone else was doing at the time." When Bill Grant, the previous athletic news director at the University of San Francisco (and himself a Compton graduate), left in 1948, Newell recommended Rozelle for the position, which included a full-ride scholarship. It would prove to be another in a series of serendipitous turns in Rozelle's career. Finishing his undergraduate education at USF, he was steeped for the first time in the challenging academic atmosphere offered by the Jesuits. And for $75 a month and all his school expenses, Rozelle worked as USF's student athletic news director at a time when the school was rising to national prominence in both basketball and football.

When the Dons basketball team marched to the National Invitation Tournament title in 1949, Rozelle was the conduit with the national media, and perfectly framed the Cinderella story for what Newell would describe as a "mesmerized Eastern press." That same year, the newlyweds Pete and Jane moved to a small two-room apartment near the campus.

In 1951, the lightly regarded Dons began the football season 4-0 and traveled to Yankee Stadium for a game against perennial Eastern power Fordham. Rozelle showed up at seven newspaper offices in the city, advancing the game and praising the Dons as one of the best football teams in the country, with a particular emphasis on USF's fleet, powerful halfback Ollie Matson. For the legendary Grantland Rice, Rozelle went a step further. He stopped by Rice's

New York apartment, and escorted him personally to the Randalls Island stadium for the game, then brought him home after USF's 32–26 win.

The glorious 9-0 season was a coda to the era of great Jesuit football teams. USF suspended its football program early in 1952, citing staggering losses, and a diminishing number of like-sized independents (both Loyola and St. Mary's had "de-emphasized" earlier) on the West Coast.

Yet again, Rozelle's timing was perfect. In Los Angeles, the Rams' publicity director Tex Maule had just returned to Texas to take a similar job with the old Dallas Texans. Tex Schramm, serving as general manager, remembered hearing about the skilled kid from San Francisco, and hired Rozelle as the publicity director for the 1952 season. On the Rams, Rozelle fell under the tutelage of Reeves and Schramm, and quickly moved beyond his role in publicity, helping the team throughout the year with its vast scouting operations.

And yet for a time, it seemed as if his career would bring him elsewhere. Even after leaving San Francisco, Rozelle continued to correspond with the San Francisco public relations executive Ken Macker, a polished, engaging sportsman who'd been a boyhood friend of Pete Newell's.

Heavily influenced by the works of public relations pioneer Edward Bernays, Macker and a generation of young executives were convinced that there was a calling in public relations much higher than the snake-oil sales pitches of publicists, press agents, and ad salesmen. They envisioned public relations serving as a modern conduit between businesses and their customers, a field that would combine social science findings and journalistic principles in a manner that would allow companies to frame their message in a more coherent and eloquent manner.

Macker had for years been hoping to start his own company, and in January 1955, the international public relations firm of P. K. Macker and Co. was launched, with headquarters in San Francisco and offices in New York and Los Angeles. Macker lured Rozelle as a partner, giving him a sizable raise (from his $6,500 with the Rams, to $9,600 a year with an annual bonus and a chance to buy a 10 percent stake in the company).

Within months, Rozelle was hard at work handling publicity for the 1956 Olympic Games in Melbourne on behalf of the Victoria Promotion Committee, the Australian government body overseeing the Games. He escorted Aussie miler John Landy around the U.S. for a series of media appearances that proved a rousing success.

By the end of the 1956 Olympics, Macker and Co. had established itself as a prestigious, growing firm, with such big-name accounts as Qantas Airlines, videotape innovators Ampex, and the international brewer San Miguel. Rozelle was a rising executive in the world of public relations, traveled frequently to New York, and was well acquainted with the advertising and television industries.

He might well have stayed at Macker, but for the call in 1957 from Bert Bell. Bridling under the constant bickering between Reeves and his partners, and dispirited by Reeves's drinking binges, Tex Schramm had resigned as the Rams' GM to accept an offer from CBS's Bill MacPhail, and moved to New York to work for CBS Sports. After Reeves had rejected all of Ed Pauley's suggestions for GM, and Pauley and the other owners had refused all of Reeves's suggestions, Bell intervened and suggested Rozelle, whom he'd remembered fondly as a gracious and extremely competent PR man. So that neither side would be seen to have the upper hand, it was determined that Bell would be the one to make the offer to Rozelle. "You're the first thing they've agreed on since Garfield was shot," said Bell.

Returning in April 1957 to the team's cozy offices on Beverly Boulevard, Rozelle immediately set about solving problems and smoothing over old disagreements. He presided over a settlement between a group of disaffected veterans threatening to hold out over training camp pay, and convinced the Rams' ownership to make some overdue concessions, by which players would receive $50 per exhibition game, have their per diem increased from $6 to $9, and receive half a year's premium for each player's health insurance, which at the time was still the sole responsibility of the player.

In place of Schramm's booming voice and occasionally brusque demeanor, Rozelle strived for inclusiveness, and brought to the offices a kind of easy, chipper professionalism. He sent handwritten Christmas notes to everyone on the team payroll, going beyond perfunctory season's greetings to mention how each person had helped the club that year, and express his appreciation for it.

Rozelle's presence stabilized the stormy ownership situation in Los Angeles. Actual relations between Reeves and the other owners didn't really improve—Pauley and Reeves wouldn't ride on the same elevator to the Coliseum press box on game days—but communication between the two camps did. Rozelle earned the good graces of both factions, and Reeves often referred to him as "the most honest man I've ever known."

Under Rozelle, every aspect of the Rams' public presentation exhibited a high-gloss polish. For the team's programs and yearbooks, he hired a gifted, versatile graphic artist named David Boss, a lanky, urbane Texan who was as enchanted as Rozelle with the romance and action of football. Around the same time, Rozelle met a bluff, likable salesman named Larry Kent, a representative for Roy Rogers, Inc., the highly successful licensing company that by the late '50s was responsible for the licensing of $30 million annually in Roy Rogers clothing, toys, games, and promotions. Through Kent, Rozelle helped set up the Rams Store, a corner storefront just a block away from the team's offices on Beverly Boulevard, which sold everything from T-shirts ($1.25) to earrings ($3.95) to highball glasses ($7.95 for a set of eight), all emblazoned with the Rams' emblem. The most popular item was a novelty called a bobble-head doll ($1.00), a six-inch-tall ceramic statuette of a smiling football player, whose oversized helmeted head bobbled on a spring.

The Rams had already become profitable by Rozelle's arrival, but his promotional and public relations savvy helped accelerate that growth. Before the Colts-Giants 1958 title game that supposedly put the NFL on the map, the Rams under Rozelle had drawn four crowds of larger than 95,000 to the cavernous Coliseum—including a record 102,368 to a 49ers game in 1957—and had become the most profitable club in pro football.

Within six months of returning to Southern California, Jane was pregnant. Anne Marie Rozelle (she would add the "e" to her first name as an adult) was born on September 28, 1958. Pete left a game to go to the hospital at halftime, with the Rams leading, and returned just in time to see Lou Groza kick a field goal, to lift the Browns to a 30–27 win late in the fourth quarter.

The world he'd grown up dreaming about had become a reality. And the distinctive culture of pro football had exerted its pull on him. Rozelle had to admit that he was transfixed with the myriad variables of competition that made up life in the NFL. "Pro football," he would say flatly, "is the most fascinating thing in the world."

In his three years as GM of the Rams, Rozelle improved the team's fortunes in virtually every way except on the field. He'd made his biggest splash by trading eleven players for the Cardinals' star running back, former University of San Francisco classmate Ollie Matson. But though Matson was a productive runner in 1958, he couldn't stop the club's decline in 1959.

The Rams were co-favorites to win the West in 1959, but the season began badly, with a narrow loss to the Giants at home, and a shocking 34–0 loss at the hands of San Francisco on the road. Though they won their next two games, the season became unhinged with three close losses during a three-game homestand, the beginning of an eight-game losing skid to end the season. Dan Reeves had been sitting in the Rams' locker room after the season's final game, a 45–26 blowout loss to the Colts. Reeves wasn't angry, only sad to be there, to have to tell Sid Gillman he was being fired. Throughout the Rams' organization, Gillman's inability to repeat the conference title of 1955 was mystifying. He was a consummate tactical coach, and many of the players liked him. The team's scouts believed they had among the best talent in the league. And while Bill Wade had been unable to replicate the brilliance at quarterback of Bob Waterfield and Norm Van Brocklin, that deficiency hardly seemed to account for the 2-10 record of a club that many tabbed as a contender.

It was an equally agonizing moment for Rozelle, for whom the entire fall had been a protracted torment. But a GM's job was to work for next year, even when the present one was in shambles. He spent long nights prepping for the 1960 draft (which the NFL secretly held in November, to compete with the earlier AFL draft). With the first overall pick, the Rams selected LSU halfback and Heisman winner Billy Cannon.

Cannon's experience that fall would foreshadow the chaotic future years of pro football. Though the NFL had for decades lived by the agreement that it would not sign players until their college eligibility had been exhausted, the challenge from the AFL prompted many GMs and personnel directors around the country to jump the gun, secretly negotiating prior to the draft, and before the New Year's bowl games, to sign players to contracts.

On November 30, Cannon—traveling under the alias of Billy Gunn—checked into the Warwick Hotel in Philadelphia for a secret negotiation with the Rams. Rozelle signed Cannon to a contract with a $10,000 bonus, a $500 check to cover travel expenses, and three one-year contracts at $15,000 per year. They agreed the undated contract would not take effect until after LSU faced Mississippi in the Sugar Bowl January 1, but even that understanding was confidential, since signing the contract would have made Cannon ineligible for the Sugar Bowl, and violated the NFL's agreement with the NCAA.

Back in Houston, Oilers owner Bud Adams was growing frustrated. He'd spent weeks trying to reach Cannon, his first-round "territorial selection" in the AFL draft. Repeated calls to Cannon's dorm room, his parents' house, his girlfriend's house had all yielded nothing. So in mid-December, he decided to take another tack, and let money do the talking.

He phoned a health club that Cannon frequented in Baton Rouge, run by Alvin Roy, a pioneer in football strength conditioning who would later work for several pro teams.

"I'm sure he wants to talk to you, Bud," said Roy. "I know he's been real busy with all his commitments."

"Well, you just tell him this," said Adams. "I don't know if he's signed with the Rams yet or he hasn't. Doesn't make any difference, they're not going to do anything about it. Just tell him I'll give him double whatever they gave him to sign with him. Here's my phone number, tell him to call me collect."

It was about 5:00 p.m. then, and after getting off the phone, Adams turned to his wife and said, "I bet you I'll get a long-distance call from Billy Cannon in the next hour." Thirty minutes later the phone rang, with an operator asking Adams if he'd accept a long-distance call from a Billy Cannon.

"Oh, I'd be happy to."

After Cannon reluctantly admitted to Adams that he had signed an agreement with the Rams, Adams explained that the NFL knew its contract was improper, and that "we can get around that." True to his word, Adams doubled the Rams' deal, offering a $20,000 bonus, and a three-year deal at $30,000 each, for a package of $110,000, to which Cannon quickly agreed.

The Oilers then conceived a stunt designed to cause the older league maximum embarrassment. They arranged to sign Cannon immediately upon the completion of the Sugar Bowl, on the Tulane Stadium field, in front of a national television audience. The signing would come at the earliest possible time that Cannon could sign after his eligibility was up. Then if the Rams claimed they'd *already* signed him, they would be admitting they'd done so improperly.

Rozelle first heard rumors about the Oilers deal when he arrived in New Orleans for the game, where his attempts to meet privately with Cannon proved fruitless. On New Year's Day, LSU played its rematch with Mississippi in the Sugar Bowl, and when the final gun sounded, an outwardly calm Rozelle hurried around the field looking for Cannon. Meanwhile, the best-known college football player in the nation walked to the end zone. There, under the goalposts, on national television, Cannon signed a contract with the Oilers.

A few minutes later, Rozelle greeted Cannon in the locker room and put his arm around Cannon's shoulders. "Well, Billy, it's going to be awfully nice having you with us in Los Angeles."

"But I just signed with the Houston Oilers," said Cannon, confirming Rozelle's worst fears.

As reporters crowded around Cannon's locker, Rozelle stood by, composed but expressing a look of deep regret. "Billy," he said softly at one point, "don't say anything you'll regret later."

The Rams sued the AFL, claiming Cannon was already under contract. The lawsuit, heard in Los Angeles County Court, eventually ruled in favor of Cannon and the Oilers, with whom he began the 1960 season. But even before

the case began, the job had begun to weigh heavily on Rozelle. His disappointment over the season, his sadness at watching his friend Gillman's firing, the
pressure to find a worthy successor, and the struggle to secure Cannon's services combined to leave him not only exhausted, but profoundly frustrated,
and unusually ambivalent about his future.

His friend John Lehman was convinced that Rozelle was considering a return to journalism, and it was obvious that the job, like the previous one, had
become a major strain on his marriage. And yet, as Rozelle boarded the plane
for Miami on January 16, his plans were clear: in a week, his wife, Jane, would
pack their swimsuits, her watercolors, and his copy of Ian Fleming's latest,
Thunderball, drop off their daughter, Anne, with Pete's parents, and join him
in Miami. From there, they'd take off to begin their much needed vacation, a
one-week getaway to Jamaica.

That was still the plan on Tuesday afternoon, January 26, when Dan Reeves
quietly sidled up to Rozelle, and asked him to step outside for a moment.

———

To say that Rozelle was a dark horse candidate for the vacant commissioner's
chair would be a misrepresentation. Until Reeves and Wellington Mara discussed him while casting about for possible compromise choices, Rozelle was
not a candidate at all. For much of the time at the Kenilworth, he was a face in
the crowd, a young GM who had to leave the room when the owners entered
into executive session. As late as the morning of his election, he was identified
as Los Angeles Rams general manager "Pete Rosele" in a stray quote in the
Miami Herald, where he appeared primarily because he was one of the few
team officials still milling around the hotel lobby. The circumstances that led
to Rozelle's election were unprecedented, unanticipated, and unforeseeable.

But once the idea was raised, it quickly gained support. Paul Brown and
Jack Mara also liked the young Rozelle and, during the lunch break that day,
they joined Reeves and Wellington Mara in asking Rozelle to step outside for a
private talk.

"Pete," Brown said, "we've been talking about this. We'd like to put your
name up as an ideal compromise candidate."

Rozelle looked at the group, eyes widening. "You've got to be kidding," he
said. "That's the most ludicrous thing I've ever heard." They convinced him
they were serious, and explained why they thought he would make a good
choice. After a few moments of reflection, Rozelle's initial response was that he
didn't think he could be elected, and he didn't want to be embarrassed by
being rejected.

"Don't worry about being embarrassed," said Paul Brown. "We won't put your name up until we're sure you're going to get elected."

Rozelle returned to his hotel room down the street at the Balmoral, where Jane had taken a bus tour of the city in the morning. With a bashful smile, he said, "This has really been a strange meeting. Guess who they're talking about as a candidate now."

"You," she said instantly. "Alvin Ray Rozelle."

While Jane didn't try to talk him out of it, over the course of the afternoon, others would. But after speaking with CBS executive Bill MacPhail, Rozelle told Brown, Reeves, and the Maras that, with some trepidation, he'd be willing to be considered. It was Brown, again, who was most reassuring. "Pete," he said, "don't worry—you'll grow into it."

Once they had a candidate, the group returned to the Kenilworth to drum up support. The first stop was Well Mara's visit to Art Rooney. Rozelle's name was so far off the radar that the Steelers' owner at first looked puzzled, before realizing Mara was talking about the Rams' bright young GM.

Rooney in turn agreed to present the Solid Seven's choice to the Eagles' Frank McNamee.

"Frank, they want to get out of here," said Rooney. "They're ready to come off Leahy. They think we should go for Pete Rozelle."

"Great," said a weary McNamee. "Who the hell is Pete Rozelle?"

"I don't really know him, either," said Rooney, "but if Well says he's okay, that's good enough for me."

That evening, as the owners reconvened in the conference room for the twenty-third ballot, Rozelle was excused so that his nomination might be discussed. With the phalanx of reporters waiting in the nearby lobby, sure to seize on any possible clue, he could hardly go there. So he went to the men's restroom across the hall from the conference room and waited. When a writer or hotel guest came in the bathroom, Rozelle would look in the mirror, adjust his tie and wash his hands, very carefully and very deliberately, waiting for the other person to finish his business and leave. Then Rozelle would stay. By his own estimate, he washed his hands thirty-five times over the next half-hour, before Carroll Rosenbloom walked into the men's room and greeted him with an outstretched hand and the words, "Hello, Mr. Commissioner."

Returning to the conference room for greetings and congratulations, Rozelle would utter the famous line, "I can honestly say I come to you with clean hands." The meeting quickly adjourned and Rozelle was rushed to an impromptu press conference.

Rozelle announced that he strongly supported expansion, and that after a year or more of transition, he would eventually hope to move the league offices to New York City.

Even as he paid his respects to Bell, he also made it clear that he was not going to try to operate in the way his predecessor had. When asked about Bell's unique operating style, his ability to keep all the league's business in his head and back pocket, Rozelle smiled and allowed, "I think I'll have files." About the challenge of succeeding Bell, he was unabashedly humble. "I hesitate calling it a challenge," he said later. "That would sound ludicrous. It is much more than a challenge and if I can come close to filling Bert Bell's shoes, I'll have to be luckier than ever before."

But the next morning, he took the gavel and, in an instantly more formal and businesslike manner than had been the case under Bell or Gunsel, led the proceedings, navigating the straits of expansion with assurance. In short order, the league ratified expansion, with Dallas coming into the league in 1960 and Minneapolis-St. Paul in 1961. Other matters were tabled, though Rozelle told the owners that he strongly supported a package television deal for the league.

"We knew within twenty-four hours," said Wellington Mara, "that we hadn't made a mistake."

At 12:25 a.m. on Friday, January 28—twelve days after the meetings started— Rozelle banged the gavel to end the 1960 annual meetings. As the owners left the room, George Halas offered a piece of advice. "Get a pullout telephone," said Papa Bear. "There's no sense answering calls at four in the morning."

Much of the national press couldn't help but jump to the conclusion that anyone so young and so pleasant would have to be a callow, ineffectual leader. The consensus was that Rozelle—"The Child Czar" in more than one tabloid headline—was little more than a place-holding figurehead. "New NFL Boss— Monarch or Mouthpiece?" asked the main headline in the February 8, 1960, edition of *The Sporting News,* with a subhead noting, "Former Tub-Thumper Seen as Spokesman; Magnates No Longer Need Dictator." "The first test," wrote Sid Ziff in the *Los Angeles Mirror News,* "may come when George Halas tries to run the works next season. Bert Bell never crossed him. Will Rozelle take a chance?"

There had always been about Rozelle an aspect of the perfect companion. Loyal, boyish, bright, and avid, he possessed a disarming manner. It would be said about him later that his most redeeming quality was his persistent likability. But this was selling him short. He possessed both a gravitas and a sense of self. The sun-dappled, fresh-scrubbed wholesomeness of his youth had matured into a more cosmopolitan assuredness. Milk shakes and ice cream gave way to Rusty Nails and cigarettes. But his face still shone with that sincere, inclusive smile. He was a nice, smart man, who embodied much of the hopes, dreams, aspirations, and sensibilities of postwar Americans.

That he had a tendency to be in the right place at the right time was undeniable. His election required so many distinct elements—Leahy's intransigence, the Eastern clubs' refusal to move the league offices out west, Halas's commitment to expansion, Brown's reluctance to a draft effort—as to be nearly accidental.

Pete Rozelle was aware that one impasse among owners had brought him back into pro football, and another one had elevated him to its highest office. He was convinced that for a commissioner to succeed, he would have to find a way to settle those stalemates. Rozelle was not soft, and not merely genial; the man who got along so well also understood how to get what he wanted from people, and would soon prove himself to be a tough executive, capable of Machiavellian maneuvering and brutally firm leadership. He was smart, assured, and insightful, bringing a degree of sophistication to the office that hadn't previously existed. And he possessed a vision of the future that pointedly did not involve cramped offices in suburban Philadelphia or long nights spent manipulating dominoes to fashion a league schedule.

After the long siege, the old heads had finally seized on a compromise of convenience. But in the same stroke, the National Football League had, almost unwittingly, delivered itself to the future.

9

The New Frontier

Forrest Gregg had just returned to Dallas after his second pro season with the Green Bay Packers, when he heard the news, in January 1959, that the team had fired coach Ray "Scooter" McLean, and hired New York Giants assistant coach Vince Lombardi. A few days later, the smart, agile offensive lineman was out shopping when he ran into fellow Southern Methodist alum and ex-Giant Tiny Goss.

"Hey, Forrest," said Goss, "y'all got a new coach."

"Yeah," said Gregg. "Vince Lombardi."

"Y'all know anything about him?"

"No, I don't. Do you?"

Goss smiled. "Yeah. He is a *real* bastard."

Gregg filed this information away along with the few other bits of information he'd been able to glean about Lombardi. In an age before media saturation, when players had little contact with their teams during the off-season, much of what a player could learn about a new coach came from word of mouth. Gregg still hadn't met Lombardi, seven months later, when he set off with teammate John Symank for the Packers' training camp at St. Norbert's College, just outside Green Bay. Driving up from Texas, they reached Milwaukee, about 120 miles from camp, by nightfall, still two days prior to the date when veterans had to report. "We decided before we made a determination to stay all night in Milwaukee and drive up on to Green Bay in the morning, we'd call [teammate] Dave Hanner. We called Dave up and said, 'Dave, what's going on?' He just said, 'Wow.' I said, 'What do you mean?' He said, 'He's working our tail off.' I said, 'We're in Milwaukee, we're thinking about whether we're going to stay or drive on in.' Dave said, 'My suggestion to you would be to drive on in.' "

Gregg and Symank arrived after one in the morning and told the dorm attendant who checked them into camp that, because it was so late, they were going to sleep in.

At seven o'clock in the morning, wake-up time throughout camp, there was a loud rap on their door, summoning the players to the 7:30 breakfast. When they arrived at the cafeteria, Packers GM Jack Vainisi spotted them, and brought them over to meet Lombardi.

"I went over there," said Gregg, "and he was kind of a short guy, had a real nice smile, very pleasant. 'Glad to have you guys here, glad you came in early. Pleased to meet you. Practice is at ten.' I hadn't been planning on even having breakfast, much less practicing. But after he said it I thought it was probably a pretty good idea."

Just that quickly, the Vince Lombardi legend was growing.

In 1960, pro football nearly doubled itself, the twelve teams of 1959 multiplying to twenty-one a year later. The financial boom and the growth of the American middle class made the explosion possible, and the sense of a new era dawning was heightened by a new commissioner, a new rival league, and, in the country at large, a presidential campaign that would bring a new president to the White House.

The tension between the sport's past and future was felt most acutely in Green Bay, Wisconsin, where a pervasive gloom surrounded the team throughout much of the '50s. While the jet-powered cosmopolitan world of postwar America was taking shape, the small central Wisconsin burg of 62,000 people seemed willfully rooted in a Rockwellian portrait of an earlier era, isolated from the bustle of modern urban life, still remarkably homogenous (only 128 blacks lived in the county in 1959) and stubbornly proud of it.

The city's claim to fame—that it was the last of the small industry towns to still have a major professional sports team—seemed increasingly tenuous by the late '50s. The NFL's only publicly held franchise was a living testament to the league's heritage, and yet there was a feeling among many in the league that the team wouldn't be able to compete for much longer. Though their per-

sonnel department, run by the sharp Jack Vainisi, had enjoyed a series of productive drafts, Green Bay had the smallest payroll in the league, and made far
less television money than most other clubs.

Green Bay's last NFL title had come during the lean, war-depleted season
of 1944. After posting a 6-5-1 mark in 1947, the Packers suffered eleven consecutive losing seasons, during which their 37-93-2 record was the worst in the
NFL. For most of that time, they played their games in City Stadium (with a
capacity of 24,500), next to Green Bay East High School, whose field was
closely surrounded by an oval handrail, meaning that players running out of
bounds at full speed knew they had to quickly slide down to avoid a jarring
and potentially injurious collision. The move into the new City Stadium (later
renamed Lambeau Field after patriarch Curly Lambeau) had drawn headlines
in 1957. Even Bert Bell, who wouldn't fly, took the train in from Philadelphia
to be on hand, but the Packers continued to lose.

Forrest Gregg, arriving in 1957, had been disappointed with what he
thought was a lack of general fitness among pro players and a lack of seriousness toward the profession that pervaded his first two seasons in Green Bay.
McLean ran light workouts for his players in the day and played long poker
games with them at night. During practices, if one of the team's veterans
thought McLean was pressing too hard, he might remark, "Long season,
coach," and McLean would, shortly thereafter if not immediately, end the
practice.

After the 1-10-1 1958 campaign, feeling that they needed to break from the
past, the Packers pursued and hired Lombardi, the top offensive assistant on
the Giants' staff. He came highly recommended from around the league, even
from a reluctant George Halas. "I shouldn't tell you this, Ole," Halas confided
to Packers president Dominic Olejniczak, "but he'll be a good one. I shouldn't
tell you because you're liable to kick the crap out of us!" In that Halas would
prove prophetic.

At St. Norbert's in 1959, Gregg saw a team instantly transformed, and a training camp environment in which none of the old rules applied. On the first day
of camp in which all the veterans participated, Lombardi's volcanic temper revealed itself. The victim was wide receiver Max McGee, who after running a
pass route, started walking back to the huddle.

"GET BACK OVER THERE!" howled Lombardi. "Mister, we don't WALK
around here—we run!"

What startled Gregg about Lombardi's tantrum wasn't the volume, or even
the relatively slight transgression that inspired it, but the target. "I had never

heard a coach, in my two years at Green Bay and in professional football, ever say anything derogatory to a wide receiver or a running back. Most of the guys who got grief were offensive linemen, defensive linemen, linebackers. I thought to myself, 'I can handle this. We're all the same.' I knew from then on, we had something different than we had before, and we got a chance. We had some good talent on the team; we just needed direction.'"

There was a daunting ferocity to Lombardi's approach that was a departure from the standard practice of his contemporaries. He possessed the stereotypical fiery temper of the old-school coaches, but none of the emotional distance. A coach "must be a pedagogue," he said. "He has to pound the lessons into the players by rote, the same way you teach pupils in the classroom." Paul Brown had much the same philosophy, but lacked the galvanizing emotionalism of Lombardi's combustible persona.

Lombardi's philosophy was one of stripped-down fundamentals, an unstinting emphasis on execution and repetition, so that the plays his teams ran were perfectly choreographed and flexible works of physical art, each with their own options and variations built in. Within that context, his contribution to the game's strategic and tactical evolution came to be known as the delayed option, or option blocking. Instead of static blocking assignments, Lombardi's system often allowed his offensive linemen the flexibility to block a man in whatever direction was convenient, then leave it up to the trailing runner to find the resulting hole once he got the ball. Lombardi called the concept "running to daylight."

Returning many of the players on the squad that won a single game in 1958, the Packers went 7-5 in 1959, and Lombardi was named Coach of the Year. He had adroitly utilized his personnel, putting Paul Hornung in as his feature halfback, in much the same manner that Frank Gifford had been in New York, and settling on the taciturn, steely Bart Starr, a late-round draft choice out of Alabama, as his quarterback. A pair of fleecings of the Cleveland Browns—acquiring defensive lineman Henry Jordan in 1959 and offensive lineman Willie Davis (shifted to defense, where he'd enjoy a Hall of Fame career) in 1960—helped solidify the defense. In 1960, the Packers won the Western Conference title, and battled the Philadelphia Eagles to the end in the NFL championship game, before losing, 17–13.

A year later, the Packers added the distinctive oval G to their helmets, and as they rose to the first of back-to-back titles, the team and the town became a kind of iconographic reminder of the power of American small towns. Starr, Hornung, backfield mate Jim Taylor, and defensive anchor Ray Nitschke were all becoming stars, but no one was bigger than the hard-driving, eminently quotable Lombardi. After the Packers routed the Giants, 37–0, in the 1961 NFL title game, Lombardi received a telegram that read: "Congratulations on a great game. It was a fine victory for a great coach, a great team, a great town. Best regards, President Kennedy."

———

While one dynasty was forming in Green Bay, another was in the works at the league's new headquarters in New York City.

Rozelle's "transitional year" in Philadelphia turned out to be little more than a spring vacation. On April 5, 1960, after adjourning the NFL meetings in Los Angeles in March (during which the Chicago Cardinals received permission to move their franchise to St. Louis), the Rozelles took an overnight flight from Los Angeles to Philadelphia, where they stayed for the next few weeks at a suite in the Warwick Hotel. By the end of May, they'd leased a six-room apartment at 16 Sutton Place in New York City.

In July, the NFL office opened its new headquarters in midtown Manhattan, on the twenty-third floor of the General Dynamics Building at Rockefeller Center. The contrast between the old and the new NFL offices wasn't limited to location. In the place of Bell's slangy authority, there was the distinctly more formal Rozelle administration, in which the commissioner, once in the office, never removed his suit coat or tie. He was joined in New York by his executive secretary with the Rams, Thelma Elkjer, a loyal, gifted assistant whose role as gatekeeper became all the more important in the new job. Rozelle arrived early and stayed late, and handled much of his correspondence in carefully worded typewritten communiqués—the drafts batted out in his distinctive all-lower-case style, then retyped by Elkjer.

In New York, Rozelle was close to the advertising, television, and publishing industries, a mass media community already galvanized by the rise of pro football and the concurrent Giants renaissance that would put them in six title games in eight seasons. Rozelle quickly solidified important friendships with key executives like Jack Landry at Philip Morris, one of the league's main advertisers, and Bill MacPhail, head of sports at CBS. Both were visionaries in their respective fields, and both would be key confidants in the decade ahead.

Landry was a hale man with ruddy complexion and a robust, cheerful demeanor who'd conceived the "Marlboro Man," which would become one of the most successful campaigns in American advertising history. At a press conference in 1962, a writer spied Rozelle smoking Marlboros and asked him if it was a coincidence that he was using a product advertised on NFL games.

"Well," said Rozelle, smiling, "before I became commissioner I smoked Viceroys."

More crucial to the league's rising prominence was MacPhail, the affable bachelor with a soft face, a sharp wit, and a longshoreman's capacity for alcohol. As the head of CBS Sports, he had indirectly prompted Rozelle's return to the NFL, by hiring Tex Schramm away from the Rams in 1957. In 1960 and 1961, MacPhail would be Rozelle's main outside ally as he confronted his most important early challenge—trying to convince the NFL owners to adopt a single-network joint television package similar in structure to the AFL's, with league members to share equally the revenue that would be realized.

Meanwhile, Rozelle began to completely revamp the NFL's relationship with the media. With his dual background in newspapers and public relations, he understood the inner workings of mass communication with a level of sophistication that his predecessor couldn't have matched. In the spring of 1960, he called the first meeting of the league's publicity directors, and gently reached an agreement with the league's aging PR man Joe Labrum that he would serve in his capacity one more year and then accept an attractive retirement package.

Shortly after the end of the 1960 season, Rozelle had a meeting with Jim Kensil, the brawny, self-assured correspondent for the Associated Press, who wrote a weekly sports media column, perhaps the first of its kind, called "The Sports Dial." By 1961, the column had grown in influence, especially in the sports television industry, and Rozelle was an avid reader. That spring, Kensil interviewed Rozelle for one of his columns and the two men proved temperamentally well matched. They spoke again two days later, by phone, about the strengths and weaknesses of the NFL's past publicity efforts. Rozelle was already intrigued, convinced that Kensil could be just the man to orchestrate the more sophisticated and aggressive approach he was seeking for the league's press relations. Kensil beat him to the punch, saying, "What you need there is somebody like me. I'd like to run your show."

The hiring raised eyebrows among the New York press corps; Kensil was a respected print man with no background in public relations, a calling still viewed with suspicion by many writers. In a letter to his friend Arnold Zeitlin, a correspondent for UPI, Kensil explained himself: "The job is mine, no strings. . . . The salary is nice. The office is great. And best of all, I like pro football better than any other sport. Honestly, it is one of the few jobs I would have quit for. I couldn't do public relations for garden tools, cosmetics or garbage disposals, but pro football is another matter. I can believe in it."

In Kensil, Rozelle would find more than a public relations conduit. He would find another true believer with a fierce conviction in the superiority of pro football as a spectator sport. In the years ahead, he became Rozelle's most trusted office adviser, confidant, and sounding board, "Mr. Inside" to the commissioner's "Mr. Outside." In that off-season prior to 1961, Rozelle and Kensil rebuilt the NFL's publicity apparatus, quickly transcending the inherent limitations of Labrum's folksy manner and modest mimeographed weekly statistical summaries. The same summer, Rozelle hired the Elias Sports Bureau, the statistical arbiter for Major League Baseball. It was a major expense, but one that almost immediately paid off, not merely because the statistics were more accurate, but because newspapers treated them with greater respect.

Kensil increased the quality of the information the NFL distributed to all media outlets. He took advantage of new breakthroughs in Teletype capability at the major wire services (distributing news stories would no longer require a typesetter to retype them for use in a local paper), sending extensive weekly NFL stats to hundreds of newspapers instead of a handful. To capitalize on the heightened interest in the game, he started giving newspaper editors a steady diet of NFL preview and statistical features, and beginning in 1961 ran a weekly "capsule preview" of each game played in the coming weekend.

Even before the 1961 season was underway, the *Pittsburgh Post-Gazette*'s Jack Sell noted that Kensil had "started a long-needed flow of information about the various players, accenting personalities rather than statistics." Kensil's "handouts," as he called them, not only provided the media with more to write about, but also did so in a professionally written format without any obvious boosterism. Some newspapers even took to simply running the press releases verbatim.

The rise of pro football broke into the broader general media in that 1960 season. When Maule collaborated with the sports photographer and illustrator Robert Riger for a coffee-table book titled *The Pros, SI* ran a cover story with a seven-page portfolio of black-and-white photographs from the book. Later in October, a CBS News special titled "The Violent World of Sam Huff" aired on its Sunday evening program *The Twentieth Century*. "Today, you will play pro football, riding on Sam Huff's broad back," intoned narrator Walter Cronkite at the start of the thirty-minute special. "You're going to be closer to pro football than you've ever been before." And during a season in which pro football was popping up all over, *Life* magazine's December 5 issue featured a gatefold cover with a dramatic, ground-level shot of a football perched on a tee, an instant before Steve Myhra kicked off to begin a game at Memorial Stadium in Baltimore. The cover blurb read: "The Great Spectator Sport: Pro Football Breaks Away for Big Gains."

For his part, Rozelle was working on his numerous relationships in television and advertising, as well as his personal connection to the nation's largest and most influential sports magazine. Rozelle's friend Tex Maule introduced the commissioner to *Sports Illustrated*'s new managing editor, André Laguerre, the former press attaché to Charles de Gaulle during World War II, and a late but staunch convert to the world of pro football.

In Rozelle's words, *Sports Illustrated* "treated pro football like it had never been treated before." The magazine, after a decade of losses, began finding itself in the early '60s, and pro football was a key element of its content change from upscale sporting magazine to a news magazine devoted largely to spectator sports. In a confidential 1962 letter to Time Inc. founder Henry Luce, Laguerre wrote, "I'm developing a strong hunch that pro football is our sport. We have grown with it, and each of us is a phenomenon of the times. We gave it more coverage last year, but I plan to extend it this fall. It seems that our reader identifies himself more with this sport than golf or fishing. College football is too diffuse and regionalized. Baseball in some quarters is considered old-fashioned or slightly non-U. Horse racing and winter sports have less broad appeal."

It would be difficult to pinpoint any single development that caused the sport's increased profile, and some had been in motion prior to Rozelle's arrival. But the confluence of elements—the Giants' stature, the '58 title game, the Packers' mystique, Rozelle's vision and Kensil's implementation of it, the sport's appeal to Madison Avenue—all contributed to pro football moving toward center stage of American sports.

There was also a sense, even in politics, that the cultural moment was right for football. Eisenhower had been a football player as well as a fan, but was better known for his love of golf. The two candidates in the 1960 presidential campaign brought their pro football fanaticism to a new level. Richard Nixon, who'd played football at Whittier College, took advantage of every opportunity to participate in football functions as vice president. In 1957, he traveled to Green Bay for the opening of Lambeau Field and two years later was in New York to present the Heisman Trophy to Billy Cannon. He was so captivated by the NFL title game in 1958, he wrote a note to Weeb Ewbank, telling him that he, like Ewbank, had worked as a child as a delivery boy for his father's grocery store. A year later, before the 1959 title game, Nixon visited the Giants' locker room prior to the game, and shook hands with each player. "Some people were getting their ankles taped, some people had on just their gray T-shirts, very few had on numbers the way you could identify them," said Pat Summerall.

"Nixon went to every person in our locker room, all of the active players, and had a conversation with everyone. Knew what kind of a year they had, if they had statistics, he knew the statistics. There was no way, unless he was a very devout fan, that he could have known all that. I thought that is one of the most amazing things I have ever seen in my life. We're getting ready for the championship game, and here's the vice president, going to every locker, knowing everybody's name."

John F. Kennedy and his brothers had long been associated with football, and the family's bruising games of touch football on the lawn of Joseph Kennedy's Hyannis Port estate were the stuff of both family and political legend—also a way to let off steam on the afternoon of the 1960 general election, as the family waited for returns to start coming in. "I think they were both always attracted to athletes," said Robert Kennedy's wife, Ethel Kennedy, of Jack and Bobby. "They had mixed it up, and they didn't complain." The family was close to Colts owner Carroll Rosenbloom, and distant relatives of the Rams' Dan Reeves, whose wife's sister was married to Ethel Kennedy's brother George Skakel. Kennedy had met Lombardi during the 1960 primary, and invited him to the inauguration in Washington (though Lombardi had to decline because of the annual league meetings).

The president had retired from touch football by the time he was elected, but Attorney General Robert F. Kennedy—who'd been an intense, if undersized, end on the Harvard varsity in 1947—was still a regular, invariably playing quarterback. RFK kept a football in his office at the Justice Department, and would often toss it during meetings with close friends, like Justice Byron "Whizzer" White, a college star at Colorado, or civil rights staffer Burke Marshall during meetings.

Jack and Bobby often built their Sundays around watching the Colts or Redskins play, and had started to take a particular interest in Lombardi's progress in Green Bay. The Kennedys certainly had much in common with Lombardi in both religion and politics, but it was more than that. "I'm sure there were a lot of other Catholic Democrats around," said Ethel Kennedy. "Jack and Bobby clearly were drawn to Vince because of his character and his handling of the men. And I think it was his spirit."

As Bert Bell had indicated when the new league announced its presence, there were plenty of players out there. The NFL's tight rosters and reluctance to give a job to all but the most proven and expensive of rookies meant that there were hundreds of players around the country with the talent to make an NFL roster yet unable to find the right opportunity. George Blanda, who'd retired after growing tired of alternating as a starting quarterback for the Bears, signed up with Houston. Don Maynard, a gifted wide receiver who'd hurt himself with fumbles while playing with the Giants in 1958, signed with the New York Titans, where he got a chance to shine. Jack Kemp, last cut by San Francisco, and Sid Gillman, fired by the Rams, both landed in Los Angeles, with Barron Hilton's Los Angeles Chargers, where both would flourish in the more wide-open offensive environment of the new league.

While the AFL was following the NFL rulebook to the letter, with the exception of the two-point conversion, there was a concerted effort to add to the passing game. For its official ball, the league used the Spalding JV-5, one fourth of an inch longer, and one fourth of an inch slimmer than the NFL Wilson model.

For Gillman, the Chargers job was a second chance at the pro level. With the Rams, he'd grown overly sensitive to criticism from his team, the fans, and the press. With the Chargers, he was free to pursue his innovative tendencies and experiment with the passing game in a way he'd never dared in the NFL (where over five seasons he ran the ball nearly 55 percent of the time). Through the inventive passing game conceived by Gillman, the Chargers took to the air more than half the time in each of his first three seasons in the league.

Though the Chargers proved an exciting aesthetic success, they were virtually ignored in Los Angeles, drawing 11,545 for their last regular season game in the 100,000-seat Coliseum. A month after the season ended, the team agreed to move to San Diego, provided the city would add an upper deck to Balboa Stadium, increasing the capacity to 34,000.

Grave circumstances existed throughout the league, with Denver, Oakland, and the New York Titans struggling to make payroll through the first season. The Broncos' entire operation was threadbare, from their drab brown-and-yellow uniforms (with notorious brown vertical stripes on their socks) to the team's offices, housed in a military-styled Quonset hut thirty yards from their practice field. The Raiders were forced to play their games across the bay in San Francisco, the first four at the aging Kezar Stadium and the last three at Candlestick Park; their home attendance averaged just 9,611 in their first season.

Bud Adams's Houston Oilers had the AFL's best team in 1960, with an offense anchored by Bears castoff George Blanda, who came out of retirement to lead the new league in passing, and Billy Cannon, who proved his worth in both football ability and box office sway. In the 1960 championship game, played at Houston's Jeppesen Stadium, the Oilers won a hard-fought game (which included 3 ejections), 24–16.

But even if the level of competition was not up to that of the NFL, and the attendance was minor league by comparison (NFL games averaged 40,106 in paid attendance, while the AFL's announced average was 16,538, though even that modest figure was highly suspect), NFL teams couldn't afford to ignore the new league. The courts struck down the NFL's early signings, with the Rams losing Cannon to Houston, and the Lions losing Johnny Robinson to Dallas. The Colts, after back-to-back titles in 1958 and 1959, assumed they'd have little problem signing their top draft choices. But by the time Don Kellett and Weeb Ewbank got serious, they'd lost four of their first five choices to the AFL, including number one pick Ron Mix, who would go on to a Hall of Fame career. It was one of the factors that led to Ewbank's firing at the end of the 1962 season.

Because the Rams' and Giants' organizations were so well entrenched, the only meaningful head-to-head battle for the loyalty of a city occurred in Dallas, whose sports fans greeted the beginning of the 1960 football season as though they were enjoying a ringside seat at a heavyweight bout, which in essence they were. The city of 700,000 was the second smallest in the NFL, larger than only Green Bay. Eight years after the low-rent Texans washed out in half a season, Dallas was getting not one but two new pro football teams. Both leagues viewed the city as a crucial foothold in the larger war. And the club's respective owners were from two of the richest, most celebrated oil baron families in the state. It seemed impossible that both could survive, and certain that someone's reputation would suffer greatly.

Carrying a season ticket order book wherever he went, Lamar Hunt set about Dallas, spreading the word about the city's AFL entry, the Texans. His plan was designed to evoke both excitement (the Texans called themselves "Football's ZING Team") and class (charging a dime more per ticket than the Cowboys, at Hunt's insistence). For kids, Hunt inaugurated the Texans' "Huddle Club," which for $1 gave a child a team T-shirt and free admission to all the games. "The Texans tried everything to get fans out to their games," wrote John Eisenberg in the fan's memoir *Cotton Bowl Days*. "They put certificates good for free tickets in balloons set loose over the city. They gave away tickets in packages of corn chips. They gave away tickets to drivers who had their windshields washed at Sinclair gas stations." Hunt also hired a few dozen young, attractive teachers to sell tickets, offering each a loaner convertible, with the woman selling the most getting to keep her car. The winner, a comely blonde named Norma Knoble, eventually married Hunt.

On Sunday, October 2, 1960, the Texans drew 37,500 to their game with the New York Titans. It was Barber Day, at the Cotton Bowl, with everyone wearing barber smocks given free admission. ("What men control the largest captive audiences of men in Dallas?" reasoned Hunt. "The barbers.") Also in the crowd were beneficiaries of the Texas Teen Salute, high school students who got in free when they showed a ticket stub from a high school game played two nights earlier, the same Friday night that the Cowboys were in the Cotton Bowl, drawing 18,500.

Meanwhile, Cowboys fans were impatient. When western star Roy Rogers and his wife, Dale Evans, rode around the field in a convertible at halftime of the Cowboys' home opener, they were pelted with programs, paper cups, and ice cubes from fans who were already upset with the home team. "I'm surprised Lamar didn't have a day where ice throwers at our games got in free to see the Texans," said Schramm, who for the rest of his life would resent Hunt for his riches, his outwardly cool demeanor, and the fact that the presence of the AFL club further complicated Schramm's already daunting job of franchise building.

The Cowboys were for all intents the NFL's first true expansion team. The league had added clubs before, but since it stabilized into its two-division format in 1933, all the franchises added had either previously existed in another league or were a combination of established teams with defunct ones. The Cowboys were created out of thin air. Clint Murchison paid a nominal $50,000 for the rights to the franchise, and $550,000 for the thirty-six players, that he drafted from the other twelve teams.

Behind diminutive quarterback Eddie LeBaron, Dallas struggled to an 0-11-1 record in its first season. Meanwhile, the 8-6 Texans had the league's Rookie of the Year and Most Valuable Player, halfback Abner Haynes, who'd gone to college at North Texas State in Denton. "I was a big Texan fan, and so were all of my friends," said Walt Garrison, then a high school star in Lewisville, later a running back with the Cowboys. "We didn't go to any Cowboy games. The Texans had Abner Haynes, who was a local guy, and they had a winning team even though they played in the AFL. Dallas fans don't care what league you play in as long as you win."

When a reporter asked Clint Murchison if the Cowboys were hurt by the Texans' underdog status, the owner was taken aback. "I'll be damned," he said. "You're the first person who I ever heard call a Hunt an underdog."

———

Partly because of the opportunities offered by the AFL, pro football in the '60s began to bear the fruits of fifteen years of fitful racial progress. By the end of the '50s, there was a sense throughout pro football that things were starting to change. While racism was still common, it was becoming less overt.

The unique problems faced by football teams in the South were a further index of what the country had—and hadn't—accomplished in race relations. In 1946, the Browns had left Marion Motley and Bill Willis behind when they visited the Miami Seahawks, since Florida state law prohibited integrated sports. When the Cleveland Browns returned to Miami for the 1961 Playoff Bowl, the consolation game for the runners-up in each conference, Paul Brown brought his entire team. But he was greeted by a hotel manager who informed him that the club's black players would have to stay elsewhere.

"No, our team stays together," said Brown firmly.

After a heated exchange, the manager stood his ground.

"I'll tell you what then," said Brown. "We'll just get back on the plane and go back home."

The hotel capitulated, a crisis was averted, and the Browns integrated Miami hotels on that evening.

But in every city, it seemed, there was another fight. Segregation in Dallas had become a national sports story at the 1957 Cotton Bowl, when the lack of any integrated hotels forced Jim Brown to be separated from his Syracuse teammates. In 1959, even before the Cowboys franchise had been officially recognized, Tex Schramm met with the powerful Dallas Citizens Council, the de facto city planners who controlled everything from zoning to racial policies. At the time, the Dallas school system was completely segregated, as were its residences, restaurants, hotels, and even city buses, where blacks were still made to ride in the back. Schramm argued that he could not hope to have a successful pro football team in Dallas if the city persisted in segregating its hotels. The Schramm petition brought the case to a head and integration to at least one of Dallas's major hotels; the Ramada Inn next to Dallas Love Field agreed to integrate, provided it wouldn't be blackballed by the Citizens Council and other hotels.

On the field, there was less room for segregation than ever before. During his first training camp with the Packers in 1959, Lombardi confronted his team about racism. "If I ever hear nigger or dago or kike or anything like that around here, regardless of who you are, you're through with me," he said. "You can't play for me if you have any kind of prejudice." Packers defensive back Willie Wood would call Lombardi "perhaps the fairest person I ever met." And his simultaneous commitment to and bullying of the players later prompted the lineman Henry Jordan's famous line, "He treats every man the same—he treats us all like dogs."

Of all the instances of racism, the most embarrassing one was in the nation's capital. By the beginning of the 1961 season, there were eighty-three blacks on the NFL's fourteen clubs—or, to be more precise, eighty-three on thirteen clubs, since the Washington Redskins, the self-professed Team of the South, which still played "Dixie" before all its home games, had abided by owner George Preston Marshall's edict not to use black players.

Even among Marshall's defenders, the best that could be said about him was that he was an opportunist rather than a racist, and that he kept his club segregated to avoid alienating the wide network of fans in the Deep South, where the Redskins barnstormed during the exhibition season, and broadcast their games during the regular season. The all-white Redskins were obviously at a competitive disadvantage due to the policy (the team suffered through a 1-12-1 record in 1961), but Marshall's vow—"We'll start signing Negroes when the Harlem Globetrotters start signing whites"—seemed steadfast in the face of public opinion.

Few were more vigilant or persistent in their critique of the blustery Marshall than the *Washington Post*'s sports columnist Shirley Povich, who brought that criticism to a kind of apex in his account of a Redskins-Browns game in 1960:

> For 18 minutes the Redskins were enjoying equal rights with the Cleveland Browns yesterday, in the sense that there was no score in the contest. Then it suddenly became unequal in favor of the Browns, who brought along Jim Brown, their rugged colored fullback from Syracuse. From 25 yards out, Brown was served the ball by Milt Plum on a pitch-out and he integrated the Redskins' goal line with more than deliberate speed, perhaps exceeding the famous Supreme Court decree. Brown fled the 25 yards like a man in an uncommon hurry and the Redskins' goal line, at least, became interracial.

By that fall, Marshall's stubbornness had become a public embarrassment. The means for intervention first occurred to Kennedy's new secretary of the interior, Stewart Udall. The city's new D.C. Stadium, where the Redskins would begin play in 1961, was built on federal land, as part of the National Capital Parks System, which as with all government buildings had clear rules forbidding discrimination in hiring. After checking first with Robert Kennedy to receive clearance from the administration to press the issue ("Go get him!" RFK told Udall. "Make him do it!"), Udall called a press conference in the spring, announcing that he had sent a warning letter to Marshall, advising the owner that the government was aware of the Redskins' reputation for practicing discrimination and to be aware of "the implications of this new regulation—and our view of its import." After a couple months of bluster from Marshall, during which Rozelle visited Washington for some private prodding, the owner finally capitulated, negotiating a compromise in late August that would allow the Redskins to play in D.C. Stadium in 1961, with the agreement that the team would be integrated by the beginning of the 1962 season.

It was a significant victory for the league, an important symbolic one for the administration, and another example in the growing tendency for the public to view the world of sports as a microcosm of the society at large.

———

As Vince Lombardi's star was rising, Paul Brown was struggling in Cleveland. The beginning of the new decade found the Cleveland Browns, the dominant team of the '50s, contending with the frustration of being merely good. It was a particularly rough adjustment for Paul Brown.

The 1961 season featured Brown's first coaching outing against Lombardi, with Green Bay hammering Cleveland, 49–17, the worst defeat Paul Brown had ever suffered in front of a home crowd. Later in the season, in a crucial showdown against the Giants, the Browns were again outplayed in front of their home fans, 37–21. Players who'd been loath to criticize Brown in the past became more outspoken. "It's not just Sam Huff, but the whole Giant defensive unit is excellent," said Jim Brown after the 1961 season. "Plus the fact that their scouting of Paul Brown's system is so good that they often know what he's going to run even before Brown does himself."

Paul Brown was still Paul Brown. His contribution to the sport was unquestioned. His attention to detail and fundamentals hadn't noticeably wavered. But something ineffable in his relationship with his team had.

It was not merely that the Browns weren't winning the championship every year. It was that the teaching atmosphere, without Collier and Ewbank, seemed less pronounced, more rote. In the absence of the respect he'd earlier been accorded, a kind of cynicism set in among the team. The Browns still gave players IQ tests at the beginning of the year, but cheating had become widespread. Some players had even taken to imitating PB's all-purpose, finger-wagging sign-off, delivered in an imperious tone, "Just so you know . . ."

What virtually all those who played for Brown during those years agree upon is that Brown was frustrated by his inability to get his most talented player, Jim Brown, to behave in the way he wanted him to. It had been an axiom of Paul Brown's philosophy that he treated all players the same. But in Jim Brown, he would find an athlete who would not be intimidated.

When halfback Bobby Mitchell came to the Browns as a rookie from Illinois in 1958, Paul Brown had him room with Jim Brown. The two men hit it off, but at times Mitchell felt like a stand-in, incurring the wrath that Paul Brown wanted to direct at his star running back, but didn't dare to. On more than one road trip, Mitchell would beseech the slow-to-rise Brown to hurry to make the team bus on time. When the two men arrived, whether a minute late or a minute early, the rest of the team was waiting. "He'd come up to us," said Mitchell, "and he'd walk right up in front of me—he wouldn't walk up in front of Jim—and he'd go off on me. 'We don't allow anyone, not one person on this team, to be late.' And Jim's standing there with his arms crossed, 'cause Jim knew he was talking to him. But he wasn't in Jim's face, you see my point?"

"Bobby had to go through it," agreed Jim Brown. "Paul Brown would relate messages sideways and Bobby was the guy because Bobby and I were always close. See, I'm not the kind of person you can holler at. You gotta explain to me what you want, and I'll try to deliver that. But I'm not gonna be hollered at. That's just not who I am. So Paul wasn't gonna be able to holler or say certain things to me. And then the whole concept, that you treat everybody equal, starts to fall apart. How the hell you gonna do that? It doesn't work, 'cause we're not all picking tobacco and making 30 cents an hour."

In 1961, the Browns were sold for the then record sum of $4.1 million. The new owner was a sly, wisecracking New York advertising executive named Art Modell, a longtime Giants season-ticket holder who was emblematic of a new breed of fan, drawn to the action of the sport as well as the collegiality of the social scene that sprung around it.

Modell met with the Maras and some other owners. He eventually put together an ownership group, and made his case to Rozelle. "I gave him my financial statement—which was a load of shit," said Modell. On January 25, 1961, staking virtually all of his holdings and leveraging himself severely, Modell bought the Browns.

One of the attractions of the team was the mystique and mastery of Paul Brown. Yet Modell was disappointed to realize, very early on—"I would say about twelve hours after the check cleared"—that he would not be welcomed by the coach. Brown met Modell's wisecracks with silence, and bridled at the owner's constant presence. Every morning during the regular season, he'd show up at the Browns' offices, at 7:30, and listen in on film study and chalk talks. At the Browns' offices, he took the large office that had previously belonged to Brown, which embittered the coach further.

Early in the 1961 season, Modell came into the locker room prior to a game. "Paul called the team together," he recalled. "I sat on a duffel bag in the back of the room as he told the players, 'Play hard . . . no mistakes. . . . Okay, let's go.' The players filed out and then Paul called me over and said, 'I'd appreciate it if you never came in here again. This is private, between myself and the players. You don't belong here and can't come back.' That hurt me. I didn't think it was necessary for him to talk to me that way."

The situation worsened later in the year. After George Preston Marshall finally consented to integrating his club, the Redskins—to much fanfare— drafted Ernie Davis with the first selection in the 1962 NFL draft, held in November 1961. He knew, though, that Davis would be tough to sign, since the Buffalo Bills had selected him in the AFL draft. Just days after the draft, Marshall dealt Davis to Cleveland for Bobby Mitchell and Cleveland's first-round pick, running back Leroy Jackson. Brown, who'd grown impatient with Mitchell's tendency to fumble on inside runs, had long coveted Davis. It was Paul Brown who dealt with Marshall; Modell didn't know anything about it until he got a call from the Redskins owner.

"What do you think of our trade?" Marshall asked.

"George, what trade?" said Modell.

"Mitchell and your No. 1 pick for our No. 1 pick."

There was silence on the line, and then Marshall said, "Aren't you running that franchise?"

Modell, still reeling, stammered out a response before Marshall cut him off. "Don't ever let that happen again," he said. "You are the owner. You own the franchise. It's *yours.*"

Had Davis been able to play that season, 1962 might have been a very different campaign for the Browns. But during a routine training camp physical, team doctors discovered he was dying of leukemia. In the midst of their real sorrow, Modell and Paul Brown argued over whether Davis should be allowed to suit up for a token exhibition game appearance, and their communication, already poor, grew nonexistent.

In Washington, the arrival of the brilliant Mitchell brought a happy ending to the Redskins' integration saga, allowing Marshall to fulfill his promise to integrate the team by 1962. It was not a comfortable season for Mitchell, who was singled out for abuse by many in the stands and the city. There were other indignities; at the team's preseason kickoff dinner, Marshall implored Mitchell to sing along to the Redskins Band's performance of "Dixie."

"I'm sorry Mr. Marshall," Mitchell dryly replied, "I don't know the words." Mitchell held up majestically, and played even better, eventually fashioning a Hall of Fame career as a flanker (and later becoming one of the first blacks to serve a consequential position in an NFL team's front office).

Despite the loss of Mitchell and the devastating illness of Davis, the Browns entered the 1962 exhibition campaign with high hopes. Furthering the idea that a renaissance was imminent was the return of Blanton Collier, who accepted his old assistant's job with the Browns after being fired at Kentucky. Brown said he'd let his new starting quarterback, Jim Ninowski, call some of the plays himself. Many players were comforted by the placating influence of Collier, who had convinced Brown to allow quarterbacks to call audibles at the line of scrimmage.

But Collier himself could see that something had changed. Though he hailed Collier upon his return, Brown never gave his old friend an office, leaving him to work out of meeting rooms and at spare desks. And the innovations installed during training camp were soon scrapped. Brown vacillated between Ninowski and Frank Ryan at quarterback, and Jim Brown failed to lead the league in rushing for the first, and only, time in his career. The Browns, unable to win more than two games in a row, were eliminated early, and after yet another loss to the Giants, 17–13, in the next-to-last game of the season, Paul Brown went into a deep funk.

The team returned to Cleveland for a short week of practice before flying to San Francisco for the Saturday season finale. The last practice, on a Friday at League Park, found Brown running the team through its paces in the midst of a snowstorm. "Instead of being on the field with us, Paul sat in his car, about twenty yards behind the offense," recalled Lin Houston. "The quarterback would go to Paul's car after every play, and Paul would roll down the window and give him the play. The players were all freezing, and Paul was in his warm car."

Two days later, sitting in the visiting owner's box at Kezar Stadium during the last game of the year, a listless 13–10 win over the 49ers, a miserable Modell turned to team business manager Harold Sauerbrei, who'd covered the Browns for the *Plain Dealer* through 1954, and then joined the team as public relations director, before becoming business manager in 1960.

"Harold, I need your advice," said Modell. "What should I do?"

Sauerbrei had long been a Paul Brown loyalist, but he'd seen the same things Modell had seen: a standoffish, increasingly alienated coach, and a broad feeling of discontent in the locker room.

"Make a change," said Sauerbrei.

Modell fretted over the decision for nearly a month. On January 16, 1963, Modell summoned Paul Brown to his office.

"Paul, sit down please," said Modell. Brown, perturbed, still unclear about the reason for the meeting, sat down impatiently. "Paul," Modell continued. "I'm going to make a change. I'm going to go in a different direction. I hope you understand. I think we have to part company. I'm going to ask you to step down as coach and general manager, and you are to be reassigned."

Brown's face was blank. Then his eyes narrowed. He said nothing, simply got up and marched out of Modell's office, before Modell could explain his reasons. Brown called his son, Mike, away on military duty, and, voice quavering, gave him the news. "He's taken my team away from me," he said.

The firing illustrated the fleeting, fluid nature of football superiority. Paul Brown's teams had traveled to the championship game in eleven of the first twelve seasons he coached, winning seven titles. Though Cleveland posted a 39-22-3 record in Brown's last five years in Cleveland, he couldn't get the team back to the title game. The rest of the league caught up, and the decisive edge Brown had for so long enjoyed had vanished.

A day after firing Brown, Modell offered the job to Blanton Collier. Collier said he'd have to consult with two people before accepting: his wife, Forman, and Paul Brown.

Collier called Brown on the phone and explained that he'd been offered the job. His friend was terse, but encouraging. "You have to take it, Blanton," Brown said. "You owe it to your family." With that, and Forman's blessing, Collier decided he would accept the job.

But soon after, Collier received a desperate call from Mike Brown, Paul's son, who pleaded with him not to accept the job, because his father—despite what he'd said—would take it personally. And indeed he did. Brown never forgave Collier, never again regarded him as a friend. "I speak to Blanton," Brown explained years later. "I don't talk to him."

Collier, in his press conference, credited Brown for his extraordinary influence, and was injured by the ensuing rift for the rest of his life.

Paul Brown, for his part, showed more pain and vulnerability than ever before. Even when he finally spoke to the press, more than a week after the firing, he seemed disconsolate. "Outside of my family," he said, "what else except football have I known in my life?"

To a great extent, Pete Rozelle's early years as commissioner would be high-lighted by his fulfillment of the quest that had eluded Bert Bell, the realization of a package television deal that would put the NFL exclusively on one net-work, and bring each team an equal share of television revenues. This became harder in the new decade, when the Baltimore Colts, making $600,000 per year from NBC, were earning nearly ten times as much from TV as some teams in the league, and CBS was threatening to drop contracts altogether with teams in several smaller markets.

By 1960, CBS held contracts for nine of the twelve NFL teams, each individually negotiated, ranging from a high of $175,000 for the New York Giants down to $75,000 for the Green Bay Packers. But NBC had struck a novel deal with the Colts and Steelers, taking the rights to the two teams and broadcasting one national game a week. The Colts, fresh off their back-to-back championships, were the most appealing team in the league. And broadcasting just one national game a week significantly reduced expenses. CBS, meanwhile, was all over the country, paying the production costs of five crews on a typical football Sunday, so as to be able to broadcast each team's game back to its own home market. The Browns had their own far-flung independent network, sponsored by Carling Beer, which stretched from Texas to the East Coast, and competed with CBS in numerous markets, along with ABC's broadcast of the AFL game of the week.

In some cities, two or three NFL games were broadcast on Sunday, often beginning at identical times. This diluted the audience and frustrated advertisers and the network alike. If the situation persisted, MacPhail told Rozelle, CBS would drop smaller markets, because without the promise of an exclusive broadcast, the rights fees paid to those clubs couldn't be justified.

MacPhail had made an informal presentation to the league owners in 1960, offering to pay $3 million a year for exclusive rights to the league's regular season broadcasts, to be divided by the NFL in any way it saw fit. The challenge for Rozelle was to convince teams like Cleveland, Pittsburgh, and Baltimore, all earning more money from other networks, that the league would be better off splitting the money equally among all the teams, a move certain to cost some clubs money in the short run.

Debates over the proposed plan had been simmering for years, with small- and big-market clubs hewing to predictable stances. At the hotel bar at the Kenilworth in 1960, Dan Rooney and Dan Reeves wound up in an unusually spirited exchange over the question.

"There's a couple of different ways we can do this," allowed Reeves.

"There's only one way we can do it," Rooney interrupted, "and that's to divide the money equally."

"That's not going to happen."

"Then there's not going to be any television in this league."

Reeves was nonplussed. "How can you say that, Dan? What would you do about it?"

"Well, when you come to Pittsburgh, there aren't going to be any Los Angeles Rams games going to L.A.," said Rooney. "We have every right in the world to do this."

"Then you won't get any money," said Reeves.

"Then neither will you."

During the course of the conversation, Reeves offered numerous variations, some similar to the Veeck and Rickey concepts, another in which all the teams started out with what they'd made the previous season, then divided all additional monies that came in a package deal. By 1961, Reeves had reluctantly come around, partially at the behest of Rozelle.

A year later, at the 1961 annual meetings, held at the Warwick Hotel in New York, Rozelle began by delivering the commissioner's annual report, in which he noted, "Much of the past year has been spent in developing a television plan for the future. The NFL has been credited with harnessing television and using it to greater advantage than any other sports activity. This position, however, will be lost without planning for the future."

Two days of extensive lobbying, with the assistance of Lombardi (trying to sway the Mara brothers with the Giants, along with other small-market clubs), led Rozelle to the brink of approval. The Giants had been extremely reluctant to join in the plan, especially the flinty Wellington Mara, until his brother, Jack, persuaded him. At the Friday meeting, it was Wellington Mara who said, "We should all share, I guess. Or we're going to lose some of the smaller teams down the line, and we've all stuck together."

After much debate, the motion passed on January 27, 1961, one day after the one-year anniversary of Rozelle's election. It allowed the commissioner to negotiate a TV contract on behalf of all the league's members, maintained the home blackout policy, and stipulated every road game each team played would be broadcast back to its own home market.

"The big-city people—Halas, Reeves, the Maras—went along," said Rozelle later. "If Green Bay lost its television money, they wouldn't have a balanced league. It was an altruistic decision on their part."

Nearly as soon as Rozelle struck the deal, he saw it invalidated. The agreement, signed with CBS in April, was rejected as a violation of antitrust law two months later by U.S. District Court Judge Allan K. Grim. A dejected Rozelle returned to New York by train, and when he greeted his daughter, Anne, at the Rozelles' Sutton Place apartment, burst into tears.

The curious reasoning of Grim's decision was that, in his 1953 ruling (allowing the league to black out telecasts of home games in home markets), he had not expressly allowed a package deal, and thus couldn't allow such an arrangement after the fact.

The league's next move was to try to push for congressional approval. The deal was aided by Carroll Rosenbloom's close relationship with the Kennedy family, as well as Rozelle's friendship with Kennedy press secretary and fellow University of San Francisco alum Pierre Salinger.

After a round of intense politicking—and a promise not to play or televise games on Saturday during the college football season to placate the NCAA—the league successfully pushed through a congressional action that provided antitrust exemption for joint TV deals. On the eve of the signing, the president held a small reception for the sponsors of the bill at the White House. Rozelle, forever gracious and inclusive, spent much of the event talking earnestly to Kennedy's personal secretary, the matronly, fifty-two-year-old Evelyn Norton Lincoln. At one point, a bemused JFK walked over to Salinger and asked, "Pierre, is the commissioner *hitting* on my secretary?" Salinger explained that it was "just like Pete" to engage the least important person in the room.

On September 30, 1961, Kennedy signed the Sports Broadcasting bill, giving pro football an exemption from antitrust statutes. And it paid off almost immediately. On January 10, 1962, CBS signed the first national TV contract with the NFL, at the same terms that had been agreed to a year earlier—$4,650,000 per season for two years.

In ensuing years, the policy of revenue sharing was viewed by many critics as a monopolistic act of market control. Ron Powers, in his history of television sports, *Supertube,* wrote that Rozelle "was in fact quietly constructing a perfect model for socialism." But the idea that a joint television deal was inherently socialistic only made sense if one viewed a sports league as purely a business enterprise, and this was to miss a good part of the essence of competitive sports.

"The whole thing was equalizing the competition on the field," said Rozelle. "The sharing of income gave everyone the tools, the money, to compete equally. Now, some don't. But management and coaching and so forth being the big difference—and players—they had the opportunity, at least, to compete equally."

Much bluster would come in later years about owners as selfless or devoted to the good of the whole. But in this single case, the decision to share revenue equally—echoing the one that the AFL made at the behest of Hunt, and the one that the world of baseball ignored despite the entreaties of Veeck and Rickey—would become a model for American sports that would allow the games to rise from the Darwinian business model in which each club struggled for the last dollar, toward a system that made the primary competition the one on the field of play.

At heart, the NFL's decision to approve a joint TV contract, whatever the intent, served to place a higher priority on an equality of *opportunity* for all competitors than on maximizing the revenue of any individual franchise. In short, pro football had established an important tenet about which, forty years later, baseball owners were still bickering.

That the entire enterprise came to dominate America's living rooms on fall weekends, changing the rhythm, tone, and nature of Sunday afternoons across the country, was still a work in progress. It would be years before professional football could plausibly boast of eclipsing Major League Baseball in overall popularity. But with the historic television deal, the last of the necessary elements was in place for the coming gridiron coup, as well as the continued survival of the Packers and other small-market teams.

In this, the efforts of Rozelle and Lombardi complemented one another. Just as Rozelle helped the NFL by pushing through revenue sharing, Lombardi's arrival in Green Bay added a dose of glamour to the league's last quaint franchise and dramatically demonstrated the power of the egalitarianism of revenue sharing. It wasn't just a concept. It was how the sport ensured it was closer to operating as a pure meritocracy than any other realm in American society. And it offered the irresistible lure of how a Green Bay—with good personnel and superior coaching—could rise up and smite the New Yorks of the world.

By the end of the 1962 season, the Packers beat the New York Giants for their second straight world title. Paul Hornung, despite missing part of the season with an injury, was becoming one of the best-known athletes in sports, with lucrative endorsement deals from Zenith, Jantzen, and Marlboro. And Lombardi had eclipsed Brown as the most visible coach in pro football, appearing on the cover of *Time* magazine's December 21, 1962, issue. The cover caption read "The Sport of the '60s."

10

The Czar

Vince Lombardi sat in the chair, tie stiffly knotted about his neck, a look of perplexed dismay creasing his face as he scanned the file that Pete Rozelle had handed him. After reviewing the two-page statement and its tersely phrased admissions—"*I also bet on the regular season games of the Packers and other teams in 1959, 1960 & 1961*"—Lombardi sighed deeply, closed the file and placed it back on Rozelle's desk.

"Well, you have no choice," the coach said. "You *have* to suspend him."

"I think I do," said Rozelle, taking another drag on a cigarette, casting a sympathetic glance across his desk.

"Well, then," said Lombardi, "let's go get a drink."

It was early April 1963, just months after Lombardi's Packers had won their second straight NFL title. That night, Lombardi and Rozelle hit the town, both seeking to dilute their burdens. Lombardi was morose over evidence of betrayal by his favorite player and the consequence it might have on the dynasty he was building; Rozelle was steeling himself for the firestorm to come when he would announce the suspension of two of the league's best-known players—1961 Most Valuable Player and Packers Golden Boy Paul Hornung, and the Detroit Lions All-Pro defensive tackle Alex Karras—and bring to an explosive conclusion his methodical, comprehensive investigation of the most serious gambling scandal in pro football since the Filchock-Hapes scandal of 1946.

The Hornung-Karras case was merely the centerpiece of Pete Rozelle's remarkable 1963. He would enjoy greater power and notoriety in later years, but the events that occurred over the fourteen-month period—from December 1962 through January 1964—would largely define Rozelle's leadership, and set in motion pro football's inexorable ascendance. By the end of that period, he'd met the greatest challenges the office had to offer, been hardened by the criticism that accompanied it, and emerged as the unmistakable leader of pro football, a callow "child czar" no more.

The chatter about different players associating with gamblers had been building throughout the 1962 season, with numerous reports from the ex-FBI agents on retainer in cities throughout the league. By early January, the suspicions were a matter of public record, with the Bears' George Halas commenting that some of the league's players were guilty of "undesirable associations." The *New York Times* ran a series of pieces under headlines like "Hoodlums Linked to Detroit Lions" and "Inquiry Widens in Pro Football." There were no point-shaving charges, as occurred with Filchock and Hapes in 1946, but instead vague suggestions of associations between gamblers and stars. Pete Rozelle knew, as had Bert Bell, that the suspicion could be as damaging as the fact.

By January 9, 1963, Rozelle had publicly confirmed that the league was beginning an investigation of unnamed players and, on that same day, met Hornung at the Plaza Hotel in New York to ask about his relations with suspected gamblers and whether he himself had gambled on football. Hornung denied that he had, and agreed to submit to a lie detector test. The next afternoon, Hornung reported to the office of John P. Daly, one of the league's security men, where the test was conducted. In a subsequent report to Rozelle, polygraph consultant Thomas J. McShane said that, after Hornung denied having bet on any NFL games or passing any information to bettors, McShane had "promptly advised Mr. Hornung that his chart clearly indicated that he was purposely withholding pertinent information, that he had lied on several critical questions, including his betting on games, having bets placed through others, furnishing information to others for betting purposes. . . . He was reminded that he did not have to say anything, but it was strongly suggested to him that it was in his best interests and the interests of professional sports that he cooperate completely and furnish all the information he could regarding the investigation at hand."

With that, Hornung buckled, and confessed that he had placed a series of bets, from the 1959 season through the 1962 preseason, with his friend Barney

Shapiro, the head of a California novelty company who had once, in the '50s, owned a small stake in a Las Vegas hotel and casino. He'd also placed bets with another friend, and had shared information with both men on the state of the Packers.

Though Shapiro was not a bookmaker, and although his bets were placed legally in Las Vegas, Hornung was still in blatant violation of Paragraph 11 of the standard player's contract, which declared that the commissioner possessed broad powers "to fine, cancel the contract or suspend indefinitely any player accepting bribes or fixing games, or having knowledge of same," but also any player "who bets on a game, or who is guilty of any conduct detrimental to the welfare of the National Football League or professional football."

On January 16, 1963, NBC's *The Huntley-Brinkley Report* aired an interview with Karras in which the burly, sardonic lineman admitted to NBC reporter Ed Burk that he'd bet on games, and bet occasionally on his own team. Rozelle had spoken to Karras two weeks earlier, but after the news program aired that evening, he summoned Karras back to New York immediately. Karras was in Rozelle's office at eleven o'clock the next morning.

There was, by then, enough evidence to discipline both players. But Rozelle pressed forward with his investigation for two more months—even as the media was bubbling with speculation about the gravity of the charges and criticism of Rozelle's own persistent lack of comment on the investigation. One of the central principles of public relations, instilled in Rozelle during his years with P. K. Macker and Co., was the value of full disclosure: don't conceal, but never rush to comment if the facts weren't clear. Nothing was more damaging to an organization's credibility than to make a partial admission, then be forced to come back later to confirm more charges. So Rozelle continued digging, pursuing leads, reinterviewing the particulars, clarifying the league's bylaws and the commissioner's powers therein. Only in April, after exhausting all angles, was he satisfied that the matter had been investigated thoroughly enough that there would be no further damaging revelations.

On the morning of April 17, he called Hornung's home in Louisville. Hornung's mother answered and said her son was away. "Is there anything I can tell Paul?" she asked.

Rozelle choked up trying to answer her, but managed to say, "No, ma'am. If you'll just have Paul call me."

Later that afternoon, he spoke with both Hornung and Karras by phone, informing each man that he would be suspended indefinitely, but could apply for reinstatement in one year.

Bunkered in the league offices, Rozelle and Kensil had spent more than two days hammering out the press release, an artfully constructed eight-page document—released just hours after he'd notified the players—which opened with the good news, offering a staunch defense of the game's integrity:

> There is no evidence that any NFL player has given less than his best in playing any game.
>
> There is no evidence that any player has ever bet against his own team.
>
> There is no evidence that any NFL player has sold information to gamblers.
>
> There is clear evidence that some NFL players knowingly carried on undesirable associations which in some instances led to their betting on their own team to win and/or other National Football League games.

Rozelle went on to announce that he'd suspended Hornung and Karras "indefinitely" and doled out additional fines to several Lions players who had bet on the 1962 NFL championship game, as well as coach George Wilson.

Rozelle's public face was one of empathetic firmness. He spoke highly of Hornung's honesty, never mentioning that the player had lied during the initial polygraph examination ("When I told Hornung of the charges, he admitted them," said Rozelle). Hornung, for his part, seemed genuinely contrite. "It was a carefree, thoughtless thing I did," he told the press. It certainly helped that Lombardi, while showing affection for his favorite player, publicly backed the commissioner and affirmed the justice of the punishment. "I am shocked and hurt," Lombardi said. "However, there was a definite violation of the player contract and constitution and bylaws of this league in regard to gambling, which is punishable by suspension. The commissioner had no alternative because, if allowed to continue, it would lead to more serious consequences."

Karras was much more critical, of both the suspension and the entire investigation. "I haven't done anything to be ashamed of," he said, "and I'm not guilty of anything." But he, too, eventually toed the line, giving up his stake in a tavern deemed undesirable by the NFL.

The public and media response, while understandably mixed in Detroit and Green Bay, was for the most part highly complimentary of Rozelle's handling of the crisis. "Commissioner Rozelle became commissioner yesterday," wrote Doc Greene in the *Detroit News*. Jim Murray in the *Los Angeles Times* recognized the commissioner's difficult position: "Rozelle had to protect the game rather than the players. He had to show the owners, the players—and the public—that pro football was a big boy now, a public trust that the public could trust."

And that, in a sense, was Rozelle's greatest accomplishment in the investigation. By suspending two of the best-known players in the league for what he himself described as an action of "no criminality," Rozelle lowered the threshold for punishable behavior and raised the bar for the level of behavior the league could expect from its players. In so doing, he raised the public level of confidence in the game itself.

About a week after the suspension, Rozelle received a handwritten note from Hornung's mother, Loretta, thanking him for his handling of the incident. "I know it was not an *easy* decision to make," she wrote, "and I, too, fully appreciate your responsibility to the League—it had to come first." He replied immediately, on April 30: "Words cannot express my deep appreciation for the most thoughtful letter I received today and just finished reading."

The fallout from the Hornung and Karras suspensions was so great that there was little discussion about the loose end that *hadn't* been tied up, Rozelle's ongoing investigation into possible gambling on games by Carroll Rosenbloom. Ultimately, there was to be no public sanction. Instead, Rosenbloom privately submitted to Rozelle a written oath that he would no longer gamble on football. (Two different Colts employees of the '60s, though, said they witnessed him placing bets on his team from the Colts' offices later on in the decade.)

The last thing Rozelle did before closing the book on the Hornung and Karras cases was to hire James Hamilton, former intelligence chief of the Los Angeles police department, as the league's full-time head of security. Hamilton would cultivate a series of contacts in each league city, and would both report and follow up on rumors regarding player conduct.

———

Throughout the previous year, many of the league's biggest problems had been resolved. In May of 1962, the NFL successfully defended itself in U.S. district court in Baltimore against the $10 million civil suit brought by the AFL. When the case was filed, Rozelle had retained the Washington, D.C., firm of Covington & Burling, among the nation's premier litigators in antitrust law. The lead partner in the case was the legendary Gerhard Gesell, among the giants of twentieth-century antitrust litigation, whose knowledge of sports was limited. He was abetted by a rising young lawyer named Hamilton Carothers, a wry, acerbic weekend athlete who understood the structure of sports, and who would become one of Rozelle's key advisers over the next twenty-five years.

In December 1962, with Dan Reeves still battling with his partners over the direction of the Rams, Rozelle suggested the structure of a sealed auction that would finally settle the impasse, and allow one side to buy the other out. It ended happily for Rozelle, with his friend Reeves submitting the highest bid and regaining sole operating control of the team, at a total price of $7.1 million.

Writing after a league meeting late in 1962, the *Los Angeles Herald Examiner*'s Bob Oates noted that, once again, "the old salts of the league have marveled at the smoothness of the operation under the young commissioner, Pete Rozelle. . . . The characteristics of all Rozelle enterprises seem to be harmony and action, two things that are not normally related."

It would be years before anyone but Rozelle's closest friends understood the pressure he was under during that span, but a fuller appreciation of his performance during the time renders it all the more remarkable.

While Rozelle's public persona was ascendant, his private life was becoming increasingly troublesome. The workload, which he'd known would be severe, proved nearly unrelenting. In the months after taking the job in 1960, he was taking over the office, moving to Philadelphia, then New York, and fighting the Billy Cannon suit; in the 1961 off-season it was tortured negotiations, within the league and on Capitol Hill, to push the joint television package through; in 1962 it was the AFL vs. NFL antitrust suit; in 1963 it was the gambling investigation.

In addition to that, Rozelle's presence was now desired, even necessary, at dozens of social events a month. The shy Jane was miscast as the wife of a public figure; she had never enjoyed the spotlight, and her drinking, which friends had first noticed during Rozelle's tenure with Ken Macker in the '50s, had grown to troublesome proportions.

"In fairness, I think Pete was married to pro football more than he was married to Jane," said his friend John Lehman. The specter of marital discord had grown so daunting by 1963 that Rozelle often found excuses to stay late. "He said he didn't want to go home," said one co-worker at the league office. "So he'd stay out as long as possible and maybe when he got home, she'd be asleep."

When Tex Schramm and his wife, Marty, visited New York, they frequently made dinner appointments with the Rozelles. "At the last minute," said Schramm, "something would always come up. 'Jane's not feeling well.' 'Jane can't make it.' After a while we began to figure it out."

The year 1963 was a particularly taxing one for the Rozelle household. Jane was hospitalized for a few days in January and June, and after another setback in late September, she was admitted to another facility for extensive treatment.

"If I can look at what my life was, from one to ten, she might have been there one and a half percent of the time," said Anne. "I mean, it was *really* small. Really small. My dad always made every school event; I don't know how he did that but he did. Then I went through a period where I was struggling in school and I remember they said, 'She can't tell time.' So he would literally clear his calendar for an entire weekend, and work all weekend long on, 'We're going to learn the time.' "

Rozelle compensated for Jane's increasing absences by frequently bringing Anne along on road trips and letting her play in the NFL offices when he went into work on Saturday mornings. In this instance, Rozelle's omnicompetent secretary, Thelma Elkjer, played an even more important role, often acting as a surrogate mother, taking the girl shopping or to dinner. He stayed in many nights, coming home from work and switching into a bathrobe, helping Anne with her homework or eating dinner in front of the TV, reading newspapers and novels and talking to MacPhail or Landry or, most frequently and at greatest length, Kensil on the phone. It was not the most ideal of worlds, but those closest to Rozelle never questioned the father's love for the daughter. At a time when men routinely eschewed the obligations of parenting, Rozelle was taking even more of it on himself.

The final straw for Rozelle came in a series of episodes in 1965, one in which Jane threatened her own daughter and a teenage nanny with a knife. Another afternoon, Thelma Elkjer patched through a call to Rozelle from his wife, calling from a midtown bar, asking him to come get her. When he went to pick up Jane, he found Anne sitting on the barstool next to her.

"That convinced him that he had to get a divorce," said friend Pete Newell. "Anne was the light of his life." In 1967, at a time when such a thing was virtually unprecedented, Pete Rozelle was awarded custody of his daughter.

————

In *White Collar,* his cultural history of the rising middle class, C. Wright Mills observed that by the '60s postwar America had become "a great salesroom, an enormous file, an incorporated brain, and a new universe of management and manipulation." The sport that best reflected that change was pro football, and the league that was best able to create and capitalize on those changes was the NFL.

In essence, the NFL didn't merely sell a game, it created a full-force public relations strategy to bring the game to America. The league's two great marketing innovations came into being at approximately the same period. Both were ideas presented by outsiders, then embraced and honed to maximum advantage by Rozelle.

One of Rozelle's annual duties as commissioner was to sell the filmmaking rights to the league's championship game. The resulting half-hour films looked like an extended version of the highlight reels shown before movies in the earlier part of the century—press box views of big plays, presented in chronological order, accompanied by marching band music, and the cloying, alliterative voice-overs so common at the time. Tel-Ra Productions, the small Philadelphia company that had retained the rights to the NFL title game films for several years, was the leader in the market. Tel-Ra also packaged several teams' highlight films, the sort of things shown at fraternity smokers and booster club meetings as a vehicle for improving a club's season ticket sales.

Into the modest bidding in November 1962 came a brash, artful Philadelphia huckster named Ed Sabol, a loud, vulgar, funny iconoclast who'd spent twenty prosperous but unhappy years working for his father-in-law's coat company. In 1956, at age forty, he cashed in his holdings and retired.

One of the avocations he'd taken up over the years was using his 16mm camera to film his son Steve's football games, and by November of 1962, Sabol had decided he wanted to get into the sports film business. Knowing that the rights to the 1961 NFL title game had been sold for $2,500, he came in with a sealed bid for $5,000 from his start-up company Blair Motion Pictures, Inc., whose credits to that point included a Caribbean vacation film, a documentary about the vain quest of a whale harpooner, and a stop-action film of a Howard Johnson's motel being constructed. After Rozelle opened the sealed bids, and discovered that the high bidder, Blair Motion Pictures, had never filmed a professional football game before, he called Sabol into his office for a consultation. Sabol made a dramatic pitch, proposing to use eight cameras instead of Tel-Ra's four, bring zoom lens and slow motion into the equation to provide more intimacy, use more dramatic music and more sharply defined narration. After two days to think about it, Rozelle went ahead and awarded the contract to Sabol, telling him, "I just hope that we get a film out of this."

The 1962 championship game, played in frigid conditions at Yankee Stadium, found the machine-like Packers, behind another superb performance from Hornung, defeating the Giants, 16–7, to win their second straight title.

The film about the game premiered for the press and Giants officials six weeks later at Toots Shor's restaurant on West 52nd Street. Sabol's film, titled *Pro Football's Longest Day,* opened with contrasting shots of tiny Green Bay and majestic New York, and documentary-style vignettes from Bart Starr,

Vince Lombardi, and Frank Gifford. Then it cut to the opening credits, with a bank of fourteen NFL team logos, disappearing one at a time as drumbeats sounded off. At the end of the cadence, only the Giants and Packers logos remained. These clashed over the NFL shield in the middle of the screen and cut to a shot of a miniature football stadium, inside of which stood two small bobble-head dolls, one in a Packers uniform and one in a Giants uniform. Over Chris Schenkel's clipped narration, written by Sabol himself, the frigid conditions became all the more vivid. The Packers' iconic Lombardi, pacing the sidelines in his camel's hair coat, took on the aspect of a general leading his troops into war. And the action that had unfolded too quickly to be fully absorbed live revealed itself to be a carefully orchestrated series of troop movements, captured in close-up and slow motion by Sabol's cameras.

After the screening, Rozelle came over to Sabol and told him it was "the best football film I've ever seen."

Sabol held on to the rights for the 1963 and 1964 championship games and, after securing the 1964 film, he came to Rozelle with a bold proposal. He suggested that the league bring Blair Motion Pictures in-house, as a promotional vehicle. In addition to shooting the championship game, Sabol could also assemble a staff that would produce highlight videos for each team, at a much cheaper cost than they were presently being charged by outside filmmakers, and help the club find a sponsor for each. At the league meetings in the spring of 1965, Sabol made his pitch, asking for a one-time investment of $20,000 per team. On the recommendation of Rozelle, the owners voted to buy Blair Motion Pictures and rename it NFL Films, putting Ed Sabol on the NFL payroll at $30,000 per year. The endeavor took flight immediately, and in 1965 many CBS affiliates, along with American Express, had bought into a syndicated weekly feature, the *NFL Game of the Week.* NFL Films began in 1965 to send two cameramen (one with a press-box-wide view of each play, another from the field for close-ups) to every NFL game. And so began the profligate documentation that would bring about the self-mythologizing of pro football.

The idea of bringing NFL Films in-house was more plausible to owners because of a project Rozelle had been working on since returning to the Rams in 1957. The Rams' partnership for licensing souvenirs, with Larry Kent and Roy Rogers, Inc., was so successful that in 1959 Kent proposed expanding it to the entire league, noting in a prospectus that pro football offered "the most exciting potential for brand name licensing that exists on the American scene."

Bert Bell had liked the idea, and appointed a committee of Rozelle, the Colts' Carroll Rosenbloom, and the Bears' George Halas. The limited partnership of National Football League Enterprises was formally created on October 1, 1959. The ambitious project put the use of all the teams' logos and emblems under the Roy Rogers umbrella, and while the partnership suffered a loss in its first full year, volume increased quickly, and by 1962 NFL Enterprises was profitable. But both Kent and Rozelle recognized that for the plan to really pay off, it would have to be brought in-house, giving the league more creative control and a greater share of the profits. In 1963, Rozelle convinced the league's owners to found National Football League Properties, Inc., "a business arm of the 14 teams, individually and collectively, in such areas as youth sports competitions, publishing, advertising and merchandising." Where previously the clubs had used several different manufacturers for their team pennants, NFL Enterprises contracted with a single company, to make pennants for all teams, assuring greater consistency, uniformity, and quality.

"We wanted fans to think of the teams as equal," explained Hamilton Carothers, the attorney from Covington & Burling who'd grown close to Rozelle during the AFL vs. NFL trial. "And we did not want a stand selling pennants, one from the New York Giants, made of silk, and another one, of the Pittsburgh Steelers, made of paper. If you could buy fancy T-shirts from the New York Giants, but crap, junky T-shirts from another team, that's no good—that hurts the league."

The first catalogue included seat cushions and bobble-head dolls, team logo baby bibs ("I'm a Little Colt") and utility bags. In New York, Saks Fifth Avenue included a "Giants Locker Room" window display during the 1963 Christmas season, featuring a full range of Giants souvenirs and a child-sized Giants uniform. In 1964, in cooperation with NFL Properties, Ford sponsored the league's "Punt, Pass & Kick" promotion. While the group's attempt to cater to girls—the NFL "Pom-Twirl and Drill Competition"—was decidedly less successful, most of the ventures were a hit. A year after bringing the entity in-house, the league realized rights payments of over $100,000 in 1965.

Kent was the can-do president of NFL Properties and, just as crucially, artist and graphic designer David Boss was hired as the design consultant. Boss, who in the late '50s had designed the Rams' slick yearbooks, had earlier been summoned by Rozelle to conceive a recruiting brochure to be distributed to potential players, called *The NFL and You.* By 1965, Boss began the Creative Services division of NFL Properties, and provided design aid to licensees, clients, and the teams themselves. In the years ahead, it would begin a series of remarkably prolific and sophisticated print projects.

It would be a few more years before NFL Properties began to turn a significant profit. But profits in either case were incidental; Rozelle viewed both

Properties and the separate entity of NFL Films as vehicles to expand the prestige and profile of the league. And in this, he succeeded spectacularly. In an increasingly fast-paced, commercialized age, the league had found a way to set itself apart. Up until the '60s, sports had been something to do, something to read about, or something to watch. With NFL Films, it became something to be experienced, and with NFL Properties it became a kind of extended lifestyle choice. Pro football wasn't just for Sundays anymore. The NFL press office increased coverage of, and interest in, the league throughout the week. And the ancillary divisions developed other ways for the game to be enjoyed: a movie about football could be as entertaining as the game itself. And those who chose to identify with a particular team could now pay for the privilege, with handsome hats, T-shirts, and other souvenirs. Pro football was escaping from its confines, and beginning to insinuate itself into the larger realm of American popular culture.

The 1963 season kicked off with the dedication of the Pro Football Hall of Fame in Canton, Ohio, and saw the continued escalation of ticket sales and television ratings, as well as legal victories. On Thursday, November 21, the U.S. Fourth Circuit Court of Appeals reaffirmed the lower court's ruling in favor of the NFL in the AFL's $10 million antitrust suit, effectively bringing to an end three and a half years of litigation. Several owners sent telegrams of congratulation, which were waiting for Rozelle when he arrived at his office, in a buoyant mood, on Friday, November 22, 1963.

Earlier that afternoon, Rozelle and Jim Kensil were just returning from their lunch at the Holland House when they heard the news that the president had been shot in Dallas. Within an hour after a choked, shaken Walter Cronkite delivered the news of the president's death on CBS, with secretaries and executives at the NFL offices walking around in tearful disbelief, Rozelle made his first decision of the crisis, and began to try to reach his friend and fellow University of San Francisco alum Pierre Salinger.

It seemed impossible. Word of the shooting had reached Salinger, Kennedy's press secretary, on a plane over the Pacific with five cabinet members bound for an economic summit in Asia. Arrangements were made for a return to Honolulu, the speediest possible refueling of the jet, and then a nonstop, full-speed flight to Washington.

The plane touched down at Hickam Field in Honolulu less than two hours after the first UPI bulletin, and Dean Rusk and Salinger left the plane to talk to the White House. After being whisked to the Pacific Command of the U.S. Air Force, Salinger returned to the jet within ten minutes, just as the refueling was finishing. The jet's door was closing when word came that the press secretary was needed once more on the phone.

Escorted by an Air Force officer, Salinger returned to the nearest phone, assuming that it was the White House with more directives. He rushed to the phone and picked it up.

"Pierre," said the harried voice on the other end of the line. "It's Pete. What should we do?"

Through Salinger, Rozelle had met Kennedy and developed a casual friendship. Through Salinger, he would make, that afternoon, the agonizing decision. Salinger never did discover how Rozelle managed to get through to him during that sliver of time in Honolulu. But in their two- or three-minute conversation, both men agreed that the president would have wanted the games to go on, and that the country would be reassured by the presence of football games on Sunday.

With Salinger's counsel, as well as the recognition that games weren't scheduled in either Dallas or Washington that weekend, the decision was made: the NFL would play. Rozelle's statement took the long view: "It has been traditional in sports for athletes to perform in times of great personal tragedy. Football was Mr. Kennedy's game. He thrived on competition."

In retrospect, of course, the decision to go ahead with the games would seem crass and misguided. And by the time Lee Harvey Oswald was killed by Jack Ruby—on national television, less than two hours before the first kickoff of that Sunday—it had become obvious that the expert PR man Rozelle had made a grievous public relations mistake.

It was exacerbated by AFL president Milt Woodward's decision that same Friday afternoon to postpone all AFL games. Commissioner Joe Foss was out of the office and out of touch, flying from one place to another. Woodward, searching for a decision, had phoned the NFL offices in the afternoon and spoken to Kensil, who said he thought they were going to play the games. Woodward said the AFL was leaning toward doing the same. But late in the afternoon, after waiting for several hours with no word from Foss, Woodward sat in his office with AFL director of publicity Jack Horrigan, scanning the telex as wires from clubs around the league poured in. At five o'clock, he said to Horrigan, "Tell 'em that Sunday's games are off. Tell the clubs and call the network. Here, let me . . . I'll call the TV people myself."

While the AFL was lauded for its restraint, Rozelle took a series of broadsides. "Rozelle's decision was probably the cheapest move ever made in the history of a sport not noted for good taste, or the grand gesture," wrote Charles McCabe in the *San Francisco Chronicle*.

On Saturday morning, teams got on planes. The Cowboys traveled to Cleveland, where Bob Lilly would recall that the baggage handlers at the airport and the porters at the hotel wouldn't handle their luggage.

But the games went on, with only minor modifications. Halftime festivities at all stadiums were canceled, and a moment of silence was observed before each kickoff. The Browns canceled a planned halftime tribute to retiring receiver Ray Renfro, and at the behest of Cleveland Browns owner Art Modell, when the PA announcers gave out-of-town scores in NFL stadiums, they refrained from using the word Dallas, referring to the franchise as "the Cowboys" instead.

In the visitor's locker room before the game, many of the Cowboys saw the live feed of Jack Ruby shooting Lee Harvey Oswald. As the team headed out onto the field, quarterback Eddie LeBaron passed the word, "Boys, put your helmets on and keep 'em on." Cleveland beat the distracted Cowboys team. "We were really kind of worried about getting killed," said Bob Lilly. "We stood there going, 'I wonder if there are any snipers around here?' We wore our helmets the whole time, and wore those big parkas."

In his biography of Vince Lombardi, David Maraniss described the scene at Milwaukee County Stadium (where the Packers played three home games each season) that Sunday as an "eerily contained and somber affair. There was no pregame introduction of the starting lineups. There were no commercial announcements on the scoreboard. The television booth was shut down; the only broadcast was on radio. The only music was the national anthem. No halftime band. The players were equally subdued. The normally raucous Willie Davis played in dazed silence at his defensive end position, no swearing that day."

At Yankee Stadium, where the Giants played the Cardinals in a crucial game for first place, fans came in with none of the carnival pregame buzz.

In the press box, prior to the game, the *New York Herald Tribune*'s Red Smith encountered Rozelle and announced crossly, "I think you're doing the wrong thing."

"Why?" asked Rozelle.

"Because it shows disrespect for a dead president of the United States who isn't even buried yet."

"There can be no disrespect where no disrespect is intended," said Rozelle.

Even in the wake of the bizarre Oswald killing, the opening moments of the Giants-Cardinals game still fulfilled some measure of the cathartic unity that Rozelle and Salinger had imagined. Recalling the scene that took place when it came time for Martha Wright to perform the national anthem, the writer Stanley Cohen remembered himself and so many others in the stadium "singing full-out, for the first time perhaps since a grade school assembly program . . . and Martha Wright's voice was lost in the swell. We sang it that way until the end, and then, in place of the customary applause that signaled the start of the game, there was only silence, a silence so deep that you felt as if you had fallen through the bottom of the world."

After the stirring, spontaneous communal outpouring of the anthem, the game began and most present would remember a somber, listless affair. Cohen recalled the feeling "that we had come together to share the burden of our grief and that the football game to be played was incidental to our purpose . . . as if it were being played very far away and in three-quarter time." Joe Pollack, the publicity man for the Cardinals, would remember it as something watched "from the other end of the telescope." Norman Mailer attended the game with George Plimpton, the two writers sitting silently for much of the contest, feeling the natural sadness and inevitable portent, recalling as hollow the disconcerting experience of watching a football game while a country was still grieving.

Yet memory can play tricks. The Giants-Cardinals game indeed had an eerily quiet beginning, and years later, players and commentators alike would remember how empty and somber the stadium was. But on that Sunday afternoon, a different truth emerged: six minutes into the second quarter, facing a crucial third-and-short play, Giants quarterback Y. A. Tittle walked to the line of scrimmage, surveyed the field, began barking numbers—and then raised both his arms in the air, delivering the plea for the crowd to quiet down so his teammates could hear his signals.

Rozelle and the NFL owners had been wrong about the timing, the fallout, the impact, and the response. But they were right about one thing: the people wanted the games.

Historians have tended to judge Rozelle harshly for his decision to play the league schedule, partly because he was so hard on himself. On numerous occasions in his later years, he would describe the decision as the greatest single regret of his commissionership.

The most frequent criticism of Rozelle, that he kept the games going for the money, was baseless. If anything, the decision cost the league television money. CBS decided not to telecast that weekend, and the NFL surrendered one fourteenth of the money it was to have made from its TV contract that year. Had games been rescheduled, and the weekend's games made up at the end of the season, the NFL would have recouped its losses.

At least two elements of that weekend's fallout Rozelle could not have fore-seen. He couldn't have known that Oswald would be shot on the morning of Sunday's games, heightening the sense of chaos within the country. More im-portantly, he could not have anticipated the role that television would play during the long weekend. The previous cataclysmic events that had been the touchstones for most American lives—the attack on Pearl Harbor, FDR's death, or the dropping of atomic bombs on Hiroshima and Nagasaki—had been experienced through radio reports. Later events, like the launching of Sputnik, were reported widely on television, but had scant accompanying vi-sual evidence. But on that weekend of November 22–24, a nation sat in front of the television, watching itself mourn, and gaining a sense of itself in a way it never had before. In that heightened context, Rozelle's decision would seem like a rash one.

The deeper criticism, that the Kennedy family was offended by Rozelle's decision to play, was based on a fallacy that assumed that anyone in John F. Kennedy's circle of grief cared at all about what the Vikings and Bears did that weekend. The Kennedy family had been friendly with Rozelle prior to the event, and would remain so afterward.

"I just don't think it was on his screen," said Ethel Kennedy, trying to recall the reaction of her husband, Robert F. Kennedy, to Rozelle's decision. "It was such a bleak time. Certainly, with this family, when anything bad happened, everybody tried to do some form of activity. And you could see it either way. People needed something to distract them."

Despite the criticism, the sharpest he'd endured during his commissionership, the year still ended triumphantly for Rozelle and the league. In early Novem-ber, *Sports Illustrated* managing editor André Laguerre made the decision to name Rozelle as the magazine's Sportsman of the Year. Laguerre himself had incurred some criticism for running a picture of Navy's Roger Staubach—rather than a memorial to JFK—on the cover of *SI* the week after the assassi-nation. So he wasn't inclined to change his mind about Rozelle just because of the unpopularity of Rozelle's decision. The honor had grown increasingly vis-ible as *Sports Illustrated* had matured, and Rozelle, as the first nonathlete to win the award, stirred plenty of interest, many letters, and much dissent. Though it would later be seen as a visionary selection, its importance at the time was more significant. "It gave me more credibility with the old guard of owners," said Rozelle. "Suddenly, I was no longer a 33-year-old kid commis-sioner." Laguerre saw then what would only become obvious later: Rozelle was revolutionizing sports as well as the role of the sports commissioner.

With Hornung on the sidelines, the Packers weren't the same team in 1963, losing the Western Conference title to Chicago. The Bears would go on to win the NFL title that season, with the sixty-six-year-old Halas lifting the championship trophy one more time, as Chicago beat the Giants, 13–10, on another frigid championship Sunday, this time in Chicago.

A week later, after Sid Gillman's Chargers routed the Boston Patriots, 51–10, in the AFL title game, a few members of the press began to consider whether the AFL champions might be on par with the NFL champs. After San Diego's victory, Gillman said, "We're the champions of the world. If anyone wants to debate it, let them play us." Even Otto Graham said he'd pick the Chargers to beat the Bears if the two teams could have met.

The talk prompted another round of merger whispers, as well as a Gillman telegram to his old boss Rozelle, which read: "PETE—EVEN POPE JOHN RECOGNIZED THE OTHER LEAGUE."

Gillman received Rozelle's reply the next day: "SID—YES BUT IT TOOK HIM TWO THOUSAND YEARS."

––––––

The coda to Rozelle's amazing 1963 came a few weeks later, in January 1964, with the first-ever open bidding for an NFL package television contract. The NFL was increasingly being viewed as one of television's most valuable properties, a perception enhanced by the league's increasingly sophisticated marketing skill. Baseball commissioner Ford Frick seemed utterly clueless by comparison. "The view a fan gets at home," he said, "should not be any better than that of the fan in the worst seat of the ballpark."

Rozelle instructed each network that was interested to submit a sealed bid at the NFL offices at 11:00 a.m., Friday, January 24. Bill MacPhail showed up for CBS, Carl Lindemann for NBC, and Roone Arledge for ABC. The first bid opened, from NBC, was for $10.3 million a season, for a package of $20.6 million. Then came ABC's bid, for $13.2 million a season, virtually tripling the annual value of the previous CBS deal, $26.4 million in all. Finally, Rozelle opened CBS's bid and announced that the network had come in with a proposal that called for $14.1 million per season, or $28.2 million. Like its competitors, CBS's bid included a plan to, for the first time, broadcast doubleheader games the last five weeks of the regular season.

"Pete was always cool," remembered Barry Frank, then a J. Walter Thompson advertising exec, later a lieutenant to Roone Arledge at ABC, who was in the room that day. "He didn't bat an eye, he just read out each bid. The mood in the room was tense, because this was the future. The NFL was so big in those days. MacPhail was almost overcome; he was so thrilled to have it." Rozelle and MacPhail headed to Toots Shor's for a celebratory toast, while the representatives of the other networks left in dejection.

MacPhail recalled later that he was so happy about the winning bid, he forgot to call his boss, Jim Aubrey. "God, was he *enraged*. He had already heard about it—in the *men's room*, for God's sake—from some guy who heard it on the radio. He was livid and he told me next time I better goddamn well remember that I worked for CBS and not the press or the next time there wouldn't *be any* goddamn next time."

The circumstances surrounding the bidding would become part of television industry legend, with rumors of a mole at ABC leaking the amount of the network's bid to someone in the NFL, and the strong belief, by Arledge, that Rozelle had worked in concert with CBS to make it possible for the established network to submit the top bid.

Decades later, Pat Summerall offered an explanation that added to the aura of mystery. Summerall was sitting with Bill MacPhail late that week, when MacPhail got a call from Rozelle. "He tells MacPhail, 'NBC's bid is higher than yours and I don't want NBC involved in broadcasting the NFL. CBS needs to up its bid.' "

The Friday of the auction, several of the league's owners were on a retreat, at Clint Murchison's Island in Spanish Key, eagerly waiting news though with no phone service to receive it. As the previous contract had been for $9.3 million over two years, expectations were high for a significant bump. Art Modell was dispatched to the Florida mainland to phone New York and get the word.

Reaching Rozelle on the phone, he asked how it had gone.

"Fourteen point one million," said Rozelle.

After a pause, Modell said, "Well, it could be worse. I had been hoping for a little more, but, hell, Pete, seven million a year isn't half bad. We can make it—"

"No, Art," said Rozelle, interrupting. "Fourteen million *per year*. Twenty-eight million for *two years*."

There was a longer pause, and Modell's next words were, "Pete, you gotta stop drinking at breakfast."

NFL teams had been making $365,000 per season in television revenues. With the new contract, each club would bring in about $1 million per season. That news was greeted back on the island with cheers and hugs. Toasts were made, to Rozelle and the brotherhood of owners, and the imminent demise of the American Football League was predicted. The elation over the expected collapse of the AFL wouldn't last long, but satisfaction with Rozelle's performance would. He had won not just the respect but, in many cases, the compliance of the fourteen willful, headstrong owners of the National Football League.

Over the next decade, pro football's popularity rode a rocket of social dynamism, fueled by years of population growth, upward mobility, television's incursion into the very center of American life, and, not incidentally, the steady and incontrovertible rise in the quality and competitiveness of the sport itself. The league still had the mind-set of an insurgent, albeit a decidedly upscale one, and Pete Rozelle still popped a cork on a bottle of champagne the morning after the final game of the World Series, announcing, "Here's to the beginning of football season." By then it was clear that his confidence, his ease, his avid attention had been rewarded. Pro football was on the way.

Even baseball was starting to take notice. As football's attendance and profile continued to rise, Major League Baseball's crowds remained largely flat, with much of the growth coming in new markets like Los Angeles, San Francisco, and Atlanta. As the movement to the suburbs quickened (there were 35 million American suburbanites in 1950 and twice that many twenty years later), cities began to stagnate, a trend frequently cited as a cause of baseball's problems.

Gabe Paul, the Cleveland Indians' president, was asked in 1964 to explain why his team had suffered such a glaring loss in attendance. He reasoned that most fans had moved out to the suburbs, and didn't want to travel to the city for games at Cleveland Stadium. Apprised of the comment, Mets manager Casey Stengel mused, "Well, I guess all the fans moved back to town for football season."

11

War

With the record-breaking CBS contract in place, the National Football League began the 1964 season poised for its greatest year ever. *Fortune* magazine, in a cover story that fall, noted that the game "is wonderfully attuned to the pace and style of American life in the 1960's. To a nation of spectators, it offers an unsurpassed spectacle. In a time of mass education, it is an educated man's game."

The success that the league enjoyed was due not just to the vision of Rozelle or the serendipity of television, but was also the culmination of a generation worth of postwar sacrifice, of the commitment of Halas and Lambeau, the indomitability of Bert Bell, the familial fidelity of the Maras and the Rooneys, and the fervent, violent struggles of hundreds of players who played football when it was professional in little more than name. By the end of the 1963 season, the game had exploded in popularity, ticket sales and public interest were at an all-time high, and the CBS deal offered the promise of record revenues to come.

And over the next two years, the entire enterprise was nearly destroyed.

What began to transpire early in 1964 and continued at a fevered, ruinous pace throughout the next thirty months was the most tempestuous period in the history of professional football. The irony is that, even as the battle critically wounded several teams, rent ownership in both leagues, and cost both the NFL and the AFL millions of dollars, the epic war *helped* pro football. The same elements that jeopardized the teams and their business plans only made the game itself more fascinating, more urgent, more pointed—and more newsworthy, with headlines coming year round instead of just in the fall. The competition between the NFL and the AFL would resonate long after the peace had been won. Decades later, when Tex Schramm talked about "the war in the '60s," he was not referring to Vietnam.

By its fourth season, the American Football League had begun to demonstrate its resilience and appeal. Though the crowds were often sparse and the playing facilities frequently subpar, the football that the AFL teams played, once its teams began to gel, was marked by a kind of inspired spontaneity, a lightness and freedom that was altogether new for professional football. The eight teams of the new league used their greatest institutional weakness, the lack of tradition, as a strength: while AFL owners honored the unwritten agreement with the NFL not to raid each other's veteran players, they moved aggressively for rookies. Because of that, the league's players were mostly young, emerging talents, or reborn journeymen making the most of a second chance. The coaches were building reputations rather than trying to preserve them, and so were less susceptible to the cautious mentality that can metastasize football at any level.

In Los Angeles, then San Diego, where Sid Gillman's imaginative pass offense was given free rein, the Chargers flipped the old cliché, using the pass to set up the run. The offense was built not around a back, but the splendid, balletic wide receiver Lance "Bambi" Alworth, whose talents were fully exploited in Gillman's system. In Dallas, Hank Stram used defenses never before tried on the pro level, and on offense developed a complex array of formations, shifts, and motion, with each new wrinkle designed to force the defense to wait, or think, one split second longer before reading its keys and deploying its forces. That there was more passing than in the NFL was a given. But there also was more daring, more teams going for it on fourth down, more fake punts, more trick plays, more busted plays preserved by impromptu laterals, more plays altogether that were drawn up in the dust on a sideline.

Because of this, and the fact that it was setting up shop in so many uncharted areas, the league developed a surprisingly loyal following. The brand of football played in the AFL was enjoyable long before it was coherent, and its strategy and tactics eclipsed the NFL's at a time when its talent level had yet to catch up. By the end of 1963, it had eight functioning franchises operating in eight sustainable markets, all being run with sound football principles. In the process, it continued to offer opportunities to players, coaches, owners, and even cities.

Len Dawson had been the fifth player selected in the 1957 draft, by the Pittsburgh Steelers. What he learned in the NFL was that, even for a highly touted rookie, opportunities were hard to come by. Dawson's confidence had waned while his skills atrophied on the bench in Pittsburgh and Cleveland, where he threw just forty-five passes over five seasons.

"I remember Paul Brown had us convinced it was bad for football," said Dawson of the AFL. "I can remember sitting in a meeting and he said, 'This league is not going to last. It's a bunch of sons of rich guys. It's a hobby with them. They don't know anything about football. The people playing there are not capable of playing in the National Football League. They'll be nothing but castoffs and they won't last more than a year or two.' That was the attitude the NFL had, and they directed at the players. So at first we're thinking, 'Well, this is a bad league.' It took us a couple of years to realize, 'Wait a minute. What's so bad about it?' Because it gives more people jobs, more coaches jobs, and it gives us maybe an opportunity to be competitive where you might make more money. So being bright as we are as football players, it took us a couple years to realize that, but we eventually did."

Texans coach Hank Stram, who had coached Dawson at Purdue as a collegian, saw him in 1961, and told him he still felt he could be a terrific quarterback, and that if he could ever get out of his NFL contract, the Texans would sign him. After his second season of inactivity in Cleveland, Dawson asked Brown for his release and, after going unclaimed by any other NFL team, signed with the Dallas Texans.

"After a while, I had serious doubts of my ability," said Dawson. "In five years in the NFL, I never played two games in a row. I never started and finished a game. I had to ask myself why. One conclusion was that I wasn't good enough."

Hank Stram was a plump, prideful, chattering man, a dandy bantam with a prematurely balding pate who had inherited from his father a haberdasher's attention to detail, never leaving the house without seeing that his shoes were shined, usually sporting one of the hundred or so suits in his closet. But he had an uncommon mastery of the technical details of football. Shocked in the early weeks of training camp by Dawson's sloppy fundamentals, Stram overhauled his quarterback's footwork, throwing motion, and follow-through. He restored Dawson's confidence and by the time the Texans began the 1962 season, Dawson had supplanted Cotton Davidson as the team's starter.

In Dallas, the battle between the Texans and Cowboys entered its third year in 1962, with no winner in sight. Neither team had established clear superiority in attendance, and both were suffering sizable financial losses. The big difference was on the field, where the Cowboys were still building for the future while the Texans were poised to challenge for the AFL title. Early in 1962, Hunt hired Don Klosterman away from the Chargers, and made him director of pro player personnel. Klosterman, the magnanimous former quarterback from Loyola Marymount (a skiing accident in the '50s ended his playing career), was a nattily dressed charmer with a devilish sense of humor and a sharp eye for talent. In the cat-and-mouse game of player recruitment, the "Duke of Bel Air" was an expert at coercion.

Just before the season opener that year, Lamar Hunt engaged in his single instance of owner meddling, making a trade against Stram's wishes. To the Oakland Raiders, who were struggling to stay in business and bereft of a quality quarterback, Hunt exchanged Cotton Davidson (who'd lost his starting job to Dawson) for the Raiders' first-round choice in the 1963 draft. Stram was furious at the time, but that November, with the woeful Raiders last in the league, the choice the Texans traded for became the first selection in the AFL draft. They chose and quickly signed the mammoth Grambling defensive tackle Junious "Buck" Buchanan, about whom Klosterman raved, "He can run a 220 in twenty seconds flat with a goat under each arm." Buchanan's selection, less than fifteen years after Tank Younger was signed as a free agent, signaled a new era for black colleges. "Once Buck went first," said longtime Grambling coach Eddie Robinson, "then the floodgates just opened wide, and everyone started coming down. Suddenly it wasn't just three or four scouts anymore."

A year later, Klosterman hired pro football's first full-time black scout, Lloyd Wells. "The Judge" was an ebullient, sly ladies' man, a Houston photographer with a long list of contacts, a taste for fine things and an angle on virtually everything. Many pro teams began looking more closely at the historically black colleges in the '60s, but Wells made regular stops at dozens of black schools, and in the space of a few years, the team selected players from Grambling, Jackson State, Southern, Prairie View, Morgan State, and Tennessee State, almost all of whom would become pro stars.

In the jargon of the war between the leagues, Klosterman was the quintessential closer, someone who could talk to college athletes, get their attention, and convince them to take a chance on the upstart league. Flying from Dallas to Minneapolis in November of 1962, he found himself seated next to Minnesota senator Hubert Humphrey, who after introductions asked him what he was going to the Twin Cities for.

"I'm going up to talk to Bobby Bell," said Klosterman.

"You'll never sign Bobby Bell," said Humphrey flatly. The All–Big 10 defensive end had been drafted by the Vikings and was a local favorite. "He's going to be our first black mayor; he is the most important player we've ever had."

Klosterman spent a week in Minneapolis with Bell, a high school quarterback and one of the great athletes of the era, and signed him away from the Vikings, whose complacency would cost them. "The Vikings and [coach] Norm Van Brocklin just sort of had this attitude like, 'Oh, don't worry about it, he'll come here,' " said Bell. "But Don Klosterman was a *salesman*. He said, 'Bobby, we really want you with us, what's it gonna take here?' " What it took in this case was Lamar Hunt approving Klosterman's offer of a five-year, no-cut contract, a rarity even in the days of big bonuses.

With the Chargers slumping to an injury-riddled 4-10 season, Dallas ran away with the AFL West in 1962, qualifying to face the two-time defending champion Oilers for the league title. On December 23, at Jeppesen Stadium in Houston, the third American Football League championship game was played, in front of a standing-room-only crowd of 37,981. Weather was bad across the country, and the game enjoyed unusually high ratings, viewed by 56 million people. They saw a sudden-death classic that lasted into the sixth period, the longest pro football game to date, as the Texans took 77:20 to defeat the Oilers, 20–17, in perhaps the first AFL contest to register on the national sports consciousness. "The AFL was born at the age of three, so magnificent was the game," wrote Shirley Povich in the *Washington Post*.

Returning home to Dallas for a celebratory Christmas Eve, Lamar Hunt found himself with a dilemma similar to the one Dan Reeves faced in Cleveland seventeen years earlier. His team had won its league championship, but lost money in the process, with little hope of financial improvement in a divided, fiercely contested market. Though the Texans had sold 1,100 more season tickets and averaged 200 more fans per game than the Cowboys in 1962, both teams were suffering from the fight. The Cowboys lost $2 million their first three years, and Hunt's losses were nearly $2.5 million.

Convinced that his team needed to be a success for the AFL to survive, he'd begun furtively scouting out other cities in the fall of 1962. His initial interest was moving a franchise to New Orleans. He even traveled there and asked his friend David Dixon, the New Orleans businessman who'd been working to bring pro football to the city, to set up a meeting with a few of the board members at Tulane. But seating at the Sugar Bowl was still strictly segregated and by the end of the year, Hunt's attention had turned to Kansas City, Missouri, which after having brought major league baseball to its westernmost frontier in 1955, was seeking a pro football franchise. On February 8, 1963, Hunt announced that he would move the franchise to Kansas City if the city would sell 25,000 season tickets and provide free use of an office space and practice field. Despite the ticket drive stalling at 15,000, the Dallas Texans left town May 14, bound for Kansas City.

Len Dawson was with his wife, Jackie, in Pittsburgh when he heard the news. "I mentioned to some friends that the team was going to Kansas City and they said, 'Kansas City, Missouri, or Kansas City, Kansas?' I said, 'You mean there's two of them?' So I had no idea which one. The thought then, particularly back east, was, 'Man, you're going to a cow town. They have horses and cattle running in the middle of the main street in the city.' "

Unreported at the time was the arrangement between the Texans and Cowboys, who had quietly agreed to buy the Texans' practice facilities and, in addition, paid $100,000 (in $10,000 annual payments over the next ten years) to Dallas for "moving expenses." The Cowboys were glad to pay to be rid of the competition and, back in Dallas, Tex Schramm celebrated, convinced he'd finally freed himself forever of his nemesis, Lamar Hunt.

While Hunt was wealthy enough to weather the Texans' losses, some of the AFL's other owners weren't. In Denver and Oakland, the early years were an exercise in cut-rate franchise survival. The Broncos had been in trouble from the start, and the Raiders only survived the 1961 season with $400,000 from Buffalo owner Ralph Wilson, who secretly loaned the money to Oakland owner Wayne Valley so that the team—and, in Wilson's mind, the league—could remain afloat. Both teams got better on the field as a prelude to fixing their bottom line, and both went to the coaching staff of the Chargers to do it.

Gillman had assembled the best coaching staff in either league in 1960. One of the assistants, Chuck Noll, would spend much of the '60s as an aide to Don Shula in Baltimore, but two other Gillman protégés, Jack Faulkner and Al Davis, saw more immediate results, each winning AFL Coach of the Year honors, in 1962 and 1963, respectively. The defensive specialist Faulkner was hired by the Broncos, and organized a bonfire of the club's laughable vertically striped socks before the 1962 season, then rallied his undermanned team to a 7-7 record during the campaign. Davis, taking over the disaster that was the Raiders a year later—they'd won three games over the previous two seasons—turned the club around to a 10-4 mark in 1963, and began infusing the team with the menacing mystique that would later become a trademark.

Dallas, Denver, and Oakland had all been concerns for the AFL, but the league's biggest problem was in New York. Almost from the opening kickoff in

1960, the Titans had been an object of widespread public ridicule, primarily because the egomaniacal owner Harry Wismer seemed lost in his own delusional world. When the Chargers called to ask the Titans to send some promotional pictures of their stars, Wismer mailed 100 8 × 10 glossies of himself.

A Chargers-Titans game in 1962 brought a crowd estimated as 12,000 by the AP and 7,500 by the *Times,* and announced by the Titans as 21,467. The home team rose up to beat the injury-depleted Chargers, but with time left in the fourth quarter, and lights visible from Yankee Stadium just across the river, Wismer refused to pay the $250 to turn the Polo Grounds lights on.

Only a $40,000 bailout from the league office (with the other seven teams pitching in) allowed the team to make payroll through the end of the 1962 season, and even then matters were made more difficult by Wismer fighting to retain control of a team he could no longer afford to put on the field.

The situation looked so desperate early in 1963 that even the league's founder was ready to give up on the nation's largest market. "I personally favored the league moving the team out of New York," said Hunt. "We had a chance to sell to somebody in Miami, and I didn't think it was worth staying in New York, playing at the Polo Grounds in front of 5,000 people. I was very shortsighted; I didn't know how strong a guy Sonny could be."

Sonny was David A. "Sonny" Werblin, one of the heads of the Music Corporation of America, and the leader of the five-man ownership group that paid $1.3 million to take over the failed franchise. Werblin had given the AFL a hand in securing its first TV deal, with ABC, in 1960. He was smooth, shrewd, connected, self-assured, and wealthy—in short, everything Harry Wismer was not. In the polished persona of Werblin, the entertainment world saw a new breed of showman, less carnival huckster than smooth executive deal maker. Werblin's contacts within the industry were a matter of legend: he had negotiated Ed Sullivan's lengthy CBS deal, as well as representing the likes of Jackie Gleason, Alfred Hitchcock, Jack Benny, and scores of others. In 1965, the show business trade paper *Variety* would say of Werblin that, in his three decades in show business, he "wielded more influence, made more money, made and broke more careers than perhaps any other show biz impresario in New York."

Werblin made an instant splash in the world of football. On April 15, 1963, he announced the launch of the Gotham Football Club, Inc., a reconstituted Titans team with a new nickname (Jets, which neatly rhymed with baseball's Mets), new colors (green-and-white, in honor of Werblin's St. Patrick's Day birthday), a new coach (recently deposed Colts leader Weeb Ewbank), and plans to move into a new stadium (Shea, which they'd share with the Mets, in Queens, right next to the site of the 1964 World's Fair).

After playing one last season in the Polo Grounds, the Jets moved aggressively in the year ahead, first by outbidding the Giants for Ohio State All-America running back Matt Snell. In the summer before the 1964 season, Werblin put his full promotional force to bear on publicizing the Jets. Each of the 3,500 children and teenagers who visited the Jets' training camp went home with an "I'm a Jet Fan" T-shirt. A 110-piece "Jetliner Band" was assembled for the games, all of the stadium ushers at Shea were fitted with green-and-white uniforms, and the team devised a model Jet airplane that rode around the sidelines. On AM radio in New York that summer, the airwaves were dominated by the Jets' radio campaign, featuring Jet-Set Janie, who asked, "Hey, what kind of a name is Weeb?"

By 1964, there were only nine former Titans still on Ewbank's roster, and that 1964 team, with sparkling wideout Don Maynard and redoubtable linebacker Larry Grantham, averaged 42,000 per home game despite a record of 5-8-1. They would have the same record the next two years, but as Ewbank refined the same system he'd had in Baltimore, he was again fashioning the nucleus of a championship football team.

As the Giants' Wellington Mara put it, "We didn't know much about Sonny Werblin when he bought the Jets. And we didn't like what we eventually found out. He was a much more formidable man than Harry Wismer, and we pretty soon sort of knew it meant trouble."

The rebirth of the Jets and the rise of the AFL was well underway by January 24, 1964, when news of the record-breaking deal between the NFL and CBS hit the streets. As Rozelle opened the three bids in his office, Joe Foss sat at the AFL offices, ready to react.

By the time a dejected Carl Lindemann returned to his NBC offices at 11:30 that morning, there was a note on his desk reading, "CALL JOE FOSS." Within hours, Lindemann and Foss were sitting in Werblin's limousine, driving around midtown Manhattan, as Werblin sketched the outline of the AFL's proposed deal: $36 million for five years, from 1965 to 1969, a five-fold increase over the annual rate that ABC was paying the AFL over the life of their contract, which had one more season before expiration. Negotiations intensified throughout the weekend, and by Monday, NBC had agreed in principle. The deal earned the AFL $7.5 million per year, barely half of the NFL's take, but the key to the equation was the number of teams in each league. While the NFL was splitting its $14.1 million per year among fourteen teams, the AFL would be divvying up its $7.5 million among only eight clubs, meaning that in terms of annual television revenue per year, the AFL would close

the gap, *would actually gain ground* on the established league. At 11:00 p.m.
Monday, just three days after the NFL deal with CBS, the AFL executives celebrated with NBC at Toots Shor's, the same spot Rozelle and MacPhail had
toasted their agreement the previous Friday.

Around NFL circles, still giddy with glee and a measure of infallibility after
the CBS deal, the news hit with a bracing force. "Well," said the Steelers' Art
Rooney, "they don't have to call us Mister anymore."

The war between the leagues meant not just more money for players. In some
instances, it signaled the beginning of a greater measure of influence, albeit
still limited, over the conditions under which they played and practiced.

This subtle shift in power was reflected in the NFL in 1963 and 1964, with
the jarring sight of the Cleveland Browns being coached by someone who
wasn't Paul Brown.

As Brown left the stage and Blanton Collier took over, many chose to
judge the new leadership by its effect on a single player, Jim Brown. The results
were immediate. After gaining just 996 yards in 1962, Brown nearly doubled
his output the next year, rushing for 1,863 yards, a new NFL record, as
Cleveland improved to a 10-4 mark (after going 7-6-1 in Paul Brown's
final season).

At the beginning, Collier stuck very close to Brown's program. "It was like
Blanton's mouth was moving, but Paul Brown was talking," said safety Ross
Fichtner. "You would not have known the difference, except for Blanton's
voice. It was as if Paul had written his script."

And yet, somehow, everything was different. Collier, who had always been
considerate, even kind, to his players, brought a new synthesis, combining his
mastery of the game's technical details, a modernistic belief in positive reinforcement (he had a master's degree in educational administration), and a
fierce emotional loyalty (he shook hands with his left hand, because it was "the
closest to my heart").

Collier proved much more able than Brown to cede some measure of autonomy to his players. On road trips, the Saturday night pregame movie continued, but the film was now chosen by team vote, rather than by the coach.
On the field, the checkoff system allowed the quarterback to audible to a different play at the line of scrimmage if the defensive formation threatened the
one called in the huddle. Collier also used a broader lexicon for pass routes, allowing more flexibility within routes and in overall patterns.

The biggest change came in blocking philosophy. Instead of Brown's static blocking assignments, Collier was a proponent of option blocking. As Browns lineman John Wooten explained it, "You come off the ball, place your head in the center of the chest of the defensive player. If he flows to either side, you immediately continue him going—you continue to help him go that way. No matter what the defensive player did, he was going to be wrong." The Browns called it the do-dad block; in Dallas it was the slip wedge. Both techniques shared the same philosophical underpinnings as Lombardi's "run to daylight," and in each instance, players received more flexibility, more freedom, within a system.

"One of the reasons that I welcomed Blanton at the time is because he gave me that ability to truly express myself in the years that he was there," said Jim Brown. "You see coaches sometimes don't want players to have input—and great players must have input. Because when players got together to discuss things, we would deal with the reality of a play, not the theory of it. Blanton had been a coach with Paul, so he knew all that stuff, and he gave us the freedom. And it was the freedom that I remember most. Loved most."

After the 1963 season, Collier sat down for his annual systematic analysis of the previous season. After screening all fourteen games, charting every player's performance in every play of every game, he began to articulate a lingering uneasiness he'd felt throughout the entire 1963 season. Collier came to the conclusion that one reason the club lacked the cohesion it needed was that it was becoming more racially divided than ever. The problem had been simmering for at least a decade, over numerous slights as large as salary inequity to a lingering resentment among the black players on the team over their exclusion at certain club-sponsored cocktail parties. "They don't invite us to the parties and events with the pretty white girls, then we won't go to those community functions, that boring, political shit, where they want to make us look like one big happy family," Jim Brown said. "If we can't go to all the stuff, the fun stuff, then we won't do the fake stuff. They room us together, we'll stay together. We'll play hard, dress right, carry ourselves with class, and be team people. But we don't have to kiss any ass, or take any attitude, to pacify some redneck from Mississippi."

That off-season, Collier summoned his team leaders and issued a directive that he would not tolerate the racial divisions that he was seeing. By confronting the problem openly, and relying on Brown and the other team leaders to solve it, Collier paved the way for a tightly knit Browns team that rolled in 1964, averaging nearly 30 points per game on the way to an Eastern Conference title. In the 1964 title game, the Browns would play host to the heavily favored Baltimore Colts, who had experienced a rebirth in the second year of new head coach Don Shula.

The game itself was a bruising draw in the first half, with neither team able to score in the cold, muddy conditions. But in the second half, the Browns' offense broke through, with Jim Brown's 46-yard run setting up the first of three Frank-Ryan-to-Gary-Collins touchdown passes. Cleveland's defense confounded Johnny Unitas and the league's highest-scoring offense, sealing a 27–0 shutout to give Cleveland its first world championship since Otto Graham's last game in 1955.

In Palm Springs, Paul Brown watched the game with his sons, suffering more or less in silence as his team, with his name, coached by his friend, defeated the Colts. Nearly two years after being fired, the pain was still too fresh. "My father would watch a little bit," said Mike Brown. "Then he'd have to get up and walk out. Then he'd come back in after a while."

The victory validated Modell's decision to fire Paul Brown and hire Collier, but it hinted at something else as well. Even as Vince Lombardi's autocratic style was engendering both fear and loyalty in Green Bay, Collier's success proved there was another way for a coach to reach modern athletes, and provided a framework in which Jim Brown could emerge not just as a star, but a team leader.

In a rudimentary way, the successful racial reconciliation of the Browns players offered a tentative first step—for management, the media, and many pro football fans—toward learning to accept the modern black athlete on his own terms. Just as there were people in Boston who couldn't abide Martin Luther King, Jr., but would learn to appreciate Bill Russell, so it was in Cleveland, where many who were bewildered by Malcolm X and notions of black power would grow to respect Jim Brown. This was not, of course, a substitute for true empathy or political enfranchisement, but it offered a hope, and a beginning toward a broader understanding.

By the mid-'60s, observers were beginning to see within pro football a reflection of the explosion of technology in American society at large. While baseball remained firmly rooted in the cumulative generational traditions known as The Book, the unwritten bible of the sport's wisdom, pro football's coaches seemed to embrace many of the new technologies of the jet age, in the hopes that they might provide some small but crucial advantage.

As far back as the '20s, technology was seen as a potential edge in the ceaseless competition of football. Bert Bell, when managing his father's hotel in Philadelphia, had noticed that desk clerks would signal to housekeeping that a room needed to be cleaned through a device known as a telautograph, which allowed a person sitting in one place to write a message on a slate, which would then be read instantly on another slate elsewhere. Bell used the device while an assistant at Penn in the late '20s, sitting in the press box to spot opponents' formations, and peppering head coach Lou Young on the Penn bench with the details.

Secure phone connections from press box to bench eventually superseded the telautograph, but it wasn't the end of sideline innovations. Lombardi devised his Polaroids-on-a-pulley system in 1953 and, in 1957, Rams GM Pete Rozelle suggested the team try out the technology of the Ampex Corp. (one of his clients during his time with P. K. Macker and Co.), which had just developed a videotape machine that allowed for instantaneous playback. This met with the approval of the film-obsessed Sid Gillman, and in the fall of 1957, Ampex shot videotape of the Rams game.

The next step, taken by the Cowboys in the early '60s, would be toward computers. At the 1960 Olympics in Squaw Valley, Tex Schramm had been fascinated with the information generated by an IBM computer, which calculated statistics, medal standings, and record times. Frustrated during his time with the Rams about how long it took to wade through the avalanche of data on college seniors, Schramm was convinced that computer technology could be used to organize the scouting data, and more reliably isolate the most salient information.

After he returned from the Olympics to start work full-time with the Cowboys, Schramm called IBM and explained what he wanted to do. That's what led him to Salam Quereishi, a computer programming expert in the Service Bureau Corporation, an IBM subsidiary in the burgeoning Silicon Valley of Palo Alto, California. Quereishi, an Indian who'd received a master's degree in mathematics at Aligarh, India, was a cricket fan who knew nothing of American football. After a halting first meeting in which Schramm's gruff manner and Quereishi's thick accent made it difficult for either man to understand the other, they moved more slowly, methodically establishing what Schramm was seeking to accomplish, and how computers might help.

Very quickly, Schramm realized he'd need to remake the scouting form to make it more standardized. For the computer to do its job, the Cowboys needed to pare away the colorful language of the scout's trade: "Quick as a cat" was out, in favor of a form that required more easily defined input. The team eventually came up with a new questionnaire that had fifteen statements, each describing a particular skill. Players were rated from a scale of 1 to 9, a 9 if they fit the scale exactly, down to 1 for not fitting it at all. And because the team was concerned with the more minute gradations on the positive side, the scale was unbalanced, so that a 3 was average.

Computers were a massively expensive undertaking, and Schramm saw that the Cowboys needed partners to share the burden of investment. He selected the Rams and 49ers, teams he knew well (but both from the Western Conference and thus not direct competitors). The 49ers' general manager, Lou Spadia, had heard Dan Reeves express an interest in the potential of computers as well, and both were amenable to making a joint investment. Over the next four years, each team would contribute more than $300,000 to developing a computer model that could evaluate players. It would be four years before the Cowboys would be ready to implement anything, but they had the prospect of a future edge. And in the meantime, they'd formed the first scouting combine, a surreptitious group code-named Troika.

By 1964, Schramm was ready to implement a system that was a synthesis of past and future. It would incorporate the old-school notions of bird-dogging and beating the bushes with the Rams-inspired thoroughness that had become the norm for the league, while adding a third element, a new mind-set that attempted to quantify every opinion.

While the raw data and analysis was shared, each team used it in its own way. Though all three clubs recognized the same five "critical factors" of football skill—"quickness and agility," "competitiveness," "character," "mental alertness," "strength and explosion"—each team weighted these attributes differently. The same was true of the positional characteristics (quarterbacks, for example, were also rated for things like poise and setup, while receivers were graded on their ability to react to the ball and run after the catch).

There would still be—there would always be—room for horse sense and intuition in the Cowboys' system. During the 1964 draft, when it took Dallas six hours to draft Mel Renfro in the second round (the team was checking on the status of his knee and seeking assurances they could sign him), Landry called it a day after Dallas had used their three picks in the sixth round. Armed with the team's master board and a gambler's sense of possibility, Schramm used a seventh-round pick to select Florida A&M wideout Bob Hayes, who months later would win the gold medal in the Olympic 100-meter dash. In the tenth round, he took a flier on Heisman Trophy–winning quarterback Roger Staubach, whose five-year tour of duty upon graduation from the Naval Academy in 1964 had scared most teams off.

And besides the intuiting and organizational intelligence of Schramm, there was also the omnipresent Gil Brandt, a driven man who became a master of the little gesture; he'd send footballs to college coaches, birthday cards with Cowboy stickers to their kids, anything to advance the cause of the Cowboys.

By the fall of 1964, the four years of intense work began to yield results. The Cowboys' executives were on hand for the first printout, as the IBM 7090-7094 computer produced its data on wide sheets of perforated paper. Among the myriad lists that were printed out for Dallas, after players were sorted according to a variety of criteria, was a list of the top fifteen prospects overall. At the top of the list was a cocksure quarterback from Alabama named Joe Namath.

In this case, Schramm knew the computer was working because it had confirmed the wisdom of the best scouts in the field. John Huarte of Notre Dame and Jerry Rhome of Tulsa had finished 1-2 in the Heisman voting in 1964, but in the fraternity of pro football, they were also-rans. Scouts and coaches had been buzzing about Joe Namath for years.

Al Davis was still an assistant with the Chargers in 1962. After an in-season scouting trip to watch an Alabama game in 1962, he came back sporting a sly, knowing grin.

"What'd you see?" asked Gillman.

"I saw a guy who tips the field," said Davis, a dose of portent added to his typical air of certitude.

"What do you mean?"

"This sonofabitch plays like he's going *downhill*," said Davis.

"Who is it?" asked Gillman.

"A kid, Namath, out of Pennsylvania."

At a Jets press luncheon in the fall of 1963, Werblin was raving about Miami quarterback George Mira, who'd just beaten Nebraska in the Gotham Bowl. A few minutes later, a writer asked Ewbank what he thought. "Well, George Mira's really an exciting football player," he said. "But I've known for a long time that those great small guys don't win a championship for you. And they're great quarterbacks—Eddie LeBaron, Frankie Albert, Fran Tarkenton—they're great ball-handlers and all that. But we're interested in a championship." And then, almost as an afterthought, Ewbank added, "The guy that would intrigue us is this junior quarterback at Alabama."

What set the young Joe Namath apart was a strong arm and one of the quickest releases in the history of the sport. The steelworker's son from Beaver Falls, Pennsylvania, also possessed an intuitive ability to read the defenses and "see" the field, combined with—at the time, before a litany of knee operations—uncommon mobility that made him a dangerous running threat.

Sonny Werblin divined something that had eluded the scouts and the computers. He realized that Namath had not only talent, but some ineffable added component of charisma and glamour that could make him something much more than just a skilled rookie quarterback with a big contract. "No one actually knows what it is," Werblin once said to a friend. "But it's people like, when Joe DiMaggio walks into a room. I don't think anyone can put their finger on what exactly it is, but there's no doubt that this guy's got it."

The Giants, with the retirement of Frank Gifford, had free-fallen to the bottom of the NFL East in 1964. They were looking first for a halfback, but had been concerned about the possibility of the Jets getting Namath. Wellington Mara, after reading reports that the Oilers had the rights to Namath—"they were giving people oil wells and gas stations at the time," said Mara—directed the team to go ahead and select running back Tucker Fredrickson. Then came the news: the rights to Namath had been traded to the Jets, in exchange for the rights to quarterback Jerry Rhome.

The Giants desperately tried to trade with the Cardinals for the rights to Namath, but St. Louis was convinced it could sign him. The Cardinals would prove no match for Sonny Werblin. After talking with two representatives from St. Louis in early December, Namath flew out for the Jets' December 6 game at San Diego. Namath had originally hoped for a $100,000 deal, but Alabama coach Bear Bryant convinced him to ask the Cardinals for $200,000, which they'd reluctantly agreed to. But at Namath's first meeting with the Jets and Werblin, the team's opening offer was $300,000. By the time Namath's lawyer, Mike Bite, was done negotiating, Namath was the owner of a Jet-green Lincoln Continental and a three-year contract, believed to be the largest in American team sports at the time, worth $427,000.

The contract, in detail, looked like this:

1965 salary	$25,000
1966 salary	$25,000
1967 salary	$25,000
1968 option year (renegotiable upward)	$25,000
Bonus (deferred)	$200,000
Lawyer's fee (10% of salary package)	$30,000
Lincoln Continental automobile	$7,000
Brother's salary, as scout, for three years	$30,000
Second brother's salary, as scout, for three years	$30,000
Brother-in-law's salary, as scout, for three years	$30,000
TOTAL	$427,000

On January 2, 1965, the day after Namath played brilliantly in Alabama's Orange Bowl loss to Texas, Werblin announced the signing to banner headlines. Namath going to an AFL club was itself big news, but it prompted many other stories—the astounding contract, the predictable response from veterans, such as the Browns' Frank Ryan, fresh off an NFL title, who said "If he's worth $400,000, then I'm worth a million."

If they had overspent, the Jets and Werblin chose the right man on which to do it. Namath was a leader with a swagger, and the combination of his mod, shambling persona along with the full effect of Werblin's promotional skills—in addition to the New York media's heightened interest in pro football—made for an irresistible story. "With that kind of salary," said Bob Hope in a monologue, "Joe Namath will be playing quarterback in a business suit."

After averaging 14,000 fans their final season at the Polo Grounds and 42,000 their first year at Shea, the Jets—with the rookie Namath starting by the third week—began selling out Shea, averaging 58,000 fans on the season.

His first home game drew 55,658, more people than attended the entire Titans' home schedule in 1962. What was also evident was the effect Namath had on the football field. Coming in during the second quarter of the Jets' second regular season game, with the Jets trailing Kansas City 7–3, he rifled a pass to Don Maynard in the middle of the field for his first completion. "A year earlier Don Maynard and Matt Snell had been waiting for something to happen," wrote Jerry Izenberg of the *Newark Star-Ledger*. "The something happened that night. A franchise that had once looked as though it had been stocked at random from the white pages of the Leonia, New Jersey, telephone book, had become a football team."

The Jets' signing of Namath, along with the NBC contract, reinvigorated the AFL, and palpably raised the stakes in the war between the leagues. Though their contract didn't originally call for payments until 1965, NBC advanced five different AFL clubs $250,000 each to help them cover signing bonuses in November of 1964, on the eve of the 1965 draft. Signing players offered a double advantage, in that it had the zero-sum result of bringing a good player into one league and out of the other, and it furthered the perception in the press that "the war" was being won. At the height of the conflict, the battle between the NFL and AFL took on tones of the Cold War, full of secrets, suspicion, and intrigue.

After the loss of players like Buck Buchanan and Bobby Bell in the 1963 draft, and Matt Snell and Southern Cal quarterback Pete Beathard in the 1964 draft, Rozelle began casting about for a way the league could respond with a more concerted effort. On a visit to his old team in the summer of 1964, he found it. In Los Angeles an invigorated Dan Reeves, back in his owner's office for a full year by then, was still obsessing on the draft, still intent on finding an edge. Well ahead of his competitors, Reeves had identified a special need in the reality of a two-league world. "We need to get an earlier start on relationships," he told Rozelle. "It should be like rushing someone in a college fraternity." Reeves had devised a plan, to be implemented by former Rams PR director Bert Rose, in which a group of Los Angeles businessmen, salesmen, advertising executives—each one having a strong background in sales or public relations—would make contact with players the Rams were interested in weeks *prior* to the draft. By establishing a relationship with a player beforehand, Reeves figured, the Rams would have a big head start on whichever AFL team would be vying for the player.

Reeves hadn't even finished explaining the idea before Rozelle, eyes sparkling with excitement, realized that if it could be done successfully in Los Angeles, it could be done throughout the league.

Rozelle asked Reeves if he could borrow Rose and put him in charge of the procedure on a league-wide basis. Thus was conceived "Operation Hand-Holding," better known as the NFL's baby-sitting program. Around the NFL office and throughout the league, a call went out for suitable execs who could strike up relationships with prospective choices prior to the draft, and help close deals when the time came. Rozelle buttonholed his friend Jack Landry at Philip Morris, who brought in many of his friends. "We didn't call them 'babysitters,' " said Rose. "We called them 'NFL representatives.' We put the program into operation in about three weeks. We had about eighty men, about thirty of whom were friends of mine and the rest who were recommended by friends. Almost all of them had the same thing in common: they were sales-oriented. They had to be, since we were asking them to sell the NFL to the best pro prospects in the country."

By November 1964, the program was in place, with more than 100 NFL "field men," each working off of a set of instructions for wooing prospective players. The brochure given to each of the baby-sitters prior to their orientation outlined "The Problem" ("the establishment of a strong competitor to the NFL in the form of a second league") and "The Solution," which theorized that "the addition of just one major sales technique" would improve the chances for signing any player an NFL club drafted. The pitch to be added would be to "mentally condition" prospective draftees to the advantages of the NFL well before the time of the draft.

The jobs offered little beyond prestige: baby-sitters were offered a choice of

$50 per day for the two weeks leading up to the draft, or a gift. The first year the gift was a Zenith radio; in 1965 it was a Tiffany silver platter with the NFL shield engraved on it, along with eight cordial glasses. The baby-sitter program included an embossed "gold card" that essentially gave the bearer the privilege to get on any United Air Lines flight with the cost billed to the league. The gold cards carried some prestige among junior and senior executives in and around New York City. Rozelle's friend Jack Landry, a baby-sitter for all three years of the program, bragged that he used his gold card to avoid a speeding ticket on the Merritt Parkway. It turned out to be an excellent investment for the NFL.

At its most extreme, the baby-sitting program was equal parts auction, fraternity rush, and velvet-gloved kidnapping. One operation found twenty-seven different players stashed away in a hotel in Detroit, and the AFL teams interested in drafting them repeatedly frustrated in trying to get through. In that same 1965 draft, the Kansas City Chiefs had high hopes for signing the dazzling running back Gale Sayers from Kansas. "Sayers, in fact, was married to a girl from K.C.," said Hank Stram, "and he told us he was definitely signing with the Chiefs, when suddenly Buddy Young of the NFL flew into town and simply made off with him." Sayers signed with the Chicago Bears.

Even after losing Sayers, the Chiefs didn't come away empty-handed in the 1965 draft. That draft included one of the war's greatest cases of signing intrigue, and certainly its most legendary, the one for Prairie View A&M wide receiver Otis Taylor. At 6-foot-3, 220 pounds, fast, strong, a physical blocker, and a marvelous athlete with dazzling long strides, Taylor was a spectacular glimpse of the future of the wide receiver position. Decades later, Klosterman would say, "When I first saw Jerry Rice, the person I thought of was Otis Taylor."

The Chiefs were confident they would sign Taylor; Lloyd Wells was a friend of the family, had known Taylor since junior high school, and had remained close to him throughout his college years. But on Wednesday, November 25, in a classic case of baby-sitter subterfuge, the Cowboys descended on the Prairie View campus and invited Taylor and teammate Seth Cartwright away to spend Thanksgiving in Dallas, with handshakes and a kind of pushy cordiality. Of course, the players *could* have insisted they were staying put, or asked to contact Wells, or the Chiefs. But Taylor, while bright, was hardly sophisticated. And the reality of the South in the mid-'60s made it highly unlikely that a twenty-one-year-old shy black college student was going to gracefully extricate himself from the situation.

While Taylor was being squired away, Wells was down in Tennessee, trying to keep tabs on another prospective Chiefs choice. Klosterman, checking with

Taylor as a matter of course, was alarmed when repeated calls to his dorm went unanswered. "So I called Otis's mother," said Klosterman, "and told her that I thought her son had been kidnapped." Wells, having heard from Klosterman, rushed back to Texas and began scouring the Houston area, calling Taylor's mother, his girlfriend, and many of his friends. He learned that Taylor and Cartwright had been taken to a Holiday Inn in Richardson, Texas, just outside Dallas, where they were being watched over by Buddy Young and another baby-sitter. When Wells tried to go see Taylor, he was recognized instantly, and the Cowboys representatives wouldn't let him through the lobby.

Wells was providing periodic reports to Klosterman, who during one call told him, "Just tell Otis his red T-bird is parked outside the Kansas City Chiefs facility, waiting for him." Late that evening, as Taylor looked out the back window of his hotel room, he saw his agitated friend, Wells, hissing to him to get ready to leave. "You don't come with me right now," said Wells, "I am going to lose my motherfuckin' job. Goddamn you!—after all the pussy I done got you! Now get down here, and let's fly to Kansas City; there's a red T-bird waiting for you."

As soon as they were convinced they could escape without detection, Taylor and Cartwright decided to make their break. They didn't even pack their luggage, but instead grabbed their jackets and silently headed out the back patio and over the fence. The next day, after signing his contract, Taylor joined the Chiefs on a trip to New York for a Jets game, then returned with the team to Kansas City and proudly drove his new red Thunderbird home to Houston.

The Chiefs, Oilers, and Jets succeeded with a mixture of canny scouting, superior recruiting and deep pockets. One other team with particular success at fighting the NFL's baby-sitters was the Oakland Raiders. Although they didn't have the financial wherewithal of other clubs, they did have coach and general manager Al Davis, who by 1965 was developing a reputation in both leagues. The *New York Times*'s Bill Wallace wrote that Davis "is the man the NFL management fears most when it comes to signing impressionable and needy collegians."

With his slicked-back hair, Brooklyn roots, and cryptic nature, Davis had both the aura and aspect of the eccentric rock 'n' roll producer Phil Spector, possessing many of the same qualities of mystery and brilliance as the other man. On the same November 1964 weekend of the Taylor heist in Texas, Davis was running the draft for the Raiders. Oakland signed Florida State wide receiver Fred Biletnikoff before officially drafting him, and spirited away the big offensive lineman Harry Schuh, staying one step ahead of the Rams' Hamp Pool (and prompting Pool's telegram to Dan Reeves, "BOO HOO, I LOST MY SCHUH") and its baby-sitters in a chase that started in New Jersey, camped briefly in Las Vegas, and wound up in Hawaii. Davis was already developing a mystique as someone who would do anything within the rules, and perhaps a few things beyond them, to win. As Schuh would recall of Davis, "He'd take his hands, run 'em through his hair, suck air through his teeth, and he'd say, 'Let me just say this, young man. Anything good in this life is worth cheating for.' "

As the civil war in pro football raged on, there was proof of pro football's gain on a wider battleground for the loyalty of American sports fans. In November 1965, Rozelle received a semi-annual report, commissioned by the NFL, from the Louis Harris and Associates polling group, titled "A Study of the Effectiveness of the Television Broadcasting of National Football League Games."

The organization conducted interviews with 3,000 households across the country (about twice the size of a normal Nielsen television survey) during a mid-October weekend, to survey the attitude of sports fans. The second page of the eighty-nine-page report consisted entirely of a two-sentence finding that would have been unthinkable even a decade earlier: "AS OF OCTOBER, 1965, FOOTBALL HAD BECOME AMERICA'S NO. 1 SPORT. THE PREVIOUS APRIL, FOOTBALL HAD FINISHED SECOND TO BASEBALL AS THE NATION'S FAVORITE PASTIME."

Harris concluded his report with the observation: "It is quite clear that the full potential of NFL football has hardly been tapped. Proper promotion and exposure should be able to greatly expand the NFL audience, and television can undoubtedly play a major role in broadening the base of fans."

It was a moment of triumph for Rozelle and the league, and the NFL did its best to trumpet the news. But the elation over the sport's ascendance was tempered throughout the rest of that year and the ensuing off-season with the cumulative fatigue and financial instability that the war between the leagues brought. Rozelle was still confident of ultimate victory and, after six years of the NFL battling the upstart AFL, the costs of war had been accepted as part of the game. But the NFL's optimism and assuredness was beginning to be tempered by frustration over the AFL's resilience and their own vulnerabilities. "We thought the AFL was in trouble," said Art Modell. "They would have lost some franchises. But hell, by then, it was becoming obvious—we would have lost some franchises, too."

As 1966 arrived, the war between the leagues entered its seventh year, more expensive and acrimonious than ever, with no end in sight.

12

A Separate Peace

For six seasons, Tex Schramm had carefully constructed the foundations for what he immodestly considered the ideal football franchise, building the Dallas Cowboys to his own exacting specifications. They were a team possessed of unusual speed and athleticism, and were also among the most intelligent teams in pro football, by virtue of the refinement of the Cowboys' aptitude testing and computer scouting program.

From the start, Schramm received a generous budget from owner Clint Murchison, as well as something he considered even more important—autonomy to construct the team his way. Schramm owned a small percentage of Cowboys stock, and usually sat in for Murchison at owners meetings, where he earned more respect than affection from his peers for his restless intelligence and relentless parsing of the league's bylaws and rulebook. William Clay Ford, the Lions' owner, referred to Schramm as "Loophole."

Before the Cowboys had the record or championships to justify it, rivals sensed an arrogance on their part that was at least partially a reflection of Schramm's self-assured insistence on doing things a certain way. At the team's training camp in Thousand Oaks, California, he brought in legendary Stanford track coach Payton Jordan, not only to help his players refine their running techniques, but to teach the Cowboys' scouts how to use a stopwatch with more precision than others.

That fine-grained attention to detail typified Schramm's fertile mind. Even in the matter of appearance, the Cowboys pointedly did things differently. By 1963, Schramm had grown dissatisfied with the Cowboys' all-white uniforms and white helmets. He wanted a look that was modern, dignified, yet clearly original. What he envisioned was a novel shade of blue, different from what had ever been seen on a football uniform. And in private sessions with the uniform supplier Rawlings, he "asked them to make me some material that had not been made before" in a color that would be at once shiny, discernibly blue, and distinctively Dallas. The unique color, ultimately called metallic blue, could look gray or silver or even light blue, depending on the time of day and light hitting it. Once Rawlings delivered the pants, Schramm summoned the helmet manufacturer Riddell and asked that they match the color to the helmet (a tricky task because of the vastly different materials and textures involved). Both companies were sworn to secrecy and, in the 1964 preseason, Dallas players came out to the Cotton Bowl in metallic blue helmets, crisp white jerseys with blue numerals, and the shiny metallic blue pants, whose texture and sheen called to mind nothing so much as the shimmering spacesuits of the Mercury 7 astronauts.

There were snags along the way, but Schramm was steadfast and Murchison backed him throughout. In *Sports Illustrated*'s 1963 pro football preview, Schramm's buddy Tex Maule picked Dallas to win its conference in only its fourth season. When the team stumbled to a 4-10 record, bringing a storm of criticism of Tom Landry, Schramm wanted to reaffirm his faith in his coach with a ten-year contract. Murchison signed off on it. When Schramm's computer scouting expenses soared to nearly a half-million dollars, Murchison agreed to pay it. But when, a few days before Thanksgiving in 1966, Clint Murchison blanched for the first time, Tex Schramm knew the war between the leagues was getting out of hand.

The buildup to the 1966 draft, held the weekend after Thanksgiving in 1965, set the two leagues on a path of mutually assured destruction. Teams were paying unheard-of sums for top-flight rookies, with contracts totaling $25 million by one estimate. The Oilers' Bud Adams wrote $850,000 in bonus checks alone, and would have written more if the Oilers' most celebrated draftee, All-America linebacker Tommy Nobis of Texas, had chosen to sign with them. Nobis was on the cover of *Life* magazine, and the subject of a national—in fact, interstellar—bidding war. Astronaut Frank Borman, a Houston resident and Oilers fan whose sons were ballboys for the team, spent two weeks in orbit with James Lovell on the historic Gemini 7 mission in December 1965. During one broadcast the astronauts beamed back on national television, Borman said, "Tell Nobis to sign with the Oilers." In the end, Nobis signed with the NFL entry, the expansion Atlanta Falcons.

In many ways, the draft had been a rousing success for the NFL. Baby-sitters were assigned much earlier than in the previous year, and it paid dividends the weekend of the draft. Ostensibly held at the Summit Hotel, just across the street from where the AFL was conducting its draft at the Waldorf-Astoria, the real NFL draft was being run a few blocks uptown, in secret, at the Lexington Hotel, known within the league as "Draft Central." There Bert Rose commanded a support staff in telephone contact with more than 100 baby-sitters, providing progress reports on each player's signability and information on any activity from the AFL. More than 300 players were listed on chalkboards, along with terse notes about each one's status—"Jets offered $225,000 and 4-yr. contract," "Tough!! Wants dough," "Giving rep a hard time," "Denver . . . will set girl friend up in beauty shop"—and teams went through the Draft Central switchboard to contact players.

Baby-sitters were assigned much earlier as the program took full effect in 1965. The NFL bragged of its high success rate and by mid-December announced that it had signed 140 of its draft choices, losing just twenty-eight to the AFL. But that number was deceptive, because many of the players taken in the early rounds by some teams hadn't been first-round caliber. "During those years," said the Cowboys' Gil Brandt, "for a lot of teams, it wasn't about drafting the best player available so much as the best signable player available."

The Cowboys were never one of the have-nots. But on the Tuesday night before the draft, Schramm was up until 4:30 in the morning, negotiating with Chicago attorney Arthur Morse, the agent for Illinois running back Jim Grabowski. Morse was determined to hear offers from both leagues, and wouldn't agree to any offer until they had. Meanwhile, the Packers had already offered a package of more than $500,000 if they selected Grabowski, and that was where Clint Murchison instructed Schramm to drop out.

When the time came for its choice, Dallas chose Iowa guard John Niland. Grabowski wound up going to the Packers, for an $850,000 contract. The unique nature of the publicly owned Packers dictated that all profits went back into the team, rather than to shareholders, meaning that when teams were spending the most money, Green Bay had the most money to spend. Schramm was a competitor at everything he did, and he hated losing a player for any reason. But losing a prized prospect like Grabowski for reasons beyond his control—he simply would have cost too much—left him furious. "That was the first time we couldn't get a player because of money," said Schramm.

By the fall of 1965, it was no longer just a few franchises. The impact was felt even in San Diego, where the Chargers, heading to their fifth AFL championship game in six seasons, were losing money. "It was all so costly," said Sid Gillman. "There were very few men who could stand the losses the owners absorbed in those years. At the draft, we'd have two blackboards, one with the names of players who would cost big money to sign, the other with those who didn't figure to come high. We always drafted from the second board."

After the season, Schramm spent several nights of contemplation in his ranch house in North Dallas, often sitting for hours in his office and looking out at his expansive front yard. Most worrisome to him were the implications of the draft. The Green Bay Packers had just won another world title, their third in five seasons. And Schramm could see that if the situation persisted, the present environment would only empower the league's strongest team, and perhaps lead to the death of some of the weaker ones.

Tex Schramm made up his mind. The battle had gone on long enough. The warrior wanted to fight for a truce.

"It was hard for me," he'd say decades later. "I wanted to kill the AFL. I still do. But from a practical standpoint, the league had to be successful first or the Cowboys' success wouldn't mean anything."

The negotiations toward a merger in 1966 were so complex and secretive, so multilayered and fragmented, that even after the dust had settled, many of the particulars still clung to differing accounts of the entire process. Fitful, furtive negotiations had been going on among owners for years. In addition to the months of back-channel negotiation in the fall of 1959, Lamar Hunt had a few meetings with George Halas in the early 1960s, including visiting the Bears owner in 1963 at his winter home, the Arizona Biltmore Hotel in Phoenix (a meeting Schramm also attended). In 1965, there were extensive negotiations between Carroll Rosenbloom and Ralph Wilson, with one round occurring at La Caravelle, the tony Washington, D.C., restaurant co-owned by Rosenbloom and Joe Kennedy. Bobby and Ethel Kennedy were dining that night and, after spotting the owners at dinner, RFK sent over a menu in which he jotted down mock accusations against the two leagues. (In fact, Kennedy supported a merger, and had offered to help with antitrust legislation after the fact.) Later in 1965, as matters were moving to a head, Schramm joined Carroll Rosenbloom and Art Modell for a meeting in Miami with Ralph Wilson. But when the indemnity price of joining the league was named—Wilson would recall the asking price as $50 million—the Buffalo owner announced the meeting and negotiations over, and walked out.

In virtually every one of these negotiations, the NFL position had been that, while it would consider a merger under certain circumstances, it wasn't interested in taking all the teams, and the two AFL clubs in NFL markets—the Jets and Raiders—would have to move. And so it was, at first, with Schramm. "My original plan was to get Oakland out of Oakland and the New York Jets out of New York," Schramm said. "I talked with Rams owner Dan Reeves in Los Angeles first. To give up New York, there had to be a major city available for the person who had the Jets. Werblin had been with MCA and was close to the Hollywood picture. Los Angeles and Hollywood would be an attraction to him. I talked to Reeves about moving out of L.A. to either San Diego or Phoenix."

But by the spring of 1966, such elaborate scenarios were no longer a realistic option. When Schramm contacted Pete Rozelle and explained that he wanted to try to strike a deal with the AFL, the two of them called Hamilton Carothers, the league's flinty, precise general counsel. Carothers explained that there was no way the leagues could come together without congressional approval, because any and every antitrust suit that the unified league would subsequently face would risk repealing the entire merger itself. While there was a widespread belief in NFL circles that at least two or three AFL franchises still hadn't proved their viability, Carothers pointed out to Rozelle and Schramm that any franchise that was killed or moved would only prompt every legislator in the state to rise up in opposition to the entire merger.

Furthermore, any negotiation with the AFL would need to be top secret, and couldn't afford leaks. "If you open it up," warned Carothers, "everyone will want to put their own conditions on it and nothing will ever get done."

So before making any contact with the AFL, Schramm contacted the Giants' Wellington Mara and the 49ers' president, Lou Spadia, to tell them what he had in mind. Both were opposed to the thought of a truce. "I do recall," said Spadia, "I didn't agree with a single thing he said. I was so opposed to it." But Spadia, as had Mara, said that he'd try to keep an open mind.

For the sake of secrecy, Rozelle agreed that Schramm, representing the NFL, should negotiate with a single person from the AFL. Schramm's counterpart would need to be someone discreet and influential within the other league, someone who could be trusted to keep the negotiations a secret. Then Rozelle let Schramm reach the inevitable conclusion himself.

"I suppose," Schramm said, an expression of mocking distaste curling his lips, "it's got to be Luh-*maahr*."

Kansas City had been slow to embrace the Chiefs, in part because of the negative experience with another itinerant owner, the confounding Charles O. Finley, who had purchased the Kansas City Athletics in 1960, and had been trying to move them ever since. "This is a horseshit town," Finley told Hunt upon their first meeting in 1963. "And no one will ever do any good here."

Hank Stram would euphemistically describe Kansas City in the '60s as "not far removed from its frontier heritage," but the truth was something more pernicious. The city, like so many American cities in the '60s, was a victim of white flight to the suburbs, and an increasingly dangerous environment around the downtown area, where the Chiefs played their home games at Municipal Stadium. This was particularly true in the heart of Kansas City, sprinkled with a series of mean little bars and dimly lit nightclubs, some of them still under Mafia control. In 1964, guard Ed Budde was brutally beaten in a bar fight, with one assailant bashing him repeatedly with a lead bolt. After surgery, Budde had a metal plate in his skull and his return was initially considered doubtful. In 1965, tight end Fred Arbanas was jumped on the street and wound up losing vision in one eye.

A tragedy finally brought the team and the town together. One of the Chiefs' early stars was Mack Lee Hill, from Texas Southern, brought to the club in 1964 by the redoubtable scout Lloyd Wells, who signed him for a $300 bonus. Late in the 1965 season, Hill ruptured a knee ligament after catching a pass against Buffalo. During knee surgery, his body reacted to the anesthesia and developed hyperthermia, rising to 108 degrees. He died on the operating table. The gravity of his death was felt in the city in a way that the Chiefs' struggles on the field hadn't been, and humanized a team that many Kansas City fans had previously held at arm's length.

Just weeks after Hill's death, the Chiefs faced a public relations crisis over comments from Don Klosterman that implied the team might move to Los Angeles. Coming on the heels of another Klosterman statement, comparing Kansas City to purgatory ("it's not exactly heaven and it's not exactly hell"), the comment exacerbated an already strained situation, and forced Klosterman's resignation. In so doing, the Chiefs finally proved they were there to stay. Though Hunt still lived in Dallas, he and his wife, Norma, had rented an apartment in Kansas City that winter, to focus their energies to a season ticket drive that lifted season ticket rolls from 9,550 in 1965 to more than 21,000 in 1966.

On April 4, Schramm called Hunt in Kansas City, and asked if he "might be able to come to Dallas to discuss a matter of mutual importance."

Hunt was returning to Texas two days later anyway, to attend an AFL owners meeting. He scheduled a layover in Dallas before continuing to Houston. On the evening of Wednesday, April 6, Hunt got off his plane at Love Field in Dallas, and walked to the statue of the Texas Ranger in the terminal's lobby. There, waiting adjacent to the statue, reading a paper, was Schramm. They shook hands and quietly moved to the door, walking into the vast Love Field parking lot, where they sat in Schramm's Oldsmobile, and spoke for about forty-five minutes.

Once inside the car Schramm delivered his message. "I think the time has come," he said, "to talk about a merger, if you'd be interested in that."

"Fine," said Hunt, evenly. "I'm interested."

Schramm made a few things clear: the NFL would want Pete Rozelle to be the commissioner of a merged league, further discussions would have to be confidential, and the NFL was finally willing to consider a merger in which all existing franchises would be accepted into the NFL. After their discussion, Schramm said he would call Hunt later in the month to talk more specifically about a framework for a deal. Much of the college signing frenzy had died down by April, and it seemed a good time for truce talks.

For two days, it was. But on April 8, at the AFL owners meeting in Houston, Commissioner Joe Foss resigned (when it became clear that he would be fired by the AFL owners if he didn't). Criticism of Foss had grown steadily over the years, and the success of the NFL's baby-sitting program, and its eleventh-hour landing of Atlanta as an expansion franchise (after the AFL had announced it would move to that city) only weakened his position.

For its new commissioner the league elected Al Davis. This was an alarming choice for leaders in both leagues. For starters, Davis was hardly loved within the AFL. Writing a year earlier in *Sports Illustrated*, Bud Shrake noted that outside of Oakland, "it is not certain where Al Davis would finish in a popularity contest among sharks, the mumps, the income tax and himself. If the voters were the other American Football League coaches, Davis probably would be third, edging out income tax in a thriller." But still chastened over the results of the 1966 draft, the majority of AFL owners decided Davis would be the perfect man to run the league in the event that the war continued.

While Davis promised to take the fight to the NFL, Hunt was secretly discussing peace with Schramm. On May 3 Schramm informed Hunt that the NFL would likely want $18 million—$2 million from each of the nine AFL teams (Miami would be the league's newest franchise in 1966)—and the expansion fee that would be charged to a tenth AFL team in 1968. Hunt asked for a week to think about it and, when they met again at Hunt's home, on May 10, he said he believed an agreement could be reached. With this hopeful sign, Schramm called Rozelle to tell him that there was a framework for a possible agreement. With an owners meeting coming the next week, Schramm and Rozelle discussed the best way to present the possibility of a merger to the rest of the league.

Since the very first stipulation set by the NFL was that Rozelle would be the commissioner of the combined leagues, there was no easy way for Hunt to tell Davis that he was working on an agreement that would cost Davis his job. So while Hunt privately mentioned some details of the negotiations to Bills owner Ralph Wilson and Patriots owner Billy Sullivan, Davis was left out of the loop.

Meanwhile, Davis was already looking ahead to the logical next battle, the 1967 draft. His first hire was Ron Wolf, a hard-bitten, slow-talking personnel man who'd assisted Davis in Oakland, and was brought to New York to oversee the league's next round of recruiting. Wolf had learned to cope with his boss's volatile nature, his temper ("I've been called 29 different kinds of motherfuckers"), and his habit of releasing information in the slightest of doses. He also knew that if Davis had a plan, it could work.

Davis also brought in fellow Syracuse alum Val Pinchbeck, who'd been working as the school's sports publicity director, the young Texas sportswriter Mickey Herskowitz, and CBS publicist Irv Kaze. With his staff in place, Davis began preparing for the AFL's response to the NFL's baby-sitter program. Within the walls of the AFL offices, where frenetic action took place, Davis was infamous for telling his charges only what they absolutely needed to know and sometimes not even that. His asides and portentous explanations added to the heightened tension, and Davis's perpetual shroud of secrecy became a running joke. When Herskowitz and Kaze would meet in the halls, one or the other would blurt out, "By Thursday, you'll understand everything." It's difficult to know what Davis might have done on his own. But such questions became a moot point, in the event, because within six weeks after taking office, the NFL provided Davis and the AFL with a plausible reason to escalate the war.

For nearly seven years, the two leagues had honored the unwritten agreement that, while they would compete for incoming rookies through their respective drafts, they would not attempt to sign the other league's veterans. That policy came to an end in May when the Giants signed the Buffalo Bills' soccer-style placekicker Pete Gogolak, who had been the second leading scorer in the AFL during the Bills' title seasons of 1964 and 1965. Gogolak kicked a pro record 28 field goals while playing out the option year of his contract in 1965. The Giants, by contrast, had made just four out of 26 field goal attempts during the 1965 season.

At the Winged Foot Country Club, the Giants' Wellington Mara had grown friendly with Fred Corcoran, the agent for Gogolak. When Corcoran told Mara his client was interested in the Giants, Mara didn't flinch. New York signed Gogolak to a three-year, $96,000 contract, the largest ever for a placekicker. It was, arguably, the single most provocative act of the decade in the war between the leagues.

The signing of Gogolak was still a closely guarded secret when the NFL owners began their spring meetings at the Shoreham Hotel in Washington, D.C., on May 16. The next day, after a morning session in which the owners argued about the merits of a league-wide scouting system, Rozelle called for a brief executive session before a lunch break.

Rozelle stood up before the group and said, "I have an announcement to make . . ."

Down near the end of the conference table, an already steaming Lombardi, who'd learned about the signing earlier that morning, looked across at Lou Spadia and Art Modell and said, "You're not gonna *believe* what you're about to hear about my best friend . . ."

As Mara sat silently by and listened, Rozelle announced the Giants' signing of Gogolak—a shock itself to most owners—then added that as there was nothing in the league's bylaws to prevent a team from signing a free agent who had played out his option, the league would permit the signing.

"This is a disgrace!" announced Lombardi. "Wellington, I can't believe that you would do something like this, to put us all into jeopardy!"

"Goddamnit," said Carroll Rosenbloom to Mara, "if you'd wanted a kicker, why didn't you just ask me? I'd have given you one."

Sitting at the table, Schramm finally understood why Rozelle had seemed so tepid about his merger plan. "What I never realized until this whole thing broke out—and I can understand because he was so much in the middle of it—is really how badly Pete wanted to beat them and didn't want a merger," said Schramm. "And I never realized that until the moment he announced he was approving the Gogolak thing."

That afternoon in Detroit, Al Davis was sitting in the insurance office of

Bills owner Ralph Wilson when the news broke. Wilson was stunned and furious about losing his star kicker, and even angrier at the NFL's precedent-setting provocation.

Davis leaned back in his chair and smiled at Wilson, and said, "We just got our merger."

"What? What are you talking about?" asked a perplexed Wilson.

"Look," said Davis. "If we go out and sign their players, we'll destroy them, and they'll come to the table."

Davis's aide Ron Wolf was in San Francisco when he got the news. He turned to his wife and said, "They have no idea what they've just done."

After news of the Gogolak signing broke, Schramm quickly called Hunt to reassure him that, despite appearances to the contrary, the NFL owners were nearing an understanding, and the senior league was acting in good faith. But since the negotiations were going on without Davis's knowledge, there was little that Hunt could do to stop Davis from his own counterattack.

Davis returned that night to the Plaza Hotel in New York, and in a cryptic interview told the *New York Times*'s Arthur Daley, "This is something I've been aware of, and I anticipated the probability. But you don't make threats at a time like this. Our answer will be in action. This is not the time to speak."

Within twenty-four hours of the report of Gogolak's signing, Davis devised a plan of response. "We pinpointed about ten players of the National Football League that we would sign them to contracts for the ensuing year if they played out their option or, this was something new, sign them to what we called 'future contracts,' even if they had a year or two left on their present contract," said Davis. "Then we decided that there was one team we would hold hostage. And if we held them hostage, we thought that their league would get the message to either leave us alone, or else let's get together. One or the other." Nearly forty years later, Davis revealed his target, which should have been obvious to any student of the works of Machiavelli. "It was the Rams," Davis said. "And the reason it was the Rams was because their owner, Dan Reeves, was beloved. And Tex and Pete had a strong affinity for Dan, had started their careers with him in Los Angeles."

The NFL owners who were worried about how Davis might respond didn't have to wait long to find out. By the time the meetings adjourned, there were reports that Sid Gillman and the Chargers had offered contracts to three New York Giants players. Weeb Ewbank, denying any coordinated campaign, said the NFL players were the ones contacting the AFL.

On the afternoon of the final session of the owners meeting, Rozelle addressed the owners in executive session and confided to the group for the first time that negotiations with the AFL had reached a critical juncture. He then gained approval for a six-man committee—Schramm, Mara, Spadia, Lombardi, Bidwill, and Rosenbloom—and instructed that group to determine their plan of action among themselves. Upstairs in one of the Shoreham suites, the group discussed the next course of action, with Mara and Spadia holding out for a continued fight. During the meeting, a glum Spadia lashed out at Lombardi, who, he said, "had promised never to vote for a merger. Our friendship ended that day."

Mara put an arm around his distraught friend Spadia. "It was bad enough when the enemy was shooting at us," he said. "Now we've got our friends shooting at us, too."

The meeting was invested with a desperate urgency, because an awareness of Mara's decision to drop the gauntlet had made the next chapter obvious: if they didn't do something to bring peace, the ensuing war, especially one in which the enemy forces were led by Davis, would mean that not all of the owners would be in the same room by 1967. As they talked among themselves, more matter-of-factly, it became clear that the only logical choice was a merger.

"The only teams that I dealt with that were anti-merger were San Francisco—I didn't blame them—and New York," said Stormy Bidwill. "Those are the only two that I remember being very anti. Everybody else may have put on a little bullshit but they wanted a merger of some kind. Now, they didn't want to give away the store, but they definitely wanted a merger."

As the meeting ended, Lombardi and Rosenbloom pulled Schramm aside and gave him a message for Rozelle. "Tell him we want to go ahead," said Lombardi.

"We want him to lead us," Rosenbloom told Schramm, before adding, "but we're *going,* with or without him."

Arriving at Rozelle's suite, Schramm sat down with his friend, who had been huddling with Marshall Leahy in another room. "We reached a decision," Schramm said. "We want the merger, and we want you to lead us in the merger. But if you're not going to lead us in the merger, then we're going to have to go ahead without you."

Rozelle, stunned and furious, rose to his feet and excused himself to go into the bathroom.

Hands on the sink, staring into the mirror, Pete Rozelle considered all that he'd fought for and all that he'd gained. A man with an oversized ego might have stormed out in a huff, or resigned. But Rozelle's next move, one Schramm would never forget, left him more convinced than ever that Rozelle was the right man to lead them.

Schramm waited in silence for a few minutes, then heard the faucet running, and Rozelle splashing water on his face. Rozelle returned to the living room of the suite, face set in determination, and, walking toward the door, said, "If that's what they want, let's go do it."

The next morning, when the committee of owners met again, this time in New York, with Rozelle present, Schramm once more expressed his desire to find some way to get the Jets and Raiders to move to other markets. Hunt hadn't agreed to such a condition (and would say later that Schramm had never mentioned it to him), but Schramm suspected the AFL wanted an agreement badly enough to capitulate.

Wellington Mara doubted that, and argued that Werblin's team was so entrenched in the city, the point was by now moot. "If I try to get the Jets to move," he said, "I'd be crucified."

At that point, it was decided that the Giants and 49ers should receive some sort of compensation, since the violation of their territorial exclusivity was against league bylaws. The figure that Schramm suggested, as a way to placate the two teams, was to simply funnel all $18 million of the AFL's indemnity payments to the two clubs, $10 million for the Giants and $8 million for the 49ers. But Mara still wasn't satisfied, arguing that it was one thing to have Joe Namath across town playing in another league but something else entirely to have Joe Namath across town as a member of the National Football League. In exchange for the Giants' acquiescence, the league awarded New York the first pick in the next draft, with a stipulation that they would take a quarterback. (The Giants could trade it only if they were trading for a starting quarterback.)

The support for a merger in principle now existed. After that meeting, the future shape of pro football depended largely on the outcome of a secret race. On one side, Schramm and Hunt were engaged in their increasingly detailed negotiations to bring about the terms for a peace. On the other side, Davis, unaware of the truce talks, was waging his concerted response to the Gogolak signing, a war of retribution on behalf of the AFL that at times threatened to make any peace impossible.

On May 23, just three days after the NFL owners meetings had adjourned, the AFL had its first response. In Oakland, the Rams' young quarterback, Roman Gabriel, met Raiders coach John Rauch at the Oakland airport, and received a bonus check for $100,000, then signed a contract for four years at $75,000 per year, for a package of $400,000. The deal, announced by the Raiders on May 26, quickly brought a retort from the Rams stating *they* had just signed Gabriel to a contract renewal.

And it was in that tense context that the events of the Memorial Day weekend played themselves out. Hunt was up in Indianapolis, to watch the Indy 500, while Schramm and Rozelle hid out in Schramm's house in Dallas, drawing up the key points of the proposed agreement, in an attempt to "finalize the terms of the plan" to present to Hunt by the end of the weekend. Meanwhile, Al Davis, amid periodic cryptic comments to his staff—"The guerrilla wins if he doesn't lose"—was working on another stage of his concerted response to the Gogolak signing.

At Davis's behest, Don Klosterman—by now the GM of the Houston Oilers—turned his attention to John Brodie, the 49ers' starting quarterback, whose contract was up for renewal. Klosterman had known Brodie for ten years, understood how fanatical the quarterback was about golfing (he'd played two years on the PGA tour) and believed he could be wooed.

"John," he told Brodie by phone, "we're in a position down here to offer you some cash. We can set things up so that if you want to, all you'll ever have to do is play golf and drink beer and gamble."

That Friday, May 28, Brodie headed to Houston along with his friend and unofficial financial adviser, a securities broker named Sonny Marx. After they checked into Room 306 of Houston's Warwick Hotel, under the name John Marx, they were visited by Klosterman and the quintessential Texan Bud Adams. Adams made an opening offer of a $500,000 contract for three seasons, and hung in there when Marx audaciously countered with the statement that Brodie should be making closer to a million. After haggling for a bit, Adams wrote out the terms on a cocktail napkin: "The AFL agrees to pay John Brodie $250,000 a season for three seasons."

With that staggering offer on the table, Brodie called 49ers general manager Lou Spadia, whom he tracked down at a hotel in Portland, just getting ready to leave for his son's graduation. In their previous conversation, just days earlier, Brodie had asked for a contract of $40,000 per year, while Spadia had held firm at $38,000.

When Spadia got the call, he was initially delighted. "John!" he said. "What are you doing in Portland?"

"I'm not in Portland," said Brodie, "I'm down in Houston."

"What are you doing in *Houston?*"

Brodie explained his trip, and the ensuing contract negotiations with the Oilers.

"Lou," he said, "they want to pay me $250,000 a year for three years."

There was a moment of silence on the line. And then Spadia said, "Gee, John . . . does that include preseason games?"

Later that night, an apoplectic Lou Spadia phoned Dallas with the news about Brodie's offer.

"And so here it is," recalled Schramm, "we've worked this all out and now we've got the Brodie situation. And so we want to get ahold of Lamar, and he's up in *fucking Indianapolis* at this race. Well, if you've ever tried to find anybody up there, it's damn near impossible. We finally got him, and I told Lamar, 'Look, I can't hold these people together. They're going to get mad and they're going to do something, and if that happens, the merger is gone. You gotta stop this sonofabitch.'"

Hunt called Bud Adams and Klosterman, to try to dissuade them from going through with the signing. By now, Davis knew some merger negotiations were going on, but wasn't aware of the particulars. He was angry at being left out of the loop, and determined that continuing his program would only increase the AFL's bargaining power.

Klosterman called Davis, who was supervising other negotiations, trying to sign Jim Ninowski from Cleveland and Sonny Jurgensen from Washington. "Lamar called," Klosterman reported to Davis, "and said he really doesn't want us to go through with this."

Davis was pensive. "Did you give him your word?"

"Yeah, I'm afraid I did."

Davis paused for a moment, considered the circumstances, and then said, "Fuck it! Sign him anyway."

Davis then called Hunt and explained that whatever he was working on, his bargaining position would be stronger with Brodie signed than it would be without his signature. In this, he was probably right. San Francisco's front office was shell-shocked, and by now resigned to the merger. In the days ahead, Lou Spadia became adamant about retaining Brodie, above all else. "I just want my quarterback," he repeated.

Hunt returned from Indianapolis late the night of May 30, and the next morning, they met at Schramm's house. Speaking from five pages of notes he compiled with Rozelle, Schramm outlined the plan. Writing on a legal pad, Hunt transcribed the specifics. When he finished, Schramm said, "There it is.

If you accept, this deal has been approved by every NFL club. If you have to alter it too much, it will blow up."

Hunt flew to New York later that day, to meet with the AFL owners, many of whom balked at the figure of $18 million. "They should pay us," said Werblin. But Hunt knew a good deal when he saw one. "I was just beginning to understand the true value of money," he said. With twenty years to pay off the total, it amounted to a payout of $2 million per team over the twenty years, with much of the money coming from accrued interest. This paled in comparison to the instantly increased value and revenues for each team in the league, as well as the reduced costs of a stabilized environment with a common draft.

Over the next few days, the negotiation got down to the fine-grained details of the agreement. Hunt called Schramm back by phone and outlined the twenty-six points with which the AFL took issue, almost all of them involving the wording of the agreements between the two New York clubs and San Francisco and Oakland. On Sunday night, June 5, meeting back in Dallas at Schramm's home, they ironed out nearly all of the remaining sticking points. By the morning of June 7, when Rozelle gained approval for the merger through a telephone poll of owners, rumors were running rampant and the press was staked out at the NFL offices. Rozelle took to taking service elevators in and out of the building to avoid detection. Carothers advised releasing the information as soon as possible, before the rumor mill damaged the fabric of the relationship.

On the evening of June 7, while Hunt was traveling to Washington for more secret meetings, Billy Sullivan sat down with Al Davis and told him he was about to be out of a job. Davis was angry, about being excluded from the negotiations, and about the terms of the agreement. "I wanted a merger," Davis said. "But I didn't like the terms of the merger. I thought it would be great because we can compete against those guys."

Later that night, on the eve of the announcement, Hunt, Schramm, Rozelle, and Kensil converged in Washington, D.C., still eluding the press. At the Sheraton-Carlton Hotel, in a suite registered under the name of Ralph Pittman, they spent much of the night banging out the wording for the press release the next day, finally finishing at 3:00 a.m. Throughout the evening and the next day, Carothers fielded phone calls from team lawyers, one who asked to vet a copy of the signed agreement. "There *is* no signed agreement," said Carothers. "It's all just notes, from Tex and Lamar."

The press release came out that afternoon, Wednesday, June 8, with young NFL interns Peter Hadhazy and Joe Browne delivering the news by hand to the AP and UPI offices. It read:

JOINT STATEMENT
NATIONAL AND AMERICAN FOOTBALL LEAGUES

The NFL and AFL today announced plans to join in an expanded major professional football league. It will consist of 26 teams in 25 cities—with expectation of additional teams in the near future.

The main points of the plan include:

- Pete Rozelle will be the commissioner.
- A world championship game this season.
- All existing franchises retained.
- No franchises transferred from present locations.
- Two new franchises no later than 1968.
- Two more teams as soon thereafter as practical.
- Inter-league pre-season games in 1967.
- Single league schedule in 1970.
- A common draft next January.
- Continued two-network TV coverage.

After sending them out to drop the news, Rozelle called CBS Sports president Bill MacPhail, who still hadn't heard the news. "Got a pencil handy?" Rozelle asked. "Then take this down . . ." He then disclosed the outline of the merger agreement.

"You can't mean it!" barked MacPhail when Rozelle reached the part about the AFL-NFL championship game, which effectively reduced the NFL championship game, for which CBS was paying $2 million a year, into a semifinal contest. "It can't be true!" Rozelle assured him that it was true, and that a press conference would be held later that day, at the Warwick Hotel in New York.

Furious, MacPhail demanded, "Why didn't you notify me that you were planning this?"

"Because," said Rozelle calmly, "it was our business and nobody else's."

As news of the agreement filtered out over the radio, New York's news and sports media geared up for the press conference. Late that afternoon, with the AFL offices abuzz with the victorious news, Val Pinchbeck, suit coat on, preparing to leave, saw an unusually subdued Al Davis sitting alone in his office.

"Aren't you going to the press conference?" Pinchbeck asked.

When Davis shook his head no, Pinchbeck asked why.

Davis looked at his assistant gravely and asked, "Remember Yalta?"

There was one matter left to be dealt with, and that was the task of convincing Representative Emanuel Celler and the House Judiciary Committee to approve the merger. As the fall wore on and the owners grew increasingly alarmed, it became clear that Celler had no intention of letting the legislation pass. At a hearing in the Rayburn House Office Building on October 11, 1966, Celler upbraided Rozelle and Hamilton Carothers, refusing to let the bill out of committee.

Rozelle, seeking a way to break the logjam, called his friend David Dixon to see if he knew a North Louisiana congressman on the committee. "For someone as sophisticated as Pete, he was rather naive when it came to politics," said Dixon. "The idea that any congressman from Louisiana was going to be able to change Emanuel Celler's mind about anything was ludicrous."

Dixon had a better idea. House Majority Leader Hale Boggs, who'd been a fraternity brother of Dixon's at Tulane, was seeking to regain some popularity after his vote in support of the civil rights bill caused his electoral majority to drop from 67 percent to 55 percent. Dixon sent his political adviser, David Kleck, up to Washington the next day, to impress upon the patrician Boggs, no sports fan, that it would help his cause to push the bill through, especially since doing so would virtually guarantee an NFL franchise in New Orleans.

The NFL had been eyeing New Orleans for its next franchise anyway. So a thinly veiled quid pro quo was offered—a franchise for New Orleans in exchange for the exemption—and Boggs went into action, circumventing Celler by attaching S. 3817 to a budget bill sure to pass in both houses.

The final approval would come October 21. Walking up the stairs of the Rotunda, when the vote looked like a sure thing, Rozelle was his usual humble self. "Congressman Boggs, I don't know how I can ever thank you enough for this. This is a terrific thing you've done."

Boggs had been a veteran of Louisiana politics too long to let such transparent politesse go unremarked. "What do you mean you *don't know* how to thank me?" he said. "New Orleans gets an immediate franchise in the NFL."

"I'm going to do everything I can to make that happen," Rozelle assured him.

At that, Boggs stopped and turned on his heels, heading back to the committee room. "Well, we can always call off the vote while you—"

Rozelle took two giant strides after Boggs, turned him gently around and said, "It's a deal, Congressman. You'll get your franchise."

"If this doesn't work out," said the patrician Boggs, by now perturbed, "you will regret this for the rest of your fucking life!"

It worked out, signed by another presidential football fan, Lyndon Baines Johnson, who'd taken to ordering highlight reels from NFL Films sent to the movie theater at the White House. The NFL and AFL got their merger and, a week later, New Orleans got its NFL franchise.

————

The "cause" of the merger would be debated for years. Both leagues seemed to be operating on twin tracks. The NFL had a hard-line commissioner determined to fight while at the same time authorizing a secret bargaining initiative from one of his closest friends, another hard-liner who had decided the time had come to merge. The AFL, formed largely because of its owners' unrequited interest in joining the NFL, had spent seven years trying to prove worthy of the older league. Then those same owners hired as commissioner a man seemingly intent on bringing down the NFL at any cost. One commissioner, Rozelle, would have lost his job if he hadn't brought about the merger, while another commissioner, Davis, lost his job because he *did* help to bring it about.

In retrospect, a few events do stand out as crucial. It was important that Schramm had opened communication lines with Hunt prior to the Gogolak signing, because establishing a baseline of good-faith bargaining would have been nearly impossible in the weeks after, with the Davis-choreographed "massive retaliation" that followed.

It was significant that the cool, deliberate Hunt was the pivot on which the AFL owners and NFL owners communicated. Men on both sides of the battle would lose their patience and bark at him, but Hunt, even-tempered through it all, was in a position to moderate the rhetoric of both sides.

And if Davis's machinations behind the scenes in the weeks after May 17 didn't help the spirit of the negotiations, they certainly hastened the endgame. The two sides had been talking for years, but the prospect of seeing the likes of Gabriel, Brodie, and the Bears' Mike Ditka in AFL uniforms brought a grave urgency to the negotiations that the older league's owners had never felt before.

After a rocky courtship, the NFL and AFL were finally engaged, and would now spend four seasons before their union was fully consummated. In dramatic terms, the merger was a false ending, for it only served to bring the combatants into closer proximity. Wellington Mara described the atmosphere at the first joint meeting as akin to that "on board the USS *Missouri.*" After six seasons of bitter one-upmanship and bloated contracts, the two leagues headed into the 1966 season as familiar enemies. The war was over, but the rivalry was destined to linger. Now, however, the coming battles would be determined on the field.

Cleveland Rams players (*top*) bundle in straw for warmth amid the brutal conditions at the 1945 National Football League championship game. Within weeks after the first postwar title game, Bert Bell (*above*, early in his tenure) was named the NFL's new commissioner, and Rams owner Daniel F. Reeves moved the champions to Los Angeles. In the spring of 1946, Reeves (*right*) arrives in Los Angeles on the Twentieth Century Limited.

Above: Paul Brown (*center*), flanked by his staff during one of his early training camps with the Cleveland Browns. Joining Brown are, from left, Howard Brinker, Blanton Collier, Weeb Ewbank, and Fritz Heisler.

Pro football integrated again in 1946, with the Rams' signing of Kenny Washington (*below left,* during training camp at Compton Junior College) and Woody Strode. The AAFC was also integrated, with the Browns' signing of the bruising fullback Marion Motley (*below right*) and Bill Willis, both future Hall of Famers.

COURTESY ST. LOUIS RAMS

COURTESY CLEVELAND BROWNS

COURTESY ST. LOUIS RAMS

Eddie Kotal (*above*), the first full-time traveling scout in the NFL, was on the road 200 days a year for the Rams and discovered such gems as Grambling graduate Tank Younger (*left*), the first player from a historically black college to play in the NFL.

After dominating the AAFC for four seasons, the Browns joined the NFL in 1950 and won the league title, with Lou Groza's field goal sealing a 30–28 championship-game win over the Rams.

Pro football comes of age: On the afternoon of December 28, 1958, in Yankee Stadium, Alan Ameche scores to lift the Colts to a sudden-death title-game win over the Giants . . .

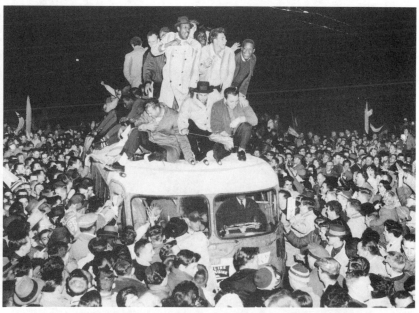

. . . and later that evening, the team returned to a joyous riot in Baltimore, where 30,000 fans greeted the Colts (in bus, after deplaning) at Friendship Airport.

Bert Bell, at his home in Narberth, working on the intricacies of the upcoming season's schedule. Bell's death in October 1959 left the league in a state of flux that would last for months.

For their new commissioner, the owners elected thirty-three-year-old Rams general manager Pete Rozelle (shown here accepting congratulations from the Bears' George Halas, the Eagles' Frank McNamee, the Redskins' George Preston Marshall, and the Eagles' Joe "Jiggs" Donoghue).

American Football League commissioner Joe Foss sits in the center, flanked by the AFL's eight owners—from left, Wayne Valley, Billy Sullivan, Harry Wismer, Bud Adams, Cal Kunz, Ralph Wilson, Lamar Hunt, and Barron Hilton—collectively known as "the Foolish Club."

Evidence of Rozelle's mastery of TV included the NFL's first joint television agreement, signed with CBS's Bill MacPhail prior to the 1962 season.

Rozelle's closest aide was Jim Kensil (*right*), with whom he composed the press release announcing that the NFL would play its games the Sunday following John F. Kennedy's assassination. Despite criticism over the decision, Rozelle was named just weeks later as *Sports Illustrated*'s Sportsman of the Year for 1963.

The NFL was years ahead of competing leagues, as indicated by two brilliant hires in the '60s. Ed Sabol (*above left*) brought his Blair Motion Pictures company in-house, where it was renamed NFL Films. The graphic artist David Boss (*right*) became the guiding creative force of NFL Properties, which marketed the game in unprecedented ways.

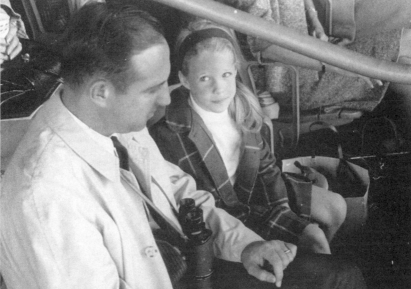

Even as Rozelle was smoothly guiding the NFL's polished ascendance, his marriage was falling apart, largely due to the alcoholism of his wife, Jane. Behind the scenes, Rozelle spent more time with his daughter, Anne (*above*, at a 1966 game), whom he quietly raised on his own.

The seven-year war with the American Football League came to an uneasy truce on June 8, 1966, when Rozelle announced that the NFL and AFL would come together. Flanking him at the press conference (*left*) were Tex Schramm and Lamar Hunt, the lead negotiators for the NFL and AFL, respectively.

In the '60s, the game changed on the field as well. The irrepressible Jim Brown, running during Cleveland's 27–0 win over Baltimore in the 1964 NFL title game, led the Browns to a title two seasons after Paul Brown had been replaced by Blanton Collier.

Tension was high prior to the first AFL-NFL world championship game, played January 15, 1967. After the Packers' 35–10 rout of the Chiefs, Rozelle presented Vince Lombardi with the trophy (*right*) that four years later would be renamed in his memory.

Two contrasts in quarterbacking styles and lifestyles: Johnny Unitas (*left*) embodied the brush-cut, nononsense self-reliance of the '50s, while Broadway Joe Namath's long hair, white shoes, and insouciant demeanor typified an entirely different era and mind-set.

Namath, holding forth by the hotel pool during the week leading up to Super Bowl III, helped engineer the biggest upset in the sport's history just days after guaranteeing it.

A year later, the AFL struck again in Super Bowl IV, as Kansas City dominated Minnesota, 23–7. The Chiefs' Otis Taylor and Len Dawson (*below left*) combined for a remarkable playoff run, and Chiefs coach Hank Stram (*below right*) was immortalized in NFL Films' highlight show of the game.

In 1970, pro football hit prime time and proved its muscle when *Monday Night Football* became a surprise hit. By 1971, the team of Howard Cosell, Don Meredith, and Frank Gifford had become celebrities in their own right, as much of a focus as the game on the field.

The Colts' graceless disposal of Johnny Unitas provided a sad final chapter to his career in Baltimore and foreshadowed even worse times in the contentious tenure of new owner Robert Irsay.

On Christmas Day 1971, the Kansas City Chiefs' Willie Lanier and Jim Lynch walk off the Municipal Stadium field after the longest game ever, a 27–24 double-overtime playoff loss to Miami.

Pomp and circumstance: Coach George Allen shows the nation's First Fan, President Richard Nixon, around the Redskins compound during Nixon's visit to pump up the morale of his beloved team in 1971.

Though the Steelers won more titles, the Cowboys were the most influential, visible team of the '70s. Tex Schramm (*above*) lifts the team's second Super Bowl trophy after the 1977 season. Along the way, Roger Staubach (handing off to Duane Thomas, *below left*) ushered in a new era for quarterbacks, and Schramm made icons of the team's cheerleaders (*below right*), shown in their debut season, 1972.

The Raiders cultivated an outlaw persona in the '70s, a reflection of their Machiavellian owner, Al Davis (*above left*), and the intimidating presence of their best players, such as Hall of Fame guard Gene Upshaw (*above right*).

On May 7, 1982, Davis and his attorney, Joseph Alioto (*right*), greet the press after the Raiders and the Los Angeles Coliseum won their case against the NFL, prompting an era of franchise free agency that would last for nearly fifteen years.

In the aftermath of the decision, the way was clear for the antics of Robert Irsay (*below left*), the Colts' owner, who evacuated the club under cover of darkness on the night of March 29, 1984, heading to Indianapolis and leaving little behind save a couple of equipment trunks (*below right*) and a stunned community wondering how it could recover its civic treasure.

After Bill Walsh (*above left*) was passed over for the Bengals job by Paul Brown, he wound up in San Francisco, where he changed the face of the pro game, winning three Super Bowls in ten seasons, including two at the expense of the Bengals and a chastened Paul Brown (*above right,* with his sons, Pete and Mike).

The one high point of a brutal decade for the league was the NFL's victory in court over the USFL, celebrated by Rozelle and attorney Frank Rothman (*left*) in July 1986. By the end of the decade, after twenty-nine years at the helm, Rozelle was ready to turn over the reins to his successor and longtime trusted legal adviser, Paul Tagliabue (*right*).

A lone Browns player watches in the surreal setting of Cleveland Stadium just a day after the Browns' plan to move to Baltimore was reported. Owner Art Modell became a pariah. Five years later, Modell (*right*) lifted the Lombardi Trophy as the owner of the Baltimore Ravens.

As the millennium dawned, a more assured Paul Tagliabue (*above*), having sagely handled the aftermath of the Browns' move, faced a range of challenges in managing the league's rapid growth and internal contradictions. Among his concerns: the continued growth and artistic creativity enjoyed by Steve Sabol (*below right*) and NFL Films, and the bottom-line aesthetic of entrepreneurial maverick Jerry Jones (*below left*).

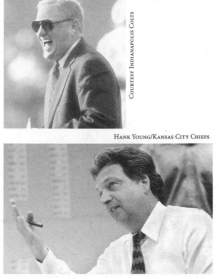

Ray Lewis of the Ravens was as much a gladiator as predecessors such as Dick Butkus, but he had a distinctly different style when taking the field for introductions.

The best of the league's administrators, such as the Colts' Bill Polian (*top*) and the Chiefs' Carl Peterson (*above*), combined football intuition with a CEO's smarts.

The NFL's place in the national culture was further confirmed late in 2001. Gathered together in Kansas City for the first weekend's games following the 9/11 attacks were, from left, Wellington Mara, Gene Upshaw, Paul Tagliabue, and Lamar Hunt.

Many felt that coaching was more important in football than in any other sport, and that coaches were more important in the modern salary-cap era than at any other time in the NFL. Old-school practitioners included the Cowboys' tough Bill Parcells (*above left*) and the Chiefs' tough-loving Dick Vermeil (*above right*), while two new-school paragons were the Ravens' combustible, technocratic Brian Billick (*below left*) and the Colts' serene, focused Tony Dungy (*below right*).

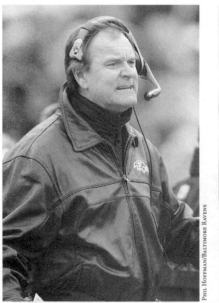

13

"The Only Thing"

s pro football rose in popularity in the '60s, almost in counterpoint to the youth movement and anti-Vietnam fervor on college campuses, it began to take on a larger symbolic meaning. For a growing group of middle-class adults, the game itself served as a kind of social touchstone, which recognized and honored—especially in the archetypes like John Unitas—the eternal verities of hard work, dedication, respect for authority, and community.

If Unitas was the embodiment of this spirit among players, Vince Lombardi was the apotheosis among coaches. In his 1963 best-seller *Run to Daylight!,* Lombardi spoke of the way the game occupied his mind during almost every waking hour. Recounting his trip to the office one morning, he noted, "There is a traffic light at the corner of Monroe and Mason and I stop behind a line of cars in the left lane. When that left-turn arrow turns green, and if everyone moves promptly, six cars can make that turn. Six days a week this traffic light is the one thing that invades my consciousness as I drive to work, that constantly interrupts that single purpose of winning next Sunday's game."

Nowhere was Lombardi's attention to detail more manifest than in the Swiss-watch precision of the brutal, beautiful Green Bay power sweep, the single play around which much of the Packers' offense was built. At coaching clinics, Lombardi would spend eight hours discussing the intricacies of the play, interrupting only for a short lunch break.

Jerry Kramer, the all-pro lineman, would remember Lombardi pounding his troops with the phrase, "Winning isn't everything, it's the only thing." Bill Curry, the erudite center who played on the Packers' 1965 world champions, recalled it differently. "Winning is not the most important thing—it's the only thing," was how Curry remembered the statement. "You might hear that every day for three weeks! Never deviated."

Whatever the exact wording, the sentiment as attributed to Lombardi became a lightning rod, as divisive a motto as Barry Goldwater's "extremism in the defense of liberty is no vice" speech during the 1964 campaign. Those who would criticize Lombardi and the institution of pro football found in the "winning is the only thing" phrase a soulless mind-set that typified everything from male chauvinism to American manifest destiny. His admirers, of course, saw something in the man and the sport that was completely different: a standard at a time when standards seemed to be slipping, a commitment to respect the game and its larger purpose, a testament to the ennobling effects of desire and willpower. There was in here, as well, an unapologetic desire for excellence. After hearing a pregame speech in which Lombardi invoked St. Paul's epistles and concluded that the key to Paul's teachings was that one must "run to win," Kramer concluded, "Vince has a knack for making all the saints sound like they would have been great football coaches."

As pro football evolved and grew more specialized, the importance of coaches continued to grow. There was a mathematical logic to this: in the age of forty-man rosters and two-platoon football, with kicking and return specialists, the significance of any single player was diluted. Stars were still important in football, but depth of quality players and degree of commitment were more important. (Nowhere was the interdependent, collaborative nature of the game more apparent than in the fortunes of the Packers' archrival, the Chicago Bears. During the late '60s, a case could be made that in Gale Sayers and Dick Butkus the Bears had the two best players in football. But the team never won its division in those years, and both Sayers and Butkus went into the Hall of Fame without ever playing a postseason game.)

By the '60s writers could speak of coaching as a profession without flinching. Lombardi with his fundamentals and fire-and-brimstone personality, and Tom Landry with his multiple schemes and corporate detachment would stand as the two archetypal figures on the NFL's stage. Iconoclastic Cowboys wide receiver Pete Gent would recall that at the beginning of each season's training camp, "Landry would come and speak, and the first thing he would explain was the history of the development of his offense and of modern foot-ball, and he would cite the Packers as the perfect example of the opposite of what we did. He'd talk about the simplicity and execution and talent of the Packers. He'd say, 'The Packers are this, and we are the opposite end, but we are willing to give up a few more mistakes, because we're going to beat them on the big play. Ultimately we will break down and give up things and we'll have a few turnovers, but we will get better and better as we execute better and bet-ter, as you know the offense more and more, it can't be stopped.' "

Landry understood and respected the philosophies of the Packers' run to daylight and the Browns' option blocking systems, and he built a defense de-signed to stop it. "The Flex" was a counterintuitive defensive system that re-quired defenders, most of whom had spent a lifetime in football being taught the virtues of absolute pursuit, to instead read a series of offensive keys. It was confounding to learn, but beautiful in execution. There was a linking, interde-pendent quality to the Flex; it was designed to prevent any big plays and shut down any available holes, or gaps, as they were known in the trade. As in most revolutionary systems that depart from the status quo in football, Landry's was aided by an extraordinary athlete at its center, the quick, explosive Bob Lilly, a defensive tackle whose physical superiority in the center of the line of scrimmage caused him to routinely be double-teamed, and occasionally triple-teamed. With Lilly at the heart of the Flex, and Don Meredith piloting Landry's multiple offense, the Cowboys were ready to challenge the Packers, and Landry's influence in the game began to approach Lombardi's.

In 1966, they were joined at the top of the coaching ranks by a third man, then in his first season as a head coach, who would eventually have an influ-ence nearly as extensive as that of Lombardi or Landry, not so much for his strategic innovation or game-coaching brilliance as for his all-consuming de-votion to the *process* of the sport.

George Allen was the longtime assistant and heir apparent to George Halas with the Bears, hired by Dan Reeves in the winter of 1966 to coach the Los An-geles Rams. After the hiring was announced, a jilted Halas brought suit, charg-ing Allen with breach of contract. In the ensuing case, it was revealed that Allen had gone behind Halas's back and solicited jobs, and had, in fact, con-tacted the Rams first. The court found for Halas, who, in a grandiloquent ges-ture, renounced all rights to Allen moments after winning the case, and said that after proving his point, Allen was free to go to the Rams.

But Papa Bear did not easily forget. At the first NFL owners meeting after the merger, Halas was eager to take up the subject of tampering with assis-tants. Standing up at the meeting, he said, "I think you know what's on my mind." Turning to Dan Reeves, Halas said, "What Dan Reeves did to me has been settled between us. We've made our peace. But as for George Allen—George Allen is a liar! George Allen is a cheat! George Allen is full of chicanery!"

At which point Lombardi turned to Reeves and whispered loudly, "Dan, it sounds like you've just got yourself a helluva head coach!"

———

Not every life has an identifiable transforming moment, an event that sets a person on the course of his life. George Allen's did. While a midshipman at Princeton in 1944, he decided he wanted to meet Albert Einstein. Allen had read that Einstein was an expert checkers player, and he became obsessed with the idea that he would call on the great man and challenge him to a game. Bringing along a fellow middie one Sunday afternoon, Allen in his dress blues knocked on the front door of Einstein's modest brick home a few blocks off the Princeton campus.

A woman answered and asked the men what they wanted.

"We're midshipmen," Allen announced, "here to see Mr. Einstein."

They were invited into the entryway and, after a few minutes, the sixty-four-year-old Einstein came down the stairs from his study. After the introductions, Allen explained, "I'd like to play you a game of checkers."

At first, Einstein demurred, but Allen was persistent, pleading for a single game.

"I don't know what you have heard," said Einstein. "There are many stories about me. But I don't play much checkers. I don't like it much."

"Well, I would just like to be able to say I played you one game."

Reluctantly, Einstein relented, then pointed out, "I do not even keep a board in my house," said Einstein. "Did you bring a board with you?"

Allen had not. And with nothing to do but give his thank-you and say his goodbyes, he turned to leave. Walking back to the campus, he began an extended, self-lacerating internal dialogue. What haunted him was not that he hadn't thought of bringing a checkerboard—in fact he'd considered it strongly and decided against it. Ultimately he had not brought it, he recalled later, because he thought "it would look a little odd if I carried a checkers board across the campus to church and into the neighborhood. I didn't want people to think I was crazy."

Allen vowed never to make the same mistake again. By the time he took the Rams job in 1966, he had long ago stopped worrying about people thinking him crazy.

As devoted to football as any man who had ever coached in the NFL before him, Allen was a man for whom the common aspects of everyday life could seem comically distant. Discussing with one writer how he met his wife, Etty, at Morningside College in 1950, he said, "She was introduced to me by the head of the speech department at a . . . what the heck kind of thing was it, it was a *play,* a play at the community theatre." A year later, he proposed by telegram, with a message that read, "AS THE 1951 FOOTBALL SEASON APPROACHES I WOULD LIKE TO HAVE YOU AS MY TEAMMATE."

Allen had been with the Rams before, as an assistant under Sid Gillman for one season in 1957. He wasn't invited back. Gillman, a man of sophisticated tastes and sardonic humor, found Allen to be an overexuberant lightweight. "Sid just didn't like him," said Jack Faulkner. "Didn't think he knew anything about football." In 1959, Allen landed an assistant's job under George Halas in Chicago, and immediately latched on to Clark Shaughnessy, by then back with the Bears as Halas's defensive coach. Shadowing Shaughnessy for three years, Allen gained a new and deeper understanding of the game. When he was promoted to the top defensive job in 1963, his impact was immediate. He became the architect of the league-leading defense that helped the Bears beat the Giants in the 1963 NFL title game, and soon became Halas's heir apparent. But the headstrong Allen was not one to patiently wait in the wings.

The people who said that Lombardi and Landry were obsessed with winning were only partly right, missing significant parts of each man's personality. But on Allen, the charge didn't seem hyperbolic. He was the logical progression of the coach as "grinder," dedicated to outwork, outsweat, outmotivate, and outplan his opposition. The off-season preparation started by Brown, the late nights obsessing over film study that began with Gillman, the acute attention to detail popularized by Lombardi, all came to roost in the personage of George Allen.

On his desk in Long Beach, where the Rams' coaches moved their offices to be next to the team's practice facility, there were no family portraits, no special gifts from his loved ones, only a single sign that read, "IS WHAT I AM DOING OR ABOUT TO DO GETTING ME CLOSER TO MY OBJECTIVE—WINNING?" It sat next to a wooden metronome, a reminder of the steady passing of time. To the Rams players, Allen declared that the building phase was over. "The future is now," he told them, and warned those hoping to make the team, "One hundred percent isn't enough. You need to give more like 120 percent."

Dan Reeves was both thrilled and secretly horrified with his new hire. A month after he took over as head coach of the Rams, Allen boldly asked Reeves if he could be named general manager as well. "I appreciate your enthusiasm," Reeves said, "but George, you're asking for my job."

In that 1966 season, Allen directed a transformation similar to the one Lombardi engineered in Green Bay in 1959. But whereas Lombardi preached simplicity, Allen was determined to take the myriad contingencies that Shaughnessy had mastered and make them accessible to his players. The defense alone had 300 different alignments and half as many audibles. Allen preferred experienced players because his system demanded it; with so much communication and on-field decision making involved, most rookies couldn't have coped with it. This was also a portent of future conflict as Reeves, the father of the modern scouting system in the NFL, began to realize he had hired a strong-willed and extremely effective coach who had absolutely no use for rookies.

In that first season, the newly purposeful Rams rose to an 8-6 record. It would be another season before they would challenge the NFL's old guard in Green Bay or new guard in Dallas, but around the league, Allen's work ethic had already raised the stakes.

Some of his peers felt he made a bit too much of his dedication. His closest assistants were convinced that, late at night, he'd take naps in his office while the projector was running, just to give his staff the idea that he was still hard at work. Coming in at 8:30 one morning, he was informed by an aide that Lombardi was on the phone. "Tell him you got me out of a meeting," said Allen.

————

Shortly after the merger was announced, Pete Rozelle appointed a committee—consisting of himself and three owners from each league (Tex Schramm, Carroll Rosenbloom, and Dan Reeves from the NFL, Lamar Hunt, Ralph Wilson, and Billy Sullivan of the AFL)—to meet and iron out the many details of the coming union. It would take eighteen full months for the merger agreement to be codified, but in the first six months, the group was preoccupied with plans for the first game between the leagues, which would match the AFL and NFL champions in Los Angeles in January 1967.

As the committee sat around a conference table in the summer of 1966, exchanging ideas about the schedule, Lamar Hunt asked about the timing of the game. "Should there be a one-week break or two before the championship game?"

"Wait," said one of the other committee members, confused about whether Hunt was talking about the league championship games or the new world championship. "Which game do you mean?"

"You know," explained Hunt. "The last game . . . the final game. The *Super Bowl.*"

There were smiles all around, and some chuckles. Hunt had thought of the name while watching his children playing with one of the hot novelties of the period, the Wham-O company's high-bouncing Super Ball. In the weeks ahead, as the group mapped out its plans in a series of meetings, it began informally distinguishing between league championship games and the finale by referring to it as the Super Bowl.

"But nobody ever said let's make that the name of the game," said Hunt. "Far from it, we all agreed it was far too corny to be the name of the new title game."

Hunt sent a letter to Rozelle, dated July 25, 1966, in which he stressed the need to come up with a title game name. "If possible, I believe we should 'coin a phrase' for the Championship Game. . . . I have kiddingly called it the 'Super Bowl,' which obviously can be improved upon."

Rozelle agreed there was room for improvement. He wasn't merely unenthusiastic about the term; he actively disliked it. League publicity director Don Weiss recalled that Rozelle "just didn't like the word 'super.' Pete was a pretty regular person, but he was a stickler on words and grammar, and 'super' was not his idea of a good word. He thought 'super' was a word like 'neat' or 'geewhiz.' It had no sophistication."

Unable to find a novel or catchy name that they were happy with, the committee announced that the game would be called "The AFL-NFL World Championship Game." Rozelle would have liked to have called the game "The Pro Bowl," but, of course, that title was already taken by the league's postseason All-Star game. When the game had been speculated about for years, it was often called a "World Series of football," which obviously wouldn't work.

Yet even before the season started, Hunt's pet term had taken on its own momentum. Headline writers, commentators, and players alike were using the term. And by January 1967 it was becoming clear that it didn't matter what the leagues tried to call the game, because "Super Bowl" had already caught on. Networks had taken to referring to the day of the game as "Super Sunday." And two weeks later in Los Angeles, on the morning of the big game, an NFL Films crew member could be heard giving a sound cue, "Super Bowl, reel one," before shooting the first reel of pregame footage at the Coliseum.

There was a curious dichotomy to the advance buildup to the first contest. So many events in the pantheon of American sports were built on generations of tradition; the World Series, the Kentucky Derby, the Indianapolis 500, the Rose Bowl were all more than fifty years old at the time. Then, suddenly, came the event that promised to be the largest of them all—the ultimate game in the nation's most popular sport—and it was the first of those sports events that had been created with the idea that its *primary* audience would be watching on television.

Television itself became another battleground. Both CBS's contract with the NFL and NBC's contract with the AFL called for exclusive broadcast rights of the league championship game. Thus a compromise was reached: for the first AFL-NFL championship game, *both* networks would broadcast the contest, spending $1 million each for the rights. They'd each spend another $1 million on promotion. In the first half of January, both networks devoted more than half of their nighttime promotional spots to the upcoming game. CBS, which would provide the video feed of the game, was charging $85,000 per minute of commercial time, about $10,000 more than NBC. NBC's announcers, Curt Gowdy and Paul Christman, made appearances on both the *Tonight* show and the *Today* show to plug the network's coverage of the game.

The 1966 season thus had a special feel, as both leagues prepared to send a representative to the first AFL-NFL championship game. In the NFL, the Packers repeated as champions, but not without an epic struggle, prevailing 34–27 over the Cowboys in the NFL championship game in Dallas.

Their opponents, appropriately enough, would be Lamar Hunt's Chiefs, who had routed the two-time defending AFL champion Buffalo Bills, 31–7, on a muddy field in Buffalo. The retooled Chiefs were clearly the class of the AFL, with a fast, oversized defensive front anchored by the mammoth Buck Buchanan, and a newly potent offense, which found Len Dawson utilizing splendid second-year flanker Otis Taylor and elusive rookie running back Mike Garrett.

All that was missing was a real sense of doubt among the public over the outcome. The AFL had been so belittled for so long that conventional wisdom held that the game wouldn't be much of a contest. The early Vegas line installed the Packers as eight-point favorites, and the spread quickly grew to 13.

Within the leagues themselves there was little *but* doubt and uncertainty, and it was this tension—the public and media sense of the game as anticlimax, combined with each league's view of the game as the culmination of a seven-year holy war—that would mark the curious blend of tension and foregone conclusion that characterized the weeks leading to the first game. For those who followed the game, the contest possessed an element of the unknown nearly unprecedented in American sports history. There hadn't been so much as a scrimmage between the two leagues in the more than seven years of the AFL's existence.

The Chiefs arrived on January 4, eleven days prior to kickoff. Green Bay arrived four days later, and then only at Rozelle's insistence. (Lombardi had wanted to fly in January 14, the morning before the game, just as the Packers would for any other road contest.) What Lombardi feared was exactly what he encountered: a large media contingent building up impossible expectations.

In one of the daily interview sessions, Lombardi slowly boiled while a reporter recited a litany of reasons why the Chiefs couldn't stay on the same field as the vaunted Packers.

"Thank you," he said, gritting his teeth after the soliloquy. "That was nice. But those people on the other side of the field don't realize that the championship has already been won. This is their chance. For seven years we've been saying they aren't as good as we are. That's fine. But suppose they are? How can I convince them in advance that the championship has already been settled? I think we'd better wait and play the game, if that's all right with the gentlemen of the press, of course." Housing the team in Santa Barbara, ninety minutes from L.A., Lombardi increased his fines for missing curfew, and pounded into his players the significance of the game, as a contest that the Packers must win to ratify all that the National Football League stood for.

The clear storyline heading into the game—the youthful Chiefs' complex approach against the experienced Packers' meat-and-potatoes attack—was largely hijacked by the boisterous antics of the Chiefs' cornerback Fred "The Hammer" Williamson, who had presented the media with a braggadocio that owed much more to Muhammad Ali's playful hazing than Jim Brown's stolid confidence. Williamson disparaged the Packers' receivers, predicted the downfall of both Carroll Dale and Boyd Dowler, and boasted of his trademark "Hammer Tackle," a swinging arm chop that he described as "a blow delivered with great velocity perpendicular to the earth's latitudes."

While Williamson entertained the media, Rozelle and his staff were meticulously setting up the game with a solemn, self-conscious evenhandedness reminiscent of nothing so much as a superpower summit. Seniority having its privileges, the Packers were designated the home team, wore their green jerseys, and got the use of the Coliseum's larger locker rooms. The six-man officiating crew would be divided equally among NFL and AFL officials, though the lead official, game referee Norm Schachter, was the NFL's best. When the Packers had the ball, they'd use the NFL's Wilson game ball ("The Duke"), while the Chiefs would use the AFL ball, the Spalding JV-5, when they had the ball. Even the pool of hospitality cars for officials and VIPs was carefully divided among NFL and CBS sponsor Ford and the NBC/AFL sponsor Chrysler.

For all that, the days before the affair were decidedly devoid of grandeur.

The event did mark the first formal occasion that would bring the AFL and NFL owners together for the first time. The Friday night party, which in later years would take on an operatic lavishness, in the first year, Rozelle recalled, was "just cold cuts at the Statler Hilton." He did give Mickey Herskowitz, one of the AFL staffers brought in to help with game preparations, a $250,000 budget to entertain the media, with outings on the Saturday prior to the game to the Santa Anita Racetrack and Disneyland. Thus began a tradition of feeding and feting the press with conscientious hospitality and an ever-present open bar. Herskowitz recalled, "Pete said, when the press left the first world championship game, he just wanted to hear them saying, 'Man, this is a lot better than the World Series.' "

Before the pregame introductions, the Chiefs' Buck Buchanan and Bobby Bell were so fired up they were crying in the tunnel waiting to take the field. The Chiefs weren't the only ones who were nervous. Frank Gifford, by now working as a sideline reporter for CBS, pulled Lombardi over for a pregame interview. "During the five minutes or so we talked," Gifford remembered, "he held on to my arm and he was shaking like a leaf."

By the 1:00 p.m. kickoff, the setting was perfect—the Coliseum on a sunny January Sunday, the grass field all the more resplendent for the $3,000 spray painting it received on the eve of the game—providing all the grandeur befitting an epic event. The game would be watched by more than 65 million people, the largest audience ever to watch a sporting event in America. Yet attendance was 63,036, leaving more than 32,000 empty seats; pro fans simply weren't used to traveling to neutral sites.

Yet for a half, fans were treated to a surprisingly competitive game. The Packers scored on their second possession, a six-play, 80-yard drive, but the Chiefs were moving the ball as well, marching across midfield on all four of their first-half possessions, as the NFL castoff and AFL star Dawson was 11-of-15 passing, employing play-action fakes and Stram's moving pocket to find open passing lanes. Green Bay led, 14–10, at the half.

The scene at halftime was tense in both locker rooms, as well as the press box, where the tight score had created a buzz of worry and excitement. NFL employee Buddy Young said out loud what others were thinking: "Old age and heat will get the Packers in the second half." In the Kansas City dressing room, the Chiefs had the look of a team that had been hoping it was good enough and had found out that perhaps it was. "I honestly thought we would come back and win it," said Stram. "We felt we were doing the things we had to do, and doing them well."

In the Packers' locker room, a peeved Lombardi told assistant coach Phil Bengston the team needed to get more pressure on the quarterback. "The coach was *concerned*," said defensive end Willie Davis. "But we also knew we couldn't stand Lombardi if we didn't win. That was always a motivation for us."

After Don Chandler's kick to the open the second half was whistled dead because NBC hadn't come back from a commercial, the second half began with Chandler's rekick, and the Chiefs took possession. On third-and-five, Dawson rolled back to pass. The Packers blitzed, a maneuver that Lombardi had often dismissed as the "weapon of weaklings." It worked splendidly in this case, as Dawson's hurried pass sailed short and was intercepted by Willie Wood, who returned it to the Chiefs' five. Green Bay scored on the next play, and again on their next possession, and the rout was on.

"It was over then," said the Chiefs' All-AFL lineman Jim Tyrer. "They wouldn't respect our run again. Our play fakes were useless. They knew we had to pass, and they just flew to the quarterback." Kansas City never threatened, and by the end, Williamson had been knocked out of the game, hammered into submission himself trying to tackle the Packers' Donnie Anderson, whose pumping knee hit Williamson's helmet. Standing over a prone Williamson, who also broke his arm in the pileup, the Packers' Fuzzy Thurston hummed a few bars of "If I Had a Hammer."

After the game, a relieved Lombardi cradled the game ball. "The players gave it to me," he said. "It's the NFL ball. It catches better and kicks a little better than the AFL ball."

When asked to assess the Chiefs, Lombardi said, "They've got great speed." Pressed further, he added, "I don't think they are as good as the top teams in the National Football League. They're a good team with fine speed but I'd have to say NFL football is tougher. Dallas is a better team, and so are several others." As silence surrounded him and writers scribbled furiously in their notebooks, a peeved Lombardi added, "That's what you've wanted me to say—now I've said it. But I don't want to get into that kind of comparison."

It was typical of the mind-set involved in the game that, afterward, Stram's two sons went to the Packers' locker room to get Lombardi's autograph. He patted Henry Stram, Jr., on the head and said, "Tell your dad his team played a good game." Stram took the news from his sons with equanimity, but when notified later of Lombardi's comments to the press, he was taken aback. "Did Vince really say we weren't that good?" he asked a group of NFL writers back at the press room in the Chiefs' hotel. "That we couldn't play at that level? Vince is a friend. Did he really say that?"

The next morning, when Lombardi walked into an NFL owners meeting in Los Angeles, he was greeted with a standing ovation.

Heading into the next season, the Packers had a clear prize in mind: no team in NFL history had won three straight titles, and Lombardi and his charges would have their second chance to accomplish it. But they were an aging team, with Hornung retiring after the 1966 season, running back Jim Taylor taken by New Orleans in the expansion draft, and center Bill Curry dealt to Baltimore. In the summer leading up to the 1967 season—the Summer of Love, of the Monterey Pop Festival, and widespread Vietnam protests—the Packers were gearing up with grim determination for a final stand. Throughout that 1967 season, the Packers had the look of a great dynasty on its last legs.

The journey to the world championship would require an extra step in 1967. With the addition of the New Orleans Saints, the NFL had grown to sixteen teams. Rather than two eight-team divisions, the league realigned into four four-team divisions—Tex Schramm's idea—in a ploy to create more division races, as well as adding an additional round to the playoffs.

Green Bay didn't dominate in 1967 as they had in earlier seasons, winning their division with a modest 9-4-1 mark. The real race occurred in the Coastal Division, where the Colts and Rams staged a furious run to the finish, with the two best records in pro football. After a stunning win in week thirteen over Green Bay (keyed by a blocked punt in the final minute), the Rams routed Baltimore, 35–10, in the season finale. It was the Colts' first loss of the year, but it knocked them out of the playoffs; both teams finished with 11-1-2 records, with the Rams' win giving them the tiebreaker advantage (the two teams had tied in an earlier game).

The Rams then traveled to Milwaukee, intent on toppling the champions, but the veteran Packers were ready, and manhandled Los Angeles, 28–7, setting up a rematch with the Dallas Cowboys for the NFL title.

The details of that NFL championship game, played December 31, 1967, in Green Bay, would become a part of American sporting legend: the morning wakeup calls to the Cowboys players, a chipper hotel desk clerk saying, "Good morning, it's your wakeup call. It's fifteen below zero." The realization that Lombardi's pet $80,000 heating system, designed to keep the field warm in any kind of weather, had seized up and frozen. "The field was exactly like playing on an ice rink," said the Cowboys' Walt Garrison. "Guys would be standing on their feet minding their own business and they'd shift their feet and the next thing they knew, they were on their ass."

The elements got the best of everyone. The officials' whistles were as useless—and as frozen—as the Packers' heating system. Early on, Cowboys running back Dan Reeves (no relation to the Rams' owner of the same name) took a vicious hit, with his facemask splitting and his upper teeth jabbing his lip. His face was bruised but it didn't bleed until several minutes later, when Reeves stood over the heater and warmed up to the point that blood began to pour out over his uniform.

On the Cowboys' bench, Garrison turned to Don Perkins and said, "We must be crazy to be out here playing."

"We're not crazy," said Perkins, looking into the stands. "Look behind you. There's about fifty thousand crazy sonuvabitches up there. They *paid* to come out here and freeze to death."

In the CBS booth overlooking the field, where play-by-play man Ray Scott carried on with his custom of calling the game with the window opened, analyst Frank Gifford noted at one point, "I think I'll take another bite of my coffee."

At first, the Cowboys seemed too stunned by the conditions to function. It didn't take the Packers' secondary long to read one of Bob Hayes's cues. On Cowboy running plays, the "Fastest Man Alive" lined up at his split end position with his hands tucked inside his pants. On pass plays, he pulled them out.

But after falling behind 14–0, the Dallas defense stiffened and turned the game around in the second quarter when Willie Townes jarred the ball from Bart Starr. Dallas end George Andrie scooped the fumble up and returned it for a touchdown. After closing to within 14–10 at the half, Dallas sprang a halfback option play on the first play of the fourth quarter, with Dan Reeves hitting Lance Rentzel for a 50-yard scoring pass to put the Cowboys ahead, 17–14.

Most great football games feature a late drive executed against the defense and the clock. The Packers faced the elements as well when they began their final march with 4:54 left on the clock, at their own 32-yard line. In addition to a Dallas defense that hadn't allowed a score for almost three quarters, they were fighting the cumulative toll of the conditions. On the final drive, the Packers' Gale Gillingham realized he no longer had any feeling in his hands. Alarmed, he began to slap them against his hip pads, just to feel a sting in his extremities. Nothing.

A series of delayed screens helped the Packers move across midfield with Starr passing crisply and his blockers giving him more time. At the two-minute warning, Green Bay was at the Dallas 39. After two more passes gained 29 yards, Starr gave the ball to Chuck Mercein on a fullback delay, again capitalizing on Dallas's relentless pursuit, and he carried the ball to the three. Anderson picked up two for a first-and-goal at the one. But after the next two plays netted no yards, and underscored the difficulty that backs were having gaining the footwork to run, Green Bay used its final timeout, on third-and-goal, at the one-yard line.

With sixteen seconds remaining, third down, and the Packers out of time-outs, the obvious choice would have been a rollout option. If Starr found a man in the end zone, he could throw for the win. If his receivers were covered he could toss the ball away and stop the clock, meaning Green Bay would still have a chance for a game-tying field goal on fourth down. This was, under the circumstances, the only sound call. But during the timeout, Starr suggested to Lombardi that he could score on a quarterback sneak, and Lombardi replied, "Run it! And let's get the hell out of here."

The call was 31 Wedge, which would call for Starr to take the snap, spin around, and hand off to Chuck Mercein. Instead, the quarterback took the ball and kept it himself, charging forward and over the line. On the line, Ken Bowman and Jerry Kramer double-teamed the Cowboys' Jethro Pugh, getting underneath his pads and pushing him far enough off the line to allow Starr to knife through the gap for the winning touchdown.

It is easy to forget, in the modern age of football, when television commentators routinely second-guess any gamble that doesn't pay off, that what made the game's finish so remarkable wasn't just the severity of the elements or the enormity of the stakes or the history between the two teams, but the sheer audacity of the final call. Had the Packers not scored on the play, there almost certainly wouldn't have been time to bring the field goal unit on for a tying kick, or even to run another play of any kind. In that event, the Packers would never have won their third straight title and their coach would have been pilloried for his blunder. Or, as Pat Summerall put it later, "If they don't score there, then Lombardi doesn't become Lombardi."

But they *did* score, and in so doing, cemented the reputation of the game as one of the greatest in league history. Inside the locker rooms after it was over, the players from both sides had the look of men who'd survived a brush with death. Dallas quarterback Don Meredith—whose usual irreverence was worn to a flat, somber eloquence—quietly described the disappointment of getting so close to the title two years in a row. In the Packers' locker room, Lombardi brought his team together and offered nothing but unqualified praise, telling them how proud he was of their effort. "I can't talk anymore," he said. "I can't say any more." He then led the team in the Lord's Prayer, before opening the locker room to the media.

But the most discussed comment afterward came from Kramer, whose memoir of the season would find its climax in the crucial block, and whose profile had been raised when a CBS camera, planning to pan to the outside to follow a receiver on a possible pass pattern, couldn't move because it was frozen to its tripod. In that stationary position, it got a perfect view of the key block and Starr's score, replayed over and over again after the game.

"There's a great deal of love for one another on this club," said Kramer afterward. "Perhaps we're living in Camelot." The idea that Camelot was in Green Bay, Wisconsin, was radical enough. A football player talking unabashedly about love was also something else altogether.

When Green Bay defeated Oakland, 33–14, two weeks later in the Super Bowl, it gave Lombardi and his team their third straight championship, and fifth in seven years. Seventeen days after the Super Bowl, Lombardi announced that he would retire from head coaching, though he would continue to run the team as general manager. His legend was ascendant, and the city of Green Bay had become fabled as a kind of embodiment of hard work and American resolve.

By the end of the year, *Instant Replay: The Green Bay Diary of Jerry Kramer* had become a best-seller, described by the *New York Times* as "the best behind-the-scenes glimpse of pro football ever produced." Its subtext was a meditation on Lombardi's appeal and power, his hold over his men. And Kramer would become not just a famous football player, but something of a full-blown celebrity, invited on talk shows, even included in Frank Sullivan's annual holiday poem in *The New Yorker* magazine ("Hail from the undersigned acclaimer/to the Packers' rugged Jerry Kramer").

With Lombardi's ascension came another round of arguments over his cultural meaning. Some were talking about him as a possible political candidate, while others seemed intent on taking him down. Leonard Shecter's profile in *Esquire* in January 1968 had been particularly harsh, implying that Lombardi was a sadist, who in his quest for perfection had lost much of his humanity.

It would all feed back into the cultural chaos of the time. The television historian Ron Powers, in describing the electronic landscape of the '60s, wrote that "CBS, the dominant carrier of professional football in the 1960s, was a passive accomplice to another payload of values that refuted most of the social revolution's aims. As seen on TV in the sixties, the National Football League leaped quickly from the status of an arcane, fringe sport to a full-blown expression of America's corporate and military ethos."

But it wasn't that simple. While a society was celebrating peace and love and community, the rising sport of the age did seem to espouse contradictory impulses of violence and aggression—yet simultaneously it embodied the same sense of community that fueled the counterculture movement. The very men that the left criticized for unchecked aggression and militarism were also those most able to work together toward a common goal. They were also, in a surprising number of instances, able to articulate those feelings, as Jerry Kramer's comments about the power of love in Camelot emphasized. Whether in Haight-Ashbury or Green Bay, the concept of Camelot was keyed to a sense of community. And at some level, the game demanded that cooperation. At a time when so much of the country was being torn asunder, even the vicarious sense of identification and community must have counted for something.

"Football requires spartan qualities to be a part of it," said Lombardi. "Sacrifice, self-denial—they're cliché words—but I believe in them with every fiber of my body. I'm not saying everybody who plays football is a spartan or denies himself. But it's a symbol of courage; it's a symbol of teamwork, which I think is a great American attribute."

By 1968, Lombardi occupied a social realm similar to that of John Wayne's, though invested with more authenticity. After Lombardi resigned his coaching duties with the Packers, Robert F. Kennedy, gearing up for the 1968 Democratic primary, sent him a cable reading, "Vince, now would you come and be my coach?" Richard Nixon himself had considered Lombardi a vice presidential candidate, until John Mitchell, investigating Lombardi's background, found out that the coach was a law-and-order Democrat, progressive on civil rights and gun control.

That previous off-season, on February 8, 1967, Lombardi was the featured speaker at the annual meeting of the American Management Association in New York City. The Rams' Jack Teele was in New York for the Saints' expansion draft, and recalled Lombardi's presence at the event. "And here he is—and no matter what we say it was a football coach talking to millionaires and scions—telling them how to run their companies. The central theme was to be the boss."

"Men want to follow," argued Lombardi to the heads of industry. "It gives them security to know there is someone who cares enough to chew them out a little bit or to correct their mistakes." Lee Iacocca, rising through the executive ranks at Ford, developed a friendship with and an admiration for Lombardi. Iacocca would recall that two of Lombardi's points—to teach his players fundamentals and demand that they play as a team—were common within the auto industry. What struck the executive was Lombardi's third tenet: "If you're going to play together as a team, you've got to care for one another. You've got to love each other. You can't just go out and say, 'I'm going to do it alone.' "

It was this interdependence, this sense of enlightened cooperation for a larger cause—among people who might not even like each other off the field—that would eventually redeem the sport for many who were bothered by the violence. And for those who had become absorbed by pro football, that idea was the game's most instructive metaphor.

"Everyone was important in the sweep," explained tight end Ron Kramer of the Packers' signature play. "It's really all of life. We all have to do things together to make this thing we call America great. If we don't, we're fucked."

14

Respect

The perception that the NFL was several cuts above the AFL didn't disappear with the merger. If anything, it intensified. Though the business war was over, there was still a sense, acutely felt on the part of those in the NFL and much of the public, that the AFL was at some level undeserving, more an invention of television than a true competitive rival of the NFL.

That first Super Bowl left a mark, and forced even those who respected the AFL to reach unpleasant conclusions about the relative merits of the two leagues. "It is a good thing it took seven years for the NFL to consent to the game," wrote Bud Shrake, *Sports Illustrated*'s lead AFL writer, after the first Super Bowl. "If it had been played the first time the AFL wanted it, the farcical result might have caused the game to be abandoned forever."

The AFL's next chance for redemption came in the preseason games between the two leagues in the summer of 1967, and while a few scores—like the revenge-minded Chiefs' 66–24 rout of Chicago—raised some eyebrows, they didn't really change attitudes, as the NFL won thirteen of the sixteen contests. Those who argued that the AFL was close to gaining parity with the NFL had even less to say after the Packers dispatched the Raiders with ease in the second Super Bowl.

The common belief by 1968 was that the AFL was so inferior, the ultimate game needed to be reworked. "We started talking in the league office that, if the game wasn't going to be competitive for several more years, we'd have to change the format once the merger was completed," said Don Weiss, then the NFL's director of publicity. "There was a feeling that it could be a long time before the AFL could field a competitive team."

That mind-set would soon receive a jolt. Though the results in the first two Super Bowls didn't show it, the American Football League was coming of age by the late '60s. Rising from the ashes of the Titans' ignominy came the glamorous, high-powered Jets, who quickly assembled under Weeb Ewbank one of the most potent passing attacks in a pass-dominated league. On the other coast, where Al Davis had returned to Oakland as general manager, the revived Raiders were a team molded in Davis's own image, an aggressive club with a gambling offensive philosophy and an intimidating defense. The Chargers and Chiefs, noted for high-scoring affairs, were among the most innovative and physically imposing teams in pro football. And if the coaching fraternity in the AFL wasn't already distinguished enough—Gillman, Stram, and Ewbank would all go to the Hall of Fame—the AFL in 1968 featured the return of a coach who *already* was a member of the Hall, Paul Brown, who returned as the coach and part owner of the expansion Cincinnati Bengals.

———

Not just in style of play but also in its social fabric, the culture of the new league was distinct from that of the NFL, particularly in race relations. The AFL was hardly an idealistic utopia of racial equality, but the topic was more contemplated, more easily confronted, and better understood than in the NFL.

The new league had been more integrated from the start, and the issue of racial justice had been explicit since January of 1965 when eighty AFL players traveled to New Orleans for the AFL All-Star Game. The twenty-one black players confronted, from the moment they arrived at the airport and tried to get taxi service, a steady stream of frank, unrepentant racism. That Saturday, January 9, many of the players were already in town, but from Bourbon Street to the French Quarter, black players were denied cab service and entrance into many of the clubs, and subjected to routine verbal abuse. At one club where the players were denied entrance, a bouncer pulled a gun on Ernie Ladd. In the lobby of the Roosevelt Hotel, the Chargers' Earl Faison heard two locals discussing him, wondering whether he was Ladd. "No," concluded one man, within Faison's earshot. "Ernie Ladd's a bigger nigger than that. That Ladd is a big nigger."

The repeated epithets and slights prompted a meeting among black players, in which they voted to boycott the game. That, in turn, prompted a hastily assembled meeting with New Orleans civic leaders, trying to quell the damage. A young black lawyer, Ernest N. "Dutch" Morial (who would later become New Orleans' first black mayor), got up in front of the players and began defending New Orleans' civil rights record, arguing that the players were overreacting, and should go ahead and play the game. Morial, an exceedingly light-skinned African-American, proved less than convincing. While he was speaking to the nonplussed players, the Jets' Winston Hill leaned over to a teammate and asked, "Who's this honky?"

A day later, Commissioner Joe Foss announced that the AFL supported the black players and that the game would be moved to Houston. It marked one of the first instances of professional athletes working together to make a social statement, and seemed to foreshadow a more open discussion of race for many of the teams. The Chiefs' white linebacker Jim Lynch recalled how struck he was by the response of his black teammates in the wake of Martin Luther King's assassination in April 1968. At the Jets' training camp that same year, the team's player association representative, linebacker Larry Grantham, stood up in front of his teammates during a players-only meeting. "Listen, I'm prejudiced," he said. "I know it. I was brought up that way. My grandmother was brought up that way, my kids, everyone else. I'm hoping to change. I'm trying to. But as far as being your player rep . . . I'll represent all of you the same, no matter what his color is."

The changed attitudes could be witnessed on the field as well, where the Chiefs installed Willie Lanier as the pro game's first starting black middle linebacker in 1968. That same year, Marlin Briscoe earned a starting quarterback job for the Denver Broncos. In the winter of 1969, the Raiders made Eldridge Dickey of Tennessee State the first black quarterback selected in the first round of a pro draft. Later that year, the rookie quarterback James Harris became the first black to start the pro season at the position, leading the Buffalo Bills into action. Harris's experience spoke not just of the distance traveled but the distance remaining. He had played college football at Grambling, and spent much of his life in segregated settings. Standing inside his first pro huddle, and calling the play to be run, it occurred to him that he'd rarely been alone with this many white people before, much less in a setting in which he was giving orders.

Into this cultural maelstrom strode the swaggering Joe Namath. By the 1968 season, his fourth in pro football, Namath had become something more than the biggest celebrity in shoulder pads. He was well on his way to his aspiration: "to be known as a good quarterback, not just a rich one."

Broadway Joe stood out in a way that few football players ever had, from his facemask, a jaunty, wide double bar with a single vertical divider, to his feet, where his signature white shoes became an icon emblematic of not merely an era but a worldview. With a reputation as sports' reigning playboy that he was all too happy to cultivate, Namath had developed a persona undeniably rebellious, yet all the while exuding an unflappable insouciance consistent with the mystique of the quarterback. As he explained once in *Sports Illustrated*, "I don't date so much as I just, you know, *run into something,* man."

Of course, there had been eligible bachelors, even sex symbols, in pro football before, Jim Brown and Paul Hornung to name two. But Brown was black, so his personality was filtered through a largely white news media that was still adjusting to the image of a black athlete who wasn't "just happy to be here." Brown's sexual magnetism and his conquests were little discussed in the media. Hornung's reputation as a ladies' man was a subject of asides and subtext, but for all his notoriety, he was an athlete living in Green Bay. Namath transcended sports, making sports fans, or at least Namath devotees, of women who previously couldn't have cared less about sports.

But there was something else at work, too, a level of coolness, and an assimilation of black social mores. The notion of Hornung as the league's dominant playboy was not unanimous. As Jim Brown explained in his autobiography, "To some of the black guys, Paul's sexual rep was funny. First off, we thought we were the great lovers. With women, with life, the white guys got all the breaks; as black dudes, we had to be power smooth. And when we'd watch a white guy who was highly acclaimed as a lover, they'd often look a little bit square. It was like watching people dance. Most black guys stay just in back of the beat, no rush. Most white guys stay just in front of it. They want to get there so fast, they get there before the beat does. Me and my partners all like Paul. We just thought he was a little ahead of the beat."

No one accused Namath of being ahead of the beat. In fact, one of his signature strengths was the ease with which the All-American who'd starred for the segregated Alabama team engaged his black teammates. The sage writer Paul Zimmerman, covering the Jets for the *New York Post* in the late '60s, blanched at Namath's reluctance to talk to the press, but marveled at his social skills. "I had seen Namath come into a dining room at training camp, check out the tables and sit down at a table composed entirely of black players," Zimmerman once wrote. "Most teams, no matter how close they are, break down into some loose kind of black-white arrangement at mealtimes. A couple of black players come in together and find a table. Then a couple more join them. Before long, it becomes an all-black table, and the one next to it becomes predominantly white. To a casual observer, it would give the appearance of a segregated dining room. But I have seen Namath plunk his tray down at one of those all-black tables, and then a few white players join him and soon it becomes a mixed table. I've seen this happen too many times to assume it's accidental. The same thing on buses. I've seen Namath integrate a little knot of black players by his presence."

While players may have been aware of Namath's racial egalitarianism, and its crucial role in bringing a team together, his persona represented something entirely different to an older generation, where he seemed to signify a larger countercultural trend threatening everything sacred in the culture. (During the season, AFL president Milt Woodward had suggested that Namath's Fu Manchu mustache was bad for the game's image, and that he should shave it off. Namath did, but only for $10,000 in a razor commercial.)

But none of this would have mattered much if Namath hadn't proved himself on the field. In 1967, he became the first quarterback to throw for more than 4,000 yards in a season. A year later, he led the Jets to their first division title.

That season's watershed game came November 17, 1968, in Oakland-Alameda County Coliseum, when the Jets, close to clinching their division, visited the Raiders, locked in a tight race with Kansas City. With kickoff at 1:00 p.m. Pacific time and 4:00 p.m. on the East Coast, the game was NBC's "national doubleheader" game, broadcast everywhere in the country save the Bay Area, where it was a casualty of the home blackout. The back-and-forth affair was extremely physical, and tightly played, and featured a desperate late drive by Namath that put the Jets ahead, 32–29, with just over a minute to play. There were still fifty seconds left in the game, the Jets leading, 32–29, with the Raiders in possession, when the clock struck 7:00 p.m. on the East Coast. At that instant, the NBC national feed of the game disappeared, just as the Raiders' Daryle Lamonica was fading back to pass. After a station break, tens of millions of fans were next treated to the opening credits of the made-for-TV movie *Heidi,* which NBC began as scheduled at 7:00 p.m. Eastern Time.

Two things quickly happened. A blizzard of angry phone calls, estimated at 10,000 to NBC's headquarters in the first hour alone, blew out the Circle-7 exchange in the heart of Manhattan. Meanwhile, unseen by most of the nation, the Raiders quickly scored two touchdowns in 19 seconds of playing time.

The headline in the *New York Daily News* the next morning said it all: "Raiders 43, Jets 32, Heidi 14."

The game turned out to be crucial for other reasons: it helped the Raiders tie for the Western Division title, and sent them into a divisional playoff with

Kansas City, where they routed the Chiefs, 41–6. Then Oakland traveled for a third game against the Jets, in the AFL championship game at Shea Stadium. This time, the Jets rallied to defeat the Raiders, 27–23, on a cold, windswept afternoon, with Namath driving the team the length of the field in the last six minutes for the winning margin. The win sent the Jets to Miami for the third Super Bowl against the Baltimore Colts, a team that many were already celebrating as one of the most imposing in NFL history.

After the Colts' near-miss in 1967, when they suffered their first loss and missed out on the playoffs on the final day of the regular season, Don Shula drove his team even harder. When Johnny Unitas tore ligaments in his right elbow in the last exhibition game, and was replaced by journeyman Earl Morrall, the Colts didn't miss a beat. With a wide complement of weapons at his disposal, Morrall passed the Colts to the league title and won the MVP award. In the 1968 NFL title game, the 13-1 Colts shut out the Cleveland Browns— the only club to beat Baltimore during the regular season—by a 34-0 score. So smothering was Baltimore's defense that the Browns never got inside the Colts' 33-yard line.

The Colts were favored by 19 points and the prospect of another mismatch was so pervasive that, in his press conference the Friday before the game, Rozelle announced the league would consider altering the structure of the postseason tournament after the merger in 1970, so that two NFL teams (presumably more evenly matched) might meet in the final. The *New York Times* headline the next day read, "Rozelle Indicates Tomorrow's Super Bowl Contest Could Be Next to Last."

But even that news was overshadowed because, from the day he arrived in Miami, a week before the game, Namath galvanized the media coverage and became the story, seizing the stage in previously unthinkable ways. On Monday, he exchanged playful barbs with the Colts' Lou Michaels at Jimmy Fazio's nightclub in Miami, and their banter almost led to a fistfight. The next day, the story of Namath and Michaels's encounter coursed through the city, and the media contingent began tailing Namath largely to the exclusion of all else. Joe Falls of the *Detroit Free Press* recalled a poolside scene early in the week: "Joe Namath is trying to read his mail by poolside surrounded by reporters. A gal in a pink bikini walks by and looks at all the writers. She says, 'Oh, poor Joe. They never let poor Joe alone.' Namath looks up at her. He doesn't say anything. His eyes say it all. The reporters shift uneasily. One of them says to Namath, 'Hey, Joe, what'd you take at Alabama—basket weaving?' Namath looks up again. 'Naw,' he says, 'that was too tough. I took journalism.' "

Namath attended the Miami Touchdown Club dinner Thursday night, to receive the organization's award as the outstanding professional football player of 1968. After a couple of drinks, his acceptance speech was even cheekier than usual. "When we won the AFL championship, a lot of people thanked the wives," he noted. "I'd like to thank all the single girls in New York, they deserve just as much credit. They're appreciated just as much." Returning to the standard patter, he said all the right things about the award not being possible without his teammates when he heard a voice from the back of the hall shout, "Namath, we're gonna kick your ass."

Namath looked out into the dark expanse and said, "Hey, I got news for you. We're gonna *win the game;* I guarantee it." He then made a few more remarks, sat down, and shortly thereafter ducked out the side door, for a ride back to the Jets' headquarters at the Galt Ocean Mile Hotel.

Word of Namath's bold pronouncement spread quickly through Miami. Guaranteeing victory was nothing new, of course—Muhammad Ali had been doing it for years—but it was still jarring in the rigid ethical structure of American team sports. Members of the Colts vowed that Namath would be in for a lesson. "Football players who are real good don't have to talk," said the Colts' menacing All-League defensive lineman Bubba Smith. Norm Van Brocklin, by now the head coach in Atlanta, was even more pointed. "I'll tell you what I think about Namath on Sunday night, after he has played his first pro football game." But Vince Lombardi, for one, saw something. He confided to columnist Jimmy Cannon the day before the game that "this kid can beat them."

In the Jets' locker room moments before kickoff, Ewbank didn't reprise the "nobody wanted you" pregame oratory with which he'd roused the Colts a decade earlier. Instead, he was businesslike and matter-of-fact. "When we win," he said to his players, "don't carry me off the field. I have a bad hip. I don't want to get hurt."

What happened next was a harmonic convergence of elements: the game's biggest star, from the nation's biggest city, cast as an underdog on the sport's biggest stage, rising to the occasion and delivering the biggest upset in pro football history.

From early on, the game had an eerie feel. The mid-afternoon start found Miami overcast, and the Colts surprisingly tight. Meanwhile, Namath, the iconoclast, played conservatively and completely within himself. After dealing with the uneven fronts and stack defensive alignments of the Chiefs, and the smothering bump-and-run of the Raiders, the Colts' conventional strong-side combination zone seemed nearly remedial to him. He knew what the defense was doing and when, and he audibled on nearly half the plays in the first half, as the Jets built a 7–0 lead over a stunned Colts club, whose offense was growing increasingly frustrated in blowing five first-half scoring opportunities.

In the third quarter, Namath coolly added to the lead, engineering two drives that resulted in field goals, to make the score 13–0. It was then that Shula put in Unitas, whose mystique alone was still enough to scare his former teammate Johnny Sample. "I told my teammates about what Unitas could do, especially under fire. I knew we'd be in trouble if he started." But Unitas's first drive failed and his second ended in an end zone interception, and by the time Baltimore got the ball again, the Jets were ahead 16–0. The Colts' lone touchdown came with 3:19 left, and after the Jets recovered the ensuing onside kick, the outcome was sealed.

Up in the press box, alongside Halas and Modell, Rozelle watched with mounting astonishment. With a few minutes left in the game, he headed down to the field level. Standing under the stands, he spied CBS's Pat Summerall, who was working the Colts' sideline for NBC, as a kind of NFL emissary. Rozelle motioned him over, and Summerall silently stood by the commissioner for a moment while they both surveyed the unthinkable. "Tell me," Rozelle said, taking a long, nervous drag on a cigarette and preparing for the trophy presentation, "everything you know about the New York Jets."

As the clock struck 0:00, Namath engaged in one last iconic gesture. Running off the field with his jubilant teammates, he lifted his index finger to the sky and headed for the locker room. The scene inside was one of ecstatic bedlam, accompanied by a savage, vengeful glee. Namath, whooping with his teammates, at first rebuffed all questions from reporters from NFL cities.

Namath would later describe the most satisfying moment of the day as coming later that night: "And when we got back to the hotel after that game, I can remember the three guys I saw: Emmitt Thomas and Buck Buchanan and Willie Lanier, three of the Chiefs. They greeted us as we got off the bus, and we *hugged,* and we felt good about it."

While the Jets and their AFL brethren partied the night away, the scene at Carroll Rosenbloom's "victory" party was more akin to a wake, with the host spending much of the party sitting behind a large rubber plant, disconsolate. Rozelle, adjusting to the shock, had gained a sense of perspective on the day's events. When one aide, on the verge of tears, expressed anguish about the implications of the loss, the commissioner was consoling. "Don't worry," said Rozelle, "this may be the best thing that ever happened to the game."

And in many ways, it was. Just as the Giants' rise had been crucial to pro football's burst of popularity in the late '50s and '60s, so it was that having a world champion in New York City further stoked interest among the advertising and media communities. The Colts players, still in shock, had constant reminders of the Jets' upset everywhere they turned. Colts center Bill Curry remembered being "subjected to the Jets on television, in commercials, on the printed page, smiling at us, singing, washing, shaving, eating soup, standing alongside cars, wearing sports clothes. The most obnoxious by far was the one in which Gerry Philbin was shown eating Manhandler soup, whatever *that* was, just stuffing his face like he was never going to have another meal in his life." Of course, each one of those opportunities was a sign of the growth of the sport as a whole. In that summer prior to the league's fiftieth season, the NFL—having outgrown the space at Rockefeller Center—moved into larger and plusher offices at 410 Park Avenue.

But before the anniversary celebration began, the league experienced one of its most turbulent off-seasons ever, challenging every one of Rozelle's recognized talents for image management, innovative leadership, adaptability and consensus building.

For all the successful diplomacy of the merger committee, the owners headed to the 1969 annual meetings without having solved the biggest merger-related problem: how to structure the unified league starting in 1970. At the February 1969 meetings, the committee made a recommendation, supported by Rozelle, to leave things just as they were. Many felt, after the Jets' Super Bowl win, that perhaps the AFL identity would be best retained. Rozelle went so far as to announce, at the beginning of the meetings, that the 16-10 alignment should stay.

When the recommendation was made at the joint league meeting, though, the effect was explosive. As Don Weiss recalled, Paul Brown "just about went berserk." Brown said that he'd signed to be in the AFL only because he had been led to believe that there would be a full merger in 1970. With the NFL possessing teams in each of the top ten television markets, while the AFL had just one, it was clear that even if TV money was distributed equally, influence wouldn't be. At the meeting, Brown stood up, argued a condensed version of his position, then provided a foreboding warning. "We will find out *legally* just what our position is regarding the specific performance clause in the merger agreement." He wasn't alone. Al Davis was more attuned than most to the competitive implications of such a split, and was determined to gain a full merger. Unable to gain the majority he needed, Rozelle was forced to adjourn the meeting without a solution, announcing that the new NFL would indeed be comprised of a thirteen-team National Football Conference and a thirteen-team American Football Conference, and thus three teams from the old NFL would have to "go over."

Suddenly, every team was fair game, though it was considered heresy to even contemplate a move on the part of the Bears, Giants, Packers, or Cowboys. And other sides were stiffening. "It would emasculate the NFL if the Browns were to leave," said Art Modell, and virtually every NFL owner felt similarly. When the owners returned for a special meeting at the league office in early May, Rozelle announced that the owners would stay there until the decision had been made.

"Oh, hell," said Rosenbloom. "We're going to be here forever." It was, in many ways, a repeat of the standoff in Miami in 1960. As a further inducement, Rozelle announced that each team that went over would receive a one-time payment of $3 million, paid by the other NFL owners. Rosenbloom, convinced that the Colts could start a new rivalry by getting in the same division with Namath and the Jets, jumped at the chance. But that was just one of three teams.

Further complicating matters was the illness of Art Modell. Diagnosed with a bleeding ulcer, he was rushed to Doctors Hospital on East End Avenue. Later that night, with the stalemate still in place, he was visited by Wellington Mara and Art and Dan Rooney.

"Gentlemen, I have decided to break this logjam," said Modell. "I will move to the American Football Conference if my friend Art Rooney will come with me, and if I can have the blessing of my dear friend Well."

Dan Rooney, standing at the foot of the bed, said, "Now just a minute. There is no way the *Pittsburgh Steelers* are going to join the American Football Conference. We have been—"

"Now, Danny," said Art Rooney, raising his hand gently. "Not so fast."

Mara smiled at his friends, and mentioned that he thought the Browns and Giants could keep their rivalry alive with annual preseason games. And Art Rooney said he'd give it some thought.

At dinner that night, Dan argued his case some more. Near midnight, they returned to the NFL's Park Avenue offices, where the siege was continuing. Dan felt that he'd finally succeeded in causing his father to see things his way. When they got to the twelfth floor, the commotion of the earlier hours had dissipated to small pockets of activity. The siege had reached thirty hours, a marathon of negotiating and stalling, and by that point, owners were sleeping in chairs, on couches. A few owners who were still awake had raided the liquor stash in Ed Sabol's small office, which the NFL Films chief used on his trips to New York.

The last clear beehive of activity was in Rozelle's office. Dan Rooney walked in, and saw the commissioner, still in a shirt and tie, looking crisp and alert. Rozelle smiled and walked over, handing Dan a small slip of paper, on which he had written:

CLEV   PITT
HOU   CINCY

Dan Rooney examined it a moment, and realized that the fight was already over. And he'd lost.

Rooney handed the slip of paper to his father who asked, "What's this?"

"That," said Dan, "is our new division."

There was no point in even trying to talk Art Rooney out of it now. The divisional alignment was too appealing. In the retooled AFC, the Steelers and Browns would go into the AFC Central, where they'd be reunited with Paul Brown and his Bengals, as well as the Houston Oilers, whose Astrodome was considered a state-of-the-art showcase facility. Besides giving both teams an attractive road game in Houston, and the continuation of their own natural home-and-home series, Rozelle had created an instantly sizzling twice-a-year rivalry pitting Brown and his Bengals against Modell and the Browns. It wasn't the old NFL, but under the circumstances, it was about as appealing a plan as possible. Once again, Rozelle had fashioned a compromise that appealed to enough people to carry the day.

In the aftermath, even Paul Brown was complimentary of his old antagonist. "As for Art Modell's decision to switch, I just feel that it's all to his credit," Brown said. "It was his decision that what is best for pro football is best for everyone."

Others saw a guiding hand. "Pete was very adept at planting suggestions," said Don Weiss. "And I think that was a case where he sort of got Art to do his bidding."

With the Central alignment set up, the rest was easy: the Broncos, Chiefs, Raiders, and Chargers, who had been with one another in the AFL West for ten years, would stay in the same division in the AFC. Baltimore would join Boston, Buffalo, the Jets, and Miami in the AFC East. It would be nearly another year before the NFC owners decided on the alignment for their new conference. In the spring of 1970, Rozelle locked up the group again and, when they still couldn't find a solution, he ordered the five most plausible plans put on separate sheets of paper. With that, his assistant Thelma Elkjer picked the winning one out of a vase.

The same 1969 off-season found Joe Namath moving at the center of the pop cultural universe. With the writer Dick Schaap, he co-wrote his autobiography, *I Can't Wait Until Tomorrow . . . 'Cause I Get Better-Looking Every Day.* He shot a movie, a motorcycle picture called *C.C. and Company* with Ann-Margret. Beneath the glitzy surface of movies and endorsements, it was proving to be a much more difficult off-season. In March, at the league meetings in Jacksonville, Namath had attended a meeting with the NFL's director of security Jack Danahy, a disciple of J. Edgar Hoover, who kept a sign in his office that read, "SECURITY NEVER SLEEPS." Danahy informed him that the FBI had been staking out Namath's restaurant and bar, Bachelors III, for gambling and other criminal activity. The warnings went unheeded until early June, when one of Danahy's contacts at the New York police department advised him that a raid on Bachelors III was imminent. At that point, Rozelle summoned Namath to a meeting and warned that he should divest himself of his business stake in the restaurant or face suspension. It was a bold, risky move on Rozelle's part, since Namath himself had been accused of no wrongdoing.

On June 6, at a bizarre morning press conference at Bachelors III, a tearful Namath announced his retirement from football. "I'm not selling," he said. "I quit. They said I'm innocent, but I have to sell. I can't go along with that. It's principle." The event prompted one of *Sports Illustrated*'s most memorable covers ("Namath Weeps") and a storm of reaction. When President Richard Nixon heard the news in the White House, he proclaimed "Good riddance!" NBC was in the midst of negotiating with advertisers for the 1969 season and, upon news of Namath's retirement, two of its largest sponsors pulled out immediately.

After Namath went off to Los Angeles for more shooting on his film, it was left to Rozelle to devise some strategy that would convince Namath to give up the restaurant and get him back in football. By then, though, Rozelle had some doubt whether Namath even *wanted* to play. He had been privy to a report alleging that, earlier in the spring, Namath had approached the Jets' surgeon, Dr. James Nicholas, with a bribe for Nicholas to declare him physically unfit to play the 1969 season, and that after Nicholas refused to cooperate, the two men exchanged heated words. (Nicholas would later deny that any such offer took place. "Joe was a close friend of mine," Nicholas said. "The report is wrong; he did nothing of the sort.")

On June 26, Namath was back in New York, for a private meeting at Rozelle's apartment in Sutton Place. Rozelle's daughter, Anne, like most ten-year-old girls in the city, was madly in love with Broadway Joe. Rozelle patiently explained to her beforehand that, while she would be able to meet Namath at another time, this meeting was not the appropriate occasion. After reluctantly promising that she'd stay in her room during the meeting, Anne burst into the living room just after she heard the doorbell ring, ran up to Namath, and jumped in his arms, before blurting, "I just want you to know that even if my daddy hates you, I still love you." With that as the icebreaker, Namath and Pete Rozelle both broke out laughing, and Anne was sent back to her room.

At the meeting, Rozelle made it clear to Namath that the league wanted him back. (Rozelle's list of talking points included the notation, "*no one picking on namath. personally like him. want him in football—biggest name we have.*") While nothing was settled that day, the two sides agreed to meet again during Namath's next break in filming. They met twice on Monday, July 14, and that week Namath decided to accept the face-saving terms of the league's compromise offer, which still required Namath to sell his stake in the restaurant, and not enter Bachelors III for the foreseeable future, but consented to allow him to invest in other Bachelors III franchises elsewhere in the country. On Friday, July 18, in a quickly arranged press conference, a beaming Rozelle announced, "Joe and I and professional football have gone through six weeks of considerable unpleasantness and I am very happy to announce that our problem is resolved."

This was Rozelle at his absolute best. Defusing an explosive situation, assuaging egos and—significantly—getting his way. Rozelle had preserved the league's reputation for toughness against gambling and, perhaps as importantly, preserved the reputation of Namath as a principled star who wanted nothing more than to play football.

As a guest on *The Mike Douglas Show* later that fall, Rozelle was asked what he wanted for his sport. "Oh, I guess I would like it, obviously, to have total integrity, and the confidence of the public," he answered. "I'd like it to be exciting, modern, 'with-it.' It has violence, certainly . . . but I think it's really more action." In the midst of all the crosstalk—Edith Piaf asking about sex the night before a game, another guest remarking upon Dick Butkus grunting at the line of scrimmage—Rozelle was never defensive, always self-effacing, and always quick to clarify the league's position. In sum, he was mastering a public relations art that had yet to be formally defined. Pete Rozelle was making sure the NFL stayed on message.

By the summer of 1969, pro football had baseball surrounded. In the persona of Lombardi, the Silent Majority on the right found a voice that exuded traditional authority in the face of cultural upheaval. And in the slangy, beatnik irreverence of Namath, the counterculture had its very own football star. In bars and living rooms, the game had surpassed baseball in popularity among mainstream sports fans. And simultaneously, "the sport of the '60s" had captured the devotion and imagination of the elite. "Football is not only the most popular sport, it is the most intellectual one," wrote William Phillips in the journal *Commentary* in 1969. "It is in fact, the intellectuals' secret vice. . . . Much of its popularity is due to the fact that it makes respectable the most primitive feelings about violence, patriotism, manhood."

The game's universe was expanding, but something else was happening as well. Within the smaller circle of avid sports fans, pro football wasn't merely growing but muscling its way to primacy, at baseball's expense. This was more than just a generational shift, signaling younger adults raised on football replacing a generation that had grown up listening to baseball on the crystal set. It showed that the NFL was reaching a vast, upwardly mobile middle class, and changing their loyalties.

Conversely, the Grand Old Game of baseball—plagued in 1968 by a historic offensive drought and slumping attendance—for the first time seemed to have become passé, quaint, an anachronism representative of little more than nostalgia for an earlier, simpler time. This was a gross oversimplification, of course, but the truth remained that while football soared, baseball floundered, prisoner to its own complacence.

"Up until now, baseball has been sacrosanct, more American than honest Abe, more Catholic than the Pope," said John Steadman of the *Baltimore News-American* in the early '70s. "So when, under Pete Rozelle, the NFL began to advertise itself as the new religion, baseball was totally unprepared to respond. They were like a punch-drunk fighter being belted around the ring. And everything the NFL did—either frontally or subliminally—was designed to disparage baseball, to get this message across: 'Hey, they're out of it. We're the ones who're relevant, the wave of the future, who have a sort of new culture sense of style.' "

This perception was shared by some within the game as well. "Baseball has become dull, not just slowed down, but *dull,*" complained Bill Veeck. "The owners recognize their failures and the loss in prestige to pro football. They're being murdered, but many won't admit it. They won't admit it because they don't know what to do about it."

In a *Sports Illustrated* article in 1967, Roone Arledge was even more pointed, writing, "Baseball is a game that was designed to be played on a Sunday afternoon at Wrigley Field in the 1920s, not on a 21-inch screen. It is a game of sporadic action interspersed with long lulls. Last year we tried rerunning plays in slow motion. It was redundant."

Both sports were still popular, but only football seemed relevant to the chaos enveloping the society. Football wasn't war, in a pure sense, but it was war in almost every metaphorical sense—gladiators in hand-to-hand combat, generals worrying over strategic battle plans, two communities sending forth their youngest and strongest representatives to settle age-old scores. Johnny Unitas called it "the closest thing there is to all-out war."

The most vivid and lasting critique of the war imagery in football came from the comedian George Carlin, who in the late '60s was still establishing himself as a biting, trenchant voice of subversive wit. His classic routine "Baseball and Football" examined the stark contrasts in the language of the two sports. "Baseball is a nineteenth-century pastoral game," Carlin noted. "Football is a twentieth-century technological struggle. Baseball is played on a diamond, in a park. *The baseball park!* Football is played on a gridiron, in a stadium, sometimes called Soldier Field or War Memorial Stadium. Baseball begins in the spring, the season of new life. Football begins in the fall, when everything is dying."

Being in tune with the chaotic times was a double-edged sword. As criticism of the war in Vietnam grew, so, too, would criticism of the institution and culture of pro football.

"I have found myself much less at ease with the violence of football than ever before," wrote longtime fan George Plimpton during his second experience with participatory journalism, in training camp with the Baltimore Colts in 1971. "The general temper of the times—the war in Indochina and the vast unrest, tipping over into brutality and rage—is itself so violent that it is impossible to accept the metaphor of football, and its popularity, without wondering whether it reflects some of the country's excesses."

The perception at the time held that pro football's audience was made up largely of the earnest mainstream determined to see the good in the country. They were Nixon's Silent Majority, the people who made Barry Sadler's "The Ballad of the Green Berets" a number one pop single in the heart of the Vietnam War. And those Americans were brought together by pro football. That much was certainly true. But it wasn't the whole truth.

Nowhere was pro football's rise more apparent or obvious than at the White House, where the nation's commander in chief, Richard Nixon, stood as the country's First Fan, a football zealot who followed the game with a rapt attention that delighted his admirers and appalled critics.

Nixon's devotion to the game was at a different order of magnitude than that of his predecessors. Along the campaign trail, he was fond of joking that he was "not heavy enough to play the line, not fast enough to play halfback, and not smart enough to be quarterback." Moving to New York City to practice law in 1963, Nixon grew even more enthralled with professional football, traveling regularly to Yankee Stadium to watch the Giants and frequently stopping by parties thrown by the Giants players. Upon accepting the Republican Party's nomination at the 1968 convention, Nixon made public his gratitude to his mother, his father, and his football coach.

ABC's producer Roone Arledge would remember the leader of the free world dropping in on ABC's broadcast of the Hall of Fame Game, in the 1971 preseason, and waiting outside the booth prior to a brief on-air chat with Frank Gifford. "You know, when Frank Gifford was playing with the Giants, I used to go to a lot of their games," Nixon told Arledge. "And, after the games, Frank would have cocktail parties at his apartment, which was right near the stadium. I used to go there quite a bit. I was invited many times. I know Frank Gifford; I'm sure he'll remember me."

Another former football player, Senator Eugene McCarthy of Minnesota, seized the football for liberals. During the 1968 primary campaign, he made the point that "Politics is like coaching football. You have to be smart enough to understand the game and dumb enough to think it's important." Elsewhere on the left, fans included members of the Black Panthers, who often frequented a bar owned by the Raiders' Gene Upshaw, and the dissident Abbie Hoffman, who was dismissive of football's left-wing critics. "They're a bunch of peacenik creeps," he said. "Watching a football game on television, in color, is fantastic."

Pro football's appeal had simply become too broad to be easily categorized. In the early '70s, when Clint Murchison's son Robert was attending Dartmouth, the school changed its nickname from Indians to Big Green. The younger Murchison, seeing the grief his university took over its old nickname, had an idea. His father's barber in Dallas was a full-blooded Cherokee who was related to Russell Means, the leader of the American Indian Movement. Wouldn't it be fun, suggested Robert, if the Murchisons offered to help Means and his followers stage a protest against the Washington Redskins, over the racial insensitivity of their nickname? Envisioning the picket signs outside of RFK Stadium, Murchison embraced the idea, and eagerly asked his barber to contact Means. And that's where the plan died. It turned out that Russell Means was a rabid football fan. And his favorite team was the Washington Redskins.

Nixon's closest friend in football was George Allen, the Los Angeles Rams coach who in the late '60s reawakened the city's love affair with its football team. Their connection was largely coincidental—Allen had been a coach at Whittier in the late '50s, and first met Nixon then. But they stayed in touch and even on the campaign trail in 1968, Nixon kept close tabs on Allen and his team.

The newest incarnation of the Rams certainly had glamour. As one of the most celebrated defenses in the game, their formidable front four was dubbed the "Fearsome Foursome," and the Rams' handsome, strapping quarterback Roman Gabriel, a part-time actor, was billed as the West Coast's answer to Joe Namath (though the parallel only went so far; Gabriel was married). Most game days in L.A., Jennifer Allen would remember the family eventually winding up at Matteo's bar, where, "after home victories, Dean Martin would greet us with cigarettes and martini in hand. . . . He'd tell my father, 'Great game, George,' then want to discuss Dad's reason for calling a draw play on third-and-long."

Starting with the tenth game of Allen's rookie season in 1966, the Rams lost just five of their next forty-four regular season games. It should have been a triumphant time for Dan Reeves, but the owner had never connected with his new coach. Reeves was perplexed by Allen's apparently joyless grasping of victory for victory's sake, and the two men grew alienated. Allen had moved the coaching offices out of the Rams' offices on Beverly Boulevard, often didn't return Reeves's calls, and had been known to fabricate stories about the owner's indifference to motivate his team.

"Dan Reeves was this very sophisticated, erudite man," said Allen's wife, Etty. "Dan loved wordplay and he loved to share a drink with friends and talk about the game. As for my husband, well, George drank milk, ate ice cream, and just started working on the next game. He was not the sort to relax over cocktails."

Upon firing Allen at the end of the 1968 season, Reeves said, "I had less fun winning with George Allen than I did losing with other coaches." But after a threatened player revolt forced Reeves to reconsider, Allen was reinstated as head coach.

After rallying round their once and future coach, the Rams were a confident team heading into the 1969 preseason, and Nixon left his retreat in San Clemente to attend not one but two of the Rams' preseason games. The Rams won their first 11 games of the 1969 season, becoming the dominant story of the season. But after clinching their division, they lost their last three regular season games, then squandered a 17–7 halftime lead on the road at Minnesota, as Joe Kapp and the Vikings rallied for a 23–20 win. After the loss, a devastated Allen was almost speechless. "I can't believe it," said Allen. "I just can't believe it. We knew we had to win."

Whatever effect it had in the society at large, Lombardi's "winning is the only thing" maxim was widely shared in pro football. A single play here or there changed not only the score of a big game, but the perception of everything that went before it. The Rams went to Miami to play Dallas (a team with its own stigma, perpetually branded as "Next Year's Champions") in the Play-off Bowl, an increasingly unpopular consolation game between conference runners-up. "You're playing for third place in the NFL," Roman Gabriel said, "which is like playing for third place in a war. There isn't any such thing. There are winners and losers, but nobody comes in third."

––––––––––

The Kansas City Chiefs knew all about such labels. Heading into the final AFL season in 1969, the Chiefs were a team with a reputation to salvage and scores to settle. For years, Joe Namath and many scouts felt that Hank Stram's team had the best talent in the league. But, for whatever reason, the franchise had made the postseason only twice, winning the AFL championship in 1962 and 1966. Still stung from their humiliating season-ending 41–6 playoff loss to the Raiders in 1968, they entered the 1969 season with a sense of purpose verging on a crusade.

That summer, at the height of the mod hairstyles, Hank Stram sent a letter to the team informing them that in the season ahead, the Chiefs would allow no long hair falling below the bottom of the helmet, no mustaches, goatees, or sideburns longer than his own. Stram had been the most fashion-conscious coach in the pros for years, and the Chiefs reflected his tastes, not merely in the variety of formations they used but in countless details of their public appearance. When traveling for a road game, the Chiefs wore tailor-made black blazers and gray slacks, white shirts and black ties, with the team's logo on the breast of the jacket. In 1968, the Chiefs began wearing fire-engine-red game pants on the road. The team's offensive huddle formed in a choir alignment, with the five interior linemen standing in the back row, backs to the line of scrimmage, mirroring the positions they would take at the line, the three receivers and two running backs standing in the front row, bending at the waist, all facing the quarterback. In these, and numerous other ways (including the manner in which they lined up for the national anthem, in numerical order), the Chiefs exuded a kind of crisp, self-conscious sense of style that was, in both its precision and its vanity, a perfect reflection of their head coach.

At a racially polarized time, the Chiefs were also noteworthy for being an integrated team that blended well together on and off the field. Through the move to Kansas City and the disappointment of Super Bowl I, the Chiefs had developed a slangy, unforced camaraderie, with the good ol' boys from the South mixing freely with the wide assortment of Southern blacks. Willie Lanier and Jim Lynch roomed together on the road, and most of the team spent their off-seasons in Kansas City, many playing on the Chiefs' barnstorming basketball team. Players of both races often mocked the dictatorial ways of Stram, whom some referred to as "Little Caesar," but to a man, they viewed their coach as utterly without prejudice. "There were some people who thought he put form over substance," said one player, "but it was clear, when it came to race, he didn't care about color, he only cared if you could play."

The team would need all the cohesion and support it could muster. After posting a 6-0 preseason record, Kansas City jumped to two easy wins on the road, over the Chargers and Patriots, to start the regular season. But in the second game Len Dawson went down with a small tear in the left knee ligament. The team sought opinions from six different specialists before they found one who recommended rest and rehabilitation, rather than season-ending surgery for Dawson. After six weeks of rest and rehabilitation, Dawson returned to rally the Chiefs to a win over Buffalo November 2. Two weeks later, he led the club into Shea Stadium just two days after the death of his father, and threw three touchdown passes to Otis Taylor in a 34–16 win, before flying to Ohio for the funeral. The Chiefs would lose twice in the last month to the Raiders, but would benefit from the AFL's expanded playoff format, in which the second-place team from each division would qualify to play the champion of the opposite division in the first round of the playoffs.

Kansas City headed to New York, for a rematch with the defending world champion Jets, winners of the AFL East. The tightly fought game was tied at 6 in the fourth quarter when Otis Taylor spoke with Dawson on the Chiefs' sidelines. As a onetime college quarterback, Taylor had a nuanced understanding of defensive coverages. Kansas City had given the Jets some trouble with its "camouflage slot" formation, in which Taylor lined up a few yards behind the line of scrimmage, between an enlarged gap between the right guard and tackle. He'd seen enough of how the Jets adapted to the formation to be convinced that if he ran a crossing pattern out of the alignment, he'd be single-covered by a strong safety who couldn't hope to keep up with him. As the Chiefs took the field following Turner's kick, Taylor sidled up to Dawson and asked excitedly, "Are you going to call it?" "Not until we get in the huddle," said Dawson. "I want everybody else to hear it."

The play developed exactly as Taylor had envisioned, yielding a 61-yard gain that devastated the Jets. On the next play, from the New York 19, Dawson found Gloster Richardson for the go-ahead touchdown, and Kansas City took a 13–6 lead. The Kansas City defense repelled two more drives, concluding the last with a Jim Marsalis interception in the end zone. The champion Jets were vanquished, and the jubilant Chiefs began looking toward a third game with Oakland, two weeks hence, in what would be the final game ever between two American Football League teams.

That game would serve as a fitting end to the league's self-contained history. The Raiders had the league's most valuable player, Daryle Lamonica; Coach of the Year, the first-year firebrand John Madden; and most potent offense, as well as a sizable home field advantage and the knowledge that they'd beaten the Chiefs in seven of their eight previous meetings.

It would be the sort of game that many of the participants would describe later as "a war." Johnny Robinson cracked two ribs on a play, Jim Marsalis left the game with a bruised kidney. Jim Lynch made one tackle with such force that he broke his belt. Daryle Lamonica tore tendons in his hand following through on a pass, his fingers tangling in the facemask of the Chiefs' onrushing Aaron Brown.

Oakland dominated the first half, but Kansas City fought back to tie the game at 7 late in the second quarter. The Raiders spent much of the third quarter in Kansas City territory as well, but couldn't convert. After Emmitt Thomas ran an end zone interception out to the six, the Chiefs found themselves pinned back deep in their own territory again, facing third-and-14 at their own two-yard-line. Avoiding the rush, Dawson scrambled and threw a high floater from his end zone toward Otis Taylor, who made a spectacular over-the-shoulder catch while tightroping along the sidelines against double coverage at the 35-yard line. The Chiefs proceeded to march down the field for a touchdown, to go up 14–7 with 3:24 left in the third quarter.

"The Chiefs would be open and flamboyant when they got ahead, but they tended to be a little conservative when the game was tighter and they were behind," said Madden. "So that was a hell of a call, and a hell of a throw by Len Dawson. Because that could have turned the game around the other way. That's a dangerous place to throw. Then Otis makes a heck of a catch on the sideline. If we knock that thing down, if we pick it off, we win the game."

Instead, the Chiefs persevered, and held on, overcoming three fourth-quarter turnovers to do so. After consecutive road wins over the defending world champions and the team with the best record in pro football, with a stifling defense that allowed just 13 points in those two games, Kansas City might have been regarded as a formidable contender. Instead, much was made of the fact that the team hadn't even won its own division. The gritty Minnesota Vikings were installed as a 13-point favorite by Jimmy "The Greek" Snyder. One headline in *Pro Football Weekly,* the newspaper that had begun publishing two years earlier and had found a rabid audience of professional fans and gamblers, noted, "If It's a Battle of the QBs . . . Kapp Has It All Over Dawson." The *New York Times*'s William Wallace predicted a 31–7 Vikings win. So the buildup to Super Bowl IV played out in eerie parallel to the previous year, with a seemingly invincible team from the NFL being put forth as prohibitive favorite, the merits of the AFL entry largely ignored in the calculation.

"They're doing it again," warned the Raiders' George Blanda during the week. "They haven't learned a thing since last year. They're underestimating the AFL all over again."

And once again, all the attention leading up to the game centered on the AFL quarterback at the eye of a media hurricane. This time, though, Len Dawson did nothing to bring it on himself.

The Chiefs were spending their first full day in unseasonably cold New Orleans on Tuesday afternoon, January 6, when NBC's *Huntley-Brinkley Report* broke a story linking Dawson and five other pro players to a Justice Department sting of a network of bookmakers, including Detroit bookie Donald "Dice" Dawson (no relation to the quarterback), whose address book included phone numbers of Len Dawson and Namath.

Seven years after the Hornung and Karras suspensions, and just months following the protracted standoff over Namath's involvement in Bachelors III, the report ignited a media frenzy beyond anything seen the year before in Miami. Rozelle was on a boat in Bimini when the news hit, and could do little but release a statement from the league office that evening, noting that the league had "no evidence to even consider disciplinary action against any of those publicly named." But hundreds of writers and reporters were already gathered in New Orleans, confronting a potentially major story with absolutely no answers.

With the media staking out the Fontainebleau Hotel, where the Chiefs were staying, it was left to Stram, Dawson, and Chiefs publicist Jim Schaaf to work out a response. Late that evening, Dawson called a press conference to make a statement. "I have known Mr. [Donald] Dawson for about 10 years," he said, "and I have talked to him on several occasions. My only conversations with him in recent years concerned my knee injury and the death of my father. On these occasions he called me to offer his sympathy. These calls were among the many I received. Gentlemen, this is all I have to say. I have told you everything I know."

Ultimately, that's all there was to the story. Neither Dawson nor the other players were ever subpoenaed, and all were cleared of any wrongdoing. Rozelle arrived in New Orleans on Wednesday, and coolly conducted an hour-long press conference in which he defended Dawson's honor as well as the league's security investigation. But the furor didn't immediately go away, and Len Dawson was left to face the biggest game of his life under a cloud of suspicion.

"He never had a tougher week in his life," said roommate Johnny Robinson. "It ate him up. From the day it all started, up to game time, he looked like he aged five years. . . . I don't think he got three hours of sleep the night before the game."

For his part, Robinson had spent much of the week in physical therapy with severely bruised ribs. Showing up the night before the game, he went to Emmitt Thomas's hotel room and, with secondary mates Jim Kearney and James Marsalis, watched films of the Vikings' offense. "It wasn't any big secret," said Robinson of the Vikings' approach. "They beat everybody they played doing the same thing. They weren't going to trick anybody—I don't think they *wanted* to trick anybody. It was, 'Here's what we're gonna do. We're not gonna run a halfback reverse pass when we can just kick your teeth in.' "

The day of the game dawned cold and overcast, with rain pelting New Orleans in the morning and a tornado warning in the area early in the afternoon. In the locker room prior to the game, the Chiefs were confident and keyed up, but not, in center E. J. Holub's description, the "blithering idiots" they were prior to Super Bowl I. The Chiefs arrived in their locker room to find a small addition to each jersey, an anniversary patch denoting the ten-year history of the AFL. "It was incredible to see the reaction of those great players," said Hank Stram. "They were so proud to wear that patch because they cared about the league. They wanted to be first-class."

When the game began, it quickly became clear that while the Vikes' under-sized 235-pound center Mick Tingelhoff may have been a worthy All-League selection in the NFL, where he was a quick-footed blocker free to operate in space, he was physically unequipped to deal with the head-on pressure and intimidation of 6-foot-7, 285-pound Buck Buchanan or 6-foot-1, 265-pound

Curley Culp, who alternated lining up right on Tingelhoff's nose in the Chiefs' odd-man fronts, largely destroying the Vikings' interior running game. Confused by the Chiefs' triple stack and intimidated by Buchanan's and Culp's alternate mauling of the outmanned Mick Tingelhoff at center, the Vikings were shut out in the first half. To say the Vikings ran a vanilla offense is to give them credit for more flavor than they mustered. In sixty-two offensive plays from scrimmage, they didn't once shift or start a play with a man into motion.

"Our whole influence was Bambi and the Chargers and the things Sid Gillman was doing, like the Raiders, and the Jets, when you got an arm like Namath; that was our culture," said the Chiefs' Jim Lynch. "The NFL was different. Their culture was the Green Bay Packers, Theirs was, 'Look, we're gonna line up and we're gonna run the Green Bay sweep. And you'd better stop us, 'cause here we come.' "

On offense, the Chiefs double-teamed the Vikings' ends, to prevent them from batting down passes, and in so doing opened passing lanes for Dawson's play-action fakes and short, crisp flares and out patterns. Kansas City drove consistently on the Vikings in the first half, building a 9–0 lead on three Stenerud field goals (the first one from 48 yards out). When the Vikings' Charlie West fumbled Stenerud's kickoff following the third field goal, the Chiefs' Remi Prudhomme recovered on Minnesota's 19, and three plays later, Mike Garrett scored from five yards out, and the Chiefs went to the half leading 16–0.

The Vikings had trailed the Rams by 10 at the half and came back to win that playoff game. But during the interminable halftime, while the Tulane Stadium crowd was being treated to a reenactment of the Battle of New Orleans that further tore up the spongy field, Vikings coach Grant apparently did nothing to adjust to the Chiefs' tactics, merely advising his team to play better. For a while they did, mounting their one sustained drive of the day, to slice the lead to 16–7.

On the next drive, with a first-and-10 at the Minnesota 46, Dawson sensed an all-out blitz and, after a short drop, flung the ball out into the flat just as he was being hit. The pass found Otis Taylor, running a quick hitch pattern, and Taylor did the rest. He broke the attempted tackle of cornerback Earsell Mackbee and sprinted down the sidelines in his long, prancing stride. Karl Kassulke had an angle on him at the 10, but Taylor's juke move and stiff arm left Kassulke on the ground. Suddenly, the Chiefs were up 23–7, and the game was all but over.

Kansas City picked off three passes in the fourth quarter (giving them 10 interceptions in three playoff games), and Aaron Brown's tackle of the previously indomitable Kapp sent the Vikings' leader to the sideline, writhing in pain. Minutes later, as the chilled New Orleans twilight subsumed what little sunlight had peeked through the densely packed clouds, the red-clad Kansas City Chiefs ran off the field, carrying Hank Stram on their shoulders, champions of the world. In the frantic locker room at Tulane Stadium, a crush of reporters came in to document the chaotic scene, along with dozens of AFL players and coaches.

Pete Rozelle presented Lamar Hunt and Hank Stram with the Super Bowl championship trophy, as Chiefs scout Lloyd Wells sat grinning in a window well against the back wall, the spot where he was sure to be in virtually every television picture of the championship podium. Redemption was all around the room. "I knew I went with the right team!" said Bobby Bell, who had chosen the Chiefs over the Vikings back in 1962. Taylor, who'd made the key offensive play in all three playoff games, spent the first fifteen minutes after the game weeping tears of joy.

Dawson, vindicated both off and on the field, received the MVP award with the same outward calm he'd exhibited all week. Then came the summons from Chiefs equipment man Bobby Yarborough.

"Hey, Lenny, come here," said Yarborough. "The phone—it's the president."

"The president of what?" asked Dawson.

"*The president,*" exclaimed Yarborough. "Nixon!"

The short conversation that ensued was a seminal moment in American sports, and spawned countless congratulatory calls and White House visits in the decades to follow. It wasn't even the first time Nixon had called the Chiefs that day. He'd rung up Stram that morning at the Fontainebleau, to tell him that he knew Dawson hadn't done anything wrong, and wished the team luck in its game that day. "I don't know if it amounted to a presidential pardon," said Stram. "But it sure made Leonard feel better."

And so the original Super Bowl series, NFL vs. AFL, ended in a 2–2 tie, and parity between the leagues that would come together the following season.

"Most people in the NFL thought that the Jets' win in Super Bowl III was a once-in-a-lifetime upset," said Steve Sabol of NFL Films. "It didn't really cause people to change their opinion. Everyone said, if they played ten times, the Colts would win eight or nine times. But after Super Bowl IV, nobody was saying that. After that, there was no doubt anymore—you had to grant that the AFL had reached parity. At the least."

Weeb Ewbank worked his way through the room, congratulating and embracing players, finally getting to where Hank Stram was standing. Ewbank gave Stram a hug, and the two coaches briefly congratulated each other on the mutual accomplishment. And both must have silently noted the irony: on the afternoon of January 11, 1970, the American Football League had finally earned the lasting respect it deserved. At that very same moment it ceased to exist.

In ten years the AFL had irreversibly altered the American sports landscape by sparking a rush to expansion that would eventually seize all sports. Major League Baseball began the decade with sixteen teams and ended with twenty-four, the National Hockey League doubled in size from six to twelve, and both the NHL and NBA would soon be challenged by rival leagues.

The AFL opened numerous new markets, in Kansas City and Denver, Buffalo and Cincinnati, Miami and San Diego. It infused pro football with a bolt of innovation. Gillman and Stram revolutionized offensive attacks, but also changed the game in the trenches, Gillman with his complex but tested blocking schemes and the myriad intricacies of his pass offense, Stram with his unbalanced line and triple-stack defense. The AFL became a fluid, active laboratory for football tactics. Super Bowl IV foreshadowed the growing complexity of the modern game.

But the league had done more than bring changes to the way the game was contested on the field. The AFL's seminal television deal paved the way for the revenue sharing that would enrich pro football—and pro football owners—for decades to come. Sonny Werblin's signing of Joe Namath started to push the sport of pro football toward the realm of celebrity culture and mass entertainment.

Most importantly, all eight members of "the Foolish Club" had made it through, meaning the AFL was the only upstart professional sports league to survive intact since baseball's American League began play in 1901. In the Raiders and the Chiefs, the Jets and the Chargers, and the league's other competitors, pro football didn't merely have ten more franchises. They'd become *teams*, with identifiable personalities and characteristics. And the world of pro football was all the richer and more complex for having grown to include them.

The Super Bowl, too, was much better for the genuine antipathy and differences between the leagues. Though the game would get bigger, the hype surrounding it more pervasive, the extra edge of rivalry brought to bear in those first four contests would never again be duplicated.

It became clear that 1970 would stand as a divide. It would mark the beginning of the third quarter-century of the NFL's history, but more than that, the complete merger of the AFL and the NFL. If the first quarter of a century of football's growth, the rag days of the NFL, had been the first act, the second quarter-century, when pro football seized the American imagination and the American marketplace, constituted the second act.

In the Chiefs' locker room, where Grambling coach Eddie Robinson stopped by to congratulate Buck Buchanan, the new world champions stood as a legacy of the efforts of Kenny Washington and Woody Strode, Marion Motley and Bill Willis. It had been less than twenty-five years since Washington signed with the Rams to reintegrate pro football, and just eight seasons after the final capitulation of pro football's last segregated team, the Redskins. But on January 11, 1970, pro football's new world champions were celebrated. It was noted that they were the first team to ever win a world title without winning its own division. But there was another, more significant milestone: the Chiefs were the first team in pro football to field a lineup in which more than half the twenty-two starters were African-American. And that, too, was a sign of the changing face of football in the '70s.

In the end the most compelling metaphor for pro football's rise in the '60s wasn't really war. The '60s enterprise that pro football most resembled was the American manned spaceflight program. Both rose to unimagined heights during the decade, both were to embrace everything that was modern about the country, and benefited from that most modern of technologies, live television. Both were spiced by a kind of thrill of danger and ultramodern promise, yet harked back to a timeless, distinctly American brand of manifest destiny. Both were branded as elaborate follies by their critics, yet captured the fancy of a large portion of the American public. And both would be splendidly marketed: Apollo as the ultimate voyage; pro football as the ultimate game. Even Nixon's postgame call to Dawson had its echoes in congratulatory postmission phone calls from JFK to the Mercury astronauts and LBJ to the Gemini astronauts.

The vision of the Apollo missions—flight director Gene Kranz pacing across the floor of mission control, talking through his headset while millions of dollars of machinery left earth's orbit—was soon mimicked on the football field, where coaches patrolled the sidelines, communicating through headsets to experts above, delegating assignments to their pilots on the field.

Finally, there was the sheer ratio of preparation to performance. Just as in the space program, in football thousands of hours of collaborative work were focused on a few hours of performance. In pro football, a season's worth of effort and organization culminated with the result of fourteen games, during which any player would play fifty or sixty snaps, each play lasting six to eight seconds. And in the sum of those compressed fragments of time was a year's harvest.

"American society was defining itself during the Cold War in a particular kind of way in relation to the Soviet Union," said the writer Gerald Early. "Some of this had to do with our ability to plan, strategize, and achieve certain kinds of goals. It's interesting that part of what the war was about was not just on the military level, it was on an engineering level, it was on a level of how a modern society is supposed to be run. And we were claiming, as a democratic capitalist society, that insofar as being able to execute certain kinds of goals, being able to plan out certain kinds of things, and achieve them, that we could do that better than they could. And what's football all about? Football is really all about preparation and about breaking down the film, coming up with a plan and a strategy and so forth. I would say during the Cold War era particularly, that those aspects of football would be something that would be important for our society and would be one other thing that would make football attractive."

Like the race to the moon, pro football was, as Rozelle took pains to say, both news *and* entertainment. *Life* magazine's review of the decade noted that the sport's "electric blend of brute force and computerlike precision helped make pro football the No. 1 spectator sport of the decade." But it was one thing to recognize that pro football had seized the decade, another to understand just how passionate and numerous its followers had become. The full impact wouldn't be known for another couple of seasons, but even by the end of the '60s, there were broad hints. One came later in January 1970, when the Nielsen organization released its ratings for the week of January 5–11, showing that 60 million people saw the final battle between the NFL and AFL. The fourth Super Bowl, the new spectacle of American sports, matching two franchises that hadn't even existed a decade earlier, had been watched by more American television viewers than saw Neil Armstrong walk on the moon.

Pro football had landed.

15

Prime Time

The unified and expanded National Football League, now comprising twenty-six teams in two thirteen-team conferences, kicked off its fifty-first season on Sunday, September 19, 1970. The future of American spectator sports arrived the following evening, at 9:00 p.m. EDT on the ABC Television Network, as the opening weekend's final game was introduced on prime-time television, not with a shot of the stadium, or the crowd, or the key players, but instead with a self-referential scene set inside a television control booth, and the voice-over of a director urgently counting down, "Five seconds to air, four, three, two, and . . . take tape!" As a jazzy riff surged forward and the opening titles flashed on the screen, *Monday Night Football* took to the air.

From Municipal Stadium in Cleveland, Ohio, where the Cleveland Browns would play host to the New York Jets, ABC's play-by-play man Keith Jackson opened the broadcast, before turning it over to his broadcast partner, Howard Cosell, standing down on the field. "It is a hot, sultry, almost windless night here," Cosell intoned, and his voice bespoke gravity, a sense of occasion. It was, to be sure, just another regular season football game. But in the electric tension of the sellout crowd and the urgency of Cosell's delivery, it was as though something more important was going on. Sports in America would never be the same.

It is easy to forget, more than thirty years after the fact, when pro football's pre-eminence seems so assured, how much of an uphill struggle Rozelle fought, throughout much of his first ten years as commissioner, to bring the NFL to prime time. Pro football's rapid ascent in the '60s did little to alter the conventional wisdom within the television industry that spectator sports were too parochial, too male, too unsophisticated to qualify as big-time entertainment.

In the short history of television, the only sport to receive a long look in prime time was boxing, which nearly died because of it. But while boxing promoters rued the consequences of overexposure, advertisers and television executives took a different lesson: sports wouldn't play in Peoria, at least not at night when the wife and kids were in front of the television. From the end of *Friday Night Fights* on NBC in 1959 to the beginning of *Monday Night Football* in 1970, there had been a bare trickle of sports shows on any of the network's prime-time schedules. The smattering of events—the Orange Bowl, or baseball's All-Star Game, or the occasional one-off prime-time broadcasts of NFL games—were viewed as anomalies.

Rozelle had argued for years that football would be a natural for a prime-time slot and that the right package of games would only increase the league's following. But his early efforts at promoting a package of Friday night games ran into stiff resistance from both the NCAA and the Alliance of High School Athletic Associations. When Congress approved the 1966 merger, it also wrote into U.S. law that the league *couldn't* play games on Friday evening. (The previous antitrust exemption, for the joint TV deal, included the proviso that the league wouldn't play games on Saturdays during the college football season.)

The prospect of a season-long Monday night package emerged in a series of conversations in the spring of 1969 between Rozelle and the innovative ABC producer Roone Arledge, whose work with ABC's NCAA college football package brought a theatrical element to the coverage of football. It was exactly what Rozelle was looking for, and after spending a few weeks discussing the details, the two men agreed upon an approach. At that point, Rozelle calmly mentioned that he must first offer the package to the league's existing network partners, CBS and NBC.

"But we made a deal!" blurted Arledge. "You can't just shop it." Rozelle patiently explained that not only would he shop it, but that he *had* to shop it.

Though Bill MacPhail sensed the possibilities of the package, he was unable to convince his superiors that CBS should break up the most powerful lineup on TV for the untested idea of pro football in prime time. When Rozelle had first presented the idea to CBS executive Bob Wood, his response was, "What!? And pre-empt Doris Day?!"

NBC might have been interested, but it already had the top-rated program of the previous two years, *Rowan & Martin's Laugh-In*, as the anchor of its

Monday night lineup, and had no interest in regularly preempting Johnny Carson and the *Tonight* show, then bringing in revenue of $28 million a year. (Carson had been miffed when NBC aired a special Monday night game in 1968, and NBC did not want to ruffle the feathers of its top star.)

With that, Rozelle told a relieved Arledge that ABC would have the package. And then, to Arledge's horror, his boss nixed the deal. ABC president Elton Rule was convinced that sports wouldn't play in prime time.

Only after the ABC rejection did Rozelle reveal his Plan B: if ABC was indeed going to pass on the package, the NFL had a deal in the works with the Sports Network, an independent production company recently purchased by Howard Hughes and renamed the Hughes Sports Network. There was no need to elaborate on the implications of that deal: awarding of a Monday Night package to the Hughes network could spark a wholesale defection of ABC stations to the new network.

The threat was underscored on a summer day in 1969. "It was a Monday morning staff meeting," said Barry Frank, then Arledge's lieutenant at ABC Sports, "and Roone was out of town, so I went to the network staff meeting for him. The guy who was the head of our station affiliates group gets up in the meeting and says, 'Guys, we've got a major problem. We're going to have to go dark on Monday nights in the fourth quarter next year.' And everybody says, 'What! Why?' He says, 'Because about 60 percent of our affiliates have agreed to take this syndicated package of Monday night football.' And [ABC vice president] Tom Moore said, 'Oh, *shit*.' So he says to me, 'I want you to get Pete Rozelle and get him on the phone and tell him I want to meet with him this afternoon.' And I did and I called Pete. And Tom went over that day. But it was a defensive move; it was not offensive, it was defensive. Nobody knew if it was going to be a big success or not."

They found out quickly. The show earned a share of over 35 percent on its opening night, en route to a consistent Nielsen rating of 18 (about 60 million homes) and a share of 31 in its first season. Reviewing the first broadcast in its Wednesday editions, the *New York Times* noted, "Executives normally tucked in bed by 11 o'clock were a little bleary-eyed yesterday morning. Teen-age youngsters also stayed up, at least in the Eastern time zone, and there were motherly mumblings about inadequate attention to homework." By early October, the broadcasts had knocked ABC's *Dick Cavett Show* off the air on Mondays, with Cavett moving to a four-night-a-week schedule through the end of the football season.

What was immediately clear, in those first weeks—especially with the use of ABC's multiple cameras—was that the games *looked* more vivid at night.

The color of a regular game took on an exquisite, saturated sheen, arc lights shimmering off the shiny headgear. The entire onfield tableau possessed a richer, more dramatic presence, accentuated by the shortened depth-of-focus of night viewing. For the fans in the stadium and players alike, the game offered the special incentive of knowing that the rest of the country's fans, and many of the rest of the league's players, were watching.

In addition to more cameras, and a separate production unit dedicated to isolation shots and slow-motion replays, ABC offered the novel presence of three commentators instead of two in the booth. Keith Jackson, the crisp, low-key ex-Marine, handled the play-by-play, with color commentary provided by Howard Cosell and Don Meredith, the inspired combination making the difference.

Cosell's brand of pointed, often trenchant, pontification—"just telling it like it is" he insisted—earned dramatic responses, both positive and negative. Many critics felt he played it both ways, stirring up a froth of hyperbole with each Monday night while at the same time bemoaning the lack of journalistic credibility in the sports media field ("What a horizontal ladder of mediocrity," mused Cosell of his competition in a 1967 interview). Many fans hated him for his erudition, his arrogance, and for the approbation he offered the boxer Muhammad Ali after he'd changed his name from Cassius Clay. Some undoubtedly disliked him for the simple fact he was Jewish. But his presence changed the environment surrounding the games.

In the booth, Jackson handled the play-by-play with his usual clipped professionalism, just a hint of his Oklahoma roots audible in some of his calls. Cosell was forever the cultural critic, investing the game and the surroundings with portent, an effort to bring context and gravity to the occasion. Meredith, on the other hand, was the Southern rascal who insisted that the game wasn't that complicated and, as a former player, possessed the authority to back that up. He also had a knack for deflating Cosell at his most grandiose.

During one game, Cosell noted, "So it's three downs and over for the Kansas City Chiefs, and that's been their wont so often tonight, at a time when they desperate—"

"Their what?" interjected Meredith.

"Their *wont.* W-O-N-T."

"Aahww, Howard . . ."

"The education of Dandy Don continues, we await the punt . . ."

The broadcasts also replaced the typical halftime fare of marching bands with a six- to seven-minute highlight package of the previous day's biggest plays, gleaned not from the burgeoning technology of videotape, but from the best of the footage compiled by the NFL Films crews that sent two cameramen to each league game. This required NFL Films to send the reel "wet," straight off the film-editing bay, to whatever city the *Monday Night Football* crew was in. There, often with no rehearsal and nothing to work with but a bare-bones play sheet, Cosell extemporaneously narrated the footage, with his own multisyllabic vocabulary and pointed intonations providing an urgent counterpoint to the sweet and empty cadences of a generation of highlights readers. From the first broadcast—when he described the scrambling Cardinals quarterback Jim Hart being "chased down by the irrepressible Deacon Jones"—it was clear that Cosell would bring something different to the package.

At a time when an easy relay of highlights was sharply limited, and when NFL Films' highlight package *This Week in Pro Football* didn't air until the following Saturday in most markets, the halftime highlights package became a powerful vehicle. Even in blowouts, the audience numbers stayed strong through the halftime package.

The impact was felt within the league as well. Like all coaches in the league, the Raiders' John Madden was invariably hard at work on Monday evenings, reviewing film and preparing scouting reports for the following week's game plan. But he began to make it a habit to have an assistant tell him when it was halftime. Then, over sandwiches and soda, the Raiders' staff would take a ten-minute break, and watch along with the rest of America. "It was the only way you could see the other teams," said Madden.

By the beginning of the show's second season, 1971, when Frank Gifford came over from CBS and replaced Jackson as the play-by-play man, the series was a bona fide hit, its cultural impact unquestioned. Howard, Dandy Don, and the Giffer were stars in their own right, treated to celebrity welcomes in any city to which they traveled.

The on-air jousting grew more ritual, and at times threatened to overshadow the game itself. The irony was that, though Cosell was more critical than many broadcasters had been in the past, he also turned out to be the most starstruck of announcers. There was something slightly off-putting about seeing the most prominent sports journalist of his generation parlay his newfound popularity into guest spots on sitcoms like *Nanny and the Professor*. Meredith understood better than his partners that the crew of broadcasters had become part of the show, and he was most adept at treating it as such. When a game seemed out of reach, Meredith would serenade the Monday night audience with the opening line of Willie Nelson's jukebox weeper "The

Party's Over," to indicate that the result was assured. *"Turn out the lights, the party's over/They say that all good things must end . . ."*

By then, *Monday Night Football* had become a legitimate cultural phenomenon. The tireless self-promotion on the part of Arledge and producer Don Ohlmeyer helped further those perceptions: after reading a story about a bowling league that had shut down on Monday nights, Ohlmeyer started pushing the notion that leagues were dying by the dozens; news of slow restaurant business prompted similar tactics. "We were like Joe McCarthy running around the country," recalled Ohlmeyer. "I have in my pocket a list of seven thousand restaurants . . ."

Not all of it was imagined. In the fall of 1970, the show business trade paper *Variety* reported that movie theater attendance was "in a real nosedive as a result of ABC's pro football." Tuesdays, rather than Mondays, became the most common day for sick calls among Detroit autoworkers.

Following ABC's example, the other networks added more isolation, more close-ups, more replays, more analysis. *Monday Night Football* opened the floodgates for other prime-time sports events. The first night World Series game came a year later, in 1971, and the Summer Olympics first went to a nightly prime-time broadcast in 1972; the NCAA basketball championship game soon followed, making its prime-time debut in 1973. Even more influential was the tone of *Monday Night Football*. Within a few years, every game had more narrative structure, a more intimate feel, a greater sense of sport as a *performance* rather than merely a game.

Monday Night Football's most lasting contribution was the unprecedented amalgam of journalism and entertainment. When "Telling It like It Is" was crossed with "Turn Out the Lights," sports began to change, and the relationship between fans and athletes, never entirely innocent, grew much more complex, with a greater self-awareness on both sides of the equation.

———

With the completion of the merger in 1970, the sport became more uniform, as corporate oversight and league-wide standardization eliminated the anomalies of earlier eras: no more botched film exchanges, no more playing games in high school stadiums, or on fields with misshapen end zones; no more teams dressing in Ramada Inns. The football that was used was the NFL football, but the older league did adopt two AFL innovations: putting players' last names on the back of all jerseys, and making the scoreboard the official game clock.

The old 16-10 alignment of the NFL and AFL was superseded by the two symmetrical thirteen-team conferences, both under the NFL umbrella.

To minimize the possibility of the Colts' plight in 1967—having the league's second-best record yet not qualifying for the playoffs—the NFL decided that each thirteen-team conference would be divided into three divisions, with the best record among nonchampions earning the fourth playoff berth as the "wild card" team, another idea conceived by Tex Schramm.

The unlikely star of the 1970 season was the new league's oldest player, forty-three-year-old George Blanda of the Raiders. Twelve years after retiring from the Bears, Blanda went on an unprecedented five-week run in which he either spelled Daryle Lamonica as starting quarterback to rally the Raiders from behind, or came on and kicked the winning field goal.

The Raiders, who'd gone to Super Bowl II, then lost the next two AFL championship games, began the 1970 season a disappointing 2-2-1, before Blanda took over for an injured Lamonica in the first quarter of the team's sixth game, against Pittsburgh, throwing three touchdown passes in a win over the Steelers. The following week, the defending champion Chiefs were caught in the web of Blanda's astonishing run, when Blanda kicked a 47-yard field goal as time ran out, earning Oakland a 17–17 tie in a wild, brawl-marred game. A week later, Blanda replaced Lamonica against Cleveland, threw a game-tying touchdown, then kicked a game-winning field goal in the last two minutes. In the following two weeks, he threw a late, game-winning touchdown against Denver, and kicked the winning field goal, with four seconds left, to beat the Chargers.

On five consecutive Sundays, Blanda had emerged from the bench, pulled his battered silver helmet over his shaggy gray hair, and rallied the Raiders to four wins and a tie. He became the most unlikely MVP but also a celebrity whose popularity within a matter of weeks transcended sports. "Now every man over 40 in the nation is young again," wrote Wells Twombly of the *San Francisco Examiner.* "Now every man in his late 30s who was dreading his 40th birthday is looking forward eagerly to the real ripening of his years." *Sports Illustrated* put him on the cover, as did *Newsweek* and *Time.* And within another year, he would be promoting Wheaties and Brut (the only two products he'd endorse, because they were the only ones—among those offered—that he actually used). As Johnny Carson started slipping Blanda's name into monologues, Blanda became synonymous with a newfound middle-aged vitality. Or, as he put it on the Brut commercial, "I can keep up with the younger guys on the field. And I like to think I can keep up with them *off* the field as well."

Even before Blanda's marvelous fall, there was, by the beginning of the '70s, a kind of mythic ambience surrounding professional football. The game was making inroads into the mainstream of American popular culture in a manner that would have been unimaginable just a decade earlier. To a certain extent, this was a result of the galvanizing personalities of Lombardi and Hornung, Jim Brown and Dick Butkus, Joe Namath and Johnny Unitas. But the cause of the game was also helped, in ways so subtle as to be incalculable, by the support apparatus developed by Pete Rozelle.

Primary among these was NFL Films, which by 1970 was producing about twenty-five hours of original material each year. While Ed Sabol's easy confidence and broad cinematic grounding helped get NFL Films off the ground, it was his son Steve's restless intelligence, and questing for something new, that would ultimately give NFL Films its signature style.

Steve Sabol inherited his mother's artistic sensibilities, but also had a boy's love for sports and action, and grew up predisposed toward grand, heroic images. For Sabol, sports was a tactile experience. He'd cut out the full-page color pictures from the '50s-era issues of *Sport* magazine and paste them to the wall. While his friends gathered after school to watch the locally taped *American Bandstand,* he would rush home to watch *Victory at Sea.* He was transfixed with the gallantry and the gravity of the old black-and-white documentaries, the sonorous tone of the show's narrator, and the bracing martial musical scores that accompanied the combat footage.

Later in life, he was drawn to dramatic artists who were capable of grand gestures: composers like Tchaikovsky and Max Steiner—whose rousing scores were crucial elements of such films as *The Caine Mutiny* and *Casablanca*—and filmmaker Leni Riefenstahl, whose triumphant 1938 documentary *Olympia* he loved. So when his father called him at Colorado College with the news of the formation of NFL Films—"I can tell by your grades that all you've been doing with your time is watching movies and playing football; that makes you perfectly qualified for this new venture"—it wasn't just nepotism. Steve Sabol turned out to be more of a natural than anyone could have imagined.

After the early success of NFL Films, the Sabols shot *This Is Pro Football,* a documentary that would attempt to capture the broad appeal of the sport and the power of NFL Films. The film began with a montage of close-in football action, made more vivid by the sounds of contact, and interspersed with close-ups of men sweating, bleeding, resting exhausted on the sidelines. Over these pictures came a rich, resonant voice, saying, in deep, measured cadences, "It starts with a whistle . . . and ends with a bang." The words, crisp, staccato, more evocative than expository, were from the pen of Steve Sabol. The voice, the deep, stentorian tones that to Steve Sabol sounded like "the fall of Dunkirk," belonged to a veteran Philadelphia newsman named John Facenda.

"He was an old, craggy-faced weather-beaten guy," recalled Steve Sabol, "who had this great, oaken delivery. I had grown up with that voice as a kid, and I remembered him doing the news. Whenever he spoke, anybody that was in the room watching the news just listened." Facenda was a casual football fan who knew little of the game's ins and outs. But Steve Sabol, who usually wrote the scripts from which he read, was frequently there coaching him. "He was an opera fan," recalled Sabol. "When we'd get to portions of the script that we really wanted to sound dramatic, he would write the word 'profundo.' "

Instead of the clanging band marches that had been the staple of football highlights, the Sabols wanted something richer and more dramatic. Steve recalled his teenage days at summer camp in the Poconos, and learning old folk songs for campfire sing-alongs, with rhythmic choruses like "What do you do with a drunken sailor, da da dadum da dadum dum dum dum." That tune was adapted into an orchestral piece by a composer named Sam Spence, who for $50,000 had scored fifteen minutes of original orchestral music for use in the film.

And then there was the cinematography. With zooms, isolation, and a vast tableau of drama, the NFL Films crews captured the intimacy of the game: fatigued and wounded men on the sideline, the intensity of a linebacker's defensive coverage audibles, the lithe acceleration of a running back moving around the corner.

When the film premiered in 1967, pro football was still far behind baseball in the matter of myth, nostalgia, and lore. The "small ball" theory of literature, oft joked about but held in some respect, maintained that golf and baseball were the true literary, intellectual pursuits. But with *This Is Pro Football* the league began to manufacture its own myth.

By then, NFL Films and Ed Sabol were beginning to merit widespread press attention. "If there is a problem with the Sabol format," wrote Tom C. Brody in *Sports Illustrated,* "it is that his shows might be too good, better than the game itself. Even the National Football League is capable of turning out an occasional stinker, sloppily played, lopsided, dull. Call [Ed] Sabol sloppy, even lopsided, but not dull. He has never been dull."

"To put it harshly, Mr. Sabol's movies are used as the shill for pro football," wrote Mel Durslag in *TV Guide* in 1969. "Their primary purpose is to call attention to the product, keeping it before the eye of the public and making it more salable to TV, which pours out millions for live coverage."

In this mission, NFL Films surely succeeded with the weekly highlights show, *This Week in Pro Football*, an hour-long review with highlights of each of the previous weekend's games, and the half-hour *NFL Game of the Week*, which focused on a more in-depth look at the most important or exciting game of the week.

That these shows found a loyal audience during the season was not all that surprising. What was a shock was the success of the third NFL Films show, *NFL Action*, which began airing in syndication in the off-season, between March and August, with a weekly half-hour of highlights. The show's primary sponsor, American Express, was at first reluctant to tread on foreign ground, airing football action in the off-season. Many of the affiliate stations, equally timid, would show it at odd hours, in the middle of the night, or at sunrise on Saturday and Sunday mornings. But the ratings *NFL Action* garnered were eye-opening, with some four million homes finding it at different times through a typical week in the off-season. Increased requests for public screenings of the shows soon poured in, from Boy Scout troops, Kiwanis meetings, and Jaycee gatherings.

This Is Pro Football proved to be the seed of a burgeoning and distinctive NFL Films look, but what would make the Sabols synonymous with a particular kind of cinematic style were two vastly different highlights films, of the third and fourth Super Bowl games.

The Super Bowl III highlights film emphasized the full range of the Sabols' cinematic powers. It opened with a montage of Joe Namath, in game action and mod civilian life—sporting the famous Fu Manchu on the sidelines, walking through a crowd of jubilant New Yorkers at the post–Super Bowl parade—and interspersed these with dozens of shots of his adoring female fans. These were the same urbane hippie chicks who'd celebrated the Summer of Love, but now, instead of burning bras or protesting the war they were waving Namath signs at Shea Stadium or sitting pretty in the stands at the Orange Bowl, wearing straw boaters adorned with the Jets' logo. Playing over the footage was a frothy tribute song to Namath, "He's Our Hero, Broadway Joe," which had been a novelty hit in New York City during the Jets' march to the title ("What a feeling, what a sight/When we see that Number 12 in green-and-white"). Nowhere was the image of the swingin' Broadway Joe—in Dan Jenkins's words "pro football's very own Beatle"—more aptly demonstrated than in the opening minutes of the film. Then the quick cutting came to an end, and the snazzy music was replaced by the funereal strumming of a guitar, as the film cut to Johnny Unitas striding the sideline, the shafts of the setting sun painting him in silhouette, looking tired and haggard. It was as if someone had juxtaposed an Andy Warhol print with *American Gothic.*

The opening montage owed a debt to the quick-cutting climax of *Bonnie and Clyde,* and eventually the NFL Films style would exert its own influence on filmmakers.

While the Super Bowl III film was undoubtedly brilliant filmmaking and superb storytelling, the film that showed the true power of how NFL Films could add depth to a game came a year later with Ed Sabol's idea for Super Bowl IV.

The night before the Chiefs and Vikings played in Super Bowl IV, Ed Sabol invited himself up to Hank Stram's suite at the Fontainebleau Hotel, telling Stram that he had something important to discuss. There, while Stram was in boxer shorts getting dressed for that evening's dinner, Sabol pitched him on wearing a small hidden microphone for the Super Bowl.

"It'll be historic!" insisted Sabol. "You'll wear a wire, no one else will know you have it on, and people will finally get to see what a coach looks like during the biggest game of the year."

"I've got an idea," said Stram. "Why don't you go over to the Roosevelt and ask *Bud Grant* to wear a wire?"

"Number one, Bud Grant isn't animated on the sidelines," said Sabol. "Number two, I don't think Minnesota is going to win the game. And number three, you don't use profanity."

"Damn right," replied Stram, who finally consented, provided that no one—not even his own players—knew he was being wired. When K.C. won going away, Sabol's brainstorm succeeded beyond his own wildest dreams, documenting the effervescent nervousness of Stram's sideline demeanor. The Sabols had wired players for sound before, but much of the grunting and play calling on the field was prosaic. In miking Stram, they found a fascinating window into the game. As the immaculately dressed, carefully toupeed Stram paced the sidelines in his red vest and black blazer, he peppered his team with affirmation, and even more nervous energy than usual. (Dawson, consulting with the hyper Stram during one timeout, thought to himself, "This guy is losing it; the pressure is really getting to him.") But other than a few play calls in the distinctive jargon of the Chiefs' offensive playbook ("65 Toss Power Trap"), Stram didn't sound that much different from any other loyal fan whose fortunes were rising and falling with a team on the field.

As before, the NFL Films treatment told the story in a way that statistics and final scores couldn't. One segment, about the Chiefs' dizzying array of multiple formations and their ability to sow confusion in the Vikings' defense, featured a shot of Vikings linebacker Wally Hilgenberg waiting to call a front and coverage in the defensive huddle, looking to the Vikings' coaches on the sidelines, palms up, hands outstretched, expressing complete befuddlement. When the Super Bowl IV film premiered at the Plaza Theatre in Kansas City in the spring of 1970, it was an instant hit, so effective that some of Stram's lines were drowned out by the laughter at earlier ones. To a national audience, it played just as well, providing an intimate glimpse of the elusive truth of life on the sidelines during the biggest game of the year.

The NFL Films style became so distinctive that the entire enterprise seemed inevitable, the *only* way to shoot a modern football film. But this was far from the case; in 1964, at just about the time Ed Sabol had pitched Rozelle on bringing Blair Motion Pictures in-house, the young director William Friedkin, who would a few years later direct *The French Connection,* shot a one-hour special for ABC called "Mayhem on a Sunday Afternoon." Part of the continuum of documentary filmmaking inspired by "The Violent World of Sam Huff," the Friedkin film was much more stylized than its predecessor, and much more dramatic. Shot in black-and-white, with veristic grit, the picture was spare, memorable, and harsh, a flat, laconic depiction of life in the NFL. The well-reviewed film could have been a blueprint for how to shoot football, but then the Sabols came along, and football movies went in a different direction.

"We are not journalists but romanticists," Steve Sabol would say later, and that distinction would make all the difference. As he would explain, "Even if we weren't owned by the N.F.L., we wouldn't be doing exposés about drugs and illegal betting. That's for Mike Wallace. Renoir would never have painted an execution. He left that to Goya."

By 1970, the Films staff was working a brutal schedule: they would typically shoot twelve games on Sunday afternoon, edit a seven-minute highlights reel for Cosell's halftime highlights Monday; produce the half-hour *NFL Game of the Week* by Tuesday, and on Wednesday, after CBS's Pat Summerall and Tom Brookshier had flown into Philadelphia to tape their on-camera segments and voice-over narration, Films would send out *This Week in Pro Football* to more than 100 stations across the country. (It would be 1977 before Major League Baseball managed to drum up a similar syndication deal, broadcasting *This Week in Baseball* with Mel Allen narrating. But even this was not a counterpart, since *This Week in Baseball* wasn't shot on film stock at all, but instead was a collection of videotape clips.)

The Sabols' imprimatur grew, from the dramatic *The Championship Chase*

("The autumn wind is a pirate, rolling in from the sea . . .") to such farcical fare as *The Football Follies,* a collection of miscues and wild plays that treated the entire enterprise as slapstick (and prompted an entire school of "sports bloopers" that never lived up to the original). One of the signature pieces of the *Follies* was *The Headcracker Suite,* a series of some of the game's most violent hits set to the music of "The Nutcracker Suite." The idea had come from a janitor at the NFL Films production facility.

The real wonder of all this was the bottom line, or the lack thereof. In a 1977 letter to Ed Sabol, Rozelle congratulated him for "fulfilling our original goal for NFL Films—to operate it as a sound business entity, but primarily as a promotional vehicle to glamorize the game and present it in its best light."

But to call Films a "vehicle" was to engage in massive understatement. In addition to running a professional football league, the NFL was operating, on the side, a full-fledged film studio, which purchased from Kodak more film stock than any other client save the U.S. Army. The league, at Rozelle's insistence, continued to treat Films with more or less benign neglect, asking only that the studio not show a loss. "You remember the quality long after you forget the price," was one of Ed Sabol's mantras, and it was used to justify every exorbitant expense that was put back into the enterprise. Rozelle protected that autonomy, and nurtured it.

While the staff was brilliant and Ed Sabol was a perfect front man, inspiring dedication in his employees, and shielding them from the talons of any meddlesome owners, Steve Sabol would become an equally irreplaceable figure. Handsome, avid, and eager, the younger Sabol was enough of a self-promoter to refer to *This Is Pro Football* as "the *Citizen Kane* of football films," and enough of a talent that the description wasn't much of an exaggeration.

"It could be argued, in fact, that even more than the live telecasts of the games themselves, the work of NFL Films has shaped America's sense of what professional football is about," wrote Ben Yagoda in the *New York Times.* "In essence, it provided the first glimpse of the sport through a cinematic eye. Its creative and technical innovations have been copied by the networks. And finally, in its unabashedly sentimental and sometimes hilariously somber treatment of the game, NFL Films has tapped into our national penchant for melodrama and made pro football into perhaps the most popular ongoing serial in America."

By the '70s, the Sabols were becoming minor football celebrities. But their counterpart in the print realm, David Boss, was still virtually unknown outside the industry. Yet the Creative Services division of NFL Properties was doing precisely the same thing in the print realm that NFL Films was doing cinematically, and—by functioning as an in-house ad agency—increasing the league's prestige and profile, with excellent conception and execution of a series of aesthetically pleasing products.

The tall, angular Boss possessed a rustic handsomeness befitting someone who spent much of his boyhood in the Texas Panhandle town of Amarillo. In 1965, after plenty of contract work in the first two years of NFL Properties, Boss was given a charge that he would describe later as trying "to convey, in creative ways, what this game was all about."

The early efforts at publications by Creative Services were done largely beneath the public radar. They were elaborate brochures focusing on the paper and printing capabilities of the paper supplier Kimberly-Clark. Ostensibly distributed within the printing industry as a calling card, the magazines served as something much more. "We used them every way possible in connection with PR," said Don Weiss. "We'd even include them in stuff like responses to fan mail. You can imagine what kind of effect that had." When Kimberly-Clark clients started requesting the annual brochures months ahead of print time, the company, and the NFL, knew they were on to something.

In anticipation of the league's fiftieth anniversary in 1969, Rozelle asked Boss to update the NFL shield logo. While keeping the general shape the same, he eliminated the thin, spindly vertical lines on the crest behind the league's initials, made the letters bolder and more stylized, and made the field of stars at the top of the crest more uniform. The result was a symbol that embodied the modern age and that, thirty-five years later, remained the single most recognizable emblem in American sports. Boss also designed a fiftieth anniversary patch, worn on all NFL uniforms during the 1969 season, and conceived a book called *The First Fifty Years*, a lavish, coffee-table treatment of the league history that would ultimately sell over 200,000 copies.

Boss also acted as a kind of de facto quality control executive overseeing all of the merchandise under the umbrella of NFL Properties. Between his oversight duty there, and his conception of different promotional campaigns, Boss was creative catalyst of the league's print entity. At a time when pop art was dominant, Boss helped inject elements of an artistic sensibility into the game. In 1965, he himself painted stylized posters for all teams, creating a series of images that brought an adult appeal. Suitable for framing, they evinced a different kind of sophistication. For the first time, one could imagine owning products with team logos that could fit seamlessly into the den of a professional with sophistication and taste. Pro football was moving off the field, and going upscale.

While most teams still used their cartoonlike or caricature-ish logos for any promotional materials or souvenirs, Boss was among the first to realize the iconic power of each team's helmet emblem. Incorporating these into pennants, team glasses, and other elements, Boss made the helmets icons in their own right.

"I think David Boss, more than any other single person, is responsible for changing the state of sports graphics in this country," said graphics executive Dave Gardner, his longtime friend and colleague. "He made pro football visually exciting. He changed it. Sports graphics had been really hokey—it was all cartoons and lowbrow humor. Nobody gave a thought to layout and design. Nobody tried to think in terms of quality. And with David, that all started to change."

In 1970, Boss began editing the league publication *Pro! Magazine,* a particularly audacious undertaking. It combined the elements of a game program (lineups, player pictures, local advertisements) with a glossy, literary football magazine, replete with color photography, illustrations, and long feature pieces.

Using the success of *The First Fifty Years* as a springboard, he presided over a publishing explosion. The NFL published dozens of books in the '70s and '80s, including Boss's magnum opus, *The Pro Football Experience,* an oversized 256-page book with double gatefold spreads, heavy-coated paper stock, and a full cloth cover, published by art book publisher Harry Abrams. At once vivid and self-important, it was the apotheosis of the Creative Services agenda, a book that wouldn't make much money but would impress virtually everyone who saw it.

Rozelle hadn't conceived NFL Properties, any more than he'd thought of the idea for NFL Films. But when presented with each opportunity, he'd had the vision to act, and did so while realizing that the revenue that could be generated by the ventures was far less important than the increase in prestige, profile, and customer loyalty that would accrue to the league and its teams. He didn't merely launch the enterprises, but guarded them jealously, protecting them from meddlesome owners peeved about the Sabols' wide editorial latitude or the division's relatively low dividends.

To his closest aides, it was clear that Rozelle paid little heed to the owners' gripes. Anything that caused people to connect with pro football, and created positive associations with the sport, could only help in the long run, regardless of how little money it might make in the short term. And so the little fiefdoms of Films and Creative Services were largely left to their own devices in Philadelphia and Los Angeles, helped in numerous intangible ways. In total, the projects helped to create a self-contained world of pro football in which fans could enter, revel in, and spend many hours of their lives—not just on Sundays and Mondays while watching games but throughout the week, and the off-season. All sports simulate a parallel universe, and baseball had the daily serial drama of a long season, the mountain of statistical data supplied by the games, and the Hot Stove League in the winter to keep fans interest. Football was a less constant presence, even during the season, was less easy to document statistically, and prior to the '60s had virtually disappeared from newspapers in the off-season.

But with the rise of the sport in the '60s, pro football became more pervasive, not merely through the domination of Sunday afternoons and Monday nights, but through the myriad ancillaries that Rozelle's forces dreamed up. The NFL had taken advantage of the game's scarcity, using Properties to brand the league and Films to glorify it.

————

While George Blanda was dominating the headlines in Oakland in the 1970 season, another old quarterback, John Unitas, was still in charge in Baltimore. Though he was benched in the early season blowout loss to the Chiefs, Unitas rallied to fashion his best season in five years and would be, for the last time in his career, at the top of his game.

Bill Curry, the Colts' center, recalled the leadership quality in Unitas. "Unitas'd come in—of course, his track record had a lot to do with it—and there was something about being in a huddle with him with a minute and forty-five seconds left, and you needed a touchdown and you were back on your own twenty-yard line. Everybody'd look over at that famous crooked nose with the scar down it. He sort of blinked his eyes behind the bar on his helmet, and you'd *know* you were going to get a touchdown. And we *would*. It was all so matter-of-fact with him. There was very seldom a pep talk. He might say to Jimmy Orr or Roy Jefferson, 'What ya got? Can you get him on an up? Can you beat him on an out? Is he playing you inside? Okay, let's try it out this time.' He'd stick his head in the huddle and call the play, *boom*. He assumed that we were going to keep a pass rush off of him, and that if we did we were going to win the game. He might say, 'Let's go, keep them out, okay?' It was all very . . . laconic. Just straightforward business. 'Let's go do it. Here we go.' "

While Unitas was still running the show by his own wits, the game was changing around him, with a burgeoning move toward the Paul Brown philosophy of coaches sending plays in from the sidelines. Brown himself was doing it with the Bengals, who won the division title in only their third season. And Landry, whose game plans had been bolstered by computer printouts of opponents' tendencies as well as the Cowboys' offensive tendencies, was doing so as well.

Super Bowl V, then, was a match-up between two teams with something to prove. The Cowboys, labeled "Next Year's Champions" for all their near-misses, would battle the Colts, still trying to live down the ignominious outcome of Super Bowl III.

It might have been a battle between two play-calling styles, but Unitas was hurt early, and spent much of the game on the bench. The game itself was played at such a high, frenetic pitch that it turned into a desperate, cosmic accident, with eleven turnovers and countless blunders. The Colts won, 16–13, on Jim O'Brien's field goal in the last minute. At the end of the game, the Cowboys' frustrated defensive tackle Bob Lilly threw his helmet some fifty feet into the air. Mel Renfro, experiencing anguish in his own way, sat on the metal benches at the foot of the Orange Bowl, staring down at the detritus of smashed cups and discarded tape. For one more year at least, the Cowboys were stuck with the label of Next Year's Champions.

But after the pitched Us vs. Them antipathy of the first four games, the battle between the two old NFL rivals lacked a bit of the customary Super Bowl fervor. "I don't want to win one for the old AFC," said Colts defensive tackle Billy Ray Smith before the contest. "I want to win one for old B.R. and the Colts. . . . We've been in the AFC for one season—how in hell can the league identify with us, and vice versa? We're still the Colts the Jets beat to a lot of people in the league. Nobody's sending us telegrams this year."

16

"God, Nixon and the National Football League"

From the first day he arrived as a quietly confident rookie at the Dallas Cowboys' training camp in Thousand Oaks, California, Duane Thomas had the look of a classic football player. The chiseled 6-foot-2, 205-pound running back had a quick first step and terrific peripheral vision. Though he hailed from little-known West Texas State University, Thomas had little trouble adjusting to the pro game. He learned the Dallas Cowboys' complex playbook quickly, carried out his assignments with verve and authority, combined both instinctiveness and intelligence as a running back, darting through holes that were obvious and discovering some that weren't. Throughout his spectacular rookie season, as he ran for nearly 1,000 yards, Thomas did everything his coaching staff or teammates could have asked.

After the Cowboys fell, 16–13, in Super Bowl V, as many of his teammates sat disconsolate or mutely subdued, Thomas spoke with a wisdom beyond his years about the disappointment of losing. "Now that it's over, I simply want to sit on the beach somewhere and watch the sun disappear into the ocean," he said. "I want to contemplate what has happened. I hope that I have been enriched by the disappointment. There is something noble in defeat. You cannot find victory unless you first understand defeat."

Thomas proved himself a terrific running back, and his success provided more evidence of the wisdom of the Cowboys' renowned scouting department. Yet thoughout that first season and into the 1971 off-season, there was an unmistakable chill of discomfort that ran through the Cowboys' front office. Tex Schramm sensed that Thomas was more complex than most football players, sensed something vaguely anti-authoritarian in his demeanor. Thomas had performed for the Cowboys, but they hadn't *reached him* yet.

Though different from many of his teammates, Thomas would prove to be not all that atypical for his time. The period of the early '70s brought an odd sense of cognitive dissonance to pro football's rise. At no other time in its history did the guiding ethos of football—teamwork, self-sacrifice, the concerted application of mental and physical discipline toward a single, united goal—seem more out of step with the larger cultural moment. The era was marked by perhaps a greater gap than had ever existed, before or since, between players and management.

In the Cowboys' case, the gap was most evident in the protracted dissatisfaction of Thomas. He was a complicated athlete, too intelligent to be dismissed as a flake, but much too much of an individualist to fit easily within the Cowboys' system. And the summer of 1971 would provide a vivid glimpse of the clash of cultures and sensibilities that would, throughout the early '70s, become prevalent in the NFL. Saddled with a bad agent, a dissolving marriage, and a contract considerably under his market value, Thomas had approached Schramm in the off-season after his rookie year, and asked to renegotiate. Schramm could be at once stubborn and likable, but on player issues he was a decided conservative, one who delighted in his reputation as a ruthless negotiator. He told Thomas that the team couldn't renegotiate his contract but only extend it, giving him a signing bonus to add more years to his contract at a similar scale.

There was little for the young running back to do; his contract bound him to the Cowboys for three more seasons—the two remaining in his contract, plus an "option" year, in which Dallas could automatically retain him at 90 percent of his previous season's salary. Any team wanting to sign Thomas after he played out his option then had to provide compensation to the Cowboys, as part of the league's decade-old "Rozelle Rule," which stipulated that if the two teams were unable to decide on fair compensation, the commissioner would decide for them. All of this had a chilling effect on player movement, and left Duane Thomas's options severely limited.

He returned to Los Angeles, where he spent the off-season rooming with free-spirit teammate Steve Kiner, in a setting that hardly could have been less compatible with the spartan existence of training camp. "We lived off of Hol-

lywood Boulevard," said Kiner of the summer of 1971. "I stayed out there
three months, but I left before the summer was over, because it was just too
much for me, too much of everything. Too much drugs, too much women,
too much craziness."

When the Cowboys' 1971 training camp opened, Thomas was nowhere to
be found, and unreachable. He finally arrived three weeks late, accompanied
by a man wearing a dashiki who called himself Ali ha ka Kabir and who requested, through Thomas, a chance to try out for the team. "Nobody had any
idea where Duane was," said Schramm, "and, suddenly, he's there with this guy
in a long robe. The two just stared at me. I wasn't sure whether to bow or run.
We refused the tryout and they left again."

On July 31, Schramm traded Thomas to New England for running back
Carl Garrett and a first-round draft choice. But after showing up at the Patriots' camp, Thomas promptly refused, during his first practice, to get into a
three-point stance prior to a play. He argued that, with the Cowboys, he had
always placed his hands on his kneepads when he was in the set position, and
that out of the Patriots' I formation set, with fullback Jim Nance directly in
front of him, he couldn't see the field from a three-point stance. After head
coach John Mazur booted Thomas off the field, the Patriots appealed to the
league for relief. Against his old friend Schramm's vigorous protestations,
Rozelle rescinded the trade and sent Thomas back to the Cowboys.

Thomas returned to Dallas and called a press conference in which he
announced that he would not speak to the media for the remainder of the
season. Before exiting, he referred to Landry as "a plastic man," director of
personnel Gil Brandt "a liar," and reserved a special venom for Schramm,
whom he called "sick, demented, and dishonest." (Apprised of the comment,
Schramm chuckled and said, "That's not bad. He got two out of three.")

Thomas was an exceptional athlete, but his troubles with management
were symptomatic of a larger trend. Raiders linebacker Chip Oliver was starting for the Oakland defense in 1969; the next season he was living in a California commune called the One World Family of the Messiah's World Crusade.
The Cardinals' Rick Sortun wrote to owner Stormy Bidwill, announcing his
retirement in a letter that began with a poem by Ho Chi Minh. When the Dolphins' Larry Csonka and Jim Kiick were on the cover of *Sports Illustrated* in
1972, Csonka was seated against the goalpost with his middle finger extended,
flipping off the camera.

Many of those who left the game were highly critical of the culture of football. The Browns' Bernie Parrish, who wrote the blistering *They Call It a*

Game, charged that the league exploited its workers for windfall profits. With the virulent broadside *Out of Their League,* the Cardinals' Dave Meggyesy, who'd been a part-time starter over eight years before quitting in 1970, argued that the sport was "a reflection and reinforcement of the worst things in American culture." In a speech to students at his alma mater, Syracuse, Meggyesy said that "symbolically and metaphysically, big-time football represents our violent culture and the mode of authoritarianism. It has as its keynote competition and militaristic, organized violence."

Weeb Ewbank, like many other old-school coaches, was simply baffled by the behavior of some of his players. In 1973, running back John Riggins staged a celebrated holdout, then finally reported to camp to sign his contract. "It was the damndest thing," said Ewbank. "He signed the contract sitting at the desk in my office. He had on leather pants and was stripped to the waist, and he was wearing a derby hat with a feather in it. It must have been what the sale of Manhattan Island was like."

Among the most pointed, and thoughtful, critiques came from the Jets' wide receiver George Sauer, one of the stars of Super Bowl III. Sauer had grown up with football—his dad was the director of player personnel for the Jets—but retired at age twenty-seven. "Football's most obvious contradiction," he would say later, "is its failure to teach character, self-discipline and responsibility, which it claims to do. I like football. It is a framework around which you can see the dynamics of a player working together with other players, which can be a beautiful thing to watch. When people enjoy what they're doing it can be ecstatic. But the way it's structured, the intrinsic values of sport are choked off. It has been de-spiritualized, the profane applied to the sacred. Its inherent worth—doing it for itself, meeting challenges, the brotherhood of a team—is denied by treating the opponent as an enemy, not an antagonist. The game can touch you as a human being if you are permitted to touch others as human beings. But this is difficult when you have a Vince Lombardi type of coach hollering at you to hate the other guy, who's really just like you in a different colored uniform."

Lombardi indeed talked about the need for football players to hate their opponents leading up to and during the game. But the coach, whose politics were an iconoclastic mix of law-and-order social conservatism with an idealistic strain of progressive liberalism, confided in one writer during his last months that "there are a lot of things I've missed out on, that I simply don't understand. My kids tell me things, and half the time I don't know what they're talking about. I'm really going to have to learn about this. I'm going to have to get out there and talk to these young people and try to find out what's going on with them."

He wouldn't have the chance. He had returned to the coaching ranks in 1969, inheriting the Redskins and becoming the toast of Washington. But he took sick before training camp in 1970, and, on September 3, he died from cancer. Not since the death of Knute Rockne had a football coach been showered with more tributes upon his passing. Left unanswered in the remembrances was how to reconcile Lombardi's ferocity, a key component of his widespread appeal, with the virulence of the critiques on modern football.

———

Lombardi had visited the ailing Dan Reeves, dying of throat cancer, in a New York hospital in 1969, but the Rams owner outlived Lombardi by seven months. When Rozelle saw his old boss, in the spring of 1971, he had taken on a ghostly pallor and was clearly in pain. He did show a spark at being rid of George Allen, whom he fired a second, and final, time after the 1970 season. In the days before his death, in April 1971, Reeves summoned his assistant and old friend Jack Teele over and whispered to him his last piece of Irish wisdom: "We spend all this money on scouting college players so that we draft the right ones," Reeves said. "We spend money scouting coaches so that we get winners. But now that the league is getting so big, with so many franchises, we need to scout *owners.*"

The words would prove prescient and reverberate through the coming decades. Though his children were interested in keeping the team, Reeves was sufficiently alienated by the final seasons with Allen that he wanted the family rid of the burden. He put the team into a trust, and it was sold in 1972 to the highest bidder.

Ultimately, the new owner of the Los Angeles Rams turned out to be the old owner of the Baltimore Colts, Carroll Rosenbloom. There had been no secret that he'd been interested in owning the Rams, but selling his club, then buying the Rams outright would have exposed him to a grievous tax hit. Instead, he *traded* the franchise to a man named Robert Irsay, who'd grown up in the Chicago suburb of Skokie, and had earned his fortune in industrial air-conditioning and heating. Irsay agreed to purchase the Rams from the Reeves estate for $19 million, then trade the club for the Colts and $4 million in cash. On July 26, 1972, the team that Rosenbloom had built into one of the cornerstones of the city's identity was dealt for the Rams.

The news hit like a shock around the league, and left Tex Schramm apoplectic. "That has to go down as one of the most ridiculous transactions in the history of professional sports," said Schramm. "Carroll knew it but you couldn't blame him for doing it. Imagine trading Los Angeles for Baltimore."

In Los Angeles, the jet-setting Rosenbloom moved seamlessly into the owner's chair. More outgoing than Reeves, he shared a passion for the game, and lived and died with the fortunes of his team. After a disappointing 1972 season, he fired ex-UCLA coach Tommy Prothro, who had been hired in 1971, and replaced him with a longtime pro assistant, the relatively unknown Chuck Knox. Bringing Don Klosterman over from the Colts as the new GM, the new Rams quickly returned to the top, going 12-2 in 1973 and starting a string of six straight division titles.

In Baltimore, it would be a much rockier ride. The Colts' front office and players had few illusions about Rosenbloom, but they never questioned his commitment to winning. In Irsay the Colts would find an uncultured, self-conscious eccentric who possessed no rapport with players, nor made any clear effort to develop one. After the engaging leadership of Rosenbloom and Klosterman, the Colts may have resented any new owner and GM, but Irsay was a meddler clearly out of his depth, and his new GM only exacerbated the inevitable tensions. Irsay brought in the acerbic personnel man Joe Thomas, who had initially introduced him to Rosenbloom. Thomas had played a major role in building the Vikings and Dolphins from expansion teams to rising powers, but he'd never run an entire football operation before, and he lacked the interpersonal skills to earn the confidence of his players, and moreover seemed utterly tone-deaf to the sensibilities of Baltimore's fans and their unique relationship with the Colts.

The Colts began the 1972 season 1-4, the most memorable game being a Unitas-Namath shootout at Memorial Stadium. Namath completed six touch-down passes and threw for 496 yards in the Jets win; Unitas was 26 of 45 for 376 yards and two touchdowns. After the fourth loss, coach Don McCafferty was fired, and replaced by John Sandusky, who was then coaching the Colts' defensive line. Later that week, some Colts players were standing around the locker room when the phone rang. Unitas got on the line and listened quietly for about twenty seconds as Joe Thomas gave him some news. Then Unitas hung up the phone. His teammates looked at him quizzically.

"I'm benched," said Unitas flatly. "They hoped I wouldn't take it as a slap in the face."

Unitas would never start another game in a Baltimore uniform, but he did have a suitably moving exit from the Memorial Stadium stage. In the Colts' final home game of the 1972 season, Marty Domres started against the Buffalo Bills. During the Colts' first drive, the stands at Municipal Stadium erupted into a sudden and sweeping applause. Above the stadium, a prop plane flew by tailing a banner that read, "UNITAS WE STAND." Domres led the team to a touchdown drive in the fourth quarter, but strained his leg as he ran for the score, and on the next series of downs, Unitas was called in to lead the Colts, prompting a round of applause that was so loud that Unitas had to yell his plays in the huddle. On the third play, he threw a wobbly pass to Eddie Hinton, who caught it and ran 63 yards for a touchdown. That prompted another explosion from the crowd, one that Unitas, for a rare time in his career, recognized with a kind of shy salute, a hesitant raising of both arms, as if at once signaling touchdown and trying to quiet the crowd.

A month later, on January 22, 1973, Joe Thomas dealt Unitas to the San Diego Chargers for $150,000. Over the next eleven days, Thomas would deal away eleven other players, earning the enduring anger of a generation of Colts fans. Few argued that Unitas wasn't on the wane, but the manner in which the affair had been handled was galling to those who cared about Unitas and the Colts, which in this case was much of the city of Baltimore.

———

George Allen landed on his feet in Washington as head coach of the Redskins, who played their games just a few minutes away from the Oval Office of Allen's biggest fan, President Richard Nixon.

Allen's arrival in Washington seemed inevitable. Several teams wooed him, and the Redskins allowed him to name his terms in a package that was unprecedented. Moving with his usual zest, Allen convinced the Redskins to build a football complex close to Dulles Airport in the Virginia countryside. The $500,000 building went up in four months, complete with modern exercise equipment and carpeted locker rooms. The two practice fields were surrounded on three sides by forest, and Allen brought his security man, Ed "Double O" Boynton, to handle the security detail. Before the first game of the 1971 season, Redskins president Edward Bennett Williams famously cracked, "When Coach Allen came to Washington, we agreed he had an unlimited budget. He's already exceeded it."

Allen would become famous for—and skillful at justifying—his obsessive work ethic. He brought a game official, decked in black-and-white stripes, with a whistle and a flag, to call penalties during practices.

Popularized around this time were Allen's "Ten Commandments of Football," the first of which was: "1) Football comes first. During the off-season, family and church should come one, two, with football third. But during the season, the competition in the NFL is so tough that we have to put football ahead of everything else."

"I can remember George Allen's first speech to us," said Redskins quarterback Billy Kilmer. "He said, 'Our enemy is the Dallas Cowboys. You've got to have hate in your heart for the Cowboys. If you don't, we can't beat 'em.' " The team quickly reflected its coach's football philosophy: well-drilled, savvy, and opportunistic on defense, sound and conservative to a fault on offense. Washington opened the season 6-0, landing Allen on the cover of *Newsweek,* before traveling to Kansas City for a showdown against a revived Chiefs team that was back to its 1969 form. Washington squandered a 20–6 lead and lost, 27–20. But despite the defeat, they were greeted by a crowd of 8,000 cheering fans at the Dulles airport that night. On the Monday after the game, Allen received a handwritten letter from another ardent fan:

> Dear George
>   I saw the game on TV yesterday. A truly great team must prove it is great in defeat as well as in victory. The Redskins showed they were a great team yesterday. You are still going to win ten.
>
>   RMN

President Richard M. Nixon did more than write notes. Later in the season, after the Redskins had lost two games in a row, Nixon visited the team's practice. Kenneth Turan and William Gildea, covering the Redskins for the *Washington Star,* chronicled the visit: "Into the [Redskins'] compound strode an ordinary, perhaps shortish fellow wearing a topcoat as a concession to the weather, followed, like Moses splitting the Red Sea, by a surging group of humanity. The man was Richard Milhous Nixon, President of the United States, who had taken time out of surely the world's most hectic schedule to make a visit that wanted words stronger than unprecedented to describe it, a visit whose sole purpose was to offer personal encouragement to his favorite team and George Allen, his favorite coach."

The team stayed in contention for the wild card race, and their December 13 Monday night showdown in Los Angeles, with the Redskins and the Rams both needing to win to stay in contention, was the climax. Washington rolled, 38–13. In the Azores, where it was early Tuesday morning when the game began, Nixon stayed awake until 4:30 local time to hear the Armed Forces Network broadcast of the game. He still got up in time for his Tuesday morning meeting with French president Georges Pompidou.

The Redskins qualified for the NFC playoffs as a wild card, and traveled to San Francisco for the first round. Nixon called Allen the night before the game and, emboldened by his friendship, casually suggested that the Redskins ought to call a flanker reverse to Roy Jefferson. Trailing 13–6, on second-and-six at the 49ers' eight-yard line, Allen called the play, and Jefferson was tackled for a 13-yard loss. Nixon would call after the game, and tell Allen that "all of Washington is proud of the team."

It wasn't just the Redskins; football predominated in the chief executive's worldview, and the most powerful man in the world lapsed easily into the role of the super-fan. In the campaign headquarters of the Committee to Re-elect the President, there was a sign that read, "Winning in Politics Isn't Everything. It's the Only Thing." During the campaign, Nixon bragged of his new "game plan" for the economy. Nixon sent Secretary of State Henry Kissinger to the Paris Peace Talks with the code name "quarterback." After suspending peace talks in May 1972, Nixon ordered the planting of mines in Haiphong harbor in Vietnam; the renewed bombing was named "Operation Linebacker."

Nixon's fandom was a mixed blessing for the league. While it certainly brought even more attention to a game that was already enjoying spectacular success, the sport's best-known fan only strengthened the belief of many that pro football was in some way a *conservative* sport, at a time when that impression must have alienated as many people as it attracted. A *Time* essayist named Champ Clark, writing in 1971, noted, "In its essence, the football audience is Middle America in the raw. It is the Silent Majority at its noisiest, relieving its frustrations in the visual excitement of the nation's most popular sport."

That view was by then prevalent in the counterculture, even among those who were themselves devotees of the game. In a *Rolling Stone* article titled "Fear and Loathing at the Super Bowl," gonzo journalist Hunter S. Thompson would explain his decision to attend the festivities surrounding Super Bowl VIII as "a crazed and futile effort to somehow explain the extremely twisted nature of my relationship with God, Nixon and the National Football League: The three had long since become inseparable in my mind."

Thompson and Nixon, diametrically opposed in their sensibilities and politics, but sharing a deep love of football, had talked about the game and little else during an hour-long interview in the back seat of a limousine during Nixon's 1968 primary campaign in New Hampshire. Afterward, Thompson assessed the candidate's level of interest in the sport thusly: "Whatever else might be said about Nixon—and there is still serious doubt in my mind that he could pass for Human—he is a goddamn stone fanatic on every facet of pro football. At one point in our conversation, when I was feeling a bit pressed for leverage, I mentioned a down & out pass—in the waning moments of the 1968 Super Bowl mismatch between Green Bay and Oakland—to an obscure, second-string Oakland receiver named Bill Miller that had stuck in my mind because of its pinpoint style & precision. He hesitated for a moment, lost in thought, then he wacked me on the thigh and laughed: 'That's right, by God! The Miami boy!' I was stunned. He not only remembered the play, but he knew where Miller had played in college."

There was one tangible consequence to Nixon's passion for the sport, and football fans would receive a lasting reward for it. For more than a decade, Nixon had been pushing the NFL to repeal its blackout rule. In the bloom of the Beltway's embrace of Allen and the Redskins in 1972, Nixon finally got congressional support for the measure. It was no secret on Capitol Hill that the congressmen around the area who couldn't get tickets to the games wanted to be able to watch them on TV. The "trial period" for the lifting of the blackout was rushed through the House in the fall of 1972. Jack Kemp, now a freshman congressman from upstate New York, the same district where the Bills had played, joked that "It passed quicker than anything since the Gulf of Tonkin resolution."

Rozelle had argued vehemently against the law, going on *Face the Nation* to engage in some of the most strident rhetoric of his commissionership. Partly due to his dire predictions, Congress passed just a limited lifting of home blackouts, which would occur only if a game was sold out seventy-two hours in advance.

In the short term, the impact of the law was pronounced. Crowds dropped in numbers, and keeping a tabulation of the "no-shows" became a weekly part of the NFL's box office report. But the NFL also broke its all-time attendance record in 1973, owing in part to complete sellouts in new stadiums like Arrowhead (where Kansas City's capacity grew by 27,000). The long-term impact was positive. It is worth remembering that until the mid-'60s, the NFL's blackout rules meant that all the NFL viewing available to fans in, say, Cleveland, during the course of a season were seven Browns road games and the NFL title game (provided, of course, that it wasn't in Cleveland). Occasional doubleheaders and the league's experimentation with prime-time games added to the menu by the late '60s; the merger and the advent of *Monday Night Football* had opened the floodgates in the '70s. In football-mad cities like Minneapolis-St. Paul, Denver, and Washington, the sellouts continued and fans who couldn't get tickets were now able to watch all of their team's games. And that, in turn, provided a serious boost to television ratings, help-ing the NFL gain another big increase in rights fees when the next TV contract was negotiated in 1974.

Football moves in eras and, in the competitive sense, the 1970 season was a carryover of the '60s, with established powers Dallas and Baltimore battling for the Super Bowl. The pivot on which the new decade turned was Christmas Day 1971. Going into that playoff weekend, the case could be made that the Cowboys and Chiefs represented the two model franchises of the NFL. The traits the two clubs shared, besides their common birthplace, were adminis-trative stability, scouting excellence, head coaches who had led them through-out their existence, and a tradition of consistency and innovation.

But on that day, the fortunes of the two clubs diverged. While Dallas knocked off Minnesota en route to its first Super Bowl title, the Chiefs were upset by the Dolphins, a young team built for the bruising realities of the '70s game. It would be fifteen years before the franchise would make the playoffs again.

Like so many epic games, this one turned on a handful of plays. But the one that best illustrated the elusive, confounding nature of the game came early in the second quarter. After Kansas City jumped to a 10–0 lead and Miami had narrowed the gap to 10–7, the Chiefs drove back down the field before their drive stalled well within field goal range of All-Pro kicker Jan Stenerud. During their preparation for the game, the Chiefs' staff had noticed while reviewing Dolphins game film that when defending a field goal attempt from a hashmark, the Dolphins tended to overload the short side of the field. So Stram installed a fake field goal play that called for deep snapper Bobby Bell to snap the ball directly to kicker Jan Stenerud, who would run a sweep to the opposite side. Len Dawson, holding for the snap, saw the Dolphins over-load the short side and made the audible to signal the fake. But a miscommu-nication among three future Hall of Famers spelled the play's demise.

"So we're on the hashmark, and we're all excited," said Stram. "It's perfect. So Lenny calls, 'two-two.' That means the ball's coming to Jan—and nobody knows how fast Jan was, especially with somebody chasing him. He ran about a four-five, four-six forty. So Jan is doing such a good job of acting that Bobby Bell, as he looks through his legs, sees Jan looking down at the spot. He thought he blew the automatic. So he snaps the ball to *Dawson*, who's totally surprised. Both guards pulled on the play. They're standing out to the right side, about ten yards downfield, looking back to see where Stenerud is. He would have gone right in for the touchdown."

Instead, Stenerud's rushed kick attempt was blocked, and the Dolphins surged back to tie the game at 10. Late in the fourth quarter, after Miami tied the game again at 24, the Chiefs' Ed Podolak, having one of the great playoff games ever, returned the ensuing kickoff 78 yards, only to be run down by the Dolphins' Curtis Johnson. After three runs into the line, Stenerud kicked the ball wide and the teams headed to overtime, where both Stenerud and Garo Yepremian missed fifth-quarter attempts, before Larry Csonka's 39-yard gain on a trap play set up Yepremian for the sixth-quarter game winner, after 82:40 of game time.

There were two Hall of Fame coaches and eleven Hall of Fame players on the field that day, and when it was all over, Willie Lanier spoke for all of them. Walking off the field, an exhausted Lanier and his longtime roommate and linebacker partner Jim Lynch were too fatigued to speak. But in the end, he wasn't haunted. "I left everything I had out there on that field," Lanier said. "That was what pro football was about, that was the game at its best."

Miami then eliminated the aging Colts in the AFC championship game, a particularly satisfying win for Shula, to advance to New Orleans to play the Cowboys in Super Bowl VI. At 1:30 in the morning, eight hours following the game, Nixon phoned Shula's house, to suggest a play for the Super Bowl, a down-and-in pass to Paul Warfield. "When the phone rang at that hour," said Shula, "I thought it was just another crazy fan." In Texas, Lyndon Johnson sent a telegram to Cowboys coach Tom Landry two days later, saying, "I will be watching the Cowboys, but I won't be sending in any plays."

By the sixth Super Bowl, with the leadership of Rozelle and Jim Kensil, and the painstaking detail work of publicity director Don Weiss, the league had developed a set of dueling all-access press interviews known as Media Day, when during the course of a four-hour period the Tuesday before the game, all the players and coaches from both teams were made available to all the media representatives (by now nearing 1,000).

Media Day would eventually grow into one of the biggest and most self-parodying aspects on the entire sports calendar, but for sheer surrealism, it would be a long time before anything could top the events of the Media Day prior to Super Bowl VI. When the Cowboys took to the field for their interviews, Duane Thomas showed up, sat down at his required seat, and was surrounded by reporters. A few opening questions yielded no reply and so for nearly fifteen minutes, Thomas and two dozen reporters just stood there, in a mute standoff. After some time had passed, Thomas asked the writer closest to him, the AP's Will Grimsley, what time it was. Grimsley wasn't wearing a watch, but nervously stared at his naked wrist for several seconds before answering that he didn't know the time. Shortly thereafter, Thomas left, though the sight of him moving his lips had brought even more reporters to the scene.

The game itself was a desultory affair, played in frigid conditions and with precious little suspense. Miami was dominated by the Cowboys' "Doomsday Defense," which bottled up the Dolphins' running game, double-covered deep threat Paul Warfield throughout, and harried quarterback Bob Griese into uncharacteristic mistakes. In the victorious dressing room, after both Clint Murchison and Tex Schramm had been escorted fully clothed into the showers, the dripping Murchison proudly announced that, "This is the successful end of our 12-year plan." Lyndon Johnson stopped by to congratulate his friend Murchison and the omnipresent Nixon made his by-now customary call to the winning coach, about which Tom Landry noted that, "He praised our offensive line."

Elsewhere in the dressing room, a blasé Thomas, flanked by adviser Jim Brown, broke his silence and consented to an interview with a nervous Tom Brookshier of CBS. It proved to be one of the more curious encounters in the history of sports television, a study in American contrasts, between white and black, old and young, square and hip, polite and defiant.

A jumpy Brookshier observed, "Duane, uh, you do things with speed but never hurry, a lot like the great Jim Brown. You never hurry into a hole. You take your time, make a spin, yet you still outrun people. Are you that fast, are you that quick, would you say?"

"Evidently," said Thomas, prompting a round of laughter from his teammates.

Though headed in different directions competitively, the Cowboys and Chiefs remained in lockstep in one of the great trends of the post-merger era, the rush to new stadiums. Many of these were the charmless circular structures shared by baseball and football teams (Philadelphia's Veterans Stadium, Pittsburgh's Three Rivers Stadium, Cincinnati's Riverfront Stadium, and St. Louis's Busch Stadium) and well-suited for neither sport.

Taking advantage of the economic boom and the new public enchantment with football, both the Chiefs and Cowboys pushed for football-only stadiums, and the results were mostly impressive. Texas Stadium, built in suburban Irving, near affluent North Dallas, offered infinitely more comfort than the Cotton Bowl. Kansas City built two stadiums, side by side—the football-only Arrowhead Stadium and the baseball-only Royals Stadium—and while the project was derided by some as a cloning of white elephants it turned out to be a bargain, the entire project having been funded for $43 million.

Both Texas Stadium and Arrowhead were built at the confluence of intersecting freeways, both were blessed with the most modern of '70s amenities, from wide, dazzling scoreboards and spacious corridors to, far above the field, glassed off in partitions of plush carpeting and wood-grained tables, some of the sport's first "luxury suites."

When the Cowboys moved into Texas Stadium in 1971, and when the Chiefs opened Arrowhead Stadium in 1972, the stadiums immediately became the envy of the league's owners. For the owners, the stadium was not merely a place to cheer the home team, but a residence in which one entertained guests. And the accoutrements and trappings of Texas Stadium and Arrowhead instantly rendered the press boxes and private booths in the older stadiums tinny and obsolete. Suddenly, the grand bowl of the Los Angeles Coliseum, the vast cement superstructures of Cleveland's Municipal Stadium and Baltimore's Municipal Stadium, even the relatively new Shea Stadium, seemed archaic.

What both Hunt in Kansas City and Schramm and Murchison in Dallas realized was that the only way to maximize the stadium experience was to broaden the stadium. Most baseball stadiums couldn't justify a capacity of more than 50,000. But a football stadium, filled just nine or ten times a year, could build thousands more seats—Arrowhead sat 78,000, Texas Stadium 64,000—and do so in a much more coherent fashion than in converted baseball stadiums.

While the sight lines at the new stadiums were invariably better (every seat at Arrowhead faced the 50-yard line), the seats more comfortable, the food more plentiful, and the facilities more accommodating, the mood at the new stadiums was more subdued. Fans were at once more comfortable and less involved. It changed the clientele for pro football, making it more corporate, more affluent, and more white. "It was very disappointing to me because it eliminated a lot of black Americans from attending the games," said the Cowboys' Mel Renfro. "It eliminated the crowd that we used to have with the excitement and the noise. It was just different, like you were playing in your living room. It was a bunch of rich people who you couldn't get excited about anything. It was just a totally different atmosphere."

The same was true in Kansas City. At Hank Stram's behest, the Chiefs became even more stylish when they opened their new stadium, wearing shiny red patent leather game shoes at Arrowhead ("You go out there first and see if they laugh," said George Daney to a teammate before the team's first game in the new shoes). Stram's sideline attire went from natty to mod, as he wore suits with epaulets, leisure suits, even—most memorably—a tailored one-piece "unisuit" outfit about which Dawson was still laughing thirty years later.

At the same time, the stadium was less intimate than Municipal, the rowdy "Wolfpack" rooting section behind one end zone further away and a little less intimidating for visiting teams.

The final characteristic that both stadiums shared was inevitable and unquestioned at the time. In Dallas and in Kansas City, as in any major new stadium of consequence in the early '70s, the field was an artificial surface.

AstroTurf had come about as something of an accident. When the Houston Astros baseball team began play in the Astrodome in 1965, the roof was installed with windows, allowing grass to grow inside. But fielders complained that they were losing balls in the glare of the dome's glass roof, and when the glass was painted to obscure the glare, the grass died. The Monsanto Company had spent much of the previous decade developing an artificial surface that would serve as a grass substitute for the cement playgrounds of urban areas. When Monsanto installed the fabric onto the playing surface of the Astrodome in 1966, they dubbed it AstroTurf, and the rush was on.

The claims of effectiveness against knee injuries hastened the rush to embrace the surface, and initially, both the league and the players joined in. "There is every indication," Rozelle said in 1968, "synthetic surfaces cut down on casualties, particularly of the knee type." By 1969, he was predicting that within five to ten years "we'll have artificial turf on all our fields." Poly-Turf, used at the Orange Bowl for the Super Bowl in 1970, was endorsed by the National Football League Players Association (earning a percentage on every square yard of the surface sold by American Biltrite). Monsanto ran an ad in the Super Bowl IV program claiming that AstroTurf could "reduce crippling knee and ankle injuries up to 80%."

But among players, the grumbling began almost instantly, as it quickly became apparent that artificial turf could not live up to the claims made for it. Temperatures on artificial fields could spike up to 30 degrees higher. And footing was far from sure—slippery on AstroTurf when it was wet, and equally unsure on Poly-Turf when it was dry. Don Shula, reviewing film of two of the Dolphins' games on the Orange Bowl Poly-Turf in 1971, spotted 114 instances of players slipping on the field. But the greater concern was the additional physical toll. Players found that they would be sore for a longer period of time after a game on artificial turf, and that even a week's practice on the surface had repercussions. By September of 1971, the Bears' star Gale Sayers was denouncing it in a *Sport* magazine story.

At Arrowhead, the Chiefs' redoubtable groundskeeper, George Toma (the "Sod God" who would be put in charge of Super Bowl fields over much of the next three decades) was spending his time cleaning bubble gum and tobacco stains on the carpet. "The thing I couldn't figure out," said Bobby Bell, "is when you've got the best grass guy in the world, they'd go to a carpet. I mean, this guy can grow grass in your *pocket*—and they wanted to get turf."

Every week, it seemed, one of the Chiefs' starters was suffering joint ailments from the constant pounding of the artificial turf. Early on in that first season, several veterans, in Len Dawson's words, "begged Stram to get some relief from the stuff. All you have to do is get a few burns on that stuff, and have it stay on your elbow, or your knee for a whole season. And in my case, a couple of times, I got blood poisoning" because festering wounds would open and, when mixed with the chemical compound used to treat the turf, would become infected.

Tom Condon, who joined the Chiefs in 1974, would recall waking up the morning after a game, with burns and abrasions having opened during the night, with the painful skinless flesh being literally stuck to the sheets. "You can't just rip the sheet off, because that starts the bleeding again," Condon said. "So you go in the shower and stand there with these sheets stuck to your arms and let the water kind of loosen them. It's disgusting."

The novelty also wore off quickly for fans in the stands. "Artificial turf has made football look strange," mused Bud Shrake in *Sports Illustrated* in 1972. "Take the foot out of the grass and put it on a carpet, and the game can seem to become an amusement, like the hotel ballroom boxing matches staged for gentlemen in dinner jackets."

Within the league itself, the push to artificial turf was myopic and misguided yet in some ways entirely understandable. The NFL was just a generation removed from a time when a team's profit or loss might hinge on the weather during a few late fall Sundays. Even before the fountains in New Orleans froze the week of Super Bowl IV, the previous decade had been marked with title games played in inclement conditions—the 1962 and 1963 title games were brutal, frigid affairs, the 1964 Browns-Colts game and the 1965 Packers-Browns contests were both played in chilled, sloppy quagmires; and the classic 1967 Ice Bowl, obviously, was the worst of all, a game that left many of the competitors with frostbite and other permanent injuries.

Of course, one of the main reasons the Ice Bowl stood out in memory was *because* of the adverse elements. And while few of those who participated were happy the game was played in such brutal weather, the game's mantle of greatness was passed down largely because of those conditions. The 1966 NFL title game, also between the Packers and Cowboys, also came down to a decisive last-minute play on the goal line, between the same two teams, but the elements were less of a factor, and that title game has been permanently eclipsed by the Ice Bowl.

The decision to play the Super Bowl in a warm-weather city was a direct reaction to the string of inclement championship games of the '60s. And the decision about which warm-weather city it would be was dictated largely, in the early '70s, by which stadium could promise synthetic turf. Don Weiss recalled that the key presentation that allowed Miami to get Super Bowl V and New Orleans to get Super Bowl VI were guarantees by the Orange and Sugar Bowls that they would have replaced their grass fields with artificial turf in time for each of the games.

But as early as 1972, Tex Maule had seen enough harrowing scenes of locker room suffering to withdraw his earlier wholehearted endorsement of the game's rush to the artificial surfaces. Writing in *Sports Illustrated*, he warned that "if it develops that there are more injuries on the manufactured fields, it is not going to be all that easy returning to grass. The cost is steep, many owners have no control over the stadiums in which their teams play— for instance, many stadiums are built to accommodate baseball as well as football—and there is always the matter of TV." After years of quagmires like the 1965 NFL title game, when numbers were virtually obscured by the mud on the field, there was a feeling that artificial turf would be an improvement simply because it made jerseys more legible.

The jerseys would indeed be easier to see; but the game itself would become less pleasurable to watch.

It wasn't the artificial turf that caused the decline of the Chiefs. Stram's Napoleonic desire to run all football operations, as well as his loyalty to the aging players who won the Super Bowl, would lead to his undoing. In their drafts from 1970 through Stram's final year in 1974, the Chiefs selected only two regular starters, wide receiver Elmo Wright and defensive end Wilbur Young.

In Kansas City, Stram had demanded, and eventually received, the right to act as a single decision maker overseeing all football decisions. He made the selections in the draft, he negotiated contracts, he made trades, and he coached the team. And he and the Chiefs would discover, too late, that the jobs had grown too large to be done well by one man, especially a man who didn't delegate responsibility. The team had lost its edge, and its fall was inevitable. In Stram's last season, the 5-9 setback of 1974, the team was still starting thirteen of the twenty-four players who had started Super Bowl IV.

And so Hank Stram, the only coach in the history of the Kansas City Chiefs, was fired after the 1974 season. The Chiefs had very nearly played in three of the first six Super Bowls; after the 1971 Christmas Day loss, it would be twenty seasons before Kansas City would host another postseason game.

Meanwhile, in Dallas, Tom Landry, the only coach in the history of the Dallas Cowboys—bolstered by a modern football organizational mechanism that divided the football duties into three clear areas of responsibility—was only halfway through a tenure that would last twenty-nine seasons. During that span, the Cowboys enjoyed one stretch in which they qualified for the playoffs in seventeen out of eighteen seasons, and enjoyed twenty straight seasons of winning records.

The teams that excelled in the '70s—the Cowboys, the Rams, the Dolphins, the Steelers, the Raiders, and the Vikings would win forty of the decade's sixty division championships—had one thing in common: a leg-up in personnel evaluation. There had been other variables in the '60s—the intrigue and subterfuge of the baby-sitters, the equalizing advantage of deep pockets (Hunt and Adams), and grand visions (Werblin). But in the '70s, with no free agency and a common draft, other variables became less relevant and personnel departments became critical. Not all of the successful teams worked with the same blueprint. Dallas had its smoothly humming computer, the Raiders were stridently anti-computer in their work, Pittsburgh split the difference between data and gut instincts. But each of these teams found an edge in scouting that would prove decisive.

———

Though the Cowboys finally won their first title in the 1971 season, their squad was aging, and it would be four more years before they'd return to the Super Bowl, with a much different cast. The quintessential team of the early '70s was the Miami Dolphins, who were quickly built into a power by Don Shula. The Dolphins' colors were snazzy but nothing else about the team's playing style evoked excitement. Playing on the Orange Bowl's bluish green Poly-Turf, the team became an extension of Shula's no-nonsense, no-mistakes asceticism. Shula had studied under an assortment of the game's best teachers, playing for Paul Brown and Weeb Ewbank, and later working for a year as an assistant under Blanton Collier at Kentucky. His years as the youngest head coach in the NFL with the Colts in the '60s were both successful and stormy. He tangled frequently with Johnny Unitas, and often made decisions that had once resided with the quarterback. By the time he got to Miami, he'd developed a commitment to execution and built a team that was designed to control the ball and not make mistakes. On defense, his assistant Bill Arnsparger made it a weekly priority to take away the opponent's most dangerous weapon. (In the 1971 playoff game in Kansas City, the Dolphins double-covered Otis Taylor on nearly every play, and the Offensive Player of the Year in the AFC was held to 12 yards on three catches.)

In 1972, Miami opened at the unveiling of Kansas City's Arrowhead Stadium, and beat the Chiefs easily, 20–10, in the rematch. Thus began an improbable march through an undefeated season. The toughest game they played that year was a 21–17 win over Chuck Noll's up-and-coming Pittsburgh Steelers in the AFC championship game. That game was played in Pittsburgh, since under the league's rotation playoff site system, the Dolphins' 14-0 record didn't guarantee them home field advantage.

Miami received scant respect prior to Super Bowl VII in the Los Angeles Coliseum. Despite an unbeaten record and their second consecutive trip to the big game, Miami was a betting underdog to George Allen's Washington Redskins. Allen's veteran-laden "Over the Hill Gang" defeated the Dallas Cowboys for the NFC title on December 31, 1972. The next morning, Allen and his family were the guests of President Nixon at the White House, though this time the chief executive suggested no plays.

The Dolphins' "No-Name Defense" was dominant, perfectly complementing the team's ball-control offense. Leading George Allen's Redskins 14–0 late in Super Bowl VII, the Dolphins lined up for a field goal that would have made the score a symbolic 17–0, to match their record. But after the attempt was blocked, kicker Garo Yepremian tried a comical pass that slipped out of his hands and into the arms of Washington's Mike Bass, who returned it 49 yards for a touchdown. The game ended 14–7, but wasn't that close.

Miami would prove to be all too representative of its era—using a conservative offense that passed sparingly, and stifling opponents with a defense that choked the run, and a zone that thwarted long passes. In so doing, they played perfectly to the thickening pace of the game, and provided a sobering reminder that though Rozelle and the league worked to highlight the excitement and aesthetic appeal of pro football, those who contested the game were preoccupied with the final result only, even if achieving that result often made for boring football. The 1972 season saw 114 fewer touchdowns than 1966, but 141 more field goals. After marching through the 1973 season with a 12-2 mark, the Dolphins dismantled the Vikings, 24–7, in what the veteran writer Wells Twombly would describe as "the dullness that was Super Bowl VIII." The blowout came at the end of a season in which, even with scoring down again, only a third of NFL games were decided by seven points or less. The Super Bowl itself was never in doubt—the Dolphins scored on their first two drives and Griese threw just seven passes the entire game. The headline in *Pro Football Weekly* was typical of the public perception of the Ultimate Contest: "Dolphins Were Super—Game a Drag."

17

America's Team

The paradox of the early Super Bowls was that even as the games themselves often disappointed, the Super Bowl's popularity continued to grow, a tribute to both pro football's new preeminence and the relentless marketing power of the league. Lacking the tradition and history of the World Series, Super Sunday compensated with pomp, circumstance, and an overarching sense of self-importance. Astronauts recited the Pledge of Allegiance, Anita Bryant sang "The Battle Hymn of the Republic," Billy Graham delivered the invocation, and the Blue Angels did the flyover. "If Jesus Christ were alive today," said Norman Vincent Peale in 1974, "he'd be at the Super Bowl."

Rozelle routinely expressed amazement at the growth of the sport and its signature game. "If someone had asked me about pro football's future when I became commissioner in 1960," he told *Playboy* in a lengthy interview, "I wouldn't even have come close to predicting what the sport has achieved in 1973 as to number of teams, television exposure and revenue, attendance and so on."

The self-effacing answer was plausible until one stopped to realize how often Rozelle repeated it, and noticed further how few things happened by accident in the NFL.

Other than the actual playing of the game, nothing was left to chance at the Super Bowl. The sites, by the mid-'70s, were selected two years in advance, and accommodations were planned to the nth degree, the thirty-five-page prep book of the first Super Bowl morphing into an overgrown manifesto of game planning. To aid in the already over-the-top buildup, the NFL standardized a two-week gap between the conference championship games and the Super Bowl, to allow more time to work out the logistical hurdles. The league brought both teams into the city where the game was being played six days prior to kickoff, and during this week of interviews, the NFL distributed a staggering amount of information to the 2,000 assembled members of the media. There were press conferences every day, taped by the league staff and brought back to the massive press facility, so that the busier journalists—as well as the lazier ones—could cover the news without leaving the room.

The Friday before the game became Rozelle's personal tour de force. At 11:00 a.m., he would march to the podium in the largest room at the media headquarters and conduct what had come to be known as his annual "state of the league" address, then take questions afterward. The overall tone resembled nothing so much as a presidential press conference, and Rozelle prepared for them in the same way. On the eve of the Friday press conference, he'd gather three or four trusted aides, and they would pepper him with the most likely questions. Come the time for the press conference, if there was something that Rozelle knew he wanted to address, one of his friends—often Pat Summerall—would be prompted to ask an early question. This deck stacking was never heavy-handed, and that was why Rozelle was so successful at it. "You ask him about a particular court case," noted one veteran writer in 1975, "and he not only tells you the judge's name but cites six other similar cases. There isn't a thing he can't answer. He never brings a note." Rozelle was never arrogant, but on these occasions he displayed an assurance that bordered on jauntiness. After finishing his prepared remarks, he'd light a cigarette, smile slyly, and say, "Fire away."

The timing of the press conference was no accident either: by Friday, teams were in their final preparations, with less time or patience for the incessant questions of the throng of press. So Rozelle's press conference served to take the heat off the teams, and fill a news void, providing something for Saturday editions, before the flood of Sunday game preview stories. It was this intuitive understanding of the media that was one of the most important and least understood of the NFL's advantages over other sports leagues. "The NFL was always the savviest PR organization of all of them, and they've always wanted to manage the news," said the *Washington Post*'s Tony Kornheiser. "They always wanted to manage the news, and they manage it better than ever. It's because the NFL has understood and mastered the way of keeping everybody at arm's length while giving you the illusion that you're *right there*. And you're not right there."

Friday nights were devoted to the league's official party, which came to be known as the Commissioner's Party. As media representatives and advertising friends of the league clamored for tickets, the function grew and grew. By January 1974, it was held at the Astrodome in Houston, with a guest list of 2,900. The crushing press hordes and two-week buildup often yielded disappointing games, and predictable criticism. But it had little impact on the viewership or ticket demand, which continued to escalate beyond that of any other single American sporting event. Eventually the sheer enormity of the press coverage not only affected the players and fans, but the press itself.

"People just go on ahead and write about the World Series," noted Roy Blount, Jr. "The Super Bowl they have to get an angle on. Try to blindside the sucker. Find the seam in its zone. Usually, after a week of free liquor and promotion, they wind up just scoffing at the $2.8 million Super Bowl–eve party, because they have to stand in line for the stone crabs behind Tony Orlando's go-fer, and file a hung-over game account that runs under the head, 'SUPER BOWL NOT SO SUPER.' "

By the mid-'70s, Rozelle was commonly regarded as the smartest, most powerful man in American sports. People routinely mentioned him as a candidate to hold higher office, and some viewed him as though he already did. The Colts' PR man Ernie Accorsi left Baltimore to join the league office in 1975. "Being around him was how I imagined the New Frontier," Accorsi said. "It was like going to Washington to work for the Kennedys."

Behind the scenes, Rozelle remained by all accounts a conscientious single parent, who went to extraordinary lengths to include his teenage daughter, Anne, in all that he could. She turned thirteen in 1971, and he brought her more often on his dinner outings, to "21" or P.J. Clarke's, introduced her to many of the women he was dating at the time. He'd take her along on weekend trips to games, leave work before dark on winter afternoons to take her sledding or skating at the Rockefeller Center skating rink.

One day in 1974, Rozelle was sitting over drinks, with Pat Summerall and Jack Landry, at the Bel Air Hotel in Los Angeles. A striking brunette walked by and the men stopped talking for a moment, in silent appreciation. Afterward, Rozelle quietly stated, "That's the one."

"That's the one what?" asked Summerall.

"That's the woman I'm going to marry. Do you know who she is?"

"No, but I can find out." Summerall knew the bartender at the Bel Air, and sidled over on a reconnaissance mission. He returned a few moments later, and sat back down in the booth.

"I'm not sure you *want* to know who she is," said Summerall, then he explained. The cosmopolitan, self-possessed, and radiantly beautiful woman was named Carrie Cooke. She was the mother of four and, though separated from her husband, still the daughter-in-law of Redskins majority partner Jack Kent Cooke.

There was a moment of silence. "Small world," offered Landry.

But Rozelle was undeterred. "Do you think I could meet her?" he asked Summerall. The courtly Summerall walked over and invited Cooke and the two women she was with to join them at his table for introductions.

Later that year, Pete and Carrie were married.

His daughter, fifteen at the time, could tell instantly that this relationship was different.

"She was absolutely perfect for him," said Anne. "If I had been him, I would have fallen for her, too, there's no question. She was beautiful, she was charming, she could make anyone feel at ease. She lit up a room when she walked into it, she was sophisticated, an excellent tennis player, acted interested in everyone she met, had a very diversified background, she'd been in nursing, modeling, race-car driving, she'd done several different things."

Rozelle's life changed quickly, beginning with a move to Harrison, New York, forty-five minutes outside the city, where Pete and Anne were joined by Carrie and her four children. He bought a regal Tudor mansion with a putting green, tennis court, swimming pool, and a perfect English library where Rozelle could scour his newspapers on the mornings he didn't take a car to the office.

With Carrie's involvement, the league inaugurated National Football League Charities, which would, in its earliest years, funnel all the profits from NFL Properties into a charitable fund, whose board included the likes of Ethel Kennedy. The league also worked with the United Way for a series of effective, heart-tugging spots run during every game (the league had stipulated that two minutes of commercial time from every game be retained by the league to use as it saw fit, to promote its own product or, as in the case with the United Way spots, to air public service messages). The premiere found the Cowboys' Roger Staubach featured with Gayla Vaughn, a seven-year-old with a congenital heart defect, and its effective imagery—of the strongest men in society reaching out to help the weak and infirm—would become a staple of NFL broadcasts for decades to come.

Around the office, Rozelle began keeping more regular hours. Though he eschewed limousines, he would take a sedan or station wagon into work, usually left the office by 6:00 p.m., and delegated more authority to the diligent,

gruff Jim Kensil (known as "The Nazi" to his staff) and the exceedingly thorough director of publicity, Don Weiss. Rozelle still lingered over details, vet-
ting and reworking the wording of press releases, approving all the designs for
the Super Bowl posters, programs, and tickets. If he seemed less driven, it was
perhaps because he'd brought the league into a period of relative stability, had
successfully ushered his daughter into her teenage years, and, in his personal
life, was finally and completely happy.

The personal happiness would last. The professional happiness would not.

On July 3, 1974, the National Football League Players Association went on
strike, and began picketing the opening of training camps, forming a line in
front of the Chargers' camp in San Diego. Each of the fifty players walking the
line, accompanied by NFLPA executive director Ed Garvey, wore a T-shirt that
read, "NO FREEDOM, NO FOOTBALL."

The antagonism between players and owners had been a long time coming—the first discussion of the possibility of a players association had occurred in 1956—and reflected the reality of a genuine shift in the marketplace.
From the perspective of veteran owners like Halas, who had guided the league
through the Depression, a world war, and challenges by the AAFC and AFL,
modern players were remarkably well paid. But in 1974, players were still making a fraction of what athletes in other sports earned. Just as the players had
feared, the signing of the merger and the common draft eliminated the large
bonuses that had elevated all players' salaries in the '60s. By 1970, the players
were cognizant of a league that was making exponentially more money than it
ever had before, while real salaries had changed only marginally since 1960.
The owners, after nearly going under during the madness of the war years,
were not inclined to share all their newly won riches with the players.

Because pro football had for so long been a poor stepchild to baseball,
some of its customs, such as paying the players nothing during training camp,
held long after ceasing to be a financial necessity. By the '60s, when players
began improving their working conditions, even modest gains were viewed as
triumphs. "Tuesday is pay-day," wrote Roman Gabriel of the training camp
grind, in his memoir of the 1969 season. "It isn't much but it's something—
something like $209 after taxes for last week's game plus $10 a day, or $70, for
expenses. I remember when we didn't get anything for eight weeks at training
camp except room and board and a few bucks for laundry. This is an improvement that the players association has made."

The NFLPA's executive director, Ed Garvey, was a sharp-edged Wisconsin
lawyer who made an issue out of Rozelle's supposed neutrality, arguing that

the executive paid by the owners couldn't be viewed as an impartial observer. This in itself was heresy to some owners. At one negotiating session, when the NFLPA's president Bill Curry was arguing the same point, an owner jumped up and said, "Damnit, don't be telling us Rozelle's not neutral. We pay him damn well to be neutral."

Though Garvey and the union were demonized by some owners, the NFLPA was never as radical as the Major League Baseball Players Association, a fact that became apparent when the ex-Brown Bernie Parrish tried to pursue a consortium of all three sports into a huge athletes union. "I talked to Jimmy Hoffa and the Teamsters," said Parrish. "They were interested in representing us if we could bring the sports together. But when we had the meeting of the representatives from all the sports, the football players screwed it up. As some baseball players told me, 'Football players act like owners.' So it didn't happen."

But the NFLPA was unified enough, by the spring of 1974, to strike. Among the demands put forth by the Players Association were elimination of the option clause and Rozelle Rule; elimination of the draft; and guaranteed salaries. But this was, in a way, assuring that there would be no bargaining at all. The draft and the Rozelle Rule were viewed as sacrosanct by the league's owners, general managers, and coaches, their existence the very cornerstone of the NFL system.

The union held firm through the first two weeks of exhibitions, but by August 13, when a federal mediator ordered a two-week "cooling-off period," the veterans voted to honor the called truce and return to camp. The strike officially ended on August 29, but the opposition was essentially crushed the moment the players came into camp. "It was a long drawn-out strike," explained the Bills' Reggie McKenzie, "and our side lost."

NFLPA president Bill Curry would admit later that the players association's list of "demands," which numbered fifty-seven in March and had reached ninety-three by the summer, was "a terrible mistake. . . . We came off arrogant." Two days after the players voted to end the strike, Bill Curry was waived by the Houston Oilers.

The NFLPA decided to carry its dispute through the courts (where *Mackey v. NFL* would attempt to overturn the Rozelle Rule) and the National Labor Relations Board (where the union would press for a federal mediator) and returned to the playing field.

But in the broader context of professional sports, where athletes in the '70s began to enjoy wide-ranging improvements, from higher pay and better working conditions to free agency and more autonomy, the players in the NFL were still behind the times. They were victimized by a variety of factors, including the merger's elimination of competition for players and the owners' intransigence in collective bargaining. The standoff created a tectonic tension that would take the better part of the next two decades to resolve.

For the owners, the headaches came in pairs. In addition to the player strike in the summer of 1974, there was the advent of another upstart league, the World Football League. Founded a year earlier by Gary Davidson, who'd launched the American Basketball Association and World Hockey Association, the twelve-city WFL began play in the summer of 1974 with a midweek playing schedule and a midsummer-to-late-fall season. Populated with owners like Toronto's John Bassett, who had been interested in owning NFL franchises, the league signed a TV deal with the independent sports network TVS, and began raiding NFL rosters.

The WFL's biggest immediate impact may have been in bringing about the dissolution of the Dolphins' back-to-back champions. Even as the Dolphins were winning Super Bowls VII and VIII, team owner Joe Robbie was penurious with raises. Reluctant to negotiate with stars Larry Csonka, Jim Kiick, and Paul Warfield, each of whom had one more year remaining on his contract, Robbie kept putting off negotiations. In mid-March, the WFL held its draft of bargaining rights to active NFL players, and Csonka, Kiick, and Warfield were selected by Bassett's franchise. In late March, the three signed a collective three-year contract for more than $3 million, to begin in the 1975 season, after the three Dolphins had fulfilled their contracts, each ending in 1974. Other players signed as well, and their lame-duck years in the NFL were often unpleasant. Paul Brown was so angered by star linebacker Bill Bergey's defection that he traded him prior to the 1974 season, though Bergey still had two years remaining on his Bengals contract.

But the new league was quickly in trouble, its first season marred by reports of inflated attendance figures and unpaid bills. The league champion Birmingham Americans had their uniforms repossessed in the locker room after winning the WFL's first championship.

The league returned in 1975 as a reorganized entry, assisted by the infusion of NFL talent. Csonka, Kiick, and Warfield seemed dispirited, consigned to a sinking ship. Gone were the wild uniforms and gaudy trappings of 1974 and, after the twelfth week of its second season, gone was the WFL.

———

The summer of 1974 would also mark the end of the career of John Unitas. His first season with the Chargers had been inglorious, as he tutored rookie Dan Fouts and took a pounding behind a porous Chargers line. For longtime fans, Unitas never looked entirely comfortable fading back in gold pants and the powder-blue jersey of the Chargers. The end came on a summer Sunday when Unitas, suffering from a sprained leg and ankle, decided he could no longer move well enough to justify continuing.

Even at the end, he displayed the love of the game that marked so many great ones. "If I could have gotten a leg transplant, I'd play another thirty years," he said. "But I couldn't move anymore. The way it was, it was like standing in the middle of a road and saying, 'Okay, Buick, run me down.'"

At the dawn of the '70s, the glamour of the quarterback position was at an all-time high—due in large part to the exploits of Unitas and Namath—but the retirement of Unitas would mark the beginning of the end of that era. The Chiefs' Len Dawson, the prototypical embodiment of onfield cool, retired after the 1975 season, along with the Redskins' Sonny Jurgensen. Namath's exit came two years later, after an ineffectual final season with the Rams. Already by 1974, Namath's physical decay had taken on a ritualistic aspect, nearly gothic in its gruesome fascination. He would strap on his heavy Lenox Hill derotation brace, limp out to the field, and then attempt to recapture his old powers. Laboring to get out from under center, he took mincing steps, gingerly setting up, completely vulnerable when the protection collapsed. That he played gamely on through the punishment only made his teammates feel worse. "He's helpless back there, a sitting duck," said teammate Steve Tannen. "He can't scramble out of trouble, and now he can't even fall right."

Quarterback remained the most important position on the football field, but it lost some of its mystique, as play-calling responsibilities gradually moved to the sidelines and press box. The rise of more complex and better-disguised coverages and zones meant that *recognizing* the defense would often become more important than anticipating it. The game had grown more complex, and some quarterbacks were privately more comfortable with *not* having the play-calling duties.

There was another reason for the decline of quarterbacks' relative stature, and that was the rise of conservative ground-based attacks throughout the league. A record ten rushers ran for over 1,000 yards in 1973, when the Dolphins *averaged* more than 210 yards rushing per game. There were fewer thrills in those bruising attacks, but the men who provided it—Larry Csonka, Franco Harris, Larry Brown—were becoming the biggest stars of the decade.

And in the mid-'70s, none were bigger than O. J. Simpson, Buffalo's star running back, who broke Jim Brown's single-season rushing record in 1973, eclipsing Brown's 1,863 yards by busting for 200 in the final game, a win over the New York Jets.

On the field, Simpson was a beautifully fluid runner, with a sixth sense for avoiding the big hit, stepping lightly, spinning away from oncoming tacklers and sluicing through the gaps opened up by his offensive line, nick-named "The Electric Company" (because, they boasted, "we turn on the Juice"). Off the field, Simpson was viewed not just as a great athlete but as an examplar of the egalitarian world of sports. Running through airports for Hertz rental cars, he became the first black celebrity to be featured in a national corporate ad campaign. *Sports Illustrated* named him runner-up for their Sportsman of the Year award in 1975 (Pete Rose won the honor). In a mid-'70s poll of grade-schoolers, commissioned by *Ladies' Home Journal,* Simpson was voted the most admired figure, by both boys and girls. He played a romantic lead opposite Elizabeth Montgomery in the police thriller *A Killing Affair,* one of the first instances of interracial romance depicted on television. He was breaking down barriers for blacks because he'd been accepted as an unthreatening superstar, a fully assimilated black man whose genial, positive presence carried none of the political, black-consciousness baggage of Jim Brown.

As had so often been the case in sports, the glory and fame enjoyed by one black served to obscure the injustices still visited upon many of the rest.

On the sidelines and in club offices, there was scant black representation in the league. Rozelle had brought in two blacks at the league office, Charlie Jackson as a security liaison and Buddy Young to handle player issues, but they were the exceptions. Among executives, coaches, and scouts, black faces were rare, with just five black assistants in the league in 1973. At a time when nearly 50 percent of the league's players were black, a black center had never started a game in the National Football League, and for years Willie Lanier was the only black middle linebacker.

For many of the other black stars in the NFL in the '70s, Simpson's success was the exception that proved the rule. There was virtually no off-field endorsement money, not merely on a national level but even in the city in which they lived, where everything from car signings to speeches to Boy Scout troops seemed to go to white players.

"I'm a premier receiver, they say, or a premier this and that," said the Chiefs' Otis Taylor in 1972. "But I'm a black man. I can't express myself, I can't do anything. People always ask me what I've endorsed. I haven't even done a dog food commercial, and that's pretty sorry for a guy who would be so happy to do one he'd eat the dog food."

In some league cities, housing barriers came down, reluctantly, due to the pressure exerted by football players. Mel Renfro had to file a lawsuit before he could integrate a section of North Dallas; the Cowboys supported him, with a great deal of reluctance. Bobby Bell of the Chiefs looked at "maybe 200 houses" before he was able to integrate the affluent Overland Park section of Johnson County, across the Missouri state line into Kansas. "When they found I was moving in, they called a neighborhood association meeting," remembered Bell. "So I went to the meeting. Of course, who they were meeting about was *me*. So I show up and say, 'I'm here for the meeting.' Guess what? All of a sudden they decided the meeting just got canceled."

By 1974, the most interesting division in football was the AFC Central, where Paul Brown's past, present, and future were tangled up in a series of incestuous rivalries. Games against his former team in Cleveland took on the aspect of crusades. And there were perhaps no fiercer rivals on opposing sidelines than Brown and his old antagonist Sid Gillman. Gillman took over a woeful 1-13 Houston squad in the middle of 1973, and won Coach of the Year honors after turning it into a dangerous 7-7 squad in 1974. That season included two galling upsets of the Bengals, each of which left Gillman looking ten years younger and Brown in a fouler mood than usual. The rising power in the league was in Pittsburgh, where the Steelers were coached by Chuck Noll, who had played for Brown at Cleveland, serving as one of the team's messenger guards shuttling in plays from the sidelines. While Noll spoke admiringly of his old coach, it was clear that he had major philosophical differences with Brown in his handling of football teams. Noll felt that calling plays "emasculates your quarterback. It's for coaches who want to be quarterbacks. Paul Brown's the oldest quarterback in the league."

The Steelers' real renaissance began in 1969, when they hired the thirty-seven-year-old Noll, the brawny, taciturn defensive specialist who had most recently been Don Shula's top assistant in Baltimore. Surveying the lack of talent in his first team, Noll made a similar call to the one made a decade earlier by Tom Landry. "In 1969, we decided we had to do certain things technically to win, and we decided to do them then, even though we knew some of the personnel couldn't do it. In other words, instead of adapting the system to the players, we just installed our system. Then we set out to fill our team through the draft."

In 1969, after identical 1-13 seasons, the Steelers and the Bears held a coin flip for the right to select first in the 1970 draft. Pittsburgh won the flip, and selected raw, strong-armed quarterback Terry Bradshaw out of Louisiana Tech.

While computers were now being used by virtually everyone in football (save the maverick Raiders, who had developed their own system and criteria under Al Davis), there was still a lack of league-wide understanding over two key questions: why players who had excelled at major-college football might not be successful in the pros, and which standouts who played against lesser college competition could excel. After Nebraska won its second straight national title in 1971, three Cornhuskers were first-round picks in the 1972 draft, but none of them—Jerry Tagge, Jeff Kinney, and Larry Jacobsen—enjoyed stellar pro careers.

The Steelers erased forty years of futility with a string of almost omniscient drafts between 1969 and 1974, drafting Joe Greene, Bradshaw, Franco Harris, and Lynn Swann in the first round, Jack Ham and Jack Lambert in the second, Mel Blount in the third, and John Stallworth and Mike Webster in the fourth. Each man wound up in the Hall of Fame.

After Franco Harris's "Immaculate Reception" to win the 1972 divisional playoff with Oakland, Pittsburgh advanced to the playoffs again in 1973, but between injuries and a burgeoning quarterback controversy, the club never had the look of a team that could challenge for the title. In 1974, a more mature Steeler unit rolled to a 10-3-1 mark and glided to an easy first-round playoff win over Simpson and the Bills, the same weekend that the Raiders were ending Miami's three-year run with an epic 28–26 win. The spent Raiders had little left the following week, and Pittsburgh won easily in Oakland, to advance to their first-ever NFL championship appearance.

Two weeks later, the Steelers took the title stifling the three-time Super Bowl–losing Vikings, 16–6, on a cold, drizzly day in New Orleans. Afterward Art Rooney, chomping on his ever-present stogie and peering serenely behind his Coke-bottle glasses, raised the Lombardi trophy presented to him by Pete Rozelle, who was moved to tears by the gravity of the occasion. The win began a string of four titles in six years for the Pittsburgh team, which would prove just as dominant in its era as the Packers had been in the '60s.

Though the beginning of the '70s would be ruled by the Dolphins, and the end by the Steelers, the decade as a whole belonged to the Dallas Cowboys. They were the league's most visible, respected, resented, and imitated team, a success financially, commercially, even aesthetically. Throughout the decade, on *Monday Night Football,* on Thanksgiving afternoons, on CBS's Sunday pregame show *The NFL Today,* in nearly every playoff season, and five of the decade's Super Bowls, the Cowboys were omnipresent.

Dallas was the team that best reflected Rozelle's ethic of corporate excellence, and the fact that his oldest friend in the sport—and closest ally in league meetings—was the Cowboys' Tex Schramm was not lost on the other owners. "If there's one team that's going to get a break," said Al Davis, "it's Dallas. On the officials' calls, on the scheduling, on the Competition Committee, on everything else relating to league matters."

But it wasn't merely perception or favoritism. With the exception of a one-year absence in 1974, Landry's team went to the playoffs every year from 1966 to 1983. And in a competitive NFC, featuring the Vikings, Redskins, and Rams, the Cowboys would represent the NFC in five of the ten Super Bowls of the '70s. The teams were smarter, faster, and more disciplined than the competition, the offensive and defensive schemes more complex, the coaching more consistent.

In the '70s, though, it was what the Cowboys did off the field that most clearly set them apart from their competition. Schramm's creation of the Dallas Cowboys Cheerleaders in 1972 brought a measure of unabashed sexuality into the game. The clean, polished Texas beauties, attired in hot pants and halter tops, were introduced in 1972 and became nationally famous in Super Bowl X three seasons later (when CBS producer Chuck Milton said "we wanted to give fans a little sex with their violence"). By 1977, they'd become pinup heroines to rival Farrah Fawcett, inspiring their own calendar and made-for-TV movie.

The team's star was Roger Staubach, the Naval Academy's Heisman Trophy–winning Vietnam vet and born-again Christian who portrayed a self-consciously wholesome image, and embodied his team's simultaneous embrace of corporate soundness and artistic style. Bright, daring, with a scrambler's electric moves and a gambler's eye for the big break, Staubach epitomized his team and his age just as completely as Otto Graham did his, and just like Graham, Staubach was criticized for being merely an on-field adjunct to his head coach's machinations. Landry drove the Cowboys to nine playoff appearances in the decade of the '70s. It was clear that Paul Brown was right: the future of football would come from the sidelines; the field generals of the Unitas, Dawson, and Namath ilk were a dying breed.

On the field Staubach was cool and calm yet flashy, an expert scrambler who was dangerous in the open field. Out of uniform, he became a kind of conservative icon, a Fellowship of Christian Athletes member who insisted on making a point of his belief in the American way. Yet there was a stubbornly headstrong quality to Staubach, at once proud and vain. Around 1975, he took to the stylistic flourish of cutting his jersey sleeves at the stripes, so more of his arms were bare. On an *NFL Today* pregame piece, Staubach took pains to tell Phyllis George, "I like sex as much as Joe Namath does. I just have it with one woman."

Even though he chafed at Landry's play calling at times, Staubach remained a good soldier, an organization man. And the organization was running at peak efficiency. Despite annually drafting near the bottom of each round, the Cowboys constantly replenished their roster. After missing the playoffs for the first time in nine years in 1974, the Cowboys' 1975 draft featured twelve players who made the active roster, and led the club to the Super Bowl.

The team's success created impossible expectations and some players questioned the fans' loyalty, prompting Staubach's famous crack that "Cowboy fans love you, win or tie." But those fans spanned the country. By 1977, the Cowboys were responsible for a quarter of all team merchandise sold by NFL Properties. Their self-published newspaper, *The Dallas Cowboys Official Weekly,* had a circulation of 100,000, half of it outside Texas.

In 1978, after the Cowboys season, an NFL films producer named Bob Ryan was overseeing the Cowboys' highlights film, one of the routine duties for the studio in the off-season, when it handled all twenty-eight team highlights videos. Ryan had noticed that at every road game in which the Cowboys played, there was a significant portion of fans rooting for the visitors. In putting together highlights of the team's 1978 season, which had ended with the Cowboys battling the Steelers, he called Dallas "America's Team." The name stuck, and only added fuel to the fire. Like the Yankees in baseball, the Celtics in basketball, or Howard Cosell in television, the Cowboys had become a galvanizing, divisive presence, both the most-liked and most-disliked entry in its field.

Writing in the *Boston Globe,* Leigh Montville argued, "The Dallas Cowboys are the team I would put in the time capsule. If the dominant sport of our generation has been pro football—and it has been—then the Cowboys are the logical choice. No team better describes football and stay-at-home Sundays of the past decade. . . . They are a team of efficiency and controversy and rhine stone glitter. They have been the best characterization of the pro football team imaginable."

The Cowboys' system generated numerous imitators, and the edge that Dallas had over the competition had narrowed considerably. But Schramm and Brandt had managed to keep the Dallas system a step or two ahead of the competition. In the '60s, Brandt was expert at manipulating the levers of military service to Dallas's advantage, often stashing a player in the National Guard rather than waive him to a competitor.

Their use of computers in scouting had evolved and grown more sophisticated. In addition to the standard measurables of height, weight, and speed, the additional five characteristics that the Cowboys analyzed in every football player, regardless of position—character, quickness, competitiveness, mental alertness, and strength and explosion—had remained constant, and was observed throughout the league. What had changed, through extensive regression analysis, were the weights that the computer gave to the numerical grade in each category. In 1965, speed had counted for 14.64 percent of a tight end's total grade. The next year it was dropped to 11 percent. In 1965, competitiveness was 7 percent of a tight end's grade, a year later it went up to 10.5 percent.

In the 1977 draft, Dallas traded up with the Seattle Seahawks (one of two expansion clubs added in 1976) for the second pick, which they used to select Tony Dorsett, the Heisman winner out of Pitt. Going into the draft there was considerable debate about whether the bigger Ricky Bell, tailback out of USC and Tampa Bay's top pick, was better than Dorsett. But the Cowboys' system rendered a clear verdict, predicting that Dorsett would enjoy a much more successful career than Bell. Only after Tampa Bay selected Bell did Dallas make the deal for the second pick. In doing so, they added the NFL's Rookie of the Year and rolled to a 12-2 regular season mark and their second world championship.

That 1977 season, though, was among the least compelling in the league's history. Scoring was down, divisional races never heated up, and despite the Cowboys' popularity the overall level of play seemed sluggish. Points per game had dropped from a high of 46.1 in 1965 to 34.4 in 1977, the lowest total in thirty-five years. Touchdowns per game were down to 4.2, the lowest since 1940; touchdown passes were down to 1.98, also the lowest since 1942. Even when the pitiful performance of expansion teams Tampa Bay and Seattle were excluded, offense was in a historic slump. The game felt more sterile than ever, and there were far too many headlines like the one in *Pro Football Weekly,* following a 10–0 Washington win over Buffalo: "Dull Redskins Beat Even Duller Bills." As if that weren't enough, there was widespread criticism of excessive violence in the game, and the alarming injury rate among starting quarterbacks—six were knocked out of action in a single day—only exacerbated the offensive drought.

Another thing that Rozelle had been fearing for a decade—the revival of Major League Baseball's popularity—had come to pass. The Red Sox' march through the 1975 season, and their classic World Series with the Reds, had ignited the charge. But it was the dawn of free agency, and George Steinbrenner's arrogant, endlessly dramatic Yankees dynasty that led to the sort of figures that distressed Rozelle.

The NFL's favored pollster, Louis Harris, presented some sobering news in September 1977: "For the first time since 1968, more sports fans in the country follow baseball than football. The margin may be only one percentage point, but the trend is unmistakably in baseball's favor, and quite significant for the fortunes of both games. When fans are asked to name their favorite sport, they still opt for football by a slim 22–21 percent. It is clear that baseball has made a real comeback." The parallel was not lost on Rozelle that, just as football had surged ahead of baseball at a time when that sport's offense was at a record low level in the late '60s, so did baseball's resurgence accompany a decline in scoring and overall excitement in football in the mid-'70s.

Super Bowl XII revealed another painful lesson of the artificial turf era—it's hard to stage a football gala indoors. The hermetically sealed atmosphere of the first indoor setting, in the Louisiana Superdome, squeezed what little life there was out of another largely forgettable Super Bowl mismatch, with the Cowboys winning, 27–10, over the Denver Broncos.

A few weeks after Super Bowl XII, Rozelle toasted his friend Schramm, and they took their customary postseason fishing trip in the Caribbean. But on this outing, there was more football discussed than usual. Both men had reached the same conclusion: it was time to go back to the drawing board; the game needed to be rescued from itself.

18

Air War

On December 28, 1975, Paul Brown led the Cincinnati Bengals onto the field at Oakland Alameda-County Coliseum, to face the Oakland Raiders in the divisional round of the AFC playoffs. The 1975 squad was his best yet, qualifying for the playoffs for the third time in the team's eight-year existence. Cincinnati went 11-3 in the regular season, losing twice to the world champion Steelers (who routinely punished the fleet Bengal receivers with bump-and-run coverage beneath a double zone), but going 11-1 against the rest of their schedule to earn the AFC wild card berth.

Cincinnati fell behind 31–14 before a late rally closed the gap to 31–28. But the upset bid came up short; after choosing to punt from midfield late in the game, the Bengals never got the ball back. Paul Brown had coached 501 football games in 41 seasons at the pro, college, and high school levels. And, as he confided to a friend, "I never got used to losing."

Four days after the loss, on New Year's Day 1976, before settling down in his home to watch Ohio State take on UCLA in the Rose Bowl, Brown called Bengals public relations director Al Heim at home. Then Brown quietly dictated the press release of his own resignation, announcing that he was retiring as head coach, effective immediately, adding the news that he would be succeeded by his well-liked assistant Bill "Tiger" Johnson. Though Brown would remain as the team's general manager in complete charge of football operations, his historic coaching career had ended.

"Take it from there," he told Heim, who was dispatched to inform the media, on a day when widespread staffing of the nation's bowl games and preparation for the coming weekend's conference championships guaranteed it would receive the least possible amount of coverage. Brown provided no additional statements and called no press conferences.

———

Though he retired from coaching, Paul Brown remained the president and general manager of the Bengals, and kept his seat on the NFL's Competition Committee. The committee was one of the by-products of the merger and Rozelle's determination to return the focus to on-field issues in the '70s. The group was handpicked by Rozelle, and given the mission of "recommending all changes in rules in the area of on the field competition." The committee was chaired by Tex Schramm and, for much of the '70s, included Brown, Don Shula, and Al Davis. Staff oversight was handled initially by Jim Kensil and then, after Kensil left to become general manager of the Jets in 1977, by new executive director Don Weiss.

In the literal, zero-sum world of pro football, where as Shula aptly put it, "You start with having to win, and you work back," the Competition Committee operated on some different theoretical plane, equal parts brainstorming session, Rules Committee, and think tank. Armed with a ream of statistics, and separated from the often ponderous financial details of the main owners meeting, the committee would meet for ten to fourteen days in late February and early March, then prepare a set of recommendations to present to the league's annual meeting each year.

For the gruff visionary Schramm, the big picture of accelerating and accentuating the game's action was of primary importance. He ran the committee with a kind of bullheadedness, arguing incessantly with his peers through the day, then drinking with them much of the night. The group brought a unique range of experiences to the job: Schramm, Brown, and Davis all owned parts of teams; Brown, Davis, and Shula had all been coaches, and had all spent time in the more wide-open AFL; Schramm and Brown both had been raised on the Bell and Rozelle credo to "Think league first." And Schramm and Davis, for their part, had found common cause because both were nearly addicted to the competitive aspects of the game. "Once Al and I were discussing the word 'devious,' " said Don Shula. "He thought it was a compliment."

But the strong personalities and shifting alliances added a creative dynamism to the group, and it wielded immense power. Though the committee's recommendations were only that, they were in fact approved more than 95 percent of the time by the league's owners.

For much of the '70s, the committee grappled with the decline in passing and scoring. Some rules brought unforeseen consequences: when the hashmarks were moved nearer the center of the field in 1972, it did open the offense up to pass to both sides of the field. But it also made field goals easier (the hashmarks now perfectly aligned with the goalposts) and gave defenses an easier time disguising their coverages. The zone defenses that swept the league forced teams into shorter passes—running backs dominated the receiving leaders, and the average yards gained per completion dipped below 13 for the first time in 36 seasons.

In 1974, more sweeping changes were instituted: a sudden death period was added for tie games in the regular season, meaning that the seven tie games of 1973 were reduced to a single tie in 1974 (if neither team scored after a full overtime period in the regular season, the game ended in a tie). Because field goals had become so common (an all-time high of nearly three per game in 1973), the goalposts were moved to the back of the end zone (a rule that had the added appeal of making the game safer, since there would be less congestion on the goal line). To further discourage field goals, failed kicks attempted outside the 20-yard-line would have the ball returned to the line of scrimmage instead of the 20.

For Paul Brown, whose Bengals teams were smallish and not particularly physical, one of the crucial issues was the abuse suffered by receivers running their routes. Prior to 1974, receivers could be hit until the ball left the quarterback's hands. The rule played into the hands of the double-zone defense, in which the two cornerbacks played tight bump-and-run coverage on their assigned wide receivers, secure in the knowledge that if a receiver got by, a safety on that side of the field would be able to punish him more. The zone began with Shula's Dolphins and later made its way around the league, and few teams played it better than the Steelers. "I call it 'the bump-hit-grab-roll-block-catch-funnel and run,' " cracked Brown prior to the committee's meeting in 1974.

A rule instituted that season put greater restrictions on a defender's ability to bump, limiting a defender to a single "chuck" on a receiver once he was three yards beyond the line of scrimmage. In the short term, this meant that receivers were no longer subjected to routine and constant hacking as they went down the field.

In practice, the Competition Committee's work often attained a clean elegance. The skimpy tie-breaking rules for divisional and conference standings of 1970 were replaced with a more intricate, rational system in 1974. When the league's rotating playoff site system was exposed, when Miami had to take its 15-0 record on the road to Pittsburgh for the 1972 AFC title game, the committee instituted a system that seeded teams according to record. In addition to preventing instances in which a conference's two best teams were drawn against each other in the first round (as happened with Miami and Kansas City in 1971), it also gave teams more of an incentive to play well late in the regular season, even after clinching a division title.

Along the way, Schramm would push through numerous minor improvements to the game: the field would become more uniform, and safer, with foam pylons replacing the flags at the corner of each end zone; a six-foot white line bordered the entire field, which kept coaches and players on the sideline further from the action, and also made out-of-bounds plays easier to spot; a play clock was added behind each end zone, allowing both the quarterback and fans to know how much time was left before the ball had to be snapped; in 1974, the referee, the head of the officiating crew, was equipped with a microphone, so that he could announce to the entire stadium (and the TV audience) a penalty, providing clarification if necessary.

In addition to the small rules changes, Schramm was the main architect of the larger changes. "Virtually all the major changes in the league were initiated by Tex," said Weiss. "It continues to amaze me how he can take an idea and formulate it. He has as fertile a mind as anybody in our league and the great ability to grasp all facets of a situation. I don't think anybody in the league is more familiar with all aspects of the operation than Tex."

Not all new ideas came from within the Competition Committee. Throughout the summer of 1976, Jim Kensil spent much of his free time at the dining room table in his house at Massapequa, building a series of charts and formulas that he wouldn't finish until the fall, a blueprint for an entirely new way of scheduling.

Whereas the league had previously made do with a pure rotation formula—home-and-home within the division, plus a cycle of conference and nonconference foes that would rotate each year—Kensil envisioned something else, a way that would not only increase the league's desire for premium match-ups but further the vision first put forth by Bert Bell in the late '40s.

Instead of merely playing other excellent teams when the rotation called for it, Kensil's schedule envisioned that the league's division winners from one season would play every other division winner the following season. Similarly, the league's fourth-place teams would play five games against other fourth-place finishers.

He called his plan "position scheduling," and in an undated memo to Rozelle, probably written in early November, Kensil wrote:

> If the 1976 season were to end with the current standings and position sched-uling were put into effect for 1977, the team's basic schedules would be set by looking up a given team on the chart below and reading vertically for its home-and-home opponents and horizontally for its single-game opponents.
>
> There would, of course, be a system for breaking ties in the standings.
>
> Also teams in a four-team division would have only 11 basic games, as would fifth-place teams in a "five."
>
> A system would be worked out, along competitive lines, to schedule the additional games needed.

Balt	Cincy	Oak	Dall	Minn	LA
NE	Clev	Denv	St.L	Chi	SF
Miami	Hou	SD	Wash	Det	Atl
Buff	Pitt	KC	Philly	GB	NO
NYJ	—	TB	NYG	—	Sea

It was not a coincidence that the idea came at a time when the league was preparing to discuss a new round of TV contracts.

On November 5, 1976, Rozelle batted out a confidential letter to Art Mo-dell and Chargers owner Gene Klein, long-standing members of the NFL's broadcasting Committee, and shared for the first time the outlines of Kensil's plan. Laying out the problem of the present scheduling system and the limited number of attractive match-ups, Rozelle wrote, "The best solution would ap-pear to be 'stacking' the schedule. This would be achieved by pitting strong against strong and weak against weak (based on previous year's standings) for the out of division games. . . . It would ensure a great increase in attractive games for TV, but also give us the strong likelihood of fantastic divisional races with many more teams staying in contention longer!"

At the same time, a strong push developed in the league toward moving from a fourteen- to a sixteen-game regular season schedule, reducing the pre-season schedule from six games to four. Rozelle added, "In the event the clubs voted to go 16-4, it would of course mean additional TV revenue. And one of the major objections to a 16 game regular season schedule (the weak having two more games to flounder and races getting locked up too early) would be greatly diminished by the 'stacked' schedule." Rozelle added, in passing, "Kensil literally drools over the large increase in 'attractive' games the stacked sked would create."

At the league's spring meetings in March, the sixteen-game schedule was approved, along with a modified form of the stacked schedule, less severe than the one originally envisioned by Kensil, but it still ensured more attractive match-ups and offered the promise of increased competition. Besides the stacked schedule and two extra weeks of meaningful regular season games, there was one other element that the league would offer, an addition conceived by Don Weiss, who pointed out that in each of the three previous seasons, a 10-4 team had failed to qualify for the playoffs. By adding a single wild card to each conference, argued Weiss, the league could add an extra weekend of playoffs, reward each of the division champions a week to rest players, and keep more teams in contention for playoff spots later in the season, all without significantly watering down the lineup of teams making the playoffs.

"The idea of parity or competitive balance or whatever you want to call it is behind just about everything that the league talked about during the '60s and '70s," said Weiss. "To try to achieve better balance, keep people in the races longer, and stuff like that. The combination of that and the smaller divisions, and the schedule devised to make the schedule more competitive and to give the weaker teams something of a break. That was all part of it, sure. And that was the end result—the end result was making your league as competitive as possible."

With all that on the table, Rozelle went into negotiations for the next TV contract confident that he could achieve a sizable increase, though he had masterfully kept expectations low, pointing out the problems in the industry and the difficulty that CBS and NBC were having competing with ABC, whose prime-time lineup was dominating television at the time.

The ensuing deal, announced in October 1977, threw everyone for a loop: a four-year, $576 million contract that the *New York Times* would describe succinctly as "the biggest deal in television history." It was not merely that each team's annual revenue from TV would double, from just over $2 million to $5.2 million. For the first time, NFL teams would be earning more revenue from the rights to telecast their games than from the ticket sales of the games themselves.

This, however, was only half the job. A few weeks after returning from his fishing trip with Rozelle, Tex Schramm flew to Hawaii and the Competition Committee meeting armed with a mandate to initiate the most sweeping changes in a generation, all in the interest of stimulating offense. In 1977, defenders had been limited to just one "chuck," or hit on receivers; when the 1978 Competition Committee met, the rule restricted that further, limiting contact to one hit within five yards of the line of scrimmage. After that point, receivers could not legally be hit until a quarterback's pass had arrived. What this would mean in the short term for the league was more unfettered movement of receivers downfield. What it meant in the long term—a revolutionary change in the way the game was played, coached, and contested—wouldn't become clear for a few years. There was little noticeable impact in 1978. Teams that were already passing (like the Chargers, where coach Don Coryell was carrying the torch of Gillman's offensive innovation) continued to do so, but most teams began the 1978 season continuing to play relatively conservative football.

By the end of the season, though, the new rules were beginning to take hold. Though the Steelers remained an intimidating, physical team, they won two more titles in 1978 and 1979 with a much more diversified attack, which relied less on Franco Harris's runs and more on Terry Bradshaw's throws to receivers Lynn Swann and John Stallworth. The Steelers' third and fourth Super Bowl wins—35–31 over the Cowboys in Miami and a rousing 31–19 defeat of the Rams in Pasadena—were wide-open affairs, much more consistent with the freewheeling game the league wanted to portray.

By 1980, the change was dramatic. Teams were passing 47 percent of the time (as compared to just 38 percent in 1977) and scoring was up to 41 points per game (from 34.4 in 1977). The end of the bump-and-run, combined with the liberalized pass-blocking rules, changed the mind-set of defenses as well. Teams switched to a more aggressive, gambling style. "We preach to our kids, 'Don't worry about getting beat on the bomb,' " said the Jets' defensive coordinator Joe Gardi during the 1981 season. "Offenses can put so many points on the board, that 14 points aren't usually going to beat you. Two-three turnovers will make up for it. Ten years ago, giving up a bomb was disastrous. Not now."

The obsession with speed was further encouraged, because now it was easier than ever to utilize it. Six track sprinters or hurdlers were taken in the first round of the 1980 draft, two of whom (world-class sprinters Lam Jones and Curtis Dickey) were among the first five overall selections.

Instead of a two-yard cushion, defenders were giving the fastest receivers a four- or five-yard cushion at the line. As this phenomenon played itself out through the league, it led to developments that would become crucial in the next phase of the sport: double-teams on the most dangerous wide receivers left single coverage on tight ends down the field and running backs coming out of the backfield, and the larger cushion given to most quick receivers, whether in man or zone coverage, meant that teams had more room to throw underneath coverages, or hit wide receivers on quick slant routes. With the new rules in place, it was only a matter of time before someone showed how best to take full advantage of them.

———————

When Paul Brown announced that Tiger Johnson would succeed him in 1976, no one was more stunned than Bill Walsh, Brown's prized offensive assistant who had been constructing the team's game plans and calling plays, without credit, for many years.

Walsh had grown up in Los Angeles, watching Southern Cal and UCLA games, and the aerial theatrics of the Rams' teams of the late '40s and '50s. Neither his crisp manner nor soft-spoken confidence could conceal the fact that he was a man of ambition. Those who knew him best realized he was one of the brightest minds in football. Even Brown, not one to shower praise on his assistants, recognized Walsh's skills. "He has ideas," Brown said approvingly, to his son, Mike.

Walsh had spent the 1966 season as an assistant with the Raiders, before leaving. He admired Al Davis, and his concepts about football, but he couldn't thrive in the Raiders' one-dimensional environment. "He is a person whose existence is consumed with what he does, and it's too much," said Walsh of Davis. "And only a few men could stay with it." Walsh was not one of them. He left the Raiders job and went to work as the head coach for the semipro San Jose Toros. In 1968, when starting the Bengals, Brown called on Walsh and eventually ceded almost total control of the passing attack, game plan, and play calling to the lanky, prematurely white-haired Californian.

Like a grad student drawing from various great thinkers to devise a new synthesis, Walsh borrowed from his earlier experiences. For a string of talented young quarterbacks and a young offensive line, Walsh brought elements of Gillman (putting more receivers into routes, spreading out the field horizontally), Davis (an unpredictable mix of play calling that isolated an opponent's weakness and exploited it at the most crucial times), and his own techniques that he'd gained from years of football (like moving a flanker in closer to the tight end, then sending him across the field on shallow drag routes that gave defenses fits). Walsh also developed, out of necessity, a habit of using shorter drops for his quarterbacks, since Cincinnati's green offensive line often couldn't hold blocks long enough to accommodate the deeper drops and longer setups of some of Gillman's and Davis's favorite patterns.

While Brown was still nominally the man in charge of play calling for the Bengals, by 1971 the plays were actually being called by Walsh, from up in the booth overlooking the stadium. Cincinnati was a stylish, finesse team that used its quickness, plenty of motion, crossing patterns, misdirection running plays, and an update of the Browns' delayed draw, a play in which the quarterback dropped back as if to pass, then handed the ball up to his blocking back.

As the Bengals rose to a series of successes in the early '70s, Walsh waited for someone to notice and give him a shot as a head coach. He was bewildered when no calls came, but consoled himself with the idea that when Brown did step down, he was the logical man to replace him.

So when he heard the news that he'd been passed over for the head coaching job for Bill Johnson, Walsh was, in his own words, "an emotional wreck." He concluded then that he would never be a head coach if he stayed in Cincinnati. As he put it, "I knew I now had to leave to have a career."

Just days after Brown's announcement, Bill Walsh sat in Paul Brown's office, with Paul and Mike Brown, and tried to explain himself.

"I have to leave," said Walsh, soon in tears over the implication.

Brown was taken aback by the unabashed emotionalism and argued that Walsh *couldn't* leave, because he was under contract in Cincinnati. Bereft and still weeping, Walsh got up and left the office.

"You wait here," said Brown, sternly. "You wait!"

But Walsh was already out the door, and on his way out of Cincinnati. It would be weeks before he began to learn the full nature of Brown's efforts to keep him. Numerous teams had called, inquiring about Walsh, and Brown had given each team a negative recommendation.

In San Francisco, Lou Spadia called after Dick Nolan left in 1975, curious if the young assistant from the area might be the right man for the 49ers job. "Paul Brown told me," said Spadia, "that, 'If I were you, I wouldn't touch him with a ten-foot pole. He'll wreck your team.' " Sid Gillman, about to embark on his last year as head coach in Houston in 1974, had called Cincinnati in the spring of 1974, to see if Walsh would work for him one year as an assistant and heir apparent, with the understanding that he could have the head coaching job in 1975. Brown declined to give permission for Gillman to talk to Walsh, then never even told Walsh about the opportunity.

After leaving Cincinnati in 1976, Walsh immediately helped transform the Chargers into one of the league's most potent offenses, and soon wound up back in the Bay Area, as the head coach at Stanford, where the undermanned Cardinal enjoyed surprising success for two seasons. The 49ers, who'd just fired their fourth coach in three years, took another look at Walsh and hired him prior to the 1979 season.

Finally receiving a chance as a head coach in the pros at age forty-seven, Walsh would soon make up for lost time. His approach would initially strike players as corporate. He used language in different ways, choosing to refer to what for decades had been known as the playbook as "our inventory of plays." The 49ers didn't have pass patterns, they had "schematics."

But there was also a component of his coaching philosophy, steeped in decades of California consciousness raising, that was more humane than the standard, the product of his years on the progressive campus at Stanford. What Walsh was attempting was not merely a new way to run an offense, but a revolutionary new way to coach a football team.

The 49ers' starting quarterback in 1979 was lightly regarded Steve DeBerg, a six-year veteran from Walsh's own alma mater, San Jose State, who had posted a 45.4 completion percentage in 1978, as the twenty-eighth-rated quarterback in the NFL. With the offensive line he inherited a shambles, Walsh shortened DeBerg's drop-back to three or five steps, and drilled him in a system in which each of his first three reads would be on one side of the field, meaning the quarterback's primary choices were within a narrower range of vision than in other offenses. With the Walsh system of timed patterns and progressive reads, and painstaking work on accelerating his drop-back, DeBerg completed 60 percent of his passes and San Francisco rose from twenty-fifth to third in the NFL in passing yards.

And yet, at the end of that first season, Walsh was both fatigued and discouraged. The 49ers went 2-14, just as they had in the previous season. DeBerg had proved a credible quarterback, especially deft at ball-handling, but he exhibited neither the touch nor the accuracy for the offense to maximize its effectiveness. And no amount of strategic innovation could make up for the team's general lack of talent. "I had no idea the team would be as bad as it was," Walsh said. "It was almost as bad as the Bengals were when we started the Bengals. So it goes without saying that I almost failed. Because it was too big a task—insurmountable, impossible, insurmountable."

Help was on the way. There are moments when the fortunes of a franchise pivot on a single game, decision, trade, or play. The Colts' fortunes rose on the price of a call to free agent Johnny Unitas; the Rams had gone into a nearly decade-long nosedive after choosing Jon Arnett instead of Jim Brown. And in the same way, the fortunes of the 49ers were forever altered by a draft-day decision, this by another team.

The 1979 draft found the Dallas Cowboys preparing for the beginning of a new era, with Roger Staubach nearing the end of his career. His understudy Danny White, who'd come over after the demise of the WFL, was the heir apparent, and the young Glenn Carano, an unpolished but physically gifted thrower from University of Nevada–Las Vegas was seen as a potential diamond in the rough. In the third round, as the Cowboys' selection came up, Tom Landry looked at the Cowboys' master list, and did something he had rarely done in his nineteen years of drafting. Instead of taking the top player on the Cowboys' chart, he went "against the board" and selected not the highest-rated player but the next-highest-ranked one, a rangy tight end named Doug Cosbie, who would go on to enjoy a productive career and provide further evidence that the Cowboys were able to find a diamond in the rough.

On the next selection, the eighty-second San Francisco chose the very player who had been on the top of the Cowboys' board, the player Dallas had passed on because, in Landry's words, "We don't really need another quarterback."

His name was Joe Montana.

By New Year's Day in Dallas, when he sealed his collegiate legend by rallying Notre Dame from a 34–12 deficit to defeat Houston in a freezing rainstorm in the Cotton Bowl, Montana had already earned the attention of NFL scouts. He was smallish for a quarterback, listed at 6-foot-1½, but barely a shade over 6-foot, with a spindly build, shaggy hair, and a big nose. Wearing his helmet, eyes twinkling out above the facemask, Montana occasionally resembled the pop crooner Barry Manilow. But what he lacked in the superficial characteristics of a first-class athlete, he more than made up for in the purest sense, in the area of touch, poise, and athletic instincts.

The team opened at 3-0 in 1980, before starting an eight-game losing streak, during which Walsh turned the starting job over to Montana. The streak was snapped with an ugly 12–0 win over the Giants in November, then followed with a 21–7 upset of a good New England team. Next the New Orleans Saints came to town, and scorched the San Francisco secondary en route to a 35–7 halftime lead. In the second half, Montana led San Francisco all the way back, tying the game at 35 in regulation, and leading them on a game-winning drive to prevail, 38–35, in overtime.

The 49ers lost their last two games of the season, to wind up 6-10. "We knew we had something," said Walsh of his realization of Montana's potential. "But we were, even at that time, who were we to think that we were gonna go anywhere? I mean, we had lost eight straight games in the second year. We might have thought *somebody* was gonna have a great quarterback, whoever gets this job next, you know."

In Montana's precocious maturity and quicksilver elusiveness there were the seeds of greatness. Walsh was able to capitalize more quickly than most of his competitors on the liberalized passing rules, using short drops, quick reads, and timed patterns. Montana internalized the patterns so completely that he possessed what Walsh would describe as "this inherent, instinctive, genetic" ability to see receivers *before* they came open on a route, throwing the ball so it would arrive just as the receiver came free. The system and the athletes complemented one another, and Walsh's system would be labeled "the West Coast offense."

The other distinctive characteristic of the West Coast offense was the "scripting" of plays. It had begun in Cincinnati when Paul Brown, eager to get a sense of the next day's game, would ask, "What are your openers?," and Walsh would provide him with a list of five or so plays that he expected to call at the beginning of the game, a list he would only veer from in a specific down-and-distance situation like third-and-short. By the time he was at San Diego, the script had grown to fifteen plays, and most games the Chargers would exhaust that list before they did anything else. In San Francisco, the script could stretch to twenty-five plays or more. "It helped our players sleep at night," said Walsh. "We could take the field without the butterflies and hypertension, the wondering, because we had a plan."

It also made the 49ers exceedingly difficult to defense. Since Landry began the sophisticated charting of opponents' offensive tendencies in the '50s, much defensive game planning involved sussing out a team's tendencies, patterns in certain down-and-distance situations. But the 49ers' script wreaked havoc with tendencies, since so many play calls had been made prior to the game, irrespective of down and distance.

In the third season, 1981, with three rookie starters in the secondary, the 49ers got off to a 1-2 start, before winning twelve of their last thirteen regular season games, to clinch home field throughout the playoffs. Montana's emerging favorite target was a slow, lanky wide receiver named Dwight Clark, who had been a tenth-round pick the same year that Montana went in the third round, and would catch eighty-five passes during the regular season. After beating the Giants, 38–24, in their opening playoff game, they played host to the Cowboys, still formidable, still glamorous, and with a score to settle after a lopsided regular season loss in San Francisco.

San Francisco seemed jittery during the rematch, giving up six turnovers, two of which led to touchdowns. With 4:54 remaining, they trailed Dallas, 27–21. Then, Montana led the 49ers on the thirteen-play drive that would solidify his pro legend. With third-and-three on the Cowboys' six-yard line, with

58 seconds to play, Montana called a sprint-out pass. A blitz flushed him further out of the pocket as he moved laterally toward the sideline. As he neared the boundary, Montana couldn't see Clark, but he knew that Clark's route called for him to be in the back of the end zone, moving in the same direction. An instant before running out of bounds he threw a sharp, high ball toward the back corner of the end zone. Staying just inside the end line, with cornerback Everson Walls shadowing him tightly, Clark leaped to catch the ball, coming down with both feet in bounds. Afterward, the Cowboys seemed stunned, and ungenerous. "Montana has to be the key," said Landry. "There really is nothing else there except the quarterback."

The 49ers would head to the Super Bowl, where waiting for Walsh would be none other than the Cincinnati Bengals, owned by Paul Brown, and resurgent themselves, having rebounded from a 6-10 mark in 1980, under the guidance of second-year coach Forrest Gregg.

The game was an uneven, if exciting affair, watched by a record crowd of 110 million Americans; bitterly cold weather across much of the country added to the audience. The 49ers would win the world championship, 26–21, and in so doing would provide the first glimpse of pro football's future.

Brown may have been grudging with praise to his competitors and former protégés, but when he delivered it, the words were sincere. The following March, during a break in the spring meetings, Brown saw Walsh and said hello. They talked for a few minutes, and inevitably fell into talk of the previous Super Bowl. "I knew what you were doing," said Brown of Walsh's play calling. "I knew what you were doing during that game . . . and I *liked* it."

So did Pete Rozelle. Pro football had quelled baseball's resurgence, and made the owners even richer. The game's offense and excitement had sprung back, its competitive balance showed signs of returning. Both Super Bowl teams had gone 6-10 the previous season, meaning that there was hope, even for longtime doormats. Not coincidentally, the sport's popularity rose to a new high.

Pro football's incursion into the mainstream of American popular culture was no longer questioned, and infrequently challenged. In 1980, the League of Women Voters scheduled two presidential debates between Jimmy Carter and Ronald Reagan on Monday nights, before an outcry from the republic of football fans—as well as a sober reconsideration on the part of realist political operatives—forced a switch. (The single debate that occurred came on a Tuesday night.)

The 49ers-Bengals Super Bowl in Detroit had earned the highest Nielsen rating of any sporting event in history, 49.1 with a 73.0 share, good numbers to bring into the negotiation with the networks later in the spring. ABC's Roone Arledge would describe sitting across from Rozelle during contract talks as having "about as much clout as the Dalai Lama has dealing with the Chinese Army." In February 1982, Rozelle sat down with his ever-present gold-plated Dunhill lighter (which he would tap lightly on a tabletop during the tensest moments of negotiations) and named his terms. The ensuing five-year, $2.1 billion deal added further luster to Rozelle's reputation, and that of pro football. With the new contract, each team's annual revenues from TV grew from $5 million to $13 million.

Taken together, the triumphant Super Bowl and another record-breaking TV deal marked another plateau in the sport's ascent. Offense had crept back up by the 1981 season, and though there were problems looming on the horizon, pro football was securely ensconced as the number one spectator sport in America.

Pat Summerall would often see his friend Rozelle, at the height of his powers during these years, and wonder how long the remarkable string might continue. "I think he had visions during that period of time of, 'Oh, boy, how much better can it possibly get?' He came down to the field before the game and it was like the Roman emperor with his entourage and the guards and the chariots. You almost expected the spears and swords to come at any minute."

19

Under Siege

Rozelle's perspective would never again seem quite so rosy, his primacy never so complete. Within months of the new TV deal, the dam broke and the NFL found itself beset on all sides, with crises, legal defeats, scandals, and strikes. These weren't PR flaps that came and went like Joe Namath's threatened retirement, but the result of deep-seated problems and fissures within the league hierarchy that would plague the NFL throughout the '80s.

Yet it's worth noting that, for all the bad news that followed, at no time during the decade was the NFL's standing as America's most popular sport seriously challenged. The game's appeal was so broad, its organizational savvy so far superior to that of its competitors that it continued, to paraphrase the old Paul Brown maxim, "to run on its own gas." The game's crown jewels stayed relatively healthy: *Monday Night Football* remained a perennial hit, even after Don Meredith's exit in 1978 and Howard Cosell's departure following the 1983 season. The Super Bowl, already a high holy day in the American civic religion, became the most important day in the calendar for the advertising industry. By the time Apple launched its Macintosh computer with the Ridley Scott–directed *1984* spot during the 1984 game, commercials were vying with the pregame and halftime entertainment as can-you-top-this spectacles.

Pro football was still king, but its imperial sense of serenity came crashing down in 1982, foreshadowing a decade of discontent most notable for a seemingly unending run of litigation from within and without, a potentially lethal challenge from yet another rival football league, widespread owner infighting, player discord that would lead to two strikes and numerous drug scandals, and myriad charges—in the midst of all the negative publicity—that the game itself had grown too corporate, too violent, too boring, or otherwise deficient in some crucial way. The turmoil would resonate into the next decade, rent the loyal fan bases in Oakland, Baltimore, and St. Louis, shake the NFL to its foundations, and eventually put a moody cap on Pete Rozelle's remarkable tenure.

––––––––

One of the central illusions of sport is that a group of athletes wearing a certain uniform can represent an entire city. And one of the wonders of sport is that the repeated exercise of that illusion, through many years and many athletes, can serve to make it a reality. The Oakland Raiders were a privately held business, but like virtually all professional sports franchises that had remained solvent long enough to become successful, they occupied a unique position in their community. The Raiders had become part of the city's identity, and succeeded in part *because* of that connection. The people of Oakland and other East Bay communities—who had supported the franchise, financed a new stadium in the '60s, and through more than a decade of sellouts helped make the Silver-and-Black one of the most recognizable franchises in the sport—could plausibly be said to possess a stake in the team that went beyond a narrow consideration of legal ownership. Too often these feelings of loyalty are dismissed, but they were at the very heart of the appeal of spectator sports in the late twentieth century.

While this would be true about any city that supported a franchise for more than two decades, it was *particularly* true of long-mocked cities like Baltimore, Cleveland, and Oakland. At some level, the football team became identified with and evoked a truth about the larger city. "You'd go anywhere in the world and you say, 'I'm from Oakland,'" recalled the actor Tom Hanks. "And people would say, 'Is that where the Oakland *Raiders* play?' And it'd be 'Yes, that's right, where the Oakland Raiders play.'"

By the time the Raiders won their first Super Bowl after the 1976 season, Al Davis had reached the pinnacle of pro football. Yet even as he found the ultimate success in the game, Davis's relationship with Pete Rozelle would thaw but never approach warmth. For this reason, the ensuing legal battle between the Raiders and the NFL was often oversimplified as the result of a personal animosity between Davis and Rozelle.

It was true that the two men were temperamentally ill-matched. Rozelle exuded the middle-class politesse of the self-effacing businessman, always deflecting credit, always flattering his opponents. He was no less willful than his foes, but almost always smoother, calmer, more assured. Al Davis had been fighting people like that his whole life.

But many would interpret Davis's battle with Rozelle as being motivated solely by revenge, that Davis still held a grudge over Rozelle being named commissioner of the merged NFL in 1966. This was a facile reading that did neither Davis nor Rozelle justice. By the summer of 1966, Rozelle was the best-known and most powerful executive in sports; Davis, by contrast, had held the job of AFL commissioner for only two months when the merger was agreed upon. Under the circumstances, it would have been unthinkable for anyone but Rozelle to be named the commissioner of a larger, unified league.

Also, it's not at all clear that Davis truly desired the commissioner's job. Once the leagues unified, much of the glamour and intrigue of the job disappeared for Davis. He would have been disenchanted with the daily challenges of the job—of consensus building and evenhanded officiating of disputes, of calmly handling crises and serving as the game's master of ceremonies. "That is not my modus operandi," said Davis later, "and I am not a commissioner. I'd rather be with a team, building a team."

What is understandable is that Davis was infuriated by the *perception*, after the merger, that Rozelle had been the mastermind to broker the ultimate deal. His own resentment of the NFL, and his increasing sense of paranoia over the league being "out to get" the Raiders, dated at least as far back as 1970, when he objected to the schedule the club was given. Rozelle, in turn, resented Davis's sponsorship of Raider defensive back George Atkinson's libel suit against Chuck Noll (who'd called Atkinson part of the league's "criminal element"). Many in the league, Tex Schramm included, viewed Rozelle's decision to remove Davis from the Competition Committee as an act of retaliation. Rozelle and Davis would never be friends. Still, it was not apparent in the late '70s that they were on a collision course that would threaten to tear the league apart. That would come later.

For much of the decade, the renegade owner who gave Rozelle the most trouble was not Davis but his close friend, Rams owner Carroll Rosenbloom.

It was Rosenbloom who pushed over the first domino in the chain of events that led to the litigious '80s, by announcing his intentions to move the Rams out of the Los Angeles Coliseum into Anaheim Stadium. But even before then, Rosenbloom had been at odds with Rozelle. When the Rams signed the Lions' wide receiver Ron Jessie, who'd just played out his option, to a contract after the 1974 season, Rozelle ruled that it should cost the Rams a number one draft pick and promising running back Cullen Bryant, Rosenbloom was enraged. Not only did he allegedly sponsor Bryant's lawsuit against the league (which ultimately resulted in Rozelle changing the compensation to an extra draft choice rather than Bryant) but he spent much of the next year rallying support for Rozelle's ouster. The centerpiece of this insurgency was a November 1975 league meeting in which Rosenbloom spent an hour in executive session ranting about Rozelle's supposed shortcomings, vowed he'd never again attend a league meeting in which Rozelle presided, and, on his way out the door, said, "I'll get even with you, either in here or out there." After Rosenbloom stormed out, all eyes in the silent room turned to Rozelle, who, sitting calmly at the end of the table, said, "Why don't we take a short recess."

But the big problem for Rosenbloom, and soon enough the league as a whole, was the Los Angeles Coliseum. Despite the Rams' run of seven consecutive division titles starting in 1973, the notoriously fickle fan base in Los Angeles quickly grew impatient with the team's inability to reach the Super Bowl. Attendance at the aging Coliseum had fallen from 76,000 in 1974 to 53,000 by 1977. Frustrated with the city's reluctance to refurbish the crumbling Coliseum in an increasingly dangerous part of downtown Los Angeles, Rosenbloom agitated for improvements, threatening to move the team to Anaheim if he didn't get them. This seemed unlikely especially to the entrenched and highly political Coliseum Commission. During a private meeting, one commissioner summed up his attitude by telling Rosenbloom, "Rosie, I think you're bluffing, man."

He wasn't, and even if he had been, such a bold challenge could only have pushed him to act. On July 28, 1978, four days after signing a letter of intent with the city of Anaheim, Rosenbloom announced that the Los Angeles Rams were moving to Anaheim. On its face, this move was no different than other moves from the heart of a city to a more accommodating suburb: Buffalo had moved its stadium to nearby Orchard Park, and the Cowboys played in suburban Irving. But the stadium in Anaheim, located just across the street from the entrance to Disneyland, was thirty-five miles south of the Coliseum, and anyone from Los Angeles—Rozelle certainly included—knew that Anaheim was in a completely different world from L.A., both culturally and geographically. For the majority of the team's longtime fan base that lived in and around the Los Angeles area, the prospect of an additional two hours or more of round-trip drive time on the glutted 405 freeway to and from the stadium was no small matter. To that end, Rozelle pleaded with Rosenbloom in a personal letter, "strongly recommending" that he not make the move to Anaheim. Rosenbloom ignored that, but did submit the move to a vote of owners, where it was approved.

In response to the Rams' move, the Los Angeles Coliseum Commission immediately appealed for the league to bring another NFL team to Los Angeles. There was little chance of this happening, though. League bylaws dictated that any move by an existing franchise into another team's territory required unanimous approval, and the Rams would be sure to oppose any move by another club into the Los Angeles area. With little hope for expansion in the near future (the league having just added Seattle and Tampa Bay in 1976), the LACC filed suit against the NFL on September 13, 1978, charging that the league's rules on franchise movements, Article IV, Section 4.3—which required unanimous agreement by club owners for the transfer of any franchise into the home territory of another franchise—was an unfair restraint of trade, in violation of the Sherman Antitrust Act.

When the owners met in special session on October 4–5 to discuss the Rams' move, Rozelle also tried, at the behest of the league's lawyers, to shore up the NFL's legal standing. Rozelle tried to push for an amendment that would change the unanimous provision to one requiring a three-fourths majority, figuring that such a rule would more likely be seen as a reasonable condition by the courts. When Rozelle put the amendment to a vote, twenty-seven teams voted in favor, but the Raiders' Davis passed, without stating a reason. Rozelle then announced that he was ruling the 27–0–1 vote unanimous, prompting Davis to bark, "If you are going to consider that unanimous, and it isn't, then I reserve the right to move the Oakland Raiders as I see fit." Davis wouldn't elaborate, but the meeting ended with a curious mixture of uncertainty and gloom.

Then, on April 2, 1979, Rosenbloom drowned off the coast of his Golden Beach, Florida, home. Just two days after Rosenbloom's death, Al Davis was quoted in the *St. Paul Pioneer Press* that "pay-TV is where it's going to be all at. It won't matter the size of the stadiums. But can you imagine two million viewers paying 10 bucks a head? That means the smart pro clubs have to be in the big TV markets. That's why we're thinking about a move to Los Angeles."

A longtime NFL owner would remark years later that "if Carroll Rosenbloom were alive, Al never would have done what he did." That may have been true, although the Raiders—whose 53,000 capacity was the second-smallest in the league—had a lease that expired after the 1979 season, and felt as though the city of Oakland was not suitably generous in its offer. (This impression was exacerbated in January, when the Oakland Coliseum Commission withdrew an offer that was on the table and substituted a less favorable one.)

On March 1, 1980, Davis signed a memorandum of agreement with the Los Angeles Coliseum Commission, which also brought the Raiders in as co-plaintiffs in the suit against the NFL. Rather than formally requesting a move, as the Rams had, the Raiders simply announced the intention of moving to Los Angeles.

On March 9, the owners voted against allowing the move to Los Angeles, 22–0–5, at a meeting that Davis didn't attend. What was startling afterward was hearing how many owners viewed Davis's greatest sin not as leaving Oakland but as ignoring the rules of the league. "I didn't like it," said Davis's old Competition Committee mate Tex Schramm, "but I'd have voted with Al if he just would have followed the rules. But then he just up and moved, and that was something I couldn't abide by. You had to respect the league."

Rozelle understood what some of the owners clearly didn't: the issue was far more than a point of order. Beyond any of the ramifications in L.A., the Raiders' move was more fundamentally a betrayal of the Oakland Raiders fans who'd supported their team for two decades, including twelve years of consecutive sellouts. "He felt very strongly that this had the potential to break faith with the fans in Oakland," said Paul Tagliabue, the Covington & Burling lawyer who would play a key role in dozens of the antitrust suits the league defended in the '70s and '80s, and who would become one of Rozelle's most trusted advisers in the process. "From that standpoint it was a critically important case . . . the fans being negatively affected by this kind of a team move added a sense of urgency from his point of view."

As fans, the Raiders' rooters could hardly be faulted. But Oakland's ticket base remained strong, through 1980 and 1981, when only a restraining order pending the outcome of the trial kept the Raiders from moving to L.A.

Howard Cosell had eviscerated Wellington Mara for moving the New York Giants across the New Jersey state line to the Meadowlands in 1976, and had been pointedly critical of Rosenbloom's move to Anaheim, but he was almost sanguine about his friend Davis's attempted move. On December 1, 1980, with the Raiders at home for a Monday night game against Denver, the fans of Oakland boycotted the game's first five minutes, holding a rally outside the stadium to protest the proposed move. Quite at odds with Cosell's reputation for candor and intellectual honesty was his comment that the crowd was arriving late due to "a traffic jam."

There was a wistful nature, then, to the city's celebration in January 1981, when the Raiders rode a wild card berth to a win in Super Bowl XV, pasting the Philadelphia Eagles, 27–10. It was difficult to embrace an owner and a team that were trying to leave.

The trial itself was a draining three-act play. The first trial ended in a hung jury; in the second trial, Raiders attorney Joseph Alioto hammered the league for its arbitrary policies on franchise moves and, in the words of former league publicist Harold Rosenthal, "had Rozelle up on the stand saying 'I don't remember,' like some Chicago alderman." On Friday, May 7, 1982—nearly four years after the Los Angeles Coliseum Commission filed suit and almost two years after the Raiders announced the intention to move—the jury in Los Angeles returned a verdict in favor of the LACC and the Raiders. In the aftermath the NFL directly filed an appeal and both parties prepared for a third trial, this to decide damages.

Even as the NFL went through the appeals process, the Raiders were playing their games in L.A. It was a curious honeymoon. The team still practiced in Oakland, and most of the players and staff retained their Bay Area residences. Meanwhile, in Los Angeles, the vision of the Raiders at the Coliseum was jarring for fans and writers alike. And the team that seemed so well suited for the East Bay in Oakland seemed utterly out of place in Southern California.

As it turned out, Davis would ultimately be victimized by his own instincts, which had blinded him to the possibilities that the league really was a joint partnership, devoted to the principles of revenue sharing. His interpretation that he *had* to move to L.A., because the power in the future would rest with the big markets and pay TV, would have been well founded in any other sport (in baseball, where the cable revenues of teams like the Yankees and Dodgers would dwarf those of teams in smaller markets, he would have been a visionary). But in pro football, adherence to the egalitarian precepts of revenue sharing, the draft, the stacked schedule, the 60–40 ticket revenue split (and, eventually, the salary cap), all served a principle of fair play, and meant that teams from small markets like Oakland and Pittsburgh could not only remain competitive but prosper.

These other truths would emerge over time. But on May 7, 1982, all that Pete Rozelle or the National Football League knew was that many of the assumptions they'd made over the nature of sports leagues and the equilibrium of their own league were, for the time being and in the absence of a successful appeal or congressional ruling, legally wrong.

It would be a long summer. Discussions of the implications of the Raiders' victory were still in the news four days later, on May 11, 1982, when the United States Football League announced its formation in a festive press conference at "21" in New York City. The USFL was the brainchild of New Orleans antiques dealer David Dixon, the longtime sports patron who worked for years to bring an NFL team to New Orleans, and who had helped Rozelle lobby for an antitrust exemption to allow the NFL-AFL merger in the fall of 1966.

Dixon had been arguing for the merits of a spring football league. He'd even made a presentation to NFL owners at an annual meeting in 1973, to use a spring league as a developmental league. From that germ of an idea, and a survey of attitudes about sports that indicated a strong interest in football even during the spring, the USFL got off the ground. Chet Simmons, one of Roone Arledge's protégés at ABC, was named the commissioner; Peter Hadhazy, who'd spent his entire adult life working at the NFL, was hired as director of football operations. The USFL, slated to start in March 1983, quickly earned a pair of national TV contracts, from ABC and ESPN, and spoke of strict payroll caps and financial sanity.

No sooner had the wave of USFL stories died down than *Sports Illustrated* featured the pro game in a rare off-season cover story. The magazine's June 14, 1982, issue featured the first all-text cover in its twenty-eight-year history, including a banner in the upper-right-hand corner reading "SPECIAL RE- PORT," and then set the lead paragraph of its story in bold black type against a stark white background. It read:

> Cocaine arrived in my life with my first-round draft into the National Football League in 1974. It has dominated my life, one way or another, almost every minute since. Eventually, it took control and almost killed me. It may yet. Cocaine can be found in quantity throughout the NFL. It's pushed on players, often from the edge of the practice field. Sometimes it's pushed *by* players. Prominent players. Just as it controlled me, it now controls and corrupts the game, because so many players are on it. To ignore this fact is to be short- sighted and stupid. To turn away from it the way the NFL does—the way the NFL turned its back on me when I cried for help two years ago—is a crime.

The first-person account of cocaine addiction came from Don Reese, who'd played in Miami and New Orleans before being waived out of the league in 1978, and included allegations that other star players, including New Orleans running back Chuck Muncie, had been users.

Though the approach was sensational, the *SI* story spoke a painful truth. Drug abuse had become a growing problem in the league, had been one at least as far back as the mid-'60s. The league, so eager to put the best face on the sport, seemed either unable or unwilling to confront the problem, but drugs had long ago started to affect the game on the field. After the strike-shortened 1982 season, in which he'd watched his defending Super Bowl champions crumble to a 3-6 record, Bill Walsh seriously considered quitting as head coach and attacking the problem as a general manager. By the fall of 1982, the problem was out in the open, fair game for comedians and no longer whispered about off the record. In the words of the respected football writer Paul "Dr. Z" Zimmerman, "The offense of the '80s is now cocaine possession."

What the league needed most after the discontented summer of 1982 was a scintillating regular season that would return the focus on football. What it got instead was a fifty-seven-day strike, the longest in the history of professional sports at that time, that struck at the heart of the season, and left NFL fans angry, betrayed, and empty.

In the previous round of negotiations, Rozelle had sagely gotten an agreement with the players association *before* signing the new television deal. But in 1982, the new TV deal was signed before negotiations started, and the record-breaking deal only emboldened the NFLPA. In March 1982, they put forth a proposal calling for a pool of money for player salaries, consisting of 55 percent of the gross of league revenues.

This was rejected out of hand, and was easier to do so because of the complex system that called for much of the salary to be based on seniority rather than the traditional individual contract bargaining handled by individual players. The strike was called after the Packers-Giants game on Monday, September 20, the season's second week. By mid-November, when a compromise was finally reached, the owners gave the players a sizable settlement package— worth $1.28 billion over the coming five seasons, with improved benefits, severance pay, and $60 million in "money now" payments, to offset much of the players' lost wages during the strike—but little real gains in terms of power.

The truncated regular season (of just nine games) and expanded playoffs (with sixteen teams) that followed made for an unsatisfying season, exacerbated by the knowledge that the strike and settlement did nothing to address the rancorous mistrust between the players and owners.

Fans were angered, but they remained fans. Ratings for the 1983 Super Bowl, in which the Redskins defeated Miami, were high. The rules changes that stimulated the offense had started to take effect. Attendance had grown to 13 million by 1983, the first post-strike season.

But there was a growing sense, among those in and closest to the game, that the league had lost its way. Rozelle didn't seem to have the confidence of his owners as much as he once did, and the owners themselves bickered more publicly than ever before. Rozelle, meanwhile, was also trying to tend to the erratic behavior of Carroll Rosenbloom's widow, Georgia, who since inheriting the team from her late husband had fired his son, Steve, tangled with GM Don Klosterman, quickly remarried, and hired the public relations firm of Rogers & Cowan to burnish her image.

And, always, there was Al Davis. After the strike-shortened 1982 season, 1983 was the Raiders' first full season in Los Angeles. With second-year running back Marcus Allen, drafted out of Southern Cal, leading the way on offense, the bruising Raiders marched to another Super Bowl title, manhandling the Washington Redskins, 38–9. By the time of the Super Bowl, January of 1984, the bad blood between Rozelle and Davis had escalated, and had spilled over to the team. On the field there was a painted football with Rozelle's signature on it, and in pregame warm-ups, the Raiders players used their cleats to scrape the name away. After the game, there was even talk that the Raiders players would boo Rozelle when he presented the trophy. But in the moments before the media came into the locker room, Davis told the club, "I don't want you booing anyone. I don't want you doing anything that would be disrespectful to the team and to the commissioner. This is not your fight. We will conduct ourselves as gentlemen."

Both Rozelle and Davis were gracious, as the Raiders celebrated their third world title in eight seasons. But very soon, it became clear that the biggest problem now was not that the Raiders were in Los Angeles. It was the repercussions of that move for other restless owners around the league.

One of 1982's most compelling films was Barry Levinson's *Diner,* a finely rendered period piece set among a group of young men living in late-'50s Baltimore. The film's most celebrated scene showed the obsessive Eddie grilling his fiancée with a quiz of Baltimore Colts trivia, which she must pass to prove her worthiness as a mate. More than the particular obsession of one fan, the film evoked the central role that the Colts played in the psyche of the city of Baltimore. Native Baltimorean Frank Deford noted that the Colts "were like a high school team for a city of a million people." By the time *Diner* was released, Baltimore's special connection with the Colts was still formidable, but the relationship had been frayed by the increasingly erratic behavior of owner Robert Irsay and the team's slumping fortunes.

Sundays at 2:00—the odd kickoff time for Baltimore Colts home games, due to a Maryland state law—were still a special occasion at Memorial Stadium, the gathering place at 33rd Street that served as a home for an ecumenical collection of fans that became known as the World's Largest Outdoor Insane Asylum. The games played here bore a distinctive look; Memorial Stadium was susceptible to a dense fog that regularly rolled in from the Chesapeake Bay, and its playing surface seemed to have more dirt than any other field in the league.

The promise of the Colts' resurgence—they won the AFC East in 1975, 1976, and 1977—was blunted by their playoff exits, the last one, in 1977, an agonizing 37–31 double-overtime loss to the Raiders. Like the Chiefs after their double-overtime home playoff loss in 1971, the Colts went into a competitive tailspin that wouldn't abate for years. In the final preseason game of 1978, Bert Jones injured his shoulder and missed almost all of the 1978 and 1979 seasons. The team collapsed along with him, and coach Ted Marchibroda was fired following the 1979 season, to be replaced by Mike McCormack, whose two-year reign in Baltimore was even less successful than his time in Philadelphia.

On November 15, 1981, during a 38–13 loss to the Eagles, Irsay marched to the coaches' booth above the field and began radioing plays down to McCormack. At the end of the season, McCormack (who would describe his coaching tenure in Baltimore as "the two most unpleasant years of my life") was fired, along with Thomas's replacement, GM Dick Szymanski.

From the rubble of that 2-14 record, Irsay brought in the taskmaster Arizona State coach Frank Kush to add discipline on the field, and installed Ernie Accorsi as GM. Accorsi had grown up a Colts fan in Hershey, Pennsylvania (and was even a consultant for the *Diner* Colts quiz). With the erratic absentee owner Irsay alienated from the community, Accorsi played a crucial role in securing the old bond between city and team. It was Accorsi who arranged a fitting farewell to Unitas in 1978, bringing him back to retire his jersey. Possessed of a sincere, weathered voice, and an Italian's resolute countenance, he often looked like a vaguely handsome man who'd just survived a sleep-deprivation experiment. And, fittingly, his years as Baltimore's GM provided their share of sleepless nights.

As the Colts slid to an 0-8-1 record in the strike-shortened 1982 season, Accorsi saw a glimpse of future promise. From the deepest wellspring of quarterback talent in more than a decade—since Jim Plunkett, Archie Manning, and Dan Pastorini went 1-2-3 in the 1971 draft—the Colts would have their choice of potential future leaders. From Miami, there was the rangy Jim Kelly, well versed in the pro-style offense of Howard Schnellenberger. From Pitt, there was Dan Marino, the top-rated quarterback heading into the 1982 season, whose stock dropped as his interception rate increased, and whose reputation was further sullied by rumors of drug usage on the postseason all-star game circuit. As Marino's profile dipped, the profile of Penn State quarterback Todd Blackledge, a less physically gifted quarterback but one seen as being more mature and more composed, rose. And Penn State's rise to a national championship in 1982 further aided his rising reputation.

Then, in Palo Alto, California, there was The Natural. John Elway, a two-sport star at Stanford, was the purest physical specimen Accorsi had ever seen. In the graduated scale that many teams used, players could be rated anywhere from 1.0 to 9.0, but for all intents and purposes, the ratings congregated between the low 4s (borderline NFL ability) to the high 7s (a potential Pro Bowl–caliber player). Elway had earned a rating as high as 8.9 from some scouts, and the Colts were sure they wanted him. Elway was less certain about the Colts. Not since 1969, when Southern Cal's O. J. Simpson faced the prospect of going to Buffalo as the top pick had a number one choice been so ambivalent. Elway requested that the Colts trade him to a West Coast team or a few other prime clubs, even threatening to pursue a baseball career instead. But Accorsi was sure that the baseball threat was a ploy, and that if the Colts could sign him, they might be able to turn around the team's fortunes. He never got the chance. Six days after the draft, Irsay—on his own—dealt Elway to Denver for Chris Hinton, the Northwestern guard who'd been the number four overall selection, part-time quarterback Mark Hermann, and two draft choices. Accorsi knew his days were numbered, and resigned after the 7-9 1983 season—then immediately went to New York to talk to his old boss Rozelle, in whom he confided that Irsay's behavior was increasingly irrational. "You need to keep an eye on him," said Accorsi.

By that time, Irsay had been using the jarring Raiders verdict to cast about for a better stadium deal, traveling to Phoenix, Indianapolis, and Jacksonville (where he was overheard telling city officials "it's not *if* I move but *when*"). On January 20, returning from a trip to Phoenix, Irsay was greeted by Maryland governor William Donald Schaefer and a horde of media, prompting an apparently drunken rant in which he stated he had "no intention of moving the goddamn team."

At the league office, there was persistent concern about what the unpre-

dictable Irsay would do. Rozelle, always one to put the best face on owner
behavior, wrote Irsay that his airport press conference "should help in mini-
mizing unwarranted speculation." But on February 7, Irsay visited the commissioner's office and complained that the negative press coverage had left
him concerned about his physical safety. Rozelle's memorandum for the
record of the meeting noted that Irsay "said he would like to move the Colts to
Phoenix . . . he would prefer to have a league vote approving the move, or at
least to move with the league's blessing, although he contended neither would
necessarily be required under current circumstances in the legal situation." At
a special privileged executive session on March 2, the league's owners met to
determine their strategy. Paul Tagliabue discussed the implications of fighting
another move with both the appeal of the Raiders verdict and the size of the
damages hanging in the balance. In the end, the league's hands were tied. The
minutes of the confidential meeting concluded that "in view of the extraordi-
narily large trial court damage award in the Los Angeles Coliseum/Raiders'
case and the current risks and confusion created by the antitrust court rulings
in California, it would be impossible to treat the Colts' possible transfer as a
League matter. . . . On that basis, the Colts' location was concluded to be a
matter for the Colts, and not the League, to decide." With the fate of the Colts
left to Robert Irsay—and with the city and state authorities left in the dark
about both his plans and his options—it was only a matter of time before Baltimore would lose its football team.

On March 28, the day after the Maryland state legislature passed a provision on eminent domain designed to legally bind the Colts to the city, Irsay
decided he had to act. Having secured a discreet deal with the city of Indianapolis, he now summoned a fleet of Mayflower moving vans to the Colts'
complex in Owings Mills, Maryland. That afternoon, he ordered some of his
assistant coaches—in the midst of pre-draft preparation—to move their own
desks and file cabinets into the vans. As a snow started to fall in the growing
twilight, Irsay grew more impatient. There was no packing, only moving. The
van with the team's records, files, trophies, and scouting information was
placed in the front. Later that night, limned in radiation lights, the convoy of
eleven trucks moved out of the complex through the wet, driving snow, past a
small, crestfallen cadre of longtime Colts fans. There was nothing they could
do by then but stand by and watch in helpless disbelief as the raw materials of
Baltimore's fabled football franchise were transported away.

There was precious little, in the wake of the Raiders ruling, that the NFL
could do, save point to the absurdity of the league's double-bound position:
"We were sued in Los Angeles for opposing the Raiders' move," noted Rozelle.

"We would have been sued in Oakland if we had approved that move. We are now being sued in Baltimore for not preventing the Colts' relocation; no doubt we would have been sued in Indianapolis if we had done so. Under current antitrust interpretations, we are literally damned if we do and damned if we don't."

Behind the scenes, the league continued to work for legislation that would overturn the moves, but this was a case of belated overstretch. Schramm and others felt the league would have been better off supporting a bill introduced by Pennsylvania senator Arlen Specter that would have set specific criteria that franchises must meet before moving, but instead the league pushed for support of a bill by Arizona senator Dennis DeConcini that would have retroactively forced teams back to their towns. It wasn't going to happen while the Raiders litigation was ongoing, and it certainly wasn't going to happen while the players were out on strike in the fall of 1982.

Irsay's greeting in Indianapolis was rapturous, but his honeymoon was relatively short-lived. In front of a crowd estimated at 20,000 that greeted the Colts at the still unfinished Hoosier Dome, Irsay's remarks were mainly for the benefit of the working press. "You people of the press have hounded my family for the last two years," said Irsay, "and my family is not about to take any more of your hounding."

Then it was left to the charms of Frank Kush, who greeted the football-starved Indianapolis fans who'd given him a standing ovation by noting, "I bet this is the last time you stand up for me, except when you want to run me out of town." As the crowd murmured, Kush added thoughtfully, "You know, it's really a pleasure to be here because we had no other place to go."

Baltimore's attempt to seize the team by eminent domain became hopeless when the team was out of the state, and suddenly, some of the league's most loyal fans were reminded how quickly things could change. The NFL's efforts to get the original Raiders verdict overturned ended on November 5, 1984, when the Supreme Court declined without comment to review the Los Angeles Coliseum Commission vs. NFL case.

There was now the new landscape: the Rams were in Anaheim, the Raiders in L.A., the Colts in Indianapolis. After 1987, the St. Louis Cardinals moved to Phoenix (where owner Bill Bidwill chose to keep the team's phone number unlisted in their new city). Only a last-gasp effort from Rozelle had managed to convince the Philadelphia Eagles' eccentric, overleveraged owner Leonard Tose to keep the club there following the 1985 season.

"I can say this because I'm not Catholic," wrote the football commentator

Beano Cook to Rozelle around this time. "At one time, a handshake was all that was needed in the NFL. Credit the nuns. Most of the owners were Catholic. They fought like hell with each other but when a deal was made, that was it. A handshake. No lawyers. You know that when Art Rooney gave his word, that was it. Same with the Mara brothers. Now nobody cares except for a few owners. In many ways, the NFL reminds me of the Roman Empire."

20

The Last Stand

ielding questions from the media in the summer of 1982, Pete Rozelle was asked about the United States Football League, which had just announced its formation but had yet to sign a single player. "What will happen," said Rozelle, "is that they *will* play. They will start to lose money. Then they will spend too much money on players and get deeper in the hole. And just about the time they are ready to go out of business, they will take a lawsuit against us. This is how it has been historically. It will happen again with this league."

By the time the USFL kicked off its first game, in March of 1983, the spring football league seemed well on the way to fulfilling Rozelle's prophecy. Despite league-wide vows of fiscal sanity in the fall, the USFL's New Jersey Generals had signed Herschel Walker, the Heisman Trophy–winning junior running back from Georgia, to the richest contract in football history. In so doing, the USFL not only threw down a gauntlet in its battle with the NFL, but also violated—by signing a player with a year of college eligibility remaining—a hallowed pact between pro and college football that had been in place since shortly after Red Grange's controversial signing with the Bears in 1925.

With the hard-won experience of the lawsuits that followed the formation of the AFL and WFL, and with the additional prospect of a sizable damage award to the Raiders and the Los Angeles Coliseum Commission in the offing, the NFL owners were in little mood for a player war. But by signing such stars as Walker, North Carolina's Kelvin Bryant, and Michigan's Anthony Carter, the USFL forced the war upon them. In 1984, the USFL lured another Heisman winner, Nebraska's Mike Rozier, as well as blue-chip quarterback Steve Young, signed to an astounding $40 million deal. Rookie contracts in the NFL had more than doubled in the space of two years, and the USFL—drafting in early January, three months before the NFL—wasn't just skimming off a few names, but were signing players in volume. In the 1984 draft alone, the Los Angeles Express signed fourteen players who had been expected to go in the first four rounds of the NFL draft.

The USFL's quality of play was instantly higher than the fly-by-night World Football League of the '70s had ever been. Most of the USFL clubs were solid (teams in Denver and Tampa Bay enjoyed attendance that approached their NFL counterparts) and many of its football coaches and administrators were well respected. The USFL had hired coaches like George Allen, Steve Spurrier, and Marv Levy. The director of football operations was Peter Hadhazy, a twenty-year veteran of the NFL office. Its administrators included such future NFL successes as Bill Polian, Carl Peterson, and Bruce Allen.

But the USFL was largely defined—some would say hijacked—by the desires and delusions of real estate tycoon Donald Trump, who purchased the New Jersey Generals in 1984, at a time when the league rashly expanded from twelve to eighteen teams, and immediately pushed for a move from the spring to the fall, where the USFL would be competing directly with the NFL. That this move was completely antithetical to Dixon's long-stated USFL charter— to play football in the spring, when there was precious little heavyweight competition for television viewers—was irrelevant to Trump's ambition.

On September 13, 1984, the USFL announced that after playing its 1985 season in the spring, it would move to a fall schedule in 1986, to confront the NFL directly. Rozelle responded in a letter to USFL commissioner Chet Simmons, "It is also becoming clearer and clearer that a treble-damage lawsuit features at least as strongly in the USFL plans as does making your league a business and entertainment success." Two weeks after Rozelle's letter, on October 18, the USFL filed a $1.69 billion antitrust suit against the NFL.

The move had come against the wishes of a valiant minority of owners who were making their way in the spring. Carl Peterson, Dick Vermeil's personnel director with the Eagles, had built the Philadelphia Stars into a league power that drew an average of 18,000 while going to the championship game in the first season and 29,000 while winning it the second. The team was planning a ticket push to the 35,000 mark, which would have put the club into the black. Instead, the USFL chose a make-or-break battle with the NFL in the fall, thereby neutralizing much of its own hard-fought gains.

"Of course that was spirited by Donald Trump and [Chicago Blitz co-owner] Eddie Einhorn, and they got a majority to vote yes on it," said Peterson. "But they also absolutely were convinced that this move would either precipitate an acquisition of some USFL teams into the NFL or we would have an antitrust case out against the NFL, because they controlled basically all the networks at that time, and that we would win hands down. And that's what these guys convinced us. Eddie Einhorn was on the baseball broadcast committee, he owned part of the White Sox with Jerry Reinsdorf, and he absolutely assured us, he said, 'It'll be done in thirty days; at the *max,* sixty days.' And of course Donald believed that. Anyway, the proof was, it took a little bit longer than that."

It would take nearly two years for the antitrust case to work itself through the courts and, in the meantime, the 1985 season found the USFL in a desperate holding pattern, trying to hang together long enough to benefit from a possible judgment. There were fewer big-money signings prior to the 1985 season, there being less big money left. Heisman winner Doug Flutie, whose NFL prospects were uncertain, became the third straight Heisman winner to join the USFL, signed by Trump's New Jersey Generals. The season was a hodgepodge of reorganization: franchises merged in Michigan and Oakland, as well as Oklahoma and Arizona. The Los Angeles Express, one of the league's flagship franchises, spent the season in shambles, and wound up moving its games from the Los Angeles Coliseum to tiny Pierce College in Woodland Hills. Teams in Philadelphia, Washington, and New Orleans all had to move, since their NFL counterparts held exclusive leases on their stadiums in the fall, and since being in a different market would increase their chances of being brought into the NFL in the event of a merger settlement. It was a particularly painful move for the Stars, who spent the 1985 season training in Philadelphia, where most of their players and staff lived, and traveled to Baltimore for home games. Amidst all the shifts, the juggled, stumbling league saw its TV ratings drop 30 percent. By the end of that third season, the league had lost a collective $200 million. But it still had one more chance, and that was to win its case against the NFL.

And in this, it seemed, the USFL had more than a puncher's chance, heightened by the thicket of contradictory antitrust rulings involving sports leagues that had accumulated through much of the '70s, as well as the possibility that the NFL's contracts with all three major TV networks would be viewed as evidence itself that the NFL was a monopoly. In the buildup to the opening of the trial in the spring of 1986, the NFL brought in a company called Legal Creative Services, which produced the makings of an exceedingly realistic mock trial—judge, courtroom, impaneled jury. The veristic conditions yielded a startling result: a unanimous decision for the USFL.

Shortly thereafter, the NFL's lead attorney on the case, Robert Fiske, met the owners in executive session at the 1986 annual meetings, and gave them a gloomy progress report on the case.

"If you were the client," asked Norman Braman of the Eagles, "what would you do—fight this or settle it?"

"I'd settle it," said Fiske, reluctantly.

There was a moment of painful silence, as the implications of that sank in with the assembled owners. At that point a voice near Rozelle spoke up. "I have a different opinion on that question," said Paul Tagliabue. "And I would like the chance to give you my answer."

If anyone understood the prospects of the USFL side or what was at stake for the NFL, it was Tagliabue. He had been steeped in the league's antitrust philosophy—articulated by Hamilton Carothers years earlier in a letter to Rozelle, that the league would spend "millions for defense, and not one red cent for tribute." In the mock trial held earlier in the year, Tagliabue had argued the USFL's side of the case (against Fiske making the NFL argument) and he understood better than any outsider why the NFL had to fight it.

"I would not settle the case," Tagliabue said. "Let's go to trial. I don't think you've got a serious exposure here. I think the case is a sham and I think there's a lot of evidence to show that it's a sham, and it's not a case where you're just going to be defending. It's a case where you have an affirmative way of characterizing what occurred that is damning in respect to their claims."

Tagliabue's stand would turn out to be a key turning point in convincing the owners to fight the case in court, and would alter the perceptions of many about the bright, formal lead counsel.

After the meeting, Tagliabue was called into a private meeting of Rozelle's inner circle, including Tex Schramm, Dan Rooney, and Wellington Mara. He expanded on his ideas, making the obvious but crucial point that settling with the USFL would set a precedent that would leave the NFL perpetually exposed to outsiders trying to sue their way into the NFL. "One consideration was that if you buckled into these people then you'd have start-up leagues and claims on an annual basis," said Tagliabue. "You couldn't encourage people to create half-assed leagues and then walk away with a lot of money one way or the other. If you felt you didn't do anything wrong, you should be prepared to stand in defense." His argument held the day, and so the NFL decided to head back to the courts again.

Fiske remained on the case but moved into a lesser role. Two days after the meetings, Rozelle phoned Frank Rothman, who'd been slated to be the lead attorney on the second Raiders antitrust case, before being offered the job as the president of MGM Studios. Two weeks earlier, the sharp, magnanimous Rothman had ended his five-year tenure as the head of production at MGM, and Rozelle brought him back into the fold.

The USFL trial was a melodramatic tour de force, a draining eleven-week ordeal that featured contradictory testimony from Trump and Rozelle, Al Davis up on the stand, testifying on *behalf* of the USFL, and Howard Cosell, expansive and combative, and by then in the midst of a long, sad decline.

The flamboyant Harvey Myerson, laying out the USFL's case, hammered home the details of a Harvard Business School speech, sponsored by the NFL Management Council, in which professor Michael Porter delivered a paper titled "How to Destroy the USFL."

Rothman had seen the way testimony about Porter's speech had swayed the mock jury, and was determined not to let it happen in the real trial. To do that, though, it wouldn't be sufficient to deny the importance of it. What was crucial was to prove that the suggestions that Porter offered—signing the top USFL stars, moving up the draft, giving ABC an inferior schedule of *Monday Night Football* games as punishment for signing with the USFL in the spring— had never been implemented on a league-wide basis. After his legal team scoured league files from throughout the '80s, Rothman had the evidence he needed. As he told the *Boston Globe*'s Will McDonough shortly after the trial, "We had evidence to show now that the Porter plan was not placed in effect and that no one used it." Coolly assured, and scrupulously accurate, Rothman patiently laid out the NFL's side, and spent as much time with Trump on the stand as possible. Rothman also argued that the USFL's move to the fall was made less for competitive benefit than to force a settlement with the NFL.

The jury had deliberated for five days when the word came that they'd delivered a verdict. Pete Rozelle was at a Chinese restaurant for lunch with Val Pinchbeck, the NFL's vice president of programming, on July 29, 1986. As they were finishing, Thelma Elkjer called the restaurant, to pass along a message that the verdict was about to be read. They paid the check and raced out to the commissioner's car. Rozelle and Pinchbeck were in the back of the car when the news headline came on . . .

The United States Football League won its court case against the NFL. Details to come . . .

As Pinchbeck sat in stunned silence, Rozelle tipped his head straight back, visibly recoiling from the news. "I remember, I was afraid maybe he was gonna have a heart attack," said Pinchbeck. In the stunned silence, Pinchbeck instructed the driver to return to the league offices: "Back to 410 Park."

In the moments that the car waded into midtown traffic, Rozelle remained in his position of frozen dejection. Then the radio station returned from its commercial break, to provide the rest of the story.

. . . The NFL was found guilty on just one of the nine counts. And the jury awarded the USFL the sum of one dollar . . .

With that, Rozelle and Pinchbeck launched off of the back seat in an excited celebration, slapping the seat backs and door frames with joy, while Rozelle gave the new directive, "Let's go down to the courthouse!"

Greeting Rothman with an embrace on the courthouse steps, Rozelle spoke of his sense of vindication. When Rozelle returned to his office, he received a call from Tex Schramm, with the Cowboys for a London exhibition against the Bears.

"Pete, I love you!" Schramm exclaimed. "We have survived! Can you believe it?"

It was left to Paul Brown, among the old-guard owners, to put the outcome in perspective. "This is the biggest threat we'd ever faced," said Paul Brown. "While I felt all along that we were in the right, I didn't have that much faith in what the jury might decide."

Weeks later, the owners held a celebration dinner at the Regency Hotel, where both Tagliabue and Rothman were presented a crystal sword, evoking the myth of King Arthur and the Knights of the Round Table. Privately at one point Rozelle confided in Tagliabue, "You know, you've made a great contribution to the league. You understand the business, you understand the people. At some point, who knows, *you* might be commissioner."

The nuances of the Raiders case and the USFL case were lost to most football fans, but the ultimate outcome would have a major impact on the shape of pro football. The Raiders decision would threaten more betrayals of the loyalty and devotion of fans that was the lifeblood of the modern game. The USFL decision, ultimately, would end for the foreseeable future the regular challenges by upstart leagues, and it would allow the NFL to continue to develop its own closed system. Yet the league's house was still not in order, and the litany of litigation would not end for another five years.

It had long been Rozelle's theory that the way to stay on top of the sports news was to stay out of the business and labor news. Not surprisingly, the repeated stories of the NFL in the courts and on strike had a withering effect. Media coverage was still widespread, but more critical, less deferential. When Jim Brown posed in a Raiders uniform for the cover of *Sports Illustrated* in 1983, as part of a far-fetched comeback bid he was considering, to rescue his all-time rushing record from Franco Harris, the cover blurb included the tagline that Brown was "just what the bor-ring NFL needs." When the *New York Times*'s David Harris wrote *The League,* an account of the behind-the-scenes board-room struggles, it was subtitled, *The Rise and Fall of the National Football League.* The media projected many of the league's off-the-field problems onto the field, and prescriptives for fixing the game were a common staple of '80s publications, from *Inside Sports* to *Esquire.*

Despite the barbs, the truth was that the NFL made significant gains in media coverage in the '80s. The advent of the national daily newspaper *USA Today* played perfectly to the serious sports fan, with more in-depth statistics and longer game stories than most local papers. A readership survey of the readers of *The Sporting News,* the longtime "bible of baseball," showed that most of its readers were bigger NFL fans. And under managing editor Mark Mulvoy, *Sports Illustrated* significantly increased its already substantial cover-age of pro football.

But the biggest change occurred on cable television, with the rise of ESPN, the all-sports cable network that began televising the NFL draft in 1982, and experienced unheard-of ratings for several hours of talking heads discussing college prospects. By the time ESPN got a share of the NFL regular season package in 1987 (eight late-season games, broadcast on Sunday nights), the network was using the NFL to prove its validity. "It was the single most important event ever," said Steve Bornstein, at the time the president of the network. "It totally legitimized the network—we had *arrived.*" ESPN's twenty-four-hour format gave a significant boost to NFL Films, whose weekly series *This Is the NFL* quickly became one of the network's most popular blocks of nonevent programming.

Back on the field, in the midst of the aerial dazzle of the 49ers' offense and the big-play theatrics of Dan Marino and the Dolphins' 1984 Super Bowl season, the game started moving in the other direction, away from pass-first philoso-phy to a more basic, fundamental approach. "Neanderthal football," as Giants coach Bill Parcells described it. Strategically, the mid-'80s was an era in which the running game—as typified by the Washington Redskins' intimidating front-line, the Hogs, and the bruising fullback John Riggins—would reassert itself. Though teams like San Francisco continued to use an undersized line and win through finesse and complexity, most teams were in the punishing mold of the Redskins, Giants, and Bears, who would combine to win four titles during the decade.

And this return to the eternal verities of the sport went beyond offensive strategy. The rush to artificial surfaces had crested and, by the mid-'80s, was beginning to roll back, with natural grass fields replacing carpets in Miami, San Francisco, Chicago, and New England. Even in sartorial terms, the league was moving backward. A generation after Joe Namath's white shoes had been synonymous with NFL style, the Bears' Jim McMahon wore black high-top cleats, prompting a no-nonsense rollback in footwear.

Even entire teams could hark back to their earlier glory days, as the Cleveland Browns did in the mid-'80s. Few franchises had the tradition of the Browns and, by 1984, few owners in pro football were as respected as Art Modell. Through the years, he was there at every practice, never meddling, but sitting in his golf cart, avidly watching, ever the fan. Modell's obvious commitment to the team helped deflect criticism when the Browns struggled, which was often.

The club hadn't won a playoff game since beating Dallas in the 1969 playoffs. After the brief, mercurial rise of Sam Rutigliano's Kardiac Kids in the late '70s—and the debilitating playoff loss to the Raiders in 1980—the Browns had fallen back in the early '80s. Saving the watered-down 1982 strike season when more than half the league was allowed into the playoffs (the Browns going with a 4-5 record), 1980 had been Cleveland's only real playoff appearance since 1972.

After beginning the 1984 season 1-7, Modell fired Rutigliano, and hired defensive coordinator Marty Schottenheimer, a former linebacker for the Patriots and Bills, and a football overachiever who'd become a highly respected defensive architect. Even at 1-7, Schottenheimer's defense was recognized as one of the best in the league, a boisterous but disciplined band of hard-hitters who could frustrate offenses with their sound, spirited play.

In Schottenheimer's vigilant intensity, the modern Browns would find a new identity. With his earnest demeanor and thick wire-rimmed glasses, Schottenheimer looked like an eighth-grade science instructor, an appearance all the more apt because he was a teacher in the truest and most traditional sense of the word. Even in the second half of the 1984 season, leading the

Browns to a 4-4 finish, Schottenheimer seemed constantly aware of the ability to educate *and* inspire his players to greater lengths. When a player would come to the sidelines after an error, the coach wouldn't haughtily ignore him, nor give him a dressing down. Instead, Schottenheimer would walk right over to the player, put an arm on each of his shoulder pads, look him directly in the eye, and say, "Young man . . ."

At the end of the 1984 season, Modell promoted Ernie Accorsi (who had been hired as an adviser shortly after leaving the Colts) to director of football operations, the team's de facto general manager. During that same off-season, Accorsi engineered the drafting of Bernie Kosar, the Miami, Florida, quarterback who'd grown up in Ohio and had a lifelong dream to play for the team. "It's not an everyday occurrence that somebody *wants* to play in Cleveland," said Modell during the 1985 preseason. "That has lent such an aura to Bernie." In Schottenheimer's first full season, the youthful Browns finished 8-8, enough to win the mediocre AFC Central. They pressed the Miami Dolphins in the playoffs, squandering a 21–3 fourth-quarter lead in a 24–21 loss.

The team was developing an identity as a tough, opportunistic, no-nonsense squad that rarely beat itself. The Browns' secondary, playing with a proprietary fervor, had taken to calling themselves the Dawgs, barking after sacks, interceptions, and other big plays. The chatter was picked up during the team's training camp and, by the middle of the 1985 season, the fans in the east end zone at Cleveland Stadium had christened the entire area as the "Dawg Pound," barking up a storm, dressed in dog collars, or waving large dog bones, throwing biscuits and all other manner of paraphernalia at opposing players. The behavior of the fans marked a new plateau in the progression of the most vociferous football fans. In the '70s, in places like Miami and Pittsburgh, fans waved white handkerchiefs or golden towels en masse, to create a visual spectacle. But the Dawg Pound was a more raucous enterprise. The elaborate costumes seemed a calculated ploy to get time on national television. But it also sparked the entire Cleveland Stadium, and soon the rickety old structure in downtown Cleveland, with its fierce winds, raucous fans, and cold weather, became one of the toughest places in the NFL for a visiting team to play. The Browns were throwbacks, reminiscent of the tough teams that Collier coached in the mid-'60s. Even their uniforms harked back to the glory days of Jim Brown.

In 1986, it all came together. The precocious Kosar blossomed as a quarterback and leader. Running back Earnest Byner was the workhorse of a versatile backfield, and the Browns' defense matured in the final quarter of the season, winning four straight to secure home field advantage throughout the playoffs. After an improbable 23–20 overtime win over the Jets, Cleveland hosted the AFC championship game on January 11, against the Denver Broncos.

The city reached a fever pitch the week of the game, and there was heavy traffic outside the Broncos' hotel on the eve of the game, horns honking through the night. Sunday dawned bitterly cold, with a piercing wind blowing in off Lake Erie, promising exactly the sort of contest for which Schottenheimer's clubs were built. After Cleveland held Denver without a touchdown for much of the game, the Browns took a seven-point lead on a late drive. The ensuing kickoff, buffeted by the wind and on the muddy field, was recovered by Denver on its own two-yard line, with five minutes left.

Against the sound of a city howling to exorcise twenty-two years of sporting demons, John Elway and his Denver teammates gathered at the back of the end zone. The scene seemed so hopeless that Elway and his teammates were actually giggling during the TV timeout. What happened next would begin to solidify Elway's reputation for magic, as well as Schottenheimer's for hard luck. Elway marched Denver 98 yards, converting on three third downs, including a third-and-18, when the ball snapped from the shotgun formation careened off the hip of Steve Watson, who'd been in motion. Elway neatly recovered it and threw a strike for a key first down, setting up the tying score. In overtime, Denver got the ball and quickly moved down the field, and Rich Karlis's kick was ruled good, though many Browns fans and players alike were convinced it had gone wide. And suddenly another enchanted season ended prematurely, just as it had for Rutigliano's Browns in 1980. But Schottenheimer's team was sounder, and would return to the title game the following season, though with equally agonizing results.

Meanwhile, a legend had been born. Though the Broncos would lose to the Giants, 39–20, in the Super Bowl, Elway's exploits would go down as a benchmark in a new chapter of the mystique of the quarterback. The change had begun in the '70s, largely in the escapability and leadership of Roger Staubach, whose persona exuded none of the battle-of-the-wits aura of a Unitas or Namath. Most prized was the sense of leading a team, not with cleverness so much as with poise and will, out of a series of crises and into the promised land. It was personified by Staubach's scrambling, and the on-the-move improvisational skills of Joe Montana. And though others would lead nearly as many comebacks, it was Elway who elevated this daredevilry to a kind of exalted art form.

It was not as though wits weren't required in the new setup. Defenses were more complex than ever, and the chore of reading those defenses and divining those disguises still fell on the quarterback's shoulders. But when the actual act of calling the plays reverted to coaches and coordinators, then the quality most prized in quarterbacks went from craftiness (like Unitas's innate, confounding ability to call a play that was different from what the defense thought he would call) to composure (like Elway's joking with teammates prior to The Drive, or Joe Montana, absurdly cool under pressure, looking at the clock with 2:00 left in Super Bowl XXIII and asking his huddled offensive teammates, during a TV timeout, "Isn't that John Candy in the stands?").

What Schottenheimer would see, across fields from Elway for more than a decade, was this unteachable, unlearnable skill on Elway's part, the ability to keep his head when all about him were losing theirs. Teams would flush Elway from the pocket, force him toward the sideline, converge toward him, and then, in an instant, watch him stop running, set his right foot, plant his left, and peg an absurdly arcing long pass across his body and across the field to a wide-open receiver streaking open 40, 50, even 60 yards down the field on the opposite sideline. It was more acrobatic, if perhaps less intellectual than the play calling of Unitas and Namath, but the shot to the heart was just as lethal.

———

Though the league emerged intact from the USFL insurgency, the 1987 annual meetings were still conducted amid an air of gloom. For the first time after decades of routine increases, the new national TV contract, a $1.4 billion, three-year deal, showed a slight dip in annual per-team revenue.

Immediately ahead was another negotiation with the NFL Players Association, determined to bargain for free agency. Meanwhile, the NFL Management Council, whose membership was dominated by hard-line owners like Tex Schramm and Tampa Bay's Hugh Culverhouse, and whose offices weren't even located at the league headquarters, geared up for another battle of wills.

When the NFLPA walked out again, it confronted a more hardened, if conflict-weary, group of owners. Lamar Hunt, always a pragmatist on these matters, had suggested to his colleagues in 1982 that the league consider hiring replacement players so that it could offer a product to television and give the veterans who were so inclined incentive to cross the picket lines. It was one of the few things that Schramm and Hunt agreed on, and it informed the Management Council's hard-line stance during the 1987 strike. "We had learned some things and were determined not to let what happened in 1982 recur," said Schramm. "We learned that, as a strike progressed, more and more players began to disagree with the wisdom of it but had no recourse or alternative because the union's leadership was so committed. We also were aware that it was very damaging to the league to go through such a long period without any games. We lost the interest of the media, the fans, and everybody else as far as pro football was concerned. There were no games, and all you read about was the strike."

After the Patriots-Jets Monday night game of September 21, the Players Association called a strike. This time the league was ready. After one weekend's games were canceled, the league scheduled games for week four with replacement players.

These replacement players received the NFL minimum of $3,125 a week, and in the cases of teams like the Giants, who hadn't actively recruited prior to the season, the collection that played was a motley assortment of out-of-shape ex-college also-rans and has-been semipro grunts. Surveying his "team" during the first scab practice in 1987, Bill Parcells remarked dryly, "I believe there are a few guys out there who the Heisman voters overlooked." The team's first game was a *Monday Night Football* matchup with the 49ers, in which they were outclassed 41–21 in front of 15,471. In the closing minutes, a camera focused for twelve seconds on defensive lineman Reggie Carr, apparently asleep on the Giants sideline.

There were fewer veterans crossing the line than expected, but with replacement games still drawing modest crowds and TV audiences, the players had no leverage. They voted to return to their teams on October 15, just twenty-four days into the strike, even though no settlement was reached. And on the same day the players returned, the NFLPA filed an antitrust case against the NFL in Minnesota federal court, seeking to overturn the league's free agent compensation system and give players full free agency.

In the short term, though, the owners' victory was complete. In Tex Schramm's words, "There *was* no agreement; they just came back." But there was little celebrating among management, as the walkout had further alienated owners from players and both groups from fans.

Rozelle himself thought the use of replacement players was a huge mistake, destroying the credibility of the league with its fans and players, as well as the networks and advertisers. For Dan Rooney, who'd toiled as a loyal part of the league structure for years, one problem was his close friend Rozelle's unwillingness to be involved directly. Hewing to his role as "impartial observer," Rozelle declined to sit in on the negotiating sessions.

Assessing the damage to the league's reputation after the fact, many in the NFL came to the conclusion that, whatever the tactical success derived from using replacement players, the larger price wasn't worth it.

"If you're going to have 'labor disruption' every five years, well, 'labor disruption' is an industry term," said Bill Polian, Buffalo's GM at the time. "When you translate that to the fan, that means that his favorite player is tarnished. His team is disrupted. But what we're in business to do is to entertain and please and involve the fans—that's what we do for a living. So if you constantly erode that bond between the fans and the players in the franchise, if it becomes labor problems and a disruption of the product on the field as opposed to rooting for the Buffalo Bills or the Oakland Raiders, or the New England Patriots, or whomever—you've broken a connection with the fans."

————

Without an agreement there wasn't even the sense of making peace that had existed after the 1982 strike. In 1987, the players returned, but remained equally adamant and disaffected about their treatment. And there were more problems than a lack of a collective bargaining agreement and meaningful free agency. The league's drug policy seemed at once harsh and inconsistent, and when Rozelle implemented a steroids-testing program, the Players Association vowed to fight it in court.

There was also the inescapable issue of race. In a league in which more than 50 percent of the players were black, the NFL had been very slow in pushing for opportunities for minorities off the field. Outside of Upshaw, head of the NFLPA, there hadn't been a high-ranking black in the league structure since the death of Buddy Young.

At the club level, there was little but frustration for savvy executives like Tank Younger in Los Angeles and San Diego, and Bobby Mitchell in Washington. They had the experience and the know-how to be general managers, but there wasn't an owner in the league willing to give them the responsibility.

Those with the long view could see progress. As a player, Younger had been the first black to make All-Pro at linebacker, and as he moved into scouting and front office work, he'd watched other positions change. "Back in the '60s, a lot of the cornerbacks were black, 'cause they could run. Then the game started changing, the offenses started changing. So defenses went from having two black cornerbacks to now they started having black strong safeties, because the big tight ends were coming out then who could run—John Mackey, Ray Chester—these kind of guys. So then offenses caught up with that, because the defenses kept a free safety—a white kid that was supposed to be smart and all that shit, but he couldn't run. So the offenses found a way to isolate some fucker who could *fly* on him. So now, you look at the defensive backfield and 90 percent of them are all black." By the beginning of the '80s, the last onfield barriers were coming down. Dwight Stephenson became the first All-Pro black center in 1983, Doug Williams became the first black quarterback to win a Super Bowl in 1988, and Art Shell became the first African-American head coach of the modern era, in 1989.

But for many blacks, the slow, sporadic litany of firsts was growing tiresome. Few spoke with more authority on the topic than Jim Brown. He, like many other players, were put off by the fuss surrounding Doug Williams's publicized Super Bowl win.

"Sometimes, all this talk about black quarterbacks makes me feel I've stepped into a time warp, landed in 1958," wrote Brown in his memoir, *Out of Bounds.* "It's almost the 1990s, people still discuss a few black quarterbacks as if they represent some meaningful breakthrough for blacks. When Doug Williams played in the Super Bowl, I kept reading that the moment was proud and historical for blacks. Is that right? To me, it sounded more like the white media working out its hangups. The story of that game wasn't Doug Williams's blackness. It was that Doug's career was nearly expired, he had the heart to keep coming back, to stay prepared, then excelled in the most pressure-filled game of his life. That had nothing to do with his blackness, and I don't buy its profundity for other black people. Blacks in the 1990s don't need any more symbols. They need equal rights. What Doug Williams did in the Super Bowl won't do shit for a cat who can't throw a football."

Though the change had come on the field and in the huddle, where black quarterbacks and middle linebackers had become commonplace, a much different story was taking place on the sidelines. In 1980, there were only fourteen black assistants in the NFL, none at the coordinator level. Only Bill Walsh's 49ers club seemed to actively recruit minorities, and by 1988, Walsh had four black coaches on his staff, including two—Dennis Green and Ray Rhodes—who would get head coaching jobs in the '90s.

But the big coaching news in 1989 was the Raiders' mid-season hiring of Art Shell, the first black head coach in the league's modern era. To the small fraternity of black coaches throughout the league, the hiring was the exception that proved the rule. The first NFL team to hire a black coach would be the one team isolated from the traditional NFL mind-set.

In Pittsburgh, Tony Dungy—lanky, poised, outwardly serene—developed a reputation as an assistant coach who was going places, a rising star moving quickly up the ladder. He retired at twenty-five, when he became the league's youngest assistant coach in 1981. Three years later, he became the league's youngest coordinator, taking over the Steelers' defense. Inheriting a squad that was a shell of the dominating defense that had been the cornerstone of the Steelers' '70s dynasty, Dungy had mastered Chuck Noll's low-key style, and enjoyed results. And yet he got no job offers, nor even any interviews.

It was at a league meeting, in the mid-'80s, talking with the wizened Giants' GM George Young, that Dungy first sensed what he was up against.

"I want to help you," said Young, somewhat bashfully. "I want to see you succeed in this business, and I think you can. But you'll never advance any farther with that beard. It's just not seen in the NFL."

The soft-spoken Dungy told Steelers owner Dan Rooney about it. "Well, in some organizations, that's probably true," said Rooney. "But we like people to be themselves. In our organization, I wouldn't worry about it. But in some organizations that's probably true."

The problem, of course, was not unique to sports. As blacks were moving into more and more central roles within sports, entertainment, and other industries—as a burgeoning black middle class was in many cases realizing the rough outlines of the American dream—there was a different story in the hallways and offices.

The actor Laurence Fishburne would recall a dinner he attended in the mid-'80s, in which he spoke to the multitalented entrepreneur Quincy Jones, the producer of the Oscar-nominated *The Color Purple*. When Fishburne asked Jones if he'd considered hiring a black director to handle the film, Jones replied that he didn't know any black directors. Fishburne later said, "I remember thinking, 'Well you *should* know some black directors. You should make it your business to know.' But I didn't say that."

And so it went in pro football in the '80s. There were some talented black coaches working their way up the ladder—not just Dungy, but Dennis Green in San Francisco, Shell in Oakland, Romeo Crennel in New York—but not many GMs, presidents, and owners knew of them.

And fewer still made it their business to know.

———

Even in the final, and best, Super Bowl of the decade, there was an undercurrent of discontent. In his tenth year as a head coach, Bill Walsh piloted the 49ers to another Super Bowl against, once again, the Cincinnati Bengals, a team coached by former Walsh assistant Sam Wyche, who had taken some of

Walsh's offensive concepts and adapted them to an even more wide-open system, this one employing the shotgun formation and, often, a hurry-up offense.

After a seesaw battle, the Bengals took a lead late in the fourth quarter, before Montana directed another precision late-game rally, nailing John Taylor in the end zone in the final minute to lift the 49ers to their third title in eight seasons (they would win a fourth the following year). But even that signal event was muted somewhat by the setting, Miami's Joe Robbie Stadium, just blocks away from the Overtown section of the city, which had suffered six days of rioting in the weeks leading up to the game.

Through the long, miserable decade, Rozelle soldiered on, grimly determined to work his old charm and resolve as many problems as possible. But much of the job's joy had been drained in the ongoing series of depositions that dominated the decade. And when Rozelle suffered a small stroke in 1987 (unbeknownst to any but his family and closest friends), even the commissioner's Friday press conference became an effort, though he rose to the occasion.

Carmen Policy was working in the front office of the San Francisco 49ers, the most successful franchise of the '80s. He saw a leader who was consumed with the tasks at hand. "I got the impression that Pete was like an airline pilot trying to steady the plane through a great deal of turbulence, and couldn't deal with having the meals and cocktails served to the passengers. And they were hungry back there!"

The league was still the number one sport, but the challenges—labor unrest and acrimony, rumors of drug abuse, owner infighting, challenges anew from upstart leagues—had seemed, after a while, more like *conditions* than challenges. For the first time in his career, Rozelle seemed tired, and without a clear vision of where to proceed next.

"I saw more frowns on Pete's face in the late '80s than I'd seen in all the years before that put together," said Don Weiss. "There were some things he just didn't want to hear about or be confronted with. A mundane thing or something with the Alumni Foundation or the Hall of Fame, unless it had a subpoena attached to it, that was intruding. And he never was like that before then. I feel sorry for the guys who came in late and never saw the real Rozelle."

That fall he had trouble sleeping. By his wife, Carrie's, estimation, he was smoking three packs of cigarettes a day, sleeping fitfully, and dreading work. He would stay awake long enough to watch the eleven o'clock news, drift off to a restless sleep, and then, eyes bloodshot, get up an hour or two later and roam the house, chain-smoking and sketching out ideas on an ever-present legal pad. Somewhere, in the quiet space of one of those long nights, Pete Rozelle reached a conclusion that had been years in the making: *I'm not going to get everything cleared up.*

Paul Tagliabue, who'd spent so much time with Rozelle during the array of litigation in the '80s, saw evidence of the same torment. "It was obvious that he was not enjoying it, and it was obvious that his wife was not enjoying his lack of enjoyment."

21

Changing of the Guard

Wednesday, March 22, 1989, looked like a particularly slow day at the Marriott Desert Springs Resort in Palm Desert, California. The third day of the NFL's annual meetings had been an uneventful one; the Competition Committee was holding off its recommendation on renewing instant replay, the most important votes—announcing the league's new steroids-testing policy, and a limit on off-season roster sizes—had already been pushed through, and the afternoon executive session agenda included little more than a report by the Management Council.

Pete Rozelle called the roll at the afternoon session, then faced the group of owners with whom he'd helped chart the course of pro football's ascendancy. Hairline receding to nothingness, face paunchy and drawn, and lacking the color of his omnipresent magnificent tan, Rozelle looked like a president of the United States at the end of his second term. He mentioned that twenty-nine years earlier, when he'd been elected commissioner, Paul Brown assured him that he'd grow into the job. "Well, Paul," he said to Brown, "I don't know how well I did, but you sure gave me enough time to do it." Then Rozelle announced that he'd decided the previous fall to announce his retirement at this meeting, and was doing so immediately. There was a moment of profound, stunned silence, followed by a standing ovation. On his way out the door to the press conference in an adjacent room, he was intercepted by Al Davis, who embraced him and wished him the best of luck. Years later, owners and others in Rozelle's inner circle were still arguing about whether Davis's gesture was a heartfelt act of reconciliation or merely a pose of Machiavellian utility. Some never could decide. "Al Davis is going to do what's best for Al Davis," allowed Tex Schramm. "On the other hand, he *is* a sentimental person."

So was Rozelle, who began weeping earlier in the day when informing his closest aides, again when informing the owners during the executive session, and once more when dropping the bombshell on the press. Concluding his brief remarks to the media with understated simplicity, he stammered, "and, uh . . . It's been a great thirty years." There were a few questions about the timing of the decision, and then someone asked him to assess his own impact on the game, but he demurred. "I'll have to take some time to think about that. I don't think I can give you an intelligent answer to that right now."

With the announcement of his exit, Rozelle rang down the curtain on the most successful commissioner's tenure in American sports. His departure also ushered in the league's most convulsive and widespread period of internal transition since the merger. In addition to Rozelle's exit, Bill Walsh had announced his retirement from pro coaching after the 49ers won their third Super Bowl in eight seasons. Rozelle's main ally and closest friend in football, Tex Schramm, was already preparing to end his thirty-year tenure as president and general manager in Dallas, as the Cowboys had changed hands earlier in the spring. But all of these changes were instantly overshadowed by Rozelle's announcement.

Wellington Mara, one of the old guard of veteran owners placed on a committee to search for a successor, said, "We will look for a man who has read the pages of history and learned those lessons, and a man who has the foresight to apply those visions to the future. We are searching for the replacement to an irreplaceable man."

Change was already in the air a month earlier, at the Indianapolis scouting combine, where 300 of the nation's best seniors—and one junior—were sprinting, working out, and submitting to physical exams and interviews. The draft class of 1989 promised the deepest collection of impact players in years, and though the first pick would be the prototypical quarterback—UCLA's Troy Aikman—there were signs elsewhere that a new era was dawning.

Tony Mandarich, the burly, pile-driving tackle from Michigan State, whose tattooed biceps began a new trend in offensive lineman body art, seemed an utterly different breed of offensive lineman, and he would be the second player taken. Oklahoma State's Barry Sanders, who won the Heisman Trophy as a junior, had received permission to enter the draft, becoming the first true underclassman ever to do so. He would go third overall.

Though the first three players taken were on offense, much of the talk in Indianapolis was about the splendid group of prospects on the defensive side of the ball. And by the end of the week, it was clear that the real talisman of the draft, the symbol of the changing times, was a Florida State defensive back named Deion Sanders.

In the five years since 1984, when the Supreme Court had struck down the NCAA's control over college football telecasts, essentially deregulating broadcasts and allowing major schools like Notre Dame and Nebraska and Florida State to appear on national television seven or eight times a season instead of only twice, a sea change had occurred in the coverage of college football. Along with the rise of the cable sports network ESPN, the deregulation of college football broadcasts meant that widespread media coverage became a constant reality at the nation's major college powers, propelling college football's stars into a much more visible position in the American sporting pantheon.

Into that harsh light of publicity stepped the flamboyant Sanders, who carefully cultivated his "Prime Time" persona at Florida State, where he showed up for his final regular season game in a limousine, sporting a top hat and tails. He was the nation's best defensive back, but he was more celebrated for his outrageous, media-savvy personality.

At the combine, Sanders exuded an air of not just cocky confidence but easy familiarity with the NFL executives in attendance. Sauntering to the start of the 40-yard-dash timing area, he spotted Al Davis in a lower row of the observation area and proclaimed, "Okay, Al, we're gonna run this *juuust* this once." It was lost on no one that just five or ten years earlier, none of the players at the combine would have had the confidence to approach Davis at all, much less to address him playfully by his first name.

Heretofore, many in professional football had been ignorant of the changes occurring in popular culture, especially the increased influence of rap music and hip-hop on mainstream America. Coaches for generations had routinely squelched the players' right to self-expression for the sake of the larger good. But with Sanders, and others like him, players were arriving on the scene who were products of that culture, and to understand them meant understanding something of the context from which they emerged. Speaking from his home on the day of the NFL draft, after Atlanta selected him fifth overall, Sanders boasted, "I'm gonna ask for so much money, the Falcons are gonna have to put me on layaway."

_____

One of the last meetings that the Arkansas businessman and diehard Cowboys fan Jerry Jones took before purchasing the club in 1989 was with Dan Burke, the CEO of Cap Cities, the company that owned ABC and ESPN and was intimately involved with programming pro football. Jones asked about the importance of NFL programming to the networks.

"Frankly, we can't do without it," Burke told Jones. "And we really need to make sure that we have a reasonable approach to it. It concerns me. If something happened to Pete Rozelle, I would wonder if that thing were going to be negotiated in a responsible way as far as the networks were concerned."

The scheduled forty-five-minute meeting stretched on for a couple of hours, as encounters with Jones tended to do. After thanking Burke and leaving, Jones walked out with a smile.

"Well, what do you think?" asked a friend.

"Two things," said Jones. "First, it really has given me encouragement toward buying the Cowboys. I'm glad to see the game is that strong television-wise. Secondly, the last time I heard my negotiator being bragged on by my opponent, I changed negotiators."

Far removed in sense and sensibility from the patrician elders of the league, the oil entrepreneur Jones was energetic, homespun, and frank, a life-long football fan who'd played on Arkansas's 1964 national championship team. Contemplating his love for the game, he remarked that "I don't know of any ticker-tape parades they give in this country for anybody other than war heroes, astronauts or winning teams." Placing much of his personal fortune on the line, Jones paid $140 million for the Cowboys, a record sum for a professional sports franchise at the time. He inherited a legendary team that had grown stale and financially unsound.

On February 28, three days after reaching an agreement with previous owner Bum Bright to buy the club, Jones came to Dallas to meet with his choice for the Cowboys' new head coach, the University of Miami's fiercely driven Jimmy Johnson, who'd been his teammate at Arkansas. They met for dinner at a Tex-Mex restaurant called Mia's, which turned out not only to be a frequent hangout for journalists (the _Dallas Morning News_'s Ivan Maisel discovered Jones and Johnson eating there), but also Tom Landry's favorite restaurant. The next day, Jones flew to Austin and gave Landry his walking papers, though only after Schramm urged him to give Landry the news in person.

At the press conference in which he introduced Johnson as his new head coach and sheepishly explained that he hadn't meant to offend anyone with his firing of Landry, Jones also clarified the degree of involvement he expected to have with his football team.

"I will sell my house in Little Rock and move to Dallas," he said. "My entire office and my entire business will be [the Cowboys'] complex. I want to know everything there is to know, from player contracts to socks and jocks and television contracts. This is my company, and I will be making all the decisions. The Cowboys will be my life."

Tex Schramm submitted his resignation on the day that the league approved the Cowboys sale, taking the job as the commissioner of the new World League of American Football, the developmental spring league that the NFL was creating to try to sell pro football in Europe. But even if there hadn't been a choice position waiting for him, Schramm wouldn't have abided working for Jones.

"You could tell right from the beginning that he didn't give a damn about history," Schramm said. "You can tell this man has absolutely no feeling for the past. You almost expected him to take the stars off the helmets." Schramm packed up his files one morning, and left the Cowboys' lavish Valley Ranch complex, which he'd envisioned and created. It would be more than fourteen years before he so much as drove by it again.

In place of Tom Landry's lofty detachment, Cowboys fans would be treated to another native Texan coaching their team, although one who was decidedly more open with his emotions. Johnson's face was round and fleshy, like a million chubby Texas good ol' boys, but he exuded a burning, consternated intensity. He had grown up in Port Arthur, right on the Gulf of Mexico, a bright but uncurious jock who loathed his classmate, the hippie chick Janis Joplin (the feeling, by all reports, was mutual), and who had learned racial tolerance and understanding from sports.

In the late '80s, Johnson's teams at the University of Miami had been highly successful and widely disliked. Football coaches had for years spoken of players executing and carrying out their assignments in terms of "expressing themselves." Johnson's Hurricanes expressed themselves with a thoroughly modern swagger; they were taunting, dominating, preening clubs, whose players oozed with a confidence that was intimidating to some and viewed as unsportsmanlike by many.

"We had a lot of black players out front," Johnson would recall later. "I think a lot of the resentment came that way. The black players knew that, and the black players knew how I felt. I don't know that there was racism involved in the resentment, but there was some ignorance involved—people who have had few dealings with other ethnic groups. I mean real relationships, not getting somebody to clean your house."

Football, of course, had always attracted hard cases, but in the decade of the '80s, the locus of national football talent had moved from the Rust Belt of the industrial Midwest (where hard-bitten coal-miners' sons had defined toughness for much of the century) to the depressed and largely rural South, where a new generation of blue-chip players, mostly black, displayed a toughness with a harder, more contemporary sheen. One of Johnson's best players at Miami had been the wide receiver Michael Irvin. Drafted by the Cowboys in 1988, Irvin had been the fifteenth of seventeen children, and had developed a deep and abiding hunger for the trappings of success ("I crave things," Irvin said) and the spotlight. Johnson brought some of this attitude, and some more of these players, with him to Dallas.

There would be no honeymoon for the new regime—Jones's graceless handling of the Landry firing made sure of that—and the first season only exacerbated the problem. Bereft of speed (Irvin tore his anterior cruciate ligament and missed the season), and lacking a pass rush, the Cowboys were below average in all phases of the game. But in the midst of the woeful 1-15 campaign, in which Jones and Johnson would be mocked as two yahoos out of their depth in the big leagues, they executed the deal that would hasten the Cowboys' rise back to the top of the NFL.

The Cowboys' most marketable player was Herschel Walker, whom Schramm had cannily drafted after the 1984 season, and signed after the USFL folded in 1986. As the spearhead of Landry's declining offense, Walker had put up two 1,000-yard seasons, but Johnson wasn't convinced he'd still be a premium back by the time the Cowboys rose again.

The Minnesota Vikings were convinced they were just one powerful running back away from a run at the Super Bowl, and coveted Walker. Their GM, Mike Lynn, was so desperate to acquire Walker that he paid a fearsome price: seven draft choices (three in the first round, three in the second, and one in the third) and five players.

While Walker and the Vikings struggled in the aftermath, the Cowboys used their newfound arsenal of picks to bring an influx of young, fresh bodies, many of whom the Cowboys' coaching staff—largely brought in from Johnson's Miami staff—had coached or coached against. Before it was all over, Emmitt Smith, Russell Maryland, Darren Woodson, and Kevin Smith all came to Dallas as part of the Walker trade.

"At the time, I knew that some kind of deal was going down on Herschel," recalled Giants GM George Young. "Right before I went to bed that night, I heard about the deal that Minnesota had given Dallas. I didn't sleep at all that night. I knew the Dallas Cowboys weren't going to be down on the bottom very long."

———

Though the NFL found itself in a far different place than it had been the last time it picked a new commissioner—after Bert Bell's death in 1959—the succession struggle following Rozelle would turn out to be at least as confounding and paralyzing as the previous one. The subsequent election would require fewer ballots (twelve rather than twenty-three), but would set daunting records for search committees (three different ones) and elapsed time (seven months, four days).

The lone recommendation of the original search committee, composed entirely of old-guard owners, was veteran administrator Jim Finks, the longtime Vikings and Saints executive. But Finks, while universally liked, was just a year younger than Rozelle, and seemed a cautious, transitional choice. After a summer of wrangling, and the drafting of another search committee, a protracted deadlock developed between those supporting Finks and a group pushing for Paul Tagliabue, the league's lead counsel. Tagliabue hardly seemed a revolutionary, but he'd stressed the need to focus on new ways of increasing revenues and promised, if elected, to break with tradition and involve himself directly in the collective bargaining process. The standoff lingered through the summer, and the drafting of a second search committee, and into the fall, with neither side—the old guard supporting Finks or the "Chicago Eleven" group of mostly new owners who were pushing for Tagliabue—willing to budge. An early October meeting in Dallas yielded no progress and, after waiting seven months to vacate the job from which he had retired, Rozelle grew increasingly impatient with the intransigence of both sides. He drafted one more committee, and told them, "You've got twenty-four hours to come up with a unanimous recommendation, or we're going to throw both names out and start over again." Finally, the supporters for Finks relented and Tagliabue was elected on the twelfth ballot.

Once again, the new commissioner was in the bathroom when he got the news: Tagliabue was shaving when Rozelle called his Washington home at 6:30 the next morning, urging him and his wife to fly to Cleveland immediately to meet the owners and press.

Paul Tagliabue and his wife, Chan, would discover very quickly that he'd experienced more than a promotion. After returning that night to a celebration dinner in D.C., he and Chan arrived home at 11:30. Their daughter, Emily, watching a movie in the den, greeted them and said, "Here's a phone number. President Reagan's in Japan and he wants you to call him."

"Yeah, right," said Tagliabue.

"No, he's called three times in the last hour," said Emily. "He keeps calling and interrupting my movie. He's going off someplace the next morning in Tokyo and is leaving his hotel. He said it's urgent that you call him as soon as you can be reached."

Tagliabue didn't know the former president, and he and Chan had never been invited for a White House dinner. But Reagan was a fan, and had wanted to congratulate Tagliabue on the position. Inevitably, the former president advised him to "Win one for the Gipper."

―――――

The task of succeeding the man generally regarded as the greatest commissioner in sports history would carry with it challenges beyond what the commissioner left on his desk. And it would prove to be a particularly hard case for Paul Tagliabue. Authoritative and confident in daily life, he had a tendency to look stiff and a bit goofy in front of TV cameras, his conservative suits and oversized tortoiseshell glasses hiding an athlete's physique, and his legalistic answers at times obscuring his deep convictions.

But if it was Tagliabue's fate to never be seen as living up to the image of Pete Rozelle, it was a burden he could bear. Tall (6-foot-5), tough, and scrupulously honest (he would later say he never remembered cheating at any contest anytime in his life), he brought a formidable intellect, an implacable persistence, and a resolute sense of duty to any task he confronted. Lacking Rozelle's light touch and easy manner, Tagliabue would have to work harder, and was prepared to do so. He'd been doing it all his life.

He came from a family of strivers. His father, Charles, was a rough-hewn, self-reliant second-generation American who started his own construction company in New Jersey. Paul was the third of four children, all boys, who grew up in a two-story walk-up in Jersey City. Charles Tagliabue's boys were encouraged, though never coddled, and taught, "If you don't want to break your back, you better learn how to work with your head."

Though Paul was recruited by Frank McGuire to become part of the New York pipeline of schoolboy talent recruited to basketball powerhouse North Carolina, he instead took a scholarship at Georgetown, where he became the school's single-season rebounding leader (a record that stood for decades, to be broken by Patrick Ewing). Next came a full academic scholarship to New

York University Law School, where he met Chan, a bright, vivacious belle from Georgia. After a three-year stint at the Pentagon, where he was intimately involved with military strategic planning for the U.S. and its NATO allies, Tagliabue accepted a job at Covington & Burling, which had been wooing him for years. After twenty years—and over fifty cases in which he'd represented the league—Tagliabue assumed the commissionership.

The baton was passed at midnight on November 6, 1989. Rozelle, batting out one last note on his Royal typewriter at the Park Avenue office, took a few minutes to commit to writing some career reflections, never published. Headed "Thinking Back on Retirement," the two-page document began with his reflections of the 1960 election at the Kenilworth, and then worked back to his time with the Rams and the University of San Francisco. In his distinctive, all-lower-case type, Rozelle wrote, "Summing up and looking back I would have to say that there has been more than a little luck involved in my career. Have often recalled something I was told in a church summer camp. Character is what you are as a person and reputation is what people think of you. If you have a bad reputation you might as well have a bad character. So always worked very hard and tried not to alienate any more than necessary. If there was a secret to my success must have been a combination of luck and remembering that summer camp admonition."

For Tagliabue, the biggest surprise of his first year was how little he had to do with the actual games themselves. "I took over on a Monday," Tagliabue said, "and then the following week the whole country was in a dither about the slate of games. I hadn't spent two minutes on anything to do with the games, and every week that would happen. You kind of say, 'How the hell does that happen?' You're in charge of the organization and you don't have anything to do with what's going on. It's still the case."

He more than compensated for that during the rest of the week. He attacked the job just as he would a complex case, throwing himself into it completely. Staffers marveled at his ability to read everything and wondered where he found the time to do so. "I think at the beginning, people were shocked by how hands-on Paul was," said executive director Don Weiss. "He became an ex officio member of every committee, from expansion to realignment—the typical lawyer's approach. If you can't meet today, well how about tomorrow, even if it is a holiday or a Saturday?"

It was quickly apparent that Tagliabue wouldn't merely carry on Rozelle's policies. Rozelle had installed a steroids-testing program, over the objections of the Players Association in 1988, the efficacy of which had been largely clouded by the players' suspicion of the methods of Dr. Forest Tennant, the head of the league's drug program. Tagliabue elicited Tennant's resignation, and began overhauling the substance abuse program.

Tagliabue also was more willing than Rozelle to use the office as a bully pulpit. When Bengals coach Sam Wyche balked at allowing a female reporter into the Cincinnati locker room, Tagliabue fined him a week's pay, the largest fine of a coach in league history. When Arizona voters rejected a referendum to recognize Martin Luther King, Jr.'s, birthday as a state holiday, Tagliabue recommended that the league move the 1993 Super Bowl, previously awarded to Phoenix, out of the state entirely. (The league did so the following spring, promising Phoenix the game in 1996 if it subsequently recognized the King holiday.) The league also gained a concession from the networks, which agreed not to discuss point spreads or other gambling-related information in pregame shows. These were symbolic gestures, for sure, but proved to be important ones, not only for the message sent to fans, but for the ones sent to the players.

Tagliabue's first major decision in the public eye came in January 1991, when Operation Desert Storm was launched just days prior to the conference championship games. The games went on, amid scattered protest that it was disrespectful to do so. The *Washington Post*'s Shirley Povich, who'd covered World War II, offered a contrasting view: "It is curious why pro football seems to have been fingered as the target for showing our solemn concern for the sacred lives of our men and women in the desert. Other businesses and activities seem to have escaped this responsibility."

The war was already well along a week later, and there was little question that the Super Bowl would go ahead as scheduled. At the press conference the Friday before the game, Tagliabue articulated the curious position the league found itself in. "We are trying to have a tone and a theme for the game," he said, "that will recognize not only that it's the twenty-fifth Super Bowl, the Silver Anniversary Super Bowl football game, but also an event that's being played against the backdrop of some very grave developments in the Middle East."

In the end, people watched for the reasons they usually watched. The Super Bowl's ratings were aided by the closeness of the game, in which the underdog Giants, playing ball-control offense, ground out a 20–19 win that wasn't clinched until Buffalo's Scott Norwood missed a field goal in the closing seconds.

Following the Giants' win over the Bills, the balance of power remained firmly planted in the NFC's Eastern Division, which beginning with the Giants' win would boast five of the next six Super Bowl champions. In 1991, it was the Washington Redskins winning it all, giving Joe Gibbs his third championship, with his third different Super Bowl quarterback, in ten years.

But even then, a new dynasty—perhaps the NFL's last, as it would turn out—was being built in Dallas. Even before their 1-15 debacle in 1989, the Cowboys took advantage of the liberalized "Plan B" free agency rules, which allowed teams to sign without compensation any player not on another team's thirty-seven-player protected list. By 1990, with their pro scouting system in place, Dallas signed Jay Novacek, a tight end from the Cardinals. Novacek would catch 59 passes in his first year in Dallas (and would soon begin a string of five consecutive Pro Bowl appearances), and with the return of a healthy Michael Irvin and the arrival of rookie running back Emmitt Smith, the Cowboys jumped from 1-15 to 7-9. A year later, Johnson guaranteed that the Cowboys would be a playoff team, and they backed up his boast, going 11-5 and upsetting the Bears in an NFC divisional playoff.

In 1992, the Cowboys opened with an upset win over the defending champion Redskins, then marched to a conference-best 13-3 record, with a defense anchored by speed rusher Charles Haley (acquired for two draft choices from San Francisco, who couldn't handle the temperamental end any longer) and Chad Hennings (an Air Force Academy graduate, and another late-round steal acquired by Schramm in his last draft). Offensively, the team's stout, punishing offensive line cleared gaping holes for the slippery fireplug Emmitt Smith. Meanwhile, the maturing quarterback Troy Aikman had lived up to his billing as a classic pro-style leader, and Michael Irvin and Alvin Harper proved a lethal wideout tandem, with Novacek punishing teams when Aikman checked down to him on intermediate routes.

Johnson's crowing locker room mantra—"How 'Bout Them Cowboys!?!" —became a rallying cry for the team, which seemed to thrive in the media spotlight that others found daunting. The Cowboys' 52–17 rout of Buffalo in Super Bowl XXVII became at the time the most watched television program in American history, viewed by an estimated 133.4 million Americans.

And it was clear, in the wake of the Super Bowl win, that it was only the beginning. As Paul Zimmerman wrote in *Sports Illustrated,* "Troy Aikman and Emmitt Smith and Michael Irvin and Ken Norton Jr. and Charles Haley—all those implements of destruction that embarrassed and humiliated a proud, battle-tested team are just starting to feel their oats. Coach Jimmy Johnson and his hair spray; Jerry Jones, the owner who hungers for the limelight. You say you're tired of them already? Gee, that's tough, because the whole gang's going to be with us for a while." America's Team was back.

Five years earlier, in 1987, during a late night negotiating session on the eve of the NFL bringing in replacement players, NFL Players Association executive director Gene Upshaw sat across from Tex Schramm and, once again, explained why the union was adamant about getting some form of free agency.

"You're not *going* to get it!" barked Schramm. "You're not going to get it in five years, you're not going to get it in ten years, you're not *ever* going to get it. Don't you see? You're the cattle, we're the ranchers!"

That philosophy informed much of the late '80s in negotiating, though there was more than simple hardheadedness at work. For executives like Schramm, who'd viewed the game as a laboratory of team building, the prospect of unfettered free agency went against all the precepts that guaranteed equality of opportunity. He may have been reactionary, but no one doubted he was sincere: Tex Schramm, and many others like him, really did believe that free agency would ruin the game of professional football.

By the end of his tenure, Pete Rozelle was beginning to disagree. He despaired at the acrimonious state of relations, and had begun to question whether his policy of trying to remain strictly above the fray had been the wisest idea. During his final months in office, he was taking a more conciliatory stance. "Maybe what Ed Garvey was talking about a few years back—that some owners found distasteful—really was a good solution after all. He had wanted 55 percent of the team revenues for the players' salaries, pensions, etc., and everyone pooh-poohed it, including myself. They would grab it today."

On the morning of Super Bowl XXIII, just two months before his retirement announcement, Rozelle brought together the Players Association and Management Council and tried to barter an agreement. But even the limited free agency plan on the table—granting players free agency after seven years in the NFL—was rejected by the Management Council. And yet in light of the free agency offered in other sports, and the series of rulings that went against the league in the '80s, free agency was clearly coming.

Among the first people to talk about the labor issue with Tagliabue after he took office was Al Davis, who said he felt that Jack Donlan (the league's lead negotiator, soon dismissed by Tagliabue) and the Management Council had, for much of the decade, showed disrespect to the Players Association, attempting to bully them. But Upshaw was not a man easily bullied. "You're dealing with an educated guy who wants to get something done," said Davis. "All of you have built up a stereotype. You've painted them as militants, when all they want is equal rights."

Though Tagliabue and Upshaw were on opposite ends of many legal battles, they had developed a warm personal relationship. In the '80s, while still at Covington & Burling, Tagliabue would see Upshaw occasionally and would invariably tell him, "Don't give up; keep pushing for a solution." Upshaw had sensed that Tagliabue could provide a break with the past, and had been pulling for his election throughout the summer of 1989. Like a wise general who knows better than anyone the horrors of war, Tagliabue was an attorney determined not to spend the next decade the way Pete Rozelle had spent the previous one.

Though Tagliabue and Upshaw had dozens of meetings in the first three years of his tenure, it was clear that both men's constituencies were waiting for the next legal outcome to dictate their strategy. It came in the federal district court in Minneapolis, where Judge David Doty presided over a suit involving Jets running back Freeman McNeil and several other NFL players. The jury trial for the McNeil case came in with a verdict on September 9, 1992, finding that the Plan B free agency system violated antitrust law by being more restrictive than was necessary to achieve competitive balance. But the damages phase of the trial offered minimal relief (with only four of the eight plaintiffs receiving damages, totaling $543,000), and the verdict left room for the NFL to adopt a slightly less restrictive plan that could lightly loosen the system and which would have to be tried in court all over again.

By then, negotiations had grown serious, and another case—this one involving All-Pro defensive end Reggie White—was being heard by Doty. In late December of 1992, Judge Doty sat both sides down in his chambers, and showed them a sealed envelope. He warned them that inside was his solution, and it was a solution that neither side would like. Though both sides would later question whether Doty's threat was an empty one—"I still don't think there was anything at all in that damn envelope," said Upshaw—it pushed both the players and management toward a compromise.

And over the next days, the two sides came to a solution that had been sitting on the table, really, for four decades. In 1953, while handing down his decision upholding blackouts of home games in the NFL, Judge Allan Grim moved far afield and noted, "In order to try to keep its teams and approximately equal strength and to protect weaker teams from stronger teams, a league theoretically might use a number of devices." Grim went on to list seven possible methods, including "(5) limit the total amount of salaries which a team can pay."

The idea became a cornerstone of a new agreement, which gave players unrestricted free agency after four years in the league. The agreement also ingeniously added an evergreen clause, which encouraged both sides to extend the contract before it expired. In the last year of the contract, the owners would lose their cap, and the eligibility for free agency would kick up from four years to six years. Suddenly, after a quarter-century of haggling, the players had achieved a sizable percentage of the gross (it would work out to around 65 percent, once the cap went into effect) and true free agency.

The agreement accomplished something that would prove even more important: by establishing a sense of proportion that guaranteed players almost two thirds of every dollar the NFL made, it made the players partners of the owners in more than rhetorical terms.

But there was still some resistance from both sides. "We had been so used to a system that had virtually no movement in terms of free agency," said Carmen Policy, then the president and CEO of the 49ers. "To accept free agency was worse than having to go through chemotherapy. Chemotherapy's supposed to cure cancer, whereas free agency's a form of cancer itself." Among some players, there was a similar distaste for a cap. The Cowboys' Irvin correctly viewed it as a move that would cost the game's biggest stars money. "Free agency with a cap is like no free agency," he said. Irvin would be the most vocal of the plan's critics, and he tangled angrily with Upshaw at a meeting in the Cowboys' locker room in May 1993.

But for a generation of players who'd been through the decades-long battle for recognition, there was no doubt that the agreement was a victory. Shortly after a spate of player criticism made the news, Upshaw received a phone message in his office from John Mackey, the head of the NFLPA in the early '70s who'd mortgaged the end of his own career to sue the NFL over the Rozelle Rule. "I read what those ungrateful S.O.B. players are saying about the new agreement," said Mackey. "Tell them they can kiss your ass. You're doing a great job."

There would still be loopholes that would have been better closed, but with the agreement, the NFL, already the nation's most popular spectator sport, added a modern economic structure that would make sense both financially and competitively. On August 12, 1994, when the Major League Baseball Players Association went out on strike, the contrast couldn't have been any greater. It called to mind the old Edward Bennett Williams quote, "The only thing dumber than a dumb football owner is a smart baseball owner."

Of course, Major League Baseball, even in its rancorous ineptitude, continued to possess one thing that the NFL didn't have, a broad antitrust exemption that could be used to block arbitrary and capricious franchise moves. It was one loophole that neither Rozelle nor Tagliabue, to their eternal regret, had been able to close.

22

Pearl Harbor

In Kansas City, Lamar Hunt still went to the games, still worried over the tiny details, still lived and died with the fortunes of his football team. But through the '70s and '80s, his once proud franchise fell into a cycle of house-cleaning, renewed promise, and dashed expectations, and the reputation of the Chiefs began to fade.

Arrowhead Stadium, the magnificent structure built as a result of Chiefs victories of the '60s, witnessed little but failure in the '70s and '80s. From 1974 to 1988, the team sold out just three games, and became better known for its turmoil: the accidental drowning death of running back Joe Delaney in 1983; the sad picket line scuffle in 1987 between striking linebacker Jack Del Rio and Chiefs great Otis Taylor, by then a scout for the team; the 1988 revelation that head coach Frank Gansz had lied about his military record.

Through it all, Hunt remained polite, supportive, and slightly withdrawn, and this ceaseless composure came to rankle his closest friends, who knew how competitive he really was.

"I've never heard him say a derogatory remark about anyone," marveled lifelong friend Buddy Rupe. "I'd call Al Davis 'the biggest asshole that ever drew a breath of air.' And Lamar would say, 'Well, at times he can be difficult.' I just want to slap him upside the head. 'He's not *difficult,* Lamar—he's a shit-head!' "

Finally, at the end of the 1988 season, in which the 4-12 Chiefs played in front of sparse crowds and more than a quarter-million empty seats, Hunt took action. He fired Gansz and GM Jim Schaff, and bumped longtime president Jack Steadman to the role of chairman of the board. In his place came the tanned, restless, and ultra-competitive outsider, Carl Peterson, who took the lofty titles of president, general manager, and chief operating officer. Despite mirrored shades, feathered hair, and tailored suits, Peterson was a football lifer with a blend of talents uniquely suited to the modern game.

In the past, most "football people" dealt with football alone, and left business concerns to an administrative staff. But Peterson was part of a new breed who, following Tex Schramm's trailblazing example, excelled at both. In Kansas City, Peterson didn't just overhaul the team's scouting apparatus, he rebuilt its community presence as well. He toured six states to drum up support and commissioned market studies to better understand the team's fan base. The existing fan base was an aging, dispirited lot, seeking credibility above all else. Rather than making any outlandish claims for his new regime, Peterson developed a series of TV commercials, shot in gritty black-and-white, that showed players working out in preparation for the new season, and closed with the phrase, "No Promises, No Excuses."

His first choice as head coach, his close friend Dick Vermeil, turned him down, choosing to stay retired. Peterson was casting about for other candidates when one of the best coaches in the NFL dropped in his lap. Marty Schottenheimer had just led the Browns to their fourth straight playoff season, particularly impressive in light of a plague of quarterback injuries. Yet after the season, Modell and Schottenheimer had clashed over his assistants, and he resigned.

Schottenheimer's fundamental approach and Teutonic resolve worked as well in Kansas City as it had in Cleveland, and the results were nearly instantaneous: the team went 8-7-1 in 1989, barely missing the playoffs, then went 11-5 in 1990, advancing to the postseason for only the second time in twenty seasons. The team's season ticket base of 26,000 in 1988 grew within four years to more than 71,000, with a waiting list of 15,000, and the Chiefs would lead the league in attendance six times during the '90s. It wasn't just the wins in Arrowhead that were different; Peterson helped transform the game day experience, bringing in a team mascot and adding rock music at key intervals (becoming perhaps the first team to pump the opening chords of the Rolling Stones' "Start Me Up" prior to kickoff), as well as moving the team's radio contract to an FM rock station that would bring a younger audience.

And like the best football coaches, Schottenheimer helped change the personality of the team. As in Cleveland, Schottenheimer's teams did things right, playing sound, bruising defense and conservative, ball-control offense. The first draft choice of the new era was the versatile edge rusher Derrick Thomas, a game-breaking linebacker who quickly became the anchor of a ferocious Chiefs defense that already had one of the game's best secondaries.

There had been talk, after the Royals' rise in the '70s and their World Series title in 1985, that Kansas City had become a baseball town. But as soon as the Chiefs placed a credible team on the field, the city swung back around again. Beginning in 1990, the team went to the playoffs seven times in eight seasons, and Arrowhead—a sterile, empty bowl for much of its history—was transformed into one of the toughest places in the league for road teams to visit. By October 6, 1991, when Kansas City played at home on *Monday Night Football* for the first time in eight years, the team was greeted by an otherworldly din that lasted throughout the 33–6 dismantling of the defending conference champion Bills. "I've never seen anything like that in my life, before or since," said Tony Dungy, then an assistant for the Chiefs.

What the team meant to the city was no less real for being so ineffable. As Mike Davis, a Kansas City attorney put it, "You'll never get 100,000 people together because you bought a Van Gogh at the Nelson Gallery. Sports is the principal unifying force in the metro area." Outside the stadium on game days, the 30,000-space parking lot became a haven for tailgating and barbecuing, while inside the raucous crowd developed an intimidating reputation, wreaking havoc on opposing teams, and causing seven false-start penalties for the Broncos' frustrated offense in a 1993 Monday night game. The team and its stadium had served as a social magnet, the kind of cohesive, mobilizing event that occurred with less regularity in sprawling modern societies. "Without the Chiefs and the Royals," said Kansas City Mayor Emanuel Cleaver, "we'd be Omaha . . . Wichita . . . Des Moines."

———

There were only twenty-seven cities that enjoyed the cachet of an NFL franchise, and many others had long clamored for the opportunity. With labor peace finally achieved, the NFL announced at its annual meetings in 1993 that it would expand, for the first time in sixteen years. The wave of politicking that the announcement set off was another indicator of the league's preeminent position in American sports. Since 1974, when the NFL selected Tampa Bay and Seattle to join the league (beginning play in 1976), the other major sports leagues had expanded numerous times: Major League Baseball had grown by four clubs, and both the NBA and NHL had added nine teams. But it was the first NFL expansion in two decades, and the suitors campaigned with a special fervor.

For the cities that had lost NFL franchises in the '80s, the expansion offered the promise of a kind of redemption. No city viewed its candidacy with greater fervor than Baltimore, still haunted by the Colts' escape in 1984. The Colts marching band had stuck together since the team left, and still gathered to play at an empty Memorial Stadium every Sunday that the Indianapolis Colts had a home game. With the prospect of the NFL's return, the city mobilized. There was already a guarantee from Maryland lawmakers that, if and when a franchise came to Baltimore, $200 million in stadium funds would be approved. The coming expansion also offered an opportunity for growing cities in the Sun Belt to make their case that they belonged on the national stage, and among the five finalists—with Baltimore and St. Louis—were three cities in the Southeast, Charlotte, Memphis, and Jacksonville.

The assumption all along had been that the league might pick one "new" market and another "old" market in tandem. But at the expansion vote in Chicago on October 26, the league could only agree on one entry, unanimously approving the Charlotte bid. On November 30, the league surprised all the remaining parties by selecting Jacksonville, the nation's fifty-fourth TV market and a group considered such a long shot that it had dropped out of the process earlier in the year.

The shock from the news was felt around the country, and most especially in St. Louis and Baltimore. The feeling of resentment was exacerbated in the latter city by Tagliabue's seemingly patronizing comments following the announcement. When asked what advice he would give a city like Baltimore, which had waited a decade for a chance at a new franchise and been denied, the commissioner curtly said, "We didn't force anybody to get involved in this process. That's a judgment call people have to make. Maybe they prefer to have a museum or plant in their town."

A bereft John Steadman, longtime writer for the *Baltimore Sun,* wrote a letter to Rozelle lashing out at the league's new leaders. "Tagliabue had every chance to correct a wrong, to wipe out much hostility in the affair Irsay, to clean up the past—and he didn't do it. . . . You ought to be so pleased to be away from it all, a bunch of cold over-bearing men who have no idea what the NFL is all about."

It would soon enough become apparent that in solving one set of problems, the league had created another.

The beginning of the 1993 season brought the advent of free agency, phased in a year ahead of the accompanying salary cap. The defending champion Cowboys opened 0-2 while star running back Emmitt Smith held out. But after he signed, Dallas went on to win twelve of its remaining fourteen regular season games, then vanquished the 49ers again in the NFC title game. In a Super Bowl rematch against the cursed Bills, making their fourth consecutive trip, Dallas marched to an easy 30–13 win.

The Cowboys were clearly ensconced as America's Team and a budding dynasty. Equally clear in the media-glutted environment of the '90s was that the Bills' repeated failure in the big game served to brand them as the ultimate losers, the butt of late-night jokes and object of a tormenting series of "How does it feel?" queries. On the Monday following Super Bowl XXVIII, the Bills' fourth straight Super Bowl loss, the David Letterman show included the list of "Top Ten Things Buffalo Bills Coach Marv Levy Said at Halftime." (No. 3: "Okay, boys—get out there and start sucking.")

Meanwhile, the second straight Super Bowl win had further elevated the reputations of Jerry Jones and Jimmy Johnson, and the Cowboys were given a good chance of becoming the first team ever to win three consecutive Super Bowls. Behind the scenes, however, others on the Cowboys' staff were beginning to sense the growing strain between the two. By March, Jones and Johnson, the jubilant revelers at two consecutive Super Bowl parties, were grim-faced at a Dallas press conference, in which they jointly announced Johnson's abrupt exit as head coach (accounts differed on whether the coach had resigned or been fired).

It was evident by Johnson's exit that Jones didn't merely want the Cowboys to succeed; it was important to him that he be seen as the primary architect of the Cowboys juggernaut. Implicit in this was his choice for Johnson's replacement. Jones had mused that "any of 500 people, probably including me" could lead the Cowboys to a Super Bowl, and he hired the deposed University of Oklahoma coach Barry Switzer, the self-proclaimed "bootlegger's boy" who'd been a graduate assistant on the 1964 Arkansas team on which Jones and Johnson had been teammates.

While Jones thirsted for the spotlight from football fans, he'd already earned plenty of attention, and grudging respect, from many of his fellow owners. Jones's manner lacked subtlety, but his fierce business instincts helped him see opportunities that others might have missed, and that fervent drive would serve more than just the Cowboys.

In 1992, in the midst of a depressed economic environment, with the TV networks claiming tens of millions of dollars of losses on their NFL coverage, Art Modell negotiated a deal for the league that would provide the networks with a $230 million rebate for the 1992 season, in exchange for extending the contract two additional years. The move garnered the support of Tagliabue, who before a special meeting to discuss the issue called it "the most important business decision that'll be made this decade." But with Jones and Philadelphia's Norman Braman leading the opposition, the rebate plan was voted down. The rejection stung Modell—who resigned after thirty years as the league's Broadcasting Committee chairman—and further established Jones as a rising presence in the league.

A year later, the wisdom of Jones's strident optimism was ratified. When the league opened negotiations for the new contract, a significant bounce had occurred in the advertising market, and a crucial new player—Rupert Murdoch's fledgling Fox network—was vying for a contract. The result was a stunning four-year, $4.38 billion deal that nearly doubled teams' television revenue again.

In the place of CBS's tradition, the league would align its most visible conference with an unknown entity. Fox was without a sports division, and a vast majority of its 139 stations were on the UHF band, but Murdoch was convinced that an NFL deal would be a ticket to the big time. He well understood that the NFL made the network instantly respectable, and the contract alone led to dozens of channel and affiliate switches, in which Fox moved to more desirable spots.

The deal ushered in a new era of business growth for the league, hastened by Tagliabue's 1991 appointment of the investment banker and former Showtime chief Neil Austrian as the new league president, overseeing the league's business interests. But most importantly, the new network deal reaffirmed the faith that Jones and others showed that, even in hard financial times, the rights to NFL broadcasts remained the most valuable commodity on television.

————

In any profound change to a complex system, the Law of Unintended Consequences will inevitably take effect. And when the NFL went to its first season with the salary cap, in 1994, the law quickly asserted itself. The league had argued for a "hard" cap, and had achieved it in principle. But one of the stipulations of the collective bargaining agreement was that any signing bonus a player received would be prorated over the life of the contract (provided the player stayed on the roster throughout that period). Signing bonuses were crucial for players, because they provided the only guaranteed money they made, and with multiple teams competing for players, the number and sizes of the bonuses skyrocketed. The teams that were best able to afford those huge bonuses weren't necessarily the clubs in the largest markets, but instead the clubs with the best stadium deals, especially those in modern stadiums with more luxury suites and revenue enhancements. Money from luxury suite rentals, concession sales, and parking fees were not part of the 60-40 home-road split, so teams with newer stadiums or better rental agreements or both enjoyed millions in extra revenue that wasn't shared with the other clubs.

No one capitalized on the new economics more quickly than Jerry Jones, who discovered a heretofore untapped revenue resource when, on August 4, 1995, he announced a ten-year, $40 million sponsorship deal with Pepsi. The league already had a soda sponsorship deal in place with Coca-Cola, but Jones skirted the legality of the conflicting deal by granting Pepsi "pouring rights" as the official soft drink of Texas Stadium. Before the fall was over, he'd signed rich stadium sponsorship deals with AT&T, American Express, and Nike, the last deal announced during a *Monday Night Football* telecast, in which Jones and Nike chairman Phil Knight walked the sidelines during halftime of the Cowboys-Giants game, upstaging a retirement ceremony for the Giants' Phil Simms. The deals seemed to strike at the heart of the league's revenue-sharing arrangement, and threatened to supersede the national deals that the league had struck. At the time, Tagliabue called the deal "short-sighted and self-serving," and within months, the league and Jones were suing each other over perceived differences. In the meantime, Jones signed Deion Sanders, who'd helped the 49ers break the Cowboys' two-year run the previous year, to a seven-year, $35 million deal with a $13 million signing bonus, and the Cowboys embarked on a quest to win their third Super Bowl in four years.

Meanwhile, in Southern California, where the pleasures and distractions of American life were unsurpassed, and where the sense of community was the most tenuous, pro football was floundering. The Rams, playing down in Anaheim, had fallen off the radar of many Los Angeles sports fans, slumping to a 23-57 record in the first half of the '90s, never recovering on the field from the absence of Eric Dickerson and the inexplicable mid-career slump of quarterback Jim Everett. Both the Rams and the Raiders needed new stadiums, but in a state battered by riots and earthquakes, the issue was a political nonstarter.

As this discontent became apparent, so did the entreaties from the jilted cities of the expansion process. Baltimore, flush with money from a state lottery and with the funding already approved to build a new stadium, had entered into negotiations with Al Davis, as well as other franchises. So had the city of St. Louis, trying for more than a decade to replace the Cardinals. Rosenbloom's widow, Georgia Frontiere (she'd since remarried), exercised an escape clause in the Rams' lease in 1994 and announced in January 1995 that the team was moving to St. Louis, which offered a package that included a domed stadium, a state-of-the-art practice facility in a lavish team complex, 100 percent of concession revenue, and numerous other perks.

The problem, however, was that the Rams didn't meet the long-standing criterion, in place since 1984, of a team that *needed* to move for its financial survival. The ensuing vote of 23–1 against the move, prompted an immediate threat of legal action by Missouri attorney general Jay Nixon, as well as the threat by the Rams that they would sue the league in the very same way that Al Davis had done a decade earlier. And so the league found itself at a crossroads. Fifteen years after the beginning of the Raiders litigation, it faced the possibility of another protracted dispute with another uncertain outcome. In the event, the owners blinked. "The main consideration," said Tagliabue, "was the potential damage exposure of vetoing a deal that guaranteed a team, at least in their view, I think the number was around $900 million over the life of the lease, so arguably the damage exposure is three times $900 million, which is a significant amount of money."

In April, the league voted again and the move was approved, in exchange for a series of financial concessions from the Rams. And so the Rams, which had spent fifty of their fifty-eight years of existence in Southern California, prepared for a move to St. Louis. Pete Rozelle, never publicly critical of the league or its owners, privately bemoaned the loss of the team of his youth. And at Rams' Horn restaurant in suburban Sherman Oaks, owner and former All-Pro lineman Don Paul put a new dish on the menu called "Lack of Ram."

Suddenly, Al Davis and the Raiders were all alone in the nation's number two market. The decade, which had begun with such promise, with the team advancing to the AFC championship game in Art Shell's first full season as head coach, had grown into a frustrating series of good-but-not-great seasons made all the more aggravating by the Raiders' inability to beat the Chiefs, once again their archrival. After winning thirteen division titles in twenty-four years, the Raiders would spend another decade trying to win another, during which they went through a stretch in which they lost eighteen of twenty games to the Chiefs. Davis grew more eccentric by the year. He had been known to show up to games wearing a black Raiders warm-up suit, then emerge from a bathroom at halftime wearing a white Raiders warm-up suit. Art Shell, despite compiling a 56-41 mark, was fired after the 1994 season.

While the Raiders hadn't replaced the Rams in the hearts of L.A.'s longtime football fans, they did have an impact in the city. The Raiders' colors and reputation resonated with many area rappers, and the L.A. neighborhood of Compton—the same Compton where Pete Rozelle had attended high school—had become the lodestar of the burgeoning West Coast rap movement, with rappers such as Ice Cube, Eazy-E, and Ice-T sporting Raiders jerseys and caps in their videos and promotional photos. As the gang warfare in L.A. waxed, then waned, the identification with the Raiders became more than a passing fad—for some it was a means of survival. In an increasingly style-conscious urban environment in which wearing red or blue could brand one as a member of the Bloods or Crips, the black-and-silver of the Raiders' jersey served as a suitable compromise, one that connoted street toughness without inciting attack or police suspicion.

But while the hip-hop community bought Raiders merchandise, it didn't buy enough tickets to offset a gradual and lengthy attendance slump. The aging Coliseum, restored to some of its earlier glory for the 1984 Summer Olympics, had by the mid-'90s fallen into disrepair. With an absence of luxury boxes and interior concourses for concession sales, the Coliseum was deemed unfit for the modern game. On June 23, 1995, the Raiders announced an agreement to move back to Oakland. The deal, eventually approved by the league, left the Los Angeles area without a pro football team for the first time in a half-century.

In addition to the Rams and Raiders moves, the Patriots had been negotiating for a possible move to St. Louis, the Buccaneers to Orlando, and the Oilers to Nashville. In each case, teams were moving out of larger markets and into smaller ones that were offering better stadium deals. What all this meant, as dramatized by the Raiders and Rams moves, was that Al Davis had been proved precisely wrong. It wasn't the market size at all that was crucial. The most crucial element to each team's relative revenue standing within the league was its stadium deal.

And within the league, there was a sense that tumultuous waters lay ahead if the league couldn't find a way to keep its franchises in place. Among those visibly alarmed was Art Modell, who said, "We can't hopscotch franchises around the country. We have built this business on the trust of fans. If we treat that as if it doesn't count, it isn't going to wash."

———

In contrast to the chaos and dissipation of Los Angeles, the '90s began with the city of Cleveland standing as one of the rocks on which the NFL's identity rested. The Dawg Pound, inaugurated in the glory days of the Browns' resurgence in the mid-'80s, was still going strong, and as the 1995 season began Modell was universally and justifiably regarded as one of the cornerstones of the NFL's old school.

Modell had suffered over the Browns' near misses as deeply as the city, and he was consumed with the idea of winning another world championship. "I'd give up ten years off my life to get to a Super Bowl," he said in 1994. The Browns' mid-'80s rise, nearly a decade old by this time, had helped revive the city's fortunes, and contributed to a renaissance of the downtown, with a new baseball stadium for the Indians, a new basketball arena for the Cavaliers, and the Rock and Roll Hall of Fame and Museum.

For years, Modell had been urging the city of Cleveland to help with renovations to Cleveland Stadium. While never threatening—he'd vowed that he would never move the team—he had become increasingly insistent about the team's need for the full gamut of stadium improvements. Cleveland mayor Mike White, with whom Modell had tangled for much of the decade, was pushing for the improvements and had even set up a referendum to extend the city's sin tax to appropriate funds for the renovations. In July, Modell declared a moratorium on talking about the vote so he could, he said, concentrate on football. Fans in Cleveland assumed that they could do the same.

Modell had still not made any statements, either public or private, to the league when, in late October after a league meeting, he stopped by Tagliabue's office and mentioned, "At some point I'm going to need to talk to you about my stadium situation." Tagliabue had said that sounded fine and invited Modell to call him anytime. But that was all the warning that he or the league received prior to Friday, November 3, 1995, when the staggering news leaked that Modell had signed an agreement to move the Browns to Baltimore.

It is difficult to overstate the impact of the move on the American sporting landscape. Coming a year after the emotional toll taken by the truncated 1994 baseball season, the news was a body blow that disoriented the internal compass of fans in Cleveland and across the country. Not since the Dodgers and Giants fled to the West Coast in 1958 had a franchise shift so jolted the sports world.

And to football fans, especially those in Cleveland, the move felt like a sneak attack, the sporting equivalent of Pearl Harbor. For those who had come of age secure in the womb of Rozelle's elaborate NFL universe, the move was much more traumatic than either the Raiders' or Colts' exits. Davis was a known rebel; Irsay was generally regarded as a buffoon, and in both of those cases, the moves came as a culmination of months, even years of public posturing. But to see Art Modell, for so long a pillar of the league's one-for-all rhetoric, picking up and heading for a better deal—without leaving the citizens of Cleveland so much as a last chance—was shocking. "I felt like I lost a close relative," said Browns legend Lou Groza, who began weeping when he heard the news, and would never again speak to Modell.

The game at Cleveland on Sunday, November 5, was a surreal exercise in public anguish, with the crowd alternately sullen and raging by turns. "It was the worst feeling I've had there, other than when Kennedy got killed," said Jim Brown, who'd been a special adviser to the team since 1993. "It was sort of like a dream out there today."

In the stands, the leader of the Dawg Pound, the portly computer parts salesman John Thompson, whose No. 98 jersey and dog mask were an ever-present sight, wore only the jersey to the game. Asked why he didn't wear the mask, the anguished Thompson replied, "You wouldn't wear a dog mask to your brother's funeral, would you?"

Houston (another team in the turmoil of a pending move) won, 37–10, and the postgame scene outside the Cleveland dressing room threatened to turn ugly. A group of a few dozen fans, standing on a nearby concourse, repeatedly shouted "Bring us Modell!" But Art Modell, for the first time in his thirty-three years of owning the Browns, was not in attendance. He would never again return to Cleveland.

The next morning Modell was in Baltimore, introduced by Mayor Kurt Schmoke as "the owner of the Baltimore Browns," and greeted with a standing ovation.

"I didn't want to hold up the city of Cleveland," said Modell years later. "I would never do something like that." This was cold comfort to the team's fans. While it was true that, in the aftermath, Modell's grievances were clearer, his means of redressing them were inconsistent with the principles he'd espoused for much of his career.

On the shores of Lake Erie, the reaction was something close to hysteria, not terribly different—in both the anguished tone of the reaction and the distraught nature of the accompanying rhetoric—from the feeling of civic betrayal heard in Rust Belt communities when auto plants or other factories shut down and moved out. If anything, the response was even more severe, because in this case, the company was one with which most of the people in the city identified with, rooted for, and, on Sundays, built their lives around.

The funereal scene at the stadium for the rest of the Browns' games that season was one of the saddest sights in football. The team played its final home game of the season December 17, beating Cincinnati, 26–10. After the contest, the Browns players circled the edge of the field, shaking hands. Meanwhile, a sign on the Cleveland Stadium scoreboard, trying to find the appropriate tone for the setting, rang particularly hollow. It read:

BROWNS FANS,
YOU ARE UNIQUE AND YOUR SUPPORT THROUGH THE YEARS
HAS BEEN EXTRAORDINARY!
IT'S BEEN A GREAT RUN.
FORMER AND CURRENT BROWNS PLAYERS AND COACHES THANK YOU.
THANKS FOR BEING PART OF SOMETHING SPECIAL. THANK YOU VERY MUCH!

The irony that Baltimore, which had the Colts snatched from it in 1984, would now be the recipient of an equally shocking move was not lost on the city's citizens. As the former governor William Donald Schaefer, by then no longer in office, wrote in a terse note to Tagliabue, "Old adage: 'what goes around comes around.' You could have avoided *all* this turmoil *if you* had only played fair."

So the three cities that lost NFL franchises in the '80s—St. Louis, Oakland, and Baltimore—had regained franchises in the '90s, at the expense of a mostly indifferent Los Angeles and an outraged Cleveland. Houston, as well, was jilted. The Oilers would leave thirty-seven years of often rabid fan support in Texas for uncharted territory in Tennessee, where they settled in Nashville and were eventually rechristened the Tennessee Titans. The era of franchise free agency had arrived. With the media crying apocalypse, angry fans clogging the league's fax system with letters of protest, and one of the most respected owners in the league receiving death threats, Tagliabue faced the greatest crisis of his tenure.

How had the best-managed sports league in the country come to such an ignoble turn? The simplest answer was that over the fifty years of postwar America, none of the three commissioners had been able to secure meaningful federal antitrust protection that would have allowed the league's owners to decide among themselves where the league's franchises could be located.

But it was also true that the owners had, in many ways, betrayed their own cause. They had bemoaned the Raiders' move in 1982, but instead of fighting for a bare-bones antitrust legislation that served to protect against future moves, the league supported broader retroactive legislation, which muddied the waters and lacked the support in Congress to pass. It was also true that at least some of the owners didn't *want* the legislation, but preferred to use the threat of a move to generate greater concessions from their current municipalities.

Out of the chaos of the Cleveland move to Baltimore, one important precedent was set. On February 8, 1996, Tagliabue announced that the NFL had reached an agreement with the city of Cleveland that guaranteed that the NFL would place an expansion team in Cleveland by 1999 and, in exchange for the city dropping any further legal action, would allow Cleveland to retain rights to the Cleveland Browns name, the team colors, nickname, and heritage. It was too little, too late, an instance of pure damage control. But it was probably the best that could be done under the circumstances, and would be a crucial element in repairing relations with outraged Clevelanders.

In Southern California in 1996, an ailing Pete Rozelle battled a series of cruel health setbacks. After nursing Carrie through a brain tumor he was diagnosed with one of his own. As his health wavered and his activities waned, he watched helplessly as the league he worked so hard to help build was cast into a state of chaos.

But almost every day, he'd come into his office, just minutes away from his house, to return calls and answer correspondence. His longtime assistant, Thelma Elkjer, who'd returned to California in 1990, answered his phones and handled his personal affairs.

Those mid-'90s years played out like a long valedictory for Rozelle. In January of 1996, when the Super Bowl celebrated its thirtieth anniversary with a gathering of the writers who had covered each of the games, Rozelle was too ill to travel. He sent along a note, which read in part, "If I was there today, just for old times sake I would turn a chair around, grab a Coke, pull out a cigarette, and wait for your questions. If you asked me a tough one, I would take a minute to light the cigarette so I could buy some time. I think you were on to my trick."

In 1996, as his health worsened, Rozelle stopped going out to functions. His last public appearance came in August, when he was onstage in San Diego to watch Jack Kemp accept the vice presidential nomination at the Republican National Convention. Standing alongside him, and shepherding him through the crowd, was another longtime friend and occasional adversary, former union leader and *Mackey v. NFL* plaintiff John Mackey.

In the fall, Rozelle spent his weekends glued to the bank of big-screen TVs in his den, receiving a select few friends. He did witness the revival of the Green Bay Packers, who in the free agency era would become a synthesis of the sport's grandest virtues, the ultimate small-market team (just 100,000 citizens in Green Bay), led by the modernistic approach of Bill Walsh protégé Mike Holmgren, and the sharp personnel moves of the hard-bitten, plainspoken

GM Ron Wolf, who in 1992 traded a first-round pick for a little-used Atlanta backup quarterback named Brett Favre.

Rozelle died on December 6, 1996, and the next month found the NFL in a kind of extended mourning. At Super Bowl XXXI in New Orleans, where the Packers beat the Patriots, both teams wore small decals, a script reading "Pete" on the back of their helmets.

And the connection—between Rozelle's vision of a sports league, and a world championship in America's biggest sport being won by a team representing a city of 100,000—was not lost on Packers president Bob Harlan.

"There are only two reasons we can exist in this market," said Harlan, in the days following Rozelle's death. "The first is that, back in the 1960s, Pete Rozelle convinced the NFL owners to share their profits. Today, 84 percent of the Packers' income comes from shared revenue. The other factor is the salary cap. It's not a 'hard cap,' and we wish it were. But it works."

By the time the Packers celebrated their title, Paul Tagliabue had stopped the bleeding in franchise free agency. At the 1996 annual meetings, the league made it clear to owners that the league would legally fight any attempted move to the Los Angeles market. With the backlash against the league and the Browns, it was becoming apparent that the days of cities assuming the entire financing for stadiums—especially football stadiums that could guarantee use only ten days a year—were largely past. New stadiums would require some combination of public and private funding, and some clubs were hard-pressed to pledge $100 million or more, without violating the league's rules against taking on excessive debt. Out of that hardship would emerge the seeds of the plan that would eventually help stop the flow of franchise moves, the league's G-3 stadium construction program, through which the league advanced clubs the money to pay for up to 50 percent of the cost of a new stadium.

It would be three years before the new Cleveland Browns took the field for their 1999 season opener against the Pittsburgh Steelers, and while it would never be quite the same for the people of Cleveland, Tagliabue and the league had done what they could to preserve the unique relationship between the community and the team. The NFL universe was once again an environment in which the most spirited competition could return to the field of play. It would take some time to recognize it as such, but out of the chaos of franchise free agency, a new golden era had begun.

23

"A Different World"

In a comfortable, unassuming office park in the Baltimore suburb of Timonium, the most celebrated quarterback in pro football history spent his days like most Americans, working for a living.

He was usually alone in the cozy two-room office, and answered his own phone. "Matco Electronics," he'd say, "this is John Unitas." He was no mere front-door greeter or community affairs representative. Unitas would have considered such work patronizing. As a vice president of the small company, which manufactured circuit boards, he filled orders, planned appointments, moved product.

And though the effects of a 1968 arm injury had left his right hand virtually useless, Unitas simply adapted, and soldiered on stoically. He couldn't shave or brush his teeth or zip a zipper or button a shirt, but he started writing, eating, and answering the phone with his arthritic left hand.

Like so many other Colts from the glory years, he had found work in Baltimore, and stayed after his career was over, even after the disappointment of several failed business ventures, and the disillusionment of the Colts leaving town in 1984.

Unitas was still working in Baltimore when the Ravens began play in 1996. He bore no grudge against Art Modell, and when the owner invited him to the games, Unitas came. He'd often stand on the sidelines, and acknowledge the roar of the crowd when his image was flashed on the huge video screen.

The Ravens were the new home team, but Baltimore's heart still belonged to the old Colts and Johnny Unitas.

When asked about the modern game, Unitas told the truth as he saw it. "It's become show business—high-five, low-five, dancing on the sidelines, slapping, you know, jumping in the stands. And television promotes it. And they're great players—take nothing away from anybody as far as the players are concerned. But all that's not necessary. Don't know what to do about it. I mean that's the way it is." Though he disagreed with their means of expression, he was careful not to seem resentful. "I don't blame the kids for getting the money," he said. "It's there to get. I mean, first time that you falter or you have a bad year, you're out of there. The owner doesn't care—there's no loyalty lost in the National Football League."

Unitas had played in a period before football players became millionaires, but even if he'd been independently wealthy, work seemed embedded in his personality. He rose above the poverty of his youth, but never forgot it. Upon losing to Unitas and the Colts in 1965, the Vikings' coach Norm Van Brocklin explained the result by saying, "We should've won, but Unitas is a guy who knows what it was to eat potato soup seven days a week as a kid. That's what beat us."

What was true in Unitas's day was equally true in the modern age. "If one truism ever existed in sports," said the Giants' longtime GM George Young, "it's that hungry players are better players. Sports is socioeconomic." At the turn of the twenty-first century, football would become, more than ever before, a story about the tenacious children of unemployment, poverty, and divorce fighting their way to a better life. Unitas and many of those who remained in the game recognized the timeless quality of the hunger of the dispossessed, that the players who made it to the pro level were often the ones most desperate to succeed.

That presented new challenges for teams, not just in interviewing but managing players. "You have to have the foresight nowadays to know where the problems are coming from, and you have to avoid them," said Bill Parcells, whose teams were noted for having a stronger surveillance and security presence than almost any other team. "It is difficult because the owners have never tried to survive in this world. This is a different culture you're dealing with here. These kids coming out of gangs, the streets, this is a whole different culture."

If the culture they were coming from was different, so was the one they were entering. For decades, of course, football players found themselves fending off the advances of sycophants, shady businessmen, unscrupulous agents, and would-be friends who would, as the Steelers' Joe Gilliam vividly put it in 1973, "seem sincere and all the time they're planning to fuck your mama and blow you up too." In the '90s, with the heightened profile of players, and the remarkable amount of money they were making, those pressures intensified and multiplied.

From 1993 to 2002, the league increased funding for its rookie seminar and player development program fourfold to help players better cope with the pressures. The change was equally dramatic among clubs. In 1992, the Chiefs became the first team to hire a full-time employee in the area of player development. A decade later, every team in the league had at least one person on the job. Their tasks included everything from financial advice to anger-management counseling, and reflected the heightened stakes for the teams.

In the modern NFL, a vast majority of coaches and administrators were white, while a vast majority of players, about 70 percent, were black. While that led to an inevitable cultural divide, it also resulted in an increased awareness of what it took to excel in the game. On the field, the racial stereotypes of blacks as gifted but undisciplined athletes, and whites as gutty, cerebral competitors often was turned on its head.

"Look, white kids are riding around in their mama's air-conditioned SUVs, eating Twinkies," said the longtime pro player and college coach Bill Curry. "The African-American kids are out there busting it in the heat, they're hungry. There are far more of these kids who come out of tough circumstances, who live and watch their mama work three full-time jobs trying to feed five brothers and sisters by herself with the grandmother helping to raise them and the great-grandmother involved too and they turn out tough, hungry, young people."

"I was at Stanford, and that's a great place to coach and it was an enjoyable place to recruit and you interacted with a great class of people," said Brian Billick, the onetime Bill Walsh assistant who became the head coach of the Ravens in 1999. "But one of the difficulties at Stanford was, you had in large part a bunch of kids who, when it's fourth-and-goal on the one-yard line against Notre Dame, know in the back of their mind, 'You know, if this doesn't work out, I'm going to be okay anyway. I'm going to go make my money, I'm going to have my career, I'm going to have my Stanford degree.' And that's all well and true, and in the bigger perspective that's the way it should be. But at that point, I want them to have a little bit more at stake. Kids from less-advantaged backgrounds take more of that perspective. 'This is my way out.' "

The players who arrived into the league in the '90s entered a world in flux. The advent of free agency and the salary cap jolted many of the game's cherished assumptions about how teams ought to be constructed, how much time that building could be expected to take, and how long it might last.

The expansion teams' quick rise was the best indicator of the radically altered world of the modern game. In the previous expansion in 1976, the Seattle Seahawks and Tampa Bay Buccaneers joined the NFL and won nine games over their first two seasons. In 1995, the Carolina Panthers and Jacksonville Jaguars joined the NFL and won thirty-five games over their first two seasons, both advancing to their conference championship games in 1996. The Packers' president and GM, Ron Wolf, who'd been there for the agonizing twenty-six straight losses at the beginning of the Tampa Bay franchise, refused to refer to Carolina and Jacksonville as expansion teams—"free agency teams" was the term he used—but by any other name, their effect was equally profound. "What they did in two years changed the whole landscape of this game forever and ever," Wolf said. "You don't have time now. If you're not successful, they kick your ass out and someone else comes in, because you have to be successful. That old adage you have to crawl before you can walk? Well, they strutted in."

Though history will record the beginning of free agency as 1993 and the first year of the salary cap as 1994, the true impact of the structure wasn't felt until a few years later, once the residual effect of earlier seasons' bonuses and contracts took their toll on successive years. The rise of the Panthers and Jags showed how quickly teams could be built. And the eventual demise of the Cowboys and 49ers, the two teams that spent much of the '90s vying for the title of Team of the Decade, showed how quickly the powers could disintegrate.

Those two teams had used lengthy contracts, creative financing—in the 49ers' case, *too* creative, resulting in a fine from the league office—and the stockpile of dominating talent they had built up in the early '90s to postpone the inevitable cap hit as long as possible. But in 1999, the hit arrived. The Cowboys, who backed into the playoffs with an 8-8 record, were a shell of their former dominating selves. Months after they'd won their third title in four seasons, wide receiver Michael Irvin was arrested for cocaine possession. Irvin's transgression turned out to be the most explosive in the larger story of the meltdown of America's Team. From late 1995 to late 1996, the NFL suspended twelve players for drug abuse, and six of them were Cowboys. In pleading not guilty to the charge of drug possession in a Dallas courtroom,

Irvin displayed an astounding amount of hubris—he showed up to his grand jury hearing in a full-length mink coat—and opened the door for a series of other sordid allegations. Through that and other trials came tales of the exploits of many of the Cowboys' players, who had rented a large mansion—"the White House," they called it—to entertain women. "We've got a little place over here where we're running some whores in and out, trying to be responsible, and we're criticized for that, too," complained a vexed Nate Newton. Players conducting extramarital affairs were nothing new (Jim Brown wrote about a similar residence, called "Headquarters," used by some of the Browns in the '60s), but widespread coverage of the event was, and further intensified the storm of coverage surrounding the club.

The 1999 season was just a stop on the way down to the first of three consecutive 5-11 seasons in 2000. By 2001, the Cowboys were a shambles, devoting more than one third of their payroll to "dead money," bonuses paid to players who were no longer with the team. The stockpile of draft choices the team built in the early '90s was gone, as was the scouting and coaching acumen of Jimmy Johnson.

And the 49ers, after a sixteen-season run in which they averaged more than twelve wins per year, and never won fewer than ten, hit a salary cap wall in 1999, dropping to 4-12. Because of choices they'd made in the mid-'90s, neither team was competitive at the end of the decade. But Dallas had added three Super Bowl trophies and San Francisco one, and both clubs felt the hardware justified the later hardships.

With the self-destruction of the great Cowboys power and the end of the 49ers' great run, the notion of the dynasty in pro football was all but over. Green Bay advanced to consecutive Super Bowls in the 1996 and 1997 seasons, winning one, before retreating later in the decade. Denver won back-to-back titles in 1997 and 1998, after which John Elway retired and the Broncos didn't win a playoff game for the next five years.

For the teams that got close but *didn't* win the Super Bowl—Buffalo, Kansas City, Pittsburgh, and Philadelphia most prominent among them—the fallout was all the more painful. Buffalo's dominating team wouldn't return to the Super Bowl after their fourth straight loss following the 1993 season, and would be forever marked—however unfairly—by their failure rather than their accomplishment. After the third Super Bowl loss, a writer saw Bills GM Bill Polian and asked if he felt depressed. "Try wounded beyond recognition," said Polian.

At first glance, it seemed as though the new economic system would make the draft less important, since there would be another method to acquire premium players. But when teams became disillusioned with the performance of their high-priced acquisitions, they came to realize that good drafts were still crucial. Not only did a draft bust hurt a club's talent level the year he arrived, but the contract he signed could impair a team's ability to sign other good players for years to come.

In this new environment, it was logical that many of the people who'd risen through the football ranks in personnel departments—Carl Peterson in Kansas City, Ron Wolf in Green Bay, Bobby Beathard in San Diego, Charley Armey in St. Louis—found themselves running not just scouting departments but entire teams. Few were better at it than Polian, the ginger-haired, hot-tempered former scout who'd built the Bills' dominant early-'90s team, then went to Carolina and turned the expansion Panthers into a championship contender in two years. After clashing with Panthers owner Jerry Richardson in the 1997 season, Polian left to take the job as president and general manager of the Indianapolis Colts, who after the brief illusory hopes of their 1995 trip to the AFC championship game had plummeted to a 3-13 season by 1997.

Polian's first big decision would be a crucial one, typifying the high stakes of the modern game: Indianapolis owned the first pick in the 1998 draft and would get to choose between two blue-chip quarterbacks. Tennessee's Peyton Manning, the son of longtime pro Archie, was a coach's player, a beast in the film room whose techniques were advanced and whose makeup seemed designed with the job of a pro quarterback in mind. Manning had been so well known for so long that some felt he'd been overrated, due to his family heritage and his prominent position as a four-year starter for the Vols. Washington State's rangy Ryan Leaf, who had the prototypical physique for pro pocket passer, was thought by most scouts to be slightly less polished but with a significantly higher upside.

Had they gone only on the game scouting of the previous fall, the Colts likely would have selected Leaf. In the months leading up to the draft, Polian spent roughly 500 hours analyzing the comparative strengths of the two quarterbacks. He and his staff watched each of Manning's 1,505 college passes and each of Leaf's 880 throws, viewing the 1997 passes twice over again. And from that epic instance of overanalysis—as well as the team's personal interviews, psychological and intelligence testing, and comprehensive physical exams—came a deeper level of understanding and, ultimately, the right choice.

"From a pure scouting standpoint, you would have taken Leaf in a heartbeat," said Polian. "Now, as it turns out, when you really got into analysis, even the physical, there were perceptions about Manning that were untrue. There were perceptions about Leaf that were untrue, but your eye sees what it sees and your ear hears what it hears, so scouts came back and said, 'Manning has a weak arm.' When you analyzed every pass they threw for the years that they were in school, that wasn't true. But no scout has the ability to do that. You can only do that in the off-season when you can put together all the film. I remember remarking to [Colts offensive coordinator] Tom Moore how astounded I was by the fact that Peyton threw a heavier ball with many more revolutions per second than Leaf. Even the physical part of it, the initial reports were wrong and the conventional wisdom and hype was one hundred percent wrong."

Indianapolis chose Manning, who started from the first game of his rookie season, winning Rookie of the Year honors. A year later, Polian's trade of Marshall Faulk to St. Louis for the draft pick that became Edgerrin James, allowed him to combine the talent of James, Manning, and wide receiver Marvin Harrison in the same explosive package. Indy went to the playoffs in 1999 and under Polian developed the look of a perennial contender. When the Bucs fired Tony Dungy after a playoff loss in 2001, Polian quickly hired him to help add stability and a solid defense to one of the most dangerous offenses in the league.

Leaf, taken with the second pick by the San Diego Chargers and signed to a five-year contract valued at $31.25 million, proved moody and petulant. He suffered three abysmal seasons in San Diego, before the Chargers swallowed the salary cap hit by releasing him in 2001. He was out of pro football a year later. But the team was still suffering the effects of the Leaf draft in 2002, when Schottenheimer took over as San Diego's head coach.

While the stakes with other picks weren't as high, divining who would succeed in professional football remained a central and complicated task with every selection. In Schottenheimer's mind, the great unknown was how each player would respond to those pressures. "If someone could provide some kind of reliable indicator of how young men would deal with these three factors—1) More adoration and recognition than they've ever been used to receiving before, 2) More unsupervised time than they've ever had in their lives, and 3) More money than they've ever had in their life—if you could find a psychological test that could give you a reliable sense of how people would respond to those three factors, you could probably eliminate about 75 percent of the mistakes in the draft."

The rise of player development led some coaches to feel that any player could be molded into a solid citizen and a conscientious football player. But experience taught coaches differently. "They usually don't change very much once they get here," said Tony Dungy. What was required to excel was an all-encompassing commitment to the game, and in virtually every case, a pro player who succeeded did so by dedicating himself to the profession.

"You can't live soft and fight hard," said the All-Pro defensive tackle Warren Sapp, whose gift of hyperbole often obscured a savage work ethic and deep-seated respect for the game. "You have to program yourself. It doesn't just happen; it ain't a switch that you turn on and turn off as you walk through the door of the complex. I mean, I live, read, eat, sleep, shit football. That's *me*. That's what I do. And if you don't do that, then this game is gonna eat you up and devour you."

In July 1999, Paul Tagliabue, making his annual tour of selected NFL training camps, stopped at the St. Louis Rams' camp in Macomb, Illinois. Addressing the players after practice, he gave his boilerplate speech. "You've got the greatest, most popular league in the world," he told the assembled players. "You've got a phenomenal opportunity. There's tremendous competitive balance. No matter where you were last year, you can win it this year. If you win it, you'll be on top of the world. Make sure you don't screw it up by doing something dumb off the field, or by letting down on the field."

The idea of winning it all seemed slightly outlandish to the Rams, the decade's losingest franchise, and who'd gone 4-12 in 1998. At the beginning of the third season of Dick Vermeil's second go-round in professional coaching, many were convinced that the Rams' hiring of Vermeil had been a mistake. Vermeil's family-type atmosphere had been unable to rescue the dysfunctional slide of troubled running back Lawrence Phillips, and his inability to mold quarterback Tony Banks into a more mature quarterback (he'd neglected off-season workouts in favor of basketball) seemed likely to spell his doom.

Though the Rams had done little to merit the sellout crowds that greeted them at the TWA Dome in their first years there, they looked outstanding in early preseason action. They'd acquired versatile running back Marshall Faulk in a draft day trade, grabbed wideout Torry Holt in the draft, and signed quarterback Trent Green, a St. Louis native, in free agency. Hopes were high in the preseason, where Green connected on twenty-eight of his first thirty-two attempts, until a late hit by Chargers safety Rodney Harrison demolished Green's left knee and knocked him out for the season. Vermeil, weeping over the injury to Green, vowed that his team would soldier on, "and we'll play good football with Kurt Warner." But the mood of any team that loses a starting quarterback in the preseason is dour, and many thought the Rams had lost their chance to make a dramatic improvement.

"I remember talking to Dick Vermeil in the season opener," said Brian Billick, then coaching his first game as the head coach of the Baltimore Ravens.
"And he was talking about hoping that this Arena League quarterback they
had could hang in long enough for them to get Paul Justin in and schooled in
the offense. I mean, no one had any idea."

Green's backup, a journeyman quarterback from Northern Iowa named
Kurt Warner, had charted an improbable course toward an NFL job. After a
middling college career, he'd signed as a free agent and been released by the
Packers in 1994 (winding up back in Cedar Falls, working out during the day,
stocking shelves at a Hy-Vee grocery store by night), spent three years with the
Arena League's Iowa Barnstormers, playing well but earning little interest
from NFL teams, before playing in the World League of American Football
and finally latching on as the number three quarterback for the Rams in 1998.
Going into the 1999 season, one scouting report said of Warner: "A 2-year
journeyman type . . . has good size and arm strength . . . shows good touch on
short to intermediate . . . has some trouble reading coverages . . . will force
some balls . . . will make a lot of mistakes."

Instead, from his first start, Warner proved to be the best quarterback in
the league. He completed 325 of 499 passes (65.1 percent) for 4,353 yards, 41
touchdowns, just 13 interceptions, and a 109.2 quarterback rating, en route to
the league's MVP award. "He's in a zone, and I've never been around anybody
who's this hot," said Vermeil late in the season. "Georgia Frontiere believes in
astrology; maybe that's the only way to explain it." The scouting report on
Warner turned out to be spectacularly wrong. The Rams, 4-12 in 1998, ripped
through the first six games without a loss, and posted a 13-3 record en route to
the number one seed in the NFC.

After two home wins in the playoffs, St. Louis went to the Super Bowl,
where they outlasted Tennessee in a 23–16 game that ended with the Titans'
wideout Kevin Dyson tackled on the St. Louis one-yard line. In the space of
four months, the least successful team of the decade had been transformed
into the best team in pro football, led by a quarterback and league MVP who'd
been considered a career backup at best.

Warner's success was more proof of the complexity of identifying talent at
pro football's most difficult position. "Most new quarterbacks don't get the
opportunity unless they're a first round pick or a high draft choice," said Vermeil. "They sit and watch somebody else do it, and they maybe never get the
chance. Certainly Kurt Warner went beyond my expectations, but I think first
off we gave him the opportunity and the other thing we gave him is the belief

he could do it. And then we backed him. I think if a kid really knows you believe in him, it gives him an opportunity to believe in himself."

Though Warner would seem to have little in common with the African-Americans who were dominating the game, one theme resonated. Even for the country kid in Cedar Falls, the game was a way out of his circumstances and toward a measure of self-esteem: "Sports were my refuge, my social life, and for a long time my salvation," he wrote in his autobiography. "Part of the reason I excelled is because I was blessed with athletic ability, but the biggest secrets of my success were the obvious ones: I worked my butt off, and I cared more about being the best than anyone else I knew."

———

By the beginning of the twenty-first century the chasm between those on the field and the rest of the football universe was widening.

"The simple fact is, when you step across the line you're in a different world," said Will Shields, the Chiefs' Pro Bowl guard. "Basically, we're gladiators that play on Sunday, we're guys that, they want you to be the nicest and sweetest people off the field, and yet on Sunday, go out and try to basically rip somebody's head off, play in and play out. And so to balance that, you can see it could be a difficult thing to do. But I've been doing it so long that it's become a habit."

The margin for error for players had decreased, and the level of criticism, through blanket coverage in the traditional media, as well as the opinion-heavy forum of talk radio and the Internet, had increased exponentially.

And so the belief that only those who played football could truly understand it, flowed in concentric circles outward from the heart of the action, even on the field. The Washington Redskins' powerful offensive line of the '80s, the Hogs, made running back John Riggins an honorary member. But when quarterback Joe Theismann asked for membership, he was denied. Nor were quarterbacks beyond petulant dismissals of their own. Apprised of a quote by kicker Mike Vanderjagt alleging that the Colts of 2002 lacked fire, Peyton Manning dismissed the comments as the ravings of an "idiot kicker."

When the Packers' coach, Mike Sherman, approached Warren Sapp after Sapp's legal but merciless blindside hit on Chad Clifton, which ended Clifton's season in 2002, Sapp's first response to Sherman was "Fuck you!" When the beef continued, Sapp repeatedly exhorted Sherman, "Put a jersey on!"

And off the field, proximity to the game was still important. After a grilling from the media following a New Orleans Saints loss in 1996, coach Jim Mora became fed up at the second-guessing of another reporter, and interjected, "You don't know when it's good or bad. You really don't know. You guys don't look at the film, you don't know what happened. You really don't know. *You think you know,* but you don't know. And—you—never—will."

When one is tested as persistently and judged as relentlessly as a professional football player—whose every assignment is part of a coordinated, interconnected thrust, each one involving a form of hand-to-hand physical combat—little is more maddening than an outsider blithely critiquing a performance. And the complexity of the modern game made any snap judgment risky.

"You know, people ask me right after the game, 'What happened on that play?' " said Bill Polian, "and I can't honestly tell them. I know the playbook, but I have to go through the film the next day, then find out from the coaches what the defensive call was, then talk to one or two of the players and ask them what *they* remember from the play—'Who did you think you were covering?' 'Who did you think had this guy?'—and then, after all that, I *might* be able to figure out what went wrong. And even then, I'm not going to publicly say who was responsible."

Thus one had the great conundrum of pro football's popularity: fans, without access to the team's playbook, scouting reports, game plans, and game films, aren't really given the tools to perfectly understand their team's actions and responses. Faced with this tremendous reservoir of insularity, there was little for the public or the media to do. The game's inherent structure resisted transparency. Football was surely the only sport where a longtime serious fan—one who knew the players by number and sight, had followed the philosophy of the coaching staff, and understood the talents of its players—could be placed in his favorite team's locker room at halftime yet still have virtually no idea what the players and coaches were discussing. Or as David Plotz put it in an essay on football in *The New Republic,* "Baseball fans think their sport is complex because they can understand it. Football fans know their sport is complex because they can't."

In the fortunes of the Baltimore Ravens in 2000, one could find many of the realities of the modern era of football brought into sharp relief. While the city had welcomed the Ravens in 1996, it did not instantly embrace them. On December 14, 1997, for the final game at Memorial Stadium, the Ravens invited seventy former Colts greats, who were dressed in vintage jerseys and introduced throughout the Ravens' 21–19 win over Tennessee. After the game, Unitas led his teammates out for one more play. He took the snap and handed off to Tom Matte, who gave the ball to Lenny Moore, who ran it in for a touchdown.

The following year, in the clumsily named PSI.Net Stadium (the title sponsor would soon go out of business in the dot-com bust), the Ravens hosted the Indianapolis Colts. Ted Patterson, the author of the memoir *Football in Baltimore,* noted the unsettling circumstances: "It was bizarre seeing the familiar blue-and-white-clad, horseshoe-helmeted Colts as the enemy in the town that had idolized and loved them with such passion; Johnny Unitas, the soul of the Baltimore Colts, stood on the sidelines and rooted against them like all the other Baltimore fans. And the former Cleveland Browns, now the Baltimore Ravens, were being cheered, while their owner, Art Modell, was still reviled in Cleveland."

In the late '90s, the league again found itself battling the public perception that many of its players were out of control. O. J. Simpson's celebrated murder case had put the subject of football players' behavior back in the news, and several other incidents intensified the scrutiny, from Irvin's drug bust to Lawrence Phillips's assault and battery charge to more serious charges: the Seahawks' Brian Blades was charged with murder in 1995, though a judge threw out his manslaughter conviction. The Panthers' Rae Carruth was charged with murdering (and later convicted of a lesser charge of conspiring to murder) the mother of his unborn child in 1999. Cases like these not only besmirched the game, but fed the belief that football players were more violent *because* they played a violent game.

It was a problem the league had seen growing for years. In 1998's *Pros and Cons: The Criminals Who Play in the NFL,* investigative reporters Jeff Benedict and Don Yaeger argued that one in five active players had committed a major crime. Though the league took issue with Benedict and Yaeger's numbers, arguing that the incidence of incarceration was less than that of a similarly aged group of men in the general public, the public perception was becoming clear.

The Carruth charges were a hot topic in January 2000, when Tagliabue, in his annual press conference two days prior to the Super Bowl, remarked, "We can't predict when players might snap, and besides, most players are really good guys." Two nights later, Ray Lewis—the first draft choice in the history of the Baltimore Ravens—would become involved in the sport's next crime drama.

Lewis was exactly the sort of player that Bill Curry had described—raised on the hard streets of Lakeland, Florida, with an absent father, a mother who worked three jobs, and the responsibility of taking care of his four younger siblings. He had attended the University of Miami, where his closest friend, roommate Marlin Barnes, was murdered. Two other close friends had died in the '90s, and Lewis had tattoos honoring each.

Upon arriving in the NFL, represented by the pugnacious agent Drew Rosenhaus, Lewis immediately became one of the best young players in the game, leading the league in tackles in two of his first four seasons. Off the field, there was much about Lewis's life to trouble his team and mainstream fans alike. The team had been growing increasingly nervous about his friendships.

On Super Bowl night, in a parking lot outside the Atlanta nightclub Cobalt, Lewis and two friends were involved in an altercation with two other men who were knifed to death. Lewis spent the off-season facing a double-murder charge, before agreeing to testify for the prosecution in exchange for a reduced charge of obstruction of justice (he'd been uncooperative and sarcastic in his early interviews with police). For his involvement in the incident and the behavior afterward, he was fined a record sum of $250,000 by Tagliabue, but allowed to return to action in the 2000 season.

With that as the backdrop, the team's defense played with a controlled fury worthy of the best defensive teams in the NFL. Their potent two-gap defensive scheme was anchored by tackle Tony Siragusa and by a punishing secondary, while the passionate, driven Lewis roamed the field in the best tradition of Butkus and Lanier. En route to winning the league's Defensive Player of the Year award, Lewis stayed largely silent during the season, though he did sound off in an as-told-to *ESPN The Magazine* cover story, in which he criticized Tagliabue for the stiff fine.

From the day Lewis was charged, his cause and character were defended by Ravens head coach Brian Billick. Tall, articulate, and self-assured, Billick was the sort of obviously intelligent man whose manner struck some people as *too* self-assured. The all-conference tight end from Brigham Young had failed to stick in tryouts with the 49ers and Cowboys before turning to coaching (and serving for two seasons in the publicity department for Walsh's 49ers). After a decade in the college coaching ranks, he returned to the pros for good for Dennis Green in Minnesota, and was perhaps the man most responsible for the widespread rush in the '90s to hands-on computer use by coaching staffs.

For all his mastery of the game's technical details, Billick's hidden strength was his undersstanding of the modern athlete, and he was the right man to lead the Ravens through the accusations and distractions of the 2000 season, when—owing largely to outrage over Lewis's behavior and the lingering resentment of Modell—the Ravens would be one of the most widely disliked teams to compete in the Super Bowl. The team's offense atrophied during the season, and quarterback Tony Banks was benched in favor of veteran backup Trent Dilfer. Billick had the good sense to adapt his own pass-first style to the talents of the team, and the Ravens ground out a series of close wins, including two road victories, the second in the playoffs, over division rival Tennessee.

In the buildup to the Super Bowl, Billick was combative and standoffish, earning a share of criticism but deflecting some of the harsh glare from the media's scrutiny of Lewis. The linebacker still faced up to the inevitable grilling on Media Day five days before the game. His lack of contrition only raised the heat. "I'm not here to please you," Lewis told the press. "If I'm an average Joe, none of you all are here. Now that's how really simple it is."

The Super Bowl featured another dominant performance from the Ravens' defense, and Lewis would be named MVP. But his most memorable moment came during the pregame introductions. After a year of personal turmoil, Lewis emerged from the tunnel of Raymond James Stadium like a rap star. He came on the field with a kind of staccato, gesticulating tribal dance, standing on his tiptoes, thrusting his hips, preening and high-stepping in a strutting, controlled rage, while cheers and boos washed over him like a baptism for his year in the wilderness. For many traditional sports fans, the gesture was not merely disquieting but offensive.

Yet no less of an expert than Jim Brown—no fan of onfield histrionics— gave him his seal of approval. "I like Ray Lewis because he's the ultimate team player," said Brown. "He's the ultimate example of a man that will study tremendously, and his being a student of the game comes out more than his physical way because in his pass defense he knows where to go. And he inspires the rest of his team."

The Ravens trounced the Giants, 34–7, completing Lewis's astonishing journey from facing a double-murder charge the weekend of one Super Bowl to being named MVP of the next one. But it was Trent Dilfer, not Lewis, who was asked to do the "I'm going to Disney World" spot that traditionally went to the game's MVP. And it was five other Ravens defenders, but not Lewis, who were featured on the cover of the following season's NFL Record and Fact Book. "After the episode in Atlanta," said NFL spokesman Greg Aiello, "we were just going to stay away from him."

The following summer, when Billick agreed to let an NFL Films crew gain unprecedented access to the Ravens' camp, for an HBO series called Hard Knocks, it gave further insight into the life of a football player. Lewis emerged as a complex character, both raffish in nature and, true to Jim Brown's words, dedicated to the game.

By the 2003 season, Lewis had become one of the most visible players in the league, a staple of NFL Films highlight packages, a constant presence in ads for EA Sports video games, and when Reebok wanted to use Lewis in an NFL apparel ad, the league consented. In the spring of 2001, he had addressed a rapt audience of players at the rookie seminar, and told them to choose their friends wisely.

More than one commentator remarked upon the large moral gap between Baltimore's previous football hero, Unitas, and its new one, Ray Lewis. But the easy generalizations shed little light. And it was ultimately left to Jim Brown to provide a sense of perspective. Asked whether the modern players could measure up to the greats of his era, he said, "I recognize that the game has to evolve, and I don't necessarily disagree with that. My car is a '69 Mercedes 280 SC—it's a classic car, and it's great for what it is. But it can't compare to all the technical things that you'll find in a 2000 car. And the kids don't want no classics. So I like the quality of the game in my day, but I recognize the brilliance of the athletes today. And I respect them."

What emerged from the Super Bowls following the 1999 and 2000 seasons was not just a fluctuating, turbulent new order in the competitive balance of the league, but something else, not quite apposite, about the match-ups.

Had the Rams and Titans stayed in Los Angeles and Houston, the two teams would have brought a history of more than ninety years in their respective cities into the game. Instead the Rams had been in St. Louis for just five seasons, and the itinerant Titans (who played in Memphis in 1997) had been playing home games in Nashville for just two seasons. It was an electrifying football game, but for longtime fans it lacked a measure of drama, because the civic identification with both teams was still in its infancy.

"Can you imagine if someone had just been in a coma for three years, and just came out of it?" said Ron Wolf in 2000. "Hey let's watch the Super Bowl—it's the *St. Louis* Rams against someone called the Tennessee Titans? You'd think you were in a foreign country. You'd think it was soccer or something."

The following year was equally jarring. It featured New York and Baltimore were vying for a title again, just as the cities had in the watershed 1958 title game. But Super Bowl XXXV didn't evoke the Giants-Colts classic (because the Ravens weren't the Colts), nor did it echo the storied showdowns between the Giants and the Browns (because Art Modell notwithstanding, the Ravens weren't the Browns, either).

In his classic study of spectator sports, *Sports Illusion, Sports Reality,* the writer Leonard Koppett identified seven key elements that distinguished spectator sports from other forms of entertainment. The second was continuity ("In sports, the relationship to earlier events is automatic, almost always present in the forefront of consciousness, and part of the melodrama that is unfolding); the fourth was coherence (for the sports fan, "everything is orderly and definite . . . sports offer an island of stability in a confusing, shifting cosmos"). But the '90s had proved just how fragile these concepts of continuity and coherence could be. So in Baltimore, St. Louis, and Cleveland, fans had football teams again. But it wasn't, couldn't ever be, quite the same.

24

Man at the Top

Nearly sixty years after the Los Angeles Rams opened their first season in California, the Los Angeles Coliseum stood in stately desolation, from every angle a reminder of a time gone by.

One could walk around the vast expanse of the Coliseum and survey the neglected grandeur of the massive cement bowl, surrounded by chain link fencing topped with barbed wire, its vast exterior walls trimmed in the faded pastels of the 1984 Olympic Games. Inside, the Coliseum still possessed its old charm, and at the peristyle end of the stadium, on the Coliseum pillars, aged in bronze, was the Coliseum's Wall of Champions. The entry for Dan Reeves read:

OWNER AND PRESIDENT
LOS ANGELES RAMS, 1941–1971
PIONEERED PROFESSIONAL SPORTS
IN THE WEST
LOYALTY, INTEGRITY AND HUMANITY
CAME WITH HIM

As pro football rode triumphantly into the twenty-first century, the same market that summoned Reeves and helped spark the first signs of postwar growth stood empty once again. And the game as Reeves experienced it—the tidy profits, the small staffs, the collegial competition among sportsman owners, and the sense of light, effortless spectacle—was virtually gone. The curious case of the Los Angeles market underscored, better than anything, how the business of football had changed.

Few expected the NFL's absence from the city to last so long. Each of the other major leagues had two franchises in the Los Angeles area, and as soon as the Raiders and Rams vacated the city, the NFL announced its intention to replace them with at least one franchise. In 1999, even as the Raiders were (again) suing the league, alleging that the NFL had sabotaged a favorable stadium deal in Hollywood Park that would have kept them in the Los Angeles area, the NFL awarded a provisional thirty-second franchise to the market, giving the city six months to secure financing for improvements to the Coliseum.

The prospect was irresistible: a refurbished Coliseum serving as the jewel of a renovated Exposition Park that already included broad sweeps of manicured lawns and cultural magnets, like the Natural History Museum of Los Angeles, the California African American Museum, and the California Science Center. But as the deadline neared, it became apparent that no real money was forthcoming. California was fighting a deepening financial crisis, and neither the city of Los Angeles nor the state of California would put forth public funds for stadium improvements. But by 1999, the National Football League was long past *giving* away franchises. While politicians charged the NFL with seeking "corporate welfare," Houston businessman Robert McNair had lined up funding for a retractable roof stadium in Houston. On October 6, three weeks after the deadline for L.A. had expired, the NFL granted its thirty-second franchise to McNair, and the Houston Texans were born, at a price of $700 million. Just a decade earlier, franchises were selling for a tenth as much.

Awarding the thirty-second franchise to Houston left Los Angeles out in the cold. It also foreshadowed a potentially epic fight in the future. In San Diego, Minneapolis, Indianapolis, and New Orleans, discussions of new stadiums for existing NFL teams all carried the implicit weight of the empty Los Angeles market. With no expansion planned in the foreseeable future, there was just one move left.

As media outlets and delivery systems multiplied in the late '90s, ratings for virtually all sports—in fact all network entertainment—dipped significantly. Yet pro football's numbers remained strong. As cable television and the Internet divided America into hundreds of narrowly defined discrete audiences, the league's primacy became even more pronounced. This led, in 1998, to another staggering television contract, an eight-year, $18.1 billion deal that would by 2005 generate $84 million per year for each club. After the deal was announced, Fox's David Hill proclaimed, "The NFL represents the only firm ground in an increasingly scary swamp. It is the one safe bet, the one thing in the network business that makes sense."

In the first decade of his tenure, Paul Tagliabue had smartly tended to that firm and fertile ground. In addition to the best labor relations agreement in pro sports, Tagliabue had secured the toughest drug- and steroids-testing programs among the leagues, and had ushered in an era of widespread revenue growth, all while keeping faith with the league's organizing principles of competitive balance. The league's successes were all the more dramatic for the context in which they occurred. Major League Baseball emerged from its World Series–killing 1994 work stoppage with its financial model more skewed than ever before, and in the following years, both the NBA and NHL lost portions of their seasons due to labor unrest.

Meanwhile, the NFL was able to keep much of the unseemly public squabbling over money out of the news, while the league's ancillary business grew markedly. This was thanks in part to the business guidance of president Neil Austrian, the investment banker who served from 1991 to 1999 as the league's chief financial officer. Austrian's late-'80s brainstorm of *NFL Sunday Ticket*—which showed out-of-market games at a premium price to satellite dish owners—finally launched in 1995 and grew quickly, generating additional revenue from fans who wanted a wider choice of games than that offered by their local TV affiliates. The same year, the NFL was the first to establish an Internet presence, with NFL.com, which would rapidly grow into one of the most popular Web addresses in sport. The league, already a leading licenser of console system video game sports simulations (EA Sports's *John Madden NFL Football* sold over 30 million units by 2004), would later become the first league to embrace fantasy sports (a crucial element in helping football pass baseball as the most popular fantasy sport), and throughout the decade remained the most popular marketer of licensed sports apparel.

Among the most important, but least understood, of the NFL's new initiatives was the league's G-3 stadium financing program, formalized in 1999, which helped stop the flow of franchise free agency and ushered in an era of widespread growth of new, revenue-rich stadiums. Through the G-3 program, the league could advance member clubs up to 50 percent (or $150 million) of the amount the club had committed as a private contribution to any public-private stadium projects.

On the strength of the league's heightened business profile and the twenty new stadiums built or refurbished since 1993, the NFL's revenues had doubled in the space of five years, to nearly $5 billion in 2002. But success has many parents, and if Paul Tagliabue no longer had to constantly cope with crises, his challenge in the twenty-first century would be to maintain the fragile equilibrium in which the league enjoyed its prosperity. That would prove, in its own way, as much of a challenge as the often traumatic previous decade had been.

———

Despite his largely successful record, Tagliabue began the second decade of his commissionership as still a largely unknown quantity to the general public, less publicized than NBA honcho David Stern, less demonized than Major League Baseball commissioner Bud Selig. Pete Rozelle's successor seemed destined to become one of those people whose public persona was largely at odds with the real person.

He was universally respected around the office, and his closest lieutenants—executive vice presidents Harold Henderson, Joe Browne, Jeff Pash, and Roger Goodell, as well as vice president of communications Greg Aiello—treated him with affectionate deference. They spoke of his essential decency, his indifference to the trappings of power, his even-handed leadership. They'd long ago stopped trying to match his fierce work rate and omnivorous reading habits. As Joe Browne told staffers, "When Paul asks you if you've read something in the *Times,* just nod your head yes, then go back to your office and find it." The owners respected him enough that by 2004 his annual compensation package was $8.5 million.

Publicly, though, Tagliabue still didn't seem to connect, and his lawyer's background often got the best of him. In interviews, he gave little insight to his own feelings, and seemed impatient with reporters who were less informed than he, which was to say virtually all reporters. In press conferences, he often spoke in platitudes, and could seem either arch or hopelessly square by turns, coming off as peevishly argumentative when fielding tough questions.

Yet Tagliabue had proven himself to the caretakers of the game, and many of those old-guard, football-first owners who'd most opposed his election in 1989 were his biggest supporters a decade later. They had learned that Tagliabue understood the eternal verities, and if he was less than adept at dazzling the press, that was a trade-off with which they were gladly willing to live. The key agreements that solidified the league's prosperity in the '90s—from the 210-page collective bargaining agreement to the complex G-3 stadium plan to the excellent drug-testing program—were achieved during long hours of meetings, involving all manner of lawyers, bankers, scientists, and financial analysts, and Tagliabue's special genius was the ability to keep those meetings from completely losing sight of the game as the core concern.

Surveying the state of the league at the end of 2001, Tagliabue was able to articulate a manifesto that was, in the best sense, an extension of the efforts of Bell and Rozelle before him.

"If you understand that you want to have every team in the league with an opportunity to win, then you have to get the players to buy into a system which has a lot of elements of sharing in it," he said. "That includes a salary cap. But you can't get the players to accept that unless you have a mirror image on the ownership side.

"Now, if you allow the revenue side of the structure to change in fundamental ways, then the whole structure will change in fundamental ways, including what the players are prepared to accept. If you end up having have-nots and haves when it comes to revenue, you end up having have-nots and haves when it comes to talent. And then you have a league with a product that is less attractive, and you've started a downward spiral. At this point, I know that as well as I know my family tree."

The year that would best demonstrate Tagliabue's leadership was 2001. It began with the potentially divisive issue of realignment, and the league's move from a six- to eight-division setup with the addition of the thirty-second franchise, the Houston Texans, in 2002. The universe of thirty-two clubs had been part of Rozelle's vision at least as far back as the summer of 1969, when in an interview with *Quarterback* magazine, he said, "If the economics of professional football were such that it would be feasible, the ideal number [of teams] would be 32. Then we could have two conferences, 16 teams in each, broken down into four four-team divisions."

But having the teams was one matter, and deciding which divisional alignments they'd go in was something else entirely. The issue provided a microcosm of the commissioner's job, of balancing the competing interests of thirty-two different owners with the game's tradition and the need for some kind of change. It had been one of Rozelle's most intractable problems in 1970, when sixty-five hours of talks at league meetings still yielded no consensus on the NFC's alignment, prompting Rozelle to call on Thelma Elkjer to draw one of five plans out of an office flower vase.

But much debate was blunted in the new round by Tagliabue's successful push to pool all teams' visiting revenues and divide them equally, thus eliminating those variables. After months of public speculation, the actual discussion went easily and the realignment plan passed unanimously. With few exceptions, teams that had been grouped together for decades remained so.

The new scheduling formula that accompanied the realignment was equally well conceived, guaranteeing teams fourteen common games with opponents within their division, and eliminating the lopsided scheduling advantage offered to fifth-place teams in previous seasons. Just weeks later, in mid-June, Tagliabue and Gene Upshaw announced that the league and NFL Players Association had reached a tentative agreement on extending the collective bargaining agreement through 2007, while mitigating one of the problems in the old agreement, the escalating minimum salary requirements based on seniority that were costing many veterans jobs.

The first weekend of the 2001 season culminated with Denver christening its new stadium with a 23–10 win over the Giants on Monday night, September 10. The following morning, at about 6:30 a.m., the Giants' charter from Denver arrived at Newark Airport. The team boarded a bus right on the tarmac, not far from where United Airlines Flight 93 was preparing for its 8:42 departure to San Francisco.

At the league office that morning, Tagliabue was on a conference call with executives of the United Way, discussing the league's charity partnership, as the planes ripped into the World Trade Center. In the wake of the third attack, on the Pentagon near the nation's capital, the conference call was cut short and Tagliabue quickly took stock of the league office, where two employees would lose spouses in the attacks. While many staffers spent the afternoon praying at St. Patrick's Cathedral a block away from the league office, Tagliabue was calling around to the extended NFL family that was closest to the attacks—Upshaw at the NFLPA headquarters in D.C., as well as the staffs of the Giants, Jets, and Redskins.

In the immediate aftermath of the attacks, there was a pronounced division of opinion within the world of sport, which would go unresolved for the next forty-eight hours. On one side, many (especially those who were physically close to the attacks) found the idea of playing games unconscionable. At Giants Stadium, the parking lot was being used as a staging area for the behemoth excavation equipment needed for the Ground Zero rescue effort. But there was a strong minority on the other side of the issue, who felt that canceling games would be an act of capitulation, a sign to terrorists that their acts had been successful. The Giants' player rep Jason Sehorn called Giants GM Ernie Accorsi on Wednesday and explained that, while the players weren't going to issue a public statement, they were unified in their opposition to games that weekend. "We're not playing," said Sehorn.

While many were inevitably looking back at Rozelle's decision to play games two days after John F. Kennedy's assassination in 1963, Tagliabue understood the larger implications. "This is not the Kennedy assassination," he told a conference call of owners. "This is not Pearl Harbor. It's worse."

His decision, written out in his home in the early morning hours Thursday and sent to the clubs that morning, was decisive, eloquent, and respectful: "This week we have witnessed despicable acts. Within our NFL family, loved ones are missing. Such events try our hearts and souls. These events and experiences will deeply affect all of us—not just for now but for years, lifetimes, generations. As a nation and as individuals, we will respond in many ways on many fronts. Supporting, respecting, grieving, learning, becoming closer, more resolute, stronger. We will carry on—not move on and forget—but carry on. . . . We will not play NFL games this weekend."

The league made a public announcement late that morning, and what happened in the ensuing hours was a dramatic demonstration of the weight of the NFL. Tagliabue's decision, in the apt words of *Sports Illustrated*'s Peter King, "gave a waffling sports world its sense of direction." Virtually every other organization fell in line. Major League Baseball announced within hours that it would not play until the following week. College football, caught in a litany of different conference reactions, wiped its Division I-A slate completely clean, with conferences that had announced they would play reversing their field and postponing. Within the afternoon, virtually every other organization in American sports, including the NHL, MLS, LPGA, NASCAR, and IRL all fell into line, canceling games, tournaments, and races in the wake of the NFL's decision.

"The NFL acted first," wrote Thomas Boswell in the *Washington Post*, "which is appropriate since it is clearly America's dominant game, as well as a worldwide symbol of the country."

When the league resumed play on Sunday, September 23, it had, for the first time ever, completely lifted its blackout rule (as an accommodation to fans still fearful about attending a public event). Tagliabue and Upshaw were in Kansas City, where the Chiefs were playing host to the New York Giants, who surely became the first visiting team in the history of Arrowhead Stadium to receive a standing ovation during pregame introductions.

Tagliabue, with his background in the Pentagon and working knowledge of the nation's security apparatus, was uniquely qualified to lead the league through the new security realities of the post-9/11 world. At a time when the leaders of every major civic organization in the country were rushing to become conversant in matters of national security and terrorism, Tagliabue *already* was an expert.

What had seemed unthinkable at first—that the league could actually move the date of the Super Bowl back a week, so as to play its entire schedule and avoid a truncated playoffs schedule and the accompanying loss of revenue—actually came to pass. The National Automobile Dealers Association, which booked 16,000 hotel rooms for the weekend following the Super Bowl in New Orleans, was initially resistant to moving their function, but finally consented, acceding to public sentiment and a financial package of $7.5 million. NADA president Phillip Brady agreed to change so as to "help the country's healing process by maintaining important traditions."

The buildup to Super Bowl XXXVI was bathed in patriotism, and the league's sense of spectacle and celebration seemed particularly appropriate for the occasion. *ESPN The Magazine*, considering the league's outsized influence, dubbed the country "NFL Nation." National Security Adviser Condoleezza Rice told an interviewer of her aspirations to become the commissioner of the NFL one day. President George W. Bush declared the game "a national security event," the first such sports event so designated, turning ultimate security responsibility over to the Secret Service, which gave it the sort of top-flight protection usually provided political conventions or U.N. General Assembly meetings.

The game itself, as well as U2's stirring halftime concert, showed the league at its best. For the third year in a row, the league crowned an unlikely champion, with Bill Belichick's New England Patriots, 12-point underdogs, rising to upset the heavily favored St. Louis Rams, 20–17.

By the end of the season, Tagliabue finally received his just due. *The Sporting News* named him, for the first time, the most powerful executive in the world of sports. And he was named Sports Executive of the Year by *Street & Smith's Sports Business Journal,* which noted that only in 2001, "as conditions evolved from difficult to horrific to grim, has the full extent of Tagliabue's leadership become apparent to those outside the NFL."

———

But Tagliabue's next challenge would be even greater. In an era littered with stories of seemingly invincible enterprises that collapsed under the weight of their own ambition, it would be his task to chart the course for the league's future, with two sets of owners attempting to pull the league in opposite directions.

By the dawn of the new century, there were two distinct models for successful sports enterprises in contemporary America.

The first, built over decades and characterized by such high-prestige entities as the NFL, the Olympics, and the NCAA basketball tournament, might be called the traditional model. Each of these events consented to an increased number of advertising breaks over the years (the NFL allowed thirty-five minutes of commercials during the game, not including the breaks during halftime). While the television timeouts were numerous, the events themselves were largely free of advertising, with the field and uniforms and interior of the venues being "clean," in the industry parlance. That allowed those watching the events to focus almost entirely on the event itself. The traditional model echoed a Rozelle maxim, repeated more than once at meetings, in which he emphasized that "while the game is being played, the product we're selling is the National Football League." In this model, the game itself was the primary "brand."

But by the '90s there was a different model emerging, one best exemplified by the NASCAR racing circuit, in which the cars being raced were *advertisements themselves*. In the English Premier Soccer League, each club's uniform included jerseys in which the team logo was dwarfed by its sponsor's emblem. The appeal to advertisers of this system was obvious. But there was also a danger, a risk that in the ever-growing quest for revenue the events and sports would become nothing more than a means to an end, existing purely as a vehicle for advertisers. Many sports trying to scrounge out that last few million increasingly succumbed to similar temptation: Major League Baseball allowed Fox, in its World Series broadcasts, and ESPN, in its telecasts, to run superimposed signage behind home plate during the games. And freed of the guiding hand and philosophy of the NCAA (which had clean venues at all its championship tournaments), college football bowl games had become glutted with in-game signage, the import of any game often obscured by what could at times seem like a four-hour corn chip commercial.

Up to the present day, the NFL has remained scrupulous about keeping commercial signage from intruding on the game. Some of the TV clutter—sponsorship tie-ins with starting lineups and statistics—was eliminated, at the NFL's behest, in the 1998 deal. As Tagliabue was proud to point out, "The playing field itself is free of commercial markings, the sidelines are free of commercial markings except to the extent the league authorizes commercial markings on the sidelines, and up to this point the commercial identification on the sideline has to do with the products that are intrinsic to the game: the uniforms, Gatorade, drinks, the Motorola headset. We've kept the commercial markings to products which are integral to the game. Those are the bright lines. We continue to have a very wide consensus in support of our resolutions that stadium signage and advertising shouldn't be visible at field level on television."

But there was greater pressure from owners for the league to market itself more aggressively. In 2000, after Austrian's exit, all the league's ancillary interests were grouped under the heading of NFL Business Ventures. Some worried that executive vice president Roger Goodell, the capable consensus builder who'd helped hammer out solutions on some of the league's thorniest issues, like expansion and realignment, was too much in the thrall of revenue building. "He uses terms like 'monetize' and 'commoditize,' " said one owner with distaste.

Meanwhile, the push for greater revenue grew insistent. Ads were already showing up on the jerseys of players in the NFL Europe league (formerly the NFL's World League of American Football), and the international broadcast of the Super Bowl sold the rights to the electronically superimposed first-down line, which in those broadcasts was a strip advertising FedEx. Neil Austrian, pondering how long the league might remain above the fray, said, "There may be some owners that, if the NASCAR model came to the league and you could put five more decals on some of these uniforms and they pay you $150 million, I can't tell you how they'd vote. I think the dollars have gotten so large that, when you pay $700-plus million for a team, you start to look for any and every way to make money. So I think it would really depend. I'd like to think that there's enough self-discipline and enough preservation of the past that they wouldn't do that, but I'm not so sure."

The battle became a constant refrain at league meetings. After one extended argument about branding, the Steelers' Dan Rooney sent Roger Goodell a football jersey mocked up with a dozen NASCAR-style corporate logos. "This," wrote Rooney to Goodell, "is what we're trying to avoid."

Ultimately, the real business tension of the new century would not be over areas where the league had historically shared revenue—in television contracts and gate receipts—but in areas where it hadn't. The fastest-growing area of income since 1998 came in unshared stadium revenue—stadium sponsorships and luxury suites and the like—that was used to calculate the salary cap but wasn't shared among league members, creating what some clubs, borrowing from the lexicon of politics, referred to as an "unfunded mandate."

The percentage of league revenues that was unshared was growing at an alarming rate, from 12 percent in 1994 to 21 percent in 2003. Some of the largest-revenue teams like the Redskins were spending less than 40 percent of their revenue on the salary cap, while others, such as the Colts, were spending more than 70 percent. The revenue gap between the top quartile of teams and bottom quartile had grown markedly in the previous years, and it seemed that, sooner or later, it would affect competition on the field.

And while the league's record on key decisions remained strong, the accumulation of outside interests and financial pressure had begun to wear on the "football people." The battleground in 2003 became the future of NFL Europe, the developmental league that served as a minor league proving ground for teams and as an international outreach program for the league. To the business leaders in the league, NFLEL didn't "monetize" sufficiently. To those directly involved with competition on the field—and who had seen the hundreds of NFLEL players make contributions on NFL rosters—complaints about the nominal costs (about $500,000 per club per season) weren't merely shortsighted, they were blind. The league eventually renewed its commitment, but by the summer of 2003, the Chiefs' Carl Peterson had grown vexed with the ongoing debate.

"This is the only place where we have a chance to develop our product," he said of NFL Europe. "We'd be out of our mind to say, 'Oh, this is too expensive,' and let it go. Unbelievable. You know, we sit in those meetings, for so long and for too many years, and we talk and we talk and we talk about *everything* but football. We talk about litigation, we talk about 'Al Davis is fucking us,' we talk about Reebok, we talk about TV—we don't talk about our product. You know, we can't forget that we play the game of football. The National Football League is the National *Football* League."

Against this backdrop of conflict over the future direction of the league, there was the runaway spectacle that was the modern Super Bowl. It was at once the league's crown jewel and its most anomalous product, the football game put on by the NFL that looked and felt least like an NFL football game.

For cultural impact, the game and the civic holiday weekend surrounding it were unrivaled. Two out of every five American households were tuned into the game. It was the weekend each year in which Americans scheduled the most at-home parties and the fewest weddings. Thanksgiving was the only day they consumed more food. The Super Bowl was the TV program most watched by men each year, of course, but also the program most watched by women, and by children, and by senior citizens, and by blacks, and by Hispanics.

It rose to this prominence on the power of the interest in the game itself. The Super Bowl's halftime show, through much of its first twenty-five years, had often been considered a forgettable dud. Rozelle's own musical taste tended to the comically bland (Mantovani among them), but even he grew fed up with the saccharine pep of Up With People, who'd played in Super Bowl IX, and returned for Super Bowl XIV. Rozelle began his postmortem meeting with his staff the day after that game by announcing, "There are three words that I don't ever want to hear again: 'Up With People.' "

Through the '80s, the game's halftime extravaganza was less obviously awful, but every bit as bland—parade float extravaganzas, stadium card shows, and B-list entertainments like a presentation featuring eighty-eight grand pianos, Chubby Checker, and the Radio City Rockettes—and that owed more to amusement-park theme shows than any meaningful adult entertainment.

But with Super Bowl XXVI in Minnesota, held in 1992 with the Redskins beating the Bills, the league faced competition. The Fox TV series *In Living Color* announced it would produce a live twelve-minute sketch that would begin the same instant the halftime show did. The following year, the NFL responded, by luring pop music's biggest name, Michael Jackson, to conduct a frenetic ten-minute halftime mini-concert. From there, the league moved quickly toward making all of the ancillary elements of the game live up to that scale of spectacle. In 1998, just minutes after the scintillating Broncos-Packers finale in Super Bowl XXXII, at a time when the crowd was transported by John Elway's ultimate triumph and the AFC's first win in fourteen years, the league felt compelled to wheel out the '70s act Three Dog Night to play a song as a *prelude* to that trophy ceremony.

In an effort to incorporate more popular musical acts into the Super Bowl pregame and halftime shows, the league often chose the unique illogic of television awards shows, drawing from numerous genres of entertainment to increase interest. The result was that music presentations, already taken out of their customary context, seemed to have no internal logic whatsoever, as in 2001 when Ray Charles's moving, beatific rendition of "America the Beautiful" was used as a lead-in to the boy-band heartthrobs the Backstreet Boys performing the national anthem.

The entire spectacle could at times come off as catering to the worst impulses of American excess. Writing about the Buccaneers' victory over the Raiders in Super Bowl XXXVII in 2003, *Slate*'s Robert Weintraub noted the schizophrenic array of acts that accompanied the game. "On the whole, the game of games seemed to play second banana to San Diego's version of the American Music Awards, starring [Celine] Dion, the Dixie Chicks, etc. If I were a Bucs fan, I'd be pretty upset that the presentation of the Lombardi Trophy, the moment that made a quarter-century of acute psychological pain worthwhile, had to wait for a performance by Bon Jovi."

"At some point," said Packers GM Ron Wolf in 2000, "the Super Bowl no longer became a game, but it became a show. And from that, football no longer became a game, it became a business."

————

And so it was that, at the height of its popularity, a sense of looming crisis pervaded the owners' meetings of the NFL. At the conclusion of the league's annual meetings in 2003, at the Arizona Biltmore, where George Halas used to spend his winters, the Bengals' Mike Brown sat down in an easy chair in a lobby outside of the owners' conference room.

Brown, in many ways an anachronism, was the most maligned and perhaps the least understood man in pro football. The team his father had owned and coached into the playoffs had, after Paul Brown's death, become something of a disgrace. The Bengals were mocked for everything from their series of poor drafts (yielding such first-round busts as David Klingler, Ki-Jana Carter, and Akili Smith) to their legendary thriftiness (bringing in the 350-pound lineman Tony Siragusa for a free agent visit, they alienated him from the start by sending him a coach-class ticket).

Mike Brown was staunchly pro-league, yet was not viewed in the public eye in the same way that other second-generation NFL owners, like Dan Rooney or Wellington Mara, were. One outraged fan established a Web site called mikebrownsucks.com, in an attempt to exert public pressure for him to step aside. What hurt Brown most, perhaps, was the misbegotten notion that he didn't *care* about winning (he'd once screamed so loudly at an Isaac Curtis touchdown in 1976, his hearing hadn't been the same since), or that he didn't know football (in a real sense, after a childhood spent in football camps, a college career as a player, and his entire adult life in administration, Brown knew little else). The criticism had left him shell-shocked. He removed his own picture and bio from the Bengals' press guide and seemed to withdraw even further from the public eye. Planning a banquet in the spring of 2003 with Cincinnati business leaders, many of whom had been critical of the organization in the past, Brown took pains to deflect any attention from himself. "The focus is not going to be on me," he told one league executive. "They would like to drive a stake through my heart."

But there were at least two sides to this story. That same spring, the Bengals hired Marvin Lewis—the gifted architect of the Ravens' record-setting defense in 2000—to be their head coach. Lewis became the third active black coach in the league, and the first since fall 2002 protests by Jesse Jackson and Washington lawyer Cyrus Mary prompted the league to reexamine its record for hiring diversity.

"I can remember my dad's generation," said Tony Dungy. "Everyone rooted for the Dodgers and everybody rooted for the Browns. The Bengals get lumped into the behind-the-times organization, no visionary thinking. Maybe that's true, but I still go back to Mike Brown and his brother and his dad in Cleveland. We wouldn't be anywhere close to where we are now without the Cleveland Browns' influence."

Contemplating the state of the league's business concerns, and his decision to name the Bengals' new stadium after his own father, rather than selling it off to a corporate sponsor, Brown spoke with an unusual firmness. "I don't see the National Football League as a strictly business operation. I see it as a sport-hyphen-business. And to me that's a different thing. Just making the most money possible is not the ultimate goal. The ultimate goal is to have a good team, to have success on the field. To have the thrill when you have a championship team and the hometown gets involved in it."

When Brown walked away, one NFL executive turned to a reporter, rolled his eyes, and whispered, "He is so out of it."

25

The Main Thing

"Me and the boys got some work to do.
You wanna come along?
It ain't like it used to be, but it'll do."

EDMOND O'BRIEN'S SYKES, IN *THE WILD BUNCH*

On a perfect August day in New Jersey, from his sparkling Sea Girt, New Jersey, home that sat just a block away from the Atlantic Ocean, a tanned and fit Bill Parcells tried to explain the lure of coaching.

"I grew up," he said, "in an environment where every day you went to the schoolyard or the playground, and every day you're playing from morning till night to find out who's best. If it was kickball, if it was basketball, if it was after dinner off the front steps of the porch, that's what it was, and I really never left that environment. [Coaching was] like an adult version of what I did as a young guy."

It was August 2001, and Parcells was prepared to spend his second full season in self-imposed retirement. He'd had offers to return, had demurred, and felt confident that "if I can make it through January," he'd be retired for good.

Then again, he'd said that after the 1999 season, when he took his New York Jets team decimated by early-season injuries and an 0-5 start, and rallied them to a strong finish in which they wound up 8-8. He knew it was perhaps his best coaching job ever, and he also knew that he couldn't possibly keep up the pace. He retired, for good he said, and commemorated the season with a book titled *The Final Season: My Last Year as Head Coach in the NFL*. For the next three years, he did some radio and TV, watched a lot of sunsets, and went to a lot of horse races. He came agonizingly close to taking the Buccaneers job in 2002, but pulled back at the last instant. He had utterly nothing to prove: he was a certain inductee into the Pro Football Hall of Fame, wealthy beyond his dreams, finally able to spend time with Judy, his wife of nearly thirty-five years. But the game still exerted its pull. He continued observing players with a keen eye, spent many nights in late night phone calls with longtime friend Al Davis.

By January 2003, Parcells was restless, divorced, and ready to step back in the fray. He didn't merely return, but chose to come back to the Cowboys, perhaps the most stressful head coaching job in the NFL, working for an owner who was notorious for his hands-on commitment, and coaching a team whose fan base was famously impatient with anything short of league-wide domination.

Parcells returned harboring few illusions about the toll that coaching took, or his own susceptibility to its stresses. It had happened to him time and time again: in training camp, he was fit and trim, with plenty of exercise and good stamina. By the end of the season, he'd have gained twenty pounds, stopped exercising, started to compulsively overeat, and would feel his body running down, victim of the accumulated stress and effort.

It had brought back Dick Vermeil, who'd retired two days after the Rams' Super Bowl win, then returned a year later to the Chiefs, after a plea from his close friend Carl Peterson. In 2004, it would lure Hall of Fame coach Joe Gibbs, out of football for over a decade, back to the Redskins.

They were aging men in a young man's game, but the signal and complex pleasures of being the leaders of men were irresistible. "There are no gray areas in this business here," said Parcells. "Your earnings aren't kind of going up, and your quarterly reports don't kind of look better. You either won or you lost."

The Steelers' patriarch, Art Rooney, once recalled riding with Vince Lombardi on a coast-to-coast flight, and hearing him talk "about how lucky you must be to win a title. Like a golfer who remembers each shot, Lombardi remembered all the breaks of the season that went in his favor, fumbles recovered, punts that rolled out of bounds instead of into the end zone."

More than ever before, those breaks and bounces determined the outcome of games in a league that had attained a new zenith in competitiveness. Once the effects of free agency and the salary cap worked their way through the system by the late '90s, talent was more evenly distributed, meaning that the margin for error was even smaller than before. The talent that a team assembled was also more transitory, meaning the course of a single season had an even greater urgency. In the new era, teams rose or fell more sharply than they had in the past.

NFL games in the new century had become consistently exciting, fluid, intense contests whose back-and-forth pace was evident even through the league's more frequent commercial breaks. The games were not merely closer, but more free-flowing. In 2002, eighteen teams won games in which they'd trailed by ten points or more at some point in the fourth quarter. That happened only twice in 1973.

The margin of error had never been thinner. With two weeks left in the 2002 season, thirteen of the sixteen teams in the AFC were still in contention for the playoffs, but none had clinched. Kansas City would lead the league in scoring that season, but its young defense blew three double-digit leads, and the club wound up 8-8, in last place in the AFC West. Had the Chiefs held on to those three leads, they would have finished 11-5, won the West, and had the conference's number one overall seed.

So much in the game couldn't be controlled—Bill Walsh was convinced that there was a 20 percent chance factor in the outcome of games—that what coaches could control they did, obsessively. So along with the added pressure of the modern game came a curious paradox. Even as coaches had less control over players off the field, they'd assumed more over players on the field. Coaching was, arguably, more important in football than any other sport. And with less distance between the best and worst teams, it was more important than ever before in the NFL.

There were numerous reasons for this. For one, players came out of college less technically sound than they had ten years earlier. "Kids aren't playing football in their backyard anymore," said the Bengals' Marvin Lewis. "They're playing it with their thumbs." Rookies needed more teaching, but in the pressurized new environment, they were also being rushed into action sooner.

While free agency gave general managers and personnel directors more influence, with the ability to acquire pro talent as well as college talent, this freedom was tempered by the knowledge that the players brought in had to fit the coach's system. And thus the coach's role, again, was paramount. "Each football team has a center of their own universe and it's their head coach," said Charley Armey, the Rams' president and GM. "The rest of us just rotate around it and if he can't make it work, it doesn't work for any of us. So we have to get him the right things to make it work."

The coaching influence extended to the field as well. In a previous era,

Super Bowls had featured a who's who of Hall of Fame and All-Pro quarter-backs. But since 1999, only one of the ten Super Bowl starting quarterbacks (the Titans' Steve McNair) had been a first-round draft choice still with his original team.

"There are two reasons why teams are getting to the Super Bowl with aver-age quarterbacks, solid quarterbacks," said Ernie Accorsi. "One is there aren't enough great ones in the league. And the coaches today dominate the game so much, there's so much more scheming, it's so much more complicated, that to me, they've almost taken players out of there. The game now has become even more complicated—the players still decide it, but to less of an extent than they used to."

———

It was late 1991, and the Browns had just fired Bud Carson as head coach. Casting about for a possible blockbuster hire, Art Modell asked one of his as-sistants, Jim Shofner, to make a run at Steve Spurrier, even then an institution at the University of Florida. Shofner was friendly with Spurrier, had coached him during his playing career with the 49ers. But Spurrier wasn't merely unin-terested, he was cheerfully derisive of the idea.

"Shof, let me tell you something," he said. "First of all, just to clear one thing up, I ain't going to *Cleveland,* all right? Secondly, you're all fuckin' crazy. We have a Skins Game every day at six o'clock." Spurrier didn't rule out ever taking a pass at a pro career, but he refused to buy into the unremitting regi-men of the pro game. "I may do it someday," he told Shofner, "but I ain't going to do it the way you do it."

More than a decade later, Spurrier brought his passing system and his un-complicated self-confidence to Washington, and vowed that he would not keep the same long hours as the rest of his competition. Spurrier's magnetism was a quick hit in the capital, and there was plenty of talk about his new ap-proach. Then the Redskins won just twelve games over two seasons, a harried Spurrier resigned at the end of the second, and that was the end of the latest less-is-more experiment in the pro coaching ranks.

While pro football players had rhythms of their life that were not that dis-similar from many wage-scale workers—a steady routine, a few business trips, an identifiable weekend—the men who coached them had jobs that had be-come incredibly stressful, and schedules that were unrelenting.

Of course, there were limits to the George Allen formula, which predicated success on outworking one's opponent, and they came in well before the logi-cal conclusion of mutually assured destruction.

If Parcells and Vermeil were old-school grinders, then Tony Dungy and Brian Billick represented the new school. Early in Marty Schottenheimer's tenure in Kansas City, when some staff meetings didn't *begin* until after midnight, Dungy and fellow assistant Bill Cowher made a pact that they would never sleep in the office. When Cowher became the head coach in Pittsburgh in 1992, he remembered that vow. Dennis Green had installed the same relatively humane system in Minnesota, where both Dungy and Billick worked as assistants. They later installed similar schedules. While the job's demands were still unyielding—"Whoever designed Christmas was not a football coach," said Billick—it had grown more bearable for some of the new breed.

But the new breed was in the minority. The reality was that the coaching profession still exacted a heavy toll. Jon Gruden, who led the Bucs to a Super Bowl in the 2002 season, famously got up at 3:17 in the morning. He was among the majority who attempted to shoehorn as much work into the day as possible, although few were as productive as Gruden.

"Coaches are an insecure group," said Parcells. "More is always better, less is not better. For the guys who aren't that confident, if you could practice Sunday morning, some coaches would be happy about that."

In the culture of competition, there was a fear of leaving any stone unturned. When he took over for Marty Schottenheimer as the Chiefs' coach in 1999, Gunther Cunningham was already famous for his work ethic. Cunningham built a remarkable personal rapport with his players, based on his melding of old-school language and temper with new-school sensitivity and compassion. But at the helm, with a fifty-three-man roster to oversee and an entire city to answer to, he became the league's leading micromanager, making sure that the shampoo and soap dispensers were full in the showers, regulating the length of the shirttails on players' practice uniforms, overseeing the team's implementation of a system of optional computer playbooks.

He was resolute and nearly successful, but never did recover from the gutshot season-ending loss to the Raiders in 1999 (the Chiefs surrendered a 17–0 lead at home, and the defeat cost them the division title and a playoff spot) and the death of Derrick Thomas, from injuries sustained three weeks later in a car accident. By the 2000 season, with a roster weighed down with dead money and a hangover from the death of Thomas, the team lost five straight in the second half to sink from the playoff race. By then, Cunningham had a haunted look. Trying to respond to adversity by working harder, he lapsed further into the abyss. On Sunday, December 24, 2000, the Chiefs played their poorest game of the year on the last day of the regular season, losing 29–13 to an indifferent Atlanta squad. On the next day, a grim Cunningham spent Christmas in his office, arriving at 5:00 a.m. to begin a systematic review of the season.

"That's just self-inflicted victimization," said Bill Walsh. "You can become so possessed at what you do and you want so dearly to be successful that you'll do anything, you'll sacrifice anything to be successful. In this case, the sacrifice is your entire existence to satisfy your own need to convince yourself you're working so hard that you will be successful. When in reality, it's just flailing at the wind, just howling at the sky."

But Cunningham's reaction was hardly unique. Walsh had seen tough coaches, under times of stress, break down into tears in front of him. In the modern environment, they were under more pressure than ever before, subjected to more media scrutiny, and working a year-round schedule that had escalated in intensity from demanding to punishing.

"We have thought a lot about this issue," said Jeff Pash, the league's executive vice president and legal counsel. "But we also know that there's no way, short of putting bars on the office doors, to keep coaches away. And if you do that, they're just going to watch film at home. It never ends."

Within two weeks of Cunningham's somber Christmas siege, Carl Peterson had fired him and coaxed his old friend Dick Vermeil out of retirement to coach the Chiefs. Vermeil had become the most famous grinder of them all. Back in the early '80s, when Vermeil and the Eagles staff were working eighteen-hour days and sleeping most nights in their offices, his director of pro player personnel, Lynn Stiles, picked up a book called *Burnout: The High Cost of High Achievement,* and noted that his boss seemed to be suffering from each of the main symptoms. Stiles placed the book on Vermeil's desk one day; two weeks later, Vermeil returned it with a note, "This doesn't apply to football coaches." But by the end of the 1982 season, a spent Vermeil announced his retirement in a tearful press conference in which he noted he was "emotionally burned-out." When he returned to coaching with the Rams fifteen years later, his kinder and gentler reputation proved mostly a facade. He still threw himself completely into his work, but had developed enough self-control to know when he'd reached the point of diminishing returns. The same would hold true in Kansas City. There were no cots in the Chiefs' offices, but Vermeil and his staff often worked past midnight during the season. He was more able to pace himself, more able to delegate. And he needed to be, because in the modern age, the pressure didn't end when the season did. "It's a six- to seven-day-a-week job in the off-season," said Vermeil. "It never used to be quite that bad.

Because now there's just, well, there *is* no off-season, there's just a time you don't play the games."

Beyond all the occupational pressures, three of the league's thirty-two coaches—Tony Dungy, Herm Edwards, and Marvin Lewis—faced an additional level of scrutiny. As the league's only black head coaches during the 2003 season, they knew that their success or failure would influence the number of doors that would open to black coaches in the future.

While the 2003 season saw a protracted controversy about whether Eagles quarterback Donovan McNabb was overrated by the media because of his race, most of the questions of racial fairness were now focused off the field. To many, the performance of black coaches held a special significance in a way that that of athletes no longer could. Because of the job's unique mixture of power, responsibility, and visibility, being a head coach in the NFL carried an added meaning, denoting not only black achievement, but also a measure of black authority in an interracial world.

"For some reason, we're all lumped together," said Kellen Winslow, the Hall of Fame tight end. "If one of us fails, we all fail as a group. If one of us succeeds, we all succeed. That's not fair, but that's the unfortunate perception."

No one bore this added burden with more grace than Dungy. But what made him so fascinating wasn't merely that he stood a fair chance of being the first black coach to lead a team to the Super Bowl, but rather that he might— as Bill Walsh had done a generation earlier—help transform the image of what a coach ought to be like.

Dungy had a deceptively serene countenance, and a soft-spoken manner that could seem utterly out of place in the violent world of football, until one examined it more closely. "One of the great lies," said Bill Polian, "is that Tony is this Caspar Milquetoast character. Nothing can be further from the truth. I mean, he's as tough as they come; he just does it in a really low voice, with no histrionics whatsoever, and you have two choices, A or B: Do what I say or be gone. Simple as that."

And in this, some things didn't change. Sooner or later, each coach had to convince his players that he could lead them. In his first year coaching the Chiefs, Vermeil said of his team, "They don't care what you know until they know that you care." Parcells offered an equally proven system, with a less empathetic manner, counseling his players during a rookie orientation with the Jets in 1999, "We're not interested in players with problems," he said. "We want you to put all the problems you have behind you. I don't need guys who have pregnant girlfriends that are calling them on the phone and all that shit. I am too old for it and I don't care about it. I want guys who can concentrate on being a football player."

What Parcells and Vermeil shared, what Billick and Dungy perpetuated, was that essential trait of commanding respect while instilling the belief in their teams that they were playing for something greater than their own paycheck. Though everyone in football was eager to point out that it was a business, the truth was that on any successful team, players spoke of care and trust, and the feeling of family.

In return for that commitment, coaches offered a unity of purpose. "The main thing," Vermeil was fond of saying, "is the main thing." It was an updated variation on Lombardi's "Winning is everything" line, with the good sense not to say it so explicitly. But it was also a mind-set that demanded focusing on the task ahead, to the exclusion of all else. No injury to any player, no matter how bad, would countenance excuses. Even focusing on it could be a sign of weakness, and so coaches were forced to take on the willful disbelief of Iraqi Minister of Information Mohammed Saeed Sahhaf, whose accounts of Iraqi military victories and boundless optimism continued, even as the 3rd Armored Division neared Baghdad.

On August 23, 2003, the Jets' Pro Bowl quarterback Chad Pennington went down in a freak injury in a preseason game, breaking several small bones in his hand. The early prognosis was that he would miss at least twelve weeks, if not the entire season. Suddenly the Jets' season of promise looked dead on arrival. When Jets coach Herm Edwards commiserated with his mentor later in the week, Vermeil told him, "Herm, you can't have a hero without a catastrophe." Edwards vowed to "leave it in God's hands," and the Jets moved forward, without excuses.

A week later, the Chiefs held their annual kickoff luncheon on the eve of their last exhibition game. Vermeil, musing on the impact of a team on a city, said, "You've got to believe . . . you've got to value the reward of trying to achieve something. Will it make a difference in your life? You bet it does. It makes a difference in a city. It makes a difference in the attitude of people going to work every day. The Chiefs have done that before and I think the Chiefs can do that again." In their season-opening win over the Chargers, Kansas City played a nearly perfect half of football, rolling to a 24–0 lead, with Priest Holmes—the free agent discard from Baltimore who'd become the most dynamic back in the league in Kansas City's system—returning from his 2002 injury and slicing through the cracks in the Chargers' defensive wall. They won going away, 27–9.

Based on the opening week's results of the 2003 season, one could have safely assumed the following: the Chiefs' defense would be vastly improved; the Buccaneers were still the soundest team in the league; the Bills were a rising power in the AFC East; the Rams would have severe quarterback troubles; the Steelers would again challenge for the AFC title; the 49ers were poised for another run in the NFC West; the Patriots wouldn't be able to survive the dissension that followed the surprising decision to release safety Lawyer Milloy; Parcells's Cowboys were still a season away from competing; the Colts hadn't shaken their offensive funk from the end of the previous season; and the Falcons, even without Michael Vick, had the look of a playoff contender. Each and every one of these assumptions would be proved wrong.

But some of those truths would take much of the season to emerge. Meanwhile, the new season played out like an exquisite serial drama, whose finish was ever in doubt. At the midway point of the 2003 season, the two teams with the best records in pro football were the Kansas City Chiefs, at 8-0, and the Indianapolis Colts, at 7-1. Both teams featured explosive offenses and improving defenses, both boasted experienced executives with a long background in personnel, and both coaching staffs were noted for their experience, player rapport, and unhysterical leadership.

But the league was so closely bunched that what set the Chiefs and Colts apart at the halfway point were slender reeds of circumstance, single plays that turned games in their favor, and unlikely victories snatched from defeat at the last moment. On October 6, the Colts staged the biggest late-game comeback in league history, rallying from a 35–14 deficit in the final four minutes to win Dungy's Tampa Bay homecoming, on his birthday. Six days later, the Chiefs came back from 17 points in the fourth quarter, on the road at Green Bay, to remain undefeated.

"The thing that most people don't understand is the level of competition in this league, and how high that is," said Billick. "The evidence to prove that is this: a 6-1 team will lose to a 1-6 team. I promise you, having been on both sides of that, you worry if you're a 6-1 team, playing that 1-6 team. And I'm not talking about worried like Florida is worried getting ready to play Cal State–Fullerton. You're legitimately worried, because you know that other club has assets, and just a couple things go wrong, and it can win. The margin for error truly is so narrow, that the top and bottom teams are not nearly as far apart as they once were." The next day, Billick's words were fulfilled. The 7-1 Colts lost a 20–7 halftime lead and let Jacksonville, a talented 1-7 team, rally to win.

If there were fewer legends in the modern NFL, perhaps it was because players and coaches alike were more often exposed, humbled in ways that an earlier generation of coaches and players hadn't been. After his Packers fell to Philadelphia in the 1960 NFL championship game, Vince Lombardi never lost another playoff game. In their six-year run in the '70s in which they won four titles, the dynastic Steelers played fifty-one games against teams with sub-.500 records, and lost just one.

But the modern NFL forbade such dominance, and sooner or later, everyone got nicked. For the previous season's Super Bowl teams, the hits came sooner. In Tampa, where the defending champion Buccaneers had begun the season like they'd finished the last, Jon Gruden's high-keyed leadership was unable to arrest a slide brought forth by age, injury, and a dangerous complacency, the collective belief by a team that it could increase its tempo and effectiveness at will. But several statement games passed without a statement from the Buccaneers, and in week 14, Tampa Bay was eliminated from the playoff race, making it five straight seasons that the Super Bowl champ from the previous season was unable to win a single playoff game in the next.

Oakland started slow and never recovered from the loss of quarterback Rich Gannon in an early-season loss to Kansas City. By the end of the season, coach Bill Callahan was dealing with festering player resentment and the Raiders, eleven months from their Super Bowl trip, were an aging, ineffective 4-12 club.

At the other end of the spectrum, the 5-11 Cowboys of 2002 were transformed quickly under Parcells, and marching toward a playoff spot. The Panthers, 1-15 in 2001, were leading the NFC South, with two big wins over Tampa Bay. And in November, the Bengals—the punch line for ineptitude in the league over the previous decade—rose up to knock off Kansas City, the league's last undefeated team, 24–19.

It was the Bengals' biggest victory in at least a decade, and it offered proof of Marvin Lewis's impact, and the transformative power of the best coaches in the business. In the jubilant locker room, the usually unruffled coach, hoarse and weeping, made a point of holding up a game ball and telling his team, "The guy I'm most thankful for is Mike Brown, because he's endured a lot for you guys . . . he had to put up with a lot of shit." Brown wasn't in the locker room when Lewis made the speech, but received the game ball later on, with Lewis's thanks for giving him and the team the opportunity to succeed. Brown was not a man of many words, but he cherished the prize as a sign of better days. He owned dozens of game balls, but the one he received from Lewis was the only one he kept in his bedroom at home.

It was only one loss for the Chiefs, but it would turn out to be an important one. The Chiefs' defense, led by coordinator Greg Robinson, favored

complex schemes designed to camouflage weaknesses. At an earlier stop in
Denver, Robinson's system had helped the Broncos win two Super Bowls, but
as the season progressed, the defense was crumbling as badly as it had in 2002.
The same Kansas City team that had been 9-0 and mentioned in the same
breath as the 1972 Dolphins was, by the end of the regular season, 13-3 and
being disparaged as defenseless impostors after a pair of 45-point scorchings
at the hands of the Broncos and Vikings. Such was the crucible of competitiveness in the modern NFL.

"I think today that competing requires more talent and more merit in
more areas than ever before," said Tagliabue late in the season. "I think it's
clear that you have to have talent in the coaching area, talent in the player personnel area, and talent in the cap-management area. If you make mistakes in
those areas the system is unforgiving both in terms of the financial consequences and the opportunity costs. Some teams are doing a better job competing in that meritocracy in those three areas. It's not a random system where
people pop up and down on a random basis. It's a merit-based system and
there are no advantages that one team can secure that another team can't secure. It's a very even playing field and an unforgiving system."

———

With the growth of sports on television came the accompanying growth of the
sports schedule. Competing leagues and sports had spread their tentacles into
an all-consuming, overlapping mass in which major sports events were held virtually every day of the year. With more than 120 major sports franchises, 117 Division I-A college football teams, and 327 Division I college basketball teams,
the calendar was clogged with an unending torrent of games, broadcasts, results,
and previews. Along the way, the notion of sports as an oasis was often lost.

Against this context of constant activity, one of the NFL's great appeals was
the built-in scarcity and compression of its action. In the space of six hours on
most fall Sundays, fans could watch their own games and monitor almost all
of the rest of that week's action, with only a single Sunday and Monday prime-
time game left. The action was immediate, surroundable, coherent and all the
more exciting because, with so few games on the schedule, each one was of
greater importance (the result of a single pro football game carried the same
competitive weight as ten baseball games).

This was one of the easily overlooked strengths of the league, and perfectly
complemented the exclusivity of its playoff structure. The two were inter-
linked, as the limited number of playoff spots invested almost every regular

season game with a tangible importance. For decades, there had been a tendency in all sports to increase the playoff field to maximize postseason revenue (more teams led to more games led to more money), and to keep more teams' fans interested throughout the season. The downside, as the NBA and NHL had learned in recent years, was that when every quality team was assured of a playoff spot, individual regular season games often held scant meaning. In basketball and hockey, the entire regular season served as little more than a very long and drawn-out qualifying heat that would eliminate less than half the league's teams for the winner-take-all playoffs. In the NFL, where home field was more important than any other sport, the advantages that accrued to playoff teams were both valuable and clearly graduated, meaning even after a playoff berth was clinched, teams had compelling reasons to keep winning to improve their seed.

In 2003, New England and Kansas City grabbed the top two AFC seeds and the bye into the second round, but the next two best teams in the conference—perhaps, in fact, in the entire league—were Indianapolis and Tennessee, both in the AFC South. When two excellent teams were in the same division, the pressure to avoid the wild card, and its three-road-game route to the Super Bowl, was tremendous. "I've never been in such a pressure cooker," the Colts' Bill Polian said in December. "We've won eleven games and might win twelve. We are still trying to clinch the division and we're not going to be in the top two seeds. It seems like we've been in the chase forever."

In the final week of the regular season in Houston, the Colts needed a win to clinch the division, but instead fell behind, 17–3, to a tough, spirited Texans team. Peyton Manning, as he'd done before, led them back with a grim efficiency, cutting the lead to seven early in the fourth quarter, then tying it with four minutes left. The defense, coming off a shellacking against Denver and with no room for error, stopped the Texans again, and Indianapolis drove into position in the waning seconds, before Mike Vanderjagt came on to kick his league-record forty-first straight field goal.

While Houston's upset hopes were dashed, other underdogs prevailed. Detroit, down 20–10 at the half and looking tentative against the Rams, jumped back in the second half and ran off 27 straight points to knock the Rams out of the number one NFC seed. In Cincinnati, where the Bengals needed a win to stay in the playoff hunt, they inexplicably collapsed against an inspired Browns team that had nothing but pride to play for.

The afternoon played out in parallel tracks of horror and amazement in the NFC North. Minnesota and Green Bay were tied for the division lead, but the Vikings held the division tiebreaker and needed only a win to advance to the playoffs. Taking a 17–6 lead over hapless Arizona into the final minutes, they seemed to have matters well in hand. The Packers were playing concurrently, and as the time melted down in Green Bay, the atmosphere at Lambeau Field was one of helpless resignation. The Packers were routing the Broncos, but a Minnesota win would eliminate the Packers from playoff contention.

With just under two minutes left in Tempe, Arizona scored on a fourth-and-goal play, with a failed two-point conversion leaving them still trailing, 17–12. When Arizona recovered the onside kick, there was a strange eruption back in Green Bay, where the majority of television sets in the new luxury boxes at Lambeau were tuned into the Vikings-Cardinals game. By this time, much of the crowd in Lambeau's lower deck was turned *away* from the field, looking up at the luxury suites, craning for a peek at the screen or even the reaction from those in the boxes.

Back in Arizona, the Cardinals started driving down the field, and got to the nine-yard line when the Vikings' defense stiffened. Two consecutive sacks dashed much of the hope, and the Lambeau faithful seemed to collectively sag. But the Cardinals scrambled to get one more play off, the last frantic snap coming with :04 showing on the clock. Arizona quarterback Josh McCown scrambled to his right and threw a dart to Nathan Poole, who came down with one foot in bounds before being pushed out of the end zone, the officials ruling it a touchdown. The result played out in a cross-country tableau of nearly instant reaction, with raucous cheering in both Tempe and Green Bay. The Packers' Brett Favre, at the end of an exhausting week in which his father passed away, paced the sideline with tears in his eyes while, back in Arizona, the stunned Vikings were dropping all over the field.

It had been another dismal season in Arizona, one that would cost head coach Dave McGinnis his job. But in an ecstatic Cardinals locker room, a red-faced McGinnis was bursting with pride. "I've never been afraid to open myself to you," said McGinnis to his team, "because you've got my heart." With his hand on Nate Poole's shoulder, he said, "I cut this man four times. And every time I did, he stood up in my office and said, 'Mac, if you need me, I'll be there.'" McGinnis brought his team together, and they let out one last collective shout. And within twenty-four hours, he was out of a job.

The league's eighty-fourth season thus ended with three of the league's doormats—3-12 Cleveland, 3-12 Detroit, and 3-12 Arizona—all rising up for key wins on the final Sunday. That week, NFL games were the top-rated program in every NFL market. The upsets also meant that, for the first time ever, every club in the league had at least four wins. On any given Sunday, indeed.

Further proof of the tight competition came in the divisional playoff weekend, January 10–11, 2004, which featured perhaps the finest quartet of games in a single weekend in playoff history, with all four decided by seven points or less, two of them in overtime.

The high-powered Rams, trailing Carolina by three at home, drove near the goal line in the final minute, but enigmatic coach Mike Martz—recklessly bold in some situations, inexplicably timid in others—chose to play for the tie instead of the win, and the Rams wound up losing in overtime. The revived Packers, fresh off an overtime win in the opening round, outplayed the Eagles on the road in Philadelphia. Facing a fourth-and-26 deep in their own territory, the Eagles were rescued once again by their redoubtable leader, Donovan McNabb, who scrambled free and found Freddie Mitchell open for a 28-yard gain, allowing the Eagles to tie the score in the final seven seconds, then win in overtime. The Patriots, riding a twelve-game win streak, were pushed to the limit by the resilient Titans, who, for much of the season, looked like the league's strongest team.

In Kansas City, where the high-flying Colts offense met the free-falling Chiefs defense, Peyton Manning rose to meet the challenge of the fierce, raucous Arrowhead crowd, and the Colts advanced, 38–31. The game was a classic modern-day NFL shootout, featuring no punts. The Chiefs had come a long way in a year, rising from 8-8 to 13-3, but the breakdown of the defense cast a pall over their first playoff game in six seasons, and a day later led to the resignation of defensive coordinator Greg Robinson. The season-ending press conference the following day, with Vermeil in a combative, emotional mood, fielding questions on the defense breakdown, was referred to later by Peterson as "perhaps the most negative press conference in history for a team that won thirteen games." But Peterson was acutely aware of Kansas City's predicament: three times in nine seasons, his teams had won 13 games and earned a first-round bye, and all three times they'd lost their first home playoff game.

That agony of dashed expectations would soon be shared in Philadelphia and Indianapolis. The savory possibility of a McNabb-Manning Super Bowl match-up spiced up the championship week previews, but 2003 was another year for defense. Carolina punished McNabb and neutralized the Eagles, sending Philadelphia to its third straight conference championship loss. In New England, as Polian grimly put it, "our quarterback picked a bad time to have a bad game." Manning seemed bothered by the Patriots' steady rush, and his receivers were consistently obstructed in their routes, allowing New England to advance to their second Super Bowl in three years.

The Colts had progressed as well, from a first-round blowout loss in the

2002 playoffs to a tightly fought championship game setback a year later. But to understand football people was to understand Bill Polian's remark that "a 41–0 loss is much easier to handle. When you lose that badly in the first round, your expectations weren't that high to begin with. The disappointment lasts only a brief time, because you realize, 'Well, we weren't good enough.' But when you get as close as we did to the big game this year, that hangover lasts."

As the Panthers and Patriots headed to Houston for Super Bowl XXXVIII, Brian Billick started scouting free agent wide receivers, Bill Polian began intense negotiations with Peyton Manning's agent, in search of a new contract that wouldn't wreck the Colts' cap status, and Carl Peterson, seeking a new defensive coordinator for the Chiefs, placed a call to Gunther Cunningham, who would soon come back to work as a coordinator for Dick Vermeil, the man who'd replaced him as head coach. The season wasn't over yet, but for thirty teams, the new quest had begun; it was time to go back to work.

———

The thirty-eighth Super Bowl lacked some of the usual pregame tension and star power. The Patriots were still viewed as a hardy band of overachievers, and the Carolina Panthers were largely unknown to much of America. For much of the first half, the game lived down to expectations, then crackled with urgency late in the half, as the Patriots capitalized on a fumble to break open the scoring, and Carolina rallied twice, to make it 14–10.

In the second half, the two teams' offenses grew increasingly daring and resourceful, and began answering big plays with big plays. The game featured the most frenetic finish in Super Bowl history, with scores on each of the last four drives and six of the last seven. After Carolina tied the game at 29 with under a minute left, the Super Bowl seemed destined for its first overtime ever. But then Carolina's John Kasay shanked the kickoff out of bounds, and the Patriots, starting at their own 40, were marched downfield by Tom Brady, who hit Deion Branch on an out pattern with 13 seconds left, putting New England in scoring position. The Patriots' Adam Vinatieri converted a 41-yard field goal to win the game, much as he had two years earlier.

For the fourth time in seven seasons, the Super Bowl had been a spellbinding game, and by its end, had become the most watched event in television history.

It was a typical performance from the remarkable Patriots. All year long— in their ability to recover from the traumatic preseason release of team leader Lawyer Milloy, their resiliency in the face of injuries, and their poise during crucial situations on the road at Indianapolis and Denver, the Patriots had shown a special resolve, proving to be a team whose whole was greater than the sum of its parts.

The Patriots' cohesion called to mind the words of the All-Pro center Bill Curry, when reflecting on the kernel of self-reliance at the heart of the ultimate team game. "There is a moment," said Curry, "in the fourth quarter, when you can't put one foot in front of the other and you've lost 14 pounds to dehydration and there's blood everywhere and you hadn't missed a play. There's not any money that is going to make you run your face into Dick Butkus. There's not a Super Bowl ring, none of that stuff. It's just some sort of instinct that says I'm indestructible and I'm going to whip this other indestructible guy here. Only then do you see a great team. All the other exterior motives don't work, at some level all you really want to do is quit. So, then, there is some little flame that never flickers and it says *you're not quitting* and it comes from inside. Then you look at the guy next to you and because you love him—you may not particularly like him off the field—but on the field you know what he is and you know what he's going to do. Then, you can't let him down, cannot let him down. That's how great teams happen. Has very little to do with moral rectitude or all the things that we love to talk about as coaches. We would like for them to be in there, but there *is* something incredibly moral at that moment when you're looking for a way to just make yourself put one foot in front of the other."

The 2003 Patriots had captured that special unity and, in answering every Panthers roundhouse with one of their own, completed their unlikely quest in one of the most stirring Super Bowls ever. Around the league, teams were examining Bill Belichick and his system with fresh eyes, looking beyond his reputation as a defensive mastermind to the method behind his personnel decisions, his draft strategy, his symbiotic partnership with personnel director Scott Pioli, the series of crises and responses that made the Patriots one of the more compelling stories in recent memory. There was also a genuine sense of awe over the Patriots' ability to run off a string of fifteen consecutive wins against a brutal schedule, in the most competitive era in league history. The accomplishment was, in its context, every bit as impressive as the Dolphins' perfect season of 1972.

Given all those factors and the drama of the game's conclusion, those who made their living in pro football found it particularly aggravating that the NFL's big game and the Patriots' grand accomplishment would, in the days immediately following the contest, be overshadowed if not totally obscured by the furor over the cultural train wreck of the Super Bowl halftime show.

And so a season that began with Britney Spears stripping down to a bustier in front of the Capitol Mall to open the NFL's Kickoff Weekend would end with the image of Janet Jackson's exposed breast dominating the aftermath of the Super Bowl. There was a certain symmetry in that, to be sure, but many who were closest to the game couldn't help but feel that somewhere along the line, the league had lost its sense of priorities.

"Why do we *do* this?" asked one frustrated club executive. "We bend over backwards and change everything around, just to draw in the people who *least care* about the game. And when that blows up in our face, we have to deal with the embarrassment."

In the end, the Jackson incident, however embarrassing it was at the time, was perhaps just that—an incident that could be easily rectified, if not so easily forgotten. Within two weeks of the game, Tagliabue announced to the membership that the concert used to launch the Kickoff Weekend festivities in the previous two seasons wouldn't be held in 2004, and that the NFL would once again reassert control over the Super Bowl halftime show.

In truth, there were bigger, more important issues on the table. The league spent much of the winter successfully fighting a challenge from Ohio State running back Maurice Clarett that would have struck down the league's rule limiting draft eligibility to athletes three years past their high school graduation. In March, Tagliabue presided over a renewal of the NFL Properties Trust master agreement, which guaranteed that licensing and apparel revenue would continue to be shared equally among all thirty-two clubs.

The argument over the Properties Trust had about it the feeling of the Spanish Civil War—a proxy battle for a much larger, more sweeping conflict to follow. A committee was appointed to discuss the broader issue of revenue sharing, and much of the league's future direction would rest on Tagliabue's ability to find common ground—in the disparate visions of Mike Brown and Jerry Jones—so as to ensure competitive balance and financial stability for the long term.

In the meantime, Tagliabue was determined not to stand pat. November 2003 brought the launch of the league's twenty-four-hour satellite channel, the NFL Network, piloted by the canny, respected Steve Bornstein, one of the key architects of ESPN's dramatic rise to power. Within months, the new network had gained access to some digital cable carriers, and it was viewed as a key part of the NFL's cable presence in the next round of TV contract negotiations. The hub of the new network, and still the most valuable single element of the league's promotional arsenal, was Steve Sabol's leviathan NFL Films, which in addition to possessing the largest sports film archive in the world also dramatically stepped up its new production schedule, and did so in a sprawling new $40 million facility, which opened in 2002.

At the end of the league meetings, Tagliabue had been receptive to the owners' offer of a three-year contract extension, which would extend his term to the end of 2007. The owners greeted this news, in the words of one league executive, "like the Democratic party in 1944, after FDR said he'd stand for one more election." Indeed, it was a tribute to Tagliabue's performance that many found it as unthinkable to imagine an NFL without him as it had once been to imagine a league without Bert Bell in his heyday, or Pete Rozelle in his.

After the draft in late April, Tagliabue turned his attention to several tracks: ongoing negotiations with the networks on a new TV package; with the Players Association on once again extending the all-important collective bargaining agreement; and discussions with the league's security forces to prevent any instances of terrorism from occurring at NFL games.

There were still numerous areas of reasonable concern for the future. But in virtually every meaningful index—the quality of its play, the level of its competition, the pay and support structure offered its players, the power and scope of its publicity apparatus, the devotion of its fans—the National Football League was not only healthy but thriving.

And even those who'd grown to accept the reality that football was a business were still struck by the way that the game could, for a while every January, render all of those business questions irrelevant, if only for a time.

"You gotta remember the cycles we go through," said Jay Zygmunt, the president of football operations for the Rams. "When we're in the playoffs, we get the game of football at its absolute best. And when you think about what guys are getting paid, guys who are making millions and millions of dollars are getting very little money for those playoff games, in terms of economic compensation. But no one cares. Everyone's making the same, it's all about the game and 'We gotta win this game.' You never hear during that time, 'Jeez, we only make X amount of dollars,' or anything like that. No one ever, ever, *ever* talks about anything but 'How do we win this game?,' 'We gotta win this game,' 'We gotta get to the Super Bowl.' You finish that cycle out with the Super Bowl and, again, you have the game of football at its best."

"The day after the Super Bowl," Zygmunt sighed, "it's the business of football at its worst. And you just—you go through it. And that's just the life cycle."

EPILOGUE

America's Game

In the fall of 1996, just weeks before his death, Pete Rozelle sat in the den of his Rancho Santa Fe home with his guest Frank Gifford. Rozelle's brain tumor was slowly killing him, and even talking required an effort, but he still enjoyed seeing his closest friends, especially on Sundays when they could sit before his bank of four TVs and dial up any game they wanted on his satellite dish, carrying the NFL's out-of-market broadcast package *Sunday Ticket*. The afternoon that Gifford visited, the pair had a light lunch and were just finishing at 1:00 p.m. Pacific Time, as the networks switched from the early games to the late games. The screens carried visions of a nation at play—stadiums filled from coast to coast, the breathless updates from studios in New York and Los Angeles providing highlights of key games, urgent voices analyzing playoff races and story lines—while Rozelle and Gifford took it all in.

It was a perfect Sunday to be a football fan, and Frank Gifford sat back in his chair, marveling not at the games so much as the man who'd helped make them so important. He looked at the bank of screens for a moment, then looked over at Pete Rozelle looking at the screens, and said softly, "Oh, Pete . . . you must be very proud."

Pete Rozelle, face wan, eyes brimming, simply smiled and nodded his head, a fan to the end.

We expect athletes to grow old; that their stardom is fleeting is part of the compact, essential to the understanding of sports. But with the men who shaped pro football in the modern age, who helped guide it to its position as the dominant spectator sport in the second half of the twentieth century, it was tempting to assume that they'd always be around, to guide the game, to quietly pull the young guns aside and remind them to "think league," or to bear witness to the earlier sacrifices of Tim Mara and Dan Reeves, Paul Brown and George Halas.

But after Rozelle's death in 1996, many of the rest quickly passed. Jim Kensil died the day of Rozelle's New York memorial service. Tex Schramm's health was fading in the spring of 2003 when Jerry Jones announced that Schramm finally would be honored in the Cowboys' Ring of Honor. A frail but spirited Schramm returned to the Valley Ranch complex for a press conference to announce the honor, but didn't live to see his actual induction. Don Weiss, even in retirement a constant presence at league meetings and Super Bowls, passed away in the fall of 2003. Shortly after Weiss's death, one longtime executive, despairing over the degree that money had come to dominate league discussions, and the loss of so many of Rozelle's inner circle from the days when football always came first, quoted Jonathan Franzen's *The Twenty-seventh City:* "What becomes of a city no living person can remember, of an age whose passing no one survives to regret?"

Even among owners, the old guard was dwindling. Wellington Mara, cheeks ruddy and eyes still twinkling at eighty-eight, ventured into the Giants' offices each day, just as his father had before him. In 2003, Lamar Hunt, seventy-one years old and still the consummate fan, timed his prostate removal surgery and extended convalescence during October, around the two Chiefs national telecasts and their bye week, so he wouldn't have to miss any games. The other surviving members of "the Foolish Club," Ralph Wilson and Bud Adams, were still on the scene and healthy. And the other second-generation owners besides Mara—Dan Rooney in Pittsburgh, Mike Brown in Cincinnati, Bill Bidwill in Arizona—were there to carry the torch. To a man, they were still vibrant.

But it was increasingly obvious to Hunt and Rooney and the rest that the fate of the game was no longer in their hands. They were too few, and they were too far past their prime. Pro football would ultimately rise or fall not on the decisions of the old guard but instead on those made by the eighteen new owners who'd joined the league in the past twenty years. Soon enough, the obligations of institutional memory would fall to the next generation—

people like Wellington Mara's son John; Lamar Hunt's son Clark; Mike Brown's daughter, Katie Blackburn—and their ability to absorb and relate the lessons passed down.

And what, exactly, were those lessons? Perhaps paramount among them is that the popularity of a sport is not predestined, and shouldn't be taken for granted.

"Baseball in 1960 was run by people who loved baseball," said the writer and Red Sox executive Bill James, "but it was run by people who, because they loved baseball so much, *assumed* that there was something 'special' about baseball which had propelled it to its predominant position in the American sports world. And because they made this assumption, they allowed the game to drift. They didn't really *think* about the game, as a commercial product; they still don't. Pete Rozelle, Lamar Hunt, George Halas and the other people who ran pro football had serious disagreements among themselves, but they all *assumed* that they had both the right and the responsibility to shape football into the best possible commercial product that could be built upon the framework of the game. If the games were boring, they assumed it was their responsibility to make them more exciting. If the games were too long, they assumed it was their responsibility to trim the fat."

The NFL's rise was surely a reflection of its time. The same things that distinguished the American way of life in the postwar era—the explosion of technology and consumerism, the rise and refinement of a corporate mind-set—also contributed to the ascendant fortunes of pro football.

It was tempting to look at the disparate state of the leagues in 2004—with Alex Rodriguez's trade to the Yankees further skewing the payroll imbalance in baseball, and a spring training full of allegations about steroid abuse, involving some of the sport's biggest stars and most hallowed records—as reason enough for the NFL's growing lead over Major League Baseball. And indeed, a Harris poll in 2003 showed that, for the first time ever, Americans named pro football as their favorite sport by a two-to-one margin over baseball (29 percent to 13 percent).

But while these developments helped shed light on the NFL's present advantage over baseball in fan appeal, the fact remained that pro football eclipsed baseball *in the '60s and early '70s,* before any of those conditions existed.

The NFL would of course not have succeeded so quickly or spectacularly if it hadn't been uniquely equipped and prepared to take full advantage of television. But there was something more at work. *The New Yorker*'s Malcolm Gladwell writes of social phenomena in terms of "tipping points," instances in which a single identifiable factor hastens a broad social change. In that context, the tipping point for pro football's eclipse of baseball may well have been the creation of NFL Films and NFL Properties in the mid-'60s. At a time when the rest of the sports world was working in small measures, with cross purposes and provincial sensibilities, the NFL began a broadly and dramatically unified set of promotional and marketing initiatives. That clarity of purpose—of the poetic mythmaking of NFL Films, of the high-toned gravity of the Creative Services branch of Properties, and the consistent quality of the licensed merchandise—created a sophisticated aura around the NFL that was unthinkable for sports entities at the time. It was not lost on some of the traditionalists that Properties and Films, two divisions that were at the heart of much of the modern-day infighting, were created not to maximize profit but to increase the league's prestige.

It was also useful to remember that pro football had not become America's favorite sport solely because of some marketing slickness, or because baseball faltered. As Rozelle would have been the first to attest, the game had started to change for the better long before he took office. It had been elevated even in the late '40s by Dan Reeves's vision, Paul Brown's innovations, a compelling and increasingly integrated cast of players, and the bold coaching initiatives throughout the league, which held that the greatest gains in football occurred not through the bludgeoning three-yard ground thrusts but through verve, imagination, and an ability to think and act on a grand scale.

Then, with the arrival of Rozelle on the scene in 1960, the game was transformed again, a terrific spectacle elevated to a fully realized alternative universe, with its own set of principles, rules, legends, and logic.

Out of the war of the '60s, and the mandate to make the game better, came not just Rozelle's vision but Tex Schramm's restless intelligence, Lamar Hunt's boundless optimism, and Al Davis's passionate brinkmanship. It was that superb blending of these philosophies and mind-sets—each one utterly committed to succeeding within football *and* the success of football in general—that helped make pro football such an evocative and compelling pursuit. At the intersection of ideas and loyalties, all the theoretical abstractions mattered—the exquisitely calibrated tie-breaking system, the symmetrical divisional setup, the eminently rational schedule rotation. And in the end, the result was simple: more people cared more about pro football than they did about other sports.

So the NFL's great triumph in the present day wasn't its $17 billion television contract or its marvelous new stadiums or even its dominance among

American sports leagues. It was that the game—the uncompromising test of brute strength and speed, tactics and willpower, the essence of its allure to players, coaches, and fans—had somehow emerged through the magnificent transformation, and greeted the twenty-first century not exactly unscathed, but still adhering to its core principles. In a profane and chaotic age, in which much of what made sports special had been sold off to the highest bidders, the game had preserved the still sacred space of its field. The spectacular edifice that Bell strived for and Rozelle made manifest had been held together and improved by Tagliabue—a brilliant engineer who anticipated many of the league's challenges and addressed them with skill and vision. The league was better conceived, better organized, and better run than its competition, and that was not incidental to its popularity.

During the filming of Oliver Stone's fabulist football drama *Any Given Sunday,* the former tight end Jamie Williams, who served as the movie's football consultant, said, "Baseball is what America aspires to be, football is what this country is."

In terms of aspiring to peace and living with violence, Williams may have been right, but when examining the support structure of the respective leagues, he had it backward. The NFL, with its egalitarian framework, was much more consistent with American aspirations of equal opportunity and pure meritocracy than any other major team sport. And Major League Baseball, for all its timeless tradition, reflected nothing so much as the growing economic stratification of modern American society.

————

Yet the league's business success often obscured the more intangible responses that the game elicited. It was true that the NFL was the country's wealthiest sports league, and its policies often served to make rich men much richer. But it was just as true—and, arguably, more important—that pro football has served, within communities and across the country, as an important social glue, a measure of the meaning of a city and its citizenry, a nation and its self-image. Through it all, the teams still carried a power and imprimatur that was impossible to valuate. It was scarcely possible to talk at length about the self-perception and identity of cities like Cleveland and Kansas City, Buffalo and Pittsburgh without mentioning the football teams. One could decry this reality, but it was a fact of modern urban life.

At the same time, it must be added that all the face-painting, tailgating, and rhythmic chanting could appear tame, perhaps even quaint, to those accustomed to the more combustible culture of European and South American soccer crowds. The possibility of violence and genuine physical danger was a reality for soccer fans throughout much of the world, yet that same menace among fans was virtually absent in big-time American sports. This was a reality open to interpretation, and some chose to view the relatively low levels of crowd violence in the United States as a sign of the country's generosity of spirit and sophisticated understanding of sportsmanship. Others, like the Australian David Hill, the head of sports at Fox, judged that "soccer fans in England and Europe are far more passionate than fans here." For better or worse, the closest American sports fans came to what the English writer Nick Hornby described as "the communal ecstasy" of a jubilant soccer crowd was in the NFL on late fall and winter Sundays, when games and seasons hung in the balance and cities mobilized to witness the action, gathering at stadiums and around televisions in countless living rooms and bars throughout each city.

And it was this level of involvement that was the league's central strength, not only in the big markets, but across the country. By the beginning of the 2004 season, the Cleveland Browns had gone forty years without winning a title. The Jets hadn't been to a Super Bowl in thirty-six years, the Chiefs thirty-five years, the Colts thirty-four years. Yet in the modern NFL, unlike much of Major League Baseball, hope could still spring eternal. In the fans' loyalty was the reminder that sports is never just entertainment, nor just a business. This was a core truth, and the league trifled with it at its own peril.

"To me, the fans are the real purists," said Ernie Accorsi, "because they have nothing to gain. They have no winning share, they get no break, they pay their way in, they put up with the discomforts, they have to live with the detachment. So with me, they're the all-time selfless, pure people. That's why I give them so much of the benefit of the doubt, even when they write me and criticize everything I'm doing, because I know, with them, there is nothing at stake here but emotion and love with their team."

The game exerted its pull from within as well. For those like Carl Peterson and Bill Polian, the allure of the Super Bowl ring continued to be a potent symbol, the talisman they'd pursued throughout their careers. John Madden said that winning one made it much easier for him to retire two years later. And if he hadn't won? "I'd probably *still* be coaching now." Will Shields, after nine Pro Bowl seasons, still looked on winning a ring as "validation, a justification for all the time and the years spent." Jack Faulkner, who came to the pros on Sid Gillman's Rams staff in 1955, would concur. Faulkner was in his forty-fifth year in pro football, working as an advance scout for the Rams, when they went on their miracle run in 1999. In December of that year, Faulkner lost his wife of fifty years. A month later, he won his first championship. He cried when the ring was presented to him the following summer, and laughed out loud when Al Davis, his fellow assistant from Gillman's legendary staff of 1960, saw him wearing it. "Look at how big that goddamn thing is," complained a mock-outraged Davis, who naturally vowed that the next Raiders ring would have to be larger.

Yet the deeper they got into football, the more that players and coaches alike learned that it wasn't about the ring, so much as the signal effort to acquire it.

On August 3, 2002, Bill Polian traveled from Indianapolis to Canton for Jim Kelly's induction into the Hall of Fame. Some of the pain from the Bills' four Super Bowl losses had diminished by then, and the induction served as a reunion of sorts for that memorable team and its diehard fans. The evening of the induction, Kelly hosted a party at a Canton hotel. Friends and family came, and many of the Bills fans who had driven from upstate New York to Canton were staying at the same hotel. At one point, a member of the Bills grabbed Polian from the ballroom and told him that many of the players were looking for him.

They'd all assembled in a small anteroom off the ballroom. When Polian walked in, he was greeted by the men with whom he'd been through the glory years in Buffalo. Not only the superstars like Kelly and Bruce Smith and Darryl Talley, but dozens of less famous players, like Kenny Davis and Kent Hull and Steve Tasker, along with Marv Levy and several of his assistants. The wives drifted off after a while, and soon there was the atmosphere not unlike the flight back from one of the Bills' many road wins, a group of thirty-five to forty men sitting in a sweeping semicircle in a small room. They sat and drank beer, reminisced, laughed, and basked in the wash of memories.

At one point, Polian was distracted by a series of flashes from a nearby doorway. He turned to look, and saw dozens of Bills fans, lined up three and four deep, straining to take pictures. Bruce Smith invited them in, and the players and coaches lined up until the crush for photographs grew so great that Kelly finally led his coaches and teammates out to the ballroom bandstand, where hundreds of fans stood snapping pictures for nearly fifteen minutes.

Later, as Polian was leaving the bandstand, a couple introduced themselves and asked if he would mind posing for a picture with them.

"Not at all," said Polian. "I'm honored. But tell me, why is there so much excitement over this? I mean, I understand Jim is who Jim is, and what he's done for Buffalo and what have you, but . . ."

The woman leaned toward Polian and said, "You must understand: that was the happiest time of our lives. We just wanted to be close to you guys again."

———

As the perceptive English writer James Lawton put it in his outsider's view of the sport, pro football "is an activity that observes many of the conventions of sport, but always the game has a meaning and a psychology that can never be contained within the parameters of the field. This, of course, can be true of other sports, but in American football the point is insistent. If all sport is a magnificent triviality, American football seems least tolerant of the limitations."

It was an observation that would have made perfect sense to Paul "Tank" Younger. The first player from a historically black college to play in the NFL had blazed some trails and been denied others—many thought he could have been the NFL's first black general manager. But as he sat in his trim bungalow in Los Angeles in the spring of 2001, his body withering but his face still bright and full of life, only months before he'd pass away, Younger's face lit up as he spoke of the sport and what it meant to him.

A visitor had asked Younger about racial progress, and its limitations. He had at once internalized all the rebukes yet seemed to lack the spoiling core of bitterness. He had seen changes on the field that reflected the larger changes in American society. The game was imperfect, but it was his game, and Younger was forever marked by his time spent in it.

"I considered it an honor to play in the league," said Younger. "And I believe that when you go on that field, you have a responsibility, not only to yourself, but to your ball club and to the fans. I believe that. You hear a lot of folks talk about coaches giving pregame talks, inspirational speeches, and all that bullshit in the dressing room prior to a game. My inspirational speech was when they played the National Anthem. That really got me fired up. It always fired me up and I wanted to go hit somebody. Shit, when they sang 'o'er the land of the free and the home of the brave,' I'm ready to go knock the *hell* out of somebody. And I feel that way today. I'll be watching a game, they play the National Anthem, goddammit, my blood starts boiling. I felt I owed a responsibility to myself, to my team, and to the fans that had plunked down their bucks to come see me play. Always felt that way."

And there was, in Younger's dedication and fans' response to it, a hint at the quality that made football the most American of games, and likely the most misunderstood. Though the NFL would continue to market itself overseas, many in the game had come to the conclusion that there was, at the bottom, something essentially untranslatable about the sport and America's obsession with it.

And perhaps that was for the best. Pro football was, in a way that baseball and basketball could never be, distinctly our own, and it defied easy characterization. "I reject the notion of football as warfare," said a character in Don DeLillo's novel *End Zone*. "Football is discipline. It's team love. It's reason plus passion."

In the end, Jacques Barzun was not necessarily wrong. To know America, one may well still have to know baseball. But to *understand* the world's only superpower at the dawn of the new century, its passion and preoccupations, idealism and contradictions, it is necessary to understand the National Football League, and its profound impact on its audience.

After Elvis Presley's death in 1977, the rock critic Lester Bangs wrote that "we will never again agree on anything as we agreed on Elvis." After a generation of ever more numerous entertainment options in modern American pop culture, in a land increasingly divided by demographics and sensibilities, narrowcasting and niche marketing, it can safely be said that we will never agree on anything the way we agree on the National Football League. Pro football is our biggest civic tent, our last genuinely *mass* entertainment.

There always remains the possibility of decay from within, or a failure to maintain faith with its fans. But for the foreseeable future, the sport will reign across the gleaming, twenty-first-century American landscape, as modern as the digital age, as timeless as the most primal urge for tribal identification, the quintessential pastime of modern America. Pro football has become the perfect symbol for the country's bustling, modernistic urgency, a splendid entertainment, a taxing and transforming profession, and a meaningful metaphor for the most American pursuit of all, those seemingly mismatched but inextricably bound ideas of competition and community.

AFTERWORD TO THE ANCHOR BOOKS EDITION

In February 2005, the New England Patriots won Super Bowl XXXIX—their second straight world championship, and third in four seasons—outlasting the Philadelphia Eagles, 24–21. Just over two months later, the National Football League announced that starting in 2006, it will move its *Monday Night Football* package from ABC, where the series had run since its inception in 1970, to ESPN.

The two events are hardly related—one took place on the field, the other in a series of boardrooms and private negotiations about as far from the game as anything involving football could possibly occur—but both offer telling revelations about the realities of pro football in the twenty-first century, hinting at the changes that are shaping the future of America's Game.

On the field, the Patriots rose to become the first dynasty built during the free agency era, a team in the truest sense, whose bedrock foundation was the strong leadership of head coach Bill Belichick and vice president of player personnel Scott Pioli. Belichick had experienced mixed success as a head coach from 1991–95 in Cleveland, but after another tenure as Bill Parcells's top assistant in New England and New York in the late '90s, he was more prepared for the demands of head coaching when Patriots owner Robert Kraft hired him in 2000. When Belichick accepted the job, he brought along longtime friend and colleague Pioli—a former Division II defensive lineman at Central Connecticut State—who had first worked for Belichick in Cleveland, and later in the '90s on the staffs of the Patriots and Jets.

The two had met in the summer of '86, when Belichick was the defensive coordinator of the Super Bowl champion Giants, and Pioli was a college student who spent his off days in the summer making the ninety-minute drive from his Washingtonville, New York home to the campus of Farleigh Dickinson University in Madison, New Jersey, just to watch the Giants training-camp practices and learn more about the game. Impressed with the student-athlete's sincere curiosity, Belichick invited him to stay for a while and observe the coaching staff at work. During his extended stay, Pioli watched practices from the field, sat in with Belichick in the film room, and absorbed the work ethic of the Giants' staff. "The thing that stood out to me as a kid who was never exposed to big-time football was the amount of work that they put into football," said Pioli. "And I don't mean the physical work of the players, I mean the time that the coaches put in, to see that you could actually spend eighteen hours a day, completely immersing yourself in football. I remember thinking to myself, this is what I *want* to be doing eighteen hours a day."

In New England, they were the two key football decision makers working under owner Robert Kraft. In 2000, Belichick and Pioli survived a 5–11 season with a club whose personnel and salary-cap structure, in which a great deal of money was tied up in just a few contracts, clearly needed to be overhauled.

Then, in the off-season of 2001, they signed twenty-four free agents, seventeen of whom made the team the next season. The group included two team captains, seven full-time starters, three special teams regulars, and two defensive backs who had seen extensive playing time in nickel-and-dime packages. The seventeen free agents—who collectively received signing bonuses totaling less than the one Seattle gave to former Patriots defensive tackle Chad Eaton the same off-season—formed the nucleus of the Patriots team that won the last nine games en route to its Super Bowl win that season.

Though they took a step back in 2002, the Patriots were the dominant team in football in 2003 and 2004. Belichick's success with defenses is well-known, but he brought more to the job than just brains. His genuine passion and his lunch-bucket sensibilities were perfectly suited for a generation of players that often grew tired and suspicious of the bloodless, cerebral "geniuses" calling the shots on many NFL teams.

For his part, Pioli was a former football player with a sharp eye for football talent, as well as a keen sense for the effect that individual players have both on the field and in the locker room. Belichick had been criticized for his tunnel vision in Cleveland—acquiring talented players who later proved to be a detriment to the team chemistry off the field—but in New England, he and Pioli took fewer risks with "problem" players, ensuring that his players bought into the team concept that he espoused.

The Patriots also changed the manner in which they entered the free agent market. When Belichick had been in Cleveland, the Browns had courted potential free agents like Andre Rison and Reggie White with limo rides and fancy dinners. But at New England, he quickly shifted gears. "That's not who we are," he said one night to Pioli, and so in New England the approach was different. On his free agent visit, Larry Izzo—the first of the Patriots' haul of the free agent signings in 2001—wound up eating pizza in the Patriots' film room; most players who visited stayed at the Residence Inn in Foxboro, rather than an upscale hotel in downtown Boston.

Along the way, the Patriots created a model for the new age that many teams were struggling to copy in 2005. The work ethic of the team was as pronounced as any of the NFL dynasties dating back at least as far as the Steelers of the '70s and perhaps even the Packers of the '60s.

It was reflected not merely in the team's staunch, nearly starless team makeup, but in many other aspects as well. The Patriots' mantra, composed by Pioli and printed in red at the bottom of each page of the team's scouting handbook, was: "We are building a big, strong, fast, smart, tough and disciplined football team that consistently competes for championships." The team was explicitly less concerned with "measurables" than they were with tangible evidence of players who excelled on the field.

Luck helped—the controversial "tuck" call in the Patriots' 2001 playoff against Oakland kept that year's run alive, and two years later John Kasey's inexplicable botched kickoff gave the Patriots the ball on their own 40-yard line at the end of their Super Bowl XXXVIII battle with the Panthers.

The best fortune of all came with the team's on-field leader, quarterback Tom Brady, who was drafted in the sixth round out of Michigan in 2000. After five years in the pros, Brady trailed only Joe Montana and Terry Bradshaw for number of Super Bowls won by a quarterback. Surely the Patriots hadn't seen that when they chose Brady. But they saw *something* in him and put a higher priority on acquiring him than any of the other teams in the league did.

In an age when players are more aware than ever of their individual value on the open market, the Patriots' success emphasized the importance of team chemistry rather than individual performance. Even the players bought into this belief, none more so than Brady, who in 2004 extended his contract for a fraction of what he might have earned as a free agent.

"The team has goals," Brady said. "The greater team goal is winning the Super Bowl. That supersedes what any player goal might be. You have to make decisions as an individual, whether you want to be part of this team or not.

And you're going to have to make sacrifices like every guy on this team makes sacrifices. I know what's important to me. I know where my priorities lie."

So did the Patriots. On the plane back from Jacksonville the evening after the Super Bowl win over the Eagles, Pioli and Belichick met to discuss roster tweaks and salary-cap status for the players under contract. The team took part in a victory parade in Boston the next day, and then, at 7:30 on Wednesday morning, Pioli and Belichick were back at work on the season ahead, taking part in a morning draft meeting.

It would be months before the rings arrived, but a new season had already begun.

———

At the league offices in New York, two matters dominated the 2005 off-season. The first was the ongoing negotiations between the NFL and the networks to renew the television contracts that were going to expire at the end of the 2005 season. The league, led by executive vice president of media Steve Bornstein, had renewed part of its TV package, extending contracts with Fox, CBS, and DirecTV in the fall of 2004. But the league was still dangling its lucrative prime-time packages on Sunday and Monday nights into the spring of 2005.

When the deal was finally nailed down in mid-April, ESPN wrested away the *Monday Night Football* franchise from fellow Disney subsidiary ABC and agreed to pay $1.1 billion per season for the right to carry the most prestigious weekly series in sports television. The Sunday night package moved to NBC, which was back in business with the NFL for the first time since 1998 and would benefit from the flexible scheduling provisions that might improve the desirability of late-season matchups. Taken together, the deals ensured that the NFL's annual television take would grow from $2.4 billion per season to $3.7 billion per season, and that the game would continue to be the dominant spectator-sport franchise on American television.

But it was how to allocate the league's growing revenues, from television and elsewhere, that formed the crux of the league's greatest challenge.

The collective bargaining agreement with the players had been scheduled to expire in 2008, though by the spring of 2005, negotiations had been going on for more than a year to renew the deal. But before such an agreement could be reached, owners would have to decide among themselves how to most equitably handle the growing revenue disparities among the teams, due largely to the increasing gap in unshared stadium revenues. It was a tricky negotiation, full of what Tagliabue liked to describe as "lots of moving parts," and he tackled it as he did most challenges, with thorough study and a series of consensus-building committee meetings in which owners tried to iron out their differences.

And they had, of course, every motivation to do so. This negotiation would almost certainly be the last time that the NFL's Tagliabue and the NFLPA's Gene Upshaw would work to extend their historic agreement of 1993. The deal had grown in stature with each passing year. As the other major sports suffered punishing losses from strikes and lockouts, the NFL and the NFLPA had spent the balance of the '90s in relative harmony, extending the CBA and working together to enforce a tougher drug- and steroid-testing program than any other major professional sports league.

There were plenty of other people involved in the negotiation, but just as they had in the early '90s, Tagliabue and Upshaw frequently sat down privately and hashed out the intricacies of a potential deal. After a one-on-one meeting that lasted nearly seven hours on April 15, they spoke again two days later, and Tagliabue mentioned George Santayana's quote, "Those who do not learn the lessons of history are doomed to repeat it." They resolved to heed Santayana's words. It seemed highly probable that the NFL and the NFLPA would once again find common ground in mutual self-interest.

So as pro football pushed toward a future that seemed in many ways different from its past—*Monday Night Football* on cable, regular season games in Mexico City, and flexible scheduling on Sunday nights—there was a sense that the caretakers of the game were truly taking care of the game.

But just as in the days of Pete Rozelle, the ultimate decision is up to the owners of the National Football League franchises. The people who own those thirty-two clubs are inheritors of one of the great enterprises in modern American society. The game has a purpose that goes far beyond business and a meaning that goes far beyond entertainment.

But history, and the fall of Major League Baseball, has shown that the NFL's status is not a birthright. If pro football falters, it won't be because its players misbehave, or its fans are fickle, or because the networks drive too hard of a bargain. It will be because, in seeking ever greater riches, the owners commit the cardinal football sin of taking their eyes off the ball.

ACKNOWLEDGMENTS

I began work on this book in the summer of 1999, and over five years have accumulated more than the usual number of debts of gratitude.

The greatest are owed to all those who took the time to talk with me about their experiences in pro football. The game possesses its own language and creates its own reality, and can be tiresome to explain to an outsider. But many people took the time and, in so doing, revealed something about the nature of the game: no one chooses a career in football because they only *sort of* like it; the game is populated by people who are passionate about their vocation. This can be seen not only on the field but in locker rooms and administrative offices, and even by the pool at resort hotels during league meetings, where I've seen people engaged in heated discussions over whether the NFL's designated inactive list is "the worst rule in the game" or another crucial tenet of the league's standard of fairness.

The main character in the NFL's rise to popularity was of course Pete Rozelle, and my ability to document something of his career and life is the result of the trust and generosity shown by Rozelle's daughter, Anne Marie Bratton, who opened up Rozelle's papers, and her home, to me. As a frequent interloper at the Bratton estate, I'm forever indebted to Anne, her husband, Doug, and their children, Miles and Alexandra, for their help and hospitality. I also appreciate the extra time taken by Rozelle's brother, Dick Rozelle, and Pete's longtime friend, John Lehman.

As for Rozelle's predecessor, there is no better source for understanding Bert Bell than his wry, delightful son Bert Bell, Jr., who provided a wealth of memories, took me on a tour of his father's Philadelphia, and helped me separate the truth from the fiction about his father's life.

The NFL's present commissioner, Paul Tagliabue, was here to tell his own story, and he did so eloquently and with tremendous patience for my novice's understanding of the law, over what turned out to be twenty-five hours of interviews in several different sessions.

At the league office, Greg Aiello and his communications staff fielded my calls and e-mails by the hundreds, and were unfailingly helpful. In addition to Greg, I'm grateful to Leslie Hammond, Brian McCarthy, Vince Casey, Pete Abitante, Randall Liu, Dan Masonson, Steve Alic, Julie Buzzard, and Alexia Gallagher for the help they provided.

I also owe special thanks to Joel Bussert, the NFL's director of player personnel (and untitled in-house historian), and Jeff Pash, the league's vice president and legal counsel, whose near-photographic memory rivals Tagliabue's own. Joe Browne, Roger Goodell, Peter Hadhazy, the late George Young, Mike Pereira, Dennis Lewin, Steve Bornstein, Hamilton Carothers, and John Beake also walked me through various stages of the league's operational structure and history.

There were nearly two dozen other sources with whom I consulted repeatedly over the past five years, and they humored me through countless follow-up questions. The late Don Weiss and the late Tex Schramm were both crucial, providing crisp reflections and insights into the game's growth in the '60s and '70s. Owners like Lamar Hunt, Wellington Mara, Dan Rooney, Art Modell, and Bud Adams spoke to me on several occasions each, demonstrating the institutional memory that helped the league succeed. The Giants' Ernie Accorsi, the Chiefs' Carl Peterson, and the Colts' Bill Polian provided a fascinating indoctrination into the game's ultracompetitive modern age, from player development to cap management. The Falcons' Rich McKay helped me understand the environment of the present-day Competition Committee. Bill Walsh, Brian Billick, Tony Dungy, Dick Vermeil, Gunther Cunningham, Marty Schottenheimer, and Jack Faulkner all gave eloquent witness to the coaching experience. (I'm especially indebted to Dungy, who let me visit him in the middle of the pressure-filled 2003 season and spend two days at his shoulder, which provided a sense of the coaching life far removed from the loud stadiums and crowded press conferences.) And Jim Brown, Gene Upshaw, Bill Curry, Pat Summerall, Frank Gifford, Bobby Mitchell, Raymond Berry, Len Dawson, and the late Tank Younger all helped me better understand the players' perspective.

At NFL Films, Steve Sabol opened the vaults so I could revisit much of his work over the past forty years and was consistently helpful in tracking down many of the lost pieces of the archival puzzle, like a full-color tape of the 1945 NFL championship game. Equally helpful were communications reps Cory Laslocky, Michelle Valkov, and Patrick Pantano, as well as director of archives Ace Cacchiotti.

Many people shared not just memories but materials, clippings, documents, correspondence, and publications. Frank Kasper, one of the NFL's "baby-sitters" during the war, sent me his fascinating collection of materials. Ed Krzemienski and Tim Brulia generously shared the fruits of their own research on the life of Joe Namath and the early years of pro football on TV, respectively. At the NFL Creative Services offices, John Wiebusch was particularly helpful. Outside the office, Roger Atkin, Dave Gardner, Herb Weitman, and Carol Boss shared recollections and evidence of the artistry of David Boss.

I received plenty of help from the PR departments of the key franchises around which I built this story. The Rams' Rick Smith has a great memory and managed the best set of team archives in the league. After Rick retired, Aaron Staenberg ably succeeded him. In Cleveland, Dino Lucarelli, the head of the thriving alumni relations group for the Browns, was an invaluable resource, pointing me to the Browns' wonderful scrapbooks and putting me in touch with several of the Browns' legends. Kevin Byrne of the Ravens arranged numerous interviews, many in the pressing environment of the regular season. I also received much-needed help from Rich Dalrymple and Brett Daniels in Dallas, Craig Kelley and Pamela Humphrey in Indianapolis, Al LoCasale in Oakland and Jack Brennan in Cincinnati. I grew up in Kansas City as a fan of the Chiefs, so I had some prior knowledge of their history, but Bob Moore of the Chiefs' PR department shared a wealth of new material that helped me flesh out the team's early years. He and his staff, including Pete Morris, Morgan Shaw, and Brad Kuhbander, were unfailingly courteous and helpful in the midst of my frequent intrusions.

I also received valuable assistance on numerous occasions from Pat Hanlon of the Giants, the esteemed Lee Remmel of the Packers, Ron Wahl of the Steelers, and Frank Ramos of the Jets, as well as Dan Edwards of the Jaguars, Greg Bensel of the Saints, Bill Johnston of the Chargers, Jim Saccomano of the Broncos, Bob Hagen of the Vikings, Reggie Roberts and later Zack Bolno of the Buccaneers, Kirk Reynolds of the 49ers, and Scott Berchtold of the Bills.

I also must thank the long-suffering Susie Stephens in Lamar Hunt's office and Kristi Bailey in Al Davis's office, both of whom I bothered on countless occasions in trying to set up interviews with those two extremely busy men.

Closer to home, as I tried to gain a more workable understanding of the game, head coach Larry Kindbom and his staff at Washington University in St. Louis gave me some insight into the inner workings of football. The chalk talks, film sessions, playbook reviews, and remedial education provided by Kindbom and his staff (especially former assistants, Ron Collins, Aaron Keen, Pedro Aruzza) were crucial in helping me gain a better understanding of the game.

This book would not have gotten off the ground without the keen eye of my agent, Sloan Harris at ICM, who understood the appeal of the project as well as the challenges it would face. He helped focus my thinking at the earliest stages and kept me on course throughout. I'm also grateful to Sloan's previous assistant Teri Steinberg and his present one, Katharine Cluverius, as well as ICM's John DeLaney, for their frequent help. The redoubtable Rick Pappas once again provided his much-needed and much-appreciated counsel.

Ann Godoff and Scott Moyers brought the project to Random House, but left before it was completed. I was grateful for their initial interest and help. In their place, Dan Menaker and Webster Younce retained faith in the book through two missed deadlines. More than anyone, it was Younce who saved me from myself and prevented the manuscript from attaining the approximate length of Churchill's six-volume history of World War II. I'm also thankful to Julia Cheiffetz, Younce's assistant; production editor Steve Messina; managing editor Benjamin Dreyer; designer Caroline Cunningham; associate production manager Erich Schoeneweiss; and Fred Chase, who copyedited the manuscript. When Younce left in the spring of 2004, he was succeeded by Mark Tavani, who in a difficult situation shepherded the book to completion. I'm also grateful to Mark's assistant, Ingrid Powell, as well as to London King and Annie Klein of the Random House publicity department.

Over the years, I was aided by a variety of underpaid researchers, including the invaluable Elizabeth Brewster, who handled the brunt of the transcriptions, as well as Shekar Sathyanarayana, Mike Wise, Andrew Satter, Chava Mandell, Chris Cramer, Candice Holliday, Sabrina Lin, Nathan Kleekamp, Ian Cornelius, Jeremy Mikecz, Kate Ashford, Ken Lee, and George Milkov. The saintly Lesley McCullough was there for the final year and provided vital work as I finished the manuscript, ranging from transcribing interviews to helping organize the endnotes to figuring out where in my basement office I'd misplaced this or that crucial document. Sharon Maslow, Jane Ward, and Lisa Dohlsein also provided transcription assistance early on.

Much of the early research was conducted at the Pro Football Hall of Fame Archives, and I'm especially grateful to Joe Horrigan, Pete Fierle, and Saleem

Choudhry for their assistance there. Steve Gietschier at the *Sporting News* archive in St. Louis was always helpful during my frequent visits, many on short notice. I spent two weeks, and could have easily spent two months, at the Library of Congress, whose staff members are invariably polite and helpful, even with questions they've heard thousands of times before. I'm also grateful for the assistance offered by David Bowser and the staff at the University City Public Library; the staff at Olin Library at Washington University in St. Louis, and the Mid-County Branch of the St. Louis County Library.

In assembling the photographs, I owe special thanks to Neil Leifer, Walter Iooss, Jr., Rod Hanna, Vernon and John Biever, Janis E. Rettaliata, Hank Young, Phil Hoffman, Bill Stover, Jennifer Allen, Cathy Kensil, Jack Landry, Jr., Paul Tepley, Terry McDonell, Fred Gaudelli, Bob Rosato, Karen Carpenter, Kevin Terrell, Scott Macrillo, Coral Petretti, Amie Trever, and Rachel Howell.

The project took much longer than I'd originally envisioned, and without the help of John Walsh and John Skipper, I'm not sure I would have been able to complete it. I will be forever in their debt.

I received shelter, sustenance, and moral support from a wide array of friends and family during my frequent cross-country travels, including my mother, Lois MacCambridge; my sister and brother-in-law, Angie and Tom Szentgyorgyi; my in-laws, Douglas, David, Danielle, and Dennis Frost, and Dominique and Cliff Parker; Rob Minter, Brian Hay, Susan Reckers, Joe Posnanski, Trey Gratwick, Mike Sutter, Sean and Elizabeth Porter, Sylvester and Angelia Givens, and Dr. Keith O. Garner. The light was always on at the home of Greg Emas and his family, where I stayed during my frequent trips to Kansas City.

Special thanks are owed to Pat Porter, Larry Schwartz, and all the others who read portions of the early manuscript. I also want to thank all those who wrote with observations and errors in the first edition, including Bill Murphy, Ken Holloway, Joe Kane, Robert Benzie, Charlie Ellis, Paul Goldberg, Jim Mooney, Richard Cottone, Bryant McEvoy, Michael Berger, former NFL lineman Gordon King, Michael Berger, Rich Dubroff, and Phil Roché. (The errors that made it through are my own. If you see any, please write me at MacCambridge@mac.com so I can make corrections in subsequent editions of this book.)

I'm also grateful for the help along the way from Arin Paske, Kelly Foster, Heather Dougherty, Kathy Stephens, Robert Draper, Vahe Gregorian, Cindy Billhartz, Gerald Early, Michael Hurd, Bill James, Robert W. Creamer, Michael Oh, Brad Garrett, Kevin Lyttle, Alex Wolff, Russell Smith, Stan Webb, Michael

Point, Kirby Moss, Carl Kuebler, Loren Watt, Hal Cox, Larry Johnson, Robert Humphrey, David Zivan, Kristin Elizondo, Teri McCarthy, Abe Peck, Chris Brown, Larry Callahan, Todd Jones, Rich Wagner, Nancy Gates, Joanne Stouwie, Jim Fiala, Ken Bertken, Bob Jacobi, Jr., and Walter Bernard.

Of course, no one suffers over a long book like a writer's family—and mine paid the price in numerous ways. I'm eternally grateful for the patience, love, and support of my wife, Danica Frost, and our children, Miles and Ella. Miles turned five this year and has been asking me since he was old enough to talk if I was done with my book yet. The answer, finally, is yes. I think.

MJM
University City, Missouri
August 2004

SOURCE NOTES

ABBREVIATIONS:

AP	Associated Press	PFW	*Pro Football Weekly*
LAT	*Los Angeles Times*	SI	*Sports Illustrated*
NYT	*New York Times*	TSN	*The Sporting News*
PFHOF	Pro Football Hall of Fame	UPI	United Press International

PROLOGUE: DECEMBER 28, 1958

ix **While the two:** Gifford int.; Summerall int.; John Steadman int.; John Steadman, *The Greatest Football Game Ever Played* (Stevensville, MD: Press Box, 1988), p. 39.

x **"We got":** Unitas int.; Berry int.

x **With that:** Justin Doherty; "The Greatest Game Ever Played?," unpublished paper, University of Wisconsin, 2000.

xi **"What happens now?":** Summerall int. on *The NFL's Greatest Games: '58 Championship*, NFL Films, 1998.

xi **Up in the booth:** Schenkel int.

xi **"John!" yelled Weeb Ewbank:** Unitas int.; Steadman, *The Greatest Football Game Ever Played*, p. 12.

xii **And in that:** Chicago Tribune Press Service, "Play-by-Play Story of 80 Yard Drive to Title by Colts," *Chicago Tribune*, Dec. 29, 1958.

xii **The rocking:** Unitas int.

xii **Moments later:** Chris Schenkel int.; Curt Smith, *Of Mikes and Men: From Ray Scott to Curt Gowdy: Broadcast Tales from the Pro Football Booth* (South Bend, IN: Diamond, 1998), p. 64.

xiii **When NBC got:** Play-by-play accounts of the game vary. The most complete version appears in John Steadman's *The Greatest Football Game Ever Played*. There's also an annotated version of Unitas's final drive in both *The Pro Football Chronicle*, by Dan Daly and Bob O'Donnell, and Tex Maule's follow-up piece about the game in the January 19, 1959, issue of *Sports Illustrated*. Even here, there's little consensus. Steadman shows Ameche's key overtime run going for 22 yards, from the Giant 42 to the 20. Maule has it as a 23-yard carry, from the 43 to the 20. Daly and O'Donnell show it as a 23-yard carry, but they have it going from the 44 to the 21. Steadman, *The Greatest Football Game Ever Played*, pp. 132–37; Dan Daly and Bob O'Donnell, *The Pro Football Chronicle* (New York: Macmillan, 1990), pp. 159–60; Tex Maule, "The Best Game Ever Played," *Sports Illustrated*, Jan. 5, 1959;

Tex Maule, "Here's Why It Was the Best Football Game Ever," *Sports Illustrated,* Jan 19, 1959.

xiii   **"What if":** Steadman, *The Greatest Football Game Ever Played,* p. 66.

xiv   **"Whoever wants":** John Bartlett and Justin Kaplan, *Bartlett's Familiar Quotations* (Boston: Little, Brown, 1992), p. 721.

xiv   **Indeed, it was:** Michener int.

xiv   **By the early:** David Harris, *The League: The Rise and Decline of the NFL* (New York: Bantam, 1986), p. 5.

xvi   **More than any:** Arthur J. Donovan and Bob Drury, *Fatso: Football When Men Were Really Men* (New York: Morrow, 1987), p. 27.

1 : GOING WEST

3   **Compact and slender:** Reeves probably got the "Irish dividends" expression from previous owner Homer Marshman, who was quoted using it in Hal Lebovitz's introduction to Joseph Hession's *Rams: Five Decades of Football* (San Francisco: Foghorn, 1987), p. 13; Susan Reeves int.; Jack Teele int.; "Bob Waterfield: Actress Jane Russell's Husband Is 1945 'Pro' Football Star," *Life,* Dec. 17, 1945; Leonard Maltin, *Leonard Maltin's 2003 Movie and Video Guide* (New York: Penguin Putnam, 2003), p. 1041.

4   **Six days before the game:** Two days before the game, the *Cleveland News* reported representatives of the Rams and the city "were going slightly berserk attempting to get the Stadium in condition for Sunday's championship." Howard Preston, "Snow and Straw Dept.: Rams Corner Both at Stadium," *Cleveland News,* Dec. 12, 1945; "Rams, City Berserk Over 'Snow Bowl,' " *Cleveland News,* Dec. 14, 1945; John Dietrich, "Snow Won't Halt Title Game," *Cleveland Plain Dealer,* Dec. 12, 1945; Herman Goldstein, "Relief from December Playoff Unlikely; Owners Still Insist on Home Schedules," *Cleveland News,* Dec. 18, 1945.

4   **On Sunday morning:** Arthur Daley, "Sports of the Times: Short Shots in Sundry Directions," *NYT,* Dec. 14, 1945; AP, "Cleveland Looks for Record Crowd," *NYT,* Dec. 14, 1945; "Cleveland 8–5 Choice Over Redskins in Pro Football Final Today," *St. Louis Post-Dispatch,* Dec. 16, 1945; William D. Richardson, "Redskins and Rams in Top Shape Today for Pro Play-off," *NYT,* Dec. 16, 1945; AP, "77,000 May Watch Pro Title Contest," *NYT,* Dec. 15, 1945.

5   **Cleveland Stadium:** Manny Eisner int.; Ed Bang column, "Between You and Me," *Cleveland News,* Dec. 17, 1945; Franklin Lewis, "Bits and Bites of Sports Chosen and Chewed," *Cleveland Press,* Dec. 17, 1945.

5   **In financial terms:** Lewis, "Bits and Bites of Sports Chosen and Chewed."

6   **NFL commissioner Elmer Layden:** The NFL's championship trophy had obscure roots. Ed Thorp was a longtime assistant to the president of A.G. Spalding & Brothers, a recognized authority on playing rules, and one of the best-known referees in the country, working both the 1925 and 1934 Rose Bowl games. A week after he died of a cerebral hemorrhage in 1934, Eagles owner Bert Bell moved that the NFL create a permanent trophy in his name. Beginning at the end of the '34 season, the "Ed Thorpe Memorial Trophy" was given to the NFL's reigning champion. Joel Bussert int.; "Ed Thorp," National Football League press release; John Wiebusch, "A Long Winter's Day," *More Than a Game* (Englewood Cliffs, NJ: Prentice Hall, 1974), p. 125.

7   **Its next president:** Carroll et al., *Total Football II* (New York: HarperCollins, 1999), p. 99; George Halas, Gwen Morgan, and Arthur Veysey, *Halas* (New York: McGraw-Hill, 1979), pp. 72–77.

8   **For most of:** Dan Rooney int.; William Henry Paul, *The Gray-Flannel Pigskin: Movers and Shakers of Pro Football* (Philadelphia: Lippincott, 1974), p. 258.

8   **"So in December 1936":** Hal Lebovitz, "Introduction," in Joseph Hession, *Rams: Five Decades of Football* (San Francisco: Foghorn, 1987), p. 12.

9   **After Carr's death:** Dan Daly and Bob O'Donnell, *Pro Football Chronicle* (New York: Collier, 2000), p. 83; George Strickler letter, PFHOF; Don Pierson int.

9 **Storck's resignation:** George Strickler letter, PFHOF; *TSN,* Nov. 19, 1942.

9 **Layden was well regarded:** Robert Peterson, *Pigskin: The Early Years of Pro Football* (New York: Oxford University Press, 1997), p. 137; Elmer Layden and Ed Snyder, *It Was a Different Game: The Elmer Layden Story* (Englewood Cliffs, NJ: Prentice Hall, 1969), p. 146; Daly and O'Donnell, *Pro Football Chronicle,* p. 66.

10 **The son of:** Dan Rooney int.; Jack Teele int.

10 **The final Sunday:** Curt Smith, *Of Mikes and Men: From Ray Scott to Curt Gowdy: Broadcast Tales from the Pro Football Booth* (South Bend, IN: Diamond Communications), p. 32.

10 **On that Sunday:** Richard Goldstein, "Football Sunday, Dec. 7, 1941: Suddenly the Games Didn't Matter," *NYT,* Dec. 7, 1980.

11 **"I honestly feel":** William Mead, *Baseball Goes to War* (Washington, D.C.: Farragut, 1985), p. 35.

11 **And although it:** *TSN,* Dec. 11, 1945.

11 **As the nation rallied:** Peterson, *Pigskin,* p. 138.

12 **But the manpower:** Walter McCallum, "Clubs Are Sliced to 25 Men Over Skins' Protest," *Washington Star,* Apr. 9, 1943; Walter McCallum, "Win, Lose or Draw," *Washington Star,* Apr. 10, 1943; John Steadman int.; John Steadman, "It Hit Sports Like a Bomb, Too," *Baltimore Evening Sun,* Dec. 6, 1991; Halas et al., *Halas,* p. 215.

12 **The owners:** Thomas B. Littlewood, *Arch: A Promoter, Not a Poet: The Story of Arch Ward* (Ames, IA: State University Press, 1990), pp. 150–51; William A. Hachten, "A Rookie with the New York Giants," unpublished manuscript, Nov. 1998; John Steadman int.; Ernie Accorsi int.

12 **So the league fought:** Layden, *It Was a Different Game,* p. 151; "One-Armed Marine to Play for Eagles While Receiving Medical Care Here," *Philadelphia Inquirer,* undated; Hall of Fame papers; NFL news release, June 2, 1994; Ted Patterson, *Football in Baltimore: History and Memorabilia* (Baltimore: Johns Hopkins University Press), p. 55.

12 **For all that:** *Official 2003 National Football League Record and Fact Book* (New York: National Football League, 2003), p. 598.

13 **"We owners":** Halas et al., *Halas,* p. 233.

13 **On June 4, 1944:** Littlewood, *Arch,* pp. 153–56.

13 **At first:** Joe Hendrickson, "Pro Football War," *Esquire,* p. 46, August 1945.

13 **But the AAFC's:** *1947 All-America Conference Record Manual* (St. Louis: Sporting News, 1947), p. 24.

14 **When the *Tribune*:** *Chicago Tribune,* Apr. 21, 1945.

14 **The off-the-cuff:** Layden, *It Was a Different Game,* p. 154.

15 **The NFL's:** Daly and O'Donnell, *Pro Football Chronicle,* pp. 27–28; Layden, *It Was a Different Game,* pp. 165–67.

15 **"Layden was forced out":** George Strickler letter to Don Pierson, Nov. 17, 1974, PFHOF.

15 **For their new:** Bell int. Harold "Spike" Claassen, *The History of Professional Football: Its Great Teams, Games, Players and Coaches* (Englewood Cliffs, NJ: Prentice-Hall, 1963) pp. 93–94; Minutes from National Football League Annual Meetings, Jan. 11–12, 1946.

15 **Then it was time:** AP, "National Pro League Backs Champs' Shift," Jan. 13, 1946; Robert L. Burnes, "The Bench Warmer," *St. Louis Globe-Democrat,* Feb. 25, 1946.

16 **Eight votes:** Unsigned press release, "Dan Reeves Moves West—Hall of Fame Report," PFHOF.

16 **"If that's your":** Ibid.

16 **This wasn't the first time:** Nineteen forty-six NFL meeting minutes; Harold Claassen, *The History of Professional Football* (Englewood Cliffs, NJ: Prentice Hall, 1963), pp. 206–7.

16 **As Reeves left:** "It's not that I love Cleveland less," Reeves explained, "but that I love Los Angeles more." "Quotes," *Los Angeles Examiner,* Jan. 15, 1946. Reeves had visited Los Angeles in 1937, and seen a burgeoning metropolis full of transplanted Easterners who were as sports-mad as fans in New York. "I've wanted to go out there ever since," he said, "and the current move is the product of long-range planning and the culmination of seven years of trying." AP, "National Pro League Backs Champs' Shift," *Chicago Tribune,* Jan. 13, 1946.

16 **The NFL's record book:** This was the disastrous year in which the league was at twenty-two teams, only to quickly contract to twelve the following season, and ten the year after; Carroll, *Total Football* II, p. 105.

17 **When Coliseum Commission chairman:** Herman Hill, "Hill's Side," *Pittsburgh Courier,* Mar. 30, 1946.

17 **Few players:** Obituaries, *TSN,* July 10, 1971; Thomas G. Smith, "Outside the Pale," *The Coffin Corner,* Vol. 11, No. 4, originally published in *The Journal of Sport History.*

18 **Jackie Robinson:** Mike Rathet and Don Smith, *The Pro Football Hall of Fame Presents: Their Deeds and Dogged Faith* (New York: Routledge, 1984), p. 210.

18 **Despite the acclaim:** Smith, "Outside the Pale."

18 **When he traveled:** Ibid.

18 **After the game:** Obituaries, *TSN,* July 10, 1971; Woody Strode, *Goal Dust: An Autobiography* (Lanham, MD: Madison, 1990), p. 134.

18 **So when Roach:** Herman Hill, "Hill's Side," *Pittsburgh Courier,* Mar. 30, 1946.

18 **"Well, fellows":** Ibid.

19 **As Harding sat down:** "Pro Grid Champs Say They Want Buddy Young," *Pittsburgh Courier,* Jan. 26, 1946.

19 **"Kenny Washington":** Herman Hill, "Hill's Side," *Pittsburgh Courier,* Mar. 30, 1946; minutes from Los Angeles Coliseum Commission meeting, Jan. 29, 1946.

19 **And so on May 4:** Strode, *Goal Dust,* p. 214.

20 **That summer:** Vincent X. Flaherty column, "Owner of Rams Comes to California to Stay," *LAT,* July 14, 1946.

20 **"That kid":** Schramm int.

2: THE ORGANIZATION MAN

21 **Standing in front of the classroom:** "Columbus Still Shows Interest in Paul Brown," *Cleveland News,* Aug. 1, 1946; Dino Lucarelli int.

21 **His voice:** Jack Clary, *Great Teams Great Years: Cleveland Browns* (New York: Macmillan, 1973), pp. 20, 32–33.

21 **"We will be":** William V. Levy, *Return to Glory: The Story of the Cleveland Browns* (Cleveland: World, 1965), p. 62.

22 **Later that morning:** Hal Lebovitz, "I'll Never Forget . . . : The Right Way . . . and the Brown Way," *Pro Magazine!,* 1980 season.

22 **"I want this team":** Arthur Daley, "A Rather Robust Darling," Sports of the Times, *NYT,* Nov. 21, 1948; Levy, *Return to Glory,* pp. 62–63.

23 **Massillon, Ohio, lay:** Michael Barone and Grant Ujifusa, *The Almanac of American Politics* (Washington, D.C.: Times Books, 2000), p. 1289.

23 **Young Paul Brown:** Paul Brown and Jack Clary, *PB, The Paul Brown Story* (New York: Atheneum, 1979), pp. 23–29; "Brown'll Remember the Kids," *Cleveland News,* May 5, 1945; Tex Maule, "A Man for This Season," *SI,* Sep. 10, 1962.

23 **"He was like a banty rooster":** Levy, *Return to Glory,* p. 44; Al Ostrow, "They Even Named the Team After Paul Brown," *St. Louis Post-Dispatch,* Nov. 6, 1959.

24 **There were rumors:** Dawson int.

24 **One key to:** After losses in each of his first three seasons to archrival Canton McKinley, Brown's Massillon Tigers beat Canton the next six seasons, compiling a record of 58-1-1 in that span. Tommy Devine, "Fans in the Huddle," *PIC* magazine, undated.

24 **"You've got to have":** Arthur Daley, "A Rather Robust Darling," Sports of the Times, *NYT,* Nov. 21, 1948.

24 **He also developed:** Mickey Herskowitz, *The Golden Age of Pro Football: NFL Football in the 1950s* (Dallas: Taylor, 1990), p. 141; Maule, "A Man for This Season."

25 **In the '30s:** Robert Smith, *Pro Football: The History of the Game and the Great Players* (Garden City, NY: Doubleday, 1963), p. 100.

25 **The T helped to civilize:** In its complexity, but also its brutality, the game served as an obvious analogue to war itself. The comparison hadn't been lost on football coaches. During World War II, Shaughnessy published a magazine-length article titled "Football in Time of War," in which he compared the charge of General Montgomery's British Eighth Army troops at El Alamein to a key play in the T formation series. "At El Alamein," wrote Shaughnessy, "the feint to the left by General Montgomery and his threat to the middle of the line prevented the Germans from shifting enough power to Montgomery's right to stop the onslaught of the British. . . . In football the play is called a fullback counter." Clark Shaughnessy and Esquire, Inc., *Football in War and Peace* (Clinton, SC: Jacobs Press, 1943) pp. 4–5; Edwin Pope, *Football's Greatest Coaches* (Atlanta: Tupper and Love, 1955), pp. 224–25.

26 **While Halas:** "Paul Brown Lays Plans for Cleveland Pro Club," *Chicago Sun,* Apr. 9, 1945.

26 **Brown was still:** Clary, *Great Teams Great Years: Cleveland Browns,* pp. 13–21; Brown, *PB,* p. 124.

27 **Once Graham was signed:** Graham int.; Lavelli int.

27 **In the Philippines:** Brown and Clary, *PB,* p. 125.

28 **"Ohio State is counting":** UPI, "Avers Attempt to Wreck Athletic Department," *Cleveland Press,* Feb. 9, 1946.

28 **"Keep in mind":** AP, "Brown Hits Back at Criticism by St. John," *Cleveland Plain Dealer,* Feb. 9, 1946.

28 **With the Rams':** Eisner int.

28 **"Regardless of":** "First Order: Browns Warned to Be Lean and Hungry," *Cleveland News,* May 29, 1946.

28 **To help him:** Bob Yonkers, "Three Cleveland Rookies Given Chance to Stick with Browns as Camp Opens," *Cleveland Press,* July 29, 1946; Kay Collier Slone, *Football's Gentle Giant: The Blanton Collier Story* (Lexington, KY: Life Force Press, 1985), pp. 160–61.

28 **At Bowling Green:** "Columbus Still Shows Interest in Paul Brown," *Cleveland News,* Aug. 1, 1946.

29 **On the third day of practice:** "Brown Passes Out First Play—It Goes Off Tackle," *Cleveland News,* Aug. 1, 1946.

29 **Brown drew from:** Mike Brown int.

29 **"There was a total":** Clary, *The Gamemakers,* p. 21.

29 **Willis was preparing:** Bob Yonkers, "Willis Tries Out with Browns, May Open Way for Negro Players in All-America," *Cleveland Press,* Aug. 6, 1946.

30 **Later in the month:** Clary, *Great Teams Great Years: Cleveland Browns,* p. 23.

30 **Brown later claimed:** Brown and Clary, *PB,* p. 129.

30 **As Dan Daly:** Daly and O'Donnell, *The Pro Football Chronicle,* p. 119.

30 **Brown never informed:** Herskowitz int.; Herskowitz, *The Golden Age of Pro Football,* p. 141.

30 **With the last two key players:** Fifteen of his players were Ohioans, and nearly all had played either for or against Brown at some point in his coaching career. "Brown Ohio," *Newsweek,* Dec. 30, 1946; Peterson, *Pigskin,* p. 155.

31 **During the Rams:** "Meat, Homes, Trucks, Girls, Etc.," *Cleveland Press,* July 15, 1946.

31 **"About $10,000 worth":** Powers quoted in Bill Leiser, "Browns Really Did Things Up Brown," *San Francisco Chronicle,* Sep. 8, 1946.

31 **The Browns outclassed their opposition:** Ron Smith, *Cleveland Browns: The Official Illustrated History* (St. Louis: Sporting News, 1999), p. 37.

31 **Dons coach Dudley DeGroot:** "The Big Difference—Motley," *Cleveland News,* Oct. 21, 1946.

32 **"There were times in games":** Ira Berkow, "The Kicker Changed the Game," *NYT,* Dec. 10, 2000.

33 **"That kind of crap":** Stuart Leuthner, *Iron Men: Bucko, Crazylegs, and the Boys Recall the Golden Days of Professional Football* (New York: Doubleday, 1988), p. 233.

33 **The team's organizational:** Ray Didinger, "A Remembrance of Paul Brown," in *A Game of Passion: The NFL Literary Companion,* John Wiebusch and Brian Silverman, eds., (Atlanta: Turner, 1994), p. 242.

33 **While Conkright's analysis:** Herman Goldstein, "Some Little Things That Made Browns Big," *Cleveland News,* Dec. 16, 1946.

33 **Cleveland's practices:** Arthur Daley, "A Rather Robust Darling," Sports of the Times, *NYT,* Nov. 21, 1948.

33 **"A coach who scrimmages":** Jack Newcombe, "Paul Brown: Football's Licensed Genius," *Sport,* Dec. 1954.

33 **As in training camp:** In the area of spouses, Brown's attention to detail was acute and unflagging. He ordered the tickets for players' wives and girlfriends separated, figuring that if they sat together, they would only trade gossip and foment resentment. Otto Graham int.; Herskowitz, *The Golden Age of Pro Football,* p. 54.

34 **During the season:** Newcombe, "Paul Brown: Football's Licensed Genius."

34 **"This is a business trip":** Bill Walsh, "Paul Brown: 60 Years of Quiet, Innovative Football," *NYT,* Aug. 11, 1991.

34 **On game days:** Lou Groza int.

34 **After the team:** Natali, *Brown's Town,* p. 55.

34 **"Is what I read":** Ibid.

34 **"We were a young team":** Terry Pluto, *When All the World Was Browns Town: Cleveland's Browns and the Championship Season of '64* (New York: Simon & Schuster, 1997), p. 24.

35 **The game itself:** "Browns Get $931 Each for Title Game," *Cleveland Press,* Dec. 20, 1946.

35 **Afterward, Brown:** Howard Preston, "Pro Title Completes the Grid Cycle for Paul Brown," *Cleveland News,* Dec. 23, 1946.

35 **After the season:** Slone, *Football's Gentle Giant,* p. 24; Jack Ryan, "Football Has Gone Scientific," *Pro Football Illustrated,* 1947.

35 **Collier's job:** Ibid.

36 **One example:** Ibid.

36 **As in every other industry:** Spadia int.

36 **"You must earn morale":** Paul Brown, "Building Morale on a Football Squad," notes from speech given at coaching clinic; Weeb Ewbank papers, University of Miami, Ohio.

37 **"We're getting":** Ryan, "Football Has Gone Scientific."

3: "LET BERT DO IT"

38 **"His mission in life":** Phil Musick, "A Football Man," in *A Game of Passion,* Wiebusch and Silverman, eds., p. 324.

39 **With the ten-team league:** Carroll et al., *Total Football II,* pp. 1751–1755; Manny Eisner int.

39 **The issue was:** Paul, *The Gray-Flannel Pigskin,* p. 258.

39 **"The owners who had":** Ray Didinger, *Great Teams Great Years: Pittsburgh Steelers* (New York: Macmillan, 1974), p. 120.

39 **So owners learned:** Minutes from National Football League meetings, PFHOF.

40 **"The schedules would always":** Musick, "A Football Man," in *A Game of Passion,* Wiebusch and Silverman, eds., p. 324.

40 **"Weak teams should play":** Untitled Bert Bell profile, undated, PFHOF.

40 **Each off-season:** Bell int.; Ed Pollock, "Bert Bell Plays Dominoes, Trying to Chart Pro Games," *TSN,* Jan. 18, 1950.

41 **For weeks on end:** Bell int.; Mike Rathet, "The Domino Theory," *Petersen's 1972 Pro Football Annual,* p. 81.

41 **His son Upton:** Upton Bell with David Chanoff, "Any Given Sunday," *Philadelphia Magazine,* Sep. 2000.

41 **Those in Bell's social circle:** Steadman int.; Bell int.; Les Biederman, "His Name's de Benneville but Otherwise He's Tough," publication unknown, Jan. 17, 1946.

41 **"If you don't think":** Harvey Pollack, "Bell of the NFL," *Sportfolio,* Jan. 1948, p. 87.

41 **"He'll go to Penn":** Bert Bell, Jr., int; Louis Effrat, "Bell's Decisions Keep Pro Football Family Happy, Rich," *NYT,* Dec. 30, 1956.

42 **Bell started at:** Anthony DiMarco, *The Big Bowl Football Guide* (New York: Putnam, 1976), p. 17; Bert Bell, Jr., int.; *Pennsylvania Gazette,* Vol. 17, May 9, 1919, pp. 729–33, University Archives and Record Center, University of Pennsylvania; *Current Biography* (New York: H. W. Wilson, 1950), p. 34.

42 **After a series of financial setbacks:** Bert Bell, Jr., int.

42 **The previous summer:** The Frankford Yellow Jackets, located on the outskirts of Philadelphia, had fallen victim to the Depression, inferior facilities, and the Pennsylvania blue laws, which prevented them from playing home games on Sunday. They were helped in November of that year when, as expected, Pennsylvania voters repealed the blue laws prohibiting Sunday sports events. Five days after the law was passed, the Eagles played their first Sunday home game. Bert Bell, Jr., int.; John Steadman int.

43 **Walking along the Jersey shore:** John Steadman, "Memories of Bell Burn Bright," *TSN,* Oct. 25, 1975; Bell with Chanoff, "Any Given Sunday."

43 **The Eagles were:** Tod Maher and Bob Gill, *The Pro Football Encyclopedia: The Complete and Definitive Record of Professional Football,* 3rd ed. (New York: Macmillan, 1997), p. 192.

43 **Bell had been particularly discouraged:** The University of Minnesota media guide has Kostka lettering in 1935, but *Total Football II* shows him playing in the NFL for Brooklyn in 1935. AP, "Back's Refusal to Sign Led to Grid Draft," *Green Bay Gazette,* Jan. 30, 1957.

43 **"Gentlemen, I've always had":** Arthur Daley, "Bell's Monument," *NYT,* Feb. 1, 1973.

44 **"People come to see":** Halas et al., *Halas,* p. 158.

45 **"Bert was a guy":** Not-for-attribution int.

45 **Historian Bob Carroll:** It became even more convoluted in 1943, when the Steelers and Eagles merged into the Steagles during the war. Bob Carroll, "How to Get from Dayton to Indianapolis by Way of Brooklyn, Boston, New York, Dallas, Hershey and Baltimore," *The Coffin Corner,* Vol. 17.

45 **Asked about the deal years later:** Musick, "A Football Man," in *A Game of Passion,* Wiebusch and Silverman, eds., p. 321.

45 **"People in Pittsburgh":** Ed Prell, "Bell Makes Believers out of Grid Magnates and Fans," *TSN,* Jan. 31, 1951.

46 **"Those guys":** Rooney int.

46 **"Pro football has":** Peterson, *Pigskin,* p. 147.

46 **More than 16 million:** James Patterson, *Grand Expectations: The United States, 1945–1974* (New York: Oxford University Press, 1996), pp. 11, 13–14, 61, 68.

47 **Upon taking the job:** Pollack, "Bell of the NFL."

47 **The challenge of the AAFC:** Littlewood, *Arch,* pp. 148–68.

47 **The AAFC possessed:** Peterson, *Pigskin,* p. 148.

49 **Bell's action was decisive:** Daly and O'Donnell, *Pro Football Chronicle,* p. 110.; Layden, *It Was a Different Game,* p. 152.

49 **Bell was convinced:** Bell would continue, throughout his tenure, to serve as a sort of public advocate, railing against the dangers of idle gossip. In *The Saturday Evening Post* in 1948, he wrote an article titled, "Do the Gamblers Make a Sucker Out of You?" which opened with an apocalyptic comparison: "I wouldn't know whether any of the nations in World War II had a poison gas in reserve that would feed upon itself if released, thereby growing more deadly and denser the farther it spread. I do know that football and all other big-gate sports are threatened by such a gas. . . . Its real name is Rumor. It's the most effective weapon the football gamblers have." AP, "Hapes and Filchock Barred Indefinitely by National League," *NYT,* Apr. 4, 1947; Bert Bell with Pete Martin, "Do the Gamblers Make a Sucker Out of You?" *Saturday Evening Post,* Nov. 6, 1948.

50 **Having won:** Patterson, *Football in Baltimore,* p. 60.; Phil Barber, "The All-America Football Conference," in *Total Football II,* pp. 527–30; Littlewood, *Arch,* pp. 132–34.

50 **Ward biographer:** Littlewood, *Arch,* p. 172.

50 **Throughout the 1947 and 1948 seasons:** Spadia int.; Maxwell Stiles, "LA Rams Told to Quit at Pro Peace Session," *TSN*, Oct. 26, 1949.; Littlewood, *Arch*, p. 173.

51 **"There's a bus outside":** Hal Lebovitz, "I'll Never Forget . . . : The right way . . . and the Brown way."

51 **By this time:** Eisner int.; Lavelli int.; Graham int.; Cleveland Browns 2004 media guide.

52 **Finally, in December 1949:** "It's Wonderful," *Time*, Dec. 19, 1949.

52 **Brown would remember:** Brown and Clary, *PB*, p. 193.

52 **For all the discussion:** David Maraniss, *When Pride Still Mattered: A Life of Vince Lombardi* (New York: Simon & Schuster, 1999), p. 105.

53 **In 1948, the Eagles:** East West Sporting Club, Inc., balance sheet, Dec. 31, 1948, PFHOF archives.

54 **The Bears' income:** Halas et al., *Halas*, p. 227.

54 **"Who wants chicken sandwiches?":** John Steadman int.; John Steadman, "Memories of Bell Burn Bright," *TSN*, Oct. 25, 1975.

4: GOING DEEP

55 **Inside the dimly lit:** Tank Younger int.; Collie Nicholson int.; Eddie Robinson int.

57 **So complete was:** Younger int.; Nicholson int.

57 **"You have to let":** Michael Hurd, "The BV Q&A: Tanks for the Memories," *Black Voices Quarterly*, Fall 2000.

57 **The success of:** While attending Georgetown in the late '20s, Reeves became impressed with an unheralded halfback from West Virginia Wesleyan, and recommended him to his older brother Eddie, then a minority owner of the Boston Redskins. The halfback's name was Cliff Battles, and he went on to become one of the league's biggest stars, leading the league in rushing in 1932. Bob St. John, *Tex! The Man Who Built the Dallas Cowboys* (Englewood Cliffs, NJ: Prentice Hall, 1988), p. 164.

57 **After hiring Kotal:** Cliff Christl and Don Langenkamp, *Sleepers, Busts and Franchise-Makers: The Behind-the-Scenes Story of the Pro Football Draft* (Seattle: Preview Publishing, 1983); not-for-attribution int.

58 **Meanwhile, the club:** St. John, *Tex!*, p. 174.

58 **At the same:** Chuck Benedict, "Pro Scouting: A Contest of Science, Luck and Wits," *Petersen's Pro Football 1962.*

59 **Facing a fifth season:** Hamilton Maule, *The Game: The Official Picture History of the NFL and AFL* (New York: Random House, 1967), pp. 130–31.

59 **Even as the losses:** Schramm int.

59 **Through a friend:** Peter Golenbock, *Cowboys Have Always Been My Heroes: The Definitive Oral History of America's Team* (New York: Warner, 1997), p. 29.

59 **The young Tex Schramm:** St. John, *Tex!*, p. 242.

60 **Reeves invited Schramm:** Marty Schramm letter to author; St. John, *Tex!*, pp. 54–55.

60 **Schramm's assignment:** Schramm int.; 1948 Rams game programs, St. Louis Rams archives.

60 **By 1949:** Schramm int.; Michael MacCambridge, *The Franchise: A History of Sports Illustrated Magazine* (New York: Hyperion, 1997), p. 58.

61 **Then, too, there were instances:** Schramm int.; Gehrke int.; St. John, *Tex!*, p. 172.

61 **Dan Reeves loved:** Mickey Herskowitz, "Different Strokes," *Pro! Magazine*, undated.

62 **Throughout the '40s:** Tom Bennett, "By Football Possessed," *Pro! Magazine*, undated.

62 **After stops:** Pope, *Football's Greatest Coaches*, pp. 223–230.

62 **As the tactics:** "I always looked upon Clark Shaughnessy as a Henry Wallace with brains," mused football writer Roger Treat after Shaughnessy went to the NFL. "A conscientious idealist who might better have followed the trail of Father Flanagan. He may never be entirely happy in the jovial thuggery of pro football, where every man has a little assassin in him." Ibid.

63 **Back at Grambling:** Nicholson int.; Eddie Robinson int. Nicholson recalled seeing the

headline "A Star Is Born," but the Rams' own meticulously kept scrapbooks contained no sign of such a headline that summer. The line quoted appeared in the *Los Angeles Times* story, Sep. 12, 1949, with the headline "Ram Eleven in Omaha for Giant Game," 1949 team scrapbook, St. Louis Rams archives.

63 **Younger lived up:** Younger int.

63 **Shaughnessy's 1949 team:** Younger int., Herskowitz, *The Golden Age of Pro Football*, p. 113.

64 **"The worst team":** In his biography of Arch Ward, Thomas B. Littlewood notes that Marshall had stated on several occasions that "our weakest teams could toy with the Browns." Littlewood, *Arch*, p. 177.

64 **As the teams headed:** Dan Rooney int.

65 **In the opener, the Browns:** Groza int.; Lavelli int.

65 **When Cleveland got the ball again:** Paul Brown, "This Was My Best," *Miami Herald*, Mar. 15, 1957.

65 **Surreptitiously, the Browns:** Groza int.; Clary, *Great Teams Great Years: Cleveland Browns*, pp. 54–63.

66 **After the game, Neale:** Clary, *Great Teams Great Years: Cleveland Browns*, pp. 34, 63.

66 **Bert Bell entered:** Ibid., p. 63.

66 **For the rest:** "The Sporting Scene: Coach," *The New Yorker*, Dec. 16, 1974.

67 **The loss to:** Howard Roberts, *The Story of Pro Football* (Chicago: Rand McNally, 1953), pp. 115–16.

67 **To those closest to:** Younger int.; Schramm int.

67 **Stydahar was a player's:** Leuthner, *Iron Men*, p. 160; Maule, *The Game*, p. 135.

67 **Reeves's other major:** Jeff Neal-Lunsford, "Sport in the Land of Television," *Journal of Sport History*, Spring 1992, p. 61.

67 **Gillette had been:** Ibid., pp. 62–63.

67 **The format of boxing:** The historian Jeff Neal-Lunsford called boxing the perfect sport for the nascent days of television: "Broadcasting equipment of the time was bulky and difficult to maneuver. Television cameras needed large amounts of light in order to produce a watchable picture, and picture clarity was a problem even under good conditions—long shots of objects tended to reduce those objects to unidentifiable specks. The *Cavalcade* solved these problems and made television engineers happy by televising boxing matches. Boxing lent itself to the existing state of television technology because it took place in a small indoor arena which could be provided with the large amount of light needed by the cameras." Ibid., p. 61.

68 **The popularity:** Benjamin G. Rader, *In Its Own Image: How Television Has Transformed Sports* (New York: Free Press, 1984), p. 41.

68 **The makers of Gillette:** Neal-Lunsford, "Sport in the Land of Television," pp. 59–60.

68 **In a postwar boom:** Reader's Digest, *America in the '40s: A Sentimental Journey* (Pleasantville, NY: Reader's Digest Association, 1998), p. 114.

68 **Sales still lagged:** Neal-Lunsford, "Sport in the Land of Television," p. 65.

68 **While boxing was:** William Johnson, *Super Spectator and the Electric Lilliputians* (Boston: Little, Brown, 1971), p. 100.

68 **And if television:** Ibid., p. 99.

68 **All this would:** Neal-Lunsford, "Sport in the Land of Television," pp. 72–73; Didinger, "A Remembrance of Paul Brown," in *A Game of Passion*, Wiebusch and Silverman, eds., pp. 251–52.

69 **By the end of the 1950 season:** Accorsi int., Gehrke int.; Schramm int.

70 **No conclusion could be reached:** Schramm int.; Halas et al., *Halas*, p. 247.

70 **"It was the lowest moment":** Didinger, "A Remembrance of Paul Brown," in *A Game of Passion*, Wiebusch and Silverman, eds., pp. 243–44.

71 **As he reached the sideline:** Graham int.; Brown and Clary, *PB*, p. 211.

71 **"It was terrible":** Shelby Strother, *NFL Top 40: The Greatest Pro Football Games Ever Played* (New York: Viking, 1988), p. 41.

71 **It was the game:** AP, "Title Contest Worth $1,116," *NYT,* Dec. 25, 1950.

71 **And when he found Brown:** Brown and Clary, *PB,* p. 212.

72 **"Sometimes, it's hell . . .":** Obituaries, *TSN,* July 10, 1971; Smith, "Outside the Pale."

72 **Similar events were occurring:** Spadia int.

72 **But by the early '50s:** Early int.

73 **As the teams:** Schramm int.

73 **The game was:** Maraniss, *When Pride Still Mattered,* p. 70.

73 **The DuMont network:** Although one confidential NFL document reported that the fee was just $75,000; Herskowitz, *The Golden Age of Pro Football,* p. 40; St. John, *Tex!,* p. 190.

73 **Greeted with:** Bert Bell, Jr., int.; Val Pinchbeck, "NFL Television History," internal league document, 1998.

74 **Television riches did not:** The next few years would be spent in a piecemeal series of local arrangements, little discussed and less documented. As the historian Richard Keller has written, "Not even God knows much about televised sport during the 1950's." Richard Keller, "Sport and Television in the 1950's: A Preliminary Survey," Emporia State University, 1982.

5: BALTIMORE

75 **"There has been a lot":** The editorial went on to place much of the blame for the league's troubles on the "brutally oppressive 'slave law' governing the drafting of new players." "Pro Football's 'Slave Law' Ought to Go," Time Out with the Staff, *Sport,* Oct. 1952.

75 **When the NFL and the AAFC:** Bert Bell, Jr., int.; Phil Barber, "The All-America Football Conference," in Carroll et al., *Total Football II,* p. 530.

76 **Somehow, the dismal Colts:** Patterson, *Football in Baltimore,* pp. 84–85.

76 **"series of underground bungalows":** Ibid., p. 86.

76 **"I will underwrite":** Comic book *Baltimore Colts,* published by American Visuals Corporation, 1950, p. 3.

76 **But after another:** "There were a lot of unemployed football players out there looking for work," recalled Art Donovan, "and about 90 percent of them seemed to be in the Colts camp kicking the living shit out of each other . . . and all we did was scrimmage. No drills. No chalk talk." Donovan and Drury, *Fatso,* pp. 119–20.

76 **A year later:** "All we want is a football team," explained the animated Baltimore lawyer William D. Macmillan, who spearheaded the efforts of the city to regain a franchise. "Fans can't come out to the Stadium to watch us count a cash settlement. It's a team we're after." John Steadman, *The Baltimore Colts Story* (Baltimore: Press Box, 1958), p. 62.

76 **Into the picture:** Daly and O'Donnell, *Pro Football Chronicle,* p. 131.

77 **None of those ideas were realized:** John Eisenberg, *Cotton Bowl Days: Growing Up with Dallas and the Cowboys in the 1960s* (New York: Simon & Schuster, 1997), pp. 20–22.

77 **Shortly after arriving:** Mickey Herskowitz, "Once Upon a Time in Dallas . . . ," from *More Than a Game,* John Weisbuch, ed. (Englewood Cliffs, NJ: Prentice-Hall, 1974), pp. 96–99); Tex Maule, "The Late, Unlamented Dallas Texans," *Pro! Magazine,* 1980; Stan Grosshandler, "A Disgrace," *The Coffin Corner,* Vol. 4, 1982; George Young int.

77 **Practices were barely organized:** Donovan and Drury, *Fatso,* p. 134.

77 **The Texans' season opened:** Jack Horrigan, "Belly Up in Dallas," *The Coffin Corner,* Vol. 7, 1985.

77 **In the following weeks:** Shrake int.

78 **Prior to the game:** Schramm int.; Golenbock, *Cowboys Have Always Been My Heroes,* pp. 17–18.

78 **And so it ended:** There was a last-minute rescue attempt by Dallas oilman Clint Murchison, Jr., but he was vacationing in South America during the week of the Millers' capitulation, and Bell declined to wait for him to return. Herskowitz, "Once Upon a Time in Dallas. . . ."

78 **While trying:** John Steadman int.; George Young int.; Patterson, *Football in Baltimore*, pp. 93–99.

78 **Sensing a settlement:** Herskowitz, "Once Upon a Time in Dallas. . . ."

78 **Though Baltimore had:** Patterson, *Football in Baltimore*, p. 97.

78 **But Bell kept leaning:** Bell even produced a sheet of estimated expenses, which factored in $210,000 for team salaries, $27,000 for the coaching staff, $2,000 for a team doctor and all doctor's bills, $900 for press meeting lunches and press box. Figuring $50,000 per game of ticket receipts—money at that point that was literally already in the bank—Bell estimated a first-year profit of just over $33,000. Baltimore estimated expenses, National Football Hall of Fame library.

79 **Bell finally settled:** Bell, Jr., int.; John Steadman int.; Maule, *The Game*, p. 50.

79 **The sales terms:** William Gildea, *When the Colts Belonged to Baltimore: A Father and a Son, a Team and a Time* (New York: Ticknor & Fields, 1994), p. 107; Herskowitz, *The Golden Age of Pro Football*, p. 179.

79 **Instead of the old:** Patterson, *Football in Baltimore*, p. 102.

79 **Paul Brown was in:** Mike Brown int.; Herskowitz, *The Golden Age of Pro Football*, p. 35.

79 **Yet beneath the surface:** Ibid., pp. 101, 104.

80 **It was the mind-set:** Ibid., p. 101.

80 **In the title game:** Shelby Strother, *NFL's Top 40: The Greatest Pro Football Games Ever Played* (New York: Viking, 1988), pp. 42–45.

80 **Brown, still coping:** Herskowitz, *The Golden Age of Pro Football*, p. 180.

80 **After a conflicted Collier:** Patterson, *Football in Baltimore*, p. 107.

80 **When he was first:** "Paul liked to control everything," said Ewbank later. "I do mean everything! And that included his assistant coaches. He didn't like somebody to leave until he was ready to let him go." Paul Zimmerman, *The Last Season of Weeb Ewbank* (New York: Farrar, Straus & Giroux, 1974), p. 275.

81 **Ewbank began:** Patterson, *Football in Baltimore*, p. 107.

81 **Art Donovan had heard:** He had won just six games during a three-year pro odyssey that brought him from Baltimore in 1950, to Cleveland (where he was traded after a short stay in training camp) and the New York Yanks in 1951, to Dallas and Hershey in 1952, and then, in 1953, back to Baltimore. Donovan and Drury, *Fatso*, p. 139.

81 **As it happened:** After Collier declined the Colts' offer, his daughter, Kay, considered the matter closed ("He had turned down the head job with the Baltimore Colts . . . and he certainly would never apply for another job"). Slone, *Football's Gentle Giant*, p. 46.

81 **Just days later:** Ibid., pp. 46–47.

81 **"The personal depth of our relationship":** Ibid., p. 49.

81 **While Brown felt:** It was particularly gratifying since, just a week earlier, in the season-ending regular season game, Detroit had continued its mastery of the Browns, winning 14–10 to run its record against Cleveland to 8-0 overall, having beaten them in two title games, two regular season games, and four exhibitions. Cleveland Browns Media Guide, 2003.

81 **While the Browns:** This prompted a line from co-owner Bob Hope, who before introducing the new coach to a Rams booster club meeting, said, "Hampton Pool? That sounds like a resting place for yachts." St. John, *Tex!*, p. 180.

82 **In those years:** Schramm int.

82 **And then, inevitably:** Reeves was not a particularly belligerent drunk, but one who enjoyed making others uncomfortable. Longtime Rams aide Chuck Benedict would remember parties where, after several drinks, Reeves "used to come over and decide he was going to sit on my lap. There was no point to it." Benedict int.

82 **"And he'd be gone":** Schramm int.

82 **After the firing:** Schramm int.

83 **There were plenty:** Faulkner int.

83 **Preparing to embark:** Sid Gillman int.; Esther Gillman int.

83 **Gillman took:** Halas had employed an aerial camera back in the '30s, and Shaughnessy had used film study to help devise the game plan that demolished the Redskins in the 1940 title game. Kevin Lamb, *Quarterbacks, Nickelbacks and Other Loose Change: A Fan's Guide to the Changing Game of Pro Football* (Chicago: Contemporary, 1984), p. 189; Dukich int.; Phil Patton, *Razzle Dazzle: The Curious Marriage of Television and Professional Football* (Garden City, NY: Dial, 1984), pp. 72–73.; Herskowitz, *The Golden Age of Pro Football*, p. 62.

84 **In his first season:** Schramm int.; conversation also mentioned in St. John, *Tex!*, p. 208.

84 **The win fulfilled:** Clary, *Great Teams Great Years: Cleveland Browns*, p. 44.

85 **The emphasis on speed:** Melvin Durslag, "Pro Football's Plenty Rough", *SI*, Nov. 28, 1955; Younger int.

85 **Reports of growing violence:** Tex Maule, "I Don't Believe There Is Dirty Football," *SI*, Jan. 27, 1957; "Savagery on Sunday," *Life*, Oct. 24, 1955; Otto Graham, "Football Is Getting Too Vicious," *SI*, Oct. 11, 1954.

86 **That led:** The ever-resourceful Fred Gehrke developed a face mask on his own with the Rams in the '40s; Gehrke int.; Mike Brown int.; Brown and Clary, *PB*, pp. 232–33; Beau Riffenburgh, "A History of Football Equipment," *The Official NFL Encyclopedia,* 4th ed. (New York: New American Library, 1986), p. 542.

86 **The other significant change:** Riffenburgh, *The Official NFL Encyclopedia*, p. 536; Donovan and Drury, *Fatso*, p. 187; Daly and O'Donnell, *Pro Football Chronicle*, p. 145.

87 **The Colts' investment:** Steadman, *From Colts to Ravens*, p. 131.

87 **While teams like:** Gil Brandt int.

88 **In the aftermath of:** Dan Rooney int.

89 **John Unitas was one:** Unitas int.; Gildea, *When the Colts Belonged to Baltimore*, p. 179; HBO documentary *Unitas*, 1999.

89 **So Unitas quickly learned:** Unitas int.; Johnny Unitas with Ed Fitzgerald, *The Johnny Unitas Story* (New York: Tempo, 1968), pp. 23–25.

89 **On many a Friday night:** Unitas int.

89 **Unitas didn't see:** Unitas int.

89 **A year later:** Gildea, *When the Colts Belonged to Baltimore*, p. 179.

90 **The lone school of consequence:** The University of Louisville's interest in Unitas was the result of a lucky break. Louisville assistant coach John Dromo had been scouting a college game at Pitt Stadium in the fall of 1950 and, needing a ride to the airport, got a lift from Unitas's high school coach, Max Carey. After failing the summer school entrance exam at Louisville, Unitas met with the registrar and appealed for a spot in the freshman class. He was ultimately admitted, and would go on to graduate in four years. Unitas int.

90 **At the Steelers':** Roy Blount, Jr., *About Three Bricks Shy . . . And the Load Filled Up: The Story of the Greatest Football Team Ever* (New York: Ballantine, 1989), p. 155.

90 **Meanwhile, Art Rooney's sons:** Didinger, *Great Teams Great Years: Pittsburgh Steelers*, pp. 171–72.

91 **Kiesling's mind:** Ibid., p. 171.

91 **On September 5:** Daly and O'Donnell, *Pro Football Chronicle*, p. 155; *Pittsburgh Press*, Sept. 6, 1955.

91 **When Kiesling called him:** Unitas int.; HBO documentary *Unitas;* Gildea, *When the Colts Belonged to Baltimore*, p. 176.

91 **"Unitas was totally ignored":** Dan Rooney int.

91 **Unitas received bus fare:** Gildea, *When the Colts Belonged to Baltimore*, p. 176.

91 **Unbeknownst to Unitas:** Dan Rooney int.

91 **With that shred of hope:** Unitas int.; Unitas and Fitzgerald, *The Johnny Unitas Story*, p. 39; Lee Greene, *The Johnny Unitas Story* (New York: Putnam, 1962), pp. 45–55.

92 **By the end of:** Carroll et al., *Total Football II*, pp. 1569–70.

92 **During that fall of 1955:** Greene, *The Johnny Unitas Story*, p. 45.

92 **In February 1956:** Ewbank was friends with Louisville coach Frank Camp, who gave Unitas an enthusiastic recommendation. Line coach Herman Ball, hired away from the Steel-

ers after the 1955 season, also vouched for Unitas's skills. Unitas int.; Greene, *The Johnny Unitas Story*, p. 72.

92 **"We took pictures":** Mickey Herskowitz, "Goodbye, Johnny U.," in *A Game of Passion*, Wiebusch and Silverman, eds., p. 376; Patterson, *Football in Baltimore*, pp. 119–20.

92 **With only one proven quarterback:** Unitas int.

93 **From the first day:** Vince Bagli and Norman Macht, *Sundays at 2:00 with the Baltimore Colts* (Centreville, MD: Tidewater, 1995), p. 71.

93 **Unitas still didn't cut:** Frank Gifford and Harry Waters, *The Whole Ten Yards* (New York: Random House, 1993), p. 187.

93 **But as would be said:** Unitas int.; Barry int.; Accorsi int.

93 **Concerned about his tendency:** Unitas int.

93 **But it was not:** Zimmerman, *The Last Season of Weeb Ewbank*, pp. 14–15.

94 **If Unitas was a diamond:** Herskowitz, *The Golden Age of Pro Football*, p. 117.

94 **The Colts were 1-2:** Gildea, *When the Colts Belonged to Baltimore*, p. 184.

94 **Ewbank would remember:** Bagli and Macht, *Sundays at 2:00*, p. 47.

94 **It was the Colts' first win:** The Browns had beaten the Colts twice in each season from 1947 through 1949, and beat the Watner-owned franchise in 1950. 2003 Cleveland Browns Media Guide.

94 **When an elated Ewbank:** Patterson, *Football in Baltimore*, p. 123.

95 **Later that week:** Gildea, *When the Colts Belonged to Baltimore*, p. 84.

6: ON ANY GIVEN SUNDAY

96 **Shortly after a rain-drenched day:** Speculation persisted later that it might have been future Cowboys owner Clint Murchison, and his partner, Bedford Wynne, who approached Bell. But nowhere in Murchison's life story is there evidence pointing to it being he, and his sons, Burke and Robert, said he'd never mentioned it to them. Mara int.; Burke Murchison int.; Robert Murchison int.; Bert Bell, Jr., int.

97 **After Steve Owen's twenty-three-year tenure:** Mara int.; Herskowitz, *The Golden Age of Pro Football*, p. 134.

97 **In 1956:** Gifford int.

97 **All over the city:** Gifford int.

97 **The dawning:** Huff int.

97 **"Mostly he is the administrator":** Red Smith, *New York World-Telegram*, undated, probably Nov. 1958.

97 **Tactically speaking:** Maraniss, *When Pride Still Mattered*, p. 161.

97 **Though they were:** Herskowitz, *The Golden Age of Pro Football*, p. 95; Gary Cartwright, "Tom Landry: God, Family and Football," in *A Game of Passion*, Wiebusch and Silverman, eds., p. 72; Maraniss, *When Pride Still Mattered*, p. 161.

98 **The antagonism was felt:** Huff int.; Gifford int.

98 **Lombardi, who came:** Maraniss, *When Pride Still Mattered*, pp. 152–54.

98 **In 1956, he took:** It was not obvious that this was a successful system, since opposing teams could always change defenses when Conerly came into the game, but the Giants were successful while using it. Ibid., p. 171.

98 **Lombardi also incorporated:** Don Smith, *Pro Football Hall of Fame All-Time Greats* (New York: Gallery Books, 1988), p. 197.

98 **"He never made a comment":** Summerall int.

98 **The cornerstone of the Landry defense:** Summerall int.

99 **In an age when offenses:** Huff int.; Sam Huff and Leonard Shapiro, *Tough Stuff: The Man in the Middle* (New York: St. Martin's, 1988), p. 50; Golenbock, *Cowboys Have Always Been My Heroes*, p. 237.

99 **For the advertising community:** Gifford int.

100 **"either juveniles":** MacCambridge, *The Franchise*, p. 22.

101 **"I believe we began":** Herskowitz, *The Golden Age of Pro Football*, p. 183.

101 **Presiding over the league's ascendance:** Effrat, "Bell's Decisions Keep Pro Football Family Happy, Rich."

101 **"We're as much concerned":** Ed Pollock, "Playing the Game," *TSN*, Feb. 1956.

101 **Early that year, when Bell collapsed:** W. C. Heinz, "Boss of the Behemoths," *Saturday Evening Post*, Dec. 3, 1955.

101 **Though he had matured:** Ibid.

102 **After more than a decade:** Philadelphia Public Library.

102 **Even in the last half:** John Dell, "Bell Gave Pro Game Players and Fans," *Philadelphia Inquirer*, Oct. 13, 1959.

102 **CBS executive Edgar Scherick:** Ron Powers, *Supertube: The Rise of Television Sports* (New York: Coward-McCann, 1984), p. 85.

102 **Many reporters would find:** Bert Bell, Jr., said, "Anytime a secretary or temp would ask, 'May I ask who's calling?,' my dad would almost run out of his office and explain that he just wanted the calls sent through. He was very concerned that no one think he was ducking him." Bert Bell, Jr., int.

103 **West Coast teams perceived:** Schramm int.

103 **"When he wanted to get something done":** Herskowitz, "For Pete's Sake," *Pro! Magazine*, undated.

103 **"The Fifties was a decade":** St. John, *Tex!*, p. 176.

103 **The number of television sets:** Powers, *Supertube*, p. 454.

104 **At CBS:** Ibid., pp. 89–90.

104 **Within much:** Johnson, *Super Spectator and the Electric Lilliputians*, p. 29.

104 **By the early '50s:** Powers, *Supertube*, p. 89.

105 **Pro football would soon change that:** Here, too, the ad executives in New York played a crucial role. Early in the '50s, at the Madison Avenue firm of Dancer Fitzgerald & Sample, the intensely energetic Edgar Scherick—from Long Island by way of Harvard—handled the Falstaff Beer account and already had success with the *Falstaff Game of the Week*, a baseball broadcast sent to non-major-league cities, with Dizzy Dean handling the play-by-play. In 1956, Scherick convinced Falstaff to move much of its business to CBS, and he followed himself later that same year, becoming the assistant to Bill MacPhail. Powers, *Supertube*, p. 69; Curt Smith, *Voices of the Game: The Acclaimed Chronicle of Baseball, Radio and Television Broadcasting—from 1921 to the Present* (New York: Simon & Schuster, 1992), pp. 143–46.

105 **In 1956, though:** Technically, only eleven of the twelve franchises had contracts with CBS that season, because the Browns still operated with their own regional network. The flagship station for the Browns' network, though, was WJW-TV in Cleveland, a CBS affiliate. Mike Brown int.; Dino Lucarelli int.; Tim Brulia, "A Chronology of Pro Football on Television: Part 1," *The Coffin Corner*, Vol. 26, No. 3 (2004).

105 **During that 1956 season:** Maraniss, *When Pride Still Mattered*, p. 169.

105 **While each team negotiated:** The full wording of Rule 4(b): "No Game shall be broadcast by television into the Home territory (i.e. within seventy-five (75) miles from the home stadium) of any other League team without the consent of such team on any day such other League team is playing a game in its home stadium; no Home game shall be broadcast by television on the day of such Game into any area included within a seventy-five (75) mile radius of the stadium in which such game is played without prior consent of the Team, the visiting team and the Commissioner. New York Giants TV contract, *CBS News*, Nov. 25, 1958.

105 **Under Bell, the television networks:** Ibid.

105 **"I never would and never have":** AP, "Players Association Doesn't Bother Bell," publication unknown, Feb. 16, 1957 (PFHOF Archives).

105 **The announcer Bob Wolff:** Smith, *Of Mikes and Men*, p. 44.

106 **The numbers were hard to argue:** NFL Record & Fact Book.

106 **Even the national press:** Weiss int.

106 **"A combination of things":** Frank Finch, "Torrid Battle Likely to Hike NFL Gate 10 pct.," *Los Angeles Times*, date unknown (PFHOF Archives).

107 **"On any given Sunday":** "Today, any team can beat another on any given Sunday, whether it be first or last," said Bell. AP, "Players Association Doesn't Bother Bell."

108 **"The scouting department":** Gil Brandt, then a scout for the Rams, concurred with Dukich's opinion that the Rams' system had Brown rated above Arnett. Brandt int.; Dukich int.

108 **The two quarterbacks that most:** Accounts vary on what happened next. Some people report that Paul Brown was crushed when he discovered he'd get neither Brodie nor Dawson, and made his selection reluctantly. Paul Brown's son, Mike, said his father wanted Brodie badly, but was less enthusiastic about Dawson, because of questions about his arm strength. Dawson himself, contacted by the Browns prior to the draft, had heard otherwise. Mike Brown int.; Len Dawson int.; Dukich int.; Brandt int.

108 **With the two quarterbacks gone:** Cleveland writer Terry Pluto insists that when the Browns' turn came, Paul Brown "never hesitated. He picked Jim Brown and then thought, 'I can get a quarterback from somewhere else.' " Pluto, *When All the World Was Browns Town*, p. 173; MacCambridge, "Jim Brown, All-Everything," *ESPN SportsCentury*, p. 190.

108 **After a touchdown run:** Jim Brown int.

108 **Huff was already a young star:** Huff and Shapiro, *Tough Stuff*, p. 31.

108 **Brown confounded:** Jim Brown and Steve Delsohn, *Out of Bounds* (New York: Kensington, 1989), p. 77.

109 **He would at once bridle:** Ibid., p. 71.

110 **All season long, the Giants:** After the Browns game, one of the members of the Giants' taxi squad, the strong-armed quarterback Jack Kemp, who'd drifted from the Lions to the Steelers to the Giants, jotted a quick note to his friend Doug Gerhart, an aspiring quarterback at his alma mater Occidental College. Kemp's letter provides a glimpse of what it must have felt like to experience that heady season firsthand. "We won again yesterday," wrote Kemp. "The greatest game I've ever seen. Gosh Doug I've never been so excited in my life. What a life. N.Y. is so great & they love the Giants now & we get big dinners free & meet all the sports personalities & it's tremendous. Also lots of money." A week later, winning the conference title would have a tangible impact on the lives of many of the players: Kemp would be voted a full share of playoff money, allowing him to put a down payment on his first house in California.; Kemp int.; Kemp letter to Doug Gerhart.

110 **In Cleveland, several players grumbled:** Pluto, *When All the World Was Browns Town*, p. 42.

110 **Weeb Ewbank made:** Donovan and Drury, *Fatso*, pp. 36–37; Patterson, *Football in Baltimore*, pp. 143–44.

111 **On fourth-and-goal at the two:** Unitas int.; Gildea, *When the Colts Belonged to Baltimore*, p. 236.

112 **The exquisite tension of overtime:** Steadman int.; Bert Bell, Jr., int.

112 **In the Giants' locker room:** Steadman, *From Colts to Ravens*, p. 149.

112 **Even the losers:** Mara int.

112 **The Colts headed home:** John Steadman, *The Greatest Football Game Ever Played: When the Baltimore Colts and the New York Giants Faced Sudden Death* (Stevensville, MD: Press Box, 1998), p. 72.

113 **When the bus was finally extricated:** Ibid., p. 73.

113 **Assessing the mob scene:** Ibid., p. 72.

114 **By the end of the '50s:** Smith, *Pro Football Hall of Fame All-Time Greats*, p. 141.

114 **In Smith's view:** Ibid., p. 122.

115 **"My interest emotionally":** Hunt int.

7: "A LIGHT BULB CAME ON"

116 **The best ideas:** Seneca, *Epistles*, 12, 11.

116 **"The NFL in the '50s":** Kemp int.

116 **Shortly thereafter:** Kemp int.; Summerall int.

117 **Minneapolis was growing:** Plaintiffs' proposed findings of fact and conclusions of law, *AFL v. NFL,* US 12599, p. 518.

117 **The Minneapolis group:** Adams int.; Halas deposition, *AFL v. NFL,* US 12599.

117 **The NFL wouldn't:** Bert Bell letter to Howsam, May 27, 1958, *AFL v. NFL,* US 12599, Exhibit 96 (J).

117 **American companies:** Patterson, *Grand Expectations,* p. 315.

117 **The league did consent:** Halas deposition, *AFL v. NFL,* US 12599.

117 **The lowly Cardinals:** While Bidwill had been among George Halas's best friends, the relationship between Halas and the Wolfners was poisonous. An irreparable split came in 1957, when the Cardinals had negotiated for the rights to play at Northwestern's handsome Dyche Stadium, just north of Chicago in Evanston, and Halas nixed the deal, producing a twenty-eight-year-old agreement—subsequently honored by Bell—that forbade the Bears to play home games south of Madison Street, or the Cardinals to play home games north of there. Walter Wolfner had vacillated for years among the choices of selling his club, moving it elsewhere, or remaining in Chicago to fight Halas and the Bears to the death. There was no reasoning with Wolfner on the subject. "You know, Halas is up there in years," Wolfner told more than one potential buyer. "He's liable to go anytime now." (As it turned out, Wolfner died in 1963; Halas died in 1985.) Summerall int.; Jack Olsen, "Unhappiest Millionaire," *SI,* Apr. 4, 1960.

118 **Born in 1932:** Hunt int.; *Fortune,* Apr. 5, 1948.

118 **From the age of six:** Much younger than his siblings, Lamar was shy but enthusiastic, and remained composed despite the pathos in the Hunt family, from the revelation that H. L. Hunt had been living and raising a completely different family, secretly, in Shreveport, to the nervous breakdown of Lamar's oldest brother, the strong-willed, preternatural oilman Hassie Hunt. Hassie's illness had a rending effect on both Hunt parents. And for the rest of the Hunt boys, it left a father who was not just absent frequently, but also heartbroken about his prized son's condition. "Hassie was the old man's favorite son," said one family friend. "And after he got so ill, it was very difficult for Mr. Hunt to get very close to any of the other boys, to be truthful." Not-for-attribution int.; Don Kowet, *The Rich Who Own Sports* (New York: Random House, 1977), pp. 77–100; E. Shrake, "The Big Daddy of Sport," *SI,* Sep. 7, 1970.

118 **He was a decent:** H. L. Hunt was a notorious gambler, known to bet vast sums on college football—maintaining a running bet of $50,000 per game with a Florida gambler named Jimmy "The Greek" Snyder in the early '50s—and he kept a dedicated, unlisted phone line in his office used solely to converse with his bookmakers. Jimmy Snyder, *Jimmy the Greek* (Chicago: Playboy, 1975), pp. 82–89.

119 **Forrest Gregg:** Forrest Gregg int.

119 **On less affable men:** Buddy Rupe int.

119 **After graduating with:** Hunt int.

119 **Late in 1958:** Ibid.

119 **He'd been negotiating:** "Lamar had more money than God," said Charlie Bidwill's son Stormy, who'd taken an active interest in the franchise from an early age and who with his brother, Bill, would eventually inherit the franchise from his mother. "Well, the only thing that he ever spent that we could figure out was that he *might* have spent some money for his clothes. Otherwise, he never spent a nickel. My mother turned to me at one point and says, 'I don't understand—I've never seen a man so cheap.'" Stormy Bidwill int.

120 **"Do you know Bud Adams?":** Murray Olderman, "Texas Gateway to Sports Expansion," *Houston Press,* Jan. 12, 1960, which credited Wolfner saying, "Of course, you realize big money in Minneapolis, Houston, Seattle, Denver and Buffalo has also been after us."

120 **Under the heading:** Lamar Hunt notes, Hunt papers, as displayed on Kansas City Chiefs history mural at Arrowhead Pavilion.

121 **When Hunt suggested:** Hunt deposition, *AFL v. NFL,* US 12599, p. 55.

121 **In his subterranean office:** Curran, *The $400,000 Quarterback,* p. 27.

121 **One of Adams's peers would later say:** Not-for-attribution int.

122 **"If I could come up with":** Adams int.; George Sullivan, *Touchdown! The Picture History of the American Football League* (New York: Putnam, 1967), p. 11.

122 **"We folks here in Minnesota":** Letter from Ole Haugsrud to Lamar Hunt, July 1959. *AFL v. NFL*, US 12599, Exhibit.

122 **Through friend and former tennis star:** Lou Sahadi, *Miracle in Miami: The Miami Dolphins Story* (Chicago: Regnery, 1972), p. 7.

122 **in New York:** Curran, *The $400,000 Quarterback*, pp. 22–23.

122 **His friend David Dixon:** Hunt deposition, *AFL v. NFL*, US 12599, pp. 54–55.

122 **On June 2:** Hunt int.; Bert Bell, Jr., int.

123 **After the meal:** Hunt deposition, *AFL v. NFL*, US 12599, p. 76.

123 **"I was at least intelligent":** Joe McGuff, *Winning It All: The Chiefs of the AFL* (Garden City, NY: Doubleday, 1970), p. 11.

123 **Bell declined:** Sahadi, *Miracle in Miami*, p. 10.

123 **On July 26:** With the news relayed by O'Brien, Hunt called Bell personally and ended any mystery. He said he'd be glad to have Bell mention the new league, but didn't want the specific cities or anyone's name used at that point. Ibid.; Hunt int.

123 **"The more football there is":** Senate Subcommittee on Antitrust and Monopoly, *Organized Professional Team Sports Hearings*, 86th Cong., 1st Sess., July 1959, S. Res. 57 on S. 616 and S. 886, p. 40.

124 **"All of you will enjoy this":** Sahadi, *Miracle in Miami*, p. 12.

124 **"I really liked Bert Bell":** Hunt int.

124 **The first meeting:** Jack Horrigan and Mike Rathet, *The Other League: The Fabulous Story of the American Football League* (Chicago: Follett, 1970), p. 15; minutes from first AFL meeting, Aug. 14, 1959.

125 **When asked to name:** Golenbock, *Cowboys Have Always Been My Heroes*, p. 11.

125 **"Everybody has been knocking":** First part of quotation, McGuff, *Winning It All*, p. 29; second part of quotation, after ellipsis, Hunt also recalled saying in interview.

125 **"What can I do?":** Sullivan, *Touchdown!*, p. 17.

125 **"If Adams and Lamar Hunt":** Jack Gallagher, Sporttalk column, "Now Is the Time for AFL to Throw in the Towel, Give Up," *Houston Post*, Aug. 31, 1959.

126 **The 1959 season:** Jimmy Breslin, "Bell Devoted Life to Game He Loved," *New York Journal-American*, Nov. 12, 1959.

126 **"A guy who needed a haircut":** Ibid.

126 **One writer said:** Red Smith, *To Absent Friends* (New York: Atheneum, 1982), p. 374.

127 **Two days after:** Bert Bell, Jr., int.; Bell with Chanoff, "Any Given Sunday."

127 **"Mr. Pauley's pitch":** Hunt deposition, *AFL v. NFL*, US 12599, pp. 154–55.

127 **The AFL had:** AFL meeting minutes, Nov. 21, 1959.

128 **"Yes!" he shouted:** Hunt int.; Adams int.

128 **While the Minneapolis group:** Finding of Facts, *AFL v. NFL*, US 12599, p. 34/(533).

128 **Conducted amid:** The Personnel Committee included Chargers GM Frank Leahy, Texans GM Don Rossi and chief scout Will Walls, Denver GM Dean Griffing, and Houston head of scouting John Breen. With college football still a one-platoon game at the time, the group selected the twenty-four best players at each position among college seniors, divided them into tiers of eight, and then drew the names out of a hat, for eight teams at each tier of each position, with each club allotted thirty-three players in all. Another draft weeks later would swell the ranks to fifty-three players per team. Hunt int.; Adams int.

128 **It would be:** Hunt int.; Ed Gruver, *The American Football League: A Year-by-Year History, 1960–1969* (Jefferson, NC: McFarland, 1997), p. 34.

129 **But the franchise:** Joe Foss and Donna Foss, *A Proud American: The Autobiography of Joe Foss* (New York: Pocket Books, 1992), p. 243; William Ryczek, *Crash of the Titans: The Early Years of the New York Jets and the AFL* (Kingston, NY: Total Sports, 2000), pp. 20–21.

129 **"They certainly":** "No Pushing Around, Senator Warns NFL," *Houston Post*, Jan. 9, 1960.

129 **But this was unfair:** Hunt int.; Bert Bell, Jr., int.

130 **"It is my contention":** Ray Gillespie, "Veeck Lashes O.B. 'Horse-and-Buggy Policies,'" *TSN*, Dec. 24, 1952.

130 **The principle that Veeck:** *The Sporting News* noted that between his TV proposals and other machinations, "Veeck caught the delegates so unprepared and so disrupted the proceedings that he forced a flurry of parliamentary rulings, points of order, two recesses and an extra session late in the afternoon of Dec. 4." Edgar J. Brands, "Minors Reject Moves to Loosen Major Ties," *TSN*, Dec. 10, 1952; Howard Green int.; Stan McIlvaine int.

130 **"Under this system":** Shirley Povich, "Veeck Still Hopes to Get His Foot in Door," *TSN*, Dec. 17, 1952.

131 **In 1953:** Schramm int.

131 **Despite his strong influence:** Bell campaigned strongly for pooling TV revenue at the league meetings in 1956 and again in 1958, and his friend Jiggs Donoghue, co-owner of the Eagles and assistant treasurer of the league, said that Bell often argued that "one of the most important things to the league was developing a package deal for television, to protect all the lower clubs. He wanted to see to it that everybody in the league got the same amount of money." Joe Donoghue, testimony, *AFL v. NFL*, US 12599, p. 1792.

131 **"It has been reported":** Statement, May 18, 1960, Rickey Papers, Library of Congress.

132 **On the plane:** It had been just weeks since Hunt had heard Branch Rickey's Continental League proposal, and he recalled how impressed he'd been with the revenue-sharing concept relating to TV broadcasts that Rickey had outlined. He decided that a new football league should certainly operate in the same manner. He wrote: "*(8) All TV and radio must be league-approved; (9) TV money will go ⅓rd to individual clubs and ⅓rd to league.*" In this, Hunt was assuming that each team would negotiate its own local TV deal, that it would keep one third of its TV revenue, then the other two thirds would go into a central pool, where it would be divided equally among all of the franchises, precisely as Rickey had outlined in his Continental League prospectus. Hunt's personal copy of papers. (In the coming months, Hunt would simplify this idea further in the coming months, eventually suggesting that the league go with a *joint* league-wide contract, negotiated with a national network by the league on behalf of all teams, then split evenly among the clubs.); Lamar Hunt int.; Lamar Hunt notes, Hunt papers, as displayed on Kansas City Chiefs history mural at Arrowhead Pavilion.

132 **After neither NBC nor CBS:** Johnson, *Super Spectator and the Electric Lilliputians*, p. 130.

133 **In a memo to Scherick:** Marc Gunther and Bill Carter, *Monday Night Mayhem: The Inside Story of ABC's Monday Night Football* (New York: Beech Tree, 1988), p. 18.

133 **Arledge would bring:** Roone Arledge, *Roone: A Memoir* (New York: HarperCollins, 2003), p. 64; Patton, *Razzle Dazzle*, pp. 63–64.

8: THE SIEGE

136 **"Too much like a policeman":** Bidwill int.

136 **"George Halas, in my presence":** Spadia int.; tabulation of voting, author unknown, St. Louis Rams archives.

136 **After another vote yielded:** "Deadlock Holds on Successor to Bell," *Houston Post*, Jan. 22, 1960.

137 **As the days dragged on:** Jimmy Burns, "Spotlighting Sports," *Miami Herald*, Jan. 23, 1960.

137 **League PR director:** Bert Bell, Jr., int.

137 **Bert Bell had once told:** Bert Bell, Jr., int.; Mara int.; Jack Brennan, "Rozelle, Others Recall Brown's Humor," *Cincinnati Enquirer*, Aug. 6, 1991.

138 **"If Jesus Christ himself":** Bidwill int.

138 **From their vantage point:** The other names considered included Giants GM Ray Walsh, Redskins GM Dick McCann, and the Steelers' longtime PR man Ed Kiley. Wellington Mara int.; "The New Commish," *Extension Magazine*, December 1960.

138 **Sitting there silently:** Wellington Mara int.

138 **"I know he's young":** Ibid.
139 **Ray Rozelle filled out:** Rozelle papers.
139 **In earlier generations:** "The Playboy Interview: Pete Rozelle," *Playboy,* Oct. 1973.
139 **Alvin Ray Rozelle:** Not-for-attribution int.; Dick Rozelle letter to author, Nov. 29, 2000.
139 **Pete grew up:** Pete's father, Ray Rozelle, the son of a farmer who settled on the outskirts of Compton late in the nineteenth century, had returned from World War I and gone straight to work, living in Lynwood, California, one of America's first true suburbs. Ray Rozelle was essentially self-educated, a man who never attended college but could master a Sunday crossword in thirty minutes. During the Depression, he kept his Pacific Market open, extending credit to numerous friends and acquaintances. Many were predictably unable to pay him back, and in the mid-'30s—after his mother refused to bail him out—his business went under. The failure was, by all accounts, a devastating event that made Ray Rozelle more taciturn, if no less hardworking. Dick Rozelle int.; Anne Marie Bratton (née Rozelle) int.; Pete Rozelle letter to Aunt Martha and Uncle Glenn, Sept. 17, 1983, Pete Rozelle papers.
139 **At the family's:** Dick Rozelle int.
139 **The childhood lesson:** Pete Rozelle was friendly, supportive, and got along, but was overmatched on the playing fields at Lynwood elementary. A teacher recommended he sit out a year of school—so as to catch up physically—and after seventh grade, he spent the 1939–40 school year in the rural Northern California hills of Ceres, at the ranch of family friends Dana and Frank Menzel. Much of that year was spent doing chores in the morning, playing basketball in the afternoon on a rim he'd put up outside the Menzels' farmhouse, and reading in the evening, especially newspapers and sports books, from *Bill Stern's Sports Stories* to the best of Clair Bee. He returned to school a year later, still smallish and kind, but with a newly robust confidence and stature. Dick Rozelle int.; Helen Rozelle int.; Leland Rozelle int.; Anne Marie Bratton int.; Pete Rozelle letter to Francis R. Ruggieri, April 4, 1988, Rozelle papers; Al Stump, "Pete Rozelle: Czar Between the Goal Posts," *Los Angeles Herald Examiner Sunday Magazine,* Nov. 2, 1969; Rozelle papers.
140 **At Lynwood Junior High:** Dick Rozelle int.
140 **Ray had bought:** Alvin [Pete] Rozelle, "Sports in Review," *Tartar Shield,* Compton College, Mar. 31, 1944.
140 **By then, Rozelle had found:** Dick Zehms, "In This Corner," *Long Beach Press-Telegram,* 1957.
140 **By high school:** Leland Rozelle int.; John Lehman int.; Max Patterson int.; Rozelle papers.
140 **Rozelle was as transformed:** John Lehman int.; Max Patterson int.; Pete Rozelle, "Winning the War on the Home Front," composition for unknown class, circa 1943, Rozelle papers.
140 **There were home movies:** Rozelle family video.
141 **"They were all climbing":** Patterson int.
141 **Rozelle, who saw:** Rozelle saw no battle, but he did meet a Japanese family during a port stay in Tokyo at the end of the war, and was invited into their home, returning to the states with numerous gifts. Dick Rozelle int.
141 **Rozelle was unfazed:** John Wiebusch, "Q&A," *GameDay Magazine,* Vol. 20, No. 3, Sep. 1989.
142 **When the team:** Lehman int.
142 **Finishing his undergraduate:** Newell int.
142 **That same year:** Paul Zimmerman, "Pete Wanted Job of Sports Editor," *LAT,* Jan. 28, 1960.
142 **In 1951, the lightly regarded:** Matson returned kicks of 94 and 90 yards for touchdowns in the game, and the press was convinced. Writing in the *New York Herald Tribune,* Harold Rosenthal joked that "Rozelle should have 'his stripes removed' for not telling the members of the fourth estate 'more' about this extraordinary runner." Kristine Setting Clark, *Undefeated, Untied, and Uninvited: A Documentary of the 1951 University of San Francisco Dons Football Team* (Irvine, CA: Griffin, 2002), p. 61.
143 **Heavily influenced by:** In a letter sent to Rozelle in May 1954, Macker discussed his plans to open his own prestige PR firm: "I am going into this—if I do—with the idea of making

it a top public relations firm, and a lifetime business. I would want you to think of it in those terms, too. I am going after only business firms and similar accounts. No political campaigns, and no short-term accounts (such as sports shows, auto shows). . . . I know you are building your future, and are not interested in a fly-by-night operation, or in taking a big gamble. I would not invite you in the organization unless I am reasonably sure—as sure as you can be in a business venture—of the possibility of success." P. K. Macker letter to Pete Rozelle, May 3, 1954, Rozelle papers.

143 **Within months:** For a fee of $82,500, Rozelle and Macker spent the nine months leading up to the games working almost entirely on increasing the Melbourne Olympic profile in the U.S. Both Rozelle and Macker logged 100,000 air miles in publicizing the effort—and during the first six months garnered more than 100,000 column inches of coverage in their clip files. Acquiring a list of all Americans traveling to Melbourne for the games, they set up a series of remote television interviews with the tourists, which they packaged into customized travelogues, interspersed with scenes of Melbourne and the games. P. K. Macker, *A PR Concept*, 1956, strategic prospectus prepared by Ken Macker and Pete Rozelle for Victoria Organizing Committee, Rozelle papers.

143 **By the end:** Bert Bell, Jr., int.; Schramm int.

144 **He presided over:** Bob Hunter, "Rams Still Unsigned," *Los Angeles Examiner*, Apr. 29, 1957.

144 **Rozelle's presence:** Rube Samuelson, "Rube Barbs: Man in Fifty Million," *Independent Star-News*, Jan. 31, 1960; Schramm int.

144 **Rozelle earned:** Bert Bell, Jr., would recall his dad receiving a call from Rozelle one evening in 1958, on the verge of resigning. But the commissioner reassured him and emphasized his support. Maureen Reeves Woodland letter to Pete Rozelle, Aug. 20, 1986, Rozelle papers; Bert Bell, Jr., int.

145 **Within six months:** "Who Is Pete Rozelle," *Los Angeles Examiner*, Jan. 27, 1960; Jerry Greene, "Rozelle's Reign a 26-year Success Story," *Orlando Sentinel*, Jan. 19, 1986.

146 **On November 30:** Bob Oates, "Rams Get Cannon 'First,' " *Los Angeles Examiner*, Dec. 1, 1959; Curran, *The $400,000 Quarterback*, p. 110; Horrigan and Rathet, *The Other League*, p. 20.

146 **"I'm sure he wants":** Adams int.

147 **A few minutes later:** Dick Peebles, "Voice of the Peebles: 83,000 Saw Cannon Sign," *Houston Chronicle*, Jan. 6, 1960; Herskowitz, "For Pete's Sake," *Pro! Magazine*, undated.

148 **"Pete," Brown said:** Rozelle papers.

149 **"Don't worry":** Mel Durslag, "A Clean Beginning," *Los Angeles Examiner*, Feb. 9, 1960.

149 **With a bashful smile:** "Pete, don't take it," said the 49ers Vic Morabito. "They'll cut you to ribbons." But Rozelle's composure was quickly returning, and he explained calmly that he felt he'd survive if elected, since he hadn't campaigned for the job and because the league faced too many problems at the moment. John Devaney, "The Inner Workings of the NFL," *Sport*, Dec. 1964.

149 **It was Brown:** Letter from Pete Rozelle to Mike Brown, Feb. 13, 1994, Rozelle papers.

149 **Rooney in turn agreed:** Mara int.

149 **By his own estimate:** Undated letter to Mike Brown, Rozelle papers.

149 **Returning to the conference room:** Rozelle was introduced to the assembled press corps, which had already stayed five days longer than they'd planned—through a spate of unseasonably cold weather, with little news to report—and were restless, cranky, and by then ravenous for news. The first question came from Louis Effrat of the *New York Times*, who asked, "Tell us, Commissioner, do you consider yourself a compromise candidate?" The question temporarily left him at a loss for words, until both he and many of the assembled reporters started laughing. Harold Rosenthal, *Fifty Faces of Football* (New York: Atheneum, 1981), p. 99.

150 **When asked about Bell's:** Art Rosenbaum column, *San Francisco Chronicle*, Jan. 28, 1960.

150 **"I hesitate calling it":** George Strickler, "Rozelle, Ram Official, New NFL Chief," *Chicago Tribune*, Jan. 27, 1960.

150 **"We knew within twenty-four hours":** Mara int.
150 **As the owners:** Doc Greene, "The Detroit News Sports Quiz: Contracts Key to Grid Peace," *Detroit News,* Feb. 2, 1960.
150 **Much of the national press:** Joe King, "New NFL Boss—Monarch or Mouthpiece?" *TSN,* Feb. 8, 1960.

9: THE NEW FRONTIER

152 **Forrest Gregg had:** Forrest Gregg int.
153 **The tension between:** Maraniss, *When Pride Still Mattered,* p. 239.
154 **Green Bay's last NFL title:** *Fabulous Fifties, Part 2,* NFL Films.
154 **Forrest Gregg, arriving in 1957:** Gregg int.
154 **After the 1-10-1 1958 campaign:** John Wiebusch, *Lombardi* (Chicago: Follett, 1971), p. 77.
154 **At St. Norbert's:** Gregg int.
154 **What startled Gregg:** Ibid.
155 **There was:** Don Phillips, *Run to Win: Vince Lombardi on Coaching and Leadership* (New York: St. Martin's, 2002), p. 92.
155 **Lombardi's philosophy:** Maraniss, *When Pride Still Mattered,* p. 79.
155 **Within that context:** Hamilton Maule, *The Players* (New York: New American Library, 1967), pp. 6–7.
156 **After the Packers routed:** Maraniss, *When Pride Still Mattered,* p. 294.
156 **Rozelle's "transitional" year:** On May 3, the Rozelles had signed a five-month lease and moved into a furnished house in Philadelphia at 2417 North 51st Street, but they stayed for less than a month before leasing their apartment in New York City. Thelma Elkjer's appointment notebooks, Rozelle papers.
156 **In July:** "PR Blood, Sweat and Security at 65," *University of San Francisco Alumnus,* Nov./Dec. 1962.
157 **"Well," said Rozelle:** Weiss int.; John Devaney, "The Inner Workings of the NFL," *Sport,* Dec. 1964.
157 **Shortly after the end:** Cathy Kensil int.; Larry Felser, "Memories," *GameDay Magazine,* Sep. 1989.
157 **The hiring raised eyebrows:** Kensil letter to Arnold Zeitlin, UPI correspondent, March 12, 1961.
157 **In Kensil:** Jim Kensil int.; Cathy Kensil int.; Larry Felser, "Memories."
158 **Kensil increased the quality:** The new wire story transmission format was known as TTS. "The league began to be more anticipatory of what people might want," said Don Weiss, who had been a colleague of Kensil's at AP (and who would himself join the league office in 1965). "Instead of being the same tired old stuff that they used to throw at you—or not throw at you as the case may be, because unless you were one of a few people, you couldn't get much of anything." Don Weiss int.
158 **Even before:** Jack Sell, "Roamin' Around" column, *Pittsburgh Post-Gazette,* Sep. 6, 1961.
158 **Later in October:** "Violent World of Sam Huff," Daly and O'Donnell, *Pro Football Chronicle,* pp. 171–73.
158 ***Life* magazine's:** *Life,* Dec. 5, 1960.
159 **For his part:** "Violent Face of Pro Football," *SI,* Oct. 24, 1960; Modell int.; Thelma Elkjer's notes.
159 **In Rozelle's words:** Pete Rozelle int. in 1995, for *The Franchise.*
159 **In a confidential 1962 letter:** Coverage inside the magazine also reflected the change: *SI* ran ten pro football stories (not counting department pieces) in 1955, thirteen in 1956, and thirteen in 1957; that number of stories had almost doubled by 1963 (and would reach thirty by the mid-'60s). MacCambridge, *The Franchise,* p. 124.
159 **There was also:** Ethel Kennedy int.; Summerall int.; Zimmerman, *The Last Season of Weeb Ewbank,* p. 31.

160   **John F. Kennedy:** Ethel Kennedy int.

160   **"I'm sure there":** Ethel Kennedy int.

160   **As Bert Bell:** Gillman int.; Gruver, *The American Football League*, pp. 38–44; Ryczek, *Crash of the Titans*, pp. 90–91.

161   **Jack Kemp:** Kemp int.; Ryczek, *Crash of the Titans*, pp. 73–74.

161   **Though the Chargers:** Mark Ribowsky, *Slick: The Silver and Black Life of Al Davis* (New York: Macmillan, 1991), p. 102.

161   **Grave circumstances:** Daly and O'Donnell, *Pro Football Chronicle*, p. 180; Curran, *The $400,000 Quarterback*, p. 100.

162   **But even if the level:** Adams int.; Hunt int.; Gruver, *The American Football League*, p. 168.

162   **"The Texans tried":** Eisenberg, *Cotton Bowl Days*, p. 37.

162   **Hunt also hired:** Hunt int.

163   **On Sunday:** Schramm int.; Curran, *The $400,000 Quarterback*, p. 157; St. John, *Tex!*, p. 257.

163   **Meanwhile:** St. John, *Tex!*, p. 257, Eisenberg, *Cotton Bowl Days*, p. 38.

163   **Behind diminutive quarterback:** Eisenberg, *Cotton Bowl Days*, p. 38.

163   **When a reporter:** Curran, *The $400,000 Quarterback*, p. 152.

164   **"No, our team":** William C. Rhoden, "When Paul Brown Smashed the Color Barrier," *NYT*, Sep. 25, 1997.

164   **But in every city:** Schramm int.; St. John, *Tex!*, p. 282; Golenbock, *Cowboys Have Always Been My Heroes*, p. 71.

164   **"If I ever hear":** Maraniss, *When Pride Still Mattered*, pp. 239–41; Arthur Daley, "Sports of the Times: The Weight of Experience," *NYT*, Dec. 28, 1966.

165   **Even among Marshall's defenders:** Thomas G. Smith, "Civil Rights on the Gridiron: The Kennedy Administration and the Desegregation of the Washington Redskins," *The Coffin Corner*, Vol. 10, originally published in *Journal of Sport History*, Vol. 14, No. 2, Summer 1987.

165   **Few were more vigilant:** Povich, "This Morning with Shirley Povich," *Washington Post*, Oct. 31, 1960.

165   **After checking first:** Alan Levy, *Tackling Jim Crow: Racial Segregation in Professional Football* (Jefferson, NC: McFarland, 1997), p. 128.

166   **The 1961 season:** Robert Deindorfer, "Has Pro Football Passed by Paul Brown?" *Sport*, June 1962.

166   **In the absence of:** Dawson int.; Bobby Mitchell int.; Didinger, "A Remembrance of Paul Brown," in *A Game of Passion*, Wiebusch and Silverman, eds., pp. 247–48; Pluto, *When All the World Was Browns Town*, pp. 25–26.

167   **When halfback Bobby Mitchell:** Mitchell int.

167   **"Bobby had to go":** Jim Brown int.

167   **In 1961, the Browns:** Modell int.

167   **Yet Modell:** Ibid.

168   **Early in the 1961 season:** Pluto, When All the World Was Browns Town, p. 46.

168   **"What do you think":** Ibid., pp. 50–51.

168   **Had Davis been:** Rosenthal, *Fifty Faces of Football*, p. 211.

169   **"I'm sorry Mr. Marshall":** Levy, *Tackling Jim Crow*, p. 136.

169   **The team returned:** Pluto, *When All the World Was Browns Town*, p. 56.

169   **"Harold, I need your advice":** Modell int.

170   **Modell fretted:** Modell didn't do anything at first. But a week after the season, he began to hear that a group of disaffected Browns, including Jim Brown, had held a private meeting to discuss their grievances with Paul Brown, and were prepared to confront Modell about the issue. Before they could do so, he intervened. Modell int.; Jim Brown int.

170   **"Paul, sit down please":** Modell int.; Pluto, *When All the World Was Browns Town*, pp. 60–63.

170   **Brown's face was blank:** Some would later charge Modell with announcing the firing during the heart of Cleveland's newspaper strike, to minimize the criticism he might receive.

But the strike had been going on for weeks. And not to be muzzled, Cleveland newspaperman Hal Lebovitz organized a group of city sportswriters to weigh in on the firing and published a twenty-four-page booklet titled *The Play Paul Brown Didn't Call*, which sold more than 50,000 copies in the ensuing months, and was so evenhanded it left both Modell and Brown angry. Pluto, *When All the World Was Browns Town*, pp. 61–62; Modell int.; Mike Brown int.

170 **A day after firing Brown:** Had Collier not taken the coaching job, he might have left anyway; the Colts' new head coach, former Browns defensive back Don Shula, had been urging him to come and work with him in Baltimore. Shula int.; Kay Collier-McLaughlin int.; Pluto, *When All the World Was Browns Town*, pp. 65–67.

170 **Collier called Brown:** Mike Brown int.; Kay Collier-McLaughlin int.

170 **But soon after:** Mike Brown int.; Kay Collier-McLaughlin int.

170 **Paul Brown:** Those closest to Brown would describe his mood as heartbroken. Days later, in a moment of reflection, Brown confided in his friend Herb Eisele, head coach at John Carroll University. "If I ever get back into coaching," he told Eisele, "I'll never let a team get away from me again." Natali, *Brown's Town*, pp. 533–34; Pluto, *When All the World Was Browns Town*, p. 63.

171 **By 1960:** Rozelle papers; Patton, *Razzle Dazzle*, p. 53.

172 **"There's a couple of":** Rooney int.

172 **A year later:** League minutes, National Football League annual meetings, Jan. 24, 1961.

172 **Two days:** Prior to that meeting, Lombardi worked the room, canvassing other smaller-market franchises, warning the Cardinals' Stormy Bidwill, "You know, you'll die with us."

"Hey, Coach," said Bidwill. "You don't have to tell me that; I know it." Bidwill int.

172 **The Giants:** Bidwill int.

172 **After much debate:** "RESOLVED, That the Commissioner of the National Football League is hereby authorized to negotiate and conclude an agreement with a national television network whereunder the league shall sell and the network shall purchase all rights of the League and its member clubs of the League. . . . Said agreement shall provide that (1) no game shall be telecast within the home territory of a member club, without the consent of such club, on the day when such club is playing a game at home and (2) every regular season Sunday afternoon games between member clubs shall, to the extent practicable, be made available to all affiliated stations of the network located within the home territory of the visiting club." League minutes, National Football League annual meetings, Jan. 27, 1961.

173 **The curious reasoning:** *Sports Illustrated*'s unsigned editorial in the August 7, 1961, issue aptly cited the apparent blind justice of the decision. Grim's ruling, argued *SI*, "has the effect of encouraging the rich to get richer and obliging the poor to remain that way, surely the opposite intent of antitrust legislation. In addition, the richer teams would inevitably become better teams, and the poorer teams would become worse teams. It seems to us too bad that a distinction before the law cannot be made between a sports association—to whose advantage (and the public's) it is to field evenly matched teams—and, say, a group of car manufacturers. Pro football, we agree, is as much business as it is sport, but it is a special kind of business and should be treated accordingly." "Grim Decision," in Scorecard, *SI*, Aug. 7, 1961.

173 **After a round:** Max Patterson int.

173 **On September 30, 1961:** Patton, *Razzle Dazzle*, p. 56.

173 **In ensuing years:** Powers, *Supertube*, p. 174.

173 **"The whole thing":** Early draft of interview transcript with the American Academy of Achievement, Rozelle papers.

10: THE CZAR

175 **Vince Lombardi sat:** Statement; "Re: Paul Vernon Hornung, Green Bay Packers, Report of Thomas J. McShane, Polygraph Expert, 1963," Rozelle papers.

175 **"Well, you have no choice":** Rozelle int. for *The Franchise*; Maraniss, *When Pride Still Mattered*, pp. 339–40.

176 **The chatter about:** AP, "Inquiry Widens in Pro Football," *NYT,* Jan. 8, 1963; UPI, "Hoodlums Linked to Detroit Lions," *NYT,* Jan. 9, 1963.

176 **By January 9:** "Memorandum of Meeting at Plaza Hotel, NYC, with Commissioner Rozelle and Paul Hornung," Jan. 9, 1963, Rozelle papers.

176 **McShane had:** "Re: Paul Vernon Hornung, Green Bay Packers, Report of Thomas J. McShane, Polygraph Expert, 1963."

177 **Though Shapiro:** Hornung's relationship with Shapiro included weekly calls during the season, with Hornung calling Shapiro collect in Las Vegas every Wednesday evening, between 7:00 and 8:00 p.m. "Shapiro would quote a pointspread to him," according to McShane's report of his interview with Hornung, "and he [Hornung] would comment on it, either going along with it by betting, or not betting at all. Shapiro would inquire as to the condition of the team at this time, and he would call Hornung back on the Saturday nights before the games to check again on the condition of the team before bets were placed. Hornung said he would furnish information to Shapiro regularly on these occasions regarding the physical condition of the Packer players." Ibid.; National Football League Players Contract.

177 **On the morning of April 17:** John Devaney, "The Inner Workings of the NFL," *Sport,* Dec. 1964.

178 **Bunkered in the league offices:** NFL release, "National Football League Commissioner's Report on Investigation."

178 **Rozelle's public face:** "Hornung, Karras Suspended for Betting," *Washington Post,* Apr. 18, 1963; AP, "Grid Bettors Out for Year," *Baltimore Sun,* Apr. 19, 1963.

178 **Karras was much more critical:** Shirley Povich, "This Morning . . . with Shirley Povich," column, *Washington Post,* Apr. 19, 1963.

178 **The public and media response:** "Judgment Day," *Newsweek,* Apr. 29, 1963; Jim Murray, "Football's Fail-Safe," column, *LAT,* Apr. 19, 1963.

179 **About a week:** Loretta Hornung letter to Pete Rozelle, undated, 1963; Rozelle letter to Loretta Hornung, dated April 30, 1963, Rozelle papers.

179 **The fallout:** There remained an unfounded rumor that Rosenbloom had bet a large sum on the 1958 championship game, then urged Ewbank, in the waning moments of overtime, to go for a touchdown rather than field goal so the Colts could cover the three-and-a-half-point spread. This would seem, self-evidently, one of the more baseless rumors in sports history. Ewbank and Rosenbloom had no contact during the final stages of the game, and even if they had, one strains to imagine how John Unitas would have responded to such a directive.

179 **Two different Colts employees:** Not-for-attribution ints.

179 **Throughout the previous:** Hunt int.; Pash int.

180 **Writing after:** Don Weiss int.; Maraniss, *When Pride Still Mattered,* pp. 325–26; Bob Oates, "Lombardi Fears Packers Past Peak," *Los Angeles Herald Examiner,* Dec. 6, 1962.

180 **"In fairness":** Tex and Dorothy Maule also lived in the same Sutton Place apartment complex, and Dorothy recalled that after the Rozelles moved to New York, Jane's problems increased. "We were invited to breakfast, and she never came out," said Maule. "They found an apartment about a street away from where we lived and moved there. I tried being friendly with her, but on several occasions he just couldn't make her show up. It was a sad story, because she was a nice person. She couldn't handle the success." John Lehman int.; Dorothy Maule int.; not-for-attribution int.

180 **When Tex Schramm:** Schramm int.

181 **"If I can look":** Anne Marie Bratton (née Rozelle) int.

181 **"That convinced him":** Newell int.

181 **In *White Collar:*** C. Wright Mills, *White Collar: The American Middle Classes* (New York: Oxford University Press, 1951).

182 **One of the:** Like so many others before him, Sabol was charmed by his first meeting with Rozelle. "He was not at all like what I expected a commissioner would be," Sabol said. "You

know—*huff huff, in and out, lay it down and let's get out.* But he was very soft-spoken, had a very friendly smile." Ed Sabol int.; Alex Ben Block, "The 27th Team," *Today/The Philadelphia Inquirer,* Dec. 10, 1972; Mark Kram, Jr., "Steve Sabol Makes History," *Philadelphia Magazine,* Sep. 1996; Tom C. Brady, "C. B. DeMille of the Pros," *SI,* Nov. 20, 1967; William Barry Furlong, "Sabol Plays Film Game into Sports Millions," *Washington Post,* May 18, 1976.

182   **The film about:** The World War II vet Sabol had recently seen Darryl Zanuck's film *The Longest Day,* about the Normandy invasion; Ed Sabol int.

183   **After the screening:** Ed Sabol int.

183   **Sabol held:** Ibid.

183   **The Rams' partnership:** On March 13, 1959, Kent sent a proposal to Rozelle, which opened: "We believe that PROFESSIONAL FOOTBALL offers the most exciting potential for brand name licensing that exists on the American scene. We believe if the program we propose is started in 1960 that within a three or four year period it can exceed the volume of business we now enjoy with ROY ROGERS. We also believe that we are uniquely suited to do this job in such a manner that in addition to making money for each of the twelve league members it will reflect credit on everyone involved and will become the strongest promotional force outside of television for each team." Larry Kent letter to Pete Rozelle, March 13, 1959, Rozelle papers.

183   **Bert Bell had liked:** Halas, back in the '30s, had agreed to license the Bears' helmet logo on one of the first bobble-head dolls in football with David Warsaw's nascent Bobbie Company; James Warsaw int.; Atkin int.

184   **The ambitious project:** A statement in early 1961 showed $31,948 in royalties and $95,009 in expenses. NFL Properties balance sheet, 1961, Rozelle papers; *1963 NFL Properties Catalog.*

184   **"We wanted fans":** Carothers int.

184   **Kent was the can-do president:** Don Smith, "Dave Boss Pioneer Award Winner," Pro Football Hall of Fame, news release, No. 10, July 1, 1992.

186   **"Pierre," said:** Salinger int.; Salinger, *P.S.: A Memoir.*

186   **Through Salinger:** Cardinals owner Stormy Bidwill, in town early for the team's game against the Giants, stopped by the NFL offices later that afternoon, like the rest of the league, seeking answers from Rozelle. "He was shaken, he was sad, like we all were," said Bidwill. "But he was also thinking in terms of 'What do we do.' He said, 'You know, Stormy, the president was very sports-minded and I wonder if he wouldn't want the world to continue and not be going into mourning forever.' " Bidwill int.; Salinger int.

186   **"It has been":** NFL press release, Nov. 22, 1963.

186   **At five o'clock:** Rosenthal, *Fifty Faces of Football,* p. 92.

186   **While the AFL:** Charles McCabe, "Czar Rozelle Whammied," "The Fearless Spectator" column, *San Francisco Chronicle,* Jan. 3, 1964.

187   **On Saturday morning:** Eisenberg, *Cotton Bowl Days,* p. 86.

187   **But the games:** Modell int.; Weiss int.; Daly and O'Donnell, *Pro Football Chronicle,* p. 191.

187   **In the visitors' locker room:** Eisenberg, *Cotton Bowl Days,* pp. 86–87.

187   **In his biography:** Maraniss, *When Pride Still Mattered,* p. 352.

187   **In the press box:** Rosenthal, *Fifty Faces of Football,* pp. 93–94.

187   **Even in the wake:** Stanley Cohen, *The Man in the Crowd: Confessions of a Sports Addict* (New York: Random House, 1981), p. 118.

188   **After the stirring:** Ibid., pp. 118–20.

188   **Joe Pollack:** Pollack int.

188   **Norman Mailer:** Plimpton int.

188   **CBS decided not:** Rozelle, in fact, briefly tried to get CBS to pay for the weekend's games, arguing that the NFL had done its part by playing the games. But after a shocked, angry response from CBS, he let the matter drop. Not-for-attribution ints.

189   **"I just don't think":** Ethel Kennedy int.

189   **Despite the criticism:** MacCambridge, *The Franchise,* p. 127.

190 **A week later:** Curran, *The $400,000 Quarterback*, pp. 93–94.
190 **The talk prompted:** Gillman int.
190 **The coda:** Gunther and Carter, *Monday Night Mayhem*, pp. 16–17.
190 **Rozelle instructed:** Johnson, *Super Spectator and the Electric Lilliputians*, p. 125.
190 **"Pete was always cool":** Frank int.
191 **MacPhail recalled:** Johnson, *Super Spectator and the Electric Lilliputians*, p. 125.
191 **The circumstances surrounding:** Ibid., p. 126.
191 **Decades later:** Summerall had remembered that CBS's Bill Paley was in the Cayman Islands; William Oscar Johnson's account, in his book *Super Spectator and the Electric Lilliputians*, had Paley at a meeting the day before the bids were made. Summerall int.; ibid., p. 125.
191 **Reaching Rozelle:** Modell int.; Johnson, *Super Spectator and the Electric Lilliputians*, p. 125.
192 **Over the next decade:** Peter Hadhazy int.; Don Weiss int.
192 **Even baseball:** Patterson, *Grand Expectations*, p. 333.
192 **Gabe Paul:** Pluto, *When All the World Was Browns Town*, p. 140.

11: WAR

193 **With the record-breaking:** Stephen Mahoney, "Pro Football's Profit Explosion," *Fortune*, Nov. 1964.
195 **"I remember Paul Brown":** Dawson int.
195 **"After a while":** Murray Chass, *Power Football* (New York: Dutton, 1973), p. 161.
196 **They chose:** Hank Stram and Lou Sahadi, *They're Playing My Game* (New York: Morrow, 1986), p. 66.
196 **"Once Buck went first":** Robinson int.
196 **A year later:** Wells int.; Younger int.; Klosterman interview transcript, *Rebels with a Cause* documentary, HBO.
197 **"The Vikings":** Bobby Bell int.
197 **With the Chargers slumping:** Some of the media that covered the title game still couldn't resist the baseball metaphor ("Triple in 11th Wins it for Texans" was the headline in the *Dallas Times-Herald*. Dick Connor, *Great Teams Great Years: Kansas City Chiefs* (New York: Macmillan, 1974), p. 22.
197 **Though the Texans:** Eisenberg, *Cotton Bowl Days*, p. 51.
197 **Hunt's attention:** At the invitation of Kansas City mayor H. Roe Bartle, Hunt secretly flew in with Jack Steadman, and as they went around meeting local businessmen, the two men referred to themselves as Mr. Lamar and Jack X.
198 **Len Dawson:** Michael MacCambridge, "Without Them, We're Wichita," *TSN*, Aug. 11, 1997.
198 **Dallas, Denver:** Oakland Raiders Media Guide; Ryczek, *Crash of the Titans*, p. 222; Curran, *The $400,000 Quarterback*, p. 127.
199 **A Chargers-Titans game:** Ryczek, *Crash of the Titans*, pp. 283, 290.
199 **Only a $40,000 bailout:** When the Titans filed for bankruptcy in February 1963, they showed some debts dating all the way back to 1960. They hadn't paid East Stroudsburg State Teachers College a $20,000 training camp bill, they owed the AFL $255,000, the Irving Trust more than $400,000. Ryczek, *Crash of the Titans*, pp. 287–88.
199 **The situation looked:** Lamar Hunt, untitled personal recollections of early days of AFL, Kansas City Chiefs archives.
199 **Sonny was:** Curran, *The $400,000 Quarterback*, p. 150.
199 **In 1965:** Ibid., p. 138.
199 **On April 15, 1963:** Patton, *Razzle Dazzle*, pp. 84–85; Zimmerman, *The Last Season of Weeb Ewbank*, p. 36.
200 **After playing one last season:** "The AFL: From Kansas City Lamar to Broadway Joe," *Pro! Magazine*, undated.

200   **Each of the 3,500 children:** Curran, *The $400,000 Quarterback,* p. 142.

200   **On AM radio:** Ibid., p. 144.

200   **By 1964:** Ramos int.; Knox int.

200   **As the Giants':** Wellington Mara int.

200   **By the time:** NBC had agreed to a deal provided that 1) the deal was signed by midnight the next Monday, January 27, and 2) no word be leaked to ABC. But Joe Foss hadn't earned the Congressional Medal of Honor for his backroom deals. So at 5:00 p.m. that Monday afternoon, he took a break from the meeting with NBC and their lawyers, and called ABC's Tom Moore from a pay phone outside the Time Life Building. Foss met Moore there, at the corner of 50th Street and Sixth Avenue, and showed him the pending NBC contract under a streetlight. Moore called ABC chief Leonard Goldenson, who said there was no way ABC could match the money. Foss, satisfied that he'd given a chance to the network that had kept the AFL alive during its early years, returned to the NBC offices and signed the deal. Patton, *Razzle Dazzle,* pp. 88–89; Johnson, *Super Spectator and the Electric Lilliputians,* pp. 133–35.

201   **Around NFL circles:** Dan Rooney int.; Bidwill int.

201   **At the beginning:** Natali, *Brown's Town,* p. 459.

201   **And yet, somehow:** Pluto, *When All the World Was Browns Town,* p. 67; Slone, *Football's Gentle Giant,* pp. 19, 142–43, 150, 156.

201   **The biggest change:** Collier had compensated for his almost total deafness by an acute observational eye for detail, not just lipreading but body language and, in football, an ability to break down the game at virtually every position to its fundamental components. "I remember an exchange he had with a receiver in a film session one time," said Browns defensive end Bill Glass. "Blanton said, 'You weren't looking at the ball, you were looking at the defender.' And the receiver had no comment. Blanton asked him, 'Do you remember what you were looking at?' The receiver said, 'No, I don't.' Blanton said, 'Look at the film,' and he ran it back. The receiver still had not commented. Blanton said, 'Watch the stripe on your helmet and you can see what you were looking at if your eyes were open.' At the last second, the stripe on the helmet bobbed away from the approaching ball and at the defender. Blanton showed the receiver in stop-action, one frame at a time . . . you could see the stripe on the helmet move just a fraction right before the ball arrived, thus making the receiver miss the pass." Slone, *Football's Gentle Giant,* pp. 39, 153, 261.

202   **"One of the reasons":** On the eve of games, Ryan and the offensive linemen would meet to go over blocking schemes. Then Dick Schafrath and John Wooten, representing the offensive line, would meet in Jim Brown's room to discuss the play list. "The three of us would talk over the plays, maybe pick six of them that we were sure would work well for the running game that week," said Schafrath. "Then I'd take those plays to Frank Ryan." Jim Brown int.; Pluto, *When All the World Was Browns Town,* p. 76.

202   **"They don't invite us":** Brown and Delsohn, *Out of Bounds,* p. 57.

202   **In the 1964 title game:** Unitas and Fitzgerald, *The Johnny Unitas Story,* p. 109.

203   **In Palm Springs:** Mike Brown int.

203   **As far back as the '20s:** Harvey Pollack, "Bell of the NFL," *Sportfolio,* Jan. 1948.

204   **Secure phone connections:** By the early '60s, Mickey Dukich, the Rams' cinematographer, began shooting game film with an anamorphic lens, to provide a wider angle for game film. Dukich int.; "85 Innovations," *Forbes,* Dec. 23, 2002; P. K. Macker and Co. brochure.

204   **Frustrated during:** Schramm int.; St. John, *Tex!,* p. 218.

204   **Very quickly:** Ibid., p. 263.; Brandt int.

205   **Computers were:** Schramm int.; Brandt int.; Spadia int.; Quereishi int.

205   **And besides:** Tex Maule, "Make No Mistakes About It," *SI,* Jan. 29, 1968.

206   **By the fall:** The computer read:

1. NAMATH, JOE	QB	ALABAMA	803
2. BUTKUS, DICK	LB	ILLINOIS	854
3. SAYERS, GALE	HB	KANSAS	851

    4. BILETNIKOFF, FRED   WR   FLORIDA STATE   776
    5. CURTIS, MIKE   LB   DUKE   801

Though his raw score wasn't as high, Namath came out on top of the particular list because of the added value placed on elite quarterbacks. As Quereishi would explain later, "Namath rates ahead . . . because he had qualities that were held in particularly high esteem by this model. . . . On another model with another set of requirements, Butkus or Sayers may have come first." Brandt, understandably proud of the Cowboys' accomplishments, was ambivalent about what the "real" first printout said, because there were a variety of master lists with different weights and measures. But Maule's story in *SI* in 1968 was accurate, according to Schramm. Maule, "Make No Mistakes About It"; Quereishi int.; Schramm int.; Brandt int.; Aaron Latham, "The Cowboys, the Indian, and the Computer That Fumbled," *Texas Monthly,* Sep. 1986.

206 **Al Davis was still:** Davis interview transcript, *Rebels with a Cause* documentary.

206 **"Well, George Mira's":** Ramos int.

207 **"No one actually":** Ibid.

207 **The contract, in detail:** From Ed Krzemienski's unpublished biography of Joe Namath, contract first reported by Dick Young of the *New York Daily News,* later reproduced in Martin Ralbovsky, *The Namath Effect* (Englewood Cliffs, NJ: Prentice Hall, 1976), pp. 16–17.

208 **On January 2, 1965:** Gruver, *History of the AFL,* p. 141.

208 **If they had overspent:** Zimmerman, *The Last Season of Weeb Ewbank,* pp. 250–51; Robert H. Boyle, "Show-Biz Sonny and His Quest for Stars," *SI,* July 19, 1965; Ramos int.

208 **"With that kind of salary":** Curran, *The $400,000 Quarterback,* p. 151.

208 **"A year earlier":** Jerry Izenberg, "And Wearing White Shoes . . . ," *Pro! Magazine,* Sep. 20, 1976.

208 **After the loss of players:** Rose int.

209 **Rozelle asked Reeves:** Larry Felser, "War Games," *Pro! Magazine,* Sep. 9, 1979.

209 **By November 1964:** The brochure sent to NFL field reps noted, "A single change or addition seldom is the complete solution to a problem. However, we feel strongly that the addition of just one major sales technique not presently pursued by the National Football League . . . would substantially strengthen our signing position with any player a member team of the league might select. . . . If we are to successfully compete in the signing field, the players we draft must, insofar as possible, be mentally conditioned to the advantages the NFL can offer *before* the time of the selection meeting." Kasper int.; Brochure for NFL Representatives, undated, pp. 1–2, Frank Kasper collection.

209 **The jobs offered:** Rozelle letter to John Commeford, June 8, 1990, Rozelle papers.

210 **"Sayers, in fact":** Stram and Sahadi, *They're Playing My Game,* pp. 76–77.

210 **Decades later:** Klosterman interview transcript, *Rebels with a Cause* documentary.

211 **"Just tell Otis":** Wells int.

211 **"You don't come":** Ibid.

211 **As soon as they:** From the hotel they went to Love Field, where they arrived at 4:45. Pulling the car up to the terminal, Wells became suspicious of two men at the Braniff gate and, fearing they were NFL reps waiting to intercept their prey, drove on to the Fort Worth airport, where he, Taylor, and Cartwright caught a 7:45 plane to Kansas City. Klosterman interview transcript, *Rebels with a Cause* documentary; Wells int.; Dick Kaplan, "The Undercover War in Pro Football," *Sport,* Aug. 1966; Hurd int.

211 **The *New York Times*'s Bill Wallace:** William Wallace, "The Decision," Sports of the Times, *NYT,* Jan. 14, 1965.

211 **With his slicked-back hair:** Ribowsky, *Slick,* pp. 148, 150.

212 **As the civil war:** It was true that the edge enjoyed by football was tenuous and somewhat circumstantial at that point. Football's edge over baseball was scant, 41 percent to 38 percent among sports fans asked to name their favorite sport. Some of the fans who'd named football their favorite sport were obviously more avid college fans than pro fans. And some of the advantage surely was seasonal; the same question in a survey six months earlier had

shown a 38 percent to 25 percent advantage for baseball. But beneath that slender edge there were volumes of information indicating that pro football's popularity was still rising. More than 40 percent of sports fans described themselves as "more interested" in pro football than they had been a few years earlier. "By far the most important and sustained drawing card in all sports today," the report noted, "are the televised games of the National Football League." Nearly half of all sports fans said they watched nearly every game on television, 40 percent said they wanted more TV doubleheaders, and 55 percent said they'd be willing to watch a game during prime-time hours. Louis Harris, "A Study of the Effectiveness of the Television Broadcasting of National Football League Games," Rozelle papers.

212 **"We thought":** Modell int.

12: A SEPARATE PEACE

214 **That fine-grained attention:** Schramm int.

214 **The buildup:** Adams int.; Felser, "War Games."

215 **More than 300 players:** Frank Kasper, a Chicago printing salesman brought into the program by George Halas's son Muggsie, had worked the previous year's draft, but met his prospect, Purdue tight end Ed Flanagan, just two days before the draft. In 1965, by comparison, Kasper contacted Purdue lineman Jerry Shay in the summer, had Shay and his girlfriend over for dinner in July, dined with his parents in August, and attended two Purdue games during the season. Shay was the seventh player taken in the 1966 draft, and signed with the Vikings that weekend. Kasper int.; Weiss int.; John R. McDermott, "'Draft Central,' N.F.L.'s Secret HQ," *Life*, Dec. 10, 1965.

215 **Baby-sitters were:** Brandt int.

215 **When the time came:** Schramm int.; Frank Luksa, "War & Peace," *Petersen's Annual Pro Football: 1970*; Tim Cowlishaw, "Segregation Among Obstacles That Failed to Deter Schramm," *Dallas Morning News*, July 22, 1991; Schramm testimony, Yazoo Smith case, No. 1643–70, p. 83.

216 **"It was all so costly":** Herskowitz, "A Lion in Winter," in *A Game of Passion*, Wiebusch and Silverman, eds., p. 33.

216 **"It was hard for me":** Cowlishaw, "Segregation Among Obstacles That Failed to Deter Schramm."

216 **The negotiations toward:** Schramm int.; Hunt int.; Wilson int.

217 **In virtually every:** "Reeves loved to go for walks," recalled Jack Teele. "On more than one occasion, we'd be out for a walk, and he'd say, 'You ever thought of Phoenix? Ever thought of living in Phoenix?' And this was during that time. 'Nice place to raise your children.' So he was thinking about it, and he told me he would be willing to do it." Teele int.; Schramm int.; Luksa, "War & Peace."

217 **Furthermore:** Carothers int.

217 **So before making:** Spadia int.

218 **"I suppose":** Schramm int.

218 **"This is a horseshit town":** MacCambridge, "Without Them, We're Wichita."

218 **Hank Stram would:** Stram and Sahadi, *They're Playing My Game*, p. 79.

218 **A tragedy finally brought:** Ibid., p. 85; McGuff, *Winning It All*, p. 100.

218 **Though Hunt still lived:** Tex Maule, "On with the Golden Game," *SI*, Sep. 15, 1966.

219 **On April 4:** Hunt int.; Schramm int.

219 **Once inside:** Schramm int.; Hunt int.

219 **For its new commissioner:** Edwin Shrake, "After Foss: A Hotter Pro War," *SI*, Apr. 18, 1966; Ribowsky, *Slick*, p. 162; William Wallace, "'War' Declared on AFL's Rival," *NYT*, Apr. 29, 1966.

220 **"I've been called":** Wolf int.

220 **For nearly seven years:** Mara informed Rozelle of the signing a day or two before the meeting and recalled that the commissioner "had no comment." Mara int.

221 **Down near the end:** Spadia int.

221 **"This is a disgrace!":** Dan Rooney int.

221 **"Goddamnit":** Modell int.; Bidwill int.

222 **Davis leaned back:** Davis int.; interview transcript, *Rebels with a Cause* documentary.

222 **Davis's aide:** Wolf int.

222 **Davis returned:** Arthur Daley, "Act of Provocation?," Sports of the Times, *NYT,* May 19, 1966.

222 **Within twenty-four hours:** "There was nothing illegal about what the Giants did," pointed out Davis's aide Scotty Stirling, who'd succeeded Davis as the Raiders' GM, but was also closely involved with war planning. "But we felt it gave us the moral wedge to go out and encourage a few people in their league to consider the same course." Jerry Izenberg, *The Rivals* (New York: Holt, Rinehart & Winston, 1968), p. 120; Davis int.; interview transcript, *Rebels with a Cause* documentary.

222 **Nearly forty years later:** Davis int.

223 **On the afternoon:** Spadia int.

223 **"It was bad":** Mara int.; Spadia int.

223 **"The only teams":** Bidwill int.

223 **As the meeting ended:** Schramm int.

223 **Arriving at Rozelle's suite:** Ibid.; St. John, *Tex!,* pp. 276–77.

224 **Schramm waited in silence:** Schramm int.

224 **The next morning:** In his later years, Schramm asserted that prior to the meeting on May 20, he had in hand an agreement from Hunt that the AFL would move both the Jets and the Raiders. Hunt said he had no recollection of that, and since they are the only two men who know the truth, it is impossible to know whether this was the case. The problem with Schramm's assertion—"my intent was always for the Jets and Raiders to move"—is that the rest of Schramm's story makes less sense. In his recollections of the time, and the contemporaneous *SI* story penned with Tex Maule, Schramm recalls that Mara in New York and Spadia in San Francisco were reluctant. But if they were faced with a plan in which the competition was moving out of town, there is no explanation for their reluctance. What's clear is that at some point, either in 1966 or earlier in 1965, there was serious discussion about the Jets moving to Los Angeles. Schramm int.; Jack Landry, Jr., int.; T. D. Werblin int.

224 **At that point:** St. John, *Tex!,* pp. 276–78.

224 **On May 23:** Roman Gabriel, *Player of the Year: Roman Gabriel's Football Journal* (New York: World, 1970), p. 107.

225 **At Davis's behest:** Spadia int.; Brodie, *Open Field,* p. 118–31.

225 **"John":** John Brodie and James D. Houston, *Open Field* (San Francisco: Houghton Mifflin, 1974).

225 **"The AFL agrees":** Adams int.

225 **When Spadia got:** Spadia int.

226 **"And so here it is,":** Schramm int.

226 **Klosterman called Davis:** Davis int.

226 **Davis then called:** Davis int.; Hunt int.; Bidwill int.; Spadia int.

226 **Hunt returned:** Hunt int.; Schramm int.; Schramm, "Here's How It Happened."

227 **Hunt flew:** Werblin int.; Hunt int.

227 **"I wanted a merger":** Davis interview transcript, *Rebels with a Cause.*

227 **Later that night:** Hunt int.; Weiss int.; Carothers int.

227 **The press release:** NFL press release, June 8, 1966; Hadhazy int.; Weiss int.; Browne int.

228 **After sending:** Al Stump, "Pete Rozelle: Czar Between the Goal Posts," *Los Angeles Herald Examiner Sunday Magazine,* Nov. 2, 1969.

228 **Furious, MacPhail demanded:** Stump, "Pete Rozelle: Czar Between the Goal Posts"; Powers, *Supertube,* p. 179.

228 **As news of the agreement:** Pinchbeck int.

229 **Rozelle, seeking a way:** Dixon int.

229 **The final approval:** Dixon int.
230 **After a rocky courtship:** And the upstarts getting equal play would take some getting used to. At the 1967 draft, the first joint draft between the leagues, many of the combatants in the subversive intrigue of the war years expressed some wistfulness for the old days. And on that afternoon, former baby-sitter Jack Landry walked into the conference room where the selection meeting was being held, and from the back of the room called out to Rozelle, "Hey, I've got a half dozen guys from Michigan State stashed in a hotel room in Yonkers. What do you want me to do with them?" Felser, "The War Years."

13: "THE ONLY THING"

231 **"There is":** Vince Lombardi, *Run to Daylight!* (Englewood Cliffs, NJ: Prentice Hall, 1963), p. 17.
232 **Jerry Kramer:** Curry would complain that the statement he heard "got bastardized into: 'Winning's not everything—it's the only thing.' I don't like that as much. That doesn't say it as well as the way I first learned it." George Plimpton and Bill Curry, *One More July: A Football Dialogue with Bill Curry* (New York: Harper & Row, 1977), p. 124; Jerry Kramer, *Instant Replay: The Green Bay Diary of Jerry Kramer* (New York: World, 1968), p. 50.
232 **After hearing:** Kramer, *Instant Replay,* p. 196.
232 **Iconoclastic Cowboys:** Golenbock, *Cowboys Have Always Been My Heroes,* pp. 230–31.
233 **Landry understood:** Eisenberg, *Cotton Bowl Days,* pp. 76–77.
233 **But Papa Bear:** Wiebusch, *Lombardi,* p. 27.
234 **"We're midshipmen":** In his reminiscence of the encounter, Allen relates that when he and his friend left, Einstein gave them a word of encouragement. "You boys ought to know, the war will end soon," he said, and then with his hands spread added, "A great boom." George Allen, *Strategies for Winning: A Top Coach's Game Plan for Victory in Football and in Life* (New York: McGraw-Hill, 1990), pp. 29–30.
234 **Allen vowed:** Jennifer Allen int.; Etty Allen int.; William Gildea and Kenneth Turan, *The Future Is Now: George Allen, Pro Football's Most Controversial Coach* (Boston: Houghton Mifflin, 1972), p. 38.
234 **As devoted to:** Gildea and Turan, *The Future Is Now,* p. 42; Jennifer Allen, *Fifth Quarter: The Scrimmage of a Football Coach's Daughter* (New York: Random House, 2000), p. 55.
235 **Allen had been:** Faulkner int.; Dukich int.; Schramm int.; Gildea and Turan, *The Future Is Now,* p. 139.
235 **On his desk:** Allen, *Fifth Quarter,* pp. 23, 95; George Allen and Joe Marshall, "A Hundred Percent Is Not Enough," *SI,* July 9, 1973.
235 **Dan Reeves:** Teele int; Hamilton Maule, *The Pro Season* (Garden City, NY: Doubleday, 1970), p. 17.
236 **In that 1966 season:** Gildea and Turan, *The Future Is Now,* p. 90.
236 **Some of his peers:** Ibid., p. 177.
236 **Shortly after:** Formal plans couldn't even begin until the antitrust exemption was secured in late October, and Rozelle's original hope to play the game at Pasadena's Rose Bowl was rebuffed by the Tournament of Roses Committee and representatives from the Big Ten and Pacific Eight conferences. So it wasn't until December 1 that the official decision was reached approving the Los Angeles Coliseum as the site for the first game. All of which meant that the league would have six weeks to organize and stage a game that would, in the future, require years of planning. Don Weiss int.; undated correspondence with Don Weiss, Rozelle papers.
236 **"Should there be":** Hunt int.; Weiss int.
236 **There were smiles:** At the Pro Football Hall of Fame, the Super Ball on display is said to belong to his daughter Sharron. But Hunt insisted, during recent interviews, that each of his children received a ball, purchased by his wife, Norma. Hunt int.
237 **"But nobody ever said":** Hunt int.
237 **Hunt sent:** Hunt letter to Rozelle, July 25, 1966, Rozelle papers.

237 **Rozelle agreed:** Weiss also recalled that Rozelle would "say things like, 'That's not right, that's correct.' It was a part of him you didn't see very often but you'd say, you know, your natural reaction to something. 'That's right' or, 'Is that right?' He'd say, 'I don't know if that is right or not, but it *is* correct.' I think that probably had something to do with [his dislike for the term 'super.' "; Weiss int.

237 **Yet even before:** When the Chiefs beat the Buffalo Bills on New Year's Day, the headline in the next day's *Kansas City Star* read "Chiefs Are Super Bowl Bound." *Kansas City Star*, Jan. 2, 1967; Hunt int.; Hunt letter to Rozelle; *NFL Films Hidden Treasures, Episode I: Super Bowls I–IV*; Weiss int.

237 **There was a curious dichotomy:** Patton, *Razzle Dazzle*, p. 99.

238 **Television itself:** *History of the Super Bowl, Volume 1: Featuring Super Bowls I Through IV*, NFL Properties souvenir magazine published for McDonald's; Connor, *Great Teams Great Years: Kansas City Chiefs*, pp. 76–79; *The Wild Ride to Super Bowl I*, HBO documentary, 2004.

238 **The 1966 season:** Golenbock, *Cowboys Have Always Been My Heroes*, pp. 322–27.

239 **"Thank you":** Marty Ralbovsky, *Super Bowl: Of Men, Myths and Moments* (New York: Hawthorn, 1971), p. 10; Wells Twombly, "Follow the Bouncing Super Bowl," Super Bowl VII program, pp. 17–18.

239 **The clear storyline:** The Chiefs were overrun with press in that week in L.A. prior to the game. Lombardi's Packers were hidden away ninety miles to the north in Santa Barbara, and all but unavailable for comment even when writers did go to their practices. Meanwhile, the Chiefs—as the upstart outsider—had tried to be as accommodating as possible. Dawson, so mobbed with reporters that he found it difficult to eat meals, recalled "it seemed as if somebody was constantly calling or talking about strategy and possible game plans and predictions. Looking back on it now, what we should have done was to shut them all off." Len Dawson and Lou Sahadi, *Len Dawson: Pressure Quarterback* (New York: Cowles, 1970), p. 97; Stram and Sahadi, *They're Playing My Game*, p. 93.

239 **For all that:** Rozelle recollections in correspondence with Don Weiss; John Wiebusch, "Q&A," *GameDay* magazine, Vol. 20, No. 3, 1989.

240 **He did give:** *The Wild Ride to Super Bowl I* documentary.

240 **Before the pregame introductions:** Connor, *Great Teams Great Years: Kansas City Chiefs*, p. 74.

240 **By the 1:00 p.m.:** Maraniss, *When Pride Still Mattered*, p. 394.

240 **The scene at halftime:** Ray Didinger, *The Super Bowl: Celebrating a Quarter Century of America's Greatest Game* (New York: Simon & Schuster, 1990), p. 48.

241 **In the Packers' locker room:** Ibid.

241 **"It was over then":** Strother, *NFL Top 40*, p. 79; Didinger, *The Super Bowl*, p. 50.

241 **After the game:** Didinger, *The Super Bowl*, p. 52.

241 **When asked to assess:** Horrigan and Rathet, *The Other League*, p. 153; McGuff, *Winning It All*, p. 184.

241 **It was typical:** Later on, when Tex Schramm saw Lamar Hunt's wife, Norma, he said, "Now you see what we've been living with all these years." McGuff, *Winning It All*, p. 186; Stram and Sahadi, *They're Playing My Game*, p. 97; Will McDonough, "Gate-Crashers and Frog's Legs," in *A Game of Passion*, Wiebusch and Silverman, eds., p. 410.

242 **The next morning:** Modell int.; Mara int.

242 **The details of that:** Gregg int.; Walt Garrison, *Once a Cowboy* (New York: Random House, 1988), p. 184; Strother, *NFL Top 40*, pp. 85–89.

243 **On the Cowboys':** Garrison, *Once a Cowboy*, p. 85.

243 **In the CBS booth:** Maraniss, *When Pride Still Mattered*, p. 420.

243 **At first:** Ibid., p. 417.

244 **With sixteen seconds:** Ibid., p. 424.

244 **It is easy to forget:** Summerall int.

244 **But they *did* score:** Gregg int.

244 **Inside the locker rooms:** Kramer, *Instant Replay*, p. 217.

245 **"There's a great deal":** Ibid.

245 **By the end of the year:** Ibid., back cover of paperback edition; Dick Schaap, *Flashing Before My Eyes: 50 Years of Headlines, Datelines and Punchlines* (New York: Morrow, 2001), p. 149.

245 **It would all feed back:** Powers, *Supertube,* pp. 67–68.

246 **"Football requires":** Lee Iacocca, "The Lesson I Learned from Vince Lombardi," in *A Game of Passion,* Wiebusch and Silverman, eds., p. 106.

246 **By 1968:** Maraniss, *When Pride Still Mattered,* p. 446.

246 **"And here he is":** Teele int.

246 **"Men want to follow":** Wiebusch, *Lombardi,* p. 98; Maraniss, *When Pride Still Mattered,* p. 398; Iacocca, "The Lesson I Learned from Vince Lombardi," in *A Game of Passion,* Wiebusch and Silverman, eds., p. 101.

247 **"Everyone was important":** Maraniss, *When Pride Still Mattered,* p. 224.

14: RESPECT

248 **That first Super Bowl:** Edwin Shrake, "Still a Long, Rough Road Ahead for the AFL," *SI,* Jan. 30, 1967.

248 **The AFL's next:** On August 23, 1967, in front of a sellout crowd of 33,041 at Municipal Stadium in Kansas City for their first interleague preseason game, against the Chicago Bears, still coached by George Halas and thus the embodiment of the NFL's old guard. The Bears were an unsuspecting football team caught in the wrong place at the wrong time. Unable to adapt to the frequent shifts on offense, the Bears came unglued in the second quarter, when Kansas City exploded for 32 points. The Chiefs maintained their intensity in the second half, and added 13 points in the last two minutes of the game. The final score sent a message heard throughout the NFL: Kansas City 66, Chicago 24.

But the game wasn't just an ambush. In addition to providing some measure of the team's and league's frustration, it hinted at some of the AFL's technical accomplishments. Stram started more plays out of the tight I formation, with tight end Fred Arbanas lining up in a string of three backs behind quarterback Len Dawson. The Bears' defense was geared toward mirroring the strength of the offense, with weak-side and strong-side designations for linebackers, cornerbacks, and safeties; by delaying revealing the strong side, the Chiefs forced Chicago to move six defenders every time Arbanas went into motion to take his spot in the line. Defensively, the Chiefs had shored up the left side of their defense, forcing four turnovers and dominating the line of scrimmage.

After the game, Lamar Hunt came to the Bears' dressing room. George Halas spotted him from across the room and said, "Lamar, have mercy on us. You really buried us." Halas was respectful and not bitter. As the coach once on the winning end of a 73–0 score, he wasn't about to ask for any quarter from an opponent. "They gave every evidence that they were as good as any team," Halas said. "They were fired up and played with great spirit. They went 100 percent on every play."

In the Chiefs' locker room, Hunt was awarded a game ball, along with the other three figures who'd received most of the criticism for the Super Bowl loss: Stram, Dawson (who threw four touchdown passes against the Bears), and cornerback Willie Mitchell.; Stram int.; Dawson int.; Stram and Sahadi, *They're Playing My Game,* pp. 104–5; Dawson, *Pressure Quarterback,* p. 104; McGuff, *Winning It All,* pp. 187–90.

248 **The common belief:** Weiss int.

249 **The new league:** Levy, *Tackling Jim Crow,* p. 141; Kemp int.

249 **The repeated epithets:** Dixon int.

250 **A day later:** As the Watts riots dominated the news the following summer, the Chiefs had their own racial incident. A black defensive back named Ron Fowlkes tangled with a white player named Doc Griffith, breaking his nose during a scrimmage. The next morning, Fowlkes attacked Griffith at a team breakfast, breaking his jaw in the process. In the context of the tension of the times, it was a potentially explosive situation. But after having

worked for years to avoid any racial divisions, Stram chose to release both players, a move applauded by his team. McGuff, *Winning It All,* pp. 95–97.

250   **The Chiefs' white linebacker:** Zimmerman, *The Last Season of Weeb Ewbank,* p. 62.

250   **Later that year:** Harris int.

250   **Into this cultural maelstrom:** MacCambridge, *ESPN SportsCentury,* p. 190.

250   **Broadway Joe:** Dan Jenkins, "Sweet Life of Swinging Joe," *SI,* Oct. 17, 1966.

251   **But there was something:** Brown and Delsohn, *Out of Bounds,* p. 100.

251   **No one accused Namath:** Zimmerman, *The Last Season of Weeb Ewbank,* p. 63; Ramos int.

252   **While players:** Namath, *I Can't Wait for Tomorrow,* p. 108.

252   **Two things quickly:** MacCambridge, *ESPN SportsCentury,* p. 202; Johnson, *Super Spectator and the Electric Lilliputians,* pp. 180–81, 233.

252   **The headline:** Patton, *Razzle Dazzle,* p. 91.

253   **After the Colts':** Jack Orr, *We Came of Age: A Picture History of the American Football League* (New York: Lion, 1969), p. 23.

253   **The Colts were favored:** William Wallace, "Rozelle Indicates Tomorrow's Super Bowl Contest Could Be Next to Last," *NYT,* Jan. 11, 1969.

253   **The next day:** "Pro! Data, Behind the Editorial Scenes," *Pro! Magazine,* Vol. 7, No. 6, Sep. 20, 1976.

253   **Namath attended:** Dave Anderson, *Countdown to Super Bowl* (New York: Random House, 1969), p. 163.

254   **Namath looked:** *Rebels with a Cause* documentary; Ramos int.; Namath, *I Can't Wait for Tomorrow,* p. 58; Anderson, *Countdown to Super Bowl,* p. 163.

254   **Word of Namath's:** Jerry Izenberg, "And Wearing White Shoes . . ." *Pro! Magazine,* Vol. 7, No. 6, Sep. 20, 1976; McDonough, "Gate-Crashers and Frog's Legs," in *A Game of Passion,* Wiebusch and Silverman, eds., p. 411.

254   **In the Jets':** McDonough, "Gate-Crashers and Frog's Legs," in *A Game of Passion,* Wiebusch and Silverman, eds., p. 411.

254   **From early on:** Ralbovsky, *Super Bowl,* p. 98.

255   **Up in the press box:** Summerall int.

255   **As the clock:** Ramos int.; Anderson, *Countdown to Super Bowl,* p. 237.

255   **Namath would later:** Lanier int.; *Rebels with a Cause* documentary.

255   **While the Jets:** Hadhazy int.

255   **And in many ways:** Plimpton and Curry, *One More July,* p. 56.

256   **When the recommendation:** Paul Brown's letter to the league included a terse analysis of the merger agreement. In a letter to the other owners, Brown voiced his opposition to retaining the old alignment:

> Simple inter-league play does not create new divisions or groupings. What I want to emphasize is that we're open to any alignment that gives everybody an equal shot at victory and profits. I'll guarantee you one thing: If the leagues retain their present identities, the NFL will continue to control the major TV markets and the AFL franchises never will be worth as much. I don't blame some of the NFL clubs for wanting to keep their cozy little four-team groupings, but at the time of the merger, when everyone was afraid of going under, the AFL paid dearly.
>
>   I don't want to ruin the effect of the Super Bowl. There will always be a Super Bowl, no matter how it's arrived at. . . . But if you leave the merger, and allow the NFL to keep sixteen teams, and the AFL to retain ten teams, the NFL will always be stronger simply because it will have sixteen of every twenty-six draft picks.

Brown and Clary, *PB,* pp. 316–17; Weiss and Day, *The Making of the Super Bowl,* p. 77.

257   **Suddenly, every team:** Jerry Green, *Super Bowl Chronicles: A Sportswriter Reflects on the First 30 Years of America's Game* (Indianapolis: Masters, 1995), p. 43.

257   **When the owners:** Brown and Clary, *PB,* p. 318.

257   **"Oh, hell":** Rooney int.; Modell int.; Schramm int.

257   **"Gentlemen, I have decided":** Modell int.; Rooney int.; Mara int.

258 **In the aftermath:** Barry Cobb, "Grid Alignment Was Even More than Designer Brown Expected," *TSN,* May 31, 1969.

258 **Others saw:** Weiss int.

258 **It would be nearly:** Ibid.

259 **The event prompted:** William Safire, *Before the Fall: An Inside View of the Pre-Watergate White House* (Garden City, NY: Doubleday, 1975), p. 552; Johnson, *Super Spectator and the Electric Lilliputians,* p. 136.

259 **Nicholas would later:** Dr. James Nicholas int.

259 **On June 26:** "That was one of the few times," she'd remember later, "that I didn't do what I was told to do, and didn't get in trouble for it." Anne Bratton (née Rozelle) int; Namath, *I Can't Wait,* pp. 34–38.

260 **As a guest:** Undated videotape of *Mike Douglas Show,* Anne Marie Bratton (née Rozelle) collection.

261 **By the summer of:** The screenwriter James Toback, upon traveling to Los Angeles to interview the retired Jim Brown in 1968, smartly captured the change in the wind: "Football had displaced baseball as the leading national sport. Boys of eight and nine in Topeka, Boise, Memphis, Buffalo, and San Francisco now dreamed of becoming Brown or Lance Rentzel or Gale Sayers; boys whose fathers thirty-five years earlier had imagined themselves Babe Ruth, Ty Cobb, or Christy Mathewson. Construction workers, call girls, politicians, actors, students, stockbrokers talked about the Jets and the Raiders, the Chiefs, Lions, Chargers, and Browns, with authentic enthusiasm; rarely exhibiting more than moderate interest in the other sports filling the American year. Baseball had become slow and dull except at the end of a season in a tight pennant race or World Series. . . . Only football constituted a full and satisfactory transformation of energy." James Toback, *Jim: James Toback's Self-Centered Memoir of the Great Jim Brown,* p. 12.

261 **"Football is not only":** William Phillips, "A Season in the Stands," *Commentary,* July 1969.

261 **"Up until now":** Smith, *Voices of the Game,* p. 302.

261 **This perception:** Ibid., pp. 300–301.

261 **In a *Sports Illustrated* article:** Johnson, *Super Spectator and the Electric Lilliputians,* p. 108.

262 **Both sports:** Thomas Morgan, "American War Game," *Esquire,* Oct. 1965.

262 **The most vivid:** George Carlin, *Brain Droppings* (New York: Hyperion, 1997), pp. 51–53.

262 **"I have found":** The Cold War rhetoric and football's militaristic technology were complementary. The briefcase full of nuclear launch codes that accompanied the president at all times was known as "the football," and the game's terminology—from the blitz to the bomb—drew deeply from military strategy.

The former Packer Bill Curry saw the movie *Patton* and was struck by the general's similarity to Lombardi. The problem, of course, came when coaches or others tried to push the parallel too far. Ron Wolf, who'd served in military intelligence before joining the personnel department of the Raiders, found any serious comparison to football and war pure folly. Recalling his days with Al Davis and the Raiders in the mid-'60s, he remembered, "We used to have it on our itinerary, it'd say 'We Go to War.' Or, you know, 'Live Bullets are Flying.' I keep hearing that all the time. Well, that's absurd—if live bullets are flying, people are *dying.* That's a different check on yourself than this thing. You're more or less pitting your mind against someone else in our game. You're certainly not committed to life or death."

Or as Otto Graham, by then coaching the Redskins in the late '60s, observed, "Football is like war without death. If nobody died in battle, people would think that was fun, too." Wolf int.; Graham int.; Maraniss, *When Pride Still Mattered,* p. 117; George Plimpton, John Gordy, and Alex Karras, *Mad Ducks and Bears* (New York: Random House, 1973), p. 292.

262 **Nowhere was pro:** Huff and Shapiro, *Tough Stuff,* p. 188; Patterson, *Grand Expectations,* p. 633.

263 **Nixon's devotion:** Nixon had made his football career, as a reserve tackle for the Whittier College Poets, a staple of his biography throughout his political career. A publicity flyer

used for his congressional campaign in 1946 noted, "He played college football ('not too successfully,' he says); maintains an intensive interest in sports." Brown and Clary, *PB*, p. 322; Fawn McKay Brodie, *Richard Nixon: The Shaping of His Character* (New York: Norton, 1981), p. 265; James Keogh, *This Is Nixon* (New York: Putnam, 1956), p. 26; Mark Harris, *Mark the Glove Boy, or the Last Days of Richard Nixon* (New York: Macmillan, 1964), p. 84; Richard Nixon, *RN: The Memoirs of Richard Nixon* (New York: Grosset & Dunlap), p. 315.

263 **ABC's producer:** Arledge, *Roone*, p. 119.

263 **Another former:** Merchant, *And Every Day You Take Another Bite* (Garden City, NY: Doubleday, 1971), p. 34.

263 **Elsewhere on the left:** Hoffman compared the unrest surrounding the 1968 Democratic convention in Chicago to a football game. Ibid., p. 59.

263 **Pro football's appeal:** Robert Murchison int.; Burke Murchison int.

264 **"after home victories":** Allen, *Fifth Quarter*, pp. 69–71.

264 **Starting with:** Schramm int.; Susan Reeves int.

264 **"Dan Reeves was":** Etty Allen int.

264 **Upon firing:** Jack Teele int.

264 **After rallying:** Maule, *The Pro Season*, pp. 158–59.

265 **Whatever effect:** Gabriel, *Player of the Year*, p. 214.

266 **At a racially polarized time:** not-for-attribution int.

266 **Kansas City headed:** Dawson int.; Taylor int.; Stram int.

267 **"The Chiefs would be open":** Madden int.

268 **Instead, the Chiefs:** Uncredited, "Vikings Are Made 13-Point Favorite," *NYT,* Jan. 7, 1970.

268 **"They're doing it again":** Strother, *NFL Top 40*, p. 79; Didinger, *The Super Bowl,* p. 105.

268 **The Chiefs were spending:** According to *Huntley-Brinkley:* "In Detroit, a special Justice Department Task Force, conducting what is described as the biggest gambling investigation of its kind ever, is about to call seven professional players and one college coach to testify on their relationship with known gamblers. Among the players scheduled to appear is Len Dawson, quarterback for the Kansas City Chiefs, who will play the Minnesota Vikings in the Super Bowl this Sunday." Though only a casual friend to Len Dawson, bookie Donald Dawson was a name known by NFL investigators. The Detroit restaurant owner had been a friend of Bobby Layne's, and during Alex Karras's testimony during the 1963 investigation, Karras strongly argued that Layne had bet on football, through Donald Dawson. Weiss int.; Didinger, *The Super Bowl,* p. 87.

268 **Seven years:** Charles Friedman, "Namath, Dawson Reported Among Those to Be Called in Gambling Inquiry," *NYT,* Jan. 7, 1970.

268 **With the media:** McGuff, *Winning It All,* p. 250.

269 **Ultimately, that's all:** But before he got through the interview, two writers, Moe Siegel of the *Washington Star* and Pat Livingston of the *Pittsburgh Press,* nearly came to blows, with Livingston strenuously defending the honor of his friend Dawson. Green, *Super Bowl Chronicles,* pp. 39–40.

269 **"He never had":** Strother, *NFL Top 40*, p. 106.

269 **For his part:** Robinson int.

269 **The day of the game:** The pregame festivities lived down to what was becoming a Murphy's Law of Super Bowl spectacles. Two hot-air balloons were scheduled to take off from the field of Tulane Stadium prior to the game. The one representing the Vikings became unmoored and drifted into the stands, crashing into an area occupied by the Sugar Bowl queen and her court, with one beauty queen suffering a broken leg in the collision. Shelby Strother, "Len's Nightmare, Len's Dream," Super Bowl XXXIV program; Jeff Miller, *Going Long: The Wild 10-Year Saga of the Renegade American Football League in the Words of Those Who Lived It* (Chicago: Contemporary, 2003), p. 346; John Garrity, "Parting Shot," *SI Presents NFL '95*; Bill McGrane int.

271 **Dawson, vindicated:** Dawson int.

271 **The short conversation:** Actually, Nixon wasn't the first president to place a phone call to an NFL champion. After the Packers routed the Giants, 37–0, to win the title in 1961, Lombardi received a call from President Kennedy. The Kennedy call, however, came later in the evening, at Lombardi's home, and was a private conversation. Klein int.; Maraniss, *When Pride Still Mattered,* p. 293.

271 **"Most people":** Steve Sabol int.

272 **The AFL opened:** Tex Maule, "Wham, Bam, Stram!," *SI,* Jan. 19, 1970, p. 10.

273 **The '60s enterprise:** The parallel between football and space exploration had been evident for more than a decade. When the air force pilot Chuck Yeager was testing the experimental X-1 at Edwards Air Force Base in California in the late '40s, he modified a leather football helmet to wear during flight, to protect him against the jostling that the X-1's pilot often incurred when the jet reached peak altitudes. Tom Wolfe, *The Right Stuff* (New York: Farrar, Straus & Giroux, 1979), p. 56.

274 **"American society":** Early int.

274 **Like the race:** Uncredited, "The Sweep of the '60s," *Life,* Dec. 26, 1969.

15: PRIME TIME

275 **From Municipal Stadium:** *Monday Night Football* telecast, Cleveland Browns vs. New York Jets, ABC, Sep. 20, 1970.

276 **Rozelle had argued:** Marc Gunther and Bill Carter, *Monday Night Mayhem* (New York: Beech Tree, 1988), pp. 26–30.

276 **"But we made a deal!":** Arledge, *Roone,* p. 103.

276 **Though Bill McPhail:** The Monday night CBS lineup featured *Gunsmoke* (number two in the Nielsen ratings in the 1969–70 season), *Here's Lucy* (number six), *Mayberry R.F.D.* (number four), *The Doris Day Show* (number ten), and *The Carol Burnett Show* (number thirteen). Cobbett Steinberg, *TV Facts* (New York: Facts on File, 1985) p. 108; undated memo, Rozelle papers.

276 **NBC might have been:** Steinberg, *TV Facts,* pp. 107–08.

277 **With that Rozelle:** Arledge, *Roone,* p. 104.

277 **The threat was underscored:** Frank int.; Edwin Shrake, "What Are They Doing with the Sacred Game of Pro Football?," *SI,* Oct. 25, 1971.

277 **They found out quickly:** Jack Gould, "TV Review," *NYT,* Sep. 23, 1970; Fred Ferretti, "Monday Football Displaces Cavett," *NYT,* Oct. 8, 1970.

278 **Cosell's brand:** With Cosell, even the routine pregame interviews took on a different cast, as Cosell's reputation as a journalist added an edge to any of the proceedings. Before week two in Baltimore, with Kansas City visiting the Colts, Cosell spent a few moments on the field interviewing Len Dawson and John Unitas. After asking Unitas about how his hyperextended left knee might affect his play, Cosell noted, "Some of the would-be experts have said you throw the short one with all the old brilliance, but the ability to throw the long one is no longer there. True or not true?"

"Well, you'd have to ask the experts," snapped the unflappable Unitas with a sardonic smile, prompting laughter even from Cosell. Videotape, *Monday Night Football* telecast, Baltimore Colts vs. Kansas City Chiefs Sep. 27, 1970; Myron Cope, "Would You Let This Man Interview You?," *SI,* Mar. 13, 1967.

278 **During one game:** *Cosell: Telling It like It Is* documentary.

279 **The on-air jousting:** Gunther and Carter, *Monday Night Mayhem,* p. 103.

280 **By then,** *Monday Night Football:* Ibid., p. 137.

280 **Not all of it:** On November 8, 1972, the situation comedy *The Bob Newhart Show* premiered an episode called "Don't Go to Bed Mad," in which the Hartleys (Newhart and Suzanne Pleshette) agreed not to go to sleep until they settled their argument over his football-watching habits, which went from Saturday afternoons to Monday nights. It was testament to the cultural pervasiveness of *Monday Night Football* that *The Bob Newhart*

Show aired on the competition, CBS. Another sure sign of *Monday Night Football*'s success were the apoplectic critiques from competitors. "I wince with embarrassment when those guys do a funny," said Bill MacPhail. "Meredith is like a buffoon, waiting to be cute. Cosell's style is good for a 15-minute show, but not for an action game. On CBS, the game is the star. ABC has lost sight of the fact that pro football is a game, not a show for three TV stars. What should we do, follow them with a team of Don Rickles, Milton Berle and Mickey Rooney?" Gunther and Carter, *Monday Night Mayhem*, p. 106; William Wallace, "Monday Night Football Hits Paydirt," *NYT*, Oct. 25, 1970; Patton, *Razzle Dazzle*, p. 111.

280 **With the completion:** Pete Rozelle, Foreword, *1970 Official National Football League Record Book.*

281 **To minimize:** Weiss int.; Schramm int.; Bussert int.

281 **The Raiders, who'd:** Wells Twombly, *Blanda, Alive and Kicking: The Exclusive, Authorized Biography* (Los Angeles: Nash, 1972), pp. 6, 32 54; Michael MacCambridge, "George Blanda, The Old Man," *ESPN SportsCentury*, p. 228.

282 **Later in life:** Steve Sabol int.; Ed Sabol int.; Levy, "Fearless Tot from Possum Trot," *SI*, Nov. 22, 1965; Ben Yagoda, "Not So Instant Replay," *NYT Magazine*, Dec. 14, 1986.

282 **After the early success:** Thomas Danyluk, "Steve Sabol," *The Coffin Corner*, Vol. 23, No. 1.

283 **"When we'd get":** Ibid.

283 **By then, NFL Films:** Tom Brody, "C.B. DeMille of the Pros," *SI*, Nov. 20, 1967.

283 **"To put it harshly":** Durslag, "They Sell Everything but the Goal Posts."

284 **In this mission:** Alex Ben Block, "The 27th Team," *Today/Philadelphia Inquirer Sunday Magazine*, Dec. 10, 1972; Durslag, "They Sell Everything but the Goal Posts."

285 **The opening montage:** Yagoda, "Not So Instant Replay."

285 **"It'll be historic":** Stram int.

285 **"Damn right":** Decades later, long after he'd left coaching, Stram would still see strangers in airports who would quote him, urging him to "Call 65 Toss Power Trap" or "Keep matriculating that ball down the field!" John Garrity, "Parting Shot," *SI Presents NFL '95*; Paul Zimmerman, "Frisked and Fleeced in New Orleans," Dr. Z's Mailbag, *CNNSI.com*, Feb. 6, 2002; Dawson quotation as related by HBO's Ross Greenburg, Greenburg int.

286 **The NFL Films:** *Mayhem on a Sunday* documentary, 1964.

286 **"We are not journalists":** Mark Kram, Jr., "Steve Sabol Makes History," *Philadelphia*, Sep. 1996; Yagoda, "Not So Instant Replay."

286 **By 1970:** Myslenski, "Q&A," *Pro! Magazine*, undated; Block, "The 27th Team," Smith, *Voices of the Game*, p. 304.

286 **The Sabols' imprimatur:** As the reach of NFL Films spread, so did its impact. It wasn't all hero worship; young producer Phil Tuckett shot the documentary *Pottstown, USA*, about the Pottstown Firebirds semipro football team, which aired on Super Bowl Sunday in 1971, and earned numerous awards. Tuckett was just one of an exemplary cast of filmmakers that were on the staff. The premier cameraman was probably Ernie Ernst, the man whose rock-steady hands with a super-slow-motion camera were most likely to capture the graceful spinning of a spiral in flight. Ernst's eye was so keen, that he was the only cameraman to catch Franco Harris's "Immaculate Reception," the incredible deflected catch that lifted the Steelers over the Raiders in the 1972 playoffs. Steve Sabol int.; Kram "Steve Sabol Makes History"; Block, "The 27th Team."; Clare Conley, "He's Having a (Foot) Ball," *Dayton Leisure*, Jan. 13, 1980.

287 **The real wonder:** Rozelle letter to Ed Sabol, Oct. 19, 1977, Rozelle papers.

287 **But to call Films:** Steve Sabol int.; Weiss int.

287 **While the staff:** Steve Sabol int.

287 **"It could be argued":** Yagoda, "Not So Instant Replay."

288 **The early efforts:** *The Gladiators; Profile of a Season*, NFL Creative Services brochures.

288 **In anticipation:** Weiss int.

289 **"I think David Boss":** Gardner int.

289 **In 1970:** *Pro! Magazine*, Vol. 1, 1970.

289 **To his closest:** Weiss int.; Sahadi int.; Arkush int.
290 **Bill Curry:** Plimpton and Curry, *One More July,* pp. 45–46.
291 **But after the pitched:** Ralbovsky, *Super Bowl,* p. 149.

16: "GOD, NIXON AND THE NATIONAL FOOTBALL LEAGUE"

292 **After the Cowboys:** Roy Blount, Jr., "The Super Bowl," advertising supplement to *SI,* Jan. 10, 1977.
293 **He returned to Los Angeles:** Golenbock, *Cowboys Have Always Been My Heroes,* p. 475.
294 **When the Cowboys':** St. John, *Tex!,* p. 105.
294 **On July 31:** Ibid., pp. 106–7.
294 **Thomas returned:** Ibid., p. 98.
294 **Thomas was an exceptional:** Blaine Newnham, "Wow, Like Let's Really Try to Win," *SI,* Oct. 12, 1970; Bidwill int.; Merchant, *And Every Day You Take Another Bite,* p. 60.
294 **Many of those:** Merchant, *And Every Day You Take Another Bite,* p. 59; Robert Lipsyte, "Out of Their League—I," Sports of the Times, *NYT,* Dec. 21, 1970.
295 **Weeb Ewbank:** Zimmerman, *The Last Season of Weeb Ewbank,* p. 185.
295 **Among the most pointed:** Merchant, *And Every Day You Take Another Bite,* p. 63.
295 **Lombardi indeed:** Paul Zimmerman, "The Good, the Great and the Ugly: Some Football Biographies Just Don't Stack Up," *CNNSI.com,* Oct. 19, 2000.
296 **Lombardi had visited:** Schramm int.; Teele int.; Benedict int.; St. John, *Tex!,* p. 161.
296 **The news hit:** St. John, *Tex!,* pp. 71–72.
297 **In Baltimore:** Tex Maule, "Nay on the Neighs, Yea on the Baas," *SI,* Aug. 14, 1972.
297 **"I'm benched":** Plimpton, *Mad Ducks and Bears,* p. 377; Patterson, *Football in Baltimore,* pp. 203–4.
298 **Allen's arrival:** Gildea and Turan, *The Future Is Now,* pp. 3, 4–5.
298 **Allen would become:** Ibid., p. 170.
298 **Popularized around:** They also included: "2. The greatest feeling in life is to take an ordinary job and accomplish something with it. 3. If you can accept defeat and open your pay envelope without feeling guilty, then you're stealing. 4. Everyone, the head coach especially, must give 110 per cent. 5. Leisure time is that five or six hours when you sleep at night. 6. No detail is too small. No task is too small, or too big. 7. You must accomplish things in life, otherwise you are like the paper on the wall. 8. A person without problems is dead. 9. We win and lose as a team. 10. My prayer is that each man will be allowed to play to the best of his ability." Allen, *Fifth Quarter,* p. 41; Gildea and Turan, *The Future Is Now,* p. 14.
299 **"I can remember":** Duane Thomas and Paul Zimmerman, *Duane Thomas and the Fall of America's Team* (New York: Warner, 1988), p. 118.
299 **Dear George:** Allen, *Fifth Quarter,* p. 125; Gildea and Turan, *The Future Is Now,* p. 229.
299 **President Richard M. Nixon:** Gildea and Turan, *The Future Is Now,* pp. 17, 261.
299 **Later in the season:** Though Nixon also was a well-known baseball fan, he rebuffed the suggestion that any support he could give might help the woeful Washington Senators. "The Senators?" asked Nixon. "It wouldn't have helped. In baseball you can't say to Harmon Killebrew, 'Come on, go out there and hit the ball.' He's already trying to hit the ball. It's more an individual effort. In football, it's more of a team effort; morale is everything. In baseball, spirit and morale are not as important. The Redskins have the right spirit." Ibid., pp. 259, 265.
299 **The team stayed:** Ibid., pp. 289, 294.
299 **In the Azores:** Merchant, *And Every Day You Take Another Bite,* pp. 35–36.
300 **The Redskins qualified:** Gildea and Turan, *The Future Is Now,* p. 316; Koppett, *The New York Times at the Super Bowl,* p. 234.
300 **It wasn't just:** Senator Edmund Muskie cracked, "We need more than a new game plan. We need a new coach." That prompted Spiro Agnew's response, "I doubt seriously if

Muskie's two yards and a cloud of dust is sufficient to impress even his fellow Democrats." Merchant, *And Every Day You Take Another Bite,* pp. 35–36; Brooks Clark, *SI,* Nov. 28, 1994; Patterson, *Grand Expectations,* p. 753; United States Air Force military history, http://www.wpafb.af.mil/museum/history/vietnam/vietnam.htm.

300 **Nixon's fandom:** *Time,* Oct. 9, 1971.

300 **That view was:** Hunter Thompson, "Fear and Loathing at the Super Bowl," *Rolling Stone,* Feb. 15, 1973.

300 **Thompson and Nixon:** Hunter Thompson, *Fear and Loathing on the Campaign Trail* (San Francisco: Straight Arrow, 1973), p. 61.

301 **There was one tangible:** Kemp int.; Carothers int.

303 **There were two:** Lanier int.

303 **Miami then eliminated:** Jeff Meyers, *Great Teams Great Years: Dallas Cowboys* (New York: Macmillan, 1974) p. 95; Dave Anderson, "Coach Nixon Sends in a Play to the Miami Dolphins," *NYT,* Jan. 4, 1972; Dave Anderson, "L.B.J. Exhorts Cowboys, but Has No Play for Them," *NYT,* Jan. 11, 1972.

303 **Media Day:** Zimmerman, "Mute but Mighty," *Sports Illustrated Presents Dr. Z's Great Moments in Super Bowl History.*

304 **The game itself:** Meyers, *Great Teams Great Years: Dallas Cowboys,* p. 93.

304 **A jumpy Brookshier:** Koppett, *The New York Times at the Super Bowl,* p. 257; Daly and O'Donnell, *Pro Football Chronicle,* pp. 224–25.

305 **While the sight lines:** Golenbock, *Cowboys Have Always Been My Heroes,* p. 469.

305 **The same was true:** Dawson int.

306 **AstroTurf had come about:** Harris, *The League: The Rise and Decline of the NFL* (New York: Bantam, 1986), p. 259; Patton, *Razzle Dazzle,* p. 126.

306 **The claims of effectiveness:** Gene Ward: "Ward to the Wise, the War Room on Park Avenue," *New York Daily News,* Dec. 8, 1968; William Johnson, "Goodbye to Three Yards and a Cloud of Dust," *SI,* Jan. 27, 1969; Astro-Turf advertisement, "82,000 Fans Didn't Pay to See This," *Super Bowl IV* game program, Jan. 11, 1970; Poly-Turf advertisement, "The grass is greener. At the Super Bowl"; *Super Bowl V* game program, Jan. 17, 1971.

306 **But among players:** There were two vastly different views about synthetic surfaces, each purist in its own self-perception. Among those who played the game, the idea of playing on a carpet felt false, corporate, insulated, and unrealistic, as odd as playing golf indoors. Alex Karras of the Lions, after a game in Houston, reported, "It kind of squishes. When there's no crowd in the Astrodome, and the place is quiet like a tomb, all you can hear is this squishing as the players run. The Texans are very proud of it; they think of it as a fancy Persian rug." Or as the Steelers' Glen Edwards aptly put it after his arms were scraped during a slide on Three Rivers Stadium AstroTurf, "That stuff be looking good, but it be burning my ass." Phil Patton, in his book on football on television, *Razzle Dazzle,* pointed out that the interiors of domes "like any stage or studio, are everyplace and no place. That is their purpose: to abolish the contingencies of climate and geography."
       But the contrary view, held by many in the league office and more than a few coaches throughout the league, was that the games were *too important* to be settled in any way other than by the teams on the field, that the exigencies of sun, rain, or snow were elements of chance that ought to be eliminated.
       After a couple more years, even Maule would relent. Plimpton, *Mad Ducks and Bears,* p. 401; Gale Sayers, as told to Ira Berkow, "I Say Artificial Turf Is Hurting Football," *Sport,* Sep. 1971; John Underwood, "New Slant on the Mod Sod," *SI,* Nov. 15, 1971; Patton, *Razzle Dazzle,* p. 123; Blount, *About Three Bricks Shy,* p. 140; Maule, *The Pro Season,* p. 87.

306 **At Arrowhead:** Bobby Bell int.

307 **Tom Condon:** John Underwood, "Just an Awful Toll," *SI,* Aug. 12, 1985.

307 **"Artificial turf has made":** Edwin Shrake, "The Day of Indignity Is Past," *SI,* Aug. 14, 1972.

308 **The decision to play:** Weiss int.

308 **But as early as 1972:** Tex Maule, "Time to Take Stock," *SI,* Sep. 18, 1972.

308 **In Kansas City:** Stram int.; Costello int.

309   **Though the Cowboys:** Blount, *About Three Bricks Shy,* p. 169.
309   **Shula had studied:** Shula int.; Taylor int.; Dawson int.
310   **Miami would prove:** Wells Twombly, "Chuck Knox Makes Nice," *Esquire,* Oct. 1974; Cohen et al., eds., *The Scrapbook History of Pro Football,* p. 303.

17: AMERICA'S TEAM

312   **The paradox:** NFL Publicity Department, *Super Bowl Notes, Quotes and Anecdotes: Games I–XXXVII,* 2004.
312   **Rozelle routinely expressed:** "The *Playboy* Interview: Pete Rozelle," *Playboy,* Oct. 1973.
312   **Other than the actual:** Weiss int.; Hadhazy int.; "The *Playboy* Interview: Pete Rozelle."
313   **The Friday before:** Kensil int; Diane K. Shah, "He Rules America on Sundays," *National Observer,* May 16, 1977.
313   **"The NFL was always";** Kornheiser int.
314   **"People just go on":** Blount, *About Three Bricks Shy,* p. 291.
314   **By the mid-'70s:** Rozelle papers; Murray, "Prologue," in *More Than a Game,* Wiebusch, p. 9, Accorsi int.
314   **Behind the scenes:** Anne Marie Bratton (née Rozelle) int.
314   **One day:** Summerall int.
315   **Rozelle's life changed:** "The *Playboy* Interview: Pete Rozelle"; Weiss int.; Anne Marie Bratton (née Rozelle) int.
315   **Around the office:** Weiss int.; Accorsi int.; Browne int.
316   **On July 3, 1974:** Harris, *The League,* p. 165.
316   **Because pro football:** Blount, *About Three Bricks Shy,* p. 237; Gabriel, *Player of the Year,* p. 67.
316   **The NFLPA's executive:** Plimpton and Curry, *One More July,* p. 100; Maraniss, *When Pride Still Mattered,* p. 354; Kramer, *Instant Replay,* p. 226.
317   **Though Garvey:** Pluto, *When All the World Was Browns Town,* p. 247.
317   **The union held firm:** Cohen et al., *The Scrapbook History of Pro Football,* p. 312.
317   **NFLPA president:** Plimpton and Curry, *One More July,* p. 98; Cohen et al., eds., *The Illustrated Scrapbook of Pro Football,* pp. 312–13.
318   **For the owners:** Joe Marshall, "Full of Sound and Fury," *SI,* Feb. 11, 1974; Harris, *The League,* p. 133; Cohen et al., *The Scrapbook History of Pro Football,* p. 297.
318   **But the new league was quickly:** Herb Gluck, *While the Gettin's Good: Inside the World Football League* (Indianapolis: Bobbs-Merrill, 1975), pp. 217–18; Mark Speck, "The Fire Burned Bright Before It Went Out," *The Coffin Corner,* Vol. 19, No. 6, 1997; Harris, *The League,* p. 168.
318   **The league returned:** *Lost Treasures,* vol. 10.
319   **The summer of 1974:** Herskowitz, "Goodbye, Johnny U.," in *A Game of Passion,* Wiebusch and Silverman, eds., p. 373.
319   **Even at the end:** Ibid., p. 379.
319   **At the dawn:** Zimmerman, *The Last Season of Weeb Ewbank,* p. 301.
319   **There was another reason:** Michael MacCambridge, "Juice," *ESPN SportsCentury,* p. 226.
320   **On the sidelines:** "The *Playboy* Interview: Pete Rozelle," p. 67.
320   **"I'm a premier receiver":** Gary D. Warner, "Otis Taylor Needs to Win," Football Digest, *Kansas City Star,* Feb. 1972.
321   **In some league cities:** Schramm int.; Bobby Bell int.; Eisenberg, *Cotton Bowl Days,* pp. 164–65; St. John, *Tex!,* pp. 292–94.
321   **By 1974:** Blount, *About Three Bricks Shy,* p. 185.
323   **Dallas was the team:** Thomas and Zimmerman, *Duane Thomas and the Fall of America's Team,* p. 124.
323   **In the '70s:** Diane K. Shah, "Sis-Boom-Bah," *Newsweek,* Nov. 7, 1977.
324   **On the field:** *Lost Treasures,* vol. 9; *Network Stars of the '70s,* NFL Films, 2000.
324   **The team's success:** Eisenberg, *Cotton Bowl Days,* p. 26.

324 **Writing in the *Boston Globe*:** Thomas and Zimmerman, *Duane Thomas and the Fall of America's Team,* p. 124; St. John, *Tex!,* p. 43.

325 **The Cowboys' system:** Steve Perkins, *Next Year's Champions: The Story of the Dallas Cowboys* (New York: World, 1969), pp. 36–37.

325 **Their use of computers:** Skip Myslenski, "The Better Way," in *The Gladiators* (Englewood Cliffs, NJ: Prentice-Hall, 1973), p. 201.

325 **That 1977 season:** Competition Committee Report, 1978, *PFW,* Dec. 12, 1977.

326 **The NFL's favored pollster:** Smith, *Voices of the Game,* p. 442.

18: AIR WAR

328 **"Take it from there":** Dave Anderson, "The Complete Control of Paul Brown," *NYT,* Jan. 2, 1976.

328 **Though he retired:** Weiss int.; Schramm int.; Harris, *The League,* p. 248.

329 **For much of:** Prior to moving the hashmarks nearer the center, a team's position in relation to the sidelines was almost as big a consideration as its position up and down the field. Teams almost automatically rotated their zone defenses to the open side of the field, since this was where most of the open territory lay. "Especially teams that ran a lot of sweeps, once they got over to one side, they were much easier to defend," said Johnny Robinson, the Chiefs' All-Pro safety. "You didn't have to cover outs and you could play inside of the receiver on that [short] side. Suddenly the hashmarks are narrowed, that side opens up, and now everything changes"; Robinson int.

329 **For Paul Brown:** Brown and Clary, *PB,* pp. 331–32; Lamb, *Quarterbacks, Nickelbacks,* p. 23; Norm Clarke, "Brown Wants 'Bump' Rule Phased Out," *St. Paul Dispatch,* Feb. 25, 1974.

330 **In addition to:** St. John, *Tex!,* p. 337.

331 **If the 1976:** Undated Jim Kensil memo to Rozelle, Rozelle papers.

331 **On November 5, 1976:** Rozelle note to Klein and Modell, Nov. 5, 1976.

331 **At the same time:** Ibid.

332 **At the league's:** Diane K. Shah, "He Rules America on Sundays," *National Observer,* May 16, 1977.

332 **"The idea of parity":** Weiss int.

332 **With all that:** NFL confidential documents, 2001.

332 **The ensuing deal:** William Wallace, "NFL Is Said to Engineer $576 Million Deal," *NYT,* Oct. 26, 1977; Harris, *The League,* p. 279.

333 **By the end:** 2004 NFL Competition Committee report.

333 **Teams switched:** Gary Smith, "The Gamblin' Man," *Inside Sports,* Jan. 1982.

333 **Instead of a two-yard cushion:** Leonard Shapiro, "Speed Kills," *Inside Sports,* Nov. 1981.

334 **"He has ideas":** Mike Brown int.

334 **Like a great student:** From Sid Gillman, the conceded father of the modern passing game, Walsh discovered surpassing complexity and imagination, but he would also see some of the same gremlins that would bedevil Clark Shaughnessy. "Sid had a system of football that was so complete, that had so much diversity to it," Walsh said. "Now, in a sense it was too diverse. It was too expansive, because you couldn't ever distill all that into specific highly timed and skilled plays—it was just too much football." Walsh int.

335 **While Brown:** Ibid.

335 **So when he:** Ibid.

335 **In San Francisco:** Spadia int.

336 **The 49ers' starting:** Lamb, *Quarterbacks, Nickelbacks,* pp. 38–39.

336 **"I had no idea":** Walsh int.

337 **"We knew":** Ibid.

338 **"This inherent, instinctive":** Ibid.

338 **"What are your":** Ibid.

339 **Afterward, the Cowboys:** Zimmerman, "Off on the Wrong Foot," *SI,* Jan. 18, 1982.

339   **Pro football's incursion:** Gunther and Carter, *Monday Night Mayhem*, p. 256.

339   **The 49ers-Bengals:** Roone Arledge remarks, Pete Rozelle memorial service, New York City, Jan. 16, 1997. Leonard Shapiro, "Rozelle All-Time League Leader," *Washington Post*, Jan. 17, 1997.

340   **"I think he":** Summerall int.

19: UNDER SIEGE

342   **While this would:** Upshaw int.; *Rebels of Oakland: The A's, the Raiders, the '70s* documentary. HBO, 2004.

343   **What is understandable:** Davis int.; Al Davis interview transcript, *Rebels with a Cause* documentary.

343   **For much of:** Weiss int.; Accorsi int.; John Crittenden, "Rams Owner Raps Yom Kippur Game," *Miami News*, Sep. 30, 1976.

344   **During a private:** Harris, *The League*, pp. 281–82; Teele int.

345   **When Rozelle put the amendment:** Weiss int.; Davis int.; Ribowsky, *Slick*, p. 278.

345   **Then, on April 2, 1979:** The memorial service that followed in California was produced by Rosenbloom's widow, the lounge singer Georgia Rosenbloom (who arrived with a grand entrance nearly an hour late). Howard Cosell delivered the eulogy, after Rozelle declined to do so, finding the entire setting unseemly. Renee Rosenbloom, the wife of Rosenbloom's son Steve, described it as the "only funeral I ever saw that could have played eight weeks in Las Vegas." Cosell, *I Never Played the Game*, p. 26; Raiders Transfer Litigation/Chronology of Pertinent Events, NFL internal document.

345   **A longtime NFL owner:** Not-for-attribution int.; Cosell, *I Never Played the Game*, pp. 53–54.

346   **On March 1:** Raiders Transfer Litigation, internal document; not-for-attribution ints.

346   **Howard Cosell had eviscerated:** Gunther and Carter, *Monday Night Mayhem*, p. 256.

347   **The trial itself:** Dave Anderson, "NFL Franchises Now Free Agents," Sports of the Times, *NYT*, May 9, 1982; Rosenthal, *Fifty Faces of Football*, p. 96.

348   **No sooner:** Don Reese with John Underwood, "I'm Not Worth a Damn," *SI*, June 14, 1982.

349   **Though the approach:** Walsh int.; Zimmerman, "An Overdose of Problems," *SI 1983 College & Pro Football Spectacular.*

350   **And, always:** In the Davis bio *Slick*, Mark Ribowsky quoted Gene Upshaw saying that the Raiders were waiting for a signal, based on how Davis's acceptance speech began, but Upshaw later denied this in a 2003 conversation with the author. "Shit, this goddamn group of mine wouldn't have understood which way he started." Ribowsky, *Slick*; Upshaw int.

350   **One of 1982's:** Frank Deford, "The Colts Were Ours . . . They Were One with the City," Scorecard, *SI*, Apr. 9, 1984.

351   **Sundays at 2:00:** "There Used to Be a Ballpark," NFL Films, Part 12.

351   **On November 15, 1981:** E. M. Swift, "Now You See Him, Now You Don't," *SI*, Dec. 15, 1986.

351   **It was Accorsi:** Accorsi int.

352   **By that time:** Patterson, *Football in Baltimore*, p. 228.

352   **At the league office:** Rozelle letter to Irsay, Jan. 27, 1984, Rozelle papers; memorandum for the record, Feb. 7, 1984, Rozelle papers; minutes of the Privileged Executive Session of the Special Meeting of the National Football League, Mar. 2, 1984, PFHOF.

353   **On March 28:** Gildea, *When the Colts Belonged to Baltimore*, p. 267.

353   **There was precious little:** Form letter sent to those complaining about Baltimore move, Rozelle papers.

354   **Irsay's greeting:** Tom Fitzpatrick, "Hoosiers' Honeymoon Sours as Colts Jekylls Turn into Hydes," Column, *Arizona Republic*, Apr. 3, 1984.

354   **Then it was:** Ibid.

354   **"I can say this":** Beano Cook, undated letter to Rozelle, Rozelle papers.

20: THE LAST STAND

356   **Fielding questions:** Will McDonough, "A Just Reward for the Upstarts," *Boston Globe,* July 31, 1986.

356   **With the hard-won:** Paul Zimmerman, "Choice Is Leftovers," *SI,* Apr. 30, 1984.

357   **On September 13:** Chet Simmons letter to Pete Rozelle, Sep. 13, 1984, Rozelle papers; Pete Rozelle letter to Chet Simmons, Sep. 27, 1984, Rozelle papers.

358   **"Of course":** Peterson int.

358   **It would take nearly two years:** Carroll et al., *Total Football II,* pp. 536–37.

359   **"If you were the client":** Not-for-attribution ints.

359   **If anyone understood:** The philosophy that Tex Schramm had distilled into the mantra, often repeated, "Pounds for defense, not one cent for tribute." Carothers correspondence with Rozelle, Rozelle papers.; Carothers int.; Schramm int.

359   **"I would not":** Tagliabue int.

359   **"One consideration was":** Ibid.

360   **"We had evidence":** Will McDonough, "How NFL Captured the Case," *Boston Globe,* Aug. 3, 1986.

361   **As Pinchbeck sat:** Pinchbeck int.

361   **With that, Rozelle:** Pinchbeck int.; St. John, *Tex!,* pp. 91–92.

361   **"Pete, I love you":** Ibid.

361   **It was left:** Craig Neff, "The Award Was Only Token," *SI,* Aug. 11, 1986.

362   **When Jim Brown:** Anonymous, "The Game Needs More Heroes, More Gladiators," *SI,* Dec. 12, 1983.

362   **"It was the single":** Steve Bornstein int.; John Walsh int.

362   **Back on the field:** Paul Zimmerman, "Passing Attacks Get Forty-Sixed," *The NFL Century,* p. 262.

363   **Even entire teams:** Modell's relationship with his players was remarkably strong, and he'd been well ahead of the curve in forming "the Inner Circle," a group of former players and drug and chemical dependency experts who regularly met with at-risk players who had a history of problems with drugs and alcohol. Modell int.; Jim Brown int.; Accorsi int.; Newsome int.

364   **At the end:** Accorsi int.; Douglas Looney, "There's a Love Fest on Lake Erie," *SI,* Aug. 26, 1985.

364   **The team was:** In the 1986 off-season, their star second-year safety Don Rodgers, a key part of an increasingly nasty and potent defense, died under bizarre circumstances, suffering a crack overdose at his own bachelor party. Even in this tragedy, the Browns proved resilient. They signed USFL castoff Felix Wright and continued their intimidating defensive style. Accorsi int.; Schottenheimer int.

366   **When the NFLPA walked out again:** St. John, *Tex!,* p. 148.

367   **After the Patriots-Dolphins:** Schramm int.; Polian int.

367   **These replacement players:** Peter King, *The Season After: Are Sports Dynasties Dead?* (New York: Warner, 1989), pp. 80–83.

368   **"If you're going to":** Polian int.

368   **"Back in the '60s":** Younger int.

369   **"Sometimes, all this talk":** Brown and Delsohn, *Out of Bounds,* p. 52.

369   **Though the change:** AP, "NFL: 'We Take the Issue Very Seriously,'" Oct. 1, 2002.

370   **"I want to help":** Dungy int.; Young int.

370   **The actor Laurence Fishburne:** Fishburne int. (1993).

371   **Through the long:** In the frequent absences of Rozelle at the league office, and with Jim Kensil gone to the Jets, more responsibility fell to Don Weiss, who was promoted to executive director. "Don really kept the league going in the '80s," said director of pro player personnel Joel Bussert. "Pete had the Raiders case, and right after that there was the USFL lawsuit, and he was just consumed with that, and understandably so. Weiss really kept the whole thing going as a football league. He really filled the role to an extent that few people realized." Bussert int.

371 **Carmen Policy:** Policy int.
371 **"I saw more":** Weiss int.
372 **Paul Tagliabue:** Tagliabue int.

21: CHANGING OF THE GUARD

373 **Wednesday, March 22, 1989:** The committee was considering a decision on Tex Schramm's ambitious plan to use an electronic device in officials' whistles that would allow the replay official in the booth, when reviewing a play, to see a mark on the screen indicating the precise instant when the whistle was blown. It was a sign of the changing times that this was another in a growing set of instances in which Schramm wouldn't get his way. "We thought it would just further complicate the matter," said Vikings GM Mike Lynn a day later. AP, "Replay for Instant Replay," *NYT*, Mar. 24, 1989.
373 **Pete Rozelle called:** John Wiebusch, "Q&A," *GameDay Magazine*, Vol. 20, No. 3, Sep. 1989; Michael Wilbon, "Rozelle Announces Retirement from NFL," *Washington Post*, Mar. 23, 1989.
373 **On his ways:** Jack Sheppard, "Rozelle Stuns NFL with Tearful Goodbye," *St. Petersburg Times*, Mar. 23, 1989; Schramm int.; Browne int.; Weiss int.; Peter King, "Rozelle Steps Down," *New York Newsday*, Mar. 23, 1989; Dave Goldberg, AP, "Rozelle Resignation."
374 **So was Rozelle:** Videotape of Rozelle press conference, Mar. 22, 1989, NFL Films archives.
374 **Wellington Mara:** Sheppard, "Rozelle Stuns NFL with Tearful Goodbye."
375 **Into that harsh light:** MacCambridge, "A Man in His Prime," *ESPN SportsCentury*, p. 279.
375 **At the combine:** Derrick Thomas int.
375 **Heretofore:** MacCambridge, "A Man in His Prime," *ESPN SportsCentury*, p. 279.
376 **"Frankly, we can't":** Jones int.
376 **"Well, what do":** Ibid.
376 **"I don't know":** Ibid.
376 **On February 28:** Golenbock, *Cowboys Have Always Been My Heroes*, p. 710.
377 **"I will sell my house":** Ibid., p. 745; Will McDonough, *The NFL Century: The Complete Story of the National Football League, 1920–2000* (New York: Smithmark, 1999), p. 280.
377 **"You could tell":** Jim Dent, *King of the Cowboys: The Life and Times of Jerry Jones* (Holbrook, MA: Adams, 1995), p. 112.
377 **"We had a lot":** Ed Hinton, "Man with a Mission," *SI Presents: That Super Season: The Dallas Cowboys Return to Glory*, 1993, p. 36.
378 **Football, of course:** Sally Jenkins, "The Mouth That Roars," *SI*, Oct. 25, 1993.
378 **"At the time":** Dent, *King of the Cowboys*, p. 119.
379 **Though the NFL:** Dave Anderson, "In the Final Hours, Pete Rozelle Reflects," Sports of the Times, *NYT*, Nov. 5, 1989; 2003 *NFL Record and Fact Book* chronology, pp. 406–7.
379 **The lone recommendation:** Rooney int.; Aiello int.; Wellington Mara int.; Policy int.; not-for-attribution int.; Peter King, "The NFL's New Boss," *SI*, Nov. 6, 1989; Rick Telander, "The Face of Sweeping Change," *SI*, Sep. 10, 1990.
379 **Paul Tagliabue:** Tagliabue int.
380 **He came from:** His paternal grandfather, Joseph Tagliabue, arrived in the United States from northern Italy in the late 1890s, and launched his own construction company in New Jersey, before dying in 1922 in a fall from a scaffold. Charles Tagliabue, Paul's father, took over the family business at age eighteen, and split from his uncle at an early age to start his own company, because the older man thought that his nephew's notion of investing money in trucks was foolish. Paul Tagliabue int.; Charles Tagliabue int.
380 **Charles Tagliabue's boys were encouraged:** Paul Tagliabue int.; Charles Tagliabue int.
380 **Though Paul:** Asked in 1990 to name a crazy period in his life, he answered, "Nothing in particular, except when I fell in love with my wife." At NYU, Tagliabue befriended future senator of Tennessee Lamar Alexander, who himself spent several holidays back in Jersey City with the Tagliabue clan. "If you say 'ma'am' to me one more time," Tagliabue's mother told Alexander on his first visit, "I'm going to smack you." Alexander int.; Telander, "The Face of Sweeping Change."

381   **The baton:** Undated notes on career, Rozelle papers; Rozelle letter to Paul Tagliabue, Sep. 11, 1990, Rozelle papers.

381   **For Tagliabue:** Tagliabue's tenure technically began Sunday, November 5, and he attended a game in Washington that evening, in which the Cowboys won their only game of the season, upsetting the Redskins, 13–3. His first workday in the New York office as commissioner was Monday, November 6. Tagliabue int.; Browne int.

381   **He more than compensated:** Weiss int.; Browne int.; Pash int.

382   **Tagliabue's first major decision:** And yet the parallels between football and war were so stark, and so embedded in the language, that it became difficult to avoid them, especially after General Norman Schwarzkopf, in addressing his troops before the initial attack, noted that "Iraq has won the toss and elected to receive." Norman Chad, "Networks Mixed Games, War with Dignity," *The National,* Jan. 21, 1991; Shirley Povich, "They Didn't Call Time in the Big One," *Washington Post,* Jan. 19, 1991; J. Adams, "Norman After the Storm," *London Sunday Times,* Sep. 27, 1992.

382   **The war was:** Press conference transcript, Jan. 25, 1991.

383   **Johnson's crowing:** By then, the Cowboys had already returned to the top of the charts among teams in NFL merchandise sales. Though they'd slumped to fifteenth in the league in 1990, selling only 2 percent of all merchandise, they were back to number one, with 16.9 percent of all sales in 1992, and would rise as high as 29 percent in 1993. Confidential league documents.

383   **And it was clear:** Paul Zimmerman, "Big D, as in Dynasty," *SI,* Feb. 8, 1993.

384   **"You're not *going*":** St. John, *Tex!,* p. 78; Upshaw int.

384   **That philosophy informed:** Upshaw int.

384   **By the end:** As early as 1982, there had been proposals on the table that would have provided the players very limited free agency, and a percentage of the gross much lower than the 55 percent they struck over in 1987. "But it didn't matter to Tex," said Bill Walsh. "He would have been opposed to it even if it was 2 percent." Walsh int.; Paul Tagliabue int.; John Wiebusch, "Q&A," *GameDay Magazine,* Vol. 20, No. 3, Sep. 1989.

384   **On the morning:** Tom Friend and Christine Brennan, "Colleagues Heap Praise on Rozelle," *Washington Post,* Mar. 23, 1989; Paul Tagliabue speech, Oct. 9, 1989, Tagliabue papers.

384   **Among the first people:** Tagliabue would remember Davis's message slightly differently. "You can't pressure Gene, though," Tagliabue recalled Davis telling him. "He's an offensive lineman, and he's been taught his whole life that if he gets hit in the head to hit back harder, but not to lose his cool." Apprised of the quote, Davis replied, "Naw, that's not what I said. But it sounds good." Davis int.; Paul Tagliabue int.

385   **Though Tagliabue:** Tagliabue found in Upshaw a reasonable counterpart. "I really like this guy," he told his friend Nick Langone. "He's one of the more practical, logical people to work with." Paul Tagliabue int.; Shell int.; Upshaw int.; Langone int.

385   **And over the next days:** *United States v. National Football League,* 116 F.Supp. 319 (E.D. Pa. 1953).

386   **The idea became:** The agreement sent shock waves through the world of sports. De facto baseball commissioner Bud Selig was on the board of the Green Bay Packers, and had repeatedly told his friend, Packers president Bob Harlan, that the NFL would "never get a cap." Harlan int.

386   **"We had been":** Policy int.

386   **But for a:** Peter King, "Put a Sock in It," Inside the NFL, *SI,* Sep. 5, 1994.

386   **There would still be:** Schaap, *Flashing Before My Eyes,* p. 284.

22: PEARL HARBOR

388   **"I've never heard":** Rupe int.

389   **In the past:** Peterson int.

389   **Schottenheimer's fundamental:** Ibid.

390 **What the team:** MacCambridge, "Without Them, We're Wichita."

391 **For the cities:** Donovan and Drury, *Fatso*, pp. 146–47.

391 **The shock from the news:** The league office would later claim he had been misquoted, and years later, Tagliabue himself would say, "I don't recall that I said it in those words." But the comment, attributed to him and not immediately corrected, had an air of condescension to it. Howard Balzer, "Why Jacksonville? T-Shirts, of Course," *PFW,* Dec. 12, 1993.

391 **A bereft John Steadman:** Letter from John Steadman to Pete Rozelle, Dec. 10, 1993, Rozelle papers.

393 **In 1992, in the midst:** But the Broadcasting Committee was still headed by the esteemed Art Modell, who had sat in on many of the negotiations, and whose experience in TV production had been a boon to the league. Modell was an old-school negotiator, who once stopped Rozelle in the street after a tense negotiation and said, "Pete, promise me right now, we'll never make a deal with the networks in which they lose money." Modell int.; Jones int.; Vito Stellino, "Tough Challenge for Tagliabue," *Baltimore Sun,* carried by the *LAT,* Mar. 21, 1992.

393 **A year later:** CBS, which claimed to have lost $200 million on the previous deal, had counted on its nearly forty-year tradition as the network of the NFL to carry the day, but Fox's $1.58 billion bid for the four-year package of NFC games was $100 million per year higher than CBS's reluctant final bid. "Seldom have two companies fought harder for the right to lose hundreds of millions of dollars," observed *Newsweek* when the deal was announced. "In Pro Football, Plus Ça Change," News of the Week, *Newsweek,* Jan. 3, 1994.

393 **The deal ushered:** Rick Korch, Steve Silverman, Ron Pollack, and Dan Arkush, "FOX Television Buys into NFL," *PFW,* Dec. 26, 1993.

394 **Meanwhile, in Southern California:** "Is L.A. Too Wimpy to Build New Stadium?," *LAT,* Feb. 22, 1994, reprinted in Jim Murray, *Jim Murray: The Last of the Best* (Los Angeles: Los Angeles Times, 1998), p. 145.

395 **The problem, however:** The Rams formally submitted to the approval process, but had little luck in convincing either Tagliabue or the other owners that a move was warranted. In the letter Tagliabue wrote to the owners assessing the necessity of the proposed move, he recommended that "the Rams' proposed relocation be disapproved by the membership. In my judgment, the relocation, on the terms presented, does not serve League interests, now or in the future." Paul Tagliabue, memorandum to principal owners, "Re: Request by the Los Angeles Rams to Transfer Their Home Playing Site to St. Louis, Missouri," Mar. 9, 1995, confidential document.

395 **In April, the league:** The Rams agreed to turn over more of their deal into the league central fund (the logic being that, had St. Louis been chosen as an expansion team, the franchise fees would have been divided equally among existing teams). Pash int.; Tagliabue int.; Teele int.

395 **Suddenly, Al Davis:** Shell was quickly hired by Marty Schottenheimer in Kansas City, where he saw the Raiders-Chiefs rivalry from another perspective. Prior to talking to the team in advance of the Chiefs' first 1995 game against the Raiders, Schottenheimer turned to Shell and said, "Art, I hope you won't take any of what I'm about to say personally," then proceeded to rip into the Raiders' philosophy, discipline, leadership, and character, reminding his club that, "if you stay in it until the fourth quarter, they'll fold." Shell int.; Schottenheimer int.; not-for-attribution int.

395 **While the Raiders:** Al Davis int.; Nelson George int.

396 **And within the league:** Steve Wulf, "Bad Bounces for the NFL," *Time,* Dec. 11, 1995.

396 **In contrast:** Modell remained ever the raconteur, full of wit and one-liners, seemingly always in the middle of a Borscht Belt stand-up act. "I fell in love with football back in 1934," he was fond of saying, "when I went to see the Brooklyn Dodgers play the New York Giants. My first favorite player on that Dodger team was Earl Lumpkin, 'cause he played without a helmet." Then Modell would wait a beat, before adding, "I think he's an owner now." Modell int.

397 **Modell had suffered:** Peter King, "Down . . . and Out," *SI,* Nov. 13, 1995.

397   **"At some point":** Tagliabue int.

398   **"I felt like":** Hal Lebovitz, for thirty-five years an ally of Modell's, typified the reaction of many in Cleveland. "He kept the Stadium going when the city didn't have the money to operate it," Lebovitz said. "By taking over the Stadium, he helped keep the Indians in town. He saved the Stouffer Hotel, which is downtown next to Terminal Tower. He did so many wonderful, charitable things. To me, there was nothing in Art Modell's manner or personality to indicate he would move to Baltimore. I knew there was trouble between Art and the city, but Art was the guy who was always blasting Al Davis and those other owners who moved their teams. I had never known Art to lie or be a hypocrite. But with this . . . by moving the team, he killed all the good works he did over all the years in one fell swoop." Groza int.; Pluto, *When All the World Was Browns Town*, p. 300.

398   **The game at Cleveland:** Bill Livingston, "Browns Are Already on Outside Looking In," *Cleveland Plain Dealer*, Nov. 6, 1995.

398   **In the stands:** King, "Down . . . and Out."

398   **Houston (another team):** Ibid.

398   **The next morning:** Timothy Heider, Tom Diemer, and Evelyn Thiess, "Deal Announced in Baltimore," *Cleveland Plain Dealer*, Nov. 7, 1995.

398   **"I didn't want":** Modell int.

398   **The funereal scene:** Ron Smith, *The Cleveland Browns: The Official Illustrated History* (Lincolnwood, IL: Sporting News, 1999), p. 202.

399   **The irony that Baltimore:** William Schaefer, letter to Tagliabue, italics in original, Nov. 16, 1995, Rozelle papers.

400   **Those mid-'90s years:** Weiss int.; Rozelle letter to Jack Landry, Jan. 6, 1994, Rozelle papers; Rozelle letter to Super 30 media club members, Jan. 24, 1996, Rozelle papers.

401   **"There are only two":** William Charland, "Pete Rozelle: Absent Hero Behind Green Bay's Success," *Christian Science Monitor*, Dec. 10, 1996.

23: "A DIFFERENT WORLD"

402   **He was usually:** Matthews int.; Unitas int.

402   **And though the effects:** John Steadman, "The Golden Arm Is on the Mend, Unitas," *Baltimore Sun*, Oct. 5, 1997.

403   **When asked:** Unitas int.

403   **Unitas had played:** Gildea, *When the Colts Belonged to Baltimore*, p. 204.

403   **"If one truism":** King, *The Season After*, p. 24.

403   **That presented:** Parcells int.

403   **If the culture:** Blount, *About Three Bricks Shy*, p. 209.

404   **"Look, white kids":** Curry int.

404   **"I was at":** Billick int.

405   **"What they did":** Wolf int.

405   **But in 1999:** Eisenberg, *Cotton Bowl Days*, p. 25; Skip Hollandsworth, "The Ringmaster of the Media Circus: Michael Irvin," *Texas Monthly*, Sep. 1996; Brown, *Out of Bounds*, p. 121.

406   **And the 49ers:** Policy int.

406   **For the teams:** Paul Zimmerman, "Big D as in Dynasty," *SI*, Feb. 8, 1993.

407   **In this new:** Polian was recruited to Indianapolis by Colts owner Jim Irsay, determined to put his own mark on the floundering team after the death of his father, Robert, in 1997. Polian int.; Jim Irsay int.

407   **Had they gone:** Polian int.; Peter King, "The Toughest Job in Sports," *SI*, Aug. 17, 1998.

408   **While the stakes:** Schottenheimer int.

408   **The rise of player development:** Dungy int.

409   **In July 1999:** Paul Tagliabue int.

409   **Though the Rams:** *Gotta Go to Work*, Rams 1999 season highlights.

410   **"I remember talking":** Billick int.

410   **Green's backup:** Gary Horton, et al., eds., *The War Room*, 1999 preseason issue.

410 **Instead, from his first start:** Michael Silver, "Hallowed Be His Game," reprinted in Special Commemorative Issue of *SI, Super Bowl Champs: The Amazing Season of the 1999 St. Louis Rams.*

410 **"Most new quarterbacks":** Vermeil int.

411 **Though Warner would:** Kurt Warner with Michael Silver, *All Things Possible* (San Francisco: Harper San Francisco, 2000), p. 23.

411 **"The simple fact is":** Shields int.

411 **"idiot kicker":** Tom Friend, "Footloose," *ESPN The Magazine,* Oct. 27, 2003.

411 **When the Packers':** *ESPN SportsCenter* broadcast, Nov. 24, 2002.

412 **"You don't know":** *Lost Treasures,* vol. 20, NFL Films, 2003.

412 **"You know, people":** Polian int.

412 **"Baseball fans think":** David Plotz, "Washington Diarist: Off Base," *New Republic,* Dec. 20, 1999.

413 **The following year:** Patterson, *Football in Baltimore,* pp. 241–42.

413 **In the late '90s:** In response to the negative publicity, the league's publicity office began publishing a recurring series of feel-good stories about players' off-field efforts for charity or education, under the shrill headline: "Dearth of Positive News? Don't Think So!" Nflmedia.com.

413 **It was a problem:** Benedict and Yaeger, *Pros and Cons,* pp. vii–xiv.

413 **Lewis was exactly:** Bob Glauber, "Lewis Not Running from the Past," *Fort Lauderdale Sun-Sentinel,* Aug. 15, 2001.

414 **From the day:** Billick had convinced his previous boss, Dennis Green in Minnesota, of the efficacy of integrating playbook, scouting reports, and tendencies in a single database. Green int.; Walsh int.; Billick int.

415 **In the buildup:** William Rhoden, "For a Day, All Paths Lead to Ray Lewis and His Past," Sports of the Times, *NYT,* Jan. 24, 2001.

415 **Yet no less:** Jim Brown int.

415 **The Ravens trounced:** At the following morning's press conference, in which MVP Lewis and his coach Billick were set to appear, Tagliabue pulled them aside prior to the event and curtly counseled them to be gracious champions. Billick grimaced and acknowledged the advice, but didn't necessarily take it to heart. Later, he would say only, "I appreciated the input; I have been doing this for a while." Paul Tagliabue int.; Billick int.; Aiello int.

416 **"I recognize that":** Jim Brown int.

417 **In his classic study:** Leonard Koppett, *Sports Illusion, Sports Reality: A Reporter's View of Sports, Journalism, and Society* (Boston: Houghton Mifflin, 1981), pp. 20–21.

24: MAN AT THE TOP

419 **But as the deadline:** "You're asking a number of taxpayers to subsidize something they'll never get to use, said state senator John Lewis (R-Orange). "It's corporate welfare." Barbara Kingsley, "Not Enough,?" *Orange County Register,* Aug. 1, 1999.

419 **As media outlets:** Richard Sandomir, "How One Network's Urgency Spelled Riches for the NFL," *NYT,* Jan. 17, 1998.

420 **Meanwhile, the NFL:** "The NFL Machine," *Business Week,* Jan. 27, 2003.

420 **Among the most:** Confidential league documents.

421 **"When Paul asks":** Browne int.; Aiello int.; Pash int.

422 **"If you understand":** Bruce Schoenfeld, "In Tough Times, NFL Chief Redefines League Leader's Role," *Street & Smith's Sports Business Journal,* Jan. 7–13, 2002.

422 **The year that would:** "Quarterback/Interview: Pete Rozelle," *Quarterback* magazine, Vol. 1, No. 1, Oct. 1969.

422 **But having the teams:** Gordon Forbes, "New Teams Mean League Must Tackle Realignment," *USA Today,* Dec. 1, 1993.

423 **Just weeks later:** A day later, the verdict came in on the Raiders' latest suit, with the league

winning handily, a jury ruling that the NFL had not sabotaged the Raiders' efforts for a new stadium in the Los Angeles area. (Though the verdict would, over a year later, be thrown out, leading to more in the latest round of Raiders litigation.)

423   **The first weekend:** Accorsi int.

423   **At the league office:** Peter King, "On the Spot," *SI*, Sep. 24, 2001.

423   **In the wake:** Tagliabue int.; King, "On the Spot."

423   **The Giants' player rep:** Accorsi int.

424   **"This is not":** King, "On the Spot."

424   **The league made:** Ibid.

424   **"The NFL acted first":** Thomas Boswell, "A Situation Much Too Serious for Any Games," *Washington Post*, Sep. 14, 2001.

424   **Tagliabue, with his:** Tagliabue int.

425   **What had seemed:** Peter Keating, "NFL Nation," *ESPN The Magazine*, Feb. 4, 2002.

425   **The buildup to:** "I find football so interesting strategically," Rice said. "It's the closest thing to war." Gregg Easterbrook, TMQ column, "I'm Pickin' Up Good Vibration," slate.com, Jan. 29, 2002.

425   **The game itself:** The Patriots might have put an end forever to Super Bowl pregame introductions when, instead of having each starter run out while introduced, the entire forty-six men on the roster ran on the field en masse. In the two seasons following, neither team chose to be introduced individually.

425   **By the end:** Schoenfeld, "In Tough Times, NFL Chief Redefines League Leader's Role."

426   **By the dawn:** Rozelle int.; Mara int.; Peterson int.

426   **"The playing field":** Tagliabue int.

427   **"He uses":** Not-for-attribution int.

427   **Neil Austrian:** Neil Austrian int.

427   **The battle became:** Goodell int.; Dan Rooney int.

427   **Ultimately:** Confidential league documents; not-for-attribution ints.

428   **"This is the only":** Peterson int.

428   **Against this:** "The fans of the team aren't there," said the *Washington Post*'s Tony Kornheiser of Super Sunday. "It's a corporate business holiday for rich Americans. It's the ultimate for being a Ford dealer or a Bud dealer. You want the fans, the fans are outside, roaming around outside trying to score a ticket. It's always been that way." Kornheiser int.

428   **For cultural impact:** Bernice Kanner, *The Super Bowl of Advertising: How the Commercials Won the Game* (Princeton: Bloomberg, 2004), pp. 2–3.

429   **Rozelle began:** Joe Browne int.

429   **The entire spectacle:** Robert Weintraub, "Last Call for Raider Nation," slate.com, Jan. 27, 2003.

430   **"At some point":** Wolf int.

430   **What hurt:** Todd Jones, "Lost Legacy," *Columbus Dispatch*, Oct. 8, 1999.

431   **"I can remember":** Dungy int.

431   **"I don't see":** Mike Brown int.

431   **"He is so":** Not-for-attribution int.

25: THE MAIN THING

432   **"I grew up":** Parcells int.

433   **"There are no":** Parcells int.

433   **The Steelers' patriarch:** Wiebusch, *Lombardi*, p. 91.

433   **More than ever:** The ten teams that played in the Super Bowl during the seasons 1998–2002 averaged 12.6 wins in their title seasons. The season following the Super Bowl, when none of the ten returned to the big game (or even won a playoff game), those same teams averaged just 7.8 wins per season.

434   **NFL games:** It took six years, 1972 to 1977, to come up with as many double-digit fourth-

quarter rallies as the NFL witnessed in 2002 alone. 2003 NFL Competition Committee report.

434 **The margin:** "When I walked into my office Sunday and saw my wife and saw my coaching staff's wives, I'll tell you, whew, it ain't worth it," Vermeil said in October, after another big lead was wiped out in a late loss. "You can't do it too long. Because you are not the only one who suffers. You're not the only one that dies, but you know that this is your responsibility. And you're conditioned—you've coached yourself how to handle it. But the other parts of your life, they aren't coached." Ivan Carter, "Playoff Dreams Slipping Away for Chiefs," *Kansas City Star*, Oct. 23, 2002.

434 **While free agency:** Armey int.

435 **"There are two":** Accorsi int.

435 **"Shof, let me":** Spurrier quotations related by Ernie Accorsi.

436 **If Parcells and Vermeil:** Parcells int.; Vermeil int.; Billick int.; Green int.; Dungy int.

436 **In the culture:** Cunningham int.; Peterson int.; Stiles int.

437 **"That's just":** Walsh int.

437 **"We have thought":** Pash int.

437 **Within two weeks:** Peterson int.; Stiles int.; Vermeil int.

438 **"For some reason":** Jarret Bell, "Dungy Welcomes Chance to Be No. 1," *USA Today*, Jan. 14, 2004.

438 **"One of the great":** Polian int.

438 **Sooner or later:** Vermeil int; Bill Parcells and Will McDonough, *The Final Season: My Last Year as a Head Coach in the NFL* (New York: Morrow, 2000), p. 12; Dungy int.; Billick int.

439 **In return:** Vermeil int.

439 **On August 23:** Ibid.

439 **A week later:** "Training Camp: Day 39," kcchiefs.com, Aug. 27, 2003.

440 **"The thing that":** Billick int.

441 **"The guy I'm":** Lewis int.; Mike Brown int.; "Sounds of the Season, 2003," NFL Network, 2004.

442 **"I think":** Paul Tagliabue int.

443 **In 2003:** John Clayton, "Upsets More Likely in AFC Playoffs," *ESPN.com*, Dec. 26, 2003.

443 **"I've never been":** "Sounds of the Season, 2003."

445 **"perhaps the most":** Peterson int.

445 **"our quarterback picked":** Polian int.

446 **"a 41–0 loss":** Ibid.

447 **"There is a moment":** Curry int.

447 **Given all those:** Jackson's bizarre halftime sideshow became the single most searched event in the history of the Internet, exceeding the number of searches for the 9/11 attacks or the 2000 presidential election or any other event since Lycos began monitoring Internet search requests in 1999. Aaron Schatz, "The Things You're Searching for: Janet Makes History," Feb. 4–5, 2004, http://50.lycos.com/.

449 **"You gotta remember":** Zygmunt int.

EPILOGUE: AMERICA'S GAME

450 **In the fall:** Gifford int.

451 **But after Rozelle's death:** Jonathan Franzen, *The Twenty-seventh City* (New York: Farrar, Straus & Giroux, 1988), p. 26.

452 **"Baseball in 1960":** James int.

452 **It was tempting:** Harris Interactive press release, "Football Widens Lead as Nation's Favorite Sport, Baseball Slips, Says U.S. Poll," Sep. 24, 2003.

454 **"Baseball is what":** *Any Given Sunday* press notes, anygivensunday/warnerbros/com/prod.html.

454 **At the same:** "What's happened here is the football teams feel they have to artificially stim-

ulate the fans," noted David Hill of football in America. "They roll out these long-dead English rock 'n' rollers like Gary Glitter and whatever, and cheerleaders, and all that is to artificially stimulate the crowd. Whereas in England, [the fans] make up their own songs. It was one of the fascinating things after John Madden watched a World Cup, he said, 'Wouldn't it be great if American fans didn't need this? If they were so passionate about their teams, they would create a song using the player's name?' So the passion that I've seen in other parts of the world does not exist here for sports." Hill int.; Nick Hornby, *Fever Pitch* (New York: Riverhead, 1992), p. 231.

455 **"To me, the fans":** Accorsi int.

455 **"I'd probably *still*":** Madden int.

455 **"validation":** Shields int.

456 **"Look at how":** Faulkner int.

456 **"Not at all":** Polian int.

457 **As the perceptive:** James Lawton, *The All-American War Game* (Oxford, U.K.: Blackwell, 1984), p. 2.

457 **"I considered it":** Younger int.

458 **"I reject":** Don DeLillo, *End Zone* (Boston: Houghton Mifflin, 1972), p. 164.

458 **After Elvis Presley's death:** Lester Bangs, "Where Were You When Elvis Died?," reprinted in *Rock and Roll Is Here to Stay: An Anthology* (New York: Norton, 2000), p. 627.

BIBLIOGRAPHIC ESSAY

In addition to the 600 hours of interviews I conducted with players, coaches, owners, administrators, and longtime observers of the game, I also had the pleasure of reading and drawing from many of the best pro football books written in the past sixty years. The "small ball" theory of American sports literature holds that golf and baseball are the true literary pursuits, but the collected works on pro football provided a much richer well than I had imagined.

As with any sport, there is much that is unreadable—the standard stultifying player biographies, the largely pedestrian team histories, the outraged deconstruction of the meaning of football by those who dislike both the game and its fans. There persists in some quarters a feeling that football people are too uniformly gung ho and achievement-oriented to write interesting books, and any number of self-justifying coaches' autobiographies would support that thesis. Yet the game has yielded numerous underappreciated literary gems, often quirky and complex, many of which have little more in common than a curious penchant for absurdly long subtitles.

An overview of the main sources I used:

General History. The best history of the National Football League has been running in weekly installments, in the pages of *Sports Illustrated,* over the past fifty years. The serious, authoritative Tex Maule set a new standard for understanding of the pro game, and his successors, including Dan Jenkins, Paul Zimmerman, Peter King, and Michael Silver have maintained that level, each with his own unique voice. Some of the best of their work is in *Pro Football: Four Decades of Sports Illustrated's Finest Writing on Professional Football* (Birmingham, AL: Oxmoor House, 1993). Much of their contemporary work, like King's *Monday Morning Quarterback* and Zimmerman's *Dr. Z's Mailbag* can be found only on si.com.

Among single-volume general histories, the most entertaining is *The Pro Football Chronicle: The Complete (Well, Almost) Record of the Best Players, the Greatest Photos, the Hardest Hits, the Biggest Scandals, and the Funniest Stories in Pro Football* (New York: Macmillan, 1990), by Dan Daly and Bob O'Donnell. It's a rollicking, readable decade-by-decade account of the pro game loosely modeled on Bill James's *The Historical Baseball Abstract,* and one of the rare books worthy of being mentioned in the same breath.

For more conventional histories, the best in recent decades have been those produced by the league. *The NFL Century: The Complete Story of the National Football League, 1920–2000* (New York: Smithmark, 1999) is a large-format coffee-table book, smartly illustrated, with Will McDonough writing the main text. (An earlier version, titled *75 Years,* was published on the occasion of the league's seventy-fifth anniversary in 1994.) Both are more comprehensive, if less dynamic, than the first title from the NFL Properties Creative Services division, *The First Fifty Years: A Celebration of the National Football League in Its Fiftieth Season* (New York: Simon & Schuster, 1969). That volume, by David Boss and Bob Oates, belongs in any pro football fan's library.

Two earlier general histories are worth noting. Harold (Spike) Claassen's *The History of Professional Football: Its Great Teams, Games, Players and Coaches* (Englewood Cliffs, NJ: Prentice Hall, 1963) was the definitive history of the league at the time of its publication, and is organized around an annual review of each season's events, and a series of informative, readable team histories. Robert Smith's *Pro Football: The History of the Game and the Great Players* (Garden City, NY: Doubleday, 1963) lacks the encyclopedic breadth of Classen's book, but provides a more coherent overview.

There is a richer vein of work on the game in specific eras. Myron Cope's *The Game That Was: A Beautifully Illustrated and Lovingly Written Account of the Great, Early Days of Pro Football* (New York: World, 1970) is one of the best works about the NFL's pre–World War II era, and includes a memorable chapter with Steelers patron saint Art Rooney.

The '40s. Robert Peterson's *Pigskin: The Early Years of Pro Football* (New York: Oxford University Press, 1997) contains the best account I've read of football in the war years, with Peterson showing just how dire the league's position grew in the early '40s. A good complement to Peterson, and the best account of the formation of the All-America Football Conference, is Thomas Littlewood's *Arch: A Promoter, Not a Poet: The Story of Arch Ward* (Ames: Iowa State University Press, 1990).

The '50s. Mickey Herskowitz's *The Golden Age of Pro Football: NFL Football in the 1950s* (Dallas: Taylor, 1990) is a handsomely illustrated account of the decade in which the game grew up, written in Herskowitz's wry Texas voice. Stuart Leuthner's oral history *Iron Men: Bucko, Crazylegs, and the Boys Recall the Golden Days of Professional Football* (New York: Doubleday, 1988) has just twenty-six subjects, but is able to delve deeply into the histories of each, to provide an illuminating series of accounts of the game in the '40s and '50s. Leuthner's book features the best, most candid interview I've seen with the Browns' legendary Marion Motley.

There are two superb documentaries on the decade: the 2001 HBO production *The Game of Their Lives: Pro Football's Wonder Years*, and the two-part NFL Films presentation *The Fabulous Fifties*.

The '60s. Bob Carroll's *When the Grass Was Real: Unitas, Brown, Lombardi, Sayers, Butkus, Namath, and All the Rest: The Best Ten Years of Pro Football* (New York: Simon & Schuster, 1993) is a careful, loving account of the game's crucial decade from one of the sport's leading historians. Carroll has brought a treasure of historical essays online in his Pro Football Researchers Association Web site (footballresearch.com), an extension of the PFRA journal *The Coffin Corner*.

This was also the decade that pro football hit the best-seller lists, thanks in part to the budding myth of Vince Lombardi and the Packers. First came Lombardi's own memoir of a week in the 1962 season, *Run to Daylight!* (Englewood Cliffs, NJ: Prentice Hall, 1963), with collaborator W. C. Heinz. Jerry Kramer's sharply rendered account of the 1967 season, *Instant Replay* (New York: World, 1968) also was a hit, and a convincing portrait of Lombardi. It wasn't just the Pack, of course. George Plimpton's *Paper Lion* (New York: Harper & Row, 1966) and Frederick Exley's somber *A Fan's Notes* (New York: Random House, 1968) gave the sport a measure of literary cachet.

Many of the best books on the game in the '60s focus on the self-contained history of the American Football League. Ed Gruver's *The American Football League: A Year-by-Year History, 1960–1969* (Jefferson, NC: McFarland, 1997) is the most thorough general history, and is smartly complemented by Jeff Miller's recent oral history *Going Long: The Wild 10-Year Saga of the Renegade American Football League in the Words of Those Who Lived It* (Chicago: Contemporary, 2003), which attempts to do for the AFL what Terry Pluto's hilarious *Loose Balls* did for the ABA, and almost pulls it off. Also worthy is Bob Curran's *The $400,000 Quarterback, or: The League That Came in from the Cold* (New York: Signet, 1969), which documents the AFL's early years. The one essential volume is the gorgeous coffee-table book *The Other League: The Fabulous Story of the American Football League* (Chicago: Follett, 1970), by Mike Rathet and Jack Horrigan. The best documentary on the history of the AFL comes in HBO's 1995 documentary *Rebels with a Cause: The Story of the AFL*, another installment in the network's *Sports of the 20th Century* documentary series.

For a unique perspective on the early years of the AFL, there's *A Proud American: The Auto-biography of Joe Foss* (New York: Pocket Books, 1992), though Foss's consistent positivism occasionally glosses over some of the tenser moments in the league. William J. Ryczek's *Crash of the Titans: The Early Years of the New York Jets and the AFL* (Kingston, NY: Total Sports, 2000) is a morbidly fascinating account of the comedy of errors that was Harry Wismer's franchise. It's hard to imagine that the same franchise, with some of the same players, was just a few years later responsible for the sport's biggest upset. The best account of Super Bowl III is Dave Anderson's *Countdown to Super Bowl* (New York: Random House, 1969), in which the respected *New York Times* writer provides an hour-by-hour account of the Jets heading up to the big game.

The 1969 season, the league's fiftieth and the last before the AFL and NFL fully merged, provided a clear line of demarcation, and two books smartly capture the sensibilities of that season. *Player of the Year: Roman Gabriel's Football Journal* (New York: World, 1970) and Tex Maule's diary of the 1969 season, *The Pro Season* (Garden City, NY: Doubleday, 1970) provide useful reminders of how small a world the NFL once was.

The '70s. A golden era for pro football publishing, partly because the game had arrived on Madison Avenue, and because David Boss's Creative Services Division at NFL Properties was publishing several volumes a year.

Dan Jenkins's best-seller *Semi-Tough* (New York: Atheneum, 1972) and its follow-up, *Life Its Ownself*, are still the funniest fictional glimpses of the pro game. Pete Gent's *North Dallas Forty* (New York: Morrow, 1973) remains among the darkest. Roy Blount, Jr., never had pro football as a beat during his time at *Sports Illustrated*, but his account of his year with the Pittsburgh Steelers, *About Three Bricks Shy of a Load: A Highly Irregular Lowdown on the Year the Pittsburgh Steelers Were Super but Missed the Bowl* (Boston: Little, Brown, 1974) is still the best season-in-the-life meditation on the game from the inside, all the better for the contrast between Chuck Noll's straight-arrow mind-set and Blount's skewed, ruminative perspective. There's also an updated paperback version, *About Three Bricks Shy—And the Load Filled Up: The Story of the Greatest Football Team Ever* (New York: Ballantine, 1989), which includes the original book, plus several essays Blount wrote about the Steelers in later years.

While Paul Zimmerman's *A Thinking Man's Guide to Pro Football* (New York: Dutton, 1970) justly earned "Dr. Z" a national following, I'm still partial to his account of the New York Jets' 1973 campaign, *The Last Season of Weeb Ewbank* (New York: Farrar, Straus & Giroux, 1974), a remarkably intimate picture of a once great team in decline and turmoil.

Two other George Plimpton titles must be mentioned. His collaboration will Bill Curry, *One More July: A Football Dialogue with Bill Curry* (New York: Harper & Row, 1977) is an engrossing, ruminative read. And *Mad Ducks and Bears* (New York: Random House, 1973), written with Alex Karras and John Gordy, is a meditation on the inglorious life of linemen.

The '80s. The decade's best football title was *Hey, Wait a Minute, I Wrote a Book* (New York: Villard, 1984), John Madden's readable account of his football career, written with Dave Anderson.

David Harris's exhaustively researched and reported *The League: The Rise and Decline of the NFL* (New York: Bantam, 1986) aptly parses the boardroom rivalries that dominated NFL politics in the decade.

Not to be missed, for its keen take on the writer's and fan's differing perspectives, is *Wait Till Next Year: The Story of a Season When What Should've Happened Didn't and What Could've Gone Wrong Did* (New York: Bantam, 1988), the highly entertaining collaboration between Mike Lupica and Oscar-winning screenwriter William Goldman. Jim Brown's *Out of Bounds* (New York: Kensington, 1989) is the rare item—a player's account of pro football that's both sensational and thoughtful.

The '90s and Beyond. The decade began with the NFL's own *The Super Bowl: Celebrating a Quarter-Century of America's Greatest Game* (New York: Simon & Schuster, 1990), a wonderful retrospective of the first twenty-four games of the series, with essays, photographs, gatefold illustrations, lineups, and play-by-play recaps for each game. For another league perspective, there was Don Weiss's *The Making of the Super Bowl: The Inside Story of the World's Greatest Sporting Event* (Chicago: Contemporary, 2003), co-written with Chuck Day, in which Weiss describes the league's early efforts to mount not just a sporting event but an entertainment spectacle. There are plenty of interesting behind-the-scenes vignettes, and a glimpse into the mind-set of Pete Rozelle, but left unanswered is the larger question of how the league balanced the integrity of the game with the constant push toward greater elements of entertainment and showmanship that surrounded it.

Whatever the merits or flaws of their research methodology, Jeff Benedict and Don Yaeger's *Pros and Cons: The Criminals Who Play in the NFL* (New York: Warner, 1998) sheds new light on a troubling issue. Tim Green's player's-eye view *The Dark Side of the Game: My Life in the NFL* (New York: Warner, 1996) seeks to demystify much of the glamorous myth surrounding the sport. Though its perception was skewed a bit by the sales hook—an interview with an active NFL player discussing his homosexuality—Michael Freeman's *Bloody Sundays: Inside the Dazzling, Rough-and-Tumble World of the NFL* (New York: Morrow, 2003) is a sharp overview of the different pressures that come to bear on the modern game.

The best account of the era of "franchise free agency" comes in Jon Morgan's *Glory for Sale: Fans, Dollars and the New NFL* (Baltimore: Bancroft, 1997). For a deeper look at one city's frustrations, there's Ed Fowler's *Loser Takes All: Bud Adams, Bad Football and Big Business* (Atlanta: Longstreet, 1997), a book that at times is more of a screed against Adams than a balanced assessment of the events that led the Oilers to move to Tennessee.

Among the key franchises I focused on in the book, four of them—the Rams, Browns, Chiefs, and Cowboys—merited their own separate volumes in the NFL's *Great Teams, Great Years* series, all published by Macmillan in the mid-'70s. Jack Clary's *Cleveland Browns* (1973), Steve Bisheff's *Los Angeles Rams* (1973), Dick Connor's *Kansas City Chiefs* (1974), and Jeff Meyers's *Dallas Cowboys* (1974) are all rewarding, and excellent introductory histories to the respective clubs, though each title is fairly screaming for an index.

Rams. No franchise has been more influential, and none has a more fascinating history than that of the much-traveled Rams. Joseph Hession's *Rams: Five Decades of Football* (San Francisco: Foghorn, 1987) is the best treatment. For the early history of the club, Bob Oates's long out-of-print *The Los Angeles Rams* (Los Angeles: Miller Gee, 1955) is essential. In addition to Roman Gabriel's *Player of the Year,* the George Allen–era Rams are also presented in Bill Libby's *Life in the Pit: The Deacon Jones Story* (Garden City, NY: Doubleday, 1970). A more complete portrait of Jones emerged later in John Klawitter's *Headslap: The Life and Times of Deacon Jones* (Amherst, NY: Prometheus, 1996). The best document of the remarkable 1999 season in St. Louis is found in Kurt Warner's autobiography *All Things Possible: My Story of Faith, Football and the Miracle Season* (San Francisco: Harper, 2000), with Michael Silver.

Browns. *PB: The Paul Brown Story* (New York: Atheneum, 1979), written by Brown and Jack Clary, was criticized for its lack of generosity of spirit at the time, but it's still an informative work, as interesting for what's left unsaid as for what's said. The best assessment of the coach's galvanizing impact on his players can be seen in Alan Natali's handsome oral history *Brown's Town: 20 Famous Browns Talk Amongst Themselves* (Wilmington, OH: Orange Frazer, 2001). Further insight into Brown can be found in the life of his onetime best friend, Blanton Collier. *Football's Gentle Giant: The Blanton Collier Story* (Lexington, KY: Life Force, 1985) is well written by Collier's daughter, Kay Collier Slone (now McCullough), and includes much of Collier's techniques and correspondence. Brown was still feared, though less revered, by the time he took over the Cincinnati Bengals. A portrait of those years can be found in Bob Trumpy's *Trump: Ten Years with the Bengals* (Virginia Beach: Donning, 1979), with Bill Mefford.

Of the franchise as a whole, Terry Pluto's *When All the World Was Browns Town: Cleveland's Browns and the Championship Season of '64* (New York: Simon & Schuster, 1997) is a richly detailed account of that club, all the more poignant for coming just two years after Art Modell moved the team to Baltimore. William V. Levy's *Return to Glory: The Story of the Cleveland Browns* (Cleveland: World, 1965) is more prosaic, but includes much valuable detail about the Browns' first two decades. Among the historical works that greeted the Browns on their return, the best is The Sporting News' *Cleveland Browns: The Official Illustrated History* (St. Louis:

Sporting News, 1999), featuring much of Tony Tomsic's marvelous photography, and *The Best of the Cleveland Browns Memories: Players, Coaches and Games* (Hinckley, OH: Moonlight, 1999).

Colts. In many ways, the Baltimore Colts were the Brooklyn Dodgers of football writing, a cherished franchise that inspired more than its fair share of literary contemplation, heightened by a wrenching move that many would equate with a loss of the entire sport's collective innocence. The late John Steadman's works—including *The Greatest Football Game Ever Played: When the Baltimore Colts and New York Giants Faced Sudden Death* (2nd ed., Stevensville, MD: Press Box, 1998), *From Colts to Ravens: A Behind-the-Scenes Look at Baltimore Professional Football* (Centreville, MD: Tidewater, 1997), and *Football's Miracle Men: The Baltimore Colts' Story* (Cleveland: Pennington, 1959)—provide a solid, authoritative perspective on the key moments of the franchise's history.

The best-written account of the Colts' relationship with Baltimore is William Gildea's *When the Colts Belonged to Baltimore: A Father and a Son, a Team and a Time* (New York: Ticknor & Fields, 1994), a richly evocative work about the ways in which the team and the town really did come together. Vince Bagli and Norman L. Macht's *Sundays at 2:00 with the Baltimore Colts* (Centreville, MD: Tidewater, 1995) provides a different perspective on the same ground, featuring interviews with thirty-one of the key figures of the Colts' years in Baltimore, from John Unitas to announcer Chuck Thompson. Then there's Art Donovan's raucous, delightful *Fatso: Football When Men Were Really Men* (New York: Morrow, 1987), written with gifted collaborator Bob Drury. The book is as responsible as any work for sparking a renewed interest in the game's characters of earlier eras. Fans of memorabilia will want to track down Ted Patterson's *Football in Baltimore: History and Memorabilia* (Baltimore: Johns Hopkins University Press, 2000), with photographs of many of the Colts souvenirs, programs, trading cards, and marginalia over the years.

Cowboys: The place to start for serious fans of the Cowboys is Peter Golenbock's leviathan oral history *Cowboys Have Always Been My Heroes: The Definitive Oral History of America's Team* (New York: Warner, 1997). There's also plenty of fascinating detail in Bob St. John's authorized biography of Tex Schramm, *Tex!: The Man Who Built the Dallas Cowboys* (Englewood Cliffs, NJ: Prentice Hall, 1988), though the book itself seems to have the disjointed narrative structure of a Charley Kaufman screenplay.

Steve Perkins's *Next Year's Champions: The Story of the Dallas Cowboys* (New York: World, 1969) is a well-rendered portrait of the Cowboys before they had the assurance gained from Super Bowl trophies. John Eisenberg's fans' memoir *Cotton Bowl Days: Growing Up with Dallas and the Cowboys in the 1960s* (New York: Simon & Schuster, 1997) conveys the pride and disappointment of those early Cowboys teams, as well as the more intimate, immediate environment at the Cotton Bowl.

The complex relationship between Tom Landry and Roger Staubach is well documented in their respective autobiographies, *Tom Landry: An Autobiography* (Grand Rapids, MI: Zondervan, 1990) and *Staubach: First Down, Lifetime to Go* (Waco, TX: Word, 1974). The best reflection of both the corporate mystique and self-importance of the franchise can be found in the team's own silver anniversary celebration, *Dallas Cowboys: The First Twenty-Five Years* (Dallas: Taylor, 1984), a lavish oversized document of the franchise written by Carlton Stowers with a foreword by James Michener. For an alternate view of this same organizational structure, there's of course Pete Gent's *North Dallas Forty* (New York: Morrow, 1973) and *Duane Thomas and the Fall of America's Team* (New York: Warner, 1988), written by Thomas and Paul Zimmerman.

The best document of Jerry Jones's impact on the team can be found in Jim Dent's *King of the Cowboys: The Life and Times of Jerry Jones* (Holbrook, MA: Adams, 1995).

Chiefs. Joe McGuff's *Winning It All: The Chiefs of the AFL* (Garden City, NY: Doubleday, 1970), written right after the Chiefs' Super Bowl win, is the best overview, by the longtime columnist of the *Kansas City Star*. It makes for a good companion piece with *Len Dawson: Pressure Quarterback* (New York: Cowles, 1970), written by Dawson and Lou Sahadi (whose ambitious magazine *Pro Quarterback* is one of the lost treasures of the early '70s). The team also produced a remarkable series of club yearbooks in the late '60s and early '70s, a golden age of football publishing. More recently, Mark Stallard's *The Kansas City Chiefs Encyclopedia* and Alan

Hoskins's *Warpaths: The Illustrated History of the Kansas City Chiefs* (Dallas: Taylor, 1999), though it has the drawback of not including any work from two photographers most associated with the team, Rod Hanna and Hank Young. More than 100 of Hanna's photographs appear in McGuff's book, while Young's own *Gameface* (Kansas City: Young, 2001) is a wonderful collection of sideline portraits over the past thirty years. Hank Stram's *They're Playing My Game* (New York: Morrow, 1986) commits the usual sins of coaches' autobiographies—all the anecdotes are a little too clean and a little too vague. More pointed is the Otis Taylor autobiography, *Otis Taylor: The Need to Win* (Champaign, IL: Sports Publishing, 2003), which in addition to its crisp recollections of Kansas City in the '60s and '70s includes a frank account of the difficulty that black players have historically had in finding careers in football after their playing days are over. No one has written about the Chiefs in the past ten years with more insight than my friend Joe Posnanski of *The Kansas City Star*. Some of his best Chiefs columns can be found in *The Good Stuff* (Kansas City: Star Publishing, 2001).

Raiders. For one of the NFL's most storied franchises, remarkably little has been written about the Raiders. Mark Ribowsky's portrait of Al Davis, *Slick: The Silver and Black Life of Al Davis* (New York: Macmillan, 1991) remains the definitive work on football's most enigmatic figure. The best book on the franchise's history is *Raiders: Collector's Edition* (San Francisco: Foghorn, 1991), by Joseph Hession and Steve Cassady.

Television. William Oscar Johnson covered TV for *Sports Illustrated* and his seminal overview of the relationship between sports and TV came in *Super Spectator and the Electric Lilliputians* (Boston: Little, Brown, 1971), a book that holds up much better than its title. Marc Gunther and Bill Carter's *Monday Night Mayhem: The Inside Story of ABC's Monday Night Football* (New York: Beech Tree, 1988) is a well-researched examination of the phenomenon, with plenty of fine-grained detail on the battles of Howard, Frank, and Dandy Don. The other two essential works on football and television are Phil Patton's *Razzle Dazzle* (Garden City, NY: Dial, 1984) and Ron Powers's *Supertube: The Rise of Television Sports* (New York: Coward-McCann, 1984). For personal memoirs, Cosell's and Gifford's reflections are less surprising or provocative than those of Roone Arledge in *Roone: A Memoir* (New York: HarperCollins, 2003).

Integration. Considering the rich scholarship on the Negro Leagues in baseball, and the dozens of books on the early stages of integration in that game, there's a shockingly small amount written about the subject in football. Alan Howard Levy's *Tackling Jim Crow: Racial Segregation of Professional Football* (Jefferson, NC: McFarland, 2003) is a welcome recent edition. Prior to that, Thomas Smith's "Outside the Pale: The Exclusion of Blacks from the National Football League, 1934–1946" and his "Civil Rights on the Gridiron: The Kennedy Administration and the Desegregation of the Washington Redskins," both originally published in the *Journal of Sport History*, were the most comprehensive accounts of the long battle to integrate the game. Arthur Ashe's *A Hard Road to Glory—Football: The African-American Athlete in Football* (2nd ed., New York: Amistad, 1993) is a good single-volume reference source, excerpting all the football writing and records from Ashe's larger classic.

It's regrettable that more interviewing wasn't done with the four men—Kenny Washington, Woody Strode, Marion Motley, and Bill Willis—who reintegrated the pro game in 1946. Strode's *Goal Dust: An Autobiography* (Lanham, MD: Madison, 1990) is the only life written among the four. Michael Hurd's *Black College Football, 1882–1992: One Hundred Years of History, Education, and Pride* (2nd ed., Virginia Beach: Donning, 1998) includes rich details of the pros' early dealings with historically black colleges and universities.

The Draft. There have really been only two books that attempted to document the draft. Hardest-to-find, but worth the trouble, is Cliff Christl and Don Langenkamp's *Sleepers, Busts and Franchise-Makers: The Behind-the-Scenes Story of the Pro Football Draft* (Seattle: Preview, 1983). Interesting, though lacking the broad perspective, is Richard Whittingham's *The Meat Market: The Inside Story of the NFL Draft* (New York: Macmillan, 1992).

Strategy. Paul Zimmerman's *The New Thinking Fan's Guide to Pro Football* (New York: Simon & Schuster, 1984) is still the best place to start, though after twenty years it could use another updating (the conscientious Zimmerman, who nearly rewrote the book in his first update, doesn't sound enthusiastic about the prospect). Peter King's underrated *Inside the Helmet: A Player's Eye View of the NFL* (New York: Simon & Schuster, 1993) is an absorbing read, especially for its detailed explanation of what a quarterback (in this case Boomer Esiason) has to do to prepare for a game each week.

Tom Bennett's *The Pro Style* (Englewood Cliffs, NJ: Prentice Hall, 1976) is the best one-stop Xs and Os overview, smartly integrating text and illustrations. Less visually appealing, but every bit as well written and illuminating, is Kevin Lamb's *Quarterbacks, Nickelbacks and Other Loose Change* (Chicago: Contemporary, 1984).

Coaching. David Maraniss's magisterial biography *When Pride Still Mattered: A Life of Vince Lombardi* (New York: Simon & Schuster, 1999) is justly celebrated for its rich, vivid portrait of Lombardi, and the distressed state of the franchise he took over in 1959. The best of the other portraits of Lombardi are Jerry Kramer's *Instant Replay* (see "The '60s") and the oral history *Lombardi* (Chicago: Triumph, 1997), both of which feature the photography of Vernon Biever.

Jack Clary's *The Gamemakers* (Chicago: Follett, 1976) begins with a profile of Paul Brown, and though the other subjects range in personality from Bum Phillips to Tom Landry to John Madden, the overall tone of the book makes a convincing case for the tremendous influence that Brown exerted on the way the game was coached.

But football coaches, the winning ones at least, are not often known for introspection and self-reflection, and thus most of the books they write tend to be archly diplomatic and self-congratulatory. Two exceptions on the pro level are Bill Parcells and Will McDonough's *The Final Season: My Last Year as a Head Coach in the NFL* (New York: Morrow, 2000) and Bill Walsh and Glenn Dickey's *Building a Champion: On Football and the Making of the 49ers* (New York: St. Martin's, 1990).

For books on coaching techniques and strategy, the most influential coaching text in the last decade has been Bill Walsh's imposing *Finding the Winning Edge*, which is prominently displayed in many college coaching offices (and tucked away in more than a few pro ones). That book was a collaboration among Walsh, Brian Billick, and James A. Peterson; Billick and Peterson later combined for *Competitive Leadership: Twelve Principles for Success* (Chicago: Triumph, 2001), which offers a frank account of the pressures of the game in the twenty-first century.

It's worth noting that three of the best books about coaching have been written by coach's daughters: *Fifth Quarter: The Scrimmage of a Football Coach's Daughter* (New York: Random House, 2000), by George Allen's daughter, Jennifer Allen; *Fields of Honor: The Golden Age of College Football and the Men Who Created It* (New York: Harcourt, 2001), by John Pont's daughter, Sally Pont (who also paints a sharp portrait of Sid Gillman during his college coaching days); and *Football's Gentle Giant: The Blanton Collier Story*, by Blanton Collier's daughter, Kay Collier Slone, now McCullough (Lexington, KY: Life Force, 1985).

Photography. The many works of Robert Riger stand out as the early standard for football photography (that's one of Riger's classic shots on the cover of this book). The two standout volumes are *The Pros: A Documentary of Professional Football* (New York: Simon & Schuster, 1960), which was written by Tex Maule, and *The Sports Photography of Robert Riger* (New York: Random House, 1995). Walter Iooss, Jr.'s, spectacular *Football* (New York: Abrams, 1986) includes a generation of the great shooter's portraits and action shots, as well as text by Dan Jenkins. Neil Leifer has yet to publish a book exclusively devoted to football, but his oversized *Sports!* (San Francisco: Collins, 1992) includes some of his most memorable football shots. The most impressive of the David Boss–edited books for Creative Services is the lavish *The Pro Football Experience* (New York: Abrams, 1973), highlighted by the gritty, intimate locker room scenes shot by Herb Weitman.

Anthologies. The best of the group is John Thorn's *The Armchair Quarterback* (New York: Scribner, 1982), which includes contributions from many of the classics of the sport, as well as such hard-to-find items as Murray Kempton's profile of Dick Butkus and the Bears (from *Esquire* in 1973), Wayne Lockwood's "Anatomy of a Game Plan" (during one of Sid Gillman's finest hours), and Gary Cartwright's sharply drawn portrait of Tom Landry. *The Fireside Book of Football* (New York: Simon & Schuster, 1964) includes a wider range of talents (from F. Scott Fitzgerald to Irwin Shaw), but draws most of its coverage from college football. The NFL has produced two literary anthologies. The first, *More Than a* Game (Englewood Cliffs, NJ: Prentice Hall, 1974) is a retrospective of the first five years of the league's "stadium magazine" *Pro!*, and features a prologue by Jim Murray. A *Game of Passion: The NFL Literary Companion* (Atlanta: Turner, 1994) delves less deeply but covers a wider range of material.

Annuals. Before sports annuals grew boring and formulaic, there were a few that had some golden eras—like Stanley Woodward's college football previews in the '50s, or the *Street & Smith's College, Pro and Prep Basketball* annuals of the late '70s. One such run was enjoyed by *Petersen's Pro Football* in the late '60s and early '70s. As edited by former Rams executive Chuck Benedict, it was a thoughtful, themed annual assessment of the game, with a strong cast of writers and photographers. The best of the recent volumes are *Sports Illustrated*'s discontinued stand-alone annuals of the mid-'90s and the comprehensive previews published today by *The Sporting News*.

Reference. *Total Football II: The Official Encyclopedia of the National Football League* (New York: HarperCollins, 1999), by Bob Carroll, Michael Gershman, David Neft, and John Thorn, is the most trusted reference work in the game. Beau Riffenburgh's *The Official NFL Encyclopedia* (4th ed., New York: New American Library, 1986) is to a great extent a hardbound version of the league's annually published *National Football League Record & Fact Book*, though it includes an essential section of chronologies for each NFL club. The later editions, though, lacked the writing breadth or conscientious design of the NFL's earlier *Official Encyclopedic History of Pro Football* (2nd ed., New York: Macmillan, 1977). The occasionally updated *The Sports Encyclopedia: Pro Football* (Grosset & Dunlap, 1999), by David Neft and Richard M. Cohen, is focused more on teams and seasons than individuals, an approach particularly well suited to football. While earlier editions date back to 1960, the latest edition includes only 1974–1998.

AUTHOR INTERVIEWS

Ernie Accorsi, Bud Adams, Greg Aiello, Senator Lamar Alexander, Bruce Allen, Etty Allen, Jennifer Allen, Hub Arkush, Charley Armey, Roger Atkin, Neil Austrian, John Beake, Bert Bell, Jr., Bobby Bell, Chuck Benedict, Raymond Berry, Charles "Stormy" Bidwill, Jr., Brian Billick, Kim Billick, Steve Bornstein, Carol Boss, Pat Bowlen, Terry Bradway, Gil Brandt, Anne Marie Bratton (née Rozelle), Jim Brown, Mike Brown, Joe Browne, Joel Bussert, Ace Cacciotti, Hamilton Carothers, Roberta Carrell, Bob Carroll, Cris Carter, Daily Childs, Jack Clary, Cris Collinsworth, Vince Costello, Bill Cowher, Robert W. Creamer, Andy Crichton, Gunther Cunningham, Bill Curry, Art Daley, Al Davis, Willie Davis, Len Dawson, Dan Dierdorf, Dave Dixon, Mickey Dukich, Tony Dungy, Gerald Early, Gregg Easterbrook, Herman Edwards, Manny Eisner, Jack Faulkner, Mal Florence, Barry Frank, Al Franken, Dave Gardner, Fred Gehrke, Mike Giddings, Frank Gifford, Esther Gillman, Sid Gillman, Bill Gleason, Roger Goodell, Otto Graham, Dennis Green, Howard Green, Forrest Gregg, Lou Groza, Jon Gruden, Peter Hadhazy, Bob Harlan, James Harris, Mike Haynes, Harold Henderson, Mickey Herskowitz, David Hill, Sam Huff, Lamar Hunt, Jim Irsay, Bill James, Jerry Jones, Lou Joseph, George Karras, Frank Kasper, Irv Kaze, Buzz Kemble, Jack Kemp, Ethel Kennedy, Cathy Kensil, Jim Kensil, Mike Kensil, Richard Kirkendall, Herb Klein, Don Klosterman, Chuck Knox, Tony Kornheiser, Jack Landry, Jr., Nick Langone, Willie Lanier, Dante Lavelli, John Lehman, Marv Levy, Dennis Lewin, Marvin Lewis, Al LoCasale, Jim Loftis, Jim Lynch, John Mackey, John Madden, Jerry Magee, Archie Manning, Wellington Mara, Dan Marino, Jim Matthews, Dorothy Maule, Bill McGrane, Joe McGuff, Stan McIlvaine, Rich McKay, Kay Collier McLaughlin, Al Michaels, James Michener, Bobby Mitchell, Art Modell, Bob Moore, Burk Murchison, Robert Murchison, Pete Newell, Ozzie Newsome, Dr. James A. Nicholas, Collie Nicholson, Michael Novak, Bob Oates, Bill Parcells, Jeffrey Pash, Max Patterson, Carl Peterson, Mary Phillips, Don Pierson, Val Pinchbeck, George Plimpton, Bill Polian, Carmen Policy, Joe Pollack, Brad Pye, Frank Ramos, Jack Ray, Dan Reeves, Jr., Susan Reeves, Lee Remmel, Greg Robinson, Johnny Robinson, Cooper Rollow, Dan Rooney, Bert Rose, Jr., Charles Rossotti, Dick Rozelle, Doug Rozelle, Helen Rozelle, Leland Rozelle, Pete Rozelle, Peter Ruocco, Buddy Rupe, Ed Sabol, Steve Sabol, Pierre Salinger, Warren Sapp, Jim Schaaf, Dick Schaap, Chris Schenkel, Marty Schottenheimer, Paul Schramka, Tex Schramm, John Semcken, Art Shell, Will

Shields, Don Shula, Michael Silver, Rick Smith, Beverly Snider, Duke Snider, Daniel Snyder, George Solomon, Lou Spadia, Tom Spock, Jack Steadman, John Steadman, Lynn Stiles, Scotty Stirling, Hank Stram, Pat Summerall, Chan Tagliabue, Charles Tagliabue, Paul Tagliabue, Jack Teele, Derrick Thomas, Bob Tisch, Dan Towler, Johnny Unitas, Gene Upshaw, Dick Vermeil, Bill Walsh, John Walsh, Al Ward, James Warsaw, Don Weiss, Herb Weitman, Lloyd Wells, T. D. Werblin, John Wiebusch, Ralph Wilson, Lamonte Winston, Ron Wolf, George Young, Paul "Tank" Younger, Paul Zimmerman, Jay Zygmunt.

Pete Rozelle, Jim Kensil, James Michener, and Dorothy Maule were interviewed by the author in 1995 for the book *The Franchise: A History of Sports Illustrated Magazine.*

INDEX